Beate I. Allert

# G.E. Lessing

# HERMEIA

Grenzüberschreitende Studien zur
Literatur- und Kulturwissenschaft

Crossing Boundaries in Literary
and Cultural Studies

Herausgegeben von
Edited by

Dietrich Harth
Achim Hölter
Monika Schmitz-Emans

Band 15
Volume 15

Beate I. Allert

# G. E. Lessing: Poetic Constellations between the Visual and the Verbal

SYNCHRON
Wissenschaftsverlag der Autoren
Synchron Publishers
Heidelberg 2018

Bibliographic information published by the Deutsche Nationalbibliothek
The Deutsche Nationalbibliothek lists this publication in the Deutsche Nationalbibliografie; detailed bibliographic data are available on the Internet at <http://dnb.dnb.de>.


Synchron Publishers GmbH, Heidelberg
www.synchron-publishers.com

Cover design by Reinhard Baumann, Munich
Cover picture: Johann Wilhelm Meil: Title vignette to Gotthold Ephraim Lessing's *Fabeln* (Berlin: Christian Friedrich Voß, 1759)
Herzog Anton Ulrich Museum, Braunschweig
Kunstmuseum des Landes Niedersachsen
Inv.-Nr. j-w-meil-ab3-0003, Photo: Museum photographer
Typesetting by Dr. Christian A. Bachmann, Berlin
Printed and bound in Germany by Strauss GmbH, Mörlenbach
ISBN 978-3-939381-97-6

# Contents

# Abbreviations

| | |
|---|---|
| Adorno GS | Theodor W. Adorno. *Gesammelte Schriften.* Ed. Rolf Tiedemann et al. 20 vols. in 23. Darmstadt: Wissenschaftliche Buchgesellschaft, 1998, |
| Erasmus ASD | *Opera omnia Desiderii Erasmi Roterodami.* Ed. J. Trapman et al. 47 vols. to date in IX *Ordines* [*Ordo* III, *Correspondence*, published separately in 12 vols.]. Amsterdam: North Holland and Brill, 1969–. |
| Erasmus CWE | Erasmus Desiderius. *Collected Works of Erasmus.* Gen. Ed. James K. McConica. 89 vols. in 85. Toronto: University of Toronto Press, 1974–. |
| Goethe GFA | Johann Wolfgang Goethe. *Sämtliche Werke, Briefe, Tagebücher und Gespräche.* Ed. Hendrik Birus et al. 40 vols. in 47. Frankfurt am Main: Deutscher Klassiker Verlag, 1985-2014. |
| Goethe GMA | Johann Wolfgang Goethe. *Sämtliche Werke nach Epochen seines Schaffens.* Ed. Karl Richter et al. 21 vols. in 34. Munich: Hanser, 1985-2014. |
| Herder FHA | Johann Gottfried Herder. *Werke in zehn Bänden.* Ed. Günter Arnold et al. 10 vols. in 11. Frankfurt am Main: Deutscher Klassiker Verlag, 1985-2000. |
| Herder SWS | Johann Gottfried Herder. *Sämmtliche Werke.* Ed. Bernhard Suphan et al. 33 vols. Berlin: Weidmannsche Buchhandlung, 1877-1913. 3rd reprint. Hildesheim: Olms, 1994. |
| Lessing FA | Gotthold Ephraim Lessing. *Werke und Briefe.* Ed. Wilfried Barner et al. 12 vols. in 14. Frankfurt am Main: Deutscher Klassiker Verlag, 1985-2003. |
| Schiller FSA | Friedrich Schiller. *Werke und Briefe.* Ed. Otto Dann et al. 12 vols. Frankfurt am Main: Deutscher Klassiker Verlag, 1988-2004. |
| Schlegel KFSA | Schlegel, Karl Wilhelm Friedrich. *Kritische Friedrich-Schlegel-Ausgabe.* Ed. Ernst Behler et al. 35 vols. in 38. Paderborn et al.: Ferdinand Schöningh, 1957–. |

# Preface

This book offers case studies on visual-verbal relations in Lessing's work from the early fables and the fable theory to the dramas and the late parables. Lessing seems to be interested in a style of presentation that can lead to disambiguation and reach the potential of the visual at its fullest.[1] He apparently struggles with probing the perfect medium and finding comfortable relations between on the one hand "Anschaulichkeit" or descriptiveness and on the other hand minimalism (especially as articulated in the concept of a "pregnant moment") in order to focus on the most consequential aspect of what is being presented. In his negotiation between a liking for the specific as well as one for the general and abstract, Lessing explicitly rejects "Allegoristerei" or the use of allegories that make an artwork rely on external information. Lessing seems to depend on select clips, condensed representations, metonymies, or *pars pro toto* expressions. He opts for diaphoric metaphors, to let go of previous meanings. This differs from Herder with his often unwieldy meanderings and a style that is instead more circular and convoluted using more epiphoric or coexisting layered metaphors to avoid deletion, forgetting, and Ekphrasis.

My interest in the work by Gotthold Ephraim Lessing and the visual has gained valuable impulses from Monika Schmitz-Emans, Alexander Košenina, Claudia Brodsky-Lacour, Monika Fick, Sabine Gross, Susan Gustafson, John McCarthy, Frederick Burwick, Liliane Weissberg, Ralf Simon, David Wellbery, Simon Richter, Richard Schade, John McCarthy, and Herb Rowland. My research has been promoted through many conferences hosted by such organizations as the *International Lessing Society*, the *American Society for Eighteenth Century Studies*, the *Modern Language Association*, the *International Herder Society*, the *Goethe Society of North America*, and the *German Studies Association*. For example, in 2015 I presented the paper "Ekphrasis und die Kunst des Verstehens: Möglichkeiten und Grenzen im Kontext Lessings" at the International Lessing Symposium on "Lessing und die Sinne" in Hannover, Germany.[2] In January 2016 I served as respondent for the panel "Laokoon at 250" at the 131st MLA Annual Convention in Austin Texas. Other venues, including invited talks, have given me opportunities to get deeper into consequential *Laokoon* debate which involved not only Lessing with his *Laokoon oder über die Grenzen der Malerei und Poesie* (1766) (a response to Winckelmann, Caylus, Shaftesbury, and Harris),[3] but subsequently

1 Lessing anticipates in that regard James Elkins, *Visual Literacy* (New York: Routledge, 2008).

2 Subsequently published in Alexander Košenina and Stefanie Stockhorst, ed., *Lessing und die Sinne* (Hannover: Wehrhahn, 2016), 161–181.

3 Lessing is often read as an admirer of English literature. See, for example Jutta Meise, *Lessings Anglophilie,* Europäische Aufklärung in Literatur und Sprache 10 (Frankfurt am Main: Peter Lang, 1997). However, Lessing was often falsely pitched against the French, since he was also an admirer of Diderot and numerous others. He was, however, critical of certain stylistic features associated with French Pictorialism.

Herder and Goethe. Herder welcomed Lessing's poetic approach to the Laokoon statue and emphasized the importance of each discipline and medium while shifting importance from the painter as already well established in the discourse on the visual more towards the poet. He suggested that the poet is equally important as the painter and can best succeed when leaving free reign to the spectator's imagination. Herder reviewed the work of Lessing favorably, commenting upon his poetic style as one that reflects on everything *in statu nascendi*, that is, as unfinished and in process, and one that nearly x-rays its own philosophical and epistemological underpinnings. One may appreciate Lessing's desire to write clearly, to avoid overabundance of details and what he calls "Schilderungssucht" as part of his objection to the style of the so-called pictorialism which was popular at the time. Pictorialism aimed at describing everything whereas Lessing argued for an approach of carefully selecting and cutting everything that may be redundant or nonessential for the image or idea to be communicated.[4] He suggests selecting the single most "pregnant" or "poignant moment" of an action in the process of representation. He likes the sculpture of the Laokoon statue for that reason. It is fruitful because it does not give away the climax of the action and makes us imagine and think. Similarly, a fable, a narrative, or a play should cut everything superfluous and summarize an entire action by means of forceful and action-packed images. All it takes is a glimpse into its constituents at work. Lessing's works experiment with metonymic contiguities and styles of visual presentation. He advocates visual writing and examines Ekphrasis, a term which is often used as the verbal description of a visual art work, a sculpture or a painting,[5] but which is also used as a rhetorical term associated with a vivid visual effect and a style "to focus and amplify emotions, with the rhetor lingering over key aspects on an image in order to persuade his audience" (Cicero, *De oratore*, Quintilian, *Institutio oratoria*). Ekphrasis in this regard is often conflated with *enargeia*, Aristotle's term not just for visual detail, but also for tropes of animation (Rhetoric 3.11.2).[6] From an intermedia perspective it has been much debated how it is possible that the medium language which has usually not been considered a visual medium can through verbal reproduction or evocation of artworks and visual phenomena itself produce images, albeit only for the audience or for spectators of a performance. It has been argued by one of the foremost theorists on Ekphrasis, Murray Krieger, that Ekphrasis provides "the most extreme and telling

4 FA 5/2, 15. For helpful introductions see Dietrich Harth, *Gotthold Ephraim Lessing. Oder die Paradoxien der Selbsterkenntnis* (Munich: Beck, 1993); Wolfgang Albrecht, *Gotthold Ephraim Lessing* (Stuttgart: Metzler, 1997); Peter J. Brenner, *Gotthold Ephraim Lessing* (Stuttgart: Reclam, 2000); and Friedrich Vollhardt, *Gotthold Ephraim Lessing* (Munich: Beck, 2016).

5 For examples, see Maria Klarer, *Ekphrasis. Bildbeschreibung als Repräsentationstheorie bei Spenser, Sydney, Lily und Shakespeare* (Tübingen: Niemeyer, 2001); Haiko Wandhoff, *Ekphrasis: Kunstbeschreibungen und virtuelle Räume in der Literatur des Mittelalters* (Berlin: De Gruyter, 2003); and Christine Ratowitsch, ed., *Die Poetische Ekphrasis von Kunstwerken. Eine literarische Tradition der Großdichtung in Antike, Mittelalter und früher Neuzeit* (Vienna: Verlag der Österreichischen Akademie der Wissenschaften, 2006); and James A. Heffernan, *Cultivating Picturacy: Visual Art and Verbal Interventions* (Waco, TX: Baylor University Press, 2006). These studies document how the visual and the verbal are often in conflict with each other.

6 G.G. Starr, "Ekphrasis," *The Princeton Encyclopedia of Poetry and Poetics*, Fourth Edition, ed. Roland Greene et al. (Princeton: Princeton University Press, 2012), 393.

instance of the visual and spatial potential of the literary medium." He builds his theoretical elaborations on Lessing's distinction between the verbal art time and the visual art of space.[7] It has been a pleasure to present on Lessing and on the *Laokoon* debate at numerous conferences and upon invitation, including as presenter in the panel "Lessing and Memory" at the 48th Annual Meeting of the American Society of Eighteenth Century Studies Conference 2017 in Minneapolis, as respondent to four papers in the panel "Laokoon at 250" at the MLA Convention 2016 in Austin Texas, as invited speaker at the symposium "Lessing und die Sinne" in Hannover 2016, as invited speaker at the festive event in the Goethe Museum in the Schloß Jägerhof Düsseldorf in June 2013, and as a presenter at the International Herder Conference at Schloß Beuggen (Rheinfelden) in October 2012.[8]

Several publications evolved from these and other talks nationally and internationally which are not reprinted here but which form the backdrop for all original chapters of this book. I presented on "Lessing's Dramatic Fragments and Heine's Dance Poem on *Faust*" at the 126th MLA Annual Convention in Los Angeles, January 2011;[9] "The Power of Abstraction and the Freedom to Cut: are Lessing's Style and Ekphrastic Approach Liberating?" at the 42nd Annual Meeting of the American Society for Eighteenth Century Studies, in Vancouver, B.C., March 2011; "From G.E. Lessing's Approach to the Poignant Moment to Contemporary Film Theory," XI Seminário de Linguistica Aplicada & VII Seminário de Tradução, Universidade Federal da Bahia, Salvador, Brazil, November 2010.[10] Further I was allowed to speak on "Conflicting Intentionalities in G.E. Lessing's Late Work" at the 41st Annual Meeting of the ASECS in Albuquerque, March 2010; "Lessing's Contribution to Eighteenth Century Discourses on Color" at the International Conference in Trans-Cultural German Studies together with the Meeting of the International Lessing Society at the University of Arizona, Tucson, March 2007; "Understatement and Minimalism in Diderot and Lessing" at the 4th Landau-Paris Symposium on Eighteenth-Century Literature on the theme "The Sketch in the 18th Century" in Paris, November 2006; "Lessing, Schiller, and the Relevance of Spiel: From Word to Impression, Metaphor to Play, Art to

---

7 Murray Krieger, *Ekphrasis: The Illusion of the Natural Sign* (Baltimore: Johns Hopkins University Press, 1992). See also Brian Cosgrove, "Murray Krieger: Ekphrasis as Spatial Form, Ekphrasis as Mimesis," Jeff Morrison and Florian Krobb, ed., *Text to Image: Image to Text, Proceedings of the Interdisciplinary Bicentenary Conference held at St. Patrick's College Maynooth (The National University of Ireland) in September 1995*, Internationale Forschungen zur Allgemeinen und Vergleichenden Literaturwissenschaft 20 (Amsterdam: Rodopi, 1997), 25-31. Most recently Sabine Gross has given an informative account of the debate between Lessing and Herder over Homer and Vergil: "Malen, Dichten, Schildern, Sehen: Lessing und Herder im Streit über Homer und Vergil." Hans Adler and Sabine Gross, ed., *Anschauung und Anschaulichkeit: Visualisierung im Wahrnehmen, Lesen und Denken* (Munich: Fink, 2016), 107-130.

8 My talk there was published as "Vom Augenblick zum Anblick: Herder und die Laokoondebatte," Ralf Simon, ed., *Herders Rhetoriken im Kontext des 18. Jahrhunderts* (Heidelberg: Synchron, 2014), 373-386.

9 Beate Allert, "Heine's *Doctor Faust:* A Ballet Poem," Lorna Fitzsimmons, ed., *Faust Adaptations from Marlowe to Aboudoma and Markland* (West Lafayette: Purdue University Press, 2017), 66-77.

10 "The Poignant Moment: From G.E. Lessing to Film Theory," *Forum for World Literature Studies* 3.3 (2011): 399-409.

Freedom," at the 121st MLA Annual Convention, Washington, D.C. in December 2005; "Horaz-Lessing-Mitchell: Ansätze zu Bild-Text Relationen und kritische Aspekte zur weiteren Ekphrasis Debatte" at the Annual Meeting of the German Society for Comparative Literature (Deutsche Gesellschaft für Allgemeine und Vergleichende Literaturwissenschaft) at the University in Potsdam, Germany, May 2005;[11] "Lessings Poetik und die Grenzen der Anschaulichkeit" at the 56th Wolfenbütteler Symposium on "Lessings Grenzen" at the invitation of the "Forschungs- und Studienstätte für Europäische Kulturgeschichte" at the Herzog August Bibliothek, Wolfenbüttel, Germany in April 2004.[12] Thanks to the colleagues who invited me to speak at these occasions, who organized these events, and to the editors and publishers of collections and journals in which my previous essays on Lessing have so far appeared: Alexander Košenina and Stefanie Stockhorst, editors of the volume *Lessing und die Sinne* (Hannover: Wehrhahn, 2016) in which my essay "Ekphrasis und die Kunst des Verstehens: Möglichkeiten und Grenzen im Kontext Lessing" was published (161-181); Ralf Simon, editor of *Herders Rhetoriken im Kontext des 18. Jahrhunderts* (Heidelberg: Synchron, 2014) with my essay "Vom Augenblick zum Anblick: Herder und die Laokoondebatte" (373-386); Galina Yermolenko, editor of *Roxalana in European Literature, History and Culture* (Burlington, VT: Ashgate, 2010) for including my essay "Roxalana in German Baroque and Enlightenment Dramas: Lohenstein, Haugwitz, Lessing, and Weisse," (89-108, 239-242). Other publications on Lessing include: "The Poignant Moment: From G.E. Lessing to Film Theory" in *Forum for World Literature Studies 3.* 3 (2011): 399-409; "Wie farbig darf die Dichtung sein? Lessings Beitrag zum Farbendiskurs im achtzehnten Jahrhundert" in *Lessing Yearbook* 37 (2008): 139-149; "Horaz-Lessing-Mitchell: Ansätze zu Text-Bild-Relationen," Monika Schmitz-Emans and Gertrud Lehnert, ed., *Visual Culture* (Heidelberg: Synchron 2008), 37-48; "Lessings Grenzen der Anschaulichkeit," Ulrike Zeuch, ed., *Lessings Grenzen,* Wolfenbütteler Forschungen 106 (Wiesbaden: Harrassowitz, 2005), 65-80; "Lessing's Poetics as an Approach to Aesthetics," Barbara Fischer and Thomas C. Fox, ed., *A Companion to the Works of Gotthold Ephraim Lessing* (Rochester, NY: Camden House, 2005), 10-30; "Reconceptualizing a Pictorial Turn: Lessing, Hoffmann, Klee and Elements of Avant-Garde Language," Marsha Meskimmon and Martin L. Davies, ed., *Breaking the Disciplines: Reconceptions in Knowledge, Art, and Culture* (London: Tauris, 2003), 187-222; "Lessing im Kontext kunsttheoretischer Debatten" in *Lessing Yearbook* 32 (2000): 371-387; "About a Burning Building in Eco and Lessing, or: How to Process Messages?" in *Lessing Yearbook* 29 (1997): 57-86.

I would like to express my deepest gratitude to the Executive Vice President for Research Suresh V. Garimella, the Deans Office of the College of Liberal Arts with Dean David A. Reingold and former Associate Dean Melissa J. Remis, and former Head of the School of Languages and Cultures at Purdue University, Madeleine Henry, for covering the subvention costs for publishing this book.

11 "Horaz-Lessing-Mitchell: Ansätze zu Text-Bild-Relationen und kritische Aspekte zur weiteren Ekphrasis-Debatte," Monika Schmitz-Emans and Gertrud Lehnert, ed., *Visual Culture* (Heidelberg: Synchron 2008), 37-48.

12 "Lessings Grenzen der Anschaulichkeit," Ulrike Zeuch, ed., *Lessings Grenzen,* Wolfenbütteler Forschungen 106 (Wiesbaden: Harrassowitz, 2005), 65-80.

I am very grateful to the Purdue Research Foundation for numerous transatlantic travel grants and conference support. I am especially thankful for the Global Synergy Grant that allowed me to host the International Herder Society Conference at Purdue University in September 2014 when I was president of the International Herder Society and for having supported the publication of the resulting book *J. G. Herder: From Cognition to Cultural Science* (Heidelberg: Synchron 2016). It helped me to better contextualize my work on Lessing here. Thanks especially to my supportive colleagues at Purdue University, the School of Languages and Cultures with Jennifer M. William, the German and Russian Department, and the interdisciplinary programs in Comparative Literature and Film, including Charles S. Ross. I should mention also the Philosophy Department at Purdue University for the kind invitation to present on "Lessing's Aesthetics" in the Illumination lecture series and to all those who supported me in teaching graduate classes in German and in Comparative Literature, including courses cross-listed with English, on topics such as Lessing, Ekphrasis, Fables, and Drama. In addition, the numerous film classes which I was able to teach at the graduate and undergraduate levels over the years have continuously helped me to develop my ideas on visuality and on the far-reaching implications of Lessing's approach. I have found it fascinating to study Lessing's approach to "poignant moments" which is relevant for montage, cinematography, and theories of film and moving images. Inspired by Lessing's approach and his poetic experiments throughout his fictional and dramatic works, I continue to pursue questions such as: when is the best moment to cut an image, what is the most effective way to present a scene, how to correlate the visual and the spatial dimensions in staging images, and how to verbalize a vision and what can we see? In other words: what are the implications and the lasting theoretical consequences of Lessing's experiments with complex poetic constellations between the visual and the verbal?[13]

Thanks to Johann S. Koch for his wonderful interest and support, his attention to details, and for publishing this book with Synchron Wissenschaftsverlag. Thanks to the three editors of the HERMEIA book series, especially for the helpful responses by Dietrich Harth. Also thanks to Christian A. Bachmann for his typesetting. Thanks to my parents Kurt and Erne Allert who often provided ideal working conditions during summers in their beautiful house in Germany. I regret that my mother did not live to see the publication of this volume. Finally thanks to my beloved husband Shaun F. D. Hughes for wonderful companionship and cheers along the way.

13 Beate Allert, ed., *Comparative Cinema. How American Students View Foreign Films* (Lewiston, NY: The Edwin Mellen Press, 2008); Beate Allert, ed., *Languages of Visuality: Crossings between Science, Art, Politics and Literature* (Detroit: Wayne State University Press, 1997), Beate Allert, *Jean Paul: Die Metapher und ihre Krise: Zur Dynamik der 'Bilderschrift' Jean Pauls* (New York: Peter Lang, 1986); and Beate Allert, ed., *J. G. Herder: From Cognition to Cultural Science/Von der Erkenntnis zur Kulturwissenschaft* (Heidelberg: Synchron, 2016).

# Introduction

## Who is G. E. Lessing and What is this Book About?

Gotthold Ephraim Lessing (1729-1781) was a prominent writer of the Enlightenment movement in eighteenth century Europe.[14] At the same time he was a stark critic of the Cartesian division of body and mind and some aspects of the major Enlightenment discourse.[15] He advocated the importance of seeing and of sense perceptions as prefigured in the visual arts, but he tried to give equal value to communication by words. He distinguishes the visual and the verbal as belonging to very separate realms, yet he tried to explore the relationships between them and their interactions in the process of being performed and then being processed by the recipients. By gaining much inspiration from interactions with contemporaries such as Moses Mendelssohn, Johann Gottfried Herder, and Denis Diderot, and by engaging with the work of theorists such as Alexander Gottlieb Baumgarten, Anthony Ashley Cooper, Third Earl of Shaftesbury, Johann Joachim Winckelmann, the Comte de Caylus, and others, Lessing questioned images and words for their distinct dimensions in space and time. What makes his work innovative and exciting is how he experimented with the intricate poetic constellations between the visual and the verbal and how he engaged with a vision for a communicative transformation. He wanted to turn audiences and readers into spectators and developed rhetorical strategies to make words visual yet also succinct and thought-provoking. He aimed at expressions that are verbally compact and developed a minimalist aesthetics for the most animating and invigorating results.

As will be illustrated in this book, Lessing finds that "Einbildungskraft" (productive imagination)[16] is the key to perception and to language, thus linking the physical act of seeing with the act of experiencing vision in complex processes of reading and rationalizing. Lessing seems to believe in the effectiveness of *Ekphrasis*, so that the visual can potentially become textual. Images can, at least under certain conditions

---

14 All other dates for individuals will be found in the index.

15 For an introduction to the Enlightenment movement, see Rolf Vierhaus, *Was war Aufklärung?* (Göttingen: Wallstein, 1995). See also Benjamin W. Redekop, *Enlightenment and Community: Lessing, Abt, Herder, and the Quest for a German Public* (Montreal: McGill-Queens University Press, 2000); Richard E. Schade and Dieter Sevin, ed., *Practicing Progress: The Promise and Limitations of Enlightenment. Festschrift for John A. McCarthy,* Internationale Forschungen zur Allgemeinen und Vergleichenden Literaturwissenschaft 106 (New York: Rodopi, 2007). For specific events in Lessing's life and his intellectual development in context, see Hugh Barr Nisbet, *Lessing: Eine Biographie*, trans. Karl S. Guthke (Munich: Beck, 2008) and the revised English original, *Gotthold Ephraim Lessing: his Life, Works, and Thought* (Oxford: Oxford University Press, 2013). All quotations from Lessing's works will be to: *Gotthold Ephraim Lessing. Werke und Briefe*, ed. Wilfried Barner et al., 12 vols. in 14 (Frankfurt am Main: Deutscher Klassiker Verlag, 1985-2003) referred to as FA (Frankfurter Ausgabe) plus volume and page number.

16 Throughout this volume, all translations within parentheses without quotation marks are mine.

which he sets out to explore, be successfully expressed by words. Translation from one medium to another comes with friction however. Ekphrasis can happen, but there are certain boundaries to be taken into account. Visuality is indeed a potential for Lessing, not only in the representation of an artwork, such as a painting or a sculpture, but also in the performing arts, in theater, and even in the writing of fiction as prefigured in the Aesopian fables. Lessing builds an approach associated with what has come to be known as "ein prägnanter Augenblick" (a pregnant or a poignant moment) in an artwork,[17] and the "stummer Schrei") (silent scream) as best shown in the ancient Laokoon statue.[18] It may represent something that we now might term a clip or rather a perfect montage. This moment evokes "Mitleid" (compassion) and highlights "Handlungen" (actions), including "innere Handlungen" (inner actions) associated with feelings, emotions, and sense perceptions at the core and the "äußern Handlungen," being outer, "sichtbare" or visible actions as presented in the plot.[19] The act of "Einbildung" (imagination and image formation) is a prerequisite for achieving

17 "Die Malerei kann in ihren coexistierenden Compositionen nur einen einzigen Augenblick der Handlung nutzen, und muß daher den prägnantesten wählen, aus welchem das Vorhergehende und Folgende am begreiflichsten wird." *Laokoon,* FA 5/2 (1990), *Laokoon: Werke 1766-1769,* ed. Wilfried Barner, 9-206 at 117. The standard translation of *Laokoon,* which will be used here with the translation within quotation marks, is Edward Allen McCormick, *Laocoön: An Essay on the Limits of Painting and Poetry,* 3rd ed. (Baltimore: Johns Hopkins University Press, 1992). ("Painting can use only a single moment of an action in its coexisting compositions and must therefore choose the one that is most suggestive [pregnant] and from which the proceeding and succeeding actions are the most easily comprehensible") (*Laocoön,* trans. McCormick 78). See also, Monika Schmitz-Emans, "Der Augenblick und das Transitorische: Lessings Medienästhetik und ihre Bedeutung für die literarische Bildinterpretation," *Die Literatur, die Bilder und das Unsichtbare. Spielformen literarischer Bildinterpretation vom 18. bis zum 20. Jahrhundert,* Saarbrücker Beiträge zur vergleichenden Literatur- und Kulturwissenschaft 7 (Würzburg: Königshausen & Neumann, 1999), 39-42.

18 "Der Meister arbeitete auf die höchste Schönheit, unter den angenommenen Umständen des körperlichen Schmerzes. Dieser, in aller seiner entstellenden Heftigkeit, war mit jener nicht zu verbinden. Er mußte ihn also herab setzen; er mußte Schreien in Seufzen mildern; nicht weil das Schreien eine unedle Seele verrät, sondern weil er das Gesicht auf eine ekelhafte Weise verstellet. Denn man reiße dem Laokoon in Gedanken nur den Mund auf, und urteile. Man lasse ihn schreien, und sehe" (*Laokoon,* FA 5/2, 29): ("The master strove to attain the highest beauty possible under the given condition of physical pain. The demands of beauty could not be reconciled with pain in all its disfiguring violence, so it had to be reduced. The scream had to be softened to a sigh, not because screaming betrays an ignoble soul, but because it distorts the features in a disgusting manner. Simply imagine Laocoön's mouth forced wide open, and then judge. Imagine him screaming, and then look") (*Laocoön,* trans. McCormick 17).

19 These are the same as the "Handlungen" in *Laokoon* which are described as "sichtbare und unsichtbare" FA 5/2, 102 ("actions, visible and invisible") (*Laocoön,* trans. McCormick 66). See further *Die Erziehung des Menschengeschlechts,* § 60: "Der erste *praktische* Lehrer.– Denn ein anders ist die Unsterblichkeit der Seele, als eine philosophische Spekulation, vermuten, wünschen, glauben: ein anders, seine innern und äußern Handlungen darnach einrichten" FA 10, 90. (The first *practical* teacher.–Since the immortality of the soul differs from a philosophical speculation, from guessing, hoping, believing: it is something else to attune one's inner and outer actions accordingly).

"Poesie" (poesy).[20] In order to do justice to the human condition and the goal of humanity, careful sense perception and reflection is needed. So is the use of adequate, "clear" but precise and differentiated language. What that means is complicated and can only be expressed poetically.

What Lessing means by the word "anschaulich" (visual or vivid), consists of a range of connotations and conditions necessary for any successful rhetoric and these he sets out to explore, at the same time not ignoring the rift which he finds unavoidable between the visual and the verbal. There are images as they exist in the realm of painting and sculpture. And there are images or metaphors in the realm of Poesie. For Lessing the media and discipline differences matter a great deal and his work is about experimenting with these important distinctions. He explores the dynamics between the visual and the verbal realms and tries to determine how to formulate what are exactly the possibilities and boundaries of images, or modes of image formation, on each side of the spectrum. This multi-directional quest has consequences for his innovative approach to Ekphrasis, visuality, metaphor, and the moving image. Lessing builds on the inclusive definition of *Ästhetik* as established by Baumgarten for whom all arts strive for the representation of nature and the beautiful within.[21] However, Lessing adds nuances to this spectrum and keeps reconsidering and reflecting on the content, the form, and the means of poetic writing with respect to various disciplines of art shifting attention from the side of production to the side of reception, reflecting on new readings of Classical texts and revising his ideas throughout his life. Imagination is at the core of poetic writing that evokes images. Lessing experiments with ekphrastic processes as a poet, playwright, and theorist of visual language. His intention is to produce vivid sense impressions so that the readers forget time while being absorbed into the visual space of the theater, or enjoying through poetic works a space of freedom. He aims at poetic language and at a style that is vivid, ideally sparking the recipients' imagination.

This notion he then further contextualizes with other ideas on poetic representation and on the creative role of illusion with respect to all the distinct disciplines of art.[22] He emphasizes the uniqueness of these disciplines according to each medium while at the same time giving imagination the central position in his approach to art and aesthetics. Horst Daemmrich noticed: "Der Begriff der Illusion nimmt in Lessings Untersuchungen ästhetischer Fragen eine zentrale Stelle ein. Dieser Sachverhalt ist besonders schwerwiegend, denn Lessing gibt keine eindeutige Definition des Begriffs" (The notion of illusion has a central position in Lessing's studies of aesthetic ques-

---

20 If "Poesie" means, among other things, "der Menschheit ihren möglichst vollständigen Ausdruck zu geben" (to give humankind their most complete expression), then it takes imagination and rhetoric to be a poet and to find adequate language in this pursuit. The definition is from Jakob und Wilhelm Grimm, *Deutsches Wörterbuch,* 33 vols. (Munich: Deutscher Taschenbuch Verlag, 1984), 13: col. 1968.

21 Alexander G. Baumgarten, *Ästhetik,* ed. and trans. Dagmar Mirbach, 2 vols., Philosophische Bibliothek 572a-b (Hamburg: Meiner, 2007).

22 Otto Haßelbeck, "Ästhetische Illusion und fiktionale Wirklichkeit," *Illusion und Fiktion: Lessings Beitrag zur poetologischen Diskussion über das Verhältnis von Kunst und Wirklichkeit,* Theorie und Geschichte der Literatur und der schönen Künste 49 (Munich: Fink, 1979), 97–118.

tions. This fact is especially important, since Lessing does not give any unambiguous definition of the term).[23] The word "illusion" refers in the context of Lessing to flexible relationships of signs and signifiers rather than to anything isolated, stable, or once and for all as if it could be fixed or determined. It has endless variable applications and possible meanings.[24]

Lessing argues that the illusion of the drama is far stronger than that of any narrative because we are not satisfied there only to "see" the character's happenings and destiny for a moment, but maintain an ongoing curiosity and an interest in the long run: "Denn da die Illusion des Drama weit stärker ist, als einer bloßen Erzehlung, so interessieren uns auch die Personen in jenem weit mehr, als in dieser, und wir begnügen uns nicht, ihr Schicksal bloß für den gegenwärtigen Augenblick entschieden zu sehen, sondern wir wollen uns auf immer desfalls zufrieden sehen" (Since the illusion of the drama is far stronger than that of a mere narrative, therefore we are much more interested in the persons of it, and we do not satisfy ourselves by seeing their destiny decided only for the current moment; instead we want to make ourselves content of it in the long run).[25] According to Lessing, *poesy* provides more time with the characters in their development in specific circumstances and hence a glimpse into their future. Theater can create more than momentary impressions of what happens to them, more than an image could, since it has a certain duration and is able to engage our imagination and thinking beyond the constrains of what is shown directly. Lessing is considered the founder of the so-called "Illusionstheater" (theater of illusion). What makes theater so intriguing, he explains, is that it draws us into a complex fictional world. It magnifies certain structures of the real as if it were a looking glass, thus revealing implicit mindsets, character traits, and communicative errors which truly exist yet are seldom noticed because they are normally not as obvious. Theater provides a kind of intensified realism and at the same time it provides more than isolated specifics. Lessing's work, as will be exemplified in this study, aims at a style of verbal minimalism in order to emancipate the recipients, to have them actively participate in a better understanding of real social interactions, and hopefully to have them change life conditions for the better. Yet there is much to explore concerning the question of the correlations between the visual and the verbal and when and where to cut.

By highlighting certain aspects of metaphoric language, Lessing's poetic style challenges previously assumed theoretical premise. He rejects what he calls "Allegoristerei" (abundant use of allegories) that draws meaning from external sources beyond the

---

23 Horst S. Daemmrich, "Illusion: Möglichkeiten und Grenzen eines Begriffs," *Lessing Yearbook* 1 (1969): 87-98.

24 On Lessing's important contributions to semiotics, see Gunter Gebauer, "Die Beziehungen von Bild und Text in Lessings *Laokoon*," Sybil Dümchen and Michael Nerlich, ed., *Text–Image, Bild–Text* (Berlin: Institut für Romanische Literaturwissenschaft Technische Universität Berlin, 1990), 17-27; Gunter Gebauer, ed., *Das Laokoon-Projekt: Pläne einer semiotischen Ästhetik*, Studien zur Allgemeinen und Vergleichenden Literaturwissenschaft 25 (Stuttgart: Metzler, 1984); David Wellbery, *Lessing's Laocoön: Semiotics and Aesthetics in the Age of Reason* (Cambridge: Cambridge University Press, 1984).

25 *Hamburgische Dramaturgie* xxxv, FA 6, 357.

given art work or text.[26] He insists on the immanent messages of both artworks and poetic texts and admits that tensions between the real and the imagined exist. They are based either side of the spectrum on possibly equally sound assumptions. Images may also be symbols for something else they cannot show directly. Lessing makes us aware of multiple possible uses of the same words and of the flexibility of language. His works draw attention to the specific contexts in which language is being used and he keeps illustrating how timing of images and of words matters. His poetic works raise philosophical questions which will lead the public to a better understanding of the implications of semiotics from the sense perceptions to thinking. Lessing interrogates the ancient concept of Ekphrasis, including its potentials and shortcomings, in trying to transfer images into words or *vice versa*. Lessing's plays do not "merely" narrate ideas; he wants to let the consequences of actions and of character traits "speak for themselves" and be suggestive beyond what is shown onstage. The plots of his dramas and prose narratives are intended to let imagination evolve ideally without the noticeable intervention of any author. The audience is invited to witness the processes of visualizing which means a complex teichoscopy is often indispensable.[27] Lessing's plays cannot do without moments of self-reflection and critical attention to the limitations of what is being seen and said. While advocating the power of poetic language, Lessing accepts silences and gaps, especially in his approach to Laokoon, as necessary and uses them as integral parts.[28]

For Lessing the word "Dichtung" (poesy) exists in a tension between the visual and the acoustic and its parameters including not only space but also time.[29] He furthermore draws attention to a visuality that according to him belongs to the dimension of space, the dimension that is prevalent in sculpture and painting. Moreover, as Lessing adds in his letters on *Laokoon, oder über die Grenzen der Malerei und Poesie* (1766) (*Laocoön: An Essay on the Limits of Painting and the Poetry*) and in the related *Paralipomena*, the concept of "Anschaulichkeit" (vividness) is a feature of poetic writing

26 "Wenn der Künstler eine Figur mit Sinnbildern auszieret, so erhebt er eine bloße Figur zu einem höhern Wesen. Bedienet sich aber der Dichter dieser malerischen Ausstaffierungen, so macht er aus einem höhern Wesen eine Puppe" (FA 5/2, 92-93): ("When the artist adorns a figure with symbols, he raises what was a mere figure to a higher being; but if the poet employs these artistic trimmings, he turns that higher being into a puppet") (*Laocoön*, trans. McCormick 60).

27 Teichoscopy, Greek *teichoscopia,* is a technique available to dramatists since Antiquity. It allows a view, metaphorically speaking, from behind a wall, of events otherwise hidden from the audience. In German this is referred to as the *Mauerschau* or *Botenbericht* (messenger report) where a messenger comes onstage to report events that took place offstage. The technique introduces elements of the plot that cannot be seen directly but only heard about. It is a practical solution to extend the visual horizon of a play imaginatively to include something beyond what is literally shown.

28 On the importance of silence in artworks see Wolfgang Kemp, "Die Kunst des Schweigens," Thomas Koebner, ed., *Laokoon und kein Ende. Der Wettstreit der Künste* (Munich: Edition Text+Kritik, 1989), 96-119.

29 *Dichtung* is literally "dense writing" and refers to both "the poetic" and to literary works in general, including the various genres of poetry and prose. Also see Victor Anthony Rudowski, "Action as the Essence of Poetry: A Reevaluation of Lessing's Argument." *PMLA* 82 (1967): 333-441.

that may well include "musikalische Bilder" (musical images).[30] These have multiple simultaneous signs, thus borrowing from the discipline of music with its tones. These are signs of simultaneity. Lessing shifts attention from the spatial to the temporal dimension. He tests the possibilities and limits of Ekphrasis. He integrates aspects of music, namely the layering of concurrent signs, into the realm of poetic writing where metaphors can similarly draw multiple meanings from each context or level of meaning. His credo is: "Je mehr wir sehen desto mehr müssen wir hinzu denken können" (The more we see the more we must be able to think about it), that is to imagine or to literally "make sense" of words or signs in the specific contexts they are being used.[31]

This study of Lessing's work focuses on a range of poetic experiments and on Lessing's nuanced approaches to them. He contextualizes concrete visions with an entire range of mental reflections on what is being seen and he experiments with poetic writing and stage productions. These may consist of what he calls *natürliche Zeichen* (natural signs) as assumed in painting, the visual realm, or consist of what he calls *willkürliche Zeichen* (arbitrary signs) which he assumes to be operating in language, the verbal realm.[32] He then proposes that *Dichtung* can bridge these two realms, the visual and the verbal, by making the arbitrary signs of language appear as if natural. To Lessing the works of the poets are able to approximate the effects of the physical responses to images produced by visual artists. Moreover, poetic images have the potential to supersede the visuality of paintings through the powerful medium of the verbal when tapped by the poets with talent and correctly, since they can produce unprecedented effects of brilliancy and amazing visions in the mind. What matters to Lessing is not only the dimension of space that dominates the visual (as he well elaborates), but also the dimension of time. Temporality and its signs possess "Gleichzeitigkeit" (simultaneity). "Töne" (tones) used to be associated exclusively with music but at least in his *Paralipomena* to *Laokoon* and the incomplete drafts and letters concerning works he had planned for the future, Lessing projects an ideal of what he calls "musikalische Bilder" (musical images) that would do more justice to the dimension of temporality in poetic language.[33] In fact he already experiments with aspects of this new idea way

30 This is a concept Lessing invented. See Beate Allert, "Ekphrasis und die Kunst des Verstehens: Möglichkeiten und Grenzen im Kontext Lessings," Košenina and Stockhorst, ed., *Lessing und die Sinne* 161-181. A similar recognition occurred to the Swiss painter Paul Klee. He notes in his diary: "Immer mehr drängen sich mir Parallelen zwischen Musik und bildender Kunst auf. Doch will keine Analyse gelingen. Sicher sind beide Künste zeitlich, das ließe sich leicht nachweisen" (*Tagebücher* § 640, 187): *"More and more parallels between music and graphic art force themselves upon my consciousness.* Yet no analysis is successful. Certainly both arts are temporal; this could be proved easily" (*Diaries* § 640, 177).

31 *Laokoon*, FA 5/2, 32: (*"The more we see, the more we must be able to imagine"*) (*Laocoön*, trans. McCormick 19).

32 See FA 5/2, 116 and *Paralipomena* 27 for a more detailed attempt to classify the signs (FA 5/2, 312-17). They will be discussed in more detail below.

33 Thomas Martinec in his essay "Musik und Sprache," *Lessing Yearbook* 41 (2014): 209-224, responds to the argument by Monika Fick and Reinhart Mayer that the Hamburg theater project could not succeed because Hamburg was in the eighteenth century a city of operas but Lessing's speech theater could not compete there. Martinec argues on the other hand that Lessing's *Hamburgische Dramaturgie*, especially Stücke XXVI and XXVII are entirely devoted to "Schauspielmusik" or to the music composed for theater performances explicitly and that it was Lessing's path-breaking contribution to help construct an aesthetics

ahead of his time and before Sergej Eisenstein, Roland Barthes, and Gilles Deleuze were to theorize on similar and related issues, including the moving image.

Despite juxtaposing paintings and texts, Lessing contributes to an entire spectrum of nuanced approaches to visuality. He develops an aesthetic that takes the possibility of the brilliance of inner images into account. As Lothar van Laak observes, Lessing gives more value to the power of "Einbildungskraft" (productive imagination) than acknowledged in earlier discussions and he also links the word imagination with the words for fantasy and fiction. Lessing is innovative in this regard because imagination requires a power of image formation and the ability to read visuality, something which became regarded as a central cognitive ability. It allows us to connect sense perceptions and images with reasoning and verbalizing.[34]

Lessing also paved the way for Johann Gottfried Herder, one of the most eloquent advocates of the importance of sense perceptions who wrote about their synesthesia, or the ability of one sense to replace or to sublimate for the lack of another. Herder draws attention to images but he does not consider Ekphrasis or the ability of images to transform themselves completely into verbalness. He draws most attention to sounds, movements, and touch, senses under the threshold of theorizing before. Whereas Herder thought of language even before it can be articulated, Lessing's approach to "Einbildungskraft" depends on appropriate verbal expression.[35] Lessing

of musical poetics which has so far been ignored. He argues that in fact there is a close bond between music and poetic writing that can already be traced in Lessing's work since 1749 (due to the "unaufhebbare[r] Zusammenhang von Poesie und Musik, der sich bereits seit 1749 in Lessings Werk abzeichnet" 210). Lessing comments that passions can well be promoted by music. To pursue this interest, Lessing interacts with the important paradigm shift that happens to take place in the discipline of music at that time. In the wake of establishing of instrumental music that emancipates itself from vocal music, language departs from music altogether and leaves a certain gap, which then eventually leads to the elevation and transformation of music itself into a language of passions itself. (211). I find Martinec's comments on Lessing's "Musikästhetik" path-breaking and would like to add his approach to so-called "musical images" as a new inter-art genre.

34 Lothar van Laak, "'Seine von sich selbst arbeitende Phantasie.' Zum Stellenwert der Einbildungskraft in Lessings *Laokoon*," Jörg Robert and Friedrich Vollhardt, ed., *Unordentliche Collectanea: Gotthold Ephraim Lessings* Laokoon *zwischen antiquarischer Gelehrsamkeit und ästhetischer Theoriebildung,* Frühe Neuzeit 181 (Berlin: De Gruyter, 2013), 309-319 at 309. Van Laak notices that Lessing uses the word "Einbildungskraft" (imagination) next to the word "Phantasie" (fantasy) with interesting contiguities of meanings. Whereas fantasy is not directly associated with seeing but rather with mental acts of contemplation and memory, both of these contribute to a concept of artistic creativity and are important matters to be considered for any artist and writer. Lessing deals with both and projects an entire spectrum of ideas and critical observations in between. Van Laak hints at the fact that Lessing in his *Laokoon* links imagination with fantasy and that therefore ultimately in Lessing's context we also find as a result a related "Produktionslogik" (logic of production) (312). He makes the point that this is something that remains to be further investigated. As far as Lessing scholarship is concerned, there has not been much consideration of his experiments with such poetic constellations. The present study will explore the intricacies between the visual and the verbal in Lessings work and investigate how images play a role in his use of language. See also Ingeborg Hoesterey, "*Laokoon* und Modernität." *Lessing Yearbook* 15 (1983): 165-176.

35 See Beate Allert, "Introduction" and Gerhard Sauder, "Sinnliche Erkenntnis: Der Kontext von Herders Abhandlung 'Vom Erkennen und Empfinden der menschlichen Seele'

paid the most attention to the eye and to seeing compared to other senses and this is especially the case in his famous *Laokoon*, where he emphasizes different kinds of visuality when comparing concrete visual artworks (sculpture and paintings) with poetic texts. He argues that the disciplines painting (Malerei) and "poetic writing" (Poesie) have distinct features and boundaries between them. While poetic writing has borders adjacent to the visual arts it is also positioned adjacent to the discipline of music and hovers in a tension in between. Lessing explores poetic constellations, interactions among the visual, the poetic (verbal), and the acoustic (music) with respect to media-specific attributes in the dimensions space and time. A sculptor or a painter must choose only one single "pregnant" moment from an entire action and it must be, he argues, one that does not give away the outcome of the action but instead invites the imagination on the part of the viewer. The poet borrows some aspects from the visual as it is also best in the verbal to be succinct and spark imagination. Whereas the signs of painting are "Körper" (bodies) in space that are aligned one after the other sequentially, the poet uses signs that are more complex because the poetic also shares features with music. The signs of music are "Töne" (tones). They can actually occur with "Gleichzeitigkeit" (simultaneity) and they are layered with multiple meanings. Such an effect can possibly also be achieved by the poet through the use of metaphors. Lessing's contributions to art and poetics are best known for their ocularcentrism but more attention needs to be paid to his discussions of verbalizing images. He is an advocate of language, especially *poesy* ("Dichtung" or the art of making language dense). The effective description or performance of something visual is for Lessing the highest achievement. His work is a conscious struggle wanting to turn readers into engaged spectators.[36] It has an impact on later movements, such as Weimar Classicism, Romanticism, Symbolism, all the way to twentieth-century phenomenology and present day theorizing on visual art.[37]

## A Preview: Poetic constellations from early to late Lessing

In Lessing's early writings, the notion of "seeing" is based on concrete life experiences, such as watching animals, plants, and people. He seems to generalize that there

(1778)," Allert, ed., *J. G. Herder* 1-16 and 135-155.

36 Peter Utz, *Das Auge und das Ohr im Text. Literarische Sinneswahrnehmung in der Goethezeit* (Munich: Fink, 1990), 39-57.

37 Lessing belongs according to his writing style and his affirmative use of metaphors to the so-called "imagists" that actually challenge the "verbalists" that are trying to do away with the visual for the sake of the verbal only. These terms are defined by Barbara Stafford in *Body Criticism: Imaging the Unseen in Enlightenment Art and Medicine* (Cambridge: The MIT Press, 1991), 472. Monika Fick astutely observes that Lessing, although drawing distinctions between painting and poetry, never ever categorically dismissed the metaphorical use of the word "Gemälde" referring to a verbal description. See her *Lessing Handbuch: Leben–Werk–Wirkung*, 4th ed. (Stuttgart: Metzler, 2016), 243. At the same time, I wish to add that Lessing ventures into exploring the vast differences between images and words and he draws, as David Wellbery noted, attention to the distinct media (*Lessing's Laocoön* 123-133).

are similar characters that exist everywhere, even as already specified in the famous fable tradition going back to Aesop. In Lessing's late works "seeing" seems more of a philosophical, abstract, and yet still poetic nature. It is associated with the process of perception and learning, cognition, finding truth, and the incomplete search to acquire knowledge. It appears to be of an almost sacred and rather individualized order, difficult to be communicated as the dialogues between Ernst and Falk illustrate. These dialogues draw awareness to the danger of words that can destroy feelings, images, and visions in the process of verbalizing them. In Lessing's late works, the so-called "visual" is then less explicable by means of Ekphrasis and it is instead associated with Socratic modesty, wisdom, and a need for privacy.

It was already known in Lessing's time that the power of *Aisthesis* (the perceived, or the perception based on the senses) was able to integrate diverse sense perceptions at the core of poetic writing.[38] This writing relies not only on images but also on words that intricately combine sense perceptions and aspects of temporality. It concerns words that, as Lessing already in the context of his early fables and then in his *Laokoon* asserts, can ideally transform into vivid sense impressions. He hints at the fact that Dryden's poetry can be more "colorful" than any "real" painting done with a brush on a canvas.[39] Lessing liberates poetic language from certain contemporary restrictions and explores the boundaries of the visual and the verbal as they interact in a wide spectrum of constellations. Lessing explores the limits of visual representation and diagnoses problems with so-called "natural signs." In this regard Lessing integrates the corporeal signs of linearity. He calls them "Zeichen" and quite literally "Figuren in dem Raume" (bodies in space) within the realm of the plastic, the visual and performing arts.[40] However, they may not be, as he illustrates in a variety of works, as immediately comprehensible as initially expected. He had already illustrated this, for example, in his comedy *Die Matrone von Ephesus* (1748-1771) where gestures and simple expressions of body language are being misread. Although in his *Hamburg*

38 See Hans Adler and Lynn Wolff, ed. *Aisthesis and Noesis: Zwei Erkenntnisformen vom 18. Jahrhundert bis zur Gegenwart* (Munich: Fink, 2013). I agree that Aisthesis had been interpreted in a reductionist way even to the point of Hegel's so-called *Kallistik* (from Greek Kalós schön) almost as if it were synonymous with *Ästhetic*, yet recent scholarship has begun to reflect upon the pre-Kantian notion of *Aisthesis* much more and become aware of Lessing's more inclusive meaning of the word, no longer as if it were serving a pregiven structure of human understanding. Recent scholars are correctly shifting emphasis on the uniqueness of aesthetic insights which, according to *Aisthesis* in more the original sense, are based upon the sensuous, the visual, the tactile, the sense- related (not the nominal or the verbally deduced). My review of this interesting and thought-provoking book by Adler and Wolff, is published in *Goethe Yearbook* 22 (2015): 311-313.

39 "Drydens Ode auf den Cäcilienstag ist voller musikalischen Gemälde, die den Pinsel müßig lassen" (*Laokoon*, FA 5/2, 114): ("Dryden's Ode for St. Cecilia's Day is full of musical pictures which leave the painter's brush idle") (*Laocoön,* trans. McCormick 76). See also Beate Allert, "Wie farbig darf die Dichtung sein? Lessings Beitrag zum Farbendiskurs im achtzehnten Jahrhundert." *Lessing Yearbook* 37 (2008): 139-149. The "Ode auf den Cäcilienstag" is "Alexander's Feast or the Power of Musique, An Ode in Honour of St. Cecilia's Day: 1697." *The Poems of John Dryden,* ed. John Sargeaunt (London: Oxford University Press, 1935), 198-200.

40 *Laokoon,* FA 5/1, 116: "Figuren und Farben in dem Raume" ("figures and colors in space") (*Laocoön*, trans. McCormick 76).

*Dramaturgy* (*Hamburgische Dramaturgie*) Lessing develops the idea "Der mitleidigste Mensch ist der beste Mensch" (The most compassionate is the most human), he raises questions on what that means.[41] He builds a sense-based aesthetics, yet focuses less on "Furcht" (fear or horror) than on "Mitleid" (pity) and "Mitleiden" (sympathy) in his own multifaceted contributions while proposing new readings of the Aristotelian principles of representation in art. Whereas in his early work Lessing seems to hint at ekphrastic hope, expressing the belief that writing can be "anschaulich" (visible and visual), especially if brief and succinct, his late works, especially *Die Parabel* and *Ernst and Falk* seem to indicate that even what seems to be a fire may be actually something else and words can undermine any grand vision; they tend to derail or lead to misunderstandings in the moment they are being expressed or institutionalized, especially if such a moment is not very well chosen well, or if history is not favorable, considering adverse circumstances.

Late in his life Lessing becomes increasingly more critical of seeing and probes questions on how to ever best conceptualize any successful visual-verbal transformations. He explores how to spark imagination through writing and through performances of plays. He had already contextualized these with a variety of suggested meanings through his earlier theoretical comments, including his elaborate treatise of the fables. Whereas in his fables and in his earlier works Lessing seems to aim at "Anschaulichkeit," an approach to an ideal concreteness and clarity of visual writing, his dramas involve various degrees of visual-verbal interactions and he no longer uses animal stories and observations taken from daily life. But during his middle period he also returns to Classical Greek texts, and translates literature from various cultures and languages which he uses in his own adaptations in the process inventing a new approach to catharsis. There are numerous dramatic productions characterized by experimenting with staging images and with writing plays that narrate stories that are based on underlying images, sculptures, and portraits. Lessing then no longer simply wants to turn his listeners in the theater into spectators of his visions. He draws attention to the complexities of perception and the subtle distinctions between acting and living, especially in a changing culture with fragile social conditions. The poet cannot make language disappear completely in the process of rhetorically savvy communication. But Lessing wants that the poet should turn arbitrary signs into natural ones and absorb the spectators into fiction. Images can sometimes appear to be fake and overdone and words may well reflect on their own fictionality, yet it is up to the spectator and the audience how much imagination they will bring to the show. Lessing aims proactively at a new "Illusionstheater" and lets the spectators ideally forget the media specific boundaries. He comments that the actors need to reflect on what they think about each "Bühnenbild" (setting) presented onstage.[42] The playwright no

---

41 Lessing formulated this dictum in a letter he wrote to Christoph Friedrich Nicolai in November 1756 (FA 11/1, 116–122 at 120) which was published in 1789 in the *Gelehrter Briefwechsel zwischen Johann Jacob Reiske, Moses Mendelssohn und Gotthold Ephraim Lessing* (FA 3 668–673 at 671). See further Hans-Jürgen Schings, *'Der mitleidigste Mensch ist der beste Mensch': Poetik des Mitleids von Lessing bis Büchner* (Munich: Beck, 1980); 2nd rev. ed. (Würzburg: Königshausen & Neumann, 2012).

42 "Wenigstens ist jedes Wort, das er dem Hamlet, wenn er die Komödianten abrichtet, in den Mund legt, eine goldene Regel für alle Schauspieler, denen an einem vernünftigen

longer maintains control over the projected illusions. Whereas in some plays the visual seems to take precedence over the verbal, especially when words tend to be superfluous, in other plays the verbal is absolutely essential in order to make sense of anything seen onstage. Images become actions rather and they are to "speak" increasingly for themselves. But only through the well-crafted dialogues which Lessing lays out before his spectators does he make us aware of the potentials and efforts he consciously puts into his variously crafted image-word constructions that create a realm of poesy that shares the dimension of space (the visual) and the dimension of time (music).

There is, I think, an interesting development in Lessing's approach to visual writing and we can trace a variety of constellations considering his experiments in this regard. His approach as documented in the early fables differs from that in the dramatic plays and from that he proposed in his theoretical treatise, *Laokoon.* If we also take into account the affiliated *Paralipomena* and the letters and notes Lessing wrote in this context, important new aspects concerning the timing of images come to the fore. We can trace Lessing's nuanced approaches to visual-verbal dynamics in a variety of works until his late parable of a burning palace, a narrative which may indicate Lessing's final stance on language in its apparent dissolution and reconceptualizing. The *Ringparabel* in *Nathan der Weise* may hold promise for another kind of visual representation in his final stance.[43] In order to find whoever may still have "the ring" that simply cannot be found in the present and seems irretrievably lost, one must recreate its radiance by means of metaphor. One must retrieve its hopefully persistent attributes which may be found where least expected. But such a remote possibility or deferral could signal perhaps that there might be a new era and a different need. Lessing ventures a *teichoscopy* and other distant imaging devices but in his late work became occupied with a "Religionsstreit" (religious quarrel).[44] He never completed his own search for intellectual freedom. Whoever claims to have the ring will have to manifest its original attributes: love, peace, and tolerance, along with other human qualities. Lessing uses rhetorical strategies suggesting through his writings and the performances of his plays how one could imagine a better time in history and more effective communications through poetry and the arts.

Lessing deals with restrictions implicit in the presentation of humans who are suffering pain and he suggested that the Laokoon figure should be presented with the mouth not widely open but just as the ancients wisely presented it, almost closed, if

Beifalle gelegen ist. 'Ich bitte euch,' läßt er ihn unter andern zu den Komödianten sagen, 'sprecht die Rede so, wie ich sie euch vorsagte; die Zunge muß nur eben darüber hinlaufen'." *Hamburgische Dramaturgie* IV, FA 6, 209 (At least each word which he puts Hamlet in the mouth when he trains the comedians is a golden rule for all actors who are interested in a decent applause. "I ask you" he has him say among other things to the comedians, "speak as I told you beforehand. 'Speak the speech, I pray you, as I pronounced it to you—trippingly on the tongue' [*Hamlet,* Act III, scene ii]. He wants them to speak without obvious artificiality and as naturally as possible.

43 *Nathan der Weise*, Act III, scene vii (FA 9, 555-562). For another edition of this text and introductory comments see Lessing, *Nathan der Weise. Die Erziehung des Menschengeschlechts*, ed. Philippe Wellnitz (Strasbourg: Presses Universitaires de Strasbourg, 2000).

44 Also known as the *Fragmentenstreit* (quarrel over the Fragments) and the *Goeze-Streit* (quarrel with Goeze). See Nisbet, *Lessing: Eine Biographie* 701-744; *Gotthold Ephraim Lessing* 537-570.

the scream was nearly silent. According to Lessing, this more subtle mode of representation draws more compassion from the spectators. But in his later works he seems to experiment with the removal of such restrictions by having Sara Sampson die onstage and speak out in pain until her last moments towards her death by poison.

Lessing has a wealth of framing devices and poetic constellations between the visual and the verbal that draw attention to words that become empty, to silences that speak, and to powerful vivid sense impressions. He seems to be increasingly in his works more critical of verbalizing emotions, since in the end his vision is allocated not only in the dimension of space, but more along with music, belonging to the invisible dimension of time. Lessing is a foremost thinker on the question how best to time images, when to cut visual representation for the sake of most poignant moments, and how to draw audiences into fiction, play, and art, so much that they are no longer readers but become imaginary spectators and compassionate humans. Recent theorists on the moving image in cinema studies, including Roland Barthes, Sergej Eisenstein, and Gilles Deleuze have gained much inspiration from Lessing and now, 250 years after the publication of *Laokoon,* Lessing continues to stimulate art theoretical debates on the nature of visual-verbal dynamics.

There has been a dominant tendency for critics so far to make Lessing responsible for having drawn a dividing line between images and words and to have interpreted his work in the light of Enlightenment logocentricity. This would then give preference to verbalness over the visual arts. It is true that Lessing emancipated "Dichtung" from strictly mimetic representation that previously always had to be based on painting and sculpture and that for Lessing the message is in part depending on the specific medium in which it is being communicated. Therefore the visual and the verbal belong to rather different media and it seems that hence images and words must be thought of as being opposed in that regard. Yet Lessing nevertheless draws attention to the time-sensitive nature of language. Meanings depend on the contexts in which words are being used. The frames of reference in which they can then be interpreted may shift with metaphoric meanings. Recent scholarship on Ekphrasis studies explores the interaction and the dynamics between the visual and the verbal and also keeps referring to Lessing for that matter. If one takes an approach of "ekphrastic hope" then one tends to believe, as apparently Lessing did, at least until his later work, in the potential of images to become words in the process of poetic "Dichtung." Poetic images can therefore still be approached in terms of "visual language" without ignoring however, some complications.

## Outline: The structure of this book

In the first section of this book I shall elaborate on Lessing's attempts to correlate images with words and show how he experiments with letting images speak when words fail or are best at their minimum. It includes chapter one on Lessing's Ekphrasis and the art of understatement, chapter two on minimalism and sketches with the focus on Lessing and Diderot, chapter three on Lessing's contribution to the fable both in terms of his theoretical treatises and his own fable writing. Chapter four is on the famous *Laokoon* (1766) and the related letters and documents that are included in the *Paralipomena* which I read as being indispensable to the entire enterprise. The fifth chapter is on drama theory and the *Hamburgische Dramaturgie* (*Hamburg Dramaturgy*), a collection of publications which Lessing called "Fermenta cognitionis" (the yeast in the cognition process).[45] They consist of play reviews, translations of performances, adaptations, and theater plans that together all form something of a theoretical base for Lessing's own work as a playwright. They reflect his position in the European theater scene at the time vis-à-vis his contemporaries.

The second section of the book deals with Lessing's experiments in staging poignant moments in Lessing's theatrical plays chronologically. It opens with chapter six on *Die Matrone von Ephesus* which challenges the notion of "natural signs" not only in the realm of art but already in reality. It questions the efficiency of gestures and body language. The chapter seven, on *Miß Sara Sampson* (1755), analyzes ambivalent emotions and complex images. Sara seems to be blind to her own dream images but nevertheless speaks endlessly until the last stunning moments of her violent death. Chapter eight links Lessing's fragments on *Faust* with his unfinished play, *Fatime* (1755–1759), since the actions of both plays draw attention to the splitting of time and the speed of the real. Chapter nine on *Minna von Barnhelm* (1767) provides a case study with the motif of unemployment after a war. It entails a twisted love story which is complicated by the psychological mechanism of staging oneself for other(s), so that even such a concrete symbol as an engagement ring can no longer be taken for face value. Chapter ten is on *Emilia Galotti*, a play that begins with an art theoretical scene between a painter and his customer discussing some portraits painter Conti has just delivered. It raises questions on the ability to do justice to images or imaginaries, whether it may be in painting, turning them into portraits, or in talking about them. It is a play that draws attention to the temporality of images and difficulties of synchronizing inner with outer images. Conti must realize that he did not succeed in turning something he perceived in nature and rendering what he saw conceptually visible in his artworks then into something one can describe accurately or even talk about, at least not with the Prince.

Part three of this book addresses Lessing's later works and their visual-verbal dynamics. It begins with chapter eleven on *Ernst and Falk* (1778) trying to unravel Lessing's complicated history as a Freemason. For example his use of the metaphor "Wolfsmilchraupe" is an example for a meaning contingent upon a range of perspectives. It is a word and an image that can have multiple meanings depending on contextual nuances. It refers to a caterpillar living on the Cypress spurge, one of a number of shrubs known as "Wolfsmilk." It is called so because of the "bite" of its poisonous white sap. As a "Raupe" (caterpillar) it has the ability to shed its skin to create a new existence for itself as a "Schmetterling" (butterfly).[46] It exemplifies in that sense the ability for qualitative change and represents in Lessing's own discourse an example for

45 Lessing, *Hamburgische Dramaturgie*, FA 6, 655.

46 The "Wolfsmilchraupe" develops into the "Wolfsmilch Ringelspinner" (Ground Lackey Moth, *Malacosoma castrensis).*

the power of Ekphrasis.[47] In this context it represents an early stage of a development, still tied to the earth, an image before the "pregnant moment" of the action, that is before it can fly from the ground to the air for another mode of existence. It stands as an example for metamorphosis and ekphrastic hope.

In his later works *Nathan the Wise* (1779) and *The Education of Humankind* (*Die Erziehung des Menschengeschlechts*, 1780) Lessing develops his ideas on liminality, borders of visual and of verbal communication, and on the importance of timing the visual. He pursues the question how the dimensions of space and of time impact what we can perceive *A Parable of a Burning Palace* (*Eine Parabel vom brennenden Palast*, 1778) illustrates the evanescence of any such building which itself could be considered as an image for language or symbolizing institutionalized "Enlightenment." It exemplifies the need to enter any of the many doors in order to see what can be gained from the inside. No metaperspective is available and it seems that in the end perhaps Lessing suggests that it is only through fairy tales, parables, metaphors, and metonymies that any vision of truth, as fragmented and volatile it may be, can be tentatively expressed. It suggests that since images are sometimes just as deceptive as words, we may be aware that there may be miracles that can neither be captured in images nor verbalized and simply told. Even though there was smoke, the building in the end was not devoured by the fire. Even if the ground plans of the building may be lost, or if the ring symbolizing the ultimate truth cannot be located in the Here and Now, Lessing suggests that truth persists. *Eine Parabel* argues that instead of searching the apparently missing ground plans what is required is, no matter whether the palace is burning or lit up otherwise, a view from the building inside and compassionate action.

In his late works Lessing turns from the dramatic writings of his middle years back to an abundance of images and symbols similar to what we found in his earlier works. Yet Lessing is not merely returning to an earlier approach to the image and metaphor as Helmut Göbel claimed with respect to *Nathan der Weise*. Instead, and this is the important difference, he inserts framing devices and draws attention to the temporality of the visual.[48] As my study will show, it is a return with a difference: Lessing is not only interested in brevity or quick effects of words that provoke visual thought and actions. His metonymic use of language in his late works is self-reflective and leaves things open for multiple framings and aspects of intertextuality. It presents not only facts but processes of visualizing, rationalizing, and action. It leads to a somber

47 Dietrich Harth (217) explains that the butterfly is an ancient symbol of the arising soul or the resurrecting human and that the caterpillar stands for a life that will be born after death in a more beautiful form: "Der Schmetterling ist ein uraltes Sinnbild der auffliegenden Seele, ja des auferstehenden Menschen. Lessing hat an anderer Steele darauf verwiesen [...] Und die Raupe steht für das Leben, das nach dem Tod [...] in schönerer Gestalt wiedergeboren wird." I think Lessing challenges any simplistic notion of equating seeing with knowing and indeed he proposes a wonderful vision of change, transformation, Ekphrastic hope, and human liberation in the context of his latest work.

48 Helmut Göbel argues with respect to *Nathan der Weise*: "Die Metaphorik, wie sie auch in den frühesten dramatischen Versuchen Lessings auftrat, kehrt hier wieder" (Lessing's metaphoricity which also occurred in his earliest dramatic attempts now returns). "Die Bildlichkeit im *Nathan*," Klaus Bohnen, ed., *Lessings Nathan der Weise*, Wege der Forschung 587 (Darmstadt: Wissenschaftliche Buchgesellschaft, 1984), 229-266 at 299. First published as chapter of *Bild und Sprache bei Lessing* (Munich: Fink, 1971), 154-195.

Socratic style as Ingrid Strohschneider-Kohrs has astutely noted.[49] Lessing's late work is marked by his awareness of multiple cultures and an open-ended search for truth. He still seems to believe in the education of humankind and the power of shared imagination and language, yet his poetic work suggests a more subtle and unimposing style to articulating the visual in the verbal.

49 Ingrid Strohschneider-Kohrs, *Poesie und Reflexion: Aufsätze zur Literatur* (Tübingen: Niemeyer, 1999), especially the chapter "Doppelreflexion und Ironie bei Lessing," 159-195. See my review of this book in *Monatshefte* 92.4 (Winter 2000): 499-500. Also see Carsten Rohde, *Doppelte Vernunft: Lessing und die reflexive Moderne* (Hannover: Wehrhahn, 2013). Rohde highlights examples from *Miß Sara Sampson*, *Minna von Barnhelm*, *Emilia Galotti*, and *Nathan der Weise* where reasoning has multiple contingencies and where Lessing makes use of various "self-reflective" strategies.

# PART I:
## Seeing and Images—Theoretical Concerns

# Chapter 1
# Lessing: Ekphrasis and the Art of Understatement

Abstract: Lessing rejects "Schilderungssucht" (the mania to describe everything in detail). Yet he did not pitch the verbal against the visual.[50] Nor did he simply reject Ekphrasis, or the notion that the visual can be effectively described, or that images can be transformed into words altogether. He was optimistic in thinking that truth can be found, although it takes an effort. He believed in a divine order in the cosmos that spanned various cultures and eras.[51] He further believed in the ability of language to be able to communicate, despite some restrictions he then tries to deal with, and to be able to transform something visual into something verbal. He was cautiously aware of certain limitations or boundaries implicit in each medium, including the visual. What is seen may be less than what is hidden.[52] Lessing has a very specific approach to "Anschaulichkeit" (vividness) that does not absorb, dissolve, or erase images into texts as some critics conclude. He aims at using a minimum of words for the most effective visual-imaginative effect. He makes original contributions to the history of the study of Ekphrasis and explores how to verbalize the visual. This has been recognized by modern art theorists including Sergej Eisenstein, Roland Barthes, Umberto Eco, Paul Klee, and Boris Groys.[53]

---

50 Inka Mülder-Bach, "Bild und Bewegung: Zur Theorie Bildnerischer Illusion in Lessings Laokoon." *Deutsche Vierteljahrsschrift für Literaturwissenschaft und Geistesgeschichte* 66 (1992): 1-30 reflects on Lessing's visual writing style and the importance of imagination for his approach aiming not only at images but rather actions. For Lessing's impact on Goethe and others, see Mülder-Bach "Sichtbarkeit und Schriftlichkeit: Goethes Laokoonaufsatz," Inge Baxmann et al., ed., *Das Laokoon-Paradigma. Zeichenregime im 18. Jahrhundert* (Berlin: Akademie Verlag, 2000), 465-479. Vilém Flusser, *Für eine Philosophie der Fotographie*, 11th ed. (Berlin: Edition Flusser, 2011, first published 1983) finds that history is marked by a "Kampf der Schrift gegen das Bild" (fight of the verbal against the visual) or conflict between text and image (10). Similarly Friederike Hassauer in *Textverluste: Eine Streitschrift* (Munich: Fink, 1992) identifies our era as one of "Textverluste" or losses of the textual as it is being increasingly replaced by images. The "visual turn" is something that has often been associated with the Enlightenment discourse but I would like to draw attention to Lessing's differentiated approach to this turn. It has, as he claims, its own important place within the verbal since the verbal has its own visual potential. Also see Gottfried Böhm and Helmut Pfotenhauer, ed. *Beschreibungskunst–Kunstbeschreibung. Ekphrasis von der Antike bis zur Gegenwart* (Munich: Fink, 1995).

51 Lessing builds on the work by Baumgarten who coined the word "Ästhetik" in 1735 and elaborated it in his *Metaphysica* (1739. 7th ed. 1779). See Hans Adler, "Was ist Ästhetische Wahrheit?" *Zeitschrift für Ästhetik und Kunstwissenschaft.* Sonderheft 15 (2016): 49-66 at 50.

52 Alain Besançon, *The Forbidden Image: An Intellectual History of Iconoclasm*, trans. Jane Marie Todd (Chicago: University of Chicago Press, 2000) offers an excellent overview of the various critical approaches to the image in philosophical discourses from antiquity to modernity.

53 At a Lessing panel titled "Laokoon at 250" chaired by Birger Vanwesenbeeck at the 2016 MLA Convention, January 9, 2016 in Austin Texas, Jonathan Blake Fine presented a paper that described Lessing's style as "anti-theoretical" and connected this with the

## 1. What is Ekphrasis? Early definitions

Ruth Webb begins her study of the meaning of Ekphrasis in the Greek rhetorical school books (*Progymnasmata*) with the observation that the definition of Ekphrasis as it is taught in modern critical discourse differs a great deal from how it was taught to students of Rhetoric in the Roman Empire. In modern theoretical discourses Ekphrasis is usually regarded as "a text or textual fragment that engages with the visual arts," but in classical times Ekphrasis was defined as "a speech that brings the subject matter vividly before the eyes."[54] The ancient definition seems much more open and does not exclusively limit Ekphrasis to "the poetic description of a pictorial or sculptural work of art" or to "words about an image" as she claims is the recent and still current understanding of the term.[55] Originally the notion of Ekphrasis focuses more on the basic need to write vividly and to involve the recipient or the public in the process, concerns also very dear to Lessing.

Although one can find both definitions of Ekphrasis applicable in the context of Lessing–he actually deals with painting and sculpture explicitly–I think that his works on Laokoon suggest that one should return to the earlier sources in Classical Antiquity and not only approach poetry or poesy as measured in comparison with the visual arts as it was usually done at his time. Christoph Buch notices that Lessing challenges in his *Laokoon* what poetic images and visual language mean and how to interpret Horace's motto *ut pictura poesis* in its broader context.[56] Lessing engages critically with such writers as Johann Christoph Gottsched and the Swiss poets and journalists, Johann Jakob Breitinger and Johann Jakob Bodmer. Their ideas by grappling with alternative interpretations of the notion of *mimesis* inspired Lessing to explore his own approach to representation by allowing imagination to gain a more constructive role in the arts and in poesy. Lessing also offered a new aesthetic approach to the sublime and to intricate questions on how to represent the beautiful, the ugly, and the painful in the realms of the visual.[57] Lessing was able to define his own path through these

anti-theoretical artist and scholar Boris Groys in his book *Einführung in die Anti-Philosophie* (Munich: Hanser, 2009). Groys, an art theorist, curator, media expert, and author, adopts numerous ideas from Lessing, including a critique of art and knowledge as commodity and the desire to have actions replace images. On the other side of the philosophical spectrum, I pointed out that for Wassily Kandinsky images are indeed already "actions" and each dot on a painting "is" already a movement.

54 Ruth Webb, *Ekphrasis: Imagination and Persuasion in Ancient Rhetorical Theory and Practice* (Burlington, VT: Ashgate, 2009), 10.

55 Webb, *Ekphrasis* 1.

56 "As painting so poetry." Horace, "De arte poetica," *Satires, Epistles and Ars Poetica,* trans. H. Rushton Fairclough, rev. ed., Loeb Classical Library 194 (1929. Cambridge: Harvard University Press, 2005), 442-489 at 480, line 361, trans. "A poem is like a picture," 481.

57 On the changing notion of mimesis throughout the 18th century, see Erich Auerbach, *Mimesis. Dargestellte Wirklichkeit in der abendländischen Literatur.* 9th ed., Sammlung Dalp 90 (Bern: Francke, 1994. On writings on *Laokoon* after Lessing, see Martin Dönike, *Pathos, Ausdruck und Bewegung. Zur Ästhetik des Weimarer Klassizismus 1796-1806,* Quellen und Forschungen zur Literatur- und Kulturgeschichte 34 (Berlin: De Gruyter, 2005), especially on Aloys Ludwig Hirt and his "Produktive Empirie" which then led to Schiller and Goethe

issues, and eventually to offer a break-through in the understanding of Ekphrasis.[58] Lessing's ideas concerning Ekphrasis are complex and interesting and have far-reaching consequences for art theory, language philosophy, film studies, image-text debates, and critical investigations into image studies and approaches to visuality.

It is often assumed that images or sense impressions precede texts and that texts strive for the mimetic power to transpose them into the realm of verbalness without the loss of "Anschaulichkeit" (vividness). For Lessing such sequencing or hierarchy is questionable. He recognizes that poetic writing has its own power of visuality which may not be based on immediately previous external sense impressions. He considers emotions as "innere Handlungen" (inner actions) that are equally important to the "äußere Handlungen" (outer actions) since they are often at the source of them. He further claims that not only actions that drive the plot are visible but actions of the mind that are sometimes albeit fleetingly expressed in facial expressions, body language, and gestures. This draws new attention to what happens onstage in the gesticulations and in signs of language and metaphor. Whereas sense impressions, ideas and visual metaphors determine the actual happenings on the surface of so-called reality and its obvious "Anschaulichkeit," there are also uncontrollable forces and hidden mechanisms of human interaction at stake. This makes visual expressions precarious and always just a touch evanescent. Thinking is needed in order to read images for their own complexity.

Already the first part of Lessing's unfinished Laokoon project consists of more than 200 pages of theoretical reflections, interspersed with poetic interludes and reviews of numerous artworks and quotations from world literature. Lessing seems to suggest, upon first glance at least, that there are unsurmountable differences between painting and poetry, the visual juxtaposed against the verbal, or vice versa. Perhaps it is one of Lessing's major achievements to have noticed that different disciplines

---

and their rejection of certain representations of strictly historical versions for the sake of symbolic ones.

58 Hans Christoph Buch, *Ut Pictura Poesis. Die Beschreibungsliteratur und ihre Kritiker von Lessing bis Lukács* (Munich: Hanser, 1972), 35-41. Buch also shows how in *Laokoon* Lessing offered on the basis of his reading of Aristotle and Johann Joachim Winckelmann, a critique of the work of Joseph Spence and Le Comte de Caylus. Lessing clarifies the battle between Gottsched and Bodmer and Breitinger by making imagination and the wonderful, as in Milton's *Paradise Lost*, the theoretical foundation upon which their difference becomes–in a Hegelian dialectic move so to speak–"aufgehoben," that is resolved. Buch writes: "Indem Lessing den Schwerpunkt der aristotelischen Mimesis von einer bloßen Kopie auf das menschlich bedeutsame Ideal verlegte, vollendete er, was Gottsched und die Schweizer begonnen hatten: den Kampf gegen die aus der Rhetorik übernommenen, mechanischen Regeln der barocken Poetik" (29) (Lessing in relocating the focus from the Aristotelian mimesis from a mere copy to the meaningful human ideal, completed what Gottsched and the Swiss had begun: the battle against the mechanical rules that had been adopted from the poetics of the Baroque). And Buch adds: "Paradoxerweise war Lessing der Boden bereitet worden von einigen jener Autoren, denen im *Laokoon* die schärfte Kritik gilt" (Paradoxically some of those critics who are most harshly criticized in the *Laokoon* have paved the ground upon which Lessing stands). The same paradox, it seems to me, is true today in Ekphrasis studies where Lessing is attacked for his approach, despite the important fact that it was indeed Lessing who paved the way for ongoing critical debates in Ekphrasis study and scholarship about visual-verbal dynamics today.

present something which is in fact rather difficult, if not impossible, to compare. Each discipline-specific perspective and each medium has its own ideal objective and its own main message. Meanings depend on various sense perceptions, historical approaches, and on the disciplines of research.

## 2. How does Lessing contribute to Ekphrasis study?

Lessing's approach to what he refers to as "Darstellung" (presentation) challenges previous modes of representation and suggests that performance itself is decisive to a point that nothing is repeated, or just enacted as if it existed before.[59] He also considers images of the mind of equal importance to the visuality of texts, but just of a different kind of vitality compared to any images on a canvas, or on a screen. This leads him, as we shall see, to an exploration of such theoretical issues concerning not only the boundaries between the visual and the verbal, but also their interactive dynamics and the process of a new concept of mimesis altogether.[60] In exploring Lessing's contribution to Ekphrasis study, I shall also highlight what I call his search for understatement. By this I mean his minimalist approach via the most effective use of expression. I believe that *Laokoon* is at the core to this approach. The art of understatement can be seen in selecting what was the "prägnanter Augenblick" (most poignant moment) of the action. It is also at work in Lessing's fables, dramas, and parables that experiment with certain aspects of the verbal-visual dynamics. What Lessing writes

59 Lessing sees a boundary for the visual since it is relegated to the dimension of space and must therefore distract itself from temporality or minimize the dimension of time which ultimately belongs to music with its simultaneous signs, to one single moment in a visual art work: "Diesen einzigen Augenblick macht er so prägnant wie möglich, und führt ihn mit allen den Täuschungen aus, welche die Kunst in Darstellung sichtbarer Gegenstände vor der Poesie voraus hat" (*Laokoon,* FA 5/2, 139): ("He [the artist] makes this single moment as suggestive as possible and describes it with all illusion which makes art superior to poetry in the portrayal of visible objects") (*Laocoön*, trans. McCormick 99). What Lessing then negotiates are degrees to which poets and playwrights must act like visual artists in making forget temporality. In addition, a poet can borrow aspects of simultaneous signs (tones) from the musician.

60 For an account of *mimesis* from antiquity to the present, see Matthew Potolsky, *Mimesis: The New Critical Idiom* (New York: Routledge, 2006). Potolsky shows that what mimesis means was much debated from the very beginning in the writings of Plato and Aristotle and has been critically contested ever since. It involves and correlates with a range of related concepts, such as representation, emulation, mimicry, catharsis, and simulation. Lessing's contribution to the debate is touched upon as an important juncture in this debate, especially in the context of his *Hamburgische Dramaturgie* (Potolsky, *Mimesis* 45-46). Particularly important is his approach to drama in terms of a catharsis or "Reinigung"(cleansing), a purging that means not only a ritual purification, a medical purge, or a notion of repressing or cutting emotions, but it may also mean establishing something of a sacrifice or the transformation into another mode of existence. Lessing states in the *Hamburgische Dramaturgie* LVIII that sometimes "diese Reinigung in nichts Anders beruhet, als in der Verwandlung der Leidenschaften in tugendhafte Fertigkeiten" (this catharsis is nothing else than the transformation of passions into moral talents and actions) (FA 6, 574).

about the image-word relations in *Laokoon* is connected to statements about the difference between paintings and poetry, images and texts; but at the same time can be seen to express concerns about overcoming binaries. Lessing suggests new types of "musical images" within the textual realm. He eventually opens up a notion of visuality within the verbal, a transformation by means of ekphrastic transfer.[61] There is room in Lessing's approach for the notion of images that can actually change their identity from one category to another and actually maintain their power in the verbal realm. What will have to be examined are the consequences or side effects along the way. Lessing's approach to the visuality of the verbal is promoted in by understatement, brevity, and "Dichtung" (poetic language). It is, however, Lessing insists, not the same as pictorial descriptiveness and ornamental speech as others had assumed.

W.J.T. Mitchell, one of the foremost theorists of visuality, has mounted a challenge to Lessing's reception. He charges Lessing with abandoning and overriding images for the sake of words and hence for a media difference between them that is so stark that the gap between them cannot be bridged by any imaginative visual-verbal dynamic. I think that his critique of Lessing's apparent "iconophobia" does not do Lessing justice since he was truly interested in seeing and preserving the visual even in the realm of the textual. Mitchell shows nevertheless that Lessing's writings on *Laokoon* have a pivotal role to play in art theoretical debates and for dealing with Ekphrasis.[62] Instead of interpreting Lessing in the tradition of the "sister arts" paradigm of mimesis, Mitchell emphasizes that the tradition of Horace repressed or ignored that underlying conflict, tension, and power struggle that exists between the visual and the verbal, images and texts. He finds Lessing's approach refreshing for articulating deep-seated differences and problems with the false equation or nominal similarity of text and image. He finds a new approach exemplified in Lessing's theoretical work. At the same time, Mitchell's approach is grounded squarely on *Laokoon* which he then reads as if Lessing was conceptualizing the visual and the verbal for the sake of a new hierarchy that would repress images under the dominance of texts.[63] Whereas I welcome his idea that Lessing's *Laokoon* is path-breaking for the theory of iconology, I believe that Mitchell has overlooked some important aspects of Lessing's approach which I think is much more favorable to images and imaging.[64]

There are fundamental questions about what Ekphrasis means and how to approach it. In his book *Picture Theory* Mitchell outlines three modalities in dealing with the ekphrastic.[65] First, there is "ekphrastic indifference" and perhaps the "common-

---

61 On approaches to multiple languages of visuality see the essays in Beate Allert, ed., *Languages of Visuality.*

62 Among his most important contributions are: W.J.T. Mitchell, *Iconology: Image, Text, Ideology* (Chicago: University of Chicago Press, 1986); *Picture Theory: Essays on Verbal and Visual Representation* (Chicago: University of Chicago Press, 1994); and *What Do Pictures Want? The Lives and Loves of Images* (Chicago: University of Chicago Press, 2005).

63 See W.J.T. Mitchell, "Space and Time: Lessing's *Laocoön* and the Politics of Genre," *Iconology* 95-115.

64 For further discussion on this topic, see Beate Allert, "Horaz–Lessing–Mitchell: Ansätze zu Bild-Text-Relationen und kritische Aspekte zur weiteren Ekphrasis-Debatte," Monika Schmitz-Emans and Gertrud Lehnert, ed., *Visual Culture* (Heidelberg: Synchron, 2008), 37-48.

65 W.J.T. Mitchell, *Picture Theory* 152-156.

place misconception" that Ekphrasis is impossible. Can any verbal description ever "reproduce" a work of painting or visual art? Second, there is "ekphrastic hope" that can arise "when the impossibility of Ekphrasis is overcome in imagination or metaphor." Such hope, Mitchell explains, means an overcoming of "difference." Stephen Cheeke positively comments this bridging from various sides of the spectrum: "[T]he hope that the word might stand in for the image, and that no one will notice the difference, or that the difference will disappear."[66] According to Cheeke, Lessing provides both in his theory in *Laokoon* and his poetic works plenty examples illustrating successful Ekphrasis. Lessing stands as a perfect example of ekphrastic hope. Cheeke adds: "More significantly perhaps, poetry opens up the static image to the temporal schema of language, to the 'sequential elements of syntax'. By saying what happens next the verbal description returns the picture of the world of narrative and agency, often revealing an ethical dimension–a moral pulse, a turn to decision, on occasion of will–that has been superseded in the still moment of the picture."[67]

Mitchell, on the other hand, calls the third mode of visual-verbal interaction "ekphrastic fear." He finds that it constitutes even in Lessing's *Laokoon* a

> moment of resistance or counter desire that occurs when we sense that the difference between the verbal and visual representation might collapse and the figurative, imaginary desire of ekphrasis might be realized literally and actually [...]. It is the moment in aesthetics when the difference between verbal and visual mediation becomes a moral, aesthetic imperative rather than (as in the first 'indifferent' phase of ekphrasis) a natural fact that can be relied on. The classic expression of ekphrastic fear occurs in Lessing's *Laocoön*, where it is 'prescribed as a law to all poets' that 'they should not regard the limitations of painting as beauties in their own art.[68]

There are several ways to overcome the differences between the verbal and the visual. It could be that Ekphrasis allows a complete transfer from one mode into another, so that what is visual can in fact become completely verbal. It could also mean that the temporal aspect becomes much more minimal, so that it is barely traceable, that the verbal and the visual become the same in one moment, depending upon the recipient or the context in which the communication takes place. It is curious, I think, that Lessing mentions his intention to conceptualize "musikalische Bilder" (musical images).[69] He wanted to integrate them into his plans for the second part of

66 Stephen Cheeke, *Writing for Art: The Aesthetics of Ekphrasis* (Manchester: Manchester University Press, 2008), 28.

67 Cheeke, *Writing for Art* 5. I find this mention of the "moral pulse" important and will return to it later.

68 Mitchell, *Picture Theory* 154-55. The German original is "verdienet den Dichtern als eine Regel vorgeschrieben zu werden. Sie müssen die Bedürfnisse der Malerei nicht zu ihrem Reichtume machen" (FA 5/2, 92): ("should be prescribed to poets as a general rule. They must not convert the necessities of painting into part of their own wealth") (*Laocoön*, trans. McCormick 60). In other words poets should not imitate the painters but be true to the needs of their own medium.

69 For more on this see Allert, "Ekphrasis und die Kunst des Verstehens," *Lessing und die Sinne* 161-181. Lessing was aware of this concept earlier. He wrote in his review of Moses Mendelssohn's *Über die Empfindungen* (1755) in *Berlinische Privilegierte Zeitung* 106 (September 4, 1755) that the object aimed for in the work of art should be "angenehme Empfindungen" (pleasant sensations). They can provide insights into "die Malerei, in die

his *Laokoon* project. We get a glimpse into the complicated nature of his projections by especially taking into account a letter which Lessing wrote to Christoph Friedrich Nicolai on May 26, 1769.[70] In addition, we gain more information by means of the posthumously published "Paralipomena" to *Laokoon,* the order of which has been the subject of ongoing debates. Lessing's unpublished writings in this regard do not solve all of the scholarly problems that could be raised. I shall argue, however, that they offer a fresh perspective on Lessing's ambitious initiative since he considers the visual and the verbal not only for their split as decidedly separate categories but he was also underway exploring their intricate relations and interactions. These concern both images and movements not only in texts but also in dramatic works and Lessing raised the concern how they work respectively considering the dimensions of space (figures, bodies, visual) and time (tones, sound acoustic). In doing so, I would like to suggest that Lessing anticipated a notion of the "movement-image" and the "time-image" as articulated much later by Gilles Deleuze in the context of his philosophical and epistemological work on cinematography.[71] Lessing began the path-breaking quest to capture time in the image, to bracket or to condense it into the so-called "prägnanter Augenblick" as presented or rather visualized in a moment of reception based on an artwork. The condensing of an entire action into one single most important moment

---

Musik, in die musikalische Malerei des Farbenclaviers, bis sogar in die noch unerfundenen Harmonien derjenigen Sinne, welchen noch keine besonderen Künste vorgesetzet sind" (into literature, into paining, into music, into the musical painting of the ocular-harpsichord, even as far as into the hitherto uninvented harmonies of those senses which do not have any specific correlating arts as of now) (FA 3, 410). For an informative reference to the color-piano of Louis-Bertrand Castel, see Joachim Gessinger, "Visible Sounds and Audible Colors: The Ocular Harpsichord of Louis-Bertrand Castel," Allert, ed., *Languages of Visuality*, 49-72 and *Auge und Ohr. Studien zur Erforschung am Menschen 1700-1850* (Berlin: De Gruyter, 1994), 115-120, 157-62, 170-175. And Lessing allows for this possibility in *Laokoon* in discussing the opening sections of Book I of Homer's *Iliad*: "Es ist unmöglich die musikalische Malerei, welche die Worte des Dichters mit hören lassen, in eine andere Sprache überzutragen" (FA 5/2, 110): ("It is impossible to translate this musical picture which the words of the poet let you also hear into another language") (*Laocoön*, trans. McCormick 72).

70 This letter has also been analyzed by Victor Anthony Rudowski, *Lessing's Aesthetica in Nuce: An Analysis of the May 26, 1769, Letter to Nicolai,* University of North Carolina Studies in the Germanic Languages and Literatures 69 (Chapel Hill: University of North Carolina Press, 1971).

71 Gilles Deleuze, *Cinema 1: The Movement-Image,* trans. Hugh Tomlinson and Barbara Habberjam (Minneapolis: University of Minnesota Press, 1986): [T]he movement which is established between the parts of a set in a frame, or between one set and another in a reframing; the movement which expresses a whole in a film or in an oeuvre; the correspondence between the two, the way in which they echo each other, in which they pass from one to the other. Because it is the same movement, sometimes composing, sometimes decomposing; these are the two aspects of the same movement. And this movement is the shot [= the movement-image], the concrete intermediary between a whole which has changes and a set which has parts, and which constantly converts the one into the other according to its two facets" (22); "Time simultaneously makes the present pass and preserves the past in itself. There are, therefore, already two possible time-images, one grounded in the past, the other in the present. Each is complex and valid for time as a whole." *Cinema 2: The Time-Image,* trans. Hugh Tomlinson and Robert Galta (Minneapolis: University of Minnesota Press, 1989), 98.

in its visual representation is to Lessing an act of art. It has also relevance to poetic writing that has the most poignant visual effects only if it leaves enough space to the imagination.

Lessing viewed paintings and poetry not as "similar" for in *Laokoon* he stresses their differences. In doing so he anticipated a long line of thinking while insisting on crucial media distinctions between the arts and related disciplines. Long before Marshall McLuhan Lessing found that in part the medium is the message.[72] Whether or not the dividing line between the visual and the verbal, images and texts, that Lessing apparently draws in his *Laokoon* treatise was meant diagnostically, in order to point out a problem, or whether it was meant as a suggestion to artists and writers not to mix up their tools and goals of expression, still remains an open question. Lessing has often been himself compared to a doorkeeper of sorts by drawing such a distinction and he was heavily criticized for his apparent efforts in trying to regulate visual-verbal relations. In any case suffice it to say here, Lessing pointed out that these relations are problematic and to some extent mutually exclusive. Part of Lessing's argument is that whereas the signs of the visual are "Körper" (bodies), figures, and colors arranged sequentially in space ("Gegenstände, die neben einander, oder deren Teile neben einander existieren"), these are usually "natürliche Zeichen" (natural signs) and he argues: "Folglich sind Körper mit ihren sichtbaren Eigenschaften die eigentlichen Gegenstände der Malerei" ("Accordingly, bodies with their visible properties are the true subjects of painting").[73] He adds that objects follow each other, or that parts of them follow each other, and these are called actions. Consequently actions are the "eigentliche" or "true" objects of dramatic art and perhaps "Dichtung."[74] Then he adds in a complicated argument to be developed later, that bodies are the signs of space that are "natural" and that tones are the signs of time that can be used arbitrarily ("willkürlich"). "Zeichen" (signs) of the poet are both visual and verbal and ideally look as if they were natural even if they are not. Such signs cannot only be the sum of previous actions but also together build the center and creative origin of future ones. The poet deals with also with "willkürliche Zeichen" (arbitrary signs) similar to the tones or signs a composer uses in music, while the sculptor or painter on the other hand employ "natürliche Zeichen" (natural signs) with the provision that they usually have a "bequemes Verhältnis" (a suitable relationship) between their signs.[75] Lessing explains the difference between these two kinds of signs and their relations in the dimensions of space and time in *Paralipomena* 8.3.1 and he notes that exceptions to the rule are possible and unusual constellations among such signs can occur.

---

72 See Beate Allert, "Lessing im Kontext kunsttheoretischer Debatten," *Lessing Yearbook* 32 (2000): 371-87 at 380-83; "Reconceptualizing a Pictorial Turn: Lessing, Hoffmann, Klee and Elements of Avant-Garde Language," Marsha Meskimmon and Martin L. Davies, ed., *Breaking the Disciplines: Reconceptions in Knowledge, Art, and Culture* (London: Tauris Press, 2003), 187-222 at 195-200; and "The Poignant Moment: From G.E. Lessing to Film Theory," *Forum for World Literature Studies* 3. 3 (Dec. 2011): 399-409 at 402-03.

73 FA 5/2, 116; *Laocoön*, trans. McCormick 78.

74 FA 5/2, 116.

75 FA 5/2, 116. See also "Paralipomenon 27" for a more detailed attempt to classify the signs (FA 5/2, 312-317) and the comments in Wellbery, *Lessing's Laocoön* 115.

> Aus dem Unterschiede der natürlichen und willkürlichen Zeichen. Die Zeichen der Malerei sind nicht alle natürlich; und die natürlichen Kennzeichen willkürlicher Dinge können nicht so natürlich sein, als die natürlichen Kennzeichen natürlicher Dinge. Es ist noch sonst viel Convention darunter. Exempel von der Wolke.[76]
>
> [On the difference between natural and arbitrary signs. Not all the signs of painting are natural; und the natural characteristics of arbitrary things cannot be as natural as the natural characteristics of natural things. In addition, there is also much convention that plays a role here. Example of the cloud].

Lessing insists that the verbal is semiotic.[77] Jason Gaiger writes: "Lessing's analysis of the different types of signs used by painting and poetry allowed his work to be reclaimed as an important contribution to semiotics, as this had been developed by figures such as Charles Sanders Peirce and Ferdinand Saussure in the late nineteenth and early twentieth centuries."[78] Monika Fick asserts that Lessing's approach to mimetic representation was utopian in not only creating a semiotics of poetic writing but also in aiming at beauty in an ideal, if not Classical sense.[79] The question is how may the creative power of imagination possibly be tapped and maintained while language

76 FA 5/2, 262. In chapter 12 of *Laokoon* Lessing discusses the problems painters face when trying to represent a scene in which some person or object is invisible. The convention is to indicate this by a cloud or mist: "Ganz wider den Geist der Dichters. Unsichtbar sein, ist der natürliche Zustand seiner Götter; [...] Nicht genug also, daß die Wolke ein willkürliches. und kein natürliches Zeichen bei den Malern ist; dieses willkürliche Zeichen hat auch nicht einmal die bestimmte Deutlichkeit, die es als ein solches haben könnte; den sie brauchen es eben sowohl, um das Sichtbare unsichtbar, als um das Unsichtbare sichtbar zu machen" (FA 5/2, 108-109): ("But this is in complete violation of the spirit of the poet! Invisibility is the natural condition of his gods; ... Thus it is not only that in painting the cloud is an arbitrary and not a natural sign, but this arbitrary sign does not even possess the definite distinctions which it could have as such, for it is used both to render the visible invisible, and the invisible visible") (*Laocoön*, trans. McCormick, 70). See also Ralf Simon, "Natürliche und willkürliche Zeichen, bequemes Verhältnis," *Die Idee der Prosa. Zur Ästhetikgeschichte von Baumgarten bis Hegel mit einem Schwerpunkt bei Jean Paul* (Munich: Fink, 2013), 62-72 and Olivier Primavesi, "Bild und Zeit. Lessings Poetik des natürlichen Zeichens und die Homerische Ekphrasis," Jürgen Paul Schwindt, ed., *Klassische Philologie* inter disciplines. *Aktuelle Konzepte zu Gegenstand und Methode eines Grundlagenfaches,* Bibliothek der klassischen Altertumswissenschaften, N.F., 2. Reihe 110 (Heidelberg: Winter, 2002), 186-211.

77 On Lessing's contribution to semiotics see Wellbery, *Lessing's Laocoön* and the essays in Gebauer, ed., *Das Laokoon-Projekt.* Hubertus Kohle identifies Lessing's semiotic practice as a break with classical theory: "Die hier implizierte semiotische Problematik in der Verbindung von *signifiant* und *signifié* führt nun aber dazu, daß die eben beschriebenen Grundlagen der klassischen Theorie aus den Angeln gehoben werden." (The implicit semiotic problematic considering here the relationship between the *signifier* and the *signified* leads to the event that the descriptive basic premises of classical theory become revolutionized). Hubertus Kohle, *Ut pictura poesis non erit: Denis Diderots Kunstbegriff. Mit einem Exkurs zu J. B. S. Chardin,* Studien zur Kunstgeschichte 52 (Hildesheim: Georg Olms, 1989), 3.

78 Jason Gaiger, "The Contemporaneity of Lessing's Aesthetics," Ritchie Robertson, ed., *Lessing and the German Enlightenment,* SVEC 2013 09 (Oxford: Voltaire Foundation, 2013), 97-117 at 105.

79 Fick, *Handbuch* 254-255.

becomes, historically speaking, increasingly more abstract.[80] It has been an important observation by Dietrich Harth that beauty in the realm of the poet differs from beauty as conceived in the physical realm of bodily signs in the visual arts, plastic or painting; "Schönheit in der Dichtung ist nicht—wie die körperlicher in der bildenden Kunst—statisch zu denken. Ihr Erscheinungsmodus ist die Zeit, und das heißt: die Bewegung."[81] (Beauty in the poetic realm is not - like that of bodily signs in the visual art - to be thought of as being static. The poetic cannot be considered anything static. Its dimension is the time, and that means movement). Harth explains that according to Lessing's *Laokoon* beauty is something transitory or "beauty in movement" ("ein transitorisch Schönes" or "Schönheit in Bewegung") onstage but moreover it taps into the active participation, into the psychic energy and compassion within the audience. Hence movement in the specific context of Lessing's approach in *Laokoon* is not only something measurable through external actions and gestures onstage; it furthermore includes the so-called "inner actions" or that which affects the sense perceptions ("Triebfedern" or driving springs) that spark and energize the emotional reactions and ultimately the empathy by the observers.

The difference between material and mental images, paintings and texts, or concretely visual graphic signs versus those belonging to verbal expression, language, had posed a variety of theoretical problems from a range of perspectives in Lessing's time. The consideration of these problems is the underlying issues in his letters and conversations with Moses Mendelssohn.[82] Among the works Lessing read carefully was Abbé DuBos, *Réflexions critiques sur la poésie et la peinture* (1719) raising questions about how perceptions differs when based on "natural signs," those a painter uses, or when based on "verbal signs" as used by a writer but structured in "arbitrary" ways. Could the poet insert a new order of naturalness? Related questions are: How could words ever have the function of "natural signs" or of such signs as we find them in sculpture and painting? Lessing omits to make a clear distinction between them and seems to leave open the question of whether or not they are virtual substitutes for what they designate. Lessing seems at first to have equated the "visual signs" with the notion of "natural signs" as his predecessors did while calling the "verbal signs" simply "arbitrary signs." But this designation, as many critics of Lessing have overlooked, is not at all Lessing's final word on the matter.[83] In the *Paralipomena* to *Laokoon,* Lessing already

80 Fick, *Handbuch* 245. Also see Joachim Jacob, *Die Schönheit der Literatur. Zur Geschichte eines Problems von Gorgias bis Max Bense,* Studien zur Deutschen Literatur 183 (Tübingen: Niemeyer, 2007), especially chapter III.4 "Die 'unbequeme' Schönheit, Lessings Laokoon," 240-286.

81 Dietrich Harth, *Gotthold Ephraim Lessing* 163.

82 Vera Forester, *Lessing und Moses Mendelssohn: Geschichte einer Freundschaft* (Hamburg: Europäische Verlagsanstalt, 2001) and my review of it in *Lessing Yearbook* 34 (2003): 213-215.

83 What he does is develop a differentiated semiotics. See Gunter Gebauer, "Die Beziehungen von Bild und Text." 17-27 Also see David Wellbery, "The Pathos of Theory in *Laokoon* Revisited," Ingeborg Hoesterey and Ulrich Weisstein, ed., *Intertextuality: German Literature and Visual Art from the Renaissance to the Twentieth Century* (Columbia, SC: Camden House, 1993), 47-63. These studies demonstrate Lessing's path-breaking contribution to semiotics and have given him credit for having offered a logical and "perfectly coherent" theoretical approach. They tend to omit, however, important tensions and open questions which Lessing was planning to deal with in his unfinished continuation to *Laokoon.*

challenged the falsely simplistic dichotomy between natural and arbitrary signs, the visual and the verbal.[84] According to Lessing's proposition, the relationship between images and texts was to be understood in terms of a problem in comparing the disciplines of art, or the so-called "Paragone-Problematik."[85] Mitchell refers to Lessing as playing a key role in modern Ekphrasis studies because he does not simply concern himself with comparison by glossing over the long stated similarity between the verbal and the visual. He pays attention to the complex power struggles and tensions that

---

Friedrich Vollhardt in the "Nachwort" to his edition of *Laokoon* comments: "Lessings verstreute, in sich nicht immer konsistente Äußerungen zum Transitorischen in der Kunst, sind bereits von den Zeitgenossen lebhaft diskutiert worden, vor allem im Blick auf die Bildenden Künste" ("Lessing's dispersed and not always consistent remarks about the transitory in art have already been discussed vividly among his contemporaries, especially regarding the Performing Arts" (*G. E. Lessing. Laokoon oder Über die Grenzen der Malerei und Poesie. Studienausgabe* (Stuttgart: Reclam, 2012), 460. And he adds that the relevance or even the avant-garde "Modernity" of his approach to the beautiful in the context of poetic theory has been long overlooked: "Dabei ist die Modernität seines literarischen Schönheitsbegriffs übersehen worden" (*Laokoon* 460-461). Vollhardt gives Lessing credit in terms of "ein wirkungsästhetisches Kalkül" or a successful calculation for what is successful in terms of a new aesthetics of reception. But what also he seems to overlook is that Lessing not only associates the beautiful with poetic language or the medium of literature. Moreover, he allows for the perception of the transitory in terms of an act of mimetic reproduction through its own original creativity while drawing attention to the characteristic, not only the beautiful.

84 Vollhardt, *Laokoon*, see the chapter "Zum Text" 275-290 and "Erläuterungen" to *Laokoon* and the "Paralipomena" 291-401.

85 The handling of the "Paragone-Problematik" is a central issue in the context of comparing the approach by Lessing with that of Diderot. Both approach the visual and the verbal with an interest in differences rather than the mere equations and similarities between painting and poetry. Hubertus Kohle finds that the "Paragone-Problematik" is actually the "Vergleich zwischen den einzelnen Gattungen" (the comparison between the various genres) (Kohle, *Ut pictura poesis non erit* 7) that is, the visual and verbal disciplines. In his review of the ut pictura poesis theme throughout history, Kohle further associates the "Paragone-Problematik" with a comparative study that encounters difficulties once the various forms of sense-related presentation became a more attentive matter of interest: "Die Künste sind eben deswegen vergleichbar, weil die unterschiedliche Form ihrer sinnlichen Darstellung (*elocutio*) keine wesentliche Rolle spielt. Dies ändert sich grundsätzlich erst im 18. Jahrhundert" (The disciplines of art or "the arts" including poetry are comparable only because each of their different forms of perceptual representation [*elocutio*, that is, the rhetorical level of performance] plays not much of a considerable role. This, however, changes fundamentally only as late as in the 18th century). Kohle, *Ut pictura poesis non erit* (3) finds Lessing at the center of this shift. Next to some art critics in France and England he raised doubt concerning the topos *ut pictura poesis*. Until then, according to the dominant discourse comparing the arts, the painter used to be privileged over the poet until with Lessing new attention was drawn to *elocutio*, rhetoric, and aspects related to sense perception. Kohle asserts that this approach is shared by Diderot and Lessing. They were innovative in raising the status of poetry to painting and also in paying attention more than anyone before had done to the material composition of each artwork. Up until the eighteenth century, inventio was considered the first and most important step in the process of mimesis whereas *elocutio* played a minor role. Now *elocutio* became an issue at the forefront. On the rise of rhetoric and its plurality in the eighteenth century see the essays in Ralf Simon, ed., *Herders Rhetoriken im Kontext des 18. Jahrhunderts* (Heidelberg: Synchron, 2014).

exist between them. However, as I indicated above, Mitchell goes one step further by arguing that Lessing actually condones the push of words to gain dominance over images, a move he claims is typical of the dominant Enlightenment logic.[86] Moreover, Mitchell argues, this constellation of images and texts in the rhetoric of the eighteenth century is a gendered one. He claims:

> Paintings, like women, are ideally silent, beautiful creatures designed for the gratification of the eye, in contrast to the sublime eloquence proper of the manly art of poetry. Paintings are confined to the narrow sphere of external display of their bodies and of the space which they ornament, while poems are free to range over an infinite realm of potential action and expression, the domain of time, discourse, and history.[87]

Mitchell is innovative in gendering the discourse associating images with the female and texts with the male. He critiques Lessing for shifting power to the text and taking it away from the female. This terminology is problematic in the context to Lessing since his work does not repress images for texts. Mitchell may be correct only to the extent that he is noticing Lessing's interest in giving poetry and poetic language a new acknowledgement in the mimesis debate. Lessing indeed adopted some aspects of the work of Edmund Burke which Mitchell lines up with what he calls "The politics of sensibility."[88] Mitchell appears to overlook, however, that images in Lessing's discourse are not only to be associated with deletion or erasure by the verbal. Even the *Laokoon* statue that appears to be still, exhibits intense motion according the way Lessing's concept of "prägnanter Augenblick" contextualizes it as a moment of an action in an artwork. It depicts not Laokoon's death, but the priest attacked by the serpents and in a state of intense pain. The outcome is open to the readers to interpret. According to Mitchell's interpretation texts are conquering images, controlling them and making history. Mitchell points to what he considers to be Lessing's "iconophobia." He suggests: "Perhaps we would be better able to listen if we had some other concept of the image to work besides Lessing's alternatives–the mute, castrated, aesthetic object, or the phallic, loquacious idol."[89] Images are, therefore, in such a notion of Ekphrasis, deleted, territorialized, and invaded by words that replace and silence them. In sum, Mitchell associates images with the female and as being threatened by words. Since Lessing seems to raise the value of the poet in comparison with the painter, in Mitchell's interpretation Lessing favors words over images. He reads *Laokoon* as an ultimately colonialist and masculinist undertaking. This approach has indeed questionable ethical dimensions which will be addressed in my alternative reading of the treatise.[90]

---

86 Mitchell, *Iconology* 114-115.
87 Mitchell, *Iconology* 110.
88 Mitchell, *Iconology* 116.
89 Mitchell, *Iconology* 113.
90 Mitchell, *Iconology* 109-111. In a more recent reference to Lessing, he says: "When Plato warns against the domination of thought by images, semblances, and opinions in the allegory of the cave, he is urging a turn away from pictures that hold humanity captive and toward the pure light of reason. When Lessing warns, in the *Laokoon*, about the tendency to imitate visual effects of visual art in the literary arts, he is trying to combat a pictorial turn that he regards as a degradation of the aesthetic and cultural properties. When Wittgenstein complains that "a picture held us captive" in the *Philosophical Investigations*, he is lamenting the rule of a certain metaphor for mental life that has held philosophy in his

Certainly Lessing contributes vitally to the ongoing discourse on visuality and Ekphrasis, but I think that he remains misunderstood in these terms because what Ekphrasis means is itself contested. Lessing experiments actively with conflict and friction in correlating images with words.[91] He raises philosophical questions about their rhetorical status among other matters. To him the ekphrastic transfer of images into texts comes not without qualification. This becomes obvious in his brilliant description of the Laokoon statue, for Lessing was a skilled practitioner with words, especially metaphor, and he incorporated visual features in his use of language while on the stage his use of *tableaux vivants* employs visuality on yet another level. Lessing became aware of the conflict that exists when images are to be narrated. I cannot agree with Mitchell's claim that Lessing's discourse on Ekphrasis is an attempt to silence images for the sake of words. Whereas it may be an Enlightenment feature to expand one's vocabulary by inventing new words and to gain control over the world by the expansion of language, one may very well question the notion whether images are indeed replaced by words. I shall build on Barbara Stafford's scholarship pointing out that the Enlightenment comes also with a new discovery of image technologies and a new power of imaging devices that promote seeing and imagining. She argues that there are not only "verbalists" among the poets, advocates, and critics of the Enlightenment, but also "imagists." I suggest Lessing was one of them.[92] Images are able to surface in the realm of metaphor selectively and as accounted for in Lessing's poetics. They appear within the verbal and have, as Lessing asserts, their own right to visuality.

## 3. Lessing's differentiated approach to the visual

Describing a visual artwork is, however, as Lessing acknowledges, an undertaking with certain challenges, especially since the observer is part of the image or participates in its construction.[93] But rather than acting as if he were a doorkeeper insisting on the divide between images and texts, Lessing diagnoses important differences depending on the media and disciplines involved and finds that there are multiple levels of language and impact visuality. He explores the rhetoric of visual effects through words, gestures, and movements. He applies some ideas from contemplating the effects of

grip." (*What Do Pictures Want* 348). It is interesting that Mitchell puts Lessing in the same context as Plato and Wittgenstein. The reference to Wittgenstein is to "Ein *Bild* hielt uns gefangen," Ludwig Wittgenstein, *Philosophische Untersuchungen. Philosophical Investigations*, ed. and trans. G.E.M. Anscombe, 2nd ed., rev. (Malden, MA: Blackwell, 1997), 1.115, 48–49.

91 On the complexity of the word "image" see Gottfried Boehm, ed. *Was ist ein Bild?* (Munich: Fink, 4th ed. 2004, first 1994) and "Jenseits der Sprache? Anmerkungen zur Logik der Bilder," Christa Maar and Hubert Burda, ed., *Iconic Turn. Die neue Macht der Bilder*, 2nd ed. (Cologne: DuMont, 2004), 28–43 and Gottfried Boehm, *Wie Bilder Sinn erzeugen. Die Macht des Zeigens* (Berlin: Berlin University Press, 2007). Also see on the iconic turn and the power of the image especially Mitchell, *Picture Theory.*

92 Stafford, *Body Criticism* 472.

93 Wolfgang Kemp, ed. *Der Betrachter ist im Bild. Kunstwissenschaft und Rezeptionsästhetik* (Berlin: Dietrich Reimer Verlag, expanded revised edition 1992).

artworks, sculptures and paintings.[94] Lessing highlights the difference between the verbal and the visual. He also establishes a realm of metaphorical visuality which will be explored further.[95] Whereas in the time leading up to Lessing, the relationship between painting and poetry was usually conceptualized in terms of their being "sister arts," or through comparisons of one another that emphasized primarily their similarities, Lessing drew new and relevant attention to distinctions. He pointed out that they are, according to their distinct media and their use of signs diverse. They should be regarded as separate because of these important differences. He argued that whereas paintings use bodies or figures in space as their signs, texts use words in time, thus being restricted to so-called "willkürliche Zeichen"(arbitrary signs) which barely resemble what they express. They are, Lessing asserts, participating in temporality and it is the specific ability of poetic language that it may be able to turn "artificial" into quasi "natural signs." The visual media, painting and sculpture by contrast must select the most poignant or "pregnant moment" of an action and ignore or bracket time completely. It is best when it can concentrate on only one single instant, framed or frozen in time. Sculptors or painters can attempt highlighting visually most effectively depending on whatever their subject matter may be and to what extent they can rely on their spectators. Poets can oscillate between borrowing signs form painting and music, hovering between the dimensions of space and time. The poet according to Lessing must also choose timing very carefully. In order to have the signs of poesy more visual, the narrative must be restricted to a minimum. However, signs may be concurrent or layered into multiple time-frames or metaphoric layers of meaning, just like the tones in music, for dissonant or for harmonious effects.

Lessing is a critic of the dominant Enlightenment discourse but contributes to it as well through his outspoken acknowledgement of productive imagination.[96] He proposes that words are contextually or environmentally defined by their specific use and argues that it is the distinctive feature of metaphors compared to other words, such as lexically defined termini in discursive language, to be are able to express something qualitatively new. Metaphors (before they turn into customary expressions or fossilized catachresis) are words that are not only mimetic but can expand one's horizon, stimulate new images, insights, and thoughts.[97] Metaphors are therefore not

---

94 See further Beate Allert, "Grenzen der Anschaulichkeit," Zeuch, ed., *Lessings Grenzen* 65-80.

95 Note that Brad Prager, *Aesthetic Vision and German Romanticism: Writing Images* (Rochester, NY: Camden House, 2007), also begins his first chapter with Lessing, arguing that Lessing's writings are "important precursors to Romantic thought, especially his 1766 essay on the subject of the *Laocoön*, which served as a foundational moment in the Romantic discourse on the perception of art" (17).

96 See John Bender and David E. Wellbery, "Rhetoricality: On the Modernist Return of Rhetoric," John Bender and David E. Wellbery, ed., *Ends of Rhetoric: History, Theory, Praxis* (Stanford: Stanford University Press, 1990), 3-19 at 19.

97 For numerous useful approaches to metaphor see the essays in Andrew Ortony, ed., *Metaphor and Thought,* 2nd ed. (Cambridge: Cambridge University Press, 1993). See also my own studies on Lessing and his use of metaphor such as "Pluralisierung der Ringe oder Ringverlust? Lessings Beitrag zur Metaphorisierung und/oder Politisierung der Sprache," Wolfram Mauser and Günter Saße, ed., *Streitschriften–Strategien des Überzeugens im Werk Lessings* (Tübingen: Niemeyer, 1993), 113-120 and "Wie farbig darf die Dichtung

only a matter of *logos* but also of *mythos,* concerning not only language, but also images from the beginning of the cognition process.[98] Lessing is undoubtedly one of the most path-breaking and provocative theorists on Ekphrasis and he experiments with the process of verbalizing something visual in language and with articulating the transfer of images into texts. In most experiments, he favors drama over prose and finds that it is best onstage to experiment with the presentation of brilliant moments or unpredictable images since in the theater multiple sense perceptions interact with the spoken words. What appears to be presented may look as if it were consisting of "natürliche Zeichen" (natural signs) and elements of nature when in fact these signs are elements of art. The most effective artwork uses its "arbitrary signs" to be recognized minimally and may well be at its best when its messages come across as if "natural" and through understatement. The suggestive power of art implicates, as Lessing is fully aware of, its own cognitive processes and these must be activated by the recipients. Lessing experiments in his works with sense perceptions, Ekphrasis, and metaphoric visuality. [99]

Lessing promotes a style consisting of understatement, of phrases that may express the point of any narrative of plot just by hinting at it, by the use of metaphor, or though contiguities only metonymically. His work has the subtle effect of producing images, or ironically their opposite, saying things by means of a minimum of words, ellipses, gaps, and by sparking the reader's, listener's, or spectator's construction of meaning according to the dictum: "Je mehr wir sehen desto mehr müssen wir uns

sein? Lessings Beitrag zum Farbendiskurs im 18. Jahrhundert," *Lessing Yearbook* 37 (2008): 139-149.

98 On cognition as conceptualized by Johann Gottfried Herder and others see the essays in: Allert, ed., *J. G. Herder.*

99 Lessing draws from a theory of sense perceptions that comes close to Herder's notion of a *fundus animae* but, as Ralf Simon explains, Lessing does not use the concept of *Aisthesis,* that is "the perceived," as a foundation for his approach although he comes very close to it: "Herder hat in seinem dem Lessing'schen *Laokoon* gewidmeten *Ersten Kritischen Wäldchen* die mangelnde Theorie der Sinnlichkeit eingeklagt, also in der Sache moniert, daß Lessings Semiotik keiner Theorie der *Aisthesis* aufruht (im Gegensatz zu den semiotischen Überlegungen Baumgartens und anderer). Rein exegetisch hätte für Lessing eine Fundierung der Semiose im dunklen Grund (*fundus animae*) durchaus nahegelegen" (Herder in his *First Critical Forest,* a work devoted among other things to a review of Lessing's *Laokoon,* complained that there seems to be a theory of the senses lacking; also taking exception to the fact that Lessing's semiotics calls up no theory of aisthesis in opposition to the semiotic deliberations by Baumgarten and others. He writes: Purely exegetically for Lessing a foundation of semiosis to be drawn from the dark ground [fundus animae] would certainly have been a closely connected thought" (Simon, *Die Idee der Prosa* 74, note 138). Baumgarten in his *Metaphysica* (1st ed., 1739), § 511 states: "Sunt in anima perceptiones obscurae ... Harum complexus FUNDUS ANIMAE dicitur" (There are in the soul obscure [*dunklen*] notions ... the totality of which notions is called THE FOUNDATION OF THE SOUL) (Baumgarten, *Ästhetik.* 2: 1072). Whereas Herder bases all the sense perceptions on a *synesthesia* that links the various senses to begin with the *fundus animae,* Lessing differentiates the various senses, tries to keep them apart, and develops a complicated approach to Ekphrasis that interprets the transfer from one sense perception to another and the shift from images to words as problematic, even at times paradoxical. This has, however, a cultural critical dimension challenging the mainstream Enlightenment discourse.

dazu denken können" ("The more we see the more we must be able to imagine").[100] Lessing claims that the most effective and emotionally stimulating language is "anschaulich" or "visual" but the question how to modify the textual for the sake of brighter visuality has ever since proven to be something of an enigma.[101] He keeps all of us concerned with the ekphrastic problem of how to describe an action or scene most effectively and how to find the best or the most poignant moment of any visual representation in an artwork, be it a sculpture, an image, or a text.

How can visual imagination be promoted? When to cut an image? How to describe something for the most effective imagination? Does it have the strongest impact when it is most detailed or when it is abstract? Lessing seems to opt for brevity and he argues that images remain most vivid if they leave room for thought. This is I think an issue of relevant urgency, especially in our own age of visual culture, or the era of extreme spectacles in which the media, photography, and image making which then lead to protest. It may seem paradoxical that a minimalist narrative style goes in tandem with the most visually effective. At least this is what Lessing claimed. He also indicated that not everything that can be shown can be told and vice versa. Verbal expression historically (both phylogenetically and ontologically speaking) tends to replace gestures and mere sounds with articulated and culturally more advanced "language" consisting of words or "Zeichen" (signs), not only of "Figuren [...] in dem Raume" (bodies in space).[102] It is hence more abstract, the more cultivated it gets. Can the verbal absorb the visual into its own medium via Ekphrasis, or do images get replaced and ultimately erased by words? Lessing seems to have some interesting suggestions.

---

100 Lessing, FA 5/2, 32; *Laocoön*, trans. McCormick 19. See also Ernesto Grassi, *Die Macht der Phantasie: Zur Geschichte abendländischen Denkens* (Königstein im Taunus: Athenäum, 1979), 260–264.

101 Prager, *Aesthetic Vision* argues that "a philosophical turn" took place with Early Romantic thinkers such as Novalis (Friedrich Leopold, Freiherr von Hardenberg), Friedrich Schlegel, Johann Gottlieb Fichte, followed by Ludwig Tieck, Joseph, Freiherr von Eichendorff, and E. T. A. Hoffmann: "Hoffmann's *Der Sandmann* (*The Sandman*, 1817) has become a standard work of visual studies" (2). Prager sets out to "demonstrate, prior constructions of the apperception of the visual arts had mainly underscored their materiality, as was the case with Lessing's *Laocoön*, which the present work treats to some length as a negative example in order to better understand that which falls apart and beneath the weight of Romantic scrutiny. The Romantics insisted that the apprehension of the material works of art (such as paintings and sculpture) were comparable to the perception of the poetic imagery, since all such apprehension is a function of the imagination and takes place therein" (2). He adds: "They thereby sublate any differences between the exterior, material world and the space of imagination" (2). I shall argue that already according to Lessing in *Laokoon*, imagination is positioned at the core of all understanding of painting and poetry.

102 Lessing, *Laokoon* FA 5/2, 116.

## 4. Consequences for Lessing's visual writing

Lessing's concept of "visual language" is not an antidote to "verbal language." Lessing does not stand for the erasure of images by words; he is not logocentric or as Mitchell would argue, an "iconoclast."[103] Mitchell further claims: "The classic expression of ekphrastic fear occurs in Lessing's Laocoön."[104] In my reading Lessing is neither afraid of images nor of emotions. He believes, in contrast to the Platonian tradition and more in line with that of Aristotle, that the emotions have to be expressed in order for catharsis to take place. He had to deal with censorship in his life and be careful what to write. His approach to language is, despite the early verdict that Lessing was an "unpoetischer Dichter" (unpoetic poet), a playwright and author across the genres who uses images and metaphors very selectively.[105] His contributions to Ekphrasis studies make us reflect on the process of visualizing and the application of certain poetic devices. His goals were that images should be maintained, stimulated, and projected via poetic genres of which he not only favored the fable and the succinct narrative, but moreover the drama with its multi-media aspects and open-ended dialogues. He ultimately also favored the parable. Lessing's efforts not only contribute to iconology and art theory but to intricate philosophical questions concerning picture theory and adequate modes of representation:

> Lessing's originality was his systematic treatment of the space-time question, his reduction of the generic boundaries of the arts to this fundamental difference. If Newton reduced the physical, objective universe, and Kant the metaphysical, subjective universe to the categories of space and time, Lessing performed the same service for the immediate world of signs and artistic media.[106]

On this aspect of Mitchell's account of Lessing's contribution to the space-time question and considering his innovative iconology from that angle, I agree. Whereas the temporal and the narrative have most often been dealt with regardless of their structural reciprocity, Lessing makes very interesting remarks about the temporal complexity of the narrative matrix, a notion which is also at the core of Paul Ricœur's theory on the narrative and to which I shall return more closely in the context of my close reading of Lessing's *Laokoon.*[107] Since I have addressed these issues elsewhere, suffice it here to mention that Lessing can well be counted instead among the so-called "imagists" as described by Barbara Stafford in juxtaposition to the "verbalists."[108] They are drawing from a pro-active approach to metaphor and a notion of images located in the

103 Mitchell, *Iconology* 115.
104 Mitchell, *Picture Theory* 154.
105 Horst Steinmetz, ed., *Lessing–ein unpoetischer Dichter. Dokumente aus drei Jahrhunderten zur Wirkungsgeschichte Lessings in Deutschland* (Frankfurt am Main: Athenäum, 1969).
106 Mitchell, *Iconology,* 96. See my response in: "Horaz–Lessing–Mitchell."
107 See Paul Ricoeur, "Narrative Time," W.J.T. Mitchell, ed., *On Narrative* (Chicago: University of Chicago Press, 1980), 165-186, esp. 167.
108 Stafford, *Body Criticism* 472. Note though, for Stafford: "Lessing's limiting and divisive strictures concerning the necessary separation of spatial and temporal activities are finally undone" (475).

"Grundbestände" (foundational elements) of words as Hans Blumenberg claimed,[109] thus insisting on the primacy of metaphor in rejection of that notion according to which they were considered only secondary similes (Quintilian).[110] Lessing's approach to metaphor builds on an Aristotelian approach according to which images precede words and remain dormant in the realm of metaphor.[111] The images get "verbalized" in text and can have an even stronger impact on the recipient than any painting could. Lessing locates visuality directly within the textuality of verbalness. He seems to assume that it is possible to transpose images into texts and that it is a feature of metaphor to be able to produce new non-mimetic images via language that is poetic. It is important to emphasize that Lessing belongs among those theorists who advocate the importance of metaphors in language, and who are intent on reviving their importance, treating metaphors not merely as dormant images, but potentially as elements decisive for creative thought. In this sense Lessing's contributions anticipate certain ideas that were much later actualized by Ludwig Wittgenstein.[112] Textual images or

109 Hans Blumenberg, *Paradigmen zu einer Metaphorologie* (Frankfurt am Main: Suhrkamp, 1998), 10. First published as: "Paradigmen zu einer Metaphorologie," *Archiv für Begriffsgeschichte* 6 (1960): 7-142 and Bonn: Bouvier, 1960. See also *Paradigms for a Metaphorology*, trans. Robert Savage (Ithaca: Cornell University Press, 2010), 3.

110 On the traditional substitution model of metaphor, see Aristotle: "A metaphor is the application of a word that belongs to another thing: either from genus to species, species to genus, species to species, or by analogy." *Poetics*, ed. and trans. Stephen Halliwell, Aristotle *Poetics*, Longinus *On the Sublime*, Demetrius *On Style*, trans. Stephen Halliwell et al., corr. ed., Loeb Classical Library 199 (Cambridge: Harvard University Press, 1999), (21)1457b, 104-105. According to Quintilian: "In totem autem metaphor brevium est similtudo, eoque distat quod illa comparatur rei quam volumus exprimere, haec pro ipsa re dicitur" (In general terms, Metaphor is a shortened form of Simile; the difference is that in Simile something is compared with the thing we wish to describe, while in Metaphor one thing is *substituted* for another). See Quintilian, *The Orator's Education* [*Institutio Oratoria*], ed. and trans. Donald A. Russell, 5 vols., Loeb Classical Library 124-127, 494 (Cambridge: Harvard University Press, 2001), 8.6.8, vol. 3, 428-429 and the discussion in Mark Johnson, "Introduction: Metaphor in the Philosophical Tradition," Mark Johnson, ed., *Philosophical Perspectives on Metaphor* (Minneapolis: University of Minnesota Press, 1981), 3-47. However, Aristotle also viewed metaphor has having creative potential ("it is metaphor, therefore, that above all produces this effect [makes us learn something]." *The "Art" of Rhetoric*, trans. John Henry Freese, Loeb Classical Library 193 (1926, Cambridge: Harvard University Press, 2006), III.x.2, 396-397. On the failure of Western philosophy (and metaphor theory) to capitalize on and to make important use of this insight, see George Lakoff and Mark Johnson, *Metaphors We Live By* (Chicago: University of Chicago Press, 1980), 190-191.

111 In *The "Art" of Rhetoric* III.x.6, 398-399, Aristotle declares that urbane speech results from the use of metaphor which "sets things 'before the eyes'" (*pro ommatōn poiei*), a process he also relates to *energeia*, the process of making actual. In III.xi.2, he explains "before the eyes" as follows: "I mean that things are set before the eyes by words that signify actuality. For instance, to say that a good man is 'four-square' is a metaphor, for both of these are complete, but the phrase does not express actuality (*energeia*), whereas "of one having the prime of his life in full bloom' does" (404-405). Note that *energeia* becomes a key term in the understanding of Ekphrasis. See Mario Klarer, *Ekphrasis: Bildbeschreibung als Repräsentationstheorie bei Spenser, Sidney, Lyly und Shakespeare*, Buchreihe der Anglia 35 (Tübingen: Niemeyer, 2001), "Der Begriff Ekphrasis," 2-8.

112 See Beate Allert, "Wie farbig darf die Dichtung sein?"

their fragments are often implicit in metaphors and metonymies that highlight *pars pro toto ("part for the whole")* relations.[113] Metaphors can also be regarded, according to Blumenberg, as "Restbestände" (leftover elements, residues) of a visual potential that may not have been realized fully in the realm of discursive language, yet which are actually valuable seeds for poetry, the composition of metaphor, and for theoretically innovative thought.[114]

Since all imagination depends in this regard on various aspects of the visual, it is thanks to those features of visuality within the realm of the verbal that language maintains its vitality and brilliance. But over time these metaphoric images are subject to an ongoing process of flattening. Jean Paul Friedrich Richter claims in his *Vorschule der Ästhetik* (2nd ed. 1813): "Wie im Schreiben Bilderschrift früher war als Buchstabenschrift, so war im Sprechen die Metapher, insofern sie Verhältnisse und nicht Gegenstände bezeichnet, das frühere Wort, welches sich erst allmählich zum eigentlichen Ausdruck entfärben mußte" (As hieroglyphs preceded letters in the process of writing, in speech the metaphors, in so far as they signify relationships and not objects, were the earlier words which slowly had to fade into denotive expression).[115] Whereas this historical process from "Bilderschrift" (the writing of images) to "Buchstabenschrift" (the writing of discursive language), or from metaphor (sense related "Ausdruck") to "Buchstaben (letters) or "Begriffe" (terminologies), cannot be avoided in the process of civilization, Jean Paul proposed, with inspiration from Lessing that it is the task of the poets to bring new life to language through innovative use of metaphor against the flux of time.[116] Since "jede Sprache [ist] in Rücksicht geistiger Beziehungen ein Wörterbuch erblasseter Metaphern" (every language [is] regarding the relationships of the minds or spirits a dictionary of faded metaphors).[117] It is the task of the poets to invigorate these by using metaphors in new constellations (neither fixed terminologies, nor pale catachreses). If they can spark the recipients' imagination metaphors can energize and rejuvenate a culture at any stage. They offer new ideas via poetry and art that then is prone to have an impact on better communication in a pluralistic society.

Visuality in the realm of the poetic verbal differs, according to Lessing, from the merely picturesque, a style which became prominent in the eighteenth century among his contemporaries, mainly in France but which Lessing challenged together with his French colleague Denis Diderot.[118] Both were critical of the so-called ***Anakreontik*** and of a style Lessing critically associated with "Schilderungssucht" (a mania to describe

113 See [Cicero] *Rhetorica ad Herennium*, ed. and trans. Harry Caplan, Loeb Classical Library 403 (Cambridge: Harvard University Press, 1954), IV.33.44-45, 340-341, describing *Intellectio* ("Synecdoche"); Quintilian, *Orator's Education*, 8.6.19-22, 3: 434-437 ("Synechdoche").

114 Blumenberg, *Paradigmen* 10; Savage, *Paradigms* 3.

115 Jean Paul (Johann Paul Friedrich Richter), *Vorschule der Ästhetik*, ed. Norbert Miller, intro. Wolfhart Henckmann, Philosophische Bibliothek 425 (Hamburg: Meiner, 1990), Course IX, § 50, 184; *Horn of Oberon: Jean Paul Richter's School for Aesthetics*, trans. Margaret R. Hale (Detroit: Wayne State University Press, 1973), 131.

116 Among the many references to Lessing in the *Vorschule*, see Course XIV § 79: Jean Paul, *Vorschule* 283, 288; *Horn of Oberon* 205, 209.

117 Jean Paul, *Vorschule* IX § 50, 184; *Horn of Oberon* 131.

118 On shared efforts between Diderot and Lessing, see for example Peter Szondi, "Tableau und coup de théatre. Zur Sozialpsychologie des bürgerlichen Trauerspiels bei Diderot.

everything) but also with "Allegoristerei," the excessive use of allegories, so that meanings can only be derived from external sources or other previous texts.[119] Lessing distances his own poetic approach clearly from such wordiness and superabundant surplus language that was also associated most often with the discourse of "Empfindsamkeit" (sentimentality). The Swiss writers Johann Jakob Bodmer and Johann Jakob Breitinger challenged any simplistic notion of *ars imitatur naturam* (art imitates nature) for the sake of a process-oriented progressive and open-ended notion of art. They were reflecting on *natura naturans* (that is nature in the process of growth), rather than *natura naturata* (that is nature as if it were completed).[120] Lessing picked up on this idea and further searched not only for "natural signs" in nature but for quasi-natural signs in art while borrowing features that are themselves elements of growth. They can, he argued, imply new possibilities of expression. Nature in art was not to be considered as given, or as a matter of fact, but rather in terms of a creative dialogic process. Since nature is viewed as growing with seasons in time and it has apparently "signs" in motion that call for open-ended productivity, Lessing argued for a notion of verbal visuality that is less wordy yet marked by succinctness, brevity, and effective minimalism. One could claim that according to the proverb: "In der Kürze liegt die Würze" (brevity is the spice of wit), Lessing found that brevity is a key ingredient of successful writing, its spice so to speak. He called for an aesthetic of minimalism and rhetoric of openness. Moreover, Lessing does not want to give up sense perception altogether for the sake of effective communication or abandon images for words. Despite his plea for brevity and poignancy, Lessing also insists that poetic verbal images can be just as bright and powerful as "Gemälde," real paintings. He suggests a visual rhetoric that is most effective via appropriate cuttings and a frugal selection of words and he argues that artworks and poetic texts should not exceed the "prägnanter Moment" in describing an action. The image should be cut off precisely before the climax of the action described; it should resemble "a still" or a film image that is metaphorically speaking framed by or focused upon the flow of the narrative or the description. It can best be provided with the most extensive potential meanings when being used in the most condensed and most thought provoking way possible. "Ekphrasis" has been succinctly defined by Murray Krieger as an attempt "to imitate in words an object of the plastic arts".[121] He was soon eager to amend his statements by adding that this

---

Mit einem Exkurs über Lessing," *Schriften*, vol. 2 (Frankfurt am Main: Suhrkamp, 1978), 205-232.

119 "Ja, diese Aftercritik in der Poesie hat zum Teil die Virtuosen selbst verführet. Sie hat in der Poesie die Schilderungssucht, und in der Malerei die Allegoristerei erzeuget" (*Laokoon*, FA 5/2, 15): ("Indeed, this spurious criticism has to some degree misled even the masters of the arts. In poetry it has engendered a mania for description and in painting a mania for allegory") (*Laocoön*, trans. McCormick 5).

120 Gottfried Willems, *Anschaulichkeit: Zu Theorie und Geschichte der Wort-Bild-Beziehungen und des literarischen Darstellungsstils*, Studien zur deutschen Literatur 103 (Tübingen: Niemeyer, 1989), esp. Chapter 7, 272-333.

121 Murray Krieger, *Ekphrasis: The Illusion of the Natural Sign* 6. James A.W. Heffernan, *Museum of Words. The Poetics of Ekphrasis from Homer to Ashbery* (Chicago: University of Chicago Press, 1993) defines *Ekphrasis* as "the verbal representation of visual representation" 3. Webb opts for: "the ability of words to spark an image in the mind" (*Ekphrasis*, 27) and Fritz Graf, "Ekphrasis: Die Entstehung der Gattung in der Antike," Gottfried Boehm

"attempt" had then to be questioned for a lack of precision. Krieger finds that the notion of "the picture-making capacity of words" has often been challenged for good reasons and he asserts that what words or metaphors create are not at all "images" in a literal sense.[122] One must not forget that textual "images" are of a different order than material paintings or sculptures, as Lessing observed.[123] The discourse on Ekphrasis has its roots in Antiquity, most often based on a consideration Homer's description of the shield of Achilles or Virgil's description of the shield of Aeneas.[124] We could ask Krieger and Lessing both: Are images to become words or words to become images and how? Will such a transfer be smooth and complete, or come with friction and complications rather? For Krieger:

> Das Problem der Ekphrasis kreist um die bildschöpferische Fähigkeit von Wörtern in Gedichten, wenn wir auch sofort einräumen müssen, daß diese Fähigkeit von der offensichtlichen Tatsache in Frage gestellt wird, daß Wörter zwar vieles andere, aber–glücklicherweise–keine Bilder sind und daß sie keine 'Fähigkeit' in irgendeinem buchstäblichen Sinn besitzen.[125]
>
> [The problematic that is Ekphrasis surrounds the picture-making capacity of words in poems, except that at once we must concede that this capacity is challenged by the obvious

---

and Helmut Pfotenhauer, ed., *Beschreibungskunst–Kunstbeschreibung: Ekphrasis von der Antike bis zur Gegenwart* (Munich: Fink, 1995), 143-155 at 143 proposes: "Ekphrasis ist mithin 'ein völlig und restlos deutlich Machen'" (Ekphrasis is among other things 'a complete, transparent creation without anything left over'), an ideal that is much more ambitious than the notion of description found in antiquity where it indicates rather a process of textualizing images, or any act of presenting quasi-visual sense impressions via narratives or verbal descriptions.

122 Krieger *Ekphrasis* 1-2. A revised version of the first chapter of *Ekphrasis* (1-28) appeared under the title: "Das Problem der Ekphrasis: Wort und Bild, Raum und Zeit–und das literarische Werk" (trans. Andrea Antor), Boehm and Pfotenhauer, ed., *Beschreibungskunst–Kunstbeschreibung*, 41-57, the English version appearing as: "The Problem of Ekphrasis: Image and Words, Space and Time–and the Literary Work," Valerie Robillard and Els Jongeneel, ed., *Pictures into Words: Theoretical and Descriptive Approaches to Ekphrasis* (Amsterdam: VU University Press, 1998), 3-20. "Wie können Wörter die Funktion des 'natürlichen Zeichens' zu erfüllen versuchen (d. h. des Zeichens, das als virtueller Ersatz für das Bezeichnete genommen werden kann), wenn Wörter offensichtlich nur arbiträre Zeichen sind, wenngleich arbiträr im Rahmen einer Konvention und oft auch eines sprachlichen Systems?" (41) "How can words try to do the job of the 'natural sign' (that is, a sign that can be taken as a visual substitute for its referent), when words are, obviously only arbitrary though conventionally arbitrary and often systematically arbitrary–signs?" (3).

123 In *Laokoon* Lessing emphasizes "daß die Malerei zu ihren Nachahmungen ganz andere Mittel, oder Zeichen gebrauchet, als die Poesie" (FA 5/2, 116): ("that in its imitations painting uses completely different means or signs than does poetry") (*Laocoön*, trans. McCormick 78).

124 See Andrew Sprague Becker, *The Shield of Achilles and the Poetics of Ekphrasis* (Lanham, MD: Rowman and Littlefield, 1995); Webb, *Ekphrasis*; Heinz Drügh, *Ästhetik der Beschreibung. Poetische und kulturelle Energie deskriptiver Texte (1700-2000)*, KULI Studien und Texte zur Kulturgeschichte der deutschsprachigen Literatur 5 (Tübingen: Francke, 2006), in particular section II: "Ekphrasis–Die Beschreibung zwischen Klassizismus und Antiklassizismus," 135-223.

125 "Das Problem der Ekphrasis" 41.

> fact that words are many other things but are not–and happily are not–pictures, and do not in any literal way, have 'capacity'.][126]

He sets out to establish what he calls the "ekphrastische Prinzip" (ekphastic principle) which he defines "in seiner engsten Bedeutung [...] zu Bezugnahme auf die versuchte verbale Nachahmung eines Objekts aus dem Bereich der bildenden Kunst, in erster Linie der Malerei und die Bildhauerei"[127] (most narrowly and closely [...] to refer to the attempted imitation in words of an object of the plastic arts, primarily painting and sculpture).[128] At the same time Ekphrasis challenges the ability of words to create images in their strictest form. Since poets are often concerned with the effort to make absent things present, the ekphrastic drive in the poet has to deal with the adverse impulse to be able to come to terms with the conflicting or different emotions: There is, according to Krieger, the poets' desire to liberate the static image (something Lessing considers to be integral to the visual arts) and this desire forces the artist to concentrate complete actions into one single "prägnanter Augenblick." And there is also the common frustration that despite the arbitrary character of the signs of language (words), there is a problem with achieving a complete illusion verbally, something which is much better handled in the realm of visual art. There seems to be an unavoidable temporality reminding us of something past or future, making us conscious of the arbitrariness of language and the tendency of words to act as polyvalent and open-ended signs which leads to the unavoidable clash between signs and the signified in the verbal realm. Nonetheless Lessing seems to claim equivalence between the external visual images in the material realm of the visual arts and the mental constructs and the image-like productions of poetic language.

Abbé DuBos had already addressed the capacity of language to evoke "visual images" by appealing to a mediation of "signs" and it was then Lessing's primary achievement to mark the media and discipline-specific differences between the visual and the verbal sign systems and to give new attributes to "Poesie" (poesy), no longer merely similar to "Malerei" (painting) but with a range of distinct attributes.[129] Lessing has often been misunderstood for allegedly advancing the verbal over the visual, as if he were ultimately to erase images by words, when in fact Lessing suggests that images can be transformed by means of Ekphrasis into poetic writing, "Poesie" or "Dichtung," which then must be "visual" or packed with "poetic images" in their own right. He argues for example that in the visual arts otherworldly or spiritual creatures are "personifizierte Abstracta" (personified abstractions) but in poetry they are "wirkliche handelnde Wesen, die über ihren allgemeinen Charakter noch andere Eigenschaften und Affecte haben, welche nach Gelegenheit der Umstände vor jenen vorstechen können" ("real, acting beings who, in addition to their general character, possess other qualities and feelings which, as circumstances demand, may stand out more prominently than the former").[130] In other words, continuity of the action can

126 "The Problem of Ekphrasis" 3.
127 "Das Problem der Ekphrasis" 42.
128 "The Problem of Ekphrasis" 4.
129 Frederick Burwick, "Lessing's *Laokoon* and the Rise of Visual Hermeneutics," *Poetics Today* 20.2 (Summer 1999): 219-272 at 222.
130 FA 5/2, 81; *Laocoön,* trans. McCormick 52.

pose a challenge and the more detailed a description the harder it may be to maintain its unique visualization.[131] Lessing is aware of complications he is then trying to probe onstage in the context of his dramatic works. The kind of visuality Lessing is calling for is not clear or colorless or without any taste, as if it were pure water as implicit in the notion of "Unbezeichnung," a term which was introduced by Lessing's contemporary Johann Joachim Winckelmann in his theoretical section on beauty ("Von dem Wesentlichen der Kunst") in *Geschichte der Kunst des Altertums* (1764).[132]

> Aus der Einheit folgt eine andere Eigenschaft der hohen Schönheit, die Unbezeichnung derselben, das ist, deren Form weder durch Punckte, noch durch Linien beschrieben werden, als die allein die Schönheit bilden [...] Nach diesem Begriff soll die Schönheit sein wie das vollkommenste Wasser aus dem Schoße der Quelle geschöpft, welches, je weniger Geschmack es hat, desto gesünder geachtet wird, weil es von allen fremden Teilen geläutert ist.[133]

> [From the unity follows another quality of high beauty, the non-descriptiveness of the same, that is, its form becomes delineated neither through points, nor through lines, as they by themselves create beauty [...] According to this idea, beauty should be like the purest possible water dipped from the depths of the spring which the less taste it has, all the healthier it is regarded as being, since it is purified of all outside particulars].[134]

Lessing engages with this text in *Laokoon* and although he contradicts Winckelmann's notion of mimesis by pointing out it is not the stoicism that causes the mouth of the suffering father in the Laokoon statue not to be wide open but instead, he argues, this is a matter of the medium itself requiring such restraint upon one "prägnanter Augenblick." He nevertheless adopts Winckelmann's idea that an artwork should draw its beauty by means of immanent features of the artwork, not by reference to any external sources, other artworks, or allegorical meanings. For Lessing, and later also to Goethe and others following this paradigm, it is not necessary to know everything that precedes or exceeds the action or the idea as presented or evoked in each present work. Lessing mentions yet another rhetorical aspect of restriction, something which I call "understatement," a concept that differs from the notion of "Unbezeichnung"

131 One should mention, however, that Lessing insists also in *Laokoon* in contrasting the poet with the painter: "Nichts nötiget hiernächst den Dichter sein Gemälde in einen einzigen Augenblick zu concentrieren. Er nimmt jede seiner Handlungen, wenn er will, bei ihrem Ursprunge auf, und führet sie durch alle mögliche Abänderungen bis zu ihrer Endschaft. Jede dieser Änderungen, die dem Künstler ein ganz besonderes Stück kosten würde, kostet ihm einen einzigen Zug" (FA 5/2, 35-36): ("Moreover, there is nothing to compel the poet to compress his picture into a single moment. He may, if he so chooses, take up each action at its origin and pursue it through all possible variations to its end. Each variation which would cost the artist a separate work costs the poet but a single pen stroke") (*Laocoön*, trans. McCormick 23-34).

132 Johann Joachim Winckelmann, *Geschichte der Kunst des Altertums* (Darmstadt: Wissenschaftliche Buchgesellschaft, 1993), 139-188.

133 Winckelmann, *Geschichte der Kunst* 150.

134 See also with a slightly different translation, Simon Richter, *Laocoon's Body and the Aesthetics of Pain: Winckelmann, Lessing, Herder, Moritz, Goethe* (Detroit: Wayne State University Press, 1992), 30-31, 56, and the discussion of "Unbezeichnung" 56-57.

(non-designation) in both Winckelmann's and Richter's readings of the term.[135] The notion of "understatement" which seems more in harmony with Lessing's thought does not necessarily mean a lack of color, an erasure of visual features for the sake of a higher "beauty," the projection of an orderly and complete universe, or simply "cutting"; it is in fact associated with several rhetorical and medium-specific strategies that are meant to emancipate the reader and spectator. Such strategies rely on certain aesthetic premises that have ethical implications, above all the promoting of sympathy and "Leidenschaften" (compassion), especially for those who, just like Laokoon, are in pain.

David Wellbery's reading of *Laokoon* explains the aesthetics of the Enlightenment in the context of its sign systems. He shows how Lessing overcomes a simplistic notion of so-called "natural signs" for the sake of linking rational reasoning with and intuitive cognition and via addressing the previously ignored deficiencies of abstract reasoning.[136] The core of Lessing's *Laokoon* is an examination of the complex of issues surrounding Ekphrasis and he experiments with what might be the most efficient and suitable approaches to visuality in the verbal. He develops his approach to "understatement" not only theoretically by saying one should avoid all "too wordy" descriptiveness or pictorialism styles in language for the sake of brevity, succinctness, and for the *prägnanter Moment.* He also shows what happens when some characters onstage say too much and when the action is such that a report simply cannot catch up with it. Lessing explains that an artist should leave things before the climax of an action to be presented but, as we shall see in his drama *Miß Sara Sampson* the action tends to go overboard. We are confronted with a character dying onstage. She is even commenting her own, slowly proceeding agony until death. It is embarrassing to watch and to be witnessing these fatal consequences of a heinous crime without apparently being able to do anything about it. Lessing lets women and underrepresented members of the society speak and what we see is not without the plea trying to win his audiences by engaging them in a number of ways as will be discussed.

Lessing thought of the realm of poetry and poetic writings as an unrestricted space for imagination which should not be limited to any sculptor or any painter.

135 Although I find Simon Richter's discussion of "Unbezeichnung" daring and stimulating, I do not agree with his conclusions completely. He associates Winckelmann's use of the term not only with the purity or immanence of an artwork but also in a gendered discourse with a negative association of femininity such as "castration." He also associates such "Unbezeichnung" or lack of designation in Lessing's context with such terms as "euphemism," a denial of death, and a removal of the "object from the order of time" (*Laocoon's Body* 57). I do not agree with these ramifications of Lessing's minimalism and with Richter's aligning Lessing with a Platonian model that, as he argues, rejects the body completely for the sake of the mind over and against all corporeality of images. Instead I find that Lessing had already in anticipation of Goethe in his approach to the *Laokoon* debate explicitly addressed the dimension of temporality while dealing with the spatial arts and in turning an interest to musical images in his *Paralipomena*. The antinomies or dualisms between painting and poetry in Richter's reading of Lessing (74–75) deserve not to be taken out of context and should be challenged in terms of Lessing's own critical and rather sophisticated discourse.

136 David E. Wellbery, *Lessing's Laocoön: Semiotics and Aesthetics in the Age of Reason* (Cambridge: Cambridge University Press, 1984), 191–227.

Whereas they have to contend only with the dimension of space and to focus on only one single poignant moment to be depicted in their visual artwork, the poets have more freedom but must also be careful not to ignore the boundaries of their own medium oscillating between the visual signs (bodies) and the acoustic ones (sounds). Lessing asserts that there is an important media difference between the visual and the verbal arts ("Malerei und Dichtung") to be taken into account, yet his comments on this issue cannot be understood simply as if he were only a doorkeeper, trying to separate the two. In his *Laokoon* Lessing is trying to find the most efficient and suitable approach to visuality and he is trying to go beyond the notion of "Nachahmung" (imitation) when he writes: "Es sey Fabel oder Geschichte, daß die Liebe den ersten Versuch in den bildenden Künsten gemacht habe: so viel ist gewiß, daß sie den großen alten Meistern die Hand zu führen nicht müde geworden" (It may be a fable or a story that Love made the first attempt in the visual and performing arts: so much is certain, that she was not tired in guiding the hand of the old masters).[137] It is the power of love, creativity and Eros personified which according to the second chapter of *Laokoon*, produces and energizes images. Lessing rejects the misused notion of "Nachahmung" that seemed to be read as if one discipline had to mimic the other. Instead he insists that the poet and the painter have each direct access to the depth of this original source. At the same time, he promotes understatement in making not only "Geschicklichkeit" (skill of the artist) the decisive matter in order to attain the "Vollkommenheit des Gegenstandes" (completeness of the object or fulfillment), but he recommends that an artist must avoid self-indulgence and step back from detailed description as well as pathos so that others may have the pleasure of finding beauty and meaning in the work themselves in their own space and as they like. Lessing avoids abundant descriptiveness and burdensome emotionality for the sake of brevity and a style that enhances the readers' awareness either for the wonderful or the horrible, as the case may be. At the same time his own style explores the boundaries between the visual and the verbal by a range of rhetorical strategies and visual-verbal sets, his description of characters and the plot of his dramatic works ranges from minimalism to exploring boundaries while dealing with intense emotions onstage and the stiffness of an audience he tries to challenge. In order to emancipate his public and to find new modes of expression, he experiments with overdone sentimentality in his early dramatic works, paradoxical constellations presenting the visual and the verbal as clashing in his middle period, and sophisticated symbolism and open-ended parables in his late work.

Throughout his works Lessing experiments with efficient and minimalist ways of representation of something that is actually projected as being still in the future. He tries to tap a source which had been long ignored, *enargeia*, as the "potency and imaginative vision," an approach that goes beyond any perceived actualization of a motion in the ekphrastic process. Christopher Collins notes that Lessing provides in *Laokoon* a proposal for a kinetic verbal image which is truly creative and thought provoking in a number of ways.[138] Collins has also pointed out, albeit not with refer-

137 FA 5/2, 22.
138 Christopher Collins, *Reading the Written Image: Verbal Play, Interpretation, and the Roots of Iconophobia* (Philadelphia: University of Pennsylvania Press, 1991), 91.

ence to Lessing, that the word "energeia" was derived from a philosophical concept associated with action (*energos*).[139] Collins asks: "If *energeia* is actualization in the form of perceptible motion we can infer that *enargeia* is the potency of a visualized object prior to act once its state of rest is exchanged for one of movement? Do we have here a distinction that applies to the verbal description of a static, as opposed to kinetic objects and therefore to the visual artifacts verbalized in *Ekphrasis*? The evidence is admittedly inconclusive but nonetheless suggestive."[140] In his work, especially his published responses to criticism of *Laokoon* and in his *Paralipomena* Lessing shifts awareness increasingly not only from addresser and addressee to referent, but also to a search for the "sensory presence" of the speakers' verbal referents, especially by promoting diegetic aspects of them. Among the consequences of this are Lessing's own quests for an art of understatement, his open-ended style of writing, that allow and promote *enargeia* as heightened *diegesis*. We could draw the conclusion based on the terminological clarification proposed by Collins that Lessing is in search of a kinetic visuality trying to tap into *enargeia,* "the process by which Ekphrasis is produced."[141] In the *Paralipomena* Lessing expresses a paradox where he talks about a "Kraft" or "force" that can help produce impressions of natural signs in poetry and poetic writing.[142] These signs appear as if natural "nur daß sie diese Zeichen selbst hinwiederum durch willkürliche ausdrücken muß" (despite the fact that these signs themselves must be expressed in turn by arbitrary signs).[143] Lessing makes us reflect on the medium, on indexical features, on acting techniques, on body language onstage, and on numerous qualities that link poetic writing with *enargeia* and "mental imagery." He brings to awareness imaginary objects so that a greater vision would come about. Lessing presents a careful approach to semiotics in his *Laokoo*n and must have felt, as Collins claims, at least at times "an unbridgeable gulf separated *picture* from *poesis.*"[144] As we shall see in the context of the *Laokoon* debate, which ultimately forms the theoretical

---

139 Lessing uses *enargeia* twice in *Laokoon*, chapter 29. He is criticizing a formulation used by Winckelmann and attributed to (Pseudo-)Longinus (FA 5/2 200-201). Lessing first quotes the appropriate passage in Greek from "On the Sublime" 15.2, where Longinus contrasts the use of *phantasia* ("visualization") by poets and orators (rhetoricians): the former use *phantasia* "to enthrall" (translating ekplēksis) while the latter use it "to present things vividly" (translating *enargeia*). See "On the Sublime, trans. W.H. Fyfe, rev. Donald Russell, Aristotle *Poetics*, Longinus *On the Sublime*, Demetrius *On Style*, trans. Stephen Halliwell et al., corr. ed., Loeb Classical Library 199 (Cambridge: Harvard University Press, 1999), 215. Then Lessing quotes the misinterpretation of this passage by Franciscus Junius (1591-1677), *De pictura veterum*, 2nd ed. Georgius Graevius (Amsterdam: Typis Regneri Leers, 1694), I.iv33, which was the source of Winckelmann's error, where Junius had substituted "Pictoriæ vero" ("painters however") for Longinus' *tēs d'èn lógois* ("that of the prose form"), associating enargeia with the painter, not the orator. In the German tradition, enargeia is translated as "Deutlichkeit" (clarity) rather than "Anschaulichkeit" (vividness).

140 Collins, *Reading* 125.

141 Collins, *Reading* 126.

142 FA 5/2 *Paralipomena* 25, 310: "Wenn also auch schon nicht die Wörter natürliche Zeichen sind, so kann doch ihre Folge die Kraft eines natürliches Zeichens haben." (Even though words are not natural signs, their impact can have the power of a natural sign).

143 FA 5/2, *Paralipomena* 25, 311.

144 Collins, *Reading* 126.

matrix for most of Lessing's later formulations on these issues, poetic language is at its best when used onstage where gestures, movements, voice and the meanings of words interact productively. This is only the case, however, if the play can turn audiences into spectators and when there are creative participants in constructing the meanings.

## 5. Lessing's move from images to actions

Even in his theory to drama, Lessing appeals to human love drawing from the Classical traditions of Ekphrasis, from previous approaches and theories on the transfer from images to words, and from the visual to the verbal realm.[145] From these traditions he adopts an approach which insists that things must be described as "anschaulich" or as visible as possible. His approach cannot be captured within the tradition of *descriptio* that relies on certain mimetic principles which for Lessing were already problematic.[146] Although in the context of his earlier writings he assumed "natürliche Zeichen" or "natural signs" in the realm of the visual while acknowledging "willkürliche Zeichen" or arbitrary signs in the realm of the verbal, he later in his life realized that even seeing requires intricate processes of deciphering and that metaphoricity and metonymic modes of "Darstellung" (presenting things) were also unavoidable in the creation images and visual references to them.

Whereas from a broad perspective all literature, poetic writing, and art is about describing and representing things, it is central for Lessing's approach that what is to be represented are not exclusively "objects" such as statues, paintings, or stable images. There are actions, relations, emotions, and movements. It is characteristic of Lessing's dynamic approach to Ekphrasis that he regards presenting something visual or verbally as involving ekphrastic hope of turning audiences into spectators and participants. He is interested not only in the transfer of images to words and the vivid verbal presentation of visible things, but in encouraging his readers and spectators to reverse the ekphrastic process. Words should become images or better even, actions again. Scripts and pictures provide vivid ideas to provide a reversed ekphrastic transfer from the verbal to the tactile. And if Ekphrasis is, as numerous critics have argued, the art of transferring images into words, or the rhetorical ability to provide sense impressions that are strong, radiant, and energetic, then it is furthermore Lessing's specific theoretical approach and praxis as a poet to animate "Dichtkunst" (poetics) and to activate the Pygmalion myth by bringing static objects, statues, images, animals and ideas alive. This implies anthropomorphism and human compassion in the processes of art in perception.[147]

---

145 See Willems, *Anschaulichkeit*, for an investigation of these notions of the visual, steeped as they are in a long rhetorical tradition.

146 See Peter Wagner, "Introduction: Ekphrasis, Iconotexts, and Intermediality–the State(s) of the Art(s)," Peter Wagner, ed., *Icons–Texts–Iconotexts: Essays on Ekphrasis and Intermediality*, European Cultures: Studies in Literature and the Arts 6 (Berlin: De Gruyter, 1996), 1-40 at 6-7.

147 On the Pygmalion myth see Oskar Bätschmann, "Pygmalion als Betrachter: Die Rezeption von Plastik und Malerei in der zweiten Hälfte des 18. Jahrhunderts," Wolfgang Kemp,

It was Lessing's hope to mobilize the audience and it is his expressed wish, as shall be documented in detail, to spark the imagination not only via outer actions but also by inner ones, since he believed that all history and each narrative derives from human character traits and human interaction in certain social conditions and ideological frameworks. The images of the mind not only reflect mimetically but also precede the external world. He wants to move by means of emotions in order to promote human empathy and compassion. He focuses on what he calls "innere Handlungen" (inner actions), sense perceptions that are inseparable from feeling and thinking, these are to be understood in the context of two complementary approaches and traditions, *aisthesis* (the perceived) and *noiesis* (the known).[148]

The aesthetics of images and texts in relation or distinction to one another, the media implicit underpinnings of all art forms and modes of communication, and the effects of rhetorical devices as well as audiences and actors, are all interwoven. The complex history of mimesis leads not only to a rhetorical turn, or the return of rhetoric, but also "visual turn" in critical theory.[149] Ralf Simon has also drawn attention to the critical strategies that involve notions of "Bildlichkeit" and "Bildkritik" in the writing of literature.[150] These approaches build on long ignored philosophical strands of *Gnoseology* going back to Leibniz.[151] They turn attention not only to the eye and seeing in isolated terms, but also in terms of those senses which lie under the threshold of perception as then conceptualized in, for example, the work of Kant, but which for Herder (and to some extent Lessing as I shall claim) were considered instrumental in an approach to cognition ("Kognition" or "Erkenntnis") drawing from *synesthesia,* the interaction among the various senses, be they acoustic, visual, tactile, etc.[152] This approach does not split thinking from feeling but remains steeped in the body, so as to speak, in the here and now of space. Ekphrasis is closely akin to the key concept of

ed., *Der Betrachter ist im Bild. Kunstwissenschaft und Rezeptionsästhetik* (Cologne: DuMont, 1985), 183-224; 2nd ed. (Berlin: Dietrich Reimer, 1992), 237-278.

148 See the essays in Adler and Wolff, ed., *Aisthesis und Noesis* and see also Susanne Knaller, "Verschiebungen im Kunstsystem. Zum Verhältnis von Sprachkunst und Bildkunst in den ästhetischen Diskursen des 18. und 19. Jahrhunderts," *Komparatistik: Jahrbuch der Deutschen Gesellschaft für Allgemeine und Vergleichende Literaturwissenschaft 2012* (Heidelberg: Synchron, 2013): 55-72. The definitions of *aisthesis* and *noiesis* are those of Richard Hibert, "Baudelaire, Baumgarten, and Sensate Knowledge," Adler and Wolff, ed., *Aisthesis und Noesis* 85-96 at 87.

149 On the notion of a rhetorical turn see Bender and Wellbery, "Rhetoricality" 3-39. See also the essays in Ralf Simon, ed., *Herders Rhetoriken* and on a "visual turn," Beate Allert, "Reconceptualizing a Pictorial Turn."

150 See, for example, Ralf Simon, *Der poetische Text als Bildkritik* (Munich: Fink, 2009) and *Die Bildlicheit des lyrischen Textes: Studien zu Hölderlin, Brentano, Eichendorff, Heine, Mörike, George und Rilke* (Munich: Fink, 2011).

151 Hans Adler and Ulrike Zeuch, ed., *Synästhesie: Interferenz–Transfer–Synthese der Sinne* (Würzburg: Königshausen & Neumann, 2002) sum up the meaning of "synesthesia" in the subtitle by linking it closely, as already Herder did, with an interference, transference, and synthesis among the sense perceptions and senses.

152 See Hans Adler, "Fundus Animae–der Grund der Seele. Zur Gnoseologie des Dunkeln in der Aufklärung," *Deutsche Vierteljahrsschrift für Literaturwissenschaft und Geistesgeschichte* 62 (1988): 197-220 and Ulrike Zeuch, *Umkehr der Sinneshierarchie: Herder und die Aufwertung des Tastsinns seit der frühen Neuzeit*, Communicatio 22 (Tübingen: Niemeyer, 2000).

*enargeia* which implies the ability of verbal presentation, orally or in writing, to make something that may be absent present via imagination in fiction, even to the extent that the reader forgets the wordiness.[153] The fictionality of the text becomes so perfect that the medium of language also seems to disappear in the action it describes. Fritz Graf correctly identifies the goal of Lessing's drama theory as being "aus Zuhörern Zuschauer machen" (to turn audiences into spectators).[154] Lessing seems influenced by the *Progymnasmata* of Nicolaus the Sophist from Myra who defines *Ekphrasis* as "descriptive speech, bringing what is described clearly (*enargôs*) before the eyes."[155] An external mode of literal seeing gets exchanged for an inner kind of metaphoric seeing that has its own colorful strong and emotionally-effective dynamic impact. It is among Lessing's notable contributions to Enlightenment discourse and to visual theory that he raised important questions on the potentials and limits of Ekphrasis with respect not only to aesthetics and metaphor but also to ethics and human interaction. Whereas some of his works expose the weaknesses of wordiness, others teach an appreciation for approximating the mute in the text without being less powerful. Lessing questions the ability of language to capture not only the essence but also the vitality of images and visual relations. He replaces static images with the representation of actions that are visually stimulating and often have open-ended meanings.

Given the choice of taking a notion of "the truth" in one hand and to opt for a way to search what truths there might be, Lessing preferred the latter. Lessing is interested in the process and the attempt to motivate his readers and spectators in such a way that they learn not only to see but also to be compassionate. He wants his contemporaries to outgrow the imperative didactic mode where teaching is completely explicit and the moral of a text already given. It is exemplary that in his fables Lessing diverges from all the other fable writers before him by explicitly letting go of any explicit moral. He makes a point in this theoretical writings that any *epimythium, promythium,* or *endomythium* as used so far in the fable tradition since Aesop would now become superfluous since the fable itself is capable of making its argument immanently, without extra frame.[156] Lessing is trying to emancipate his readers from the confines of the text and to spark imagination by leaving room for contemplation. He further explores in his *Fabeln* how to go beyond mere description by performing actions textually and semiotically. He insists that a poet should not only use the signs that have a "bequeme[s] Verhältnis" (a suitable relationship), but also those signs whose relationship might be described as belonging to a "unbequemes" (uncomfortable re-

153 Rüdiger Singer, "Intermediale Anschaulichkeit: *Enargeia* als rhetorisches Wirkungsideal von Text, Bild und actio." Adler and Gross, ed., *Anschauung und Anschaulichkeit* 157-177.

154 Fritz Graf, "Ekphrasis: Die Entstehung der Gattung in der Antike," Boehm and Pfotenhauer, ed., *Beschreibungskunst–Kunstbeschreibung* 143-155 at 145.

155 "The *Preliminary Exercises* of Nicolaus the Sophist," *Progymnasmata: Greek Textbooks of Prose Composition and Rhetoric,* trans. George A. Kennedy, Writings from the Greco-Roman World 10 (Atlanta: Society of Biblical Literature, 2003), 129-172 at 166.

156 The following definitions are taken from Laura Gibbs, "Introduction," *Aesop's Fables,* ed. and intro. Laura Gibbs. Oxford World's Classics (Oxford: Oxford University Press, 2002), ix-xxi: *epimythium,* "something that comes after the story ... added by the teller of the fable to make sure the point is absolutely clear" (xiv); *promythium,* "a moral that actually comes before the fable" (xiv); *endomythium,* "the moral inside the story" (xv) or *paramythium.*

lationship) with its signs that cannot be captured in terms of allegory or anything pregiven or textually prescribed. He explains in his "Abhandlungen zur Fabel" why he does not like allegories compared to fables He favors fables that are not allegorical but rather symbolic since these have, as he argues "Anschaulichkeit." vividness on their own. No explanations, commentaries, or explicit morals are needed. He argues that a fable should ideally not be allegorical ("kann unmöglich allegorisch sein"). If a fable were allegorical, then it would need to be tied to previously given literary sources or external information. Its message would then not be intrinsically provided but only indirectly referred to. Such a fable would be less helpful to emancipate the reader than a fable that leaves space for imagination and has everything needed to understand implicit.[157] While Lessing finds that allegories are usually geared towards a general truth, he demands that fables should be rather specific since he is interested in abbreviated yet direct modes of communication. He likes expressions of immediacy such as metaphors that suggest new equations and links between heterogeneous elements thereby expanding our inner space. The aim of Lessing's approach is to promote critical thinking and rationality. He is in search of simplicity while at the same time probing the questions: How to promote cognition in contemplation ("Erkenntnis in Betrachtung")? How to make language best "anschaulich" (vivid, visual) in such a way that it can move and have emotional impact (affect)? He wants to avoid allegory so that what is presented is not only similar to any intended meaning intended but that the illusion of the art is intact and a range of possible meanings can be specified:

> Vielleicht aber meint jemand, daß die Allegorie hier nicht auf der Ähnlichkeit zwischen den *bestimmten* Subjekten oder Prädikaten der Fabel und den *allgemeinen* Subjekten oder Prädicaten des Satzes, sondern auf der Ähnlichkeit der Arten, wie ich diese Wahrheit, itzt durch Bilder der Fabel und itzt vermittels der Worte des Satzes erkenne, beruhe. Doch das ist so viel, als nichts. Denn käme hier die Art der Erkenntnis in Betrachtung, die ich vermittels der Handlung der Fabel von dieser oder jener Wahrheit erhalte, die Handlung allegorisch nenne: so würde in allen Fabeln ebendieselbe Allegorie sein, welche doch niemand sagen will, der mit diesem Worte nun einzigen Begriff verbindet. Ich befürchte, daß ich von einer klaren Sache viel zu viel Worte mache. Ich fasse daher alles zusammen und sage: die Fabel, als eine einfache Fabel, kann unmöglich allegorisch sein.[158]

> [Perhaps someone thinks that the allegory here is not based on the similarity between the *specific* subjects or predicates of the fable and the *general* subjects, or on predicates of the sentence but on the similarity between the specific methods of how I recognize this truth exactly, whether through images of the fable and through the words of the sentence.

157 "Die anschauende Erkenntnis ist von sich selbst klar. Die symbolische entlehnet ihre Klarheit von der anschauenden. Das Allgemeine existieret nur in dem Besondern, und kann nur in dem Besondern anschauend erkannt werden. Einem allgemeinen symbolischen Schlusse folglich alle die Klarheit zu geben, deren er fähig ist, das ist, ihn so viel als möglich zu erläutern; müssen wir ihn auf das Besondere reduzieren, um ihn in diesem anschauend zu erkennen" (The cognition of the visual manifests itself clearly. The general exists only in the specific and can only been visually cognized in the specific. In order to give a general symbolic deduction all the clarity which it is capable of, that is in order to explain it as much as possible, we must reduce it to the specific so that then we can understand through it visually). "Von dem Wesen der Fabel" (About the Essence of the Fable), FA 4, 372.

158 "Abhandlungen I: Von dem Wesen der Fabel," FA 4, 345-76 at 350-351.

But this is as much as nothing. Then there would be here the method of cognition in contemplation, and if someone would want to call the action allegorical merely because of the visual cognition which I obtain supplied through the action of the fable of this or that truth: then in all fables there would be always the same such allegory, which yet nobody will want to say, who associates with this word only a single denotation. I am afraid that I make too many words of a simple matter. Thus I summarize and say: the fable, if it is a simple fable, cannot possibly be allegorical].

Lessing is skeptical about the use of allegory and in search of modes of expression that can liberate meanings from an outdated need wanting to give a general "moral" ("Lehre"). Instead of such overt didacticism he suggests to offer more specific, nuanced and perspectival subtle imperatives instead. He experiments with various modes of visuality by drawing attention to the intricacies of the visual and the verbal. He acknowledges the need to use words, even when sense perceptions are more effective and when silences are there to remain. He often aims at a condensing of complicated narratives into distilled effective moments onstage but he also speaks against oversimplification. He offers poetic texts that are "anschaulich," or that present an idea as already "evident" through the story, thus trying to avoid or to circumvent any traditional flattening of images for the sake of logical reasoning. He contradicts or critiques a notion of Ekphrasis that would require poets to imitate painters and impose imitation. Instead Lessing asserts the right of each:

Ein poetisches Gemälde ist nicht notwendig das, was in ein materielles Gemälde zu verwandeln ist; sondern jeder Zug, jede Verbindung mehrerer Züge, durch die uns der Dichter seinen Gegenstand so sinnlich macht, daß wir uns dieses Gegenstandes deutlicher bewußt werden, als seiner Worte, heißt malerisch, heißt ein Gemälde, weil es uns dem Grade der Illusion näher bringt, dessen das materielle Gemälde besonders fähig ist, der sich von dem materiellen Gemälde am ersten und leichtesten abstrahieren lassen. [Kap. XV] Nun kann der Dichter zu diesem Grade der Illusion, wie die Erfahrung zeiget, auch der Vorstellungen anderer, als sichtbarer Gegenstände erheben. Folglich müssen notwendig dem Artisten ganze Classen von Gemälden abgehen, die der Dichter vor ihm voraus hat. Drydens Ode auf den Cäcilientag ist voller musikalischen Gemälde, die den Pinsel müßig lassen. Doch will ich mich in dergleichen Exempel nicht verlieren, aus welchem man am Ende doch wohl nicht viel mehr lernet, als daß die Farben keine Töne, und die Ohren keine Augen sind.[159]

[A poetic painting is not necessarily something which is to be transformed into a material painting; but each move, each link between several moves, through which the poet makes his object sensible so that we become more clearly aware of his object, as well as of his words, can be called painterly can be called a painting, because it brings us closer to the degree of illusion which the material painting is especially capable of, which can be abstracted most immediately and easily from the material painting. [Chap. XV] Now as experience shows, the poet is able to raise also the imagination of other than visual objects to this degree of illusion. Consequently the artists must lack an entire class of paintings which the poet has available in addition. Dryden's "Alexander's Feast" (Ode on St. Cecilia's Day) is full of musical paintings which leave the brush idle. However, I do not want to get lost in such examples from which one may not learn more than the fact that colors are not sounds and the ears not eyes].

159 FA 5/2, 113–114. For a different translation see *Laocoön*, trans. McCormick 74–76.

In his theoretical treatise on the fable, *Von dem Wesen der Fabel: Fabelbuch* (About the Essence of the Fable: Fable Book) Lessing explores rhetorical strategies that involve Ekphrasis and builds poetic strategies on sense perceptions. If an understatement means to express something via hinting at meanings only, via leaving something open and gesticulating rather than presenting everything in detail, then wit, irony and humor are ways to experiment with such visual poetics. As Lessing insisted in contradistinction to Antoine Houdar de La Motte,[160] one should not *Gewürze würzen (spice spices).*[161] For Lessing there is no need to overindulge in language or in imagery, they should be sparse. For him to underscore or to contextualize visual impressions means ideally to keep their descriptions simple, to a minimum. Yet Lessing also advocates a certain level of abstraction. He refers to a notion of the beautiful and the magnificent which is always a matter of movement. He argues that the fable must be accessible by the reader and ideally turn any reader into an imaginative spectator.[162] Lessing insists that writing should be "anschaulich" (visual), evoke vivid impressions of the mind, and promote critical thinking. Lessing never lets go of the dictum: "Je mehr wir sehen, desto mehr müssen wir hinzu denken können."[163] This means not only as he suggested in the context of his fables to make a plot simple to keep the story as brief and succinct as it can possibly be. He furthermore advocates language that is characterized by images that are metaphoric. They are to be not formulaic as if they were merely catachreses or fixed terminologies.[164] All images, metaphors or metonymies make us consider the contexts in which they are used, the environment. They are time-sensitive. If the sentence "the more we see the more we must be able to imagine" is to be taken seriously, then it means also that Lessing invites readers and spectators to imagine beyond what is shown, and to find intuitively features that go beyond the verbal. Lessing seems to favor seeing among all other senses. However, he also

160 Author of Fables nouvelles, dédiées au Roy ... avec un discours sur les fables (Paris: Grégoire Dupuis, 1719).

161 Lessing, "Die Erscheinung," the first entry to Book One of his *Fabeln,* FA 4, 302.

162 John Richardson, *Fables from the German of Lessing* (York: C. Etherington, 1773), translates "Gewürze würzen" as "beautify beauty" (3). The anonymous translator of *Fables and Epigrams; with Essays on Fable and Epigram from the German of Lessing* (London: John and H.L. Hunt, 1825) is closer to the mark with "add fragrance to spices" (1). It is, in other words, something can be overdone or exaggerated and the plea not to do so hints at Lessing's approach towards understatement and to his idea that poetic language is itself "visual" to begin with.

163 FA 5/2, 32.

164 Gabriel Trop has recently pointed out: "Lessing's treatises about fables and the fables themselves, collected in 1759, under the title *Fabeln. Drei Bücher. Nebst Abhandlungen mit dieser Dichtungsart verwandten Inhalts* may be regarded as a manifesto for and a practical implementation of a conception of art in which the relationship between aesthetic form and cognition becomes one of paramount importance." "The Fable as Aesthetic Exercise: Lessing's Philosophy of Poetic Form," *Lessing Yearbook* 43 (2016): 55-76 at 55-56. I agree completely with this statement. Whereas Gabriel Trop explores how Lessing "evaluates the aesthetic form of the fable to the extent that it stimulates a cognitive operation traditionally belonging to conceptual thought, namely the binding of the particular to the general, or the process through which the human being comes to perceive, cognize, and articulate a general truth" (56), my study here focuses on metaphor and aspects of the visual through the verbal.

recognizes that what can be shown onstage through gestures, body language, mime, visual presentation and in the performance must always depend precisely on the timing of images, their movements. Lessing is thus drawing attention to the dimension of simultaneous signs, metaphors, and metonymies, similar to the signs of concurrent sounds in music. He anticipates the approach by the painter Wassily Kandinsky who claims that a point is always a movement.[165]

165 Wassily Kandinsky, *Punkt und Linie zu Fläche. Beitrag zur Analyse der malerischen Elemente*, intro. Max Brill, 7th ed. (Bern: Benteli Verlag, 1955), 21–56.

# Chapter 2
# Minimalism and Sketches: Diderot and Lessing

Abstract: This chapter focuses first on aspects concerning Ekphrasis theory that emerge in the interaction between Lessing and Dennis Diderot. He was not only known in France but all over in Europe as a prolific art critic, writer, and philosopher. Diderot was the co-founder of the *Encyclopédie ou dictionnaire des sciences, des arts et des métiers* (1751-1772) and served as this encyclopedia's editor until 1759. In this monumental effort Diderot supports the Enlightenment idea that by naming things one can expand one's horizon, gain knowledge, and become more literate but also better find one's own position in the world. He was critical of the painterly style or the movement of "Pictorialism" widely popular, especially in France. Lessing's ideas were often misunderstood as anti-French but are more accurately understood as being close to Diderot's. They shared a critical approach trying to turn images into actions, into something more dynamic onstage.

## 1. Diderot's innovations and Lessing's fascination with Diderot

What fascinates Lessing most about Diderot is his innovative stance as an expert in the visual arts and the way in which he provides astonishing examples of Ekphrasis in his copious verbal descriptions of works of art. These descriptions have their own fascination in that they actualize the most nuanced sense perceptions, demonstrating a new awareness for landscapes, literally and metaphorically, the environment, and the newest scientific and intellectual developments. In his contributions (1759-1781) to the biweekly newsletter, *Correspondence littéraire,* Diderot had responded to the charge of Friedrich Melchior Grimm, the newsletters' German expatriate editor, to describe the exhibits of the *Académie royale de peinture et de sculpture* (The Royal Academy of Painting and Sculpture) in the form of lectures and he did so most vividly.[166]

His most extensive treatments were his accounts of the *Salons of 1765 along with an "Essais sur la Peinture"* (Essays on Paintings), and the *Salon* of 1767.[167] His commentaries on the art works that he views provide a vivid impressions of these images but since the circulation of the *Correspondences littéraire* outside of Paris was fewer than 20 copies, his writing was not accessible to the general public and did not appear elsewhere in print during his lifetime. For those who did not have the opportunity to see the paint-

166 Friedrich Melchior Grimm, *Correspondence littéraire,* ed. Maurice Tourneux, 16 vols. (Paris: Garnier frères, 1887-1882).

167 The *Salon de 1765,* the *Essais sur la Peinture,* and the *Salon de 1767* have been translated as: *Diderot on Art.* I: *The Salon of 1765 and Notes on Painting,* II: *The Salon of 1767*, trans. John Goodman, intro. Thomas Crow (New Haven: Yale University Press, 1995).

ings as they were exhibited, Diderot's writings about them offered surrogate descriptions, being masterpieces of ekphrastic writing, sometimes in dense and sometimes in flowery language, sometimes critical, and sometimes full of admiration. He created the fiction of a reporter who was capable of giving the public his personal advice and expert interpretation. His approach was formulated as if he was the curator of an art museum who walked his audience past the paintings giving them a tour and describing of what he saw one work after another:

> I'll describe the paintings for you, and my descriptions will be such that, with a bit of imagination and taste, you'll be able to envision them spatially, disposing the objects within them more or less as we see them on the canvas.[168]

For example, one of the oil paintings displayed in the Salon of 1765 by Jean-Baptiste Greuze portrays a girl crying over a dead bird ("Une jeune fille qui pleure son oiseau mort").[169] It draws attention to an emotional scene, one that could be interpreted not only on a realist but also on a symbolic level. In his fictional *Salon* report, Diderot recounts an imaginary dialogue between the curator and the young girl. The dialogue reveals that the bird died of neglect. The reason is that the young girl was so distraught over her lover's visit the previous day which then apparently resulted in the loss of her bird, as well as of her virginity.[170] The contiguity of these fragments of narration is suggestive. The picture of the dead bird in this context has now multiple meanings depending on the speaker and on each point of view in the conversation.

In the *Salon* of 1767 Diderot has a long section devoted to the landscape paintings of Claude-Joseph Vernet.[171] He offers an ekphrastic description of what can be seen by his fictional narrator during a walk through an unnamed landscape close to the sea. He is accompanied by his friend, the Abbé. The "real" landscape is described each stop along the way. It is being presented as if it had been composed by Vernet and each scene described corresponds to one of Vernet's paintings which in this narrative context then gets verbally (or visually in a metaphorical realm) "exhibited." Hubertus Kohle describes the style of this section as one of "understatement" for its effectiveness:

> Nun ist dieses Vorgehen kaum als Mittel zu interpretieren, die monotone Abfolge von Bildkritiken einfach zu variieren, selbst wenn der Autor mit kokettem Understatement solches manchmal behauptet.[172]

---

168 Diderot, *On Art* I: 6. For important theoretical reflections considering Diderot's description of Greuze's painting, see Monika Schmitz-Emans, "Das visuelle Gedächtnis der Literatur:Allgemine Überlegungen zur Beziehung zwischen Texten und Bildern," Manfred Schmeling and Monika Schmitz-Emans, ed., *Das Visuelle Gedächtnis in der Literatur* (Würzburg: Königshausen & Neumann, 1990), 17-34 at 23.

169 National Gallery of Scotland in Edinburgh. There is also a reproduction of this painting on the cover of: Kristina Bonn, *Vom Schönen: Schönheitskonzeptionen bei Lessing, Goethe und Schiller* (Bielefeld: Aisthesis, 2008).

170 Diderot, *On Art* I: #110, 97-100 at 98-99.

171 Diderot, *On Art* II: 86-128.

172 Kohle, *Ut pictura poesis non erit* 111.

> [Now this strategy can barely be interpreted as a means simply to vary the monotonous sequence of image reviews, although the author sometimes claims this via charming understatement].

Diderot uses wit and humor, features that also characterize Lessing's art of understatement. In 1760 in the foreword to his translation of two of Diderot's plays, Lessing writes: "Das wahre Lächerliche ist nicht was am lautesten lachen macht, und Ungereimtheiten sollen nicht bloß unsere Lunge in Bewegung setzen" (What is truly ridiculous is not what makes us laugh the loudest, and incongruities should not just make our lungs move).[173] Lessing highlights the comical aspects of life, even if they are not the most explicit material of any comedy. They are subtle and momentary and unexpectedly emerge even under serious circumstances. Wilfried Barner, the editor and commentator on Lessing's translations of plays by Diderot, seems to suggest that for both Diderot and Lessing there was a link between the philosophical and the pedestrian, the so-called "Problemdenker" (thinker of problems) and the "Schweifende" (flanêur or pedestrian) (FA5/1, 543). Diderot's narrator appears to walk leisurely from one painting to another and from one topic to another. He connects things that may be normally regarded as distinct or heterogeneous.[174]

Diderot's narrator asks in *The Salon of 1767:* "Why does a beautiful sketch accord greater pleasure than a beautiful painting?" Since his writing is often in the form of dialogues, an answer is at once suggested by the fictional respondent: "Because it has more life and fewer forms. The more forms one introduces, the more life disappears."[175] He adds: "Why is it that a young student incapable of making even a mediocre painting can make a marvelous sketch? Because such sketches thrive on enthusiasm and genius while paintings demand work, patience, prolonged study, and extensive technical experience."[176] Philosophical questions are being raised: "Who knows that of which nature herself personified seems to be unaware?" He asks how "to introduce the forms of advanced age" into the poetic while "conserving the liveliness of youth?"[177] In other words: How to do justice to temporality, although it changes everything in nature (and in its representation) and this tends to dampen the liveliness of images? The respondent finds that it is a more effective way to represent nature in general by highlighting only selectively a few features of it. Ignoring details that are for the moment irrelevant are signs of good taste. Rather than aiming at a complete

173 FA 5/1, 16. It should be noted that laughter as represented in eighteenth century literature gained much inspiration from the paintings of William Hogarth approaching social criticism and empathy via caricatures. On this issue see Jochen Bedenk, *Verwicklungen. Wilhelm Hogarth und die deutsche Literatur des 18. Jahrhunderts (Lessing, Herder, Schiller, Jean Paul)* (Würzburg: Königshausen & Neumann, 2004).

174 FA 5/1, 543. "Der 'Problemdenker' und der von einem zum anderen 'Schweifende'–hier sind erste Ansätze jener Wahlverwandtschaft spürbar, von der man später im Hinblick auf Lessing und Diderot immer wieder gesprochen hat." (The problem-thinker and the one who roams freely from one thing to another–here are noticeable the first aspects of this elective affinity concerning which one has later so often talked about with respect to Lessing and Diderot).

175 Diderot, *On Art* II: 212.

176 Diderot, *On Art* II: 212.

177 Diderot, *On Art* II: 212.

and all too intimate representation of nature or of any aspect of life, it seems best to keep things at a distance and in perspective and to provide something of an "sketch" ("ésquisse"). In doing so, one is fortunately avoiding any pedantic claims to "know" things that are so incredibly hard to guess anyhow.

Despite this modesty the approach is generous. The narrator draws anyone curious and gently mocks those who seem overly secure in what they assume to be factual knowledge. Soon the reader notices that the discourse is gendered, that nature is referred to as if it were a feminine voice. To the respondent the narrator attributes a masculine voice.[178] The fictional author explains that he does not want to dissect nature but to allow for eroticism and longing. He adds: "Perhaps we find sketches so attractive only because, being somewhat indeterminate, they allow more liberty to our imagination, which sees in them whatever it likes. It's the same as with children looking at clouds, and we're all children to some degree."[179] Such liberty to our imagination is mediated by means of silences, gaps, and free spaces. Similarly, Diderot writes in his *Salon of 1765:*

> Sketches frequently have a fire that the finished paintings lack; they're the moment of the artist's zeal, his pure verve, undiluted by any carefully considered preparation, they're the painter's soul freely transferred to canvas. The poet's pen, the skilled craftsman's pencil, seem so frolic and just to amuse themselves. Rapid sketches characterize everything with a few strokes. The more ambiguity there is in artistic expression, the more comfortable the imagination.[180]

It is interesting that Diderot writes as if speaking and that his preference of the sketch over paintings is accompanied by a preference for orality over written styles of language. On one hand, Diderot argues for sketches on the basis of their affinity with youth, their incompleteness, and he considers sketches as the most creative beginning stages of artworks. He invents voices in his Salon contributions that associate sketches with the notion of residues, remnants, and signs of decay. At various times the narrator shows a liking for ruins and similarly for sketches that have more to do with the effects of destruction over time. Whether linked with images of youth or with old age, they share a distance to the present, a certain abstraction, something non-central and marginal. They are described either as the creation of a genius or of a wise person. Time can be personified as master agent. In other words, they draw attention not only to space but to the dimension of time. Diderot writes: "Another thing that would make ruins still more effective is a strong image of transience" and he adds:

> Well, well the powerful men of the earth who believed they built for the ages, who erected such superb residences for themselves, and who in their folly anticipated an uninterrupted series of descendants, heirs to their names, their titles, and their opulent way of life, nothing remains of their work, of their enormous expenditure, of their grand visions but debris serving to shelter some of the most indigent and unfortunate members of the human race, much more useful as ruins than ever they were in their initial splendor.[181]

---

178 See Monika Schmitz-Emans, *Die Literatur, die Bilder und das Unsichtbare* 59-87 on Diderot's *Salons*.
179 Diderot, *On Art* II: 213.
180 Diderot, *On Art* I: 104.
181 Diderot, *On Art* II: 217.

Here we meet Diderot not only as an art critic and writer of an aesthetics of minimalism for the sake of taste and style but also as a politician, a writer for social justice, a humanist who says he prefers people over buildings, the "human race" over "palaces of splendor." A tension is created that juxtaposes culture with nature. Complete pictures belong to culture along with splendid palaces yet these are to be contrasted with sketches which belong to "the human race" where life happens yet time flies.[182] The liking of the sketch may also have much to do with the rising of a middle class public, with a new bourgeois spectatorship and audience, and with new imaging technologies that make it more and more difficult to distinguish between an original and a cheap copy.[183] Whereas the sketch often meant the beginning initial first stage of a painting, it became interesting as it playfully pretends to reveal the most authentic, the least mannerist, the least affected expression by the artist and thus allows apparently insights into nature "as is" in dynamic terms, in its genesis, growth, or becoming. Also, as Diderot asserts, it gives glimpses into the artist's soul without mediation and censorship. At the same time, because it seems to be only a first unpolished expression the craftsperson or author cannot be held responsible for certain mimetic expectations that often dictated was considered valuable in the art world. By promoting the sketch, Diderot contributes to the emancipation of the audience and links aesthetics with a politics.

## 2. The shared preference of the sketch over the painting

The sketch is a genre much neglected both in art history and literary criticism. What makes it undoubtedly an interesting genre is that it paradoxically resists culture and rhetoric in its established forms for the sake of apparent nature and apparent spontaneity while at the same time using rhetorical and artistic devices in order to claim an immediacy which is in fact impossible. Truth becomes approached via fiction. This

182 Daniel Brewer, "Diderot and the Culture of Belatedness," Frédéric Ogée and Anthony Strugnell, ed., *Diderot and the European Culture*, SVEC 2006:09 (Oxford: Voltaire Foundation 2006), 183-196, finds reading Diderot an "exercise in belatedness" (187) because of a fraught and complex reception history. Diderot was concerned about how he would be seen by posterity, but he could not decide if that was something that should be taken seriously, or just laughed off (196).

183 Richard C. Sha, *The Visual and Verbal Sketch in British Romanticism* (Philadelphia: University of Pennsylvania Press, 1989) comments: "To try and solidify class distinctions, the gentry began to denigrate reproductions. In short, decorators argued that such images were tainted threefold by commerce, technology, and vulgarity. In the late eighteenth century, however, developments in printing technology would make the mass production of such drawings not only cheaper, but also more faithful to the original. In fact, technological advancements in image reproduction now made it feasible for reproductions to pass for the originals, thereby once again blurring lines between aristocratic originals and vulgar reproduction. The key technological development was the introduction in England of aquatint around 1771, which improved the ability to render tones, gradations from light to shade" (32). For further comments on the Romantics' engagement with the fragment, see Christopher A. Strathman, *Romantic Poetry and the Fragmentary Imperative: Schlegel, Byron, Joyce, Blanchot* (Albany: State University of New York Press, 2006), 3-27.

insight was reflected among artists and critics of the eighteenth century thus challenging simple mimetic assumptions, among them the notion that images can remain to be considered "natürliche Zeichen" (natural signs), whereas words are removed from nature and must be understood as belonging to a sign system that is more complex or full of "willkürliche Zeichen" (arbitrary signs). Although Lessing refers to a complex semiotic process, he does not give up entirely a belief in the magic of recalling natural signs in the realm of "Dichtung" (poesy). Reality itself in the eighteenth century had become less transparent than it had seemed before.[184] The attitude towards the tradition of mimesis is marked by a major paradigm shift towards the recognition of abstraction, seeing shadows, and optical effects in everything seen. While in the wake of rationalism, encyclopedic efforts were made to name, to catalogue, and to register all phenomena, a new sensibility drew attention to senses, feelings, and emotions that had a tendency to be ignored. Poetic language seemed promising as a way out to counteract discursive language with its perpetual flattening of images. The eighteenth century in Europe is marked by many changes that all had an impact on ways how images were being resurrected and not only avoided and how literary texts had to be read, not only with a high degree of cognition and logical understanding but also with creative imagination and with what we would call today perhaps visual literacy.

As Richard C. Sha in *The Visual and Verbal Sketch in British Romanticism* documents, the sketch became a rising genre in the eighteenth century and one which gained popularity in the nineteenth. By concentrating on its history in England, Sha finds that by the time the sketch was fully established in the movement of Romanticism, it already had lost its critical edge. Yet in eighteenth century Germany and France, it still had its luminal function, precisely at the margin of the discourses on the visual and the verbal and between high, bourgeois and low culture, and it still had much critical and creative potential especially in the context of the work of Diderot and Lessing. A sketch could say everything already or nothing at all; it could be art or be naïve. It was a way to express the most authentic, original, and be a visual representation closest to nature and be critical to culture. At the same time, a sketch could be rhetorical and most effective by pretending not only to be rhetorical but also to be "natural."

One may find that a sketch is subversive for entering visual art while being at the same time something of a temporary expression. The fictionalizing of truth and the impossibility of presenting truth in its purest and unfiltered form lies at the core of those attempts to gain objectivity despite the loss of the things in themselves and the undeniable insight that all things are mediated, never completely detached from subjectivity. They are prone to personal taste and evaluation. Fictionalized naturalness, as practiced in the discourses of the sketch, has much to do with questioning the traditional idea that images were natural signs. While the sketch expresses from one point of view a resistance to form, rhetoric, and established art, it may be from another point of view a new art form altogether. It is important in these contexts that there were rising new socio-political conditions which go hand in hand with the invention of new imaging technologies and new modes of reproduction. The sketch created

184 On this paradigm shift see Gottfried Willems, *Anschaulichkeit* and Claudia Albes and Christiane Frey, ed., *Darstellbarkeit. Zu einem ästhetisch-philosophischen Problem um 1800* (Würzburg: Königshausen & Neumann, 2003).

a new ideal of minimalist art or proposed the kind of art that is perfectly capable of hiding its artificiality. It is able to perform, if you like, a perfect kind of Ekphrasis since it would appear to make something visual through verbalness without using its normally typical artificial signs. The effect of naturalness stands as a newly established ideal, abbreviated perfection.

In an early review which appeared in the periodical *Das Neueste aus dem Reiche des Witzes* (The Newest from the Realm of Wit) in June 1751, Lessing argues that the most important thing about art is, as already Charles Batteux had shown in his essay "Einschränkung der Schönen Künste auf eine einzigen Grundsatz" (Reduction of the Fine Arts into one single Principle), that one should return to the earliest source of all arts.[185] Therefore sometimes translations may "weit getreuer geraten" (happen to be more truthful) than what the "Sinn des Verfassers" (sense or intention of the author) may have been.[186] They may capture an essence that was lost in earlier publications or editions, even the authors' own explicit claims. In this same issue Lessing also addresses Diderot in print for the first time with a review of his *Lettre sur les sourds et muets* which will be discussed in more detail shortly.[187]

Lessing had a keen interest in Diderot's works which he liked for their apparently "free" or "natural" style, as much as for their content dealing with the suppressed and the impact of social class and gender inequality. Reviewers of Diderot's plays had found it remarkable that he not only provided successful character descriptions in these works but also that the way he described living conditions made such perfect sense that the main issue was no longer restricted to the ultimate question whether or not a character was a criminal. It was more important what led to these actions portrayed. In 1760 appeared *Das Theater des Herrn Diderot* in which Lessing published his translation of Diderot's essay *Sur la poesie dramatique* which Diderot had published in 1758 as an appendix to his play *Le Père de famille* along with a translation of that play. It also included an earlier piece *Le Fils naturel ou les Épreuves de la vertu* first published anonymously in 1757.[188] Several letters to and from Lessing suggest that he had already prepared his own translations of these plays by Diderot in 1759.

---

185 Charles Batteux, *Les Beaux Arts réduits à une même principe* (Paris: Chez Durant, Libraire, 1746). See FA 2, 125.

186 FA 2, 126.

187 [Denis Diderot], *Lettre sur les sourds et muets A l'Usage de ceux qui entendent & qui parlent. Addressée à M*** ([Paris]: n.p. 1751).

188 Selections from *Das Theater des Herrn Diderot* are published in the Frankfurt edition of Lessing's works: "Diderot: Dramatische Dichtkunst," FA 5/1, 124-234; "Der Hausvater" FA 5/1, 23-125. In November 1757 after its author had served a jail sentence for atheism and materialism, Diderot's play *Le Fils naturel ou les Épreuves de la Vertu, Comédie en cinq Actes, et en Prose, avec l'Histoire véritable de la Pièce* (Amsterdam [Paris]: n.p., 1757) appeared in print, and exactly one year later, *Le Père de famille. Comédie en cinq Actes, et en Prose, avec un Discours, sue la Poésie dramatique* (Amsterdam [Paris]: n.p. [Michel Lambert], 1758). *Le Fils naturel* was subject to a charge that it may have plagiarized or had adopted elements from *Il vero amico* (The True Friend) by Carlo Goldoni (1707-1793) which had appeared in 1750.This charge was refuted in 1759. Both of these plays by Diderot were performed in anonymous German translations in Frankfurt am Main by Konrad Ackermann's troupe of players. See Nisbet, *Lessing: Eine Biographie* 360; *Gotthold Ephraim Lessing*, 271-272. Konrad Ackermann is characterized by Nisbet as being "a pioneer of the new realism" (*Lessing:*

In his 81st *Literaturbrief* of February 7, 1760, Lessing vents his frustration at the current state of the German theater: "Wir haben kein Theater. Wir haben keine Schauspieler. Wir haben keine Zuhörer" (We have no theater. We have no actors. We have no audience).[189] Just as Diderot challenged his public in France, Lessing set out to challenge the conditions in the German theater of the time. Nobody, neither an artist, nor a poet, should impose one's own thought and emotions on the public. What they should do, however, he insisted, was to spark interest in real character descriptions, their inner circles and *milieu*. He set out to address aspects of their social conditions, moods, and the vexed intellectual climate with the hope to create something new. It has been argued that Lessing's works, such as the comedy *Minna von Barnhelm* (1767), the "Bürgerliches Trauerspiel" (bourgeois tragedy) *Emilia Galotti* (1772), and the "Dramatisches Gedicht" (dramatic play or "poem") *Nathan der Weise* (1779) reflect the influence of Diderot's dramatic theory.[190] These works diverge from expected norms of genre and mix comical and social-critical elements with tragedy and high drama. They have something preliminary and open-ended, and their sketch-like features are prefigured in Diderot's *Salons*. Lessing explicitly acknowledges the influence of Diderot's thinking on his own and we may find that Diderot had more influence on the German stage than he did on that in France. There he was critical, as Lessing was, of the fashionable plays of *pictorialism* which often were marked by what Lessing terms "Schilderungssucht." Whereas Lessing acknowledged how much he felt indebted to Diderot, he also drew from others and made his own innovations.[191]

---

*Eine Biographie* 278; *Gotthold Ephraim Lessing*, 208). His troupe had been responsible for the first performance of *Miß Sara Sampson* in 1755.

189 FA 6, 698–706 at 700.

190 See for example Louise Crowther, *Diderot and Lessing as Exemplars of a Post-Spinozist Mentality*, MHRA Texts and Dissertations 78 (London: Manley, 2010), 34–38.

191 In the preface to the second edition of his translation of Diderot which appeared in 1780 with his name on the title page, Lessing writes: "Ich bin ersucht worden, dieser Übersetzung öffentlich meinen Namen zu geben. Da es nun vorlängst unbekannt zu sein aufgehöret hat, daß ich wirklich der Verfasser derselben bin; da ich mich des Fleißes, den ich darauf gewandt habe, und des Nutzens, den ich daraus gezogen, noch immer mit Vergnügen erinnere: so sehe ich nicht, warum ich mich einer Anforderung weigern sollte, die mir Gelegenheit giebt meine Dankbarkeit einem Mann zu bezeugen, der an der Bildung meines Geschmacks so großen Anteil hat. Denn es mag mit diesem auch beschaffen sein wie es will: so bin ich mir doch zuwohl bewußt, daß er, ohne Diderots Muster und Lehren, eine ganz andere Richtung würde bekommen haben. Vielleicht eine eigenere; aber doch schwerlich eine, mit der am Ende mein Verstand zufriedener gewesen wäre. Diderot scheint überhaupt auf das deutsche Theater weit mehr Einfluß gehabt zu haben, als auf das Theater seines eigenen Volks." (FA 5/1, 15) (I have been asked to give this translation publicly my name. Since it has recently stopped to be unknown that I am really the author of it; since I remember with pleasure the diligence which I have spent on it and the benefit which I have drawn from it: so I do not see why I should deny such a request which would give me the opportunity to express my gratitude to a man who has such great part in the development of my taste. In whatever state that may be, I am well aware that it would have taken a rather different direction without Diderot's modeling and teaching, perhaps a direction more of my own but barely one that would have made my mind more content. Generally speaking, Diderot seems to have made far more of an impact on German theater than on the theater of his own people). For a helpful study of Diderot's work, see Derek

Romira M. Worvill finds that it is a difficult question to answer why Lessing's earlier writings, before 1760, appear to show Diderot's influence. She also finds it hard to explain how Lessing came up with some apparent affinities.[192] She finds that Lessing incorporated visually expressive scenes and thus used elements of Diderot's approach in his own theory and practice "before he came across the theatrical writings of his French contemporary"(3). Worvill calls this "one of the unsolved puzzles of literary history" and pursues it to a certain extent when exploring also theories of art and literature forming the background to Diderot's work. She asserts the notion of "Diderot's innovations," while nevertheless showing in detail how the concept of the "painterly sign" developed by Roger de Piles,[193] the concept of an "invisible poet developed by Antoine Houdar de la Motte," and the idea of a "hidden spectator" proposed by Paul Landois.[194] All these provide fruitful influences for Diderot's approach to the theater and also influenced Lessing. Worvill elaborates on synthesis and innovation in Diderot's dramatic writings and emphasizes the importance of illusion. [195] The third section of her study is about what she calls "Lessing's assimilation of the new theatrical code."[196]

---

R. Connon, *Innovation and Renewal: A Study of the Theatrical Works of Diderot*, Studies on Voltaire and the Eighteenth Century 258 (Oxford: The Voltaire Foundation, 1989).

192 Worvill, *'Seeing' Speech* 2 argues that "a number of features generally considered hallmarks of Diderot's theater aesthetic are also present in Lessing's thinking and dramatic style before 1757." She shows that already in *Theatralische Bibliothek* of 1754 Lessing expresses a need for mixing virtue and vice in "wahre Komödien" (true comedies) (FA 3, 279). Worvill comments that Lessing writes so that these plays should approximate true life with specific events and experiences yet with universal appeal. The notion of "seeing" is used both in a concrete and in an abstract sense. One may add that in Lessing's two completed tragedies of the 1750s, *Miss Sara Sampson* and *Philotas*, he uses tableau-like scenes, thus aiming at what he reflects as "Anblick" (spectacle) (*Philotas*, Scene 6) (FA 4, 28).

193 See further Kohle, *Ut pictura poesis non erit* 43-46.

194 Landois' *Silvie, Tragédie en prose* (Paris: Chez Perrault fils, 1742) is internationally considered to be the first "bourgeois tragedy."

195 One must acknowledge Martin Fried's contribution in this context since he explored the paradox explored by Diderot that in order to be successful, a still-life painter must not just ignore the spectator: "It was necessary to obviate him, to deny his presence, to establish positively insofar as that could be done that he had not been taken into account [...] Diderot's conception of painting rested ultimately on the supreme fiction that the beholder did not exist, that he was not really there, standing in front of the canvas." Michael Fried, *Absorption and Theatricality: Painting and Beholder in the Age of Diderot* (Chicago: University of Chicago Press, 1980), 103. Yet the existence of pictures already presupposes viewers. See Worvill, *'Seeing' Speech* 79.

196 Worvill, *'Seeing' Speech* 113-209. Whereas such critics as Robert Heitner, "Concerning Lessing's Indebtedness to Diderot," *Modern Language Notes* 65 (1950): 82-88, Roland Mortier, *Diderot en Allemagne, 1750-1850* (Paris: Presses universitaires de France, 1954), and Theodorus C. Van Stockum, "Lessing und Diderot," *Neophilologus* 39 (1955): 191-202, examined aspects of Diderot reception in the work of Lessing, they and others tend to focus their studies on Lessing's translations of Diderot, his interest in a middle genre, and Lessing's application of Diderot's theory of conditions. According to Worvill, *'Seeing' Speech* they tend to underestimate the significance of the statements made by Lessing in 1780 and limit Diderot's role in Lessing's development to that of an ally in the shared rejection of French neo-classicism (19-23).

One may question however whether Lessing assimilated to the ideas by Diderot or to what extent they had a dialogue that had an impact on both innovators. Lessing shares with Diderot a plea for a careful, non-imposing mode of expression that does not give away all the details and refuses to offer explanations or conclusions. He does not believe in being able to solve all the puzzles being presented in real life or onstage. He perhaps also favors the spoken over the written word, thus drawing attention to multiple voices. Lessing's art of understatement or Diderot's minimalism are interrelated in that they do not pretend to provide a complete and polished product. In denying that, the artist or author is then allowed to be excused from certain traditional criteria that were expected from good art or poetic writing and from standards set by Aristotelian norms. Implicit could be a critique of such "high" artworks and writings that may have lost their life due to oppressive form, exaggerated ornament, and imposing rules. For example, Lessing abolishes the use of Alexandrine verse in his dramas for a more natural speech onstage while paying attention to rhythm, musical harmony, and a sense of order. As already mentioned above, he does away with "the moral" or the concluding section of the fable, a genre he contributes to while deconstructing its form. He raises awareness for the fragmentary visibility of truth, for the problem with any final yet premature conclusions, and he brings to attention such arbitrary structures that are often imposed on us in the realm of art and literature. Instead of being natural or simply out there, they are in fact culturally coded and in their totality simply a matter of social convention. Lessing in his late works prefers open endings and parables similar to the scope Diderot associated with the sketch that can capture whatever is quintessential. Lessing shared with Diderot an approach that believed in the ability of successful Ekphrasis and one which also favored minimalism. Lessing published reviews and translations of a number of works by Diderot, including a series of critical essays and plays.[197] He too thought about the question what the most effective iconographic and rhetorical strategies might be. Diderot had already written several treatises on the complexity of correlating sense perceptions, such as his *Lettre sur les aveugles* (Letter on the Blind) (1749)[198] and the *Lettre sur les sourds et muets* ("Letter on the Deaf and the Mute", 1751).[199]

Lessing was interested in the content of these works, but in addition he commented about Diderot's writing style, as if his rhetorical mode was a kind of handwriting, similar to the painter's stroke with a brush. Diderot's style as Lessing describes it (in a continued ekphrastic process that turns the writing again into a visual description) has "broken lines," consisting of digressions, and is marked by discontinuity. In his review of the *Lettre sur les sourds et muets*, Lessing comments: "Er [Diderot] schweift überall aus, er springt von einem auf das andere." (He digresses everywhere; he jumps from one thing to another).[200] Lessing does not blame Diderot for this; on the contrary in a letter also from 1751, he characterizes him as "einer von den Weltweisen" (one of the

---

197 Lessing, *Das Theater des Herrn Diderot,* 2 vols. (Berlin: Christian Friedrich Voß, 1760-1761); 2nd ed. 2 vols. (Berlin: Christian Friedrich Voß und Sohn, 1781).

198 [Denis Diderot], *Lettre sur les Aveugles A l'Usage de Ceux qui Voyent* (London [Paris]: n.p., 1749).

199 Lessing, FA 2, 127-40, 698.

200 FA 2, 127.

wise cosmopolitans) and concludes his positive evaluation by calling Diderot "einer von [...], welche sich mehr Mühe geben, Wolken zu machen, als sie zu zerstreuen" (someone [...] who puts more effort into creating clouds than into dispersing them).[201] In this context Lessing is an advocate of clouds. They are as necessary and productive in art as they are in nature.

One may argue that this review was actually a mirroring or a projection of Lessing's own writing style defended in the context of a review of the work of Diderot. He too rebelled against the presumed criticisms others might have had and rejected an overdone style of particularizing everything and dissolving visions into miniature fractions. Lessing noticed that such a style of writing can evoke a sense of uncertainty and that jumping from one thing to another may express more than just boredom or a mere lack of focus or decision, arguments that may have held against him too. Diderot's *Lettres* highlighted incongruities among sense perceptions and logical ideas and he questioned the tensions and incompatibilities between them. How can it be that seeing, touch, and hearing can interfere and be mutually exclusive at times? In his review of the *Lettre sur les sourds et muets*, Lessing refers to Diderot's "Ungebundenheit" (boundlessness)[202] in his use of language, suggesting that images are liberated from mimetic expectations and not firmly tied up to previously established fields of meaning. They can be understood sometimes as if they were free floating words, fluid metaphors that have multiple meanings depending on waves and currents. Lessing is impressed with how Diderot makes the reader aware of certain "Versetzungen" (displacements) of thoughts and in doings so shifting their focus from one frame of reference to another,[203] making the reader learn how to think conceptually and metaphorically.

Problems of perception, cognition, and the origin of ideas in images and sense impressions, these were all topics highly discussed in eighteenth-century discourses. Of particular interest was the question how sense perceptions contributed to reflection and thought. Also the correlation among the senses and the processes from sensation to perception and thinking were frequently discussed in writings on medicine, philosophy, and literature. William Cheselden, an English surgeon and author of *The Anatomy of the Humane Body* (1713), a standard medicine textbook for the next century, had made a successful cataract operation on a young boy who was blind but after the operation could see again, although he had some difficulties at first concerning the correlation between the visual and the tactile senses.[204] Journals and newspapers such as the *Philosophical Transactions* spread the news about the Cheselden case widely

---

201 FA 2, 698.

202 FA 2, 127.

203 FA 2, 127. Hans Adler, "Sind Anschauungen ohne Begriffe blind?" Adler and Gross, ed., *Anschauung und Anschaulichkeit* 27–44, challenges the Kantian axiom that thoughts without content are empty and that images without words are blind, by instead shifting interest to Herder and eventually to the work of Olaf Breidbach who in his book, *Neurale Ästhetik. Morpho-Logik des Anschauens* (Munich: Fink, 2013) tracing "Anschauung" or seeing to a pre-discursive stage and to cognition, neuroscience, and language philosophy. We may find that such relevant issues already underlie the critical Lessing-Diderot debate against the normative thinking of their time.

204 William Cheselden, *The Anatomy of the Humane Body Illustrated with Twenty-three Copper-Plates of the most Considerable Parts; All Done after the Life* (London: N. Cliff and D. Jackson, 1713).

throughout Europe. Contributors to this long ongoing debate had been initially John Locke with his epistemology making sense perception basic to all experience, then the Irish priest and philosopher George Berkeley who in his *Essay towards a New Theory of Vision* (1709) found that the eye and the hand are separated by differing "ideas" that are each specifically associated with the appropriate organ of perception.[205] As I have demonstrated elsewhere, Berkeley came to conclusions that are particularly important for metaphor theory when he claimed that everything is contextual just as are metaphors in language.[206] There were subsequently important contributions by such French writers as Voltaire, Condillac, La Mettrie, Buffon, and Diderot who had their own reflections to add to the debate although it was Diderot who had the strongest influence on Lessing in this context.

John O'Neal has argued that Diderot's major contribution to this discourse in the *Lettre sur les aveugles and its philosophical implications* was to add to the philosophical debate the discovery that "confusion" is simply not only a matter of a disability. He argues: "Diderot is no different in his thinking from his European contemporaries, except he adds his own idiosyncratic turn to the notion of confusion, radicalizing it as no one else would".[207] And O'Neal is perceptive in his account of Diderot's innovations in this debate:

> He paradoxically uses the state of confusion both as a behavior to be avoided through analytic methodology and as a necessary condition for enlightenment. Moreover, he would make of it a state to be maintained and not always to be avoided. Taking an inherently philosophical position, he believed that confusion ultimately defines our humanity and that it could lead us to a new realism. [208]

Diderot, in other words characterized disability as something we are all inflicted with and he suggests in fact that everyone should learn from those with noticeable disabilities because such people may in fact be even more closely connected to what is "real" than those who seem to function normally. O'Neal further comments: "The equality of the blind and the sighted becomes more pronounced when Diderot turns to the well-known blind English mathematician, Nicholas Saundersen."[209] O'Neil distinguishes various notions of confusion in Diderot's discourse and finds that one kind of confusion, according to Diderot, is not at all marginal or curable, something restricted to only a concern to some in society; rather it is profound, general, and unavoidable to some extent, despite all the progress towards Enlightenment. Diderot, in the discourse of Lessing, thus stands as an advocate of clouds that have their own beauty.

---

205 George Berkeley, *An Essay towards a New Theory of Vision* (Dublin: Aaron Rhames [...] for Jeremy Pepyat, 1709).

206 Beate Allert, "Theorizing Visual Language in George Berkeley and Jean Paul." *Studies in Eighteenth Century Culture* 27 (1998): 307-342.

207 John O'Neal, "Diderot and the Enlightenment's poetics of confusion in the *Lettre sur les aveugles,*" Ogée and Strugnell, ed., *Diderot and European Culture,* 159-169 at 160.

208 O'Neal, "Diderot" 160.

209 O'Neal, "Diderot"160. Nicholas Sanderson was a blind English mathematician who became a fictional character so to speak in Diderot's own writings where he stands as an icon connecting disability with genius and superior talent.

To the question by William Molyneux in response to Locke how it is possible that a man who was blind, even after having his eyesight restored, still had difficulties to distinguish a cube from a square, Diderot suggested that this person was still not relying on sight as much as on the sense of touch because he did what he was still accustomed to. Tactile and visual sense perceptions differ and their correlation may be a matter of habit or learning. Diderot did not believe that there was an innate mental capacity to distinguish shapes, as Locke had thought, but that even perception and reasoning were matters of a cultural conditioning. In other words, the boy who was blind and suddenly had his vision restored but still could not distinguish a globe from a sketch was perfectly defendable for Diderot. Molyneux and Locke had thought that it was a matter of innate senses but in their accounts they did not take habit and culture sufficiently into account.[210] If seeing is culturally conditioned and has to be learnt, then it is not naturally given, but rather a matter of habit and numerous other circumstances. If reading was a matter of cultural training, then how would it be possible to share truly new ideas? The conclusion drawn was that the modes of seeing had to be changed in order to show the public something new. Diderot and Lessing consequently shift awareness to the medium and the recipients. Language can have effects on the reader, whether by means of syntax, semantics, and context-specific metaphor, yet Lessing followed Diderot in arguing that a minimal representation is to be preferred to an overly elaborate one. As we shall see in his late work, however, Lessing is no longer asking about sketches and new beginnings but also about consequences, multiple signification systems interacting, and future criteria to detect truth. He shifts attention from aesthetics to ethics.

## 3. Poetic consequences and how to energize the audiences

Diderot had next to Shakespeare probably the strongest influence on Lessing concerning theater and the use of dramatic language. Language was considered metaphoric at the core, so that images were not imposed or secondary to it, but embedded in its deep structure. All language onstage had to appear more "natural" than was usual in the Aristotelian theater tradition which certainly also had an impact on Lessing, although he did away with the classical Alexandrine meter for the sake of a much less stilted iambus.[211] The goal was not to show the artificiality of the theater, but to bring

---

210 On more aspects and contributors to this discussion see: M.J. Morgan, *Molineux's Question: Vision, Touch and the Philosophy of Perception* (Cambridge: Cambridge University Press, 1977), Jean-Bernard Mérian, *Sur le problème de Molyneux*, ed. Francine Markovits (Paris: Flammarion, 1984) and Utz, *Das Auge und das Ohr*, esp. 18-25.

211 On Lessing and Aristotle, see Eun-Ae Kim, *Lessings Tragödientheorie im Licht der neueren Asistotelesforschung*, Epistemata 374 (Würzburg: Königshausen & Neumann, 2002) and Thomas Martinec, "Lessing und Aristoteles? Versuch einer Grenzbestimmung in Lessings Interpretation des aristotelischen Tragödienansatzes," Zeuch, ed., *Lessings Grenzen*, 82-100. Also see Martinec, *Lessings Theorie der Tragödienwirkung. Humanistische Tradition und aufklärerische Erkenntniskritik*, Untersuchungen zur deutschen Literaturgeschichte 116 (Tübingen: Niemeyer, 2003).

it closer to life, not necessarily to endorse it as it is but in a more subtle undertaking to influence the people and how they feel, not only how they think. Diderot's ability to describe paintings in his *Salons* as if you were walking with him through an art gallery offered rich material of presenting "visual writing" and this in turn led to a vividness and mobilizing of imagination by the readers who were to be engaged both intellectually and emotionally. They were allowed to experience something real through art and art became the spectacle though which to understand real life better. Mimetic assumptions were being challenged and even reversed and this also had consequences also for drama production. Theoretical links were drawn between the modes of writing and the modes of presenting visual things onstage. Two professions got to collaborate, those of the storyteller and the dramaturge.

Hubertus Kohle gives a helpful account of Diderot's innovations for the drama and it is one of his observations that it was thanks to Roger de Piles and Abbé Diderot that the *ut pictura poesis not erit* tradition was revolutionized. A new double meaning of the notion of Mimesis was invented: In the Aristotelian approach, nature contains within itself a complete repertoire of all imaginable possibilities so that any new action or act of cognition is unthinkable because such things are virtually always prefigured, However the segmentation of the world of phenomena into an uncountable number of individuations is however only "reality" for the superficial observer; these apparitions are compared to the much more real abstract reality of the formal principle only of lesser importance ("uneigentlich"). What really matters with Diderot according to Kohle is that imitation is not only tied to what is naturally given, not only conditioned by "the factual," or to things "das [...] durch die Materialisierung korrumpierte Faktische" (that are corrupted by the absorbing materialization). Moreover, *imitatio* is tied to "das universelle Ideale" (the universal ideal).[212] Consequently, the activity of an artist is not primarily an active creative one, but also an active mirroring one of a more critical nature. The product is never a pure construction of the subject; moreover it echoes something "objective" that was potentially given already. Kohle concludes that the arts are comparable because the different forms of the sense related presentations (*elocutio*) are less important than their shared ideals.

This is precisely what changed in the eighteenth century when artists in France and Germany began to question the hierarchy between *inventio* and *elocutio* and the transparency of any "objective" world for the sake of a more reception-oriented approach. What follows is a necessary of semiotic distinction: "Die hier implizierte semiotische Problematik der Verbindung von *signifiant* and *signifié* führt nun aber dazu, daß die eben beschriebenen Grundlagen der Klassischen Theorie aus den Angeln gehoben werden" (The thus implied semiotic problem of the correlation between the significant and the sign and signified leads to the fact that these described premises of the classical theory are being unhinged).[213] Kohle continues his assessment of Lessing's contribution in this broader context in summarizing first the main points of Diderot's aesthetic theory as follows: a) The sense of beauty becomes rooted in the "Spiel" or "play" among the various modes of perception and cognition; b) whatever the "beau" or "beautiful" is, it becomes de-substantialized and works in terms of functions (*rap-*

212 Kohle, *Ut pictura poesis non erit* 2.
213 Kohle, *Ut pictura poesis non erit* 3.

*ports*); c) the forms of expression are brought in the context of the historical process, so that the relationship between "pensée" (thought) and the articulated (expression) are also seen from a historical perspective; d) the example of the drama helps define the autonomy of the poetic text as a form of an inner coherence; and e) the resulting hermeneutic of the poetic text leads to a new understanding of the spectator, who is now being conceptualized in a much more active role than in literature before.[214]

It remains to be examined, however, to what extent Lessing followed the tradition of Ekphrasis that believed in a verbalizing of the visual, or whether he should be placed among the critics of Ekphrasis who see a problem with the idea that such a transfer could be easy and complete. It seems that whereas he uses *tableaux vivants* in several of his plays, he also maintains the notion that the verbal and the visual differ sharply and that a friction and tension exists in the process of any such semiotic transformation. Both Diderot and Lessing did, I agree, not follow the neo-classical tradition of their contemporaries but believed instead that drama is capable of making the signs of language become visual with the help of the actors and spectators. Lessing favors action that is not shown from the beginning to the end but similar to Diderot's tour in the *Salons*, leaves things open to the imagination by audiences whom he tries to transform into spectators. They were to learn seeing things described with their own inner eyes and fully experience the impact. Lessing writes in *Laokoon*:

> Kann der Künstler von der immer veränderlichen Natur nie mehr als nur einen einzigen Augenblick, und der Maler insbesondere diesen einzigen Augenblick auch nur aus einem einzigen Gesichtspunkte, brauchen; sind aber ihre Werke gemacht, nicht bloβ erblickt, sondern betrachtet zu werden, lange und wiederholter maβen betrachtet zu werden: so ist es gewiβ, dass jener einzige Augenblick und einzige Gesichtspunkt dieses einzigen Augenblicks, nicht fruchtbar genug gewählet werden kann. Dasjenige aber nur allein ist fruchtbar, was der Einbildungskraft freies Spiel lässt. Je mehr wir sehen, desto mehr müssen wir uns dazu denken können. Je mehr wir darzu denken, desto mehr müssen wir zu sehen glauben.[215]

> [If the artist can never make use of more than one single moment in ever-changing nature, and if the painter in particular can use this moment only with reference to a single vantage point, while the works of both painter and sculptor are created not merely to be given a glance but to be contemplated–contemplated repeatedly and at length: so it is certain that this single moment and the point from which it is viewed cannot be chosen with too great a regard for its effect. But only that which gives free rein to the imagination is effective. The more we see the more we must be able to imagine. And the more we add in our imaginations, the more we must be able to think we see].[216]

Lessing draws attention to processes of reflection on seeing and the fact that seeing often already means interpreting and vice versa. The artist must chose the most "pregnant" moment for representation in visual art in order to compensate the temporal limitations imposed on the spatial arts. Lessing and Diderot share a liking for such expression in the visual and in the verbal that is minimalist and that does not prescribe too much to the spectator and reader. At the same time, they both rely on

---

214 Kohle, *Ut pictura poesis non erit* 89.
215 FA 5/2, 32.
216 *Laocoön*, trans. McCormick 19.

"energeia" or what Aristotle refers to as "bringing-before-the-eye."[217] What mimesis meant changed in the course of the eighteenth century and has been much debated.[218] While both Lessing and Diderot challenge several traditions, including that of traditional mimesis, they both contribute to a type of expression that does not abandon the image for empowering the word instead. Even on the way from *Mythos to Logos*, something of the initial image can remain in language and metaphors are, as Walter Benjamin asserts, a matter for "Schwellenkunde" (a science of thresholds).[219] It may well capture the visual in the verbal, elements of unfinished thought as they emerge in poetic writing and in literature much more than they would in discursive "Begriffe" (the language of terminologies). Accordingly, words do not have to overwrite images, repress, or territorialize them; they can co-exist in intricate ways as both Lessing and Diderot are well aware (despite those critics who falsely conflate their advocacy for minimalism with an anti-visual stance), although the medium matters. The almost "silent scream" of the Laokoon figure is more effective than if the mouth of Laokoon were wide open. By acknowledging that, Lessing does not silence the scream but instead draws awareness to the potential of that scream, to that which goes before or beyond any normal expression. Similarly to what Diderot did for the blind in his letters on the mute and on the blind, he shifts attention not only to the medium of the arts, but also to what remains unrealized not only in art but already in reality, perhaps due to pain, due to a human disability, or due to censorship, a reality which Lessing also dealt with when he shifted his discourse from the pulpit to the stage in order to pursue his own rights. Painting is the art of space. Music is the art of time. Poetic writing oscillates with a tension between them and works both with the linearity and sequences of the visual arts as well as with the multiple-layers and simultaneities of the acoustic. Lessing places much importance on performance, the action with the visual and the verbal that involves the spectator and audience. He favors dialogue, as does Diderot. The visual artist cannot present more than one single moment out of the flux of time and the artist must choose "the most pregnant moment."

Herder gives in his *Kritische Wälder* (Critical Forests) a succinct description of Lessing's style which, as he points out, consists for example in contrast to the writings by Winckelmann in rather fragmented excursions. Lessing presents to us in his writings not only a finished product but provides glimpses into the artwork, its genesis, its own mechanisms, theoretical underpinnings, and technical devices. He writes: "Lessings Schreibart ist der Styl eines Poeten, d.i. eines Schriftstellers, nicht der gemacht hat, sondern der da machet, nicht der gedacht haben will, sondern uns vordenket, wir sehen sein Werk werdend, wie das Schild Achilles bei Homer."[220] (Lessing's mode of

---

217 See above p. 55 or Collins note 138.

218 Stephen Bann, *The True Vine. On Visual Representation and Western Tradition* (Cambridge: Cambridge University Press, 1989). Also see Norman Bryson, especially his chapters "Diderot and the Word" and "Diderot and the Image," *Word and Image. French Painting of the Ancien Régime* (Cambridge: Cambridge University Press, 1981), 154-178, 179-203.

219 On this see Winfried Menninghaus, *Schwellenkunde: Walter Benjamins Passage des Mythos*, edition Suhrkamp, N.F. 349 (Frankfurt am Main: Suhrkamp, 1986) and Azade Seyhan, "Visual Citations: Walter Benjamin's Dialect of Text Image," Allert, ed., *Languages of Visuality* 229-241.

220 Herder, HFA 2, 67.

writing is the style of a poet, that is, a writer who has not done, but in the process of doing, who does not claim to have thought, but thinks ahead of us, we see his work while it is in process to becoming completed, just like the shield of Achilles in Homer). He evokes the ancient definitions of what Ekphrasis means by thus giving us a visual notion of what we see in front of our eyes as the text evokes images in our mind. Herder continues his commentary: "Er scheint uns die Veranlassung jeder Reflexion gleichsam vor Augen zu führen, stückweise zu zerlegen, zusammen zu setzen: nun springt die Triebfeder, das Rad läuft, ein Gedanke, ein Schluß giebt dem anderen, der Folgesatz kommt näher, da ist das Produkt der Betrachtung [...] sein Buch ist ein fortlaufendes Poem, mit Einsprüngen und Episoden, aber immer unstät, immer Arbeit, im Werden".[221] (He seems, metaphorically speaking, to bring in front of our eyes the cause of each reflection, to dissect it piece by piece, to reconstruct it: now the driving force, the wheel runs, a thought, a conclusion gives momentum to the next, the concluding sentence gets nearly approximated, there is to be the product of observation [...] his book is a continuous poem with digressions and episodes but always restless, in motion, always working in the process of becoming).

Lessing's own writing style reflects his approach to the visual arts that is also one that is process-oriented and a matter of analyzing steps and causes as much as results or possible consequences. It is, as far as Lessing's own approach to theater is concerned, characterized by welcoming the productive imagination of the viewer, by limiting the painterly onstage as much as possible for the sake of giving freedom to the spectator. Lessing is wondering, what would be the most "pregnant moment" of the artwork and why the artist chose to keep the mouth of the father in the Laokoon statue almost closed as if he were to express an "almost silent scream." The reasons Lessing gives for his position have to do primarily with the limits of the medium. He argues that the signs painting uses for its reproductions are much different from the signs poetic language uses. The visual expression uses figures and colors in space and the verbal expression uses articulated sounds in time. Painting and the visual arts are limited to what is visible but the figures and colors in space which they are to signify actually move and go quickly beyond the visible. How then, this is the question, to present the invisible via the most effective expression in art? Lessing explains that not only in visual art but also in writing what matters is freedom to the imagination of the works' recipients. When he draws a line between the visual and the verbal in *Laokoon,* he does it not to exclude the visual from the verbal since he allows metaphor (similar to Diderot's sketches) back into the realm of poetic writing or fiction. Nor does Lessing once and for all exclude the temporal form the visual arts. He recognizes that their territory is space but his concept of the "pregnant moment" which has to be chosen by the visual artist for the moment of representation indicates that what Lessing tries to mobilize is a kind of seeing that goes beyond the present. Whereas Lessing shuns away from the use of allegories whose temporality is often all too coded and prescribed, he emancipates the visual from the verbal and the verbal from the visual respectively. He challenges a kind of Ekphrasis that relies on tradition. Lessing celebrates poetic language between the spatial and the temporal, the visual arts and

221 Herder, HFA 2, 67.

music. Its performance allows multiple voices and layering of meanings, plus open endings.

Lessing and Diderot both questioned pictorialism and the rococo style; they favored the aesthetic theories of Shaftesbury, Mendelssohn or the empiricist Locke, among others. Lessing in his *Laokoon* was critical of Baumgarten's categorical approach, but also of the Comte de Caylus whose pictorialism goes too far into the excesses of flowery style.[222] Lessing was also critical of the Classicist Winckelmann whose formulas "edle Einfalt" (noble simplicity) and "stille Größe" (silent grandeur) have to do with such ideals of high art that lead to a totalizing notion of unified perfection.[223] Also, Winckelmann ignores media distinctions between the visual and the verbal and does not share Lessing's intense desire to gain an inclusive, educated audience. Both Diderot and Lessing shared a minimalist approach and a certain political agenda with respect to the visual and the verbal that has a liberating effect in making the reception a part of production and showing that the production is already in the hands of the public. They created new scenarios for the artist and the spectator, the author and the reader, and invited interaction among them in order to advocate free imagination and critical thinking by the general public. There are these similarities between Diderot and Lessing considering their process-oriented, open-ended approach to visuality, their plea for understatement and minimalism, and their attempt to make language itself "visual" by questioning visibility at the same time.

Lessing in his later work introduced more complex levels of metaphoricity, multiple frames, digressions, and layering devices into his fictional dialogues. In his *Laokoon,* Lessing may have drawn a border between the visual and the verbal by aligning the verbal more with music than with the visual arts, thus allowing for features of simultaneity which are excluded in the visual arts for the sake of presenting one single "pregnant moment." Also in the verbal, Lessing attempts to present moments that can be already be considered "stills," as Eisenstein later called them, quasi arrested or framed moments that speak for action before and afterwards. Lessing seems often to exclude the temporal from the visual, but more precisely, he excludes what one normally considers temporal and shows a gap between various kinds of chronology, be they inner and outer time. These are not congruent when experienced. He interrogates in his later works the temporal by focusing on the fleeting moments that should have been fruitful but since they were missed what followed had devastating consequences. Lessing is trying to explore the liminalities of the visual and the spatial by shifting to the powerful dimension of temporality.

---

222 See Beate Allert, "Lessing's Poetics as an Approach to Aesthetics," Fischer and Fox, ed., *Companion* 104-130.

223 "Die edle Einfalt und stille große der griechischen Statuen ist zugleich das wahre Kennzeichen der griechischen Schriften aus den besten Zeiten" (The noble simplicity and quiet grandeur of the Greek statues is also the true hallmark of Greek writings from their best period). See Johann Joachim Winckelmann, *Gedanken ueber die Nachahmung der griechischen Werke in der Malerey und Bildhauerkunst,* 2nd enlarged ed. (1756), reprinted in Elfriede Heyer and Roger C. Norton, ed. and trans., *Reflections on the Imitation of Greek Works in Painting and Sculpture, complete German text* (La Salle, IL: Open Court, 1987), 1-69 at 36-39; "Gedanken ueber die Nachahmung der griechischen Werke," Walther Rehm, ed., *Kleine Schriften, Vorreden, Entwürfe,* 2nd ed. (Berlin: De Gruyter, 2002), 27-89 at 45.

As indicated above, Lessing draws attention to a pregnant moment before the climax in an action and he often leaves either the beginning or the ending open. His parable of the burning palace to be discussed in a following chapter is exemplary in revealing more than one chronology. Those who are searching for the ground plans, debating where the original might be located at the same time the palace is in fact burning, respond in a way that is clearly inadequate. So do those who run immediately to extinguish the fire not knowing yet that what appears as a fire is only an optical illusion, some strange phenomenon in nature. Indeterminacy remains and readers are left with multiple options to interpret this paradoxical parable.[224] It consists of various "epiphoric metaphors" or metaphors that do not replace any underlying meanings but add layers of meaning.

These then resemble already superimposed clips in a film, a kind of montage, images assembled and fluid in such a way that what was previous works simultaneously. By exploring the limits of the visual and the verbal, Lessing experimented in his own distinct way. Lessing was fully aware that one-dimensional linearity no longer suffices and that metaphor is unavoidable. Lessing notes: "Es ist nicht wahr, daβ die kürzeste Linie immer die Gerade ist" (It is not true that the shortest line is always the directly linear one).[225] This insight drawing attention to the importance of context was to become also influential for the film producer and critic Eisenstein. He was to develop a related idea when he writes: "The copulation (perhaps we had better say the combination) of two hieroglyphs of the simplest series is to be regarded not as their sum, but as their product, i.e. as a value of another dimension, another degree each, separately, corresponds to an object, to a fact, but their combination corresponds to a concept."[226] The search for a new creative dimension that goes beyond linear writing and beyond flat and culturally coded images is a concern already at the core of the daring minimalist approach to the visual in the fables and the *Hamburgische Dramaturgie* and the aesthetics of understatement in Lessing's *Laokoon*. As s we shall see, he admits in his late work that discrepancies and open questions remain and are to be part and parcel of any sensible vision for a diversified humanity.

---

224 For a close reading see Beate Allert, "About a Burning Building in Eco and Lessing: Or How to Process Messages?" *Lessing Yearbook* 29 (1997): 57–86.

225 *Die Erziehung des Menschengeschlechts* § 91 (FA 10, 98).

226 Sergej Eisenstein, *Film Form* (Orlando: Harcourt Brace Jovanovich, 1969), 30.

# Chapter 3
# Fables as Visual Texts but Brevity Matters

Abstract: This chapter examines Lessing's approach to visual language as found in the fable, a genre that fascinated Lessing and occupied him throughout his life both practically by translating and contributing fables to the long standing tradition himself and theoretically by writing extensive treatises about them. This activity helped shape Lessing's ideal of "Anschaulichkeit" (vividness) as attributed not only to oral but also to written language. Furthermore Lessing contributed decisively to the development and history of this genre. This chapter explores how Lessing is setting out on his investigation on visual language by learning from the ancient fable tradition. He is an admirer of Aesop's fables but aims at a style of narrative that could do without any explicit moral for the sake of its own integral message.

## 1. What is a Fable? The basics before Lessing

From the very beginning of printing, booksellers reaped rewards by publishing collections of short moral narratives associated with Aesop. He was said to be a slave and a story teller who lived in ancient Greece in the sixth century BCE and made it up the social latter due to his excellent work. He was called "the father of the fable" and Lessing had enormous respect for him.[227] Erwin Leibfried notes in his survey of the fable in German that between the years 1470 and 1600 there were published more than 686 editions of Aesop's fables.[228] Also in England there were hundreds of such editions printed, beginning with William Caxton, *The Book of the Subtyll Historyes of Aesop* published in 1486. In the Greek rhetorical tradition the word "fable" is defined as follows: "A Fable (*mythos*) is a fictitious story giving an image of truth."[229] During the early modern period "the fable" became a fantastic story, something fictional used as a

227 See Ben Edwin Perry, "Introduction," Babrius and Phaedrus, *Fables*, ed. and trans. B.E, Perry, Loeb Classical Library 436 (Cambridge: Harvard University Press, 1965), xxxv–xlvi. The standard work on the Aesopian fable is: Ben Edwin Perry, *Aesopica: A Series of Texts Relating to Aesop or Ascribed to Him or Closely Connected with the Literary Tradition that Bears his Name*, new ed. (Urbana: University of Illinois Press, 2007), but to make full use of this volume requires a knowledge of Greek and Latin. A modern edition of the Greek text containing 358 fables with parallel French translation is: Aesop (Ésope), *Fables*, ed. Émile Chambry, 7th Printing (1927. Paris: Les Belles Lettres, 2012) and the most comprehensive collection in English translation (600 fables keyed to the numbering systems of Perry and Chambry) is: *Aesop's Fables*, trans. Laura Gibbs.

228 Erwin Leibfried, *Fabel*, 4th ed., Sammlung Metzler 66 (Stuttgart: Metzler, 1982), 58.

229 Alius Theon, *Exercises*, chap. 4, *Progymnasmata*, trans. Kennedy, 23.

"bîspiel," or an example in order to present a moral or to demonstrate an idea.[230] This was mostly achieved by giving a negative example of what could happen if the norms of appropriate behavior were violated. By the eighteenth century, the fable was interpreted as a *Gattung* (genre) and became the focus of extensive theorizing, especially reflecting on criteria which determine its nature, form, and impact.[231] The term is used to refer specifically to narratives in which animals, plants, and concrete objects play decisive roles. They get humanized so to speak in a process of anthropomorphism.

Heinrich Steinhöwel was the first to comment on the fable in German. He gave five criteria for the form in his edition of Aesop (1477): First, a fable should describe only invented cases ("fabeln synt nit geschehene ding, sondern allein mit worten erdichtete ding"); second, it should contain non-human figures and things that act as if human although they are not; third, it must be delightful ("lustig syent ze hören"); fourth, it must teach something ("sich dar uß ze beßern"); and fifth, it should present the world as it appears to the humans considering their behavior and character traits ("die sitten der menschen und ihr wesen beschreybent").[232] When he came to write about the fable in his *Versuch einer Critischen Dichtkunst* (Essay on Critical Poetics), first published 1730, Johann Christoph Gottsched identified the potential for moral instruction as the most important characteristic of the fable: "Ich glaube derowegen

---

230 One should note however that the fable was not to be confused with the genre of the *exemplum* which insisted on truth in contrast to the fictional fable. See Kurt Erlemann, Irmgard Nickel-Bacon and Anika Loose, *Gleichnisse–Fabeln–Parabeln,* UTB 4134 (Tübingen: Francke, 2014), 72-81 and Klaus Grubmüller, "Fabel, Exempel, Allegorese: Über Sinnbildungsverfahren und Verwendungszusammenhänge," Walter Haug and Burghart Wachinger, ed., *Exempel und Exempelsammlungen,* Fortuna vitrea: Arbeiten zur literarischen Tradition zwischen dem 13. und 16. Jahrhundert 2 (Tübingen: Niemeyer, 1999), 58-76. See also the essays in Peter Hasubek, ed., *Die Fabel: Theorie, Geschichte und Rezeption einer Gattung* (Berlin: Erich Schmidt, 1982); Theo Elm and Peter Hasubek, ed., *Fabel und Parabel: Kulturgeschichtliche Prozesse im 18. Jahrhundert* (Munich: Fink, 1994).

231 For a historical overview of the development of fabel theory, see Jayne Elizabeth Lewis, *The English Fable: Aesop and Literary Culture 1651-1740,* Cambridge Studies in Eighteenth-Century English Literature and Thought 28 (Cambridge: Cambridge University Press, 1996), Thomas Noel, *Theories of the Fable in the Eighteenth Century* (New York: Columbia University Press, 1975), Monika Schrader, *Sprache und Lebenswelt: Fabeltheorien des 18. Jahrhunderts,* Germanistische Texte und Studien 38 (Hildesheim: Olms, 1991), and Max Staege, *Die Geschichte der deutschen Fabeltheorie,* Sprache und Dichtung 44 (Bern: Paul Haupt, 1929). Herbert Kaiser, "Die Pädagogisierung der Fabel am Ende des 18. und zu Beginn des 19. Jahrhunderts," Hasubek, ed., *Die Fabel* 163-179, examines the ways in which the fable became in a sense trivialized as it was integrated into various pedagogical programs for teaching children. There were some counter voices such as Jean Jacques Rousseau, who in 1762 insisted that: "The time of faults is the time for fables" (*Émile*, trans. Barbara Foxley, Everyman's Library 518 [London: Dent, 1955 (1911)], 210). See also the chapter "Rousseau and the Fable in Education," Noel, *Theories* 102-113. Rousseau goes further to say that the fable does not need a moral at the end because the moral should be implicit in the story: "Why then add the moral at the end, and so deprive him [the reader] of the pleasure of discovering it for himself" (210). Kaiser adds that the fable should be a "Mittel zur Reflexion von Erfahrung, d.h. zur gesellschaftlichen Erkenntnis" (177) (a medium for reflection, that is, towards social cognition). Each fable should motivate people to think.

232 Heinrich Steinhöwel, *Vita Esopi Fabulatoris* (Ulm: Johannes Zanier, c. 1476), quoted in Reinhard Dithmar, ed., *Texte zur Theorie der Fabeln, Parabeln und Gleichnisse* (Munich: Deutscher Taschenbuch Verlag, 1982), 56-66 at 58.

eine Fabel am besten zu beschreiben, wenn ich sage: sie sey die Erzählung einer unter gewissen Umständen möglichen, aber nicht wirklichen vorgefallenen Begebenheit, darunter eine nützliche moralische Wahrheit verborgen liegt" (Consequently I believe to describe the fable best, when I say: it is the narration of a possible, but not really happened event, under which hidden lies an applicable moral truth).[233] Fable writing in the eighteenth century mainstream tradition emphasized the particular "Lehre" or didactic message that was to be illustrated. The fable was intended as something appropriate for children in order to teach them certain ideas or behavioral patterns. Yet concurrently the word "fable" was also used as a technical term in literary studies.[234] In this sense–not how Lessing used the term–it refers in general to any plot of an epic or of a dramatic text, or was used just to the central motifs of an action presented therein which have a didactic purpose. Hence the word "fable" could mean rather different things in the discourses and poetic practices of the eighteenth century. Lessing applied the word to refer to a specific literary genre, one characterized as both being merely poetic and as something supposed to reveal a specific and noteworthy *Wahrheit* (truth) or *Weisheit* (wisdom). Lessing departed from Gottsched who emphasized the aspect of utility. Gottsched's approach was allegorical and prescriptive. The fable is a matter of logical construction and its means include much allegorical ornamentation. This is a notion expanded on by Breitinger in giving the fable a broader base and by making "das Wunderbare" or the marvelous the declared goal.[235] Each fable should have something new, strange, and extraordinary in its message. But what Lessing did

233 This is the opening of § 9 of Part 4: "Von den dreyen Gattungen der poetischen Nachahmung und inbesonderheit von der Fabel," Johann Christoph Gottsched, *Versuch einer Critischen Dichtkunst,* 4th ed. (Leipzig: Bernhard Christoph Breitkopf, 1751), 150-151 at 150. Also see Dithmar, *Texte zur Theorie der Fabeln* 110-111 at 110. On Gottsched and the fable Staege, *Geschichte* 23-25; Schrader, *Sprache und Lebenswelt* 31-44.

234 See Klaus Scherpe, *Gattungspoetik im 18. Jahrhundert: Historische Entwicklung von Gottsched bis Herder,* Studien zur Allgemeinen und Vergleichenden Literaturwissenschaft 2 (Stuttgart: Metzler, 1968), 37-38, 41-43, 113-117. For approaches to and uses of the Fable in the early modern period, see: Ernst Heinrich Rehermann and Ines Köhler-Zürich, "Aspekte der Gesellschafts- und Kirchenkritik in der Fabeln von Martin Luther, Nathanael Chytraeus and Burkhard Waldis," Hasubek, ed., *Die Fabel* 27-42; Elfriede Moser-Rath, "Die Fabel als rhetorisches Element in der katholischen Predigt der Barockzeit," Hasubek, ed., *Die Fabel* 59-75; Christoph Siegrist, "Fabel und Lehrgedicht: Gemeinsamkeiten und Differenzen," Hasubek, ed., *Die Fabel* 106-118; and P. M. Mitchell, "Aspekte der Fabeltheorie im 18. Jahrhundert vor Lessing," Hasubek, ed., *Die Fabel* 119-134.

235 Johann Jakob Breitinger, *Von der Esopischen Fabel* (1740) in Dithmar, *Texte zur Theorie der Fabeln* 114-116 at 114: "Die Fabel ist in ihrem Wesen und Ursprung betrachtet nichts anders, als ein lehrreiches Wunderbares. Dieselbe ist erfunden worden, moralische Lehren und Erinnerungen auf eine verdeckte und angenehm-ergezende Weise in die Gemüthern der Menschen einzuspielen, und diesen sonst trockenen und bitteren Wahrheiten durch eine künstliche Verkleidung in eine reizende Maßke, einen so gewissen Eingang in das menschliche Herz zu verschaffen, daß es sich nicht erwehren kann, ihren heilsamen Nachdruck zu fühlen" (The fable is, considering its essence and origin, nothing but something didactic and wonderful. It has been invented to transpose moral teachings and memories via subtle and pleasantly enjoyable ways into the minds of people. Hence it creates from these otherwise dry and bitter truths through an artful camouflage a delightful mask so that it may find a certain entrance into the human heart which it cannot resist so that it may feel its healing influence).

not like is that it also had to be the allegory of "a similar action" camouflaged under the dressing of a moral. An instructive message dominated everything else.[236] It was his idea to liberate fables from any preconceived formula and that what the moral was to be should not be spelled out explicitly in order to give freedom to philosophical speculation. He admitted that sometimes the pleasure of story-telling was already enough of a cause and interestingly thought of it as a matter of healing.

## 2. Lessing's theoretical reflections on the Fable

Initially Lessing published three fables in 1747, along with other verse in the Hamburg periodical *Ermunterungen zum Vergnügen des Gemüts*: "Die Nuß und die Katze" (The Nut and the Cat) (5th issue), "Die Füchse und die Bäre" (The Foxes and the Bears) (6th issue), and "Die Sonne" (The Sun) (7th issue).[237] He published three more verse fables in the October 1751 issue of *Das Neueste aus dem Reiche des Witzes*, "Der Tanzbär" (The Dancing-Bear), "Der Adler und die Eule") (The Eagle and the Owl) and "Morydan".[238] In the first volume of *Schriften*, 6 vols. (1753-1755), he published a selection of his poetry including a section of 14 fables in prose and verse.[239] At the same time he was interested in how others approached these narratives and began reviewing such collec-

236 The fable should be exactly what it says to be merely a story and a message, nothing more. It ought not to act as *Verhüllung* (cloaking or concealment) for any hidden truth or message: "Richer sagt: die Lehre solle unter dem allegorischen Bilde versteckt (caché) sein. Versteckt! welch ein unschickliches Wort! In manchem Rätsel sind Wahrheiten, in den *Pythagorischen Denksprüchen* sind moralische Lehren versteckt; aber in keiner Fabel. [...] Sein Vorgänger de la Motte hatte sich um ein gut Teil feiner erklärt; er sagt doch nur, verkleidet (deguisé). Aber auch verkleidet ist noch viel zu unrichtig [... ] weil auch verkleidet den Nebenbegriff einer mühsamen Erkennung mit sich führet. Und es muß gar keine Mühe kosten, die Lehre in der Fabel zu erkennen [...]. Wollte man mit aller Gewalt ein ähnliches Wort hier brauchen, so müßte es anstatt 'verkleiden' wenigstens 'einkleiden' heißen" (FA 4, 360) (Richer says: The moral must be hidden under an allegorical image. Hidden! What an inappropriate word! In some riddles are truths, in the *Pythagorian Reflections* there are moralistic messages hidden, but in no fable [...] His predecessor De La Motte explained it a good deal more precisely; he says only 'disguised'." But 'disguised' is still far too incorrect, because its meaning is associated with cumbersome recognition. And it must not be cumbersome to recognize a message in a fable. If one wants to use a similar word by all means then it would have to be instead of 'disguised' something like 'dressed up'). The references are to David Henry Richer, *Fables nouvelles mises en verse* (Paris: Étienne Ganeau, 1729) and De La Motte, *Fables nouvelles* (1719).

237 FA 1, 57-58, 64, 94-95. These are written in the elaborate verse style of La Fontaine.

238 FA 2, 248-249.

239 FA 2, 625-634. Seven of these were to make it into the Lessing's own fabel collection published in 1759 (FA 4, 297-411): "Die Gans" (The goose), 1.14; "Die Sperlinge" (The sparrows), 1.17; "Die Springer im Schache" (The knights in a chess game, ending shortened), 1.29; "Der Löwe mit dem Esel" (The lion with the donkey, ending shortened), 2.7; "Der Esel mit dem Löwen," (The donkey with the lion, new ending), 2,8: "Die Esel" (The donkeys), 2.10; "Die Eiche" (The oak tree, ending shortened), 3.15. "Der Löwe mit dem Esel" is based on Phaedrus, *Fabulae* 1.11 (Babrius and Phaedrus, *Fables*, 204-205), and "Die Esel," loosely based on Aesop 112.

tions beginning in 1749 with the anonymous *Neue Fabeln und Erzehlungen in gebundener Schreibart* (Hamburg: Conrad König, 1749).[240] Then followed in 1751 a review of the German translation of the *Moralske Fabler* of Ludvig Holberg,[241] 323 stories in prose, a volume Lessing actually much disliked.[242] He continued to review other collections.[243] Although the fable is, as most commentators emphasize, a genre that wants to teach something and that it has to do so in a very simple, direct and non-ambiguous manner, it seems to be Lessing's innovation to challenge such a monologic and by eventually cutting the explicit moral of the fable, to give more freedom of interpretation to the reader.

Above all Lessing developed a great admiration for the collection of fables by Aesop: *Aesopica*.[244] Dietrich Harth comments: "Die Fabel hingegen–ob in Vers oder in Prosa–guckt von unten auf die Welt, spricht eine Art Sklavensprache, schlicht und nüchtern, aber listenreich. Der von Lessing genannte Äsop steht für eine uralte, auf orientalische Quellen zurückgehende Gattung, in der die kleine Weisheit sich des Kostüms der Tierwelt bedient."[245] (The fable however–whether in verse or prose–looks at the world from below, speaks a kind of slave's language, is simple and sober but clever. Aesop whom Lessing refers to stands for an ancient genre that goes back to oriental sources in which the little wisdom makes use of the costume of the animal world). A formative step in the development of Lessing's theory of the fable and his

---

240 *Berlinische Privilegierte Zeiting* 57 (May 13, 1749), FA 1, 687-689.

241 Ludvig Holberg, *Moralske fabler* (Copenhagen: Author, 1751).

242 Ludvig Holberg, "Moralske fabler," *Værker i tolv bind,* ed. F.J. Billeskov Jansen (Copenhagen: Rosenkilde & Bagger, 1969-1971), 9: 283-465. Lessing's review of the German translation by Johann Adolf Scheibe, *Moralische Fabeln mit beygefügten Erklärungen* (Copenhagen: Franz Christian Mumme, 1751) appeared in the *Berlinische Privilegierte Zeitung* 58 (May 5, 1751) (FA 2, 88-90). In this review Lessing finds the fables "überhaupt erbärmlich" (generally wretched) and of 232 examples only thirty-two are alright. Furthermore: "Er hat sie in ungebundner Rede abgefaßt, welches wir weder billigen noch tadeln wollen" (FA 2, 89). (He has written them in unrhymed prose which we neither approve nor criticize). Regardless of the prose, Lessing had no pleasure in reading Holberg's fables and his criticism culminates in the sentence: "Niemand hat die Fabel schändlicher gemißhandelt als dieser Holberg!" (FA 2, 799) (Nobody has mistreated the fable more disgracefully than this Holberg!)

243 These include: Johan Friedrich Christ, *Fabularum veterum Aesopiarum libri duo* (Leipzig: Breitkopf, 1748) in the *Berlinische Privilegierte Zeiting* 96 (August 12, 1749) (FA 1, 693); Florens Arnold Consbruch, *Poetische Erzählungen* (Frankfurt am Main: Johann Friedrich Fleischer, 1750) Berlinische Privilegierte Zeiting 56 (May 9, 1750) (FA 1, 700-701): *Claude-François-Félix Boulenger de Rivery,* Fables et conts (Paris: Duchesne, 1754) in the *Berlinische Privilegierte Zeiting* 28 (June 3, 1755 (FA 3, 376-377); F.W. Gleim, *Lieder, Fabeln und Romanzen* (Leipzig: David Iversen, 1758), *Bibliothek der schönen Wissenschaften* 3.2 (1758) (FA 4, 117-129); John Gay, *Fabeln* (Hamburg: Grund und Holle 1758), *Bibliothek der schönen Wissenschaften* 3.2 (FA 4, 121-124), *Briefe, die neueste Litteratur betreffend,* 4-7 Briefe (1759), FA 4, 460-470.

244 See his comments on the Greek text of Aesop based on the edition, *Fabularum Aesopicarum collectio*, ed. Johann Gottfried Hauptmann (Leipzig: Johann Christian Martinus, 1741) in a manuscript from the period 1757-1759 published as *Über den Aesopus* (FA 4, 415-423). He also planned to write a history of the Aesopic fables, but the work was never finished except for a draft, FA 4, 972.

245 Dietrich Harth, *Gotthold Ephraim Lessing. Oder die Paradoxien der Selbsterkenntnis.* Becksche Reihe 631: Autoren (Munich: Beck, 1993), 22.

approach to writing his own narratives was his decision to undertake a translation of Aesop's Fables. With Instructive Morals and Reflections, Abstracted from all Political Considerations, Adapted to all Capacities; and design'd to promote Religion, Morality, and Universal Benevolence (London: Osborn, 1740), by the English Novelist, Samuel Richardson.[246] Richardson too, in his first significant publication under his own name that appeared a year before his first major novel *Pamela,* was interested in maximizing financial gain by making the Aesopian canon popular. He based his collection on the expensive and cumbersome folio edition of Roger L'Estrange that had first appeared as *Fables, of Aesop and other eminent mythologists: with morals and reflections* (London: R. Sare et al., 1692 and later editions) and reduced the number of fables from 500 to 240. He printed the volume in an easy to handle duodecimo format, and included 24 plates containing ten small engravings each that illustrate the fables included. He also played down L'Estrange's Jacobite biases in the reflections on the fables but did not eliminate them entirely.[247] He edited L'Estrange's text lightly, making a few additions of his own to the "Reflections" on the fables he selected.[248] He succeeded in making the volume attractive to many readers, especially younger ones as it remained the best-selling collection of Aesop in English for the rest of the century.

If Richardson had been motivated by financial considerations to prepare an edition of Aesop, Lessing's impetus to translate this collection was only marginally commercial but above all driven by a true fascination with and appreciation of Aesop's approach. Nisbet comments in his biography that Lessing at that time was in financial straits and that an undertaking such as the translation of Richardson's work promised rewards. Richardson was well known based on the dissemination of his novels, all of which were available in German translation.[249] Lessing saw in the attractiveness of Richardson's presentation the potential of a book for children. He adopted the idea, yet omitted Richardson's preface and the description of the life of Aesop with which L'Estrange and Richardson had begun their volumes. Instead, Lessing added a preface of his own and kept the illustrations but increased the number of plates to forty, six illustrations per page. Each fable is followed by "a moral" and "a reflection" and each has a separate heading. Although writing a fable is not the most direct way to express an idea, it seemed to him the most efficient or the most succinct mode of

246 For more recent editions, see: *Äsopische Fabeln mit moralischen Lehren und Betrachtungen. Aus dem Englischen übertragen und mit einer Vorrede von Gotthold Ephraim Lessing nach der Ausgabe von Samuel Richardson*, ed. Walter Pape (Zürich: Diogenes, 1999). The Preface is also in FA 3, 772-774 and Samuel Richardson, "Aesop's Fables," Alexander Pettit, ed., *Early Works, The Cambridge Edition of the Works of Samuel Richardson 1* (Cambridge: Cambridge University Press, 2012), 99-320.

247 For details see Alexander Pettit, "General Introduction," xxxi-xciv at lxi-lxxviii.

248 All omissions and additions are tracked in Pettit's notes to his edition, 639-687.

249 H.B. Nisbet, *Lessing: Eine Biographie 300; Gotthold Ephraim Lessing: His Life, Works, and Thought* 225. The full title that was given to the volume emphasizes the importance of Richardson's contribution above that of Aesop: *Hrn. Samuel Richardsons Verfassers der Pamela, der Clarissa, des Grandisons Sittenlehre für die Jugend in den auserlesenden Aesopischen Fabeln mit dienlichen Betrachtungen zur Beförderung der Religion und die allgemeinen Menschenliebe vorgestellet* (Leipzig: Weidemann, 1757). The volume proved very popular with editions in 1761, 1773, 1783, 1786, 1788, 1806 (*Äsopische Fabeln* 373).

communication. The potential of the fable to become widely popular had been noted even in ancient times:

> [L]ike those who give an excellent dinner with rather modest food, he [Aesop] uses humble subjects to teach great lessons, and after setting out his tale rounds it off with a "Do this" or a "Don't do that. "He also was more devoted to truth than the poets. They give their own stories forced appearance of plausibility, while he, by promising a story that everyone knows to be untrue, tells the truth precisely in not undertaking to tell the truth.[250]

The link between Aesop's fable approach and the story telling by Philostratus demonstrates that the classical interpretation thought of Aesop as clever and successful. His fables were much liked, precisely because they claimed that what they said was merely fictional. This modesty on one hand and the coding strategy on another allowed the author to venture into a kind of social criticism and astuteness one could never have found outside of the secure realm of fiction. In addition to the fables of Aesop Lessing gained in his own collection impulses from the fables by the Roman poets Phaedrus and Claudius Aelianus, especially *De natura animalium.* In sum, Lessing was particularly attracted to the work of Aesop because he found it most concise and least wordy.[251]

Lessing did not confine his knowledge of Aesop to Richardson's collection, but also studied, for example, the Greek text in Hauptmann's edition of 1741.[252] He was interested in the fact that these stories and the wisdom associated with them originated not necessarily in scholarly works of the most educated class of people. They had their roots in simple observations and down to earth life experience. He enjoyed their humor and their intellectual resistance to hierarchy. He liked that they were able of transmitting general wisdom and contributing to the wider moral education without being imposing from above.

---

250 Philostratus, *Life of Apollinius of Tyana, ed.* and trans. Christopher Jones, 3 vols., Loeb Classical Library 16-17, 458 (Cambridge: Harvard University Press, 2005-2006), Book V: 14.2-3 (2: 24-25).

251 But he was not interested in brevity for the sake of brevity. In his review of Christ's *Fabularum veterum Aesopiarum,* he criticizes the form of the fables in the medieval collections attributed to a certain Romulus which Christ "so erzählt, wie sie der Dichter erzählt haben möchte, dessen Arbeit dieses Sammlers abgekürzt, oder vielmehr verstimmelt haben" (FA 1, 693) (narrates in such a way as the poet, whose work these collectors have abbreviated or much rather mutilated, wants to have it narrated) (see also Lessing's "Romulus und Rimicius" published in 1773, FA 7, 417-446). In this review Lessing praises certain stylistic features in the fable which "he would later condemn" (Pizer, "Lessing and the Fable," Fischer and Fox, ed., *A Companion to the Works of Gotthold Ephraim Lessing* 89-104 at 91). Christ offered what he considered "abridged versions" of classical fables and he was a master of brevity in style. This is what Lessing found refreshing at first. His pedagogy was hidden rather than overt, and the point of the fable was less to teach or to be useful in a direct mode (*prodesse*) than to entertain (*delectare*). The fable was meant to offer delightful insights, to make people think on their own, reflecting Horace, *Ars Poetica,* line 333: "Aut prodesse volunt aut delectare poetae" (Poets aim either to benefit or to amuse), *Satires, Epistles and Ars Poetica,* 478-479).

252 On Lessing and Aesop see: Hans-Lothar Markschies, "Lessing und die äsopische Fabel," *Wissenschaftliche Zeitschrift der Karl-Marx-Universität Leipzig.* Gesellschafts- und Sprachwissenschaftliche Reihe 4.1/2 (1954-1955): 129-142; Rpt. Peter Hasubek, ed., *Fabelforschung,* Wege der Forschung 572 (Darmstadt: Wissenschaftliche Buchgesellschaft, 1983), 129-164.

In 1759 Lessing published his own *Fabeln: Drey Bücher. Nebst Abhandlungen* (Fables: Three Books. With Treatises) containing a total of 90 fables.[253] This collection of brief narratives could hardly be more different than that of Richardson's. Most of the fables in the first and third books are original compositions by Lessing; the second book contains more stories adapted from Aesop and Phaedrus. These short narratives convey general statements through specific examples or representations of "truth." The fables are didactic but in contrast to the Richardson and the majority of collections before his, Lessing omits "the Moral" and "the Reflection" leaving these open for the readers. He trusted that the "Lehre" is sufficiently contained in the narratives themselves as already provided without having to make them more explicit or even redundant as used to be the norm. Dietrich Harth made an important observation on Lessing's development in this regard: "Wollte der junge Lessing mit seinen frühen Versfabeln in Übereinstimmung mit der Tradition noch 'lehren', so ging ihm bald auf, daß sich das nur um den Preis der Freiheitsminderung auf Seiten des Lesers realisieren ließ."[254] (Young Lessing according to the tradition, still wanted to 'teach' but soon became aware that this was only doable with the cost of decreasing the freedom on the side of the reader). Whereas the *fabula docet* traditionally allows only one application or one singular "moral," Lessing was soon about trying to find more complex fables that had multiple wisdoms to unravel and that created new freedom to the recipients.

In dealing with the fable Lessing enjoys that the poetic and the ethical alike both dwell within the same territory. He comments: "Es gefiel mir auf diesem gemeinschaftlichen Raine der Poesie und Moral" (I liked this field shared by poesy and morality).[255] The Fable aims for an "anschauende Erkenntnis" (visually based knowledge).[256] Fables lead, as Lessing further explains, to a type of understanding capable of connecting something specific and concrete with something abstract. Lessing adds that fables use a language that is "von sich selbst klar" (clear on its own).[257] He also considers symbolic fables that draw their clarity from the outside, from allegorical and externally given meanings that may precede the given text. He insists that in their basic form fables, however, are always able to rely on their own autonomous messages and that that they already contain everything needed within in order to be fully understood given a bit of imagination. Their meanings are imminent, easily explanatory or evident, and they can be intuitively understood. Whereas "[d]ie symbolische entlehnet ihre Klarheit von der anschauenden" (symbolic texts borrow their clarity from the visual), fables can at times be "identical" with it.[258] Ideally they

253 Berlin: Christian Friedrich Voß, 1759. FA 4, 295-411. See Sieglinde Eichner, *Die Prosafabel Lessings in seiner Theorie und Dichtung*, Bonner Arbeiten zur deutschen Literatur 25 (Bonn: Bouvier, 1974); Ronald M. Mazur, "Gotthold Ephraim Lessing's Fables: Theory and Practice," Alexej Ugrinsky, ed., *Lessing and the Enlightenment* (Westport, CT: Greenwood Press, 1986), 53-57; Günter Jahn, *Lessings Fabelabhandlungen: Ein Elementarbuch der Didaktik und Methodik* (Bielefeld: Aisthesis, 2000); Fick, *Handbuch* 195-213; John Pizer, "Lessing and the Fable," Fischer and Fox, *A Companion to the Works of Gotthold Ephraim Lessing* 89-104.

254 Harth 22.

255 FA 4, "Vorrede," 298-301 at 298.

256 FA 4, "Abhandlungen I, 345-376 at 361. See further Eichner, *Die Prosafabel Lesings* 68-75, 241-264.

257 FA 4, 372.

258 FA 4, 372. See also Schrader, *Sprache und Lebenswelt* 95.

end up borrowing nothing allegorical. Instead they literally "become" visual in their own (one should add ekphrastic) way. The textual completely visualizes everything it tries to communicate. Lessing uses fables to assert the identity of creatures, humans, and animals. He claims in his theoretical comments that understanding them does not require much instruction since they work via intuition and feeling; they are easily shared. At the same time he knew very well of the fables satirical and social-critical dimensions.

> In der Fabel wird nicht eine jede Wahrheit, sondern ein allgemeiner moralischer Satz, nicht unter die Allegorie einer Handlung, sondern auf einen einzeln Fall, nicht versteckt oder verkleidet, sondern so zurückgeführet, daß ich nicht bloß einige Ähnlichkeiten mit dem moralischen Satz in ihm entdecke, sondern diesen ganz anschauend darin erkenne.[259]

> [In the fable not every truth but a general moral sentence is neither hidden nor camouflaged under the allegory of an action, but deduced from a specific example, so that I not only discover some similarities with the moral sentence in it, but also understand it fully just by looking at it and meditating].

Since the language of the fable is imminent and apparently evident, it does not hide or represent things in and through allegory; it simply "shows" things as they are presented in the story that already implicates its moral which is truth itself, as individualized as it may appear.[260] As Lessing explains in his many comments on the fables, this is a genre of fiction that serves as the basis for more complex narratives. The fable is a kind of fiction that claims not to refer to something via the use of symbols, but via rhetorical features that are "anschaulich," that is, clear or concrete. He introduces metaphors, for example character traits that are represented via equations rather than indirectly via hinting to similarity. A fox does not only act in a clever way; in the story he "is" clever and exemplifies that character trait without any "as-if" similitude or added commentary. Lessing explains that parts of something may express more than referring to themselves; they signify other parts as well, or can speak for the whole. Such rhetorical features of abbreviation (metonymy, litotes, and epigram) he introduces by means of a series of examples. Meanings as they are established in fable are, as he claims, obvious or evident even without lengthy explications or allusions to external texts. Since their understanding depends not only on what is said, but also on what remains unsaid, everything necessary is already communicated. In other words, Lessing is fully aware of gaps in the communication process and accepts them, not as a lack of clarity, but in trying to welcome them in explaining them necessarily as a part of it.

---

259 FA 4, 369, emphasis in original.

260 For Lessing the fables are the shortest way to make a cohesive statement about something essential or about an asect of truth. They cannot be anything but fictional and metaphorical. When speaking of Aesop's imitators or plagiarists, Lessing says that they have not truly experienced what they are writing about. They lack authenticity because they merely conjure up ideas, not even concrete examples that would be more telling. They may not be based on any concrete incidences which for him have to be at the core of each successful fable ("haben sich dergleichen Vorfälle meistens erdichtet, oder auch wohl an ganz und gar keinen Vorfall, sondern bloß an diese oder jene allgemeine Wahrheit" (FA 4, 345) (have most of the time invented such events, or thought perhaps not at all of any specific such event, instead only of this or that universal truth).

## 3. Lessing's experiments with the visual-verbal ("Anschaulichkeit")

The fable helped Lessing to establish his key notion of communicating truth via fiction and in part via silence.[261] Lessing was attracted to the fable for its "anschauliche Darstellung einer Wahrheit" (visual presentation of a truth) without being too wordy.[262] The suggestion of action, including moments of silence, not pictorial description, gives the fable its strength. Lessing does not imply a rejection of images for the sake of texts, as some recent critics have claimed.[263] Visuality and sense perception are not cancelled out in Lessing's poetics. His fables work with such features as reduction, condensation, *pars pro toto* relations, and contiguity. Though Lessing was an expert on Aesop's *Fables,* he departed from the form for new type of visuality within the genre's conventions of verbal representation.

Lessing tells a fable in which a fallen oak tree appears so much taller all of a sudden when dead rather than before when it was standing there alive.[264] The point is that things can sometimes best be understood or appreciated for size retrospectively or from a distance of time. This fable may also be a direct homage to Aesop who did not have much appreciation during lifetime. Fiction can show reality in ways nature may not be able to. One is often incapable of comprehending the importance of a tree until it is cut. We often do not know the beauty, the meaning, or the value of something until it is destroyed or gone.

When Lessing came to translate Richardson's Fable 83, "A Fox and a Bramble," he followed the English quite closely.[265] At the same time he also consulted the Greek text in Hauptmann's *Fabularum Aesopicarum collectio* and as a result emended the obstacle faced by the fox from a hedge to a fence (*Zaun*) and the reason for the fox's grasping the bramble becomes in order to prevent his falling rather than as the result of the bushes giving way. Now it is the fox's own fault that he is injured by the brambles. He grabs the brambles to try to prevent his falling, instead of just jumping over the fence. He seems to show a lack of courage. Was it the bramble that ripped his paws bloody? Or is it rather the fox that should be blamed?[266] Both interpretations are valid.

---

261 Helmut Koopmann, "Lessing: Das Allgemeine im Besonderen. Aufklärung als Denkfigur und Fabeltheorie," Elm and Hasubek ed., *Fabel und Parabel* 51-63 at 57 identifies the fable as the most basic of literary genres. It is complete in saying something general, although it is at the same time based on something specific, based on individual experience. However, it is incomplete considering its potential for multiple readings, depending often on dialogue or multiple voices in the narration.

262 Schrader, *Sprache und Lebenswelt* 100.

263 See Beate Allert, "Lessing im Kontext kunsttheoretischer Debatten, *LessingYearbook* 32 (2000): 371-387, esp. 371-374.

264 FA 4, 334. See further below.

265 "Der Fuchs und der Brombeerstrauch" *Sittenlehre für die Jugend* (1757), 127-128; *Äsopische Fabeln* 129-130. Richardson's rendition, *Aesop's Fables* (Fable 83) (1740) 67; (2012) 196-97, is a lightly edited version of L'Estrange's translation (Fable 102), *Fables, of Aesop (1692), 97.*

266 He gives the reasons for these changes in "Über den Aesopus," FA 4. 415. Gibbs, *Aesop's Fables* 147 translates as: "A fox climbing up over a fence was about to slip and fall, so she reached out and grabbed hold of a bramble bush."

> Ein Fuchs ward hart verfolgt und wollte sich über einen Zaun retten. Um nun keinen allzu gefährlichen Sprung wagen zu dürfen, hielte er sich an einem Brombeerstrauche fest, dessen Dörner ihm häufig in den Füßen steckenblieben. Als er herab war, fing er seine Pfoten unter gewaltigen Verwünschungen des Brombeerstrauchs, an zu lecken. Nicht so böse, *Reinecke,* sagte der Strauch: man hätte denken sollen, du, dessen Herz voll Bosheit ist, müßtest besser Bescheid wissen, als daß du dich an jemand anhieltest, der selbst auf nichts als Unheil bedacht ist.[267]

This fable is then followed by the *Lehre* (moral) and the *Betrachtung* (reflection). How Lessing handled this fable in his own collection is a demonstration of how his approach to the fable had changed since his own early efforts and how different it was from the way Richardson and others handled these texts. Fable 22 in book two of his collection is titled "Der Fuchs" (The Fox):

> Ein verfolgter Fuchs rettete sich auf eine Mauer. Um auf der andern Seite gut herab zu kommen, ergriff er einen nahen Dornenstrauch. Er ließ sich auch glücklich daran nieder, nur daß ihn die Dornen schmerzlich verwundeten. Elende Helfer, rief der Fuchs, die nicht helfen können, ohne zugleich zu schaden![268]

> [A fox being chased escaped on to a wall. In order to come safely down the other side, he grabbed a nearby bramble bush. Luckily he was able to get down the other side, only that the thorns painfully wounded him. Wretched helpers shouted the fox that are unable to help without simultaneously doing harm!].[269]

Lessing has cut the fable short omitting the response of the bramble to the fox's outrage. This is all rejected by Lessing and in his notes on this fable "Über den Aesop," he retells the story to the point where the fox speaks with the bush:

267 *Äsopische Fabeln* 129-130. "A Fox close pursued, took a Hedge; the Bushes gave way, and in catching hold of a Bramble to break his Fall, the Prickles ran into his Feet; upon this, he laid himself down, and fell to licking his Paws, with bitter exclamations against the Bramble. Good Words, *Reynard,* says the Bramble, one would have thought, that you, whose Heart is bent on Mischief, had known better Things, than to lay hold on that for Relief, which catches at every thing else for Mischief" (Richardson, "Aesop's Fables" 196-197). This fable is number 8, "Vulpes et Sentes" in Hauptmann Fabularum Aesopicarum collectio 8-9. See now Perry, *Aesopica* #19, 329, Chambry #31; *Fables,* trans. Gibbs, #306, 147. The detail that the bramble is one who "catches at every thing else" is explained in Gibbs, *Aesop's Fables* #500, 231 (=Perry, *Aesopica* #171, 387-388).

268 FA 4, 324.

269 The first translation of Lessing's *Fabeln* was John Richardson, *Fables: From the German of Mr. Lessing* (1773) which omitted the five concluding essays. A second anonymous translation appeared as: *Fables and Epigrams* (1825). This translates the fables in a rearranged order (omitting book 2, #18, "Zevs und das Schaf") and giving prose versions of 10 of Lessing's verse narratives: "Der Sperling und die Feldmaus" (Translated as "The Sparrow and the Bat," 55-56) (FA 2, 78, with the Coda, FA 2, 793): "Der Adler und die Eule" (FA 2, 248): "Die Tanzbär" (FA 2, 248); "Der Hirsch und der Fuchs" (FA 2, 626): "Die Sonne" (FA 1, 94-95): "Das Muster der Ehen" (FA 2, 628); "Der Löwe und die Mücke" (FA 2, 629); "Die Füchse und die Bäre" (FA 1, 64).

Hier sollte sich die Fabel enden, und die Moral sollte die sein, welche in folgender Sentenz des P. Syrus enthalten ist.
Quam miserum auxilium est, ubi nocet, quod sustinet.[270]

[Here the fable ought to end, and the moral should be that which is contained in the following aphorism by Publilius Syrus:
How wretched is help when it injures that to which it provides support].[271]

This is the perfect point to end the fable since everything is already obvious. For Lessing further moralizing was superfluous. He loved enigmatic style that made people think rather than giving them all the details and possible readings or perspectives. In doing so the fables often meant less rather than more. For example considering this fable the fox that was expected to be clever yet was shown as being stupid. He expected help where it was not to be expected. It was therefore not only the mistake of the thorn bush offering false help but the fox too was to blame. Self-reliance is a virtue and dependencies on others may be an obstacle.

## 4. Examples from Lessing's Fables

Lessing referred to the first fable of the third book of his collection, his original composition "Der Besitzer des Bogens" (The Owner of the Bow), to illustrate why he was critical of any mere ornaments in a story that should be short and distinct as expected from any fable.[272] This one deserves to be read closely for its presentation of what might be called an example for Lessing's minimalist aesthetics:

Ein Mann hatte einen trefflichen Bogen von Ebenholz, mit dem er sehr weit und sehr sicher schoß, und den er ungemein wert hielt. Einst aber, als er ihn aufmerksam betrachtete, sprach er: "Ein wenig zu plump bist du doch! Alle deine Zierde ist die Glätte. Schade!–Doch dem ist abzuhelfen; fiel ihm ein. Ich will hingehen und den besten Künstler Bilder in den Bogen schnitzen lassen.–Er ging hin; und der Künstler schnitzte eine ganze Jagd auf den Bogen; und was hätte sich besser auf einen Bogen geschickt, als eine Jagd? Der Mann war voller Freuden. "Du verdienest diese Zierraten, mein lieber Bogen!"–Indem will er ihn versuchen; er spannt, und der Bogen–zerbricht.[273]

[A man had had a splendid ebony bow, with which he shot very far and very accurately, and which he considered tremendously valuable. One time however, when he looked at it

270 FA 4, 415.
271 Publilius Syrus, *Sentences,* ed. and trans. Guillaume Flamerie de Lachapelle (Paris: Les belles Lettres), 118-119.
272 FA 4, 403: "Freilich geht es dem la Fontaine, und allen seinen Nachahmern, wie meinem Mann mit dem Bogen; der Mann wollte, daß sein Bogen mehr als glatt sei; er ließ Zieraten darauf schnitzen; und der Künstler Verstand sehr wohl, was für Zierarten auf einen Bogen gehörten; er schnitzte eine Jagd darauf: nun will der Mann den Bogen versuchen, und er zerbricht" (Of course it happens to La Fontaine and all of his imitators, just like my man with the bow; the man wanted that his bow should be more than smooth; he had decorations carved unto it; and the artist knew quite well what kind of decorations are suitable for a bow; he engraved a hunt; now the man wants to try the bow, and it breaks).
273 FA 4, 329.

attentively he said: "You are a little bit too plump, aren't you! All your ornament is the sheen. Too bad! –But that can be remedied occurred to him. I shall go and have the best artist carve pictures on the bow.– He went and the artist carved an entire hunting scene on the bow; and what could have been more suitable on a bow than a hunt? The man was full of joy. "You deserve these embellishments, my dear bow!" –At the same time he wants to try it out; he draws, and the bow–breaks].

Lessing's fable here is obviously a plea for simplicity instead of baroque extravagance. The man had a powerful and accurate bow, yet falsely thought that it could be improved by having pictures carved on it. Then it would look better, he thought, and he went to an artist to have that done retroactively. Images in this context are add-ons, ornaments, merely decorative. After the artist then carved pictures of a hunting scene on the bow, the owner was pleased for its new embellishments when he it looks at it at first. Yet when he actually tries to use the bow, it breaks. The fable is poking fun of such images that are pointless, secondary, ornamental features only. This is the context where we see Lessing's anti-visual stance.

When applied to language, the fable implies a rejection of that notion of superficial "metaphor" as defined by Quintilian merely as a shortened simile, or as a derived secondary language structure. This notion had already been challenged by the Italian philosopher Giovanni Battista Vico who gave metaphor a new meaning. He thought of it as vital and elementary.[274] Also Johann Gottfried Herder redefined what metaphors are and thought of them as indispensable and as a creative potential. Lessing seems to affirm such a notion of non-ornamental energetic metaphors and, as this fable illustrates, he opts for images or metaphors as being primary and metonymic. Lessing's "Poesie" has no ornamental or additional images added to a main structure in order to embellish it; instead metaphors and metonymies are for Lessing at the core of meaning and it is his plea to avoid abundant wordiness.

Lessing's idea was to be much later developed in greater detail by Friedrich Nietzsche, who said that "Wahrheiten" (truths) were also "Metaphern" (metaphors) and "Illusionen, von denen man vergessen hat, daß sie welche sind" (Illusions that have ceased to be recognized as such).[275] Nietzsche compared these metaphors to coins whose faces have become worn down but are nevertheless still valid as legal tender. It is the ways they are used and how they are interpreted in the processes of reception that give them their meaning. Lessing is critical of images that are only ornamental or painted additionally, as if painted only for embellishment; instead he treats images as "Dichtung" (dense writing) that is basic and visual from the core. The engravings provide nothing to the dynamics and ultimate beauty of the bow. Lessing's fable indicates that beauty is more complex a terms than rather being superficial. And obviously the lack of any pragmatic wisdom on the part of the owner of the bow illustrate that the engravings are the cause for the broken bow. The owner should have been content with the simple yet effective bow he had and enjoyed its sheen. Instead he

274 See further: Marcel Danesi, *Vico, Metaphor, and the Origin of Language, Advances in Semiotics* (Bloomington: Indiana University Press, 1993), esp., chapter 6, "From Precepts to Concepts: The Metaphoricity Hypothesis" 121-142.

275 Friedrich Nietzsche, "Über Wahrheit und Lüge im außermoralischen Sinn," *Werke in drei Bänden,* ed. Karl Schlechta (1954-1956, reprint Darmstadt: Wissenschaftliche Buchgesellschaft, 1997), 3: 309-322, esp. 314.

wanted a more beautiful object, but art in this sense is then soon to be associated with displeasure. In his attempt to "beautify" the bow, the owner weakens and destroys it. It is obvious or "anschaulich" in Lessing's sense that the addition of an ornamental engraving of an entire hunting scene to the bow does not make it more beautiful. The bow was already beautiful in terms of its hue, its sheen, its smoothness–and in terms of its utility. Lessing indicates that if images belong to a second order of surplus features they should be omitted. This fable could be read as an example of Lessing's criticism of the image at large. But clearly there is more at the core of visuality. Lessing values simplicity over redundancy.

The fable relies on the "anschauende Erkenntnis" (visual knowledge) already referred to, and on a sense of the beautiful that is closely connected with metaphor and an understanding of the specific. Lessing links "Poesie" with this sense of the beautiful as the dynamic, as a force. His image of the bow is reminiscent of the shield of Achilles described in Homer's *Iliad* and as to give a verbal description of an artwork that produces images in the mind of the readers even more radiant than any painted images could show. It is a passage at the core of all Ekphrasis which Lessing also illustrates in the context here. He draws attention to the importance of ethics in the context of "Poesie."

Another of Lessing's original fables, "Die eherne Bildsäule" (The Statue of Brass),[276] which opens the second book of his collection, also deserves attention in this light:

> Die eherne Bildsäule eines vortrefflichen Künstlers schmolz durch die Hitze einer wütenden Feuersbrunst in einen Klumpen. Dieser Klumpen kam einem anderen Künstler in die Hände, und durch seine Geschicklichkeit verfertigte er eine neue Bildsäule daraus; von der erstern in dem, was sie vorstellete, unterschieden, an Geschmack und Schönheit ihr gleich. Der Neid sah es und knirschte. Endlich besann er sich auf einen armseligen Trost: "Der gute Mann würde dieses, noch ganz erträgliche Stück, auch nicht hervorgebracht haben, wenn ihm nicht die Materie der alten Bildsäule dabei zu Statten gekommen wäre."[277]

> [The brass statue of an outstanding artist melted through the heat of a raging conflagration into a lump. This lump came into the hands of another artist, and through his skill he created a new statue from it, different from the first in what it represented, but equal to it in taste and beauty. Envy saw it and ground his teeth. Then he thought of a paltry compensation: "The good man would not have produced this rather tolerable piece, had not the stuff of the old statue played a role in it"].

Two statues are being compared. The first one is created by an artist and considered "vortrefflich" (excellent). It gets destroyed in a fire that reduces it to a shapeless lump of metal. A trauma, war, or a horrible catastrophic event must have happened that is not mentioned in detail but that led to the destruction of this precious artwork. There is a sign or some sort of evidence of this event and what was there before remains a memory piece something of a remnant. The second statue is a completely different art work and it cannot replace the one that is gone, yet it consists of the same material.

276 There is clearly an echo here of the wondrously decorated "zwei eherne Säulen" made by Hiram of Tyre for King Solomon's temple (I Kings 7:13-22). For a rhetorical analysis see Eichner, *Die Prosafabel Lessings* 207-208.

277 FA 4, 315.

Lessing claims a persistency of the image against all odds. Despite the demolition of the precious artwork he insists that even if the sculpture was broken, some elements of its structure have remained. This residue gets into the hands of another artist who then creates a second statue from it. In terms of subject matter the new work belongs to another era completely different from the first, but it is considered, at least according to the narrator, to be "equivalent" in terms of taste and beauty. It may even contain material traces of the previous and has been considered as Lessing's argument against plagiarism for many artists that build their own works on the knowledge of previous eras.

Everything of the first statue has been destroyed, except for a visual residue in the public memory. A lump of metal has become the raw material for something entirely new but qualitatively equivalent. At work in this narrative is something that could perhaps be described as an informed public opinion; art as it is always related to memory and other artworks of distant times and places interacting as part of a critical discourse.[278] If Lessing was against allegories as mentioned above, it should be noted that there is no indication of whether or not the second artist was aware of the original statue or whether an appreciation of the new work and its understanding in the eyes of the public depend on any knowledge of how it may still be remotely related to that artwork before. What is important in this context is, according to Lessing, the opinion of the spectators who label and evaluate it. The opinion of only one such observer is revealed through the voice of "Envy" who can only be considered as a partial participant in the statue's reception. He is preoccupied with his own view of things, his own self-related perspective. While he seems content that the first artist should have been held in excellent esteem, he would rather deny any positive judgment to the newcomer. He has no generosity, but at the same time cannot deny that the new artwork holds some power. He admits no more than that it is "noch ganz erträglich" (still rather tolerable). Instead of admitting that the second artwork is wonderful and perhaps even better than the first, the critic who represents envy holds his applause to protect the common public opinion and so as not to ruffle any feathers. Perhaps he is merely a traditionalist who thinks that outstanding artworks are all a thing of the past. He does not want to believe that the beauty of this second statue is entirely the work of a contemporary artist and attempts to diminish the surprising yet obvious dynamic of the new innovative artwork.[279] What is important is that this fable by Lessing gives a clear example why the reception of any art work should stand on its own merits and not have to compete with any possible earlier versions and possible comparable things regardless of the specific material and genre. He insists that each work has its own immanent features that should determine in fact its importance. What he tells us he does so by way of metaphors and subtle hints specifically designated by the context in which they are applied. They are not, as in the case of allegories, deduced from

278 This is very much the point of Richard Brilliant in his *My Laocöon. Alternative Claims in the Interpretation of Artworks* (Berkeley: University of California Press, 2000).

279 "Envy" tries to undercut the beauty of what he sees by resorting to a "paltry consolation," a kind of murky Thomism that denies the artist's ability to create anything new. See Joseph Margolis "Medieval Aesthetics," Berys Gaunt and Dominic McIver Lopes, ed., *The Routledge Companion to Aesthetics* (London: Routledge, 2001), 27-36, esp. 31-35.

elsewhere or drawn from previous traditional meanings. Lessing is indeed a critic of convoluted fables, complex and digressive writing styles, and has his own rhetoric of the image that deserves a closer look.

## 5. How short should the fables be? Consequences for Lessing's approach to the image

What interests me particularly is how Lessing experiments with fables in the context of exploring modes of Ekphrasis and possibilities and limits of understatement. Lessing argues: "Alle Zieraten aber sind dieser Kürze entgegen; denn ohne sie würde sie noch kürzer sein können: folglich streiten alle Zieraten, in so fern sie leere Verlängerungen sind, mit der Absicht der Fabel." (All ornaments work against such brevity, because without them it could be even shorter; consequently all ornaments, as long as they are just empty bulk, fight against the intention of the fable).[280] He thinks about ways to simplify communication and finds that brevity can best be achieved if one can refer to well-known animals that evoke a natural understanding.[281] His argument is as follows: "Eben mit zur Erreichung dieser Kürze, braucht die Fabel gern die allerbekanntesten Tiere; damit sie weiter nichts als ihren einzigen Namen nennen darf, um einen ganzen Charakter zu schildern, um Eigenschaften zu bemerken, die ihr ohne diese Namen allzuviel Worte kosten würden." (Exactly in order to achieve such brevity the fable uses the most familiar animals; so that it may just mention only their singular name in order to illustrate their complete character, in order to make notice of character traits that would cost without these names way too many words).[282] What Lessing likes most about the early fables by Aesop is their directness and how easily they can be understood without any commentary. He pokes fun at fables that have their messages ornamented too much. Although he explicitly enjoyed La Fontaine for his delightful playfulness, he was not entirely happy with the "leicht auf Umwege führende Erzehlungsart des LaFontaine" (the mode of narration of La Fontaine which easily leads to detours).[283] Lessing pursues neither "die Mittelstraße des Phädrus" (the middle road of Phaedrus), nor what he describes as the style "der zierlichen Kürze des Römers, aber doch in Versen" (of neat brevity as by the Romans, albeit in verses).[284] He defends his preference for prose over verse because he believes that "ein Genie seiner angeborenen

280 FA 4, 402. Also see Ralf Simon, *Die Idee der Prosa*. This book includes a very important chapter on Lessing (955-981) acknowledging that even for Lessing the signs of painting are no longer "natural" as previously assumed and that artificiality and hence rhetoric are part and parcel of reality (77).

281 "La Fontaine legt es einem ganz anderen Kunstrichter in den Mund, daß die Kürze die Seele der Fabel sei" (FA 4, 401) (La Fontaine puts this in the mouth of another literary critic [Olivier Patru] the statement that brevity is the soul of the fable).

282 FA 4, 402.

283 FA 4, 404. On Lessing's complex relationship to La Fontaine, see Karl August Ott, "Lessing und La Fontaine: Von dem Gebrauche der Tiere in der Fabel," *Germanisch-Romanische Monatsschrift* N.F. 9 (40) (1959): 235-266; Rpt. Hasubek, ed., *Fabelforschung* 165-206.

284 FA 4, 404.

Sprache, sie mag sein, welche es will, eine Form erteilen kann, welche er will" (that any genius may use his or her native language, whichever it may be, and whichever form it may have, as he or she pleases).[285] He also believes that the study of fables can have an important role to play in the education of children because of what he sees as "den *heuristischen* Nutzen der Fabeln" (the *heuristic* usefulness of the fables).[286]

In order to make the most of this he opts for a principle of reduction which does not require too much allegorical information or "eine weitläufige Kenntnis des Besonderen und aller individuellen Dinge, auf welcher die Reduktion geschehen kann" (a far-fetched knowledge of all the individual things based on which this reduction could happen).[287] He asserts that the narrative should contain

> ... den Samen aller übrigen Wissenschaften, sogar die moralischen nicht ausgenommen. Und es ist kein Zweifel, er wird mit diesem Samen der Moral, den er in der Geschichte der Natur gefunden zu haben glaubet, nicht auf die bloßen Eigenschaften der Tiere, und anderer geringern Geschöpfe, sondern auf die Äsopischen Fabeln, welche auf diese Eigenschaften gebauet werden, gesehen haben.[288]

> [... the seedling for all other sciences even includes the moral. And there is no doubt, he [the student] will have seen with respect to this seedling of the moral which he believes to have found in the history of nature not only the mere attributes of animals, and other less developed creatures, but the Aesopian Fables which have been built upon these attributes].

What matters to him most is that the fables allow the students to find, to invent, and to be creative on their own whenever these stories make sense to them in various contexts. The fable can be seen as positioned at the core of Lessing's entire approach to literature. He claims that poetic language should be "anschaulich" (visual) and appeal to the senses while at the same time he praises this genre for being short and

285 FA 4, 405.

286 FA 4, 408, emphasis as in the original. The title of the fifth essay is: "Von einem besondern Nutzen der Fabeln in den Schulen" (About a Particular Usefulness of Fables in Schools).

287 FA 4, 409. Lessing defines this Principle as follows: "[N]icht, daß ich damit suchte, alle Schüler zu Dichtern zu machen; sondern weil es unleugbar ist, daß das Mittel, wodurch die Fabeln erfunden worden, gleich dasjenige ist, das allen Erfindern überhaupt das allergeläufigste sein muß. Dieses Mittel ist das *Principium der Reduktion*" (FA 4, 408) (Not that I was thus trying to make poets out of students, but because it is undeniable that the method by which fables were invented is the same as commonly used by all innovators in general. This method is the *Principle of Reduction*). Lessing borrows this principle from Christian Wolff, *Philosophia practica universalis,* Part 2, new edition (Frankfurt am Main: Officina libraria Rengeriana, 1739), Ch. 2 "De modo" (Concerning Genre), § 310 "Fabulae inveniuntur ope principii reductionis" (Fables are contrived through the action of the Principle of Reduction), 282–83. Wolff takes the term from his *Psychologia Empirica* (Frankfurt am Main: Officina libraria Rengeriana, 1738), Part 1, Sect. 3, chap. 4, § 472, 365, where it is defined as: "*Principium reductionis* appello artificium, quod objectum aliquod, de quo quid quæritur, reduco ad illud notionem quondam communem habens, ut ea, quæ de hoc nobis innotuere, vi notionis communis ad aliud quoque applicari possint." (I call the theoretical premise, the principle of reduction, that I reduce any object, from which anything is required, to another notion having at times a commonality, so that these [notions], which are become known by us from that, are able to be applied by force of the common notion also to something else).

288 FA 4, 409.

succinct.[289] He experimented with it as a practical way to express stories that document an insight. They usually entail something that could not be said in any more direct or more efficient way. In a sense, the fable exemplifies metaphorical language that is unavoidable ("unhintergehbar") and cannot be shortcut by any more direct language.[290]

Lessing used the fable to explore the boundaries between the visual and the verbal and it was his desire to challenge stereotypes or general formulas. He is interested in specific human character traits, features of behavior that are shown not by looking at people or animals but by watching their actions in context. Although Lessing started out in terms of brief fables that work via equation, wit, and irony, he finds in the long run that fables are at their best when nothing is rejected or advocated blatantly, no ready-made idea gets advertised or illustrated. Instead, what needs to be accomplished by any good fable is, as he argues, that a specific event or action is "shown" in such a way that it "speaks" for more than itself. It promotes inductive reasoning, careful evaluation of facts, and ultimately a sense of tact and Socratian wisdom, modest and self-reflective.

Nisbet argues that the "stylistic minimalism" which Lessing attributed to Aesop's fables was "based, it is often alleged, on a misapprehension on Lessing's part" and he adds "for the supposedly Aseopic brevity he cultivated is not an authentic feature of the fable, but only of the abridged form in which many fables were transmitted by medieval compilers such as the Greek monk, Maximus Planudes.[291] Even more so, it puzzles me why Lessing wanted to achieve more brevity in the fables and why he was searching for the most compact style, even at times projecting it on his sources. In my reading, this has much to do with his own time in history and his wish to emancipate the public. He cultivated the question when it should be the best time for any writer or to leave a text or an artwork, to cut it as short as possible. Although he only fully developed this topic in the context of *Laokoon,* already in the context of the fables he realizes that silences and pauses are just as important as words. Less can mean more. And his fables became increasingly more complex.

---

289 He addresses this most directly in his third essay, "Von der Einteilung der Fabel," (About the Types of Fable) where he says, for example: "Diese Präzision und Kürze, worin er ein so großes Muster war, fanden die Alten der Natur der Fabel auch so angemessen, daß sie eine allgemeine Regel daraus machten" (FA 4, 398) (This precision and brevity with respect to which he [Aesop] was such a great model, was considered so appropriate in describing the nature of the fable by the ancients so that they made a general rule based on it). The "rule" Lessing refers to is a quotation from Theon's *Exercises,* chap. 4: "[I]n fables the style should be simpler and natural, and in so far as possible artless and clear," *Progymnasmata,* trans. Kennedy, 24. In addition Lessing observes: "Er [La Fontaine] wußte es, daß die Kürze die Seele der Fabel sei" (FA 4, 399). (He [La Fontaine] knew it, namely that brevity is the soul of the fable).

290 Lessing asserts that metaphors are primary language structures and anticipates Nietzsche's notion of metaphors as being at the core of language and not only decorative or added on later when he states that metaphors express "Die Wahrheit" or "the truth" as directly and as accessibly as possible at best. Metaphors have become unavoidable since images are defined by conventions. Cf. Friedrich Nietzsche, "Über Wahrheit und Lüge" 314.

291 Nisbet, *Lessing: Eine Biographie* 295–298; *Gotthold Ephraim Lessing* 265.

It seems that when discovering the Aesopian fables Lessing found himself just at a philosophical crossing between deductive reasoning as prevalent at the time in France and inductive reasoning as it came from England along with a new awareness for the empirical, for sense perceptions, instrumental optics, and diverse scientific approaches to light, optics, and energy. He found that fables could serve as heuristic instruments of perception in the realm of fiction that then allowed insights into reality without much burdensome inheritance of already traditional literary sources. Given this wide spectrum of helpful impulses and sources Lessing could draw from, it is important to contextualize his own specific contributions to the fable on the background of several ongoing discussions surrounding this genre at his time. Debates include the idea of free talking versus didacticism, the notion of a specific genre versus the idea of mixing them, the goal to present a or several summarized actions of a plot, and what its message or "Lehre" may be, hidden or overt. It is a shared observation in scholarship that Lessing wrote many fables containing animal and plant motifs, especially trees.[292] Here is one that draws attention to the importance of a tree and to recognize it. I read it as a fable suggesting that one should not underestimate its size and importance for bees and humans:

> In den hohlen Stamm eines wilden Apfelbaumes ließ sich ein Schwarm Bienen nieder. Sie füllten ihn mit den Schätzen ihres Honigs und der Baum ward stolz darauf, daß er andere Bäume gegen sich verachtete. Da rief ihm ein Rosenstock zu: Elender Stolz auf geliehenen Süßigkeiten! Ist deine Frucht darum weniger herbe? In diese treibe den Honig hinauf, wenn du es vermagst; und dann erst wird der Mensch dich segnen.[293]
>
> [A swarm of bees landed in a hollow trunk of a wild apple tree. They filled it with the treasures of their honey and the tree was so proud as a result that he despised all other trees by comparison. Then a rose bush exclaimed: Miserable pride based on borrowed sweetness! Is your fruit any less bitter? Draw the honey into and through it, if you are able to do so; only then will humanity bless you!].

It is one of the many fables that poke fun at false pride and arrogance. Lessing indicates on one level of the narrative that plagiarism is not welcome and especially not when someone borrows from someone else and expects praise for it. His fable is also a means to justify his own borrowing and his fair crediting of others who inspired him. A related fable is 2.21, "Die Traube" (The Grape) in which a hungry fox consoles himself that the grapes he has been trying to reach in vain are sour.[294]A sparrow overhears him and is puzzled as the grapes do not look sour. Trying one and finding it sweet it summoned a hundred of its brothers to also come and taste and they soon

---

292 See *Fabeln* 1.15 "Die Eiche und das Schwein" (The Oak and the Pig) (FA 4, 308); 2.25, "Der Wilde Apfelbaum" (The Wild Apple Tree) (FA 4, 326); 3.15 "Die Eiche" (The Oak) (FA 4, 334).

293 FA 4, 326. This fable is adapted from number 173 "Rusticus et Frutex "in Hauptmann, *Fabularum Aesopicarum collectio* 131-132. See now Perry, *Aesopica* #299, 438-439, Chambry #85; Fables, trans. Gibbs, #463, "The Man and the Tree without Fruit" 212-213. There is no comment on it in "Über den Aesopus."

294 On the broader ramifications of the still life with the grapes and on "Zeuxis and the Grapes" in a wide range of literatures and paintings see Bann, *The True Vine.* Bann omits to point out Lessing's important contribution to this debate.

reduced the grapes to such a state that they no longer appealed to the fox.[295] And in a move that is not usual in his fable collection he provides a *promythium* (a moral which precedes the narrative):

> Ich kenne einen Dichter, dem die schreiende Bewunderung der kleinen Nachahmer weit mehr geschadet hat, als die neidische Verachtung seiner Kunstrichter.[296]
>
> [I know a poet to whom the screeching admiration of the small imitators has done much more harm than the envious contempt of his art critics].

The grapes may be tasty to the sparrow but this does nothing to assuage the fox's hunger. The poet's imitators may be effusive in the zeal in which they imitate the master's style, but this helps him even less than the envious refusal of the literary establishment to recognize the value of his work. It seems that Lessing projected before Goethe the innovative idea that art can be auto-referential, can reveal its own becoming and that this leads into the inner core of poetic production. It models the creation of texts and artworks that then can stand, like any individual, without any external frames, completely on their own. Again the image of a tree is exemplary in this regard. Book 3.15, "Die Eiche" is a fable about a large oak draws attention to the size of the tree not by looking up to it but unfortunately by recognizing it only when the tree lies blown over after a destructive storm:

> Der rasende Nordwind hatte seine Stärke in einer stürmischen Nacht an einer erhabenen Eiche bewiesen. Nun lag sie gestreckt, und eine Menge niedriger Sträuche lagen unter ihr zerschmettert. Ein Fuchs, der seine Grube nicht weit davon hatte, sahe sie eines Morgens darauf. Was für ein Baum! rief er. Hätte ich doch nimmermehr gedacht, daß er so groß gewesen wäre.[297]
>
> [The raging wind from the north had demonstrated its strength in a stormy night on a lofty, sublime oak tree. Now, it lay flat on the ground and a lot of small bushes lay crushed under it. A fox that had his burrow not far from it saw this the following morning. What a tree! He exclaimed. Never would I have thought that it has been that tall].

With this fable Lessing draws attention to the impact of time, to the size of the tree as something that is not stable but completely dependent on the observers. The fact that the fox only recognizes the size of the tree retroactively when it lies fallen and dead, indicates that often artworks are not appreciated in their own time but can only be understood posthumously in hindsight. Lessing makes temporality an important aspect of visuality, a topic which he will later develop in the context of his theoretical treatise on the Laokoon statue. The poet is dependent on his or her own time, yet has a right to be independent from prior expectations and free to create something new. Lessing

---

295 This fable is loosely based on number 156, "Vulpes et Uva," in Hauptmann, *Fabularum Aesopicarum collectio* 118. See now Perry, Aesopica #13, 327-28, Chambry #32; Fables, trans. Gibbs, #255, 125, and Phaedrus, *Fabulae* 2.3 (Babrius and Phaedrus, *Fables* 302-305). His "Nachahmung" (imitation) of the Hauptmann's Fable 156 is in "Über den Aesopus" (FA 4, 419).

296 FA 4, 324. In "Über den Aesopus" the poet referred to as "einen großen Dichter" (419, 9) is according to the commentary in the Frankfurt edition by Gunter E. Grimm, obviously ("offenkundig") Friedrich Gottlieb Klopstock (FA 4, 1011).

297 FA 4, 334.

adopted certain aspects of fable theory from others but used the fable differently than his predecessors and contemporaries. There are numerous connections to and similarities with the works of some others, especially the philosophical premises of Christian Wolff.[298] Lessing was not primarily a philosophical writer approaching ideas through consistent terminologies. He was primarily a poet wanting to make his images cut and polished like a stone that has many sides and edges but has its own "Gestalt" or inner consistency. Lessing also had an affinity with Herder who similarly treasured the genre fable.[299] He considered it the basis for all poetry and fiction writing:

> Ist Fabel die Darstellung einer in Handlung gesetzten Lehre, so ist sie der Grund *aller* Dichtkunst, mithin der Rede wohl wert.[300]

> [Since the fable is the representation of amoral set into action, consequently it is the foundation of *all poetic art,* and hence well worth being talked about].

Lessing is in the eyes of Herder "dem wir die beste Theorie der Fabel zu danken haben" (the one to whom we owe the best theory of the fable).[301] Lessing's approach to the fable contributes to a philosophical debate and to a new approach to the rhetoric of "Veranschaulichung" (poetic visual language). Lessing drew attention to sense related features in language, to rhythm, movement, and sound, anything including metaphor, syntax, and onomatopoeia that could rhetorically enhance vividness. It seems that Lessing knew textual visualcy (or the potential to visualize something via

---

298 See Eichner, *Die Prosafabel Lessings* 49-83 on Wolff's influence on Lessing. Lessing not only–rejects allegorical cognition but also, in Eichner's words "symbolische Erkenntnis" (71). She associates the word "symbol" with "Erkenntnisformen der Wissenschaft" (forms of scientific cognition) and "Denkoperationen begrifflicher Zeichen" (thinking operations concerning discursive signs) whereas Lessing pursues "anschauende Erkenntnis" (visual– and intuitive–cognition) in the processes of knowledge formation and science.

299 Herder too was interested in fable theory and like others of his contemporaries used Lessing's approach as a starting point. See "Lessing's Aesopian Fables and the Anti-Lessing," Noel, *Theories* 85-101. Herder's fables are found in two manuscript collections, the first from 1773 containing 52 fables and a second containing an additional 28 collected under the title "Alte Fabeln. Mit neuer Anwendung" in SWS 29, *Herders poetische Werke*, ed. Carl Redlich, 5 vols. (Berlin: Weidmann, 1885-1889), 5: 379-416, 737-740. He published only nine fables during his lifetime, three uncollected which had appeared in *Der Teutsche Merkur vom Jahr 1776* (May 11, 1776): 201-203 (SWS 29, 5: 60-62) and six which had appeared in various places and which were subsequently included in the 1773 manuscript (nos. 3, 6. 17, 26, 27, 28). Herder responded to Lessing's fable theory first in an essay unpublished during his lifetime from 1767, "Aesop and Lessing" (FHA 4 [1994]). *Schriften zu Philosophie, Literatur, Kunst und Altertum 1774-1787,* ed. Jürgen Brummack and Martin Bollacher, 1311-1322), then in the third section "Von der aesopischen Fabel" of "Über Bild, Dichtung und Fabel," first published in 1787 (FHA 4, 631-677 at 648-669) and finally in the essay "Fabel," *Adrastea* 2.3 (1802) (FHA 10 [2000], *Adrastea*, ed. Günter Arnold, 235-241, 242-255). See further "Herder and the Romantic Turn," Noel, *Theories* 122-39 and Jürgen Brummack, "Herders Theorie der Fabel," Gerhard Sauder, ed., *Johann Gottfried Herder: 1744-1803,* Studien zum achtzehnten Jahrhundert 9 (Hamburg: Meiner, 1987), 251-266.

300 Herder, "Fabel," FHA 10, 242.

301 Herder, "Fabel," FHA 10, 242.

text) from the power of *enargeia.*[302] Lessing had, as Herder acknowledged, a keen sense for when best to stop a narrative so that the readers could visualize imaginatively and think further.[303]

Finally, the fables often require wit in order to be understood, that is, the ability to connect aspects that are not related or only remotely so. He establishes a notion of contingent and unpredictable truth that depends on each individual point of view and on specific circumstances. At times it may therefore not be "clear" and remain enigmatic, non-obvious, and transient. Fables are often metonymical, indicating only moments of a story but never tell the whole thing. Whereas it is among the tasks for the fable writer to find the perfect cut-off point in presenting poignant images, or to describe scenes that have the action of the story culminate, it is among the tasks of the reader to unravel the entire implicit story and its potential intricacies, no matter how brief it may appear at first. Lessing turned to the fable for an "anschauliche Darstellung einer Wahrheit in Dichtung" (a visual description of a truth through fiction).[304] Graphic and mental pictures, as well as concrete sense perceptions, are not overwritten or substituted by verbal images or metaphors, nor are they are cancelled out in Lessing's poetics. The metaphors are, as Lessing insists, as primary and as basic as any images are, even in painting and sculpture. He thought about temporal images or remnants thereof within the genre's conventions of verbal representation and tried to achieve something more "visual" mainly via the use of contiguities. These are featured in metonymies or *pars pro toto* illustrations. These can possibly avoid ornamentations that used to be typical for any pictorial style. Lessing faced limitations with such a metonymic experiment later when he uses various narrative frames, and pursues a quest for symbolic truth. Lessing developed his liking for fairytales and ultimately turned from fables to parables which stretch towards infinite conclusions and leave endings wide open. Already in his fables and essays about that genre Lessing anticipates key ideas which he later elaborates, especially in his *Laokoon.* These ideas he then tests from various perspectives throughout his subsequent dramatic and fictional works from multiple angles of the visual-verbal spectrum and with shifting roles from fabulist to poet, from critic to language philosopher and connoisseur of the fine arts.

---

302 *Enargeia* in distinction to *energeia* refers, in the definition by Christopher Collins, *Reading the Written Image* (125) to "the potency, stasis, and imaginative vision associated with the graphic arts and descriptive writing." In the narrative of a fable this means that the point of the story or its climax should not be given but left open to the reader or listener who then actively participates in the construction of meaning.

303 For a further comparison and a shared goal by Lessing and Herder with respect to the audience, see Redekop, *Enlightenment and Community.*

304 Schrader, *Sprache und Lebenswelt* 100.

# Chapter 4
# Lessing's *Laokoon* and *Paralipomena*

Abstract: This chapter focuses on the most salient features of Lessing's theoretical approach to the distinct modes of visual and verbal representation. In his comparison between "Malerei" (painting, visual art) and "Poesie" (poesy or poetic writing) he finds that the message depends in each distinct case on the medium and on the discipline, the very specific contexts in which they are being used. Lessing discusses ideas about the ancient statue of Laokoon and his theoretical conclusions. These proved to be of vast art theoretical and discourse analytical consequences for centuries to come. Correspondences and notes collected in *Paralipomena* have now become indispensable for any convincing interpretation of Lessing. Lessing does away with the long-held emphasis on similarity between the arts. Instead he focusses on the crucial distinctions them and invites us to explore the complex dynamics between the visual and the verbal. He outlines their differences carefully giving more attention to the poet and writer than had been done before in comparison to the painter and sculptor. He then develops a rather different proposal for "musikalische Bilder" (musical images) while raising questions such as: How can the visual become verbal or a description have lively visuality? How to possibly transform images into words? How can words be used most effectively so that they evoke images which capture the most significant moment of the action?

## 1. Lessing's *Laokoon* treatise of 1766: The basics

*Laokoon: Oder über die Grenzen der Malerei und Poesie (Laocoön: or on the Boundaries between Painting and Poetry),*[305] first published 1766 in Berlin by the publisher Christian Friedrich Voß, is Lessing's elaborate, successful but unfinished contribution to an ongoing

305 Lessing FA 5/2, 13-206. Also included in this volume are the *Paralipomena zum Laokoon* (*Paralipomena to Laokoon*), 207-321, "Entwürfe im Umkreis des Laokoon" (Drafts in the Context of Laokoon), 323-349, and "Briefe Antiquarischen Inhalts" (Letters of Antiquarian Content), 351-582) with their Paralipomena 583-618 followed by commentaries, 619-1214. Spellings "Laocoon," "Laocoön," and "Laokoön" are also encountered and I shall use Laokoon here except in citations. The standard translation of *Laokoon* used here is by McCormick, *Laocoön: An Essay on the Limits of Painting and Poetry*. See also H.B. Nisbet, "Laokoon in Germany. The Reception of the Group since Winckelmann," *Oxford German Studies* 10 (1979), 22-63, and Baxmann et al., ed., *Das Laokoon-Paradigma: Zeichenregime im 18. Jahrhundert* (Berlin: Akademie Verlag, 2000); Robert and Vollhardt *Unordentliche Collectanea*. Friedrich Vollhardt's "Studienausgabe" of *Laokoon* (2012) contains additionally selections from the *Paralipomena*, esp. the letter to Christoph Friedrich Nicolai of 26 May, 1769 (FA 11/1, 608-611, #489). It is particularly important for commentaries and appendices (273-467) and recent scholarship.

art-theoretical debate.[306] His comments on the Laokoon statue resulted in elaborate responses by Herder, Goethe, Schiller, Moritz, and many others to follow. There is an extensive reception history in Germany, including contributions by most major literary figures of the eighteenth century.[307] Lessing's essay focuses on the famous Laokoon statue from Antiquity. Some of its remnants and reconstructions, as has been much debated by art historians, can still be seen in the Vatican.[308] Lessing's treatise on this sculpture is about the possibilities and limits of painting and poesy, of images and texts, and about the dynamic interactions between them. It contributes to the visual-verbal debates in the wider art theoretical and philosophical controversies of Lessing's time. It probes possibilities of message transfers from one mode of perception to another, for example from a visual image into a narrative that can be characterized as creating vivid sense impressions, or images into a performance that allows the audience to forget about time and be emotionally moved. Moreover, Lessing's treatise is about aspects of cognition that involve not only the visual but also the acoustic. Lessing tries to establish a new concept of visual writing or verbal visualcy as a result of an emancipated public as projected into the future. He daringly probes the boundaries of theater with attention to language, rhetoric, and imagination. He experiments with media specific approaches from a variety of points of view. These coexist with tension but without cancelling each other. His *Laokoon* is itself a poetic construct with multiple layers of discourse, as if it were itself the shield of Achilles, "werdend," a work in progress. Lessing ventures into the realm of a semiotics that deals with exceptions. He examines not only "bequeme" (comfortable) but also "unbequeme" (uncomfortable) relations between "Zeichen" (signs). In the visual realm he calls signs "Körper" (bodies) belonging to the dimension of space, while in the verbal realm he calls signs "Töne" (sounds), belonging to the dimension of time. Lessing argues that the visual belongs to the dimension of space and that the acoustic belongs to the dimension of time. Related signs can be in movement. Signs of the visual arts (bodies or figures) occur sequentially in space. But the verbal signs of poesy can occur, like the tones in music rather, concurrently or on more than one or even multiple levels.

Lessing's keen interest in the question of how to articulate the differences between painting and poetry dates back to a statement Diderot had made which impressed Lessing sufficiently to quote it in 1751 in his review of the *Lettre sur les sourds et muets*

---

306 FA 5/2, 9-206, 627-863. While the term "Poesie" is often translated as "poetry" that term in English is too restrictive. Lessing includes lyric, epic, and drama under that heading. I translate it here as "poetic writing" (poesy). Lessing's *Laokoon* and the related *Paralipomena* contain in essence Lessing's theory of the visual, the verbal, and ekphrasis.

307 See for example Hugh Barr Nisbet, "Laokoon in Germany" 22-63; Wolfgang Düsing, "Wandlungen des Literaturbegriffs in der *Laokoon*-Debatte zwischen Lessing und Herder," Peter-André Alt et al., ed., *Prägnanter Moment. Festschrift für Hans-Jürgen Schings* (Würzburg: Königshausen & Neumann, 2002), 63-78; Monika Schrader, *Laokoon–"eine vollkommene Regel der Kunst": Ästhetische Theorien der Heuristik in der zweiten Hälfte des 18. Jahrhunderts: Winckelmann, Mendelssohn, Lessing, Herder, Schiller, Goethe* (Hildesheim: Georg Olms, 2005); Robert and Vollhardt, *Unordentliche Collectanea* (2013).

308 On this famous artwork see Bernhard Andreae, *Laokoon und die Kunst des Pergamon. Die Hybris der Giganten* (Frankfurt am Main: Fischer Taschenbuch Verlag), 1991; Thomas Koebner, ed., *Laokoon und kein Ende: der Wettstreit der Künste* (Munich: Text + Kritik), 1989; Horst Althoff, *Laokoon. Stoff und Form*, $2^{nd}$ expanded ed. (Basel: Francke Verlag, 2000).

(Letter on the Deaf and the Mute): "[D]aß jede Kunst der Nachahmung ihre Hieroglyphen habe und daß es zu wünschen sei, daß ein kundiger und zärtlicher Schriftsteller ihre Vergleichung unternehmen wollte." (That each mimetic art has its own hieroglyphs and that one may wish that a knowledgeable and sensitive writer would venture to compare them).[309] Lessing's *Laokoon* is such an undertaking. It consists of staging in the context of a narrative that serves as a theoretical treatise an intricate dispute between an art theorist, a writer, and an enthusiastic recipient. What makes Lessing's *Laokoon* so important for Ekphrasis studies is that Lessing develops the arguments based on specific artworks. His treatise has mostly been interpreted as a critical turn against Horace's famous phrase *ut pictura poesis* (as the picture so the poem).[310] Lessing highlights the uniqueness of "Dichtung" (*poesy* or dense writing) that borders not only to the visual art (sculpture or painting) with its dimension space but also to the acoustic with its dimension time. He challenges the notion of similarity between images and texts while drawing attention to the importance of the diverse media, the visual and the verbal. Lessing's efforts consist to a large extent of exploring the various conceptual frameworks, methodologies, and procedures that characterize painting on one hand, poetic writing on the other. He is responding creatively to old questions and exploring new ideas about visual-verbal dynamics drawing new attention to the art of the poet which should be equally effective and vividly powerful than that of a sculptor or painter. Lessing points out that a poem such as Dryden's "Alexander's Feast" (Ode to St. Cecilia) is capable of surpassing the visual intensity or brightness of any painting on the canvas. He adds that such a marvelous "Anschaulichkeit" or such an intense visual effect from the poem or the poetic text is not any result due to mimesis. It is itself based on the power of language, poesy, and imagination. Poesy and painting each have their own type of visuality. The great potential of visualcy in its variety works not only in the visual arts, in paintings and sculptures, but moreover in the verbal, in the poetic realm. There the visual has its own hieroglyphs, its own forces, and its own access and tools. It can make productively use of a diverse and fascinating imaginary.

Lessing's aesthetic theory in *Laokoon* is based on the intricate debate he had with art theorists and critics of his time. He discussed such ideas especially with two friends and they used to meet in Berlin 1758: Christoph Friedrich Nicolai and Moses Mendelssohn.[311] Nicolai reports how they discussed Mendelssohn's 1757 essay *Betrachtungen über die Quellen und Verbindungen der schönen Künste und Wissenschaften* (Reflections on the Sources and Connections of the Fine Arts and Belles-Lettres).[312] In this essay

309 FA 2, 134. For a different translation see Nisbet, *Gotthold Ephraim Lessing* 303.

310 Horace, "De arte poetica," line 361, *Satires, Epistles and Ars Poetica* 480.

311 On Lessing's important friendship with Moses Mendelssohn, see Amos Elon, *The Pity of it All: The German-Jewish Epoch 1743-1933* (New York: Picador, 2002), 37-40, 62-64.

312 Published anonymously in the *Bibliothek der schönen Wissenschaften und der freyen Künste* I.2 (1757): 231-268. Reprinted in Moses Mendelssohn, *Gesammelte Schriften. Jubiläumsausgabe,* 24 vols. in 35 (Stuttgart: Friedrich Frommann Verlag [Günther Holzboog], 1929 [1971]-2005), vol. 1, 165-190. This essay was revised as "Ueber die Hauptgrundsätze der schönen Künste und Wissenschaften" published in Mendelssohn's *Philosophische Schriften,* 2 vols. (Berlin: Christian Friedrich Voß, 1761; rev. ed. 1771), vol. 2, 95-152. Reprinted in *Gesammelte Schriften,* vol. 1, 425-452.

Mendelssohn raises the issue of the relationship between the visual and the verbal arts. Lessing followed this approach in his *Laokoon,* exploring the broad fields of art theory and what we would now call "aesthetics" through the lens of his own perspective as a writer and poet, making use of poetic language in drawing attention to the importance of imagination and silence as artistic devices. In his essay, which is composed of numerous dialogues and digressions, Lessing tries to comprehend the complexities of the various disciplines of art by focusing on "Poesie," that is, the poetic art that he claims is at the center of all literary endeavors. It is through his concept of "Poesie" (poesy) in his *Laokoon* that Lessing makes his contributions to art theoretical discussions.

In 1735, the philosopher Alexander Gottlieb Baumgarten had first proposed that the word "aesthetics" be given to the knowledge derived from the senses, specifically the sense-perception of beauty, as opposed to knowledge exclusively acquired in a logical fashion through reason. He treated this matter much more fully in the two volumes of his *Aesthetica* (1750-1758).[313] It was an insight later also further dealt with by Immanuel Kant in his *Kritik der Urteilskraft* (Critique of Judgment) published later in 1790. Lessing tried to understand a set of rules for a poetic theory and was especially inspired by his friend Mendelssohn. In December 1756 Mendelssohn had his "Betrachtungen" (Reflections) published. It is about the interpretation of the Laokoon statue as first articulated by Johann Joachim Winckelmann, a path-breaking art historian and expert of the visual arts. As Monika Schrader points out, it was Lessing's other friend from Berlin, Christoph Friedrich Nicolai, who in his commentary on Lessing's letters remarks that "der erste Keim" (the first seedling) to Lessing's involvement with the Laokoon problematic must be traced in the correspondence between Lessing and Mendelssohn.[314] Lessing does not use the word "Ästhetik" and Baumgarten, who has been credited for having invented this word, is only mentioned once in Lessing's *Laokoon,* in the preface.[315] I think we can understand Lessing's approach to art theory less in terms of aesthetics in the modern sense, that is, philosophical theorizing on the fine arts and the beautiful, than through an investigation of his *poesy* or poetic writing and with attention to the ethical consequences, the intended result: compassion.

Lessing's *Laokoon* makes us see to this effect and wonder about someone suffering and in pain. The response is not exclusively on beauty but on variable sense perceptions that are usually associated with pain, the unpleasant, if not the ugly. Lessing comments that the sculptor of the Laokoon group representing the father with his

313 "§. CXVI. Sunt ergo *noētá cognoscenda facultate superiore obiectum logices, asthētá episēmēs aisthētikēs siue*AESTHETICAE." Alexander Gottlieb Baumgarten, *Meditationes philosophicae de nonnullis ad poema pertinentibus* (Halle: Literis Ioannis Henrici Grunerti, 1735), 39. Reprint, *Reflections on Poetry*, ed. and trans. Karl Aschenbrenner and William B. Holtner (Berkeley: University of California Press, 1954): "Therefore things known are to be known by the superior faculty as the object of logic; *things perceived* [are to be known by the inferior faculty, as the object] of the science of perception, or aesthetic" (78). Baumgarten's "Aesthetica" is a neo-Latin coinage. For a brief history of the issues involved, see Alan Goldman, "The Aesthetic," Gaunt and Lopez, ed., *The Routledge Companion to Aesthetics* 181-192. See also Luc Ferry, *Homo Aestheticus: The Development of Taste in the Democratic Age,* trans. Robert de Laoiza (Chicago: University of Chicago Press, 1993).

314 Monika Schrader, *Laokoon–"eine vollkommene Regel der Kunst"* 37.

315 Lessing asserts that he will draw the evidence for his arguments from the original texts, and not, like Baumgarten did in his *Aesthetica, rely on a dictionary of quotations* (FA 5/2, 15).

sons attacked by snakes must have restrained the ugly before it became "Ekel" (disgust). In showing Laokoon's mouth not widely open, but just at the moment before the climax of the action and before the expected scream, he gives more space to the recipients to the artwork. Only by giving such a minimalist account of the action could the artwork spark such a lively impression and call forth the compassion by the viewers.[316] Lessing accordingly opts for minimalism in order to leave space for the readers' imagination also. The related *Paralipomena* contain important philosophical and art theoretical implications. Lessing explains the attributes, mechanisms, and "inner forces" ("Sprungfedern") that lead to poesy ("Poesie"). It is possible, he claims, that in verbal descriptions the visual persists, or it gets newly and vividly evoked. If a description is truly poetic, it will call forth the imagination of depth and action. It will not only be a visual thing thus drawing attention also to other senses and the dimension of temporality, hence movement.[317]

Baumgarten was only one of a large number of thinkers who made attempts, as the eighteenth century progressed, to theorize "das Schöne" (the beautiful) and Lessing entered this debate by claiming that "Poesie" (poetic art) and "Malerei" (painting) both produce pleasure in the individual. In his fictional account of this triangle, it is the philosopher (Mendelssohn) who recognizes that the source of this pleasure is "Schönheit" (beauty) which has "allgemeine Regeln, die sich auf mehrere Dinge anwenden lassen" (general rules applicable to a number of things).[318] It is the "Kunstrichter"

---

316 The complex question what "das Schöne" or "the beautiful" means in the eighteenth century has been thoroughly explored by Carsten Zelle in his book *Die doppelte Ästhetik der Moderne. Revisionen des Schönen von Boileau bis Nietzsche* (Stuttgart: Metzler, 1995). He mentions Lessing numerous times but especially on pages 260-261 he comments on his *Laokoon* (1766, Kap. 23-25). He correctly states that Lessing introduced the notion of "the ugly" as an aesthetic category and as a matter consequential for the philosophy of the arts ("Das Häßliche stand zwar als ästhetische Kategorie spätestens seit Lessings Laokoon auf der Tagesordung der Kunstphilosophie"). One should add that Lessing shifts attention not only from "the beautiful" to something "ugly" but rather to something which is unpleasant ("unangenehm"). Lessing shows the beautiful body of Laokoon in pain but this does not make him ugly. According to Lessing the artist restricted the visual representation of suffering so that the presentation does not impose itself upon the viewer. Zelle omits to say that Lessing makes a shift, as I argue, from aesthetics to ethics, from spectatorship and the gaze to a concerned looking and compassion. Something related was noticed by Kristina Bonn, *Vom Schönen. Schönheitskonzeptionen bei Lessing, Goethe und Schiller* (Bielefeld: Aisthesis, 2008), esp. 28-43. Also very insightful is Jane Forsey, "The Aesthetic Force of the Unpleasant" in *Eventual Aesthetics* 5.1 (2016): 15-24 where she writes that Kant neglected "the unpleasant" which he mentions in passing when writing mainly on his approach to the beautiful. Forsey explains that "the unpleasant" is much more leading to action than the beautiful or the ugly or even disgust. Lessing is in this regard still to be discovered for an aesthetic that goes far beyond the Kantian analysis of the judgement of the beautiful, the ugly, and disgust. Forsey writes: "The unpleasant stands between the ugly and disgusting–neither inviting us to linger nor driving us away–as an aesthetic response that is uniquely motivating" (18-19). This approach, (this was not mentioned by Forsey), is newly to be accredited to G. E. Lessing.

317 See Benjamin Bennett, *Beyond Theory: Eighteenth-Century German Literature and the Poetics of Irony* (Ithaca: Cornell University Press, 1993), chapter 3: "Lessing's Laokoon: The Poetics of Experience" 116-161, esp. 154-158.

318 FA 5/2, 13; *Laocoön*, trans. McCormick 3.

(art critic, that is, Lessing in this context) who in this fictional account notices that some of these rules apply more to painting, others more to the poetic texts. Lessing in response sets out to explore the nature and distribution of these rules as others have interpreted them. He challenges the tradition of *ut pictura poesis* (as painting, so poetry) by questioning the traditional superiority of *Malerei* over *Dichtung.* He tries to establish equal rights among the so-called "sister arts" while pointing out their distinct but equal capabilities. Lessing shifts importance not simply from the visual realm to that of the verbal, or from one genre to another. He experiments with visual poesy, making it to play newly discovered potentials within the verbal and especially in dramatic art, onstage.

For example, he tests the suggestive power of language through the use of metaphors, metonymies, and other poetic strategies beginning with the fable all the way to the open-ended parable. For Lessing, it was *poesy,* or the perspective of the poet (a position that included all the genres of the arts of writing) at the core of a broader investigation into the various disciplines of art. It was via his medium, writing as a poet and playwright, through which Lessing approached all the other questions on aesthetics in any modern sense. Lessing uses the word "Poesie" in his theoretical writings not as matter of cognition only, as Baumgarten did, nor merely as a genre as Aristotle presented it in his *Poetics.*[319] Lessing gives "poetic art" a new position in art theory. He associates with poesy with a vital force that connects all arts. Similar to Mendelssohn Lessing concentrated his intellectual efforts on attempting to understand *poesy.* He located it not only next to painting or plastic art but adjacent also next to music.

*Laokoon* is the culmination of Lessing's Ekphrasis theory. He asserts the importance of the media and discipline specific approaches to what we understand as truth. Lessing explains why he has chosen a minimalistic approach in the development of his argument. In order to present something with "Anschaulichkeit" or vividly the dimension of time has to be temporarily forgotten, bracketed for the sake of the here and now. He aims at viewers' experiencing space exclusively. The sculptor must have contracted the entire action of the complex and multifaceted action surrounding Laokoon into one single "prägnanter Augenblick" (pregnant, fruitful, or poignant moment) in the artwork. This moment as represented in the Laokoon statue depends completely on the dimension of space where in Lessing's approach "Zeichen" or signs are so-called "Körper im Raum" (bodies in space). As the visual belongs to the dimension of space, its signs appear one after the other, sequentially. The poet can present an idea and make it visually most effective by also adhering to the dictates of space, albeit only to a certain degree. Brevity is helpful in order to reach succinct images. He warns against overabundant allegories, the need of previous texts or external sources. Lessing argues that *poesy* belongs both to the dimension of space, yet to some extent also to the dimension of time as shared with music. Poesy oscillates and participates in both

319 In the *Poetics* Aristotle had commented upon various forms and genres of poetry ranging from epic poetry to tragedy and comedy to dithyrambic poetry, as well as considering the music of the flute and of the lyre, characterizing all of these as genres of poetry and as modes of imitation. He associated them not only with various senses but also with various media. See *Poetics,* ed. and trans. Halliwell (1-4)1447a-1449a, 28-45.

the adjacent conceptual frameworks, painting on one hand, music on the other. From music it can borrow the notion of signs as times with their pluralistic simultaneity. He insists that each discipline must be regarded with respect to its unique features. Painting adheres to the dimension of space, music to the dimension of time. Poets have a certain amount of freedom to select their tools and capacities from in between. *Poesy* is, as Lessing comes to discover, spatial yet also an art of temporality, not only bound to the singularity of sequential signs in space. It can use to its advantage what he then calls metaphor.

*Laokoon* offers his ekphrastic description and commentary on the famous statue in the Vatican collection by depicting the Trojan Priest of Apollo and his two sons being encircled and attacked by snakes.[320] The story, according to which the statue must have been created, dates back to antiquity, existing in at least three separate versions, the most familiar being that of Virgil in the *Aeneid* (Book II: 13-249).[321] The statue was discovered in 1506 just outside of Rome and then installed by Pope Julius II in the Belvedere Courtyard of the Vatican, where it remains today. There it (or at least some of it) was apparently seen by Winckelmann during a visit to Rome in 1760. His lengthy and foundational response to the statue is found in *Gedanken über die Nachahmung Griechischer Werke in Malerei und Skulptur* (Thoughts on the Imitation of Greek Works in Painting and Sculpture. 1755).[322] Winckelmann's *Gedanken* raised a number of questions which were debated for the rest of the century, next by Lessing and then by Goethe who entered the fray in 1798.[323]

Whereas most interpretations have interpreted Lessing as drawing a dividing line between the visual and the verbal, I want to show how Lessing attempted to test these boundaries for Ekphrasis and to establish awareness for visual verbalness in poesy. Lessing explores the intricate dynamics existing between painting, poesy, and music. How to compare images with words or how to describe the constellations in between?

---

320 Brilliant, *My Laocoön* 44-45. To what extent this attack was fatal and for whom it may have been intended is left open-ended, although questions such as these animated much of the discussion in the reception history. Also left open are many questions about the history of the artwork itself and the form it must originally have had. Horst Althaus, Laokoon. *Stoff und Form*, $2^{nd}$ ed. (Tübingen: Francke Verlag, 2000) documents the history and whereabouts of the art work and its fragments. An arm which was found in 1905 in Rome has been confirmed as being authentic and has led to an alternative presentation of the torso. For the older reconstruction with Laocoon's right arm outstretched, see the reproduction in Richter, *Laocoon's Body* 15, and for the modern reconstruction with right arm bent, Richter, *Laocoon's Body* 28.

321 Virgil, *Eclogues, Georgics, Aeneid I-VI,* ed. H. Rushton Fairclough. rev. G.P. Goold. Loeb Classical Library 68 (Cambridge: Harvard University Press, 1999), 316-333.

322 Winckelmann, *Gedanken* 32-37; "Gedanken" 43-44.

323 Goethe, "Über *Laokoon*," GFA 1: 18 (1998), *Ästhetische Schriften 1771-1805*, ed. Friedmar Apel: 489-500, 1253-58; Simon Jan Richter, "The End of Laocoon: Pain and Allegory in Goethe's 'Über Laokoon,'" *Goethe Yearbook* 6 (1992): 123-141. See also David Wellbery, "Das Gesetz der Schönheit: Lessings Ästhetik der Repräsentation," C.L. Hart Nibbrig, ed., *Was Heißt "Darstellen"* (Frankfurt am Main: Suhrkamp, 1994), 175-204; Gwen Raaberg, "Laokoon Considered and Reconsidered: Lessing and Comparative Criticism of Literature and Art," Ugrinsky, ed., *Lessing and the Enlightenment* 67-110; Thomas Koebner, ed., *Laokoon und kein Ende;* Brilliant, *My Laocoön* 50-61; Bonn, *Die Schönen* 29-43; Fick, *Handbuch* 232-261.

The remnants or pieces of a sculpture seem to have a life of their own. They may that be understood as being just as ephemeral as words, spoken or even committed to writing. There are images or mental impressions which they call up. Lessing's initial argument is to pay attention to the material and physical media distinctions which barely allow any trace of similarity between a concrete artwork, its visualcy, and that of a narrative, drama, or poetic text. Then it was Lessing's achievement to sharpen his own and his readers' imaginations and to find tools through poesy that could educate and mobilize the public towards ethical actions. In his dramas, as we shall later see, he experimented with images and words and with the dimensions of space and time when he suggested the innovation of "musical images."

## 2. *Laokoon* reception: Is Lessing's approach anti-visual?

Lessing's *Laokoon* has been acknowledged as important and path-breaking in many respects by David Wellbery, Murray Krieger, James Heffernan, Frederick Burwick, and, as already mentioned, Stephen Cheeke.[324] These experts on the visual all find in one way or another that Lessing had a decisive role in determining what Ekphrasis means today, sometimes also through other genres of poetic writing which Lessing used in his works. Whereas Wellbery makes a strong argument for Lessing's cohesive *Laokoon* treatise in determining the strength of poesy and in achieving a strong argument for visual effectiveness through verbalness, successful Ekphrasis in other words, he moreover finds that "Lessing's distinctions between poetry and painting (actually the plastic arts in general) constitute a global model of aesthetic signification, a remarkably penetrating and articulate development of the aesthetic semiotics which Baumgarten first imagined and which Meier and Mendelssohn began to work out."[325] Wellbery adds that Lessing distinguishes poetry and painting regarding the material constitution of their signs, their syntax, and their contents but that he does not abandon the doctrine *ut pictura poesis* altogether. He notes that in his discourse it is "relocated on a higher level of generality." By considering multiple levels of language and the potential for poesy to turn its arbitrary signs into apparently "natural" ones, Lessing stands as a founder of successful Ekphrasis.

Krieger, as the subtitle of his book *Ekphrasis: The Illusion of the Natural Sign* indicates, challenges Lessing's contributions questioning the notion of any "natural signs" in poesy and doubting successful Ekphrasis in *Laokoon.* He argues that Lessing is mostly advocating media distinctions between the visual and the verbal but also highlighting differences between the various poetic genres. Lessing contributed actively as a poet and playwright to many poetic genres throughout his life. In the realm of dramatic art he discovered the option that a playwright can to do without the invisibilities of language, thus undercutting the actual challenges of any convincingly successful

324 Wellbery, *Lessing's Laocoon;* Krieger, *Ekphrasis; Heffernan, Museum of Words;* Frederick Burwick, "Ekphrasis and Theories of Reading Visual Representation," Wagner, ed., *Icons–Texts–Iconotexts* 78-104; Cheeke, *Writing for Art;* Webb, *Ekphrasis.*

325 Wellbery, *Lessing's Laocoon* 7.

Ekphrasis process. Heffernan notes: "Lessing reminds us of drama's special role, a natural-sign role as a visual art (a 'moving picture') and, by implication, concedes the greater mimetic distance that occurs in non-dramatic poetry. For the dramatic mode of representation is not altogether dependent on the invisibilities of language, as the lyric and narrative modes are."[326] Heffernan explores the poetics of Ekphrasis from Homer to Ashbery and positions Lessing at a juncture belonging to two diverse strains of thought, while claiming on one hand "universal unitemporality of art" and introducing the notion that "the artist" that can depict only one moment in a picture, while with the other hand referring to Homer as a positive example for poets since he "represented nothing but progressive actions."[327] According to Heffernan, Lessing seems to be deconstructing or complicating his own earlier argument critically. Apparently Lessing's approach is "useful and highly applicable" but Heffernan concludes: "when Lessing says that just 'one picture' is represented in the disputation passage, he radically equivocates" and he adds "The work of poetic conversion here–the turning of spatial composition into verbal narrative–is impossible to discern or define."[328] Heffernan charges Lessing with ambivalence, or with a displacement of certain premises, drawing from and reinterpreting or claiming adaptation of ancient sources for his own version of Ekphrasis.

Burwick, similarly to Cheeke, gives Lessing full credit when interpreting his multiple and indeed complex contributions which all build interestingly upon his *Laokoon* treatise of 1766 later and then from an entire gamut of angles on Ekphrasis and related issues throughout other poetic and dramatic works. He also approaches the results of Lessing's contributing to Ekphrasis through various applicable lenses of Lessing's readers. Among them are such brilliant readers and writers as De Quincey, Wordsworth, and Keats who all drew from Lessing's Laokoon important inspiration for their works. They refer to the spatiality of visual art and the temporal in poetic language as depicted in Lessing's *Laokoon.* Lessing allows his readers and spectators (and in the following Burwick citation Lessing approached through the lens of De Quincey) to draw moments of "permanence" from "the evanescent" thus creatively participating in this lively debate and making Ekphrasis reassuringly happen. Burwick writes: "Lessing's point that the language of the evanescent moment can be of great use to the dramatic poet, for in the drama such passages 'make parts, or steps, in a natural process the *whole* of which is given, and are effaced either by more tranquil sentiments, or by the catastrophe, so that attempt is made to give permanence to the evanescent'."[329]

Brad Prager argues: "Although Lessing was not a Romantic, his writings were precursors to Romantic thought, something particularly noticeable in the essay, *Laokoon.*"[330] He notes that this work by Lessing entails assertions about vision and art

---

326 Murray Krieger, *Ekphrasis, The Illusion of the Natural Sign* (Baltimore: Johns Hopkins University Press, 1992),

327 James A.W. Heffernan, *Museum of Words: The Poetics of Ekphrasis from Homer to Ashbery.* (Chicago: University of Chicago Press, 1993), 14.

328 Heffernan, *Museum of Words* 14.

329 Frederick Burwick, *Mimesis and its Romantic Roots* (Pennsylvania: Pennsylvania State University Press, 2001, 118. Emphasis on *whole* as in Burwick.

330 Prager, *Aesthetic Vision* 17.

yet most notably develops important philosophical ideas in response to the ancient Laokoon statue and Winckelmann's earlier account of it. Instead of looking directly, Lessing tends to "favor aesthetic experience as it is said to occur in the mind's eye."[331] He seems to question not only what we see in front of our eyes but also how we process in our mind that towards critical thinking. One can read Lessing as a challenge to the divide between the exterior art work and the interior mind of the observer and as a critic of the Kantian divide. Lessing, more on the side with Herder, acknowledges the importance of sense perceptions as they precede verbal understanding in the cognition process.

As I shall illustrate in the following chapters, Lessing wanted to turn readers into spectators, for example by making drama more accessible and applicable to the public of his own time. It was his goal in writing about the Laokoon statue to show how images could be used to mobilize the audiences for ethical actions. He realized that images can transform themselves through poesy. Language is poetic if it can capture what links sense perceptions, emotions, and thoughts. Language uses arbitrary signs, yet it can approximate "natural" signs–if it becomes poesy. The poet can tap into the physical sense perceptions through the imaginative power of words. These become metaphorically speaking the beginning of inner and outer "actions" ("Handlungen"). The poignant moment of the Laokoon statue has philosophical and aesthetic consequences. Poesy marks a potential beginning of a public that has compassion. Lessing creates a direct link from what used to be aesthetics to ethics. His *Laokoon* involves Ekphrasis, the transformation of something visual into something verbal and impact emotionally and intellectually. Yet poesy cannot exclude the temporal and this has also some incalculable consequences.[332]

In a letter to Gleim Lessing wrote: "I can only think with my pen on paper," thus reflecting on his own medium as a writer.[333] Ernst Gombrich explained: "But Lessing's intimate friends had always known that you needed only to expect him to do one thing and he would do another which he considered more important."[334] Lessing was critical of himself, of the German theater, of many French playwrights, and certainly also of some visual artists. But he did not pitch the latter against the poets in general. Gombrich championed Shakespeare as "the only human being to whom Lessing conceded the title of a genius."[335] Along those lines I think that Lessing's *Laokoon* was not written against the painter and the sculptor. It was not only to draw more attention to the writer and the poet as some critics claimed. It is indeed a work about the visual as the verbal, something which can only be achieved via Ekphrasis and through activating the audience. In the footsteps of Shakespeare, Lessing demonstrated how to tap

---

331 Prager, *Aesthetic Vision* 17.

332 Friedrich Vollhardt's 2010 "Studienausgabe" of *Laokoon* makes us aware that this work was unfinished. Lessing planned additional parts that should involve a new genre of "musikalische Bilder" (musical images), a concept that would have violated the strict borders between the art forms established in the first part. There were also plans Lessing had begun to formulate in his *Paralipomena* concerning a third part of the *Laokoon* project.

333 E. H. Gombrich, "Lessing: Lecture on a Master Mind." *Proceedings of the British Academy* 45 (1957): 133-156 at 135.

334 Gombrich, "Lessing" 134; Mitchell, *Iconology* 107-109.

335 Gombrich, "Lessing" 134.

into creative imagery through sounds and words and how to possibly establish helpful guidelines for others, poets and artists. Wellbery compares Lessing's *Laokoon* with works by Baumgarten, Meier, and Mendelssohn and claims that Lessing sets new standards in terms of what to remember and what to forget when aiming at textual impact on the senses. He offers useful steps towards a coherent semiotics dealing with distinct signs and the various signification systems of the visual and verbal disciplines.[336]

Nisbet draws attention to what he stresses as a complicated and perhaps ambivalent relationship Lessing had with his contemporary Winckelmann. He claims that it was primarily Winckelmann whom Lessing in his *Laokoon* wanted to challenge. Nisbet writes: "Lessing could not but acknowledge the brilliance of Winckelmann's achievements."[337] Yet he argues for certain inconsistencies in Lessing's *Laokoon* and characterizes Lessing's attitude towards Winckelmann as "fundamentally polemical" despite his "uncharacteristic restraint."[338] Lessing was, one should add, not primarily an art historian or art critic as Winckelmann. I think Lessing was genuinely curious about what gave the Laokoon stature such strength of emotional impact. It was according to Lessing not the subdued scream of the stoic Laokoon figure as Winckelmann had explained but instead the artist's ability to confine his representation of the action within the limitations of the discipline-specific conditions. Had the mouth been more widely open, the spectators would no longer have any freedom to imagine. Then the poignant moment would have been lost for a visual of imposing, propaganda style.

I think that Lessing was not polemical as Nisbet claims. Lessing liked Winckelmann and admired his work, perhaps similar to the fallen oak tree in his fable "Die Eiche" (The Oak) when it lay stretched out on the ground and then finally was recognized as being so much bigger and more magnificent than when alive. In fact Lessing

336 Ernest W. B. Hess-Lüttich, "Medium–Prozeß–Illusion: Zur rationalen Rekonstruktion der Zeichenlehre in Lessings *Laokoon*," Gebauer, ed., *Das Laokoon-Projekt* 103-136, gives an accurate account of Lessing's idea of paintable and unpaintable facts that nevertheless can potentially be presented as "poetisches Gemälde" (poetic painting) (117). What I miss in all of these interesting contributions on Lessing's semiotics is the discussion of Lessing's approach to temporality and sense perception, ideas that are closely related and even, in my reading at least, at the core of Lessing's contribution to the *Laokoon* debate as subsequently amended by Herder's and Goethe's own contributions. In fact I think that some important observations that Ernst Osterkamp makes about Goethe in this context already apply to Lessing. See Ernst Osterkamp, *Im Buchstabenbilde: Studien zum Verfahren Goethescher Bildbeschreibungen,* Germanistische Abhandlungen 70 (Stuttgart: Metzler, 1991). What Goethe calls "der eigentliche Lebenspunct des Dargestellten" (the actual life focus of the presentation) is related to Herder's idea of "ewiger Anblick" (eternal glance) but also to Lessing's "prägnanter Augenblick" (poignant moment). What makes these moments poetic in a sense is that they assume an aspect of a view of the whole, a glimpse of something complete putting the specific into a broad–perhaps sublime and cosmic–perspective.

337 Nisbet, *Lessing: Eine Biographie* 407; *Gotthold Ephraim Lessing* 308. Nisbet mentions how Lessing was deeply touched by Winckelmann's tragic death and how he was truly an admirer of his accomplishments professionally as an art historian and expert of the visual.

338 Nisbet, *Lessing: Eine Biographie* 414, 423; *Gotthold Ephraim Lessing* 313, 320. See also: Victor Anthony Rudowski, "Lessing contra Winckelmann," *The Journal of Aesthetics and Art Criticism* 44.3 (1986): 235-243 and Bengt Algot Sørensen, "Lessings Laokoon und Winckelmann," *Lessing Yearbook* 36 (2004/2005): 69-78.

had much regret and grief at the horrible news of Winckelmann's death when he was heinously murdered on his way traveling in Trieste June 1778, just two years after Lessing's *Laokoon* was published. Lessing may have wondered then, as is reflected in his *Paralipomena* and later works, whether that he had perhaps overlooked something important about his friend's ideas. It took him a long time to process certain theoretical issues concerning the unfinished Laokoon project, as he then proclaims, until he found his own position as a poet yet modestly learning from the visual artist as well as the musician. He remained committed to his appreciation of poesy which for him had some advantages in bringing the temporal to the visual, yet he always avoided any dogmatism about what he found on his own or about what he personally believed in.

Simon Richter juxtaposes Lessing's approach with that of Winckelmann. Winckelmann is regarded as an advocate for the body, beauty, and the visual arts. Lessing is regarded as an advocate of the spirit, a writer concerned with or even obsessed with pain, and characterized as anti-visual.[339] Richter argues that "Lessing's semiotic aesthetics is primarily a denial of materiality empowered by a fascinated abhorrence of death (the sexuality is located in the fascination)." He adds that "Lessing's euphemism, beneath its veil, is a form of violence directed toward the body, a kind of grave desecration. What is finally most surprising is that euphemism's original and confounding violence occurs not on the side of painting, where one would expect it, but on the side of language and poetry, thus calling into question the crucial distinction on which the Laokoon is based."[340] I ask: Was Lessing really pitching the poetic realm of abstraction against the visual realm of concreteness? Isn't he more about concrete poesy, one that is focused on the specific and minimalist in expression? Richter extrapolates the antinomies he establishes in his interpretation of Lessing and further and develops them in gendered terms. He interprets Lessing as a Platonist. Yet if Lessing's work was only to contradict Winckelmann who celebrated the human body, as Richter claims, one should not ignore that Lessing is not about a denial of death but about a hope for eternity. Laokoon's body does not produce "Ekel," abhorrence, or disgust for Lessing but it is "unangenehm" ("unpleasant") and this puzzling feeling promotes emotions and thoughts. It is in my reading far from a rejection of the body. Richter draws his claims, which I find hard to follow, from Lessing's comment that the sculptor of the Laokoon statue had to give restraint to showing emotions. Richter reads Lessing as if he were an advocate of repressed pain and hence anti-visual.[341]

However, if Winckelmann celebrated the body and beauty, Lessing appears to be interested in the sublime but also in measured beauty. The depiction of pain is not excluded in his account of the action. But the action is much bigger than as depicted and it draws us to the Laokoon for compassion. Lessing may well have been a forerunner of the Romantics giving creative imagination a new importance.[342] I think it was Lessing's achievement to have *poesy* based, as soon later Goethe acknowledged,

339 Simon Richter, *Laocoon's Body and the Aesthetics of Pain: Winckelmann, Lessing, Herder, Moritz, Goethe* (Detroit: Wayne State University Press, 1992).

340 Richter, *Laocoon's Body* 68.

341 Richter, *Laocoon's Body* 63 passim.

342 Prager, *Aesthetic Vision* in his chapter "Interior and Exterior: G.E. Lessing's *Laocoon* as a Prelude to Romanticism" 17–33.

on physicality, on perceptions of the senses, and on the honest credo that there is a universal life force in nature. Lessing's efforts are for the sake of the reader's and spectators' imaginary space, in search of a new and compassionate public. This move towards poesy is more than strictly philosophical or theoretical. It is not dogmatic, didactic, romantic, or classicist. It may participate in these concerns or movements, yet Lessing mostly links in his approach as documented in *Laokoon* and the related *Paralipomena* aesthetics with ethics. He is writing as far as I can see without polemics against Winckelmann. Lessing is celebrating and critically depicting life, the poetic next to the other arts, and hoping that all the arts, including the previously underestimated poesy, may bring forth human compassion.

## 3. Lessing's more subtle implications: Visual texts

Lessing approaches poetry not as a genre but in the context of an inclusive "Dichtung" that is "dense writing" as a kind of poetic writing that borrows signs from music in order to achieve its media specific written verbal images or metaphors. He argues that despite these boundaries something fluid takes place or spills over from one territory or dimension to the other. In the 27$^{th}$ *Paralipomena* with his letter to Christoph Friedrich Nicolai of May 26$^{th}$ 1769, he projects a sequel for his *Laokoon* which should have ended with a study of drama that would fully integrate the features of painting and poetic writing.[343] Lessing took into account that sometimes "andeutungsweise" (by suggestion that is through allusions, contiguities, metaphors, or metonymies) important links between the different sign systems can occur.[344] His suggestion of such things as "musikalische Gemälde" (musical pictures)[345] has barely been touched on in all the many debates on *Laokoon* and in my reading it is a compelling example of the fact that Lessing just cannot be understood in terms of simple dualisms and antinomies. He is, one must argue in his defense of some blind spots, not an opponent of Winckelmann and a harsh critic of the fine arts, but most emphatically a honest connoisseur of the arts altogether and the artists' true friend. What he suggests is not that that words cannot replace images but that they can have, especially when performed onstage and in poetic dialogue, claim their own impact through an alternative visualcy.

343 FA 5/2, 312-17; Rudowski, *Lessing's Aesthetica in Nuce.*

344 See *Laokoon,* FA 5/2, 116-17.

345 FA 5/1, 114; (*Laocoön,* trans. McCormick 76). Note that earlier Lessing said: "Es ist unmöglich die musikalische Malerei, welche die Worte des Dichters mit hören lassen, in eine andere Sprache überzutragen" (FA 5/2, 110): ("It is impossible to translate this musical picture which the words of the poet present into another language") (*Laocoön,* trans. McCormick 72). It would be more accurate to translate this: "It is impossible to transpose this musical painting, which the words of the poet allow to be heard along the way, into another language." So I would like to correct this notion by pointing out that Lessing actually hints at the possibility that the words of the poet may be able to allow for ekphrasis, that is let musical paintings "speak" but only poetically, in the language of the poet, and not without the use of multiple levels of discourse, such as in metaphors.

Lessing suggests an approach to "Darstellung" (representation) in the arts emphasizing modesty, careful restriction, and tact. This is not to be confused with the concept of "Unbezeichnung" which Lessing knew from his close reading of Winckelmann and as mentioned by Nisbet and Richter, albeit with different connotations.[346] Lessing argues: "Dasjenige aber nur allein ist fruchtbar, was der Einbildungskraft freies Spiel läßt. Je mehr wir sehen, desto mehr müssen wir hinzu denken können" ("But only that which gives free rein to the imagination is effective. The more we see, the more we must be able to imagine").[347] I would like to add that Lessing's comment is not only about efficiency but also about fruitfulness or the potentials beyond the visible. What is implicit in the message for those who can read it considering the use of creative metaphor? Lessing draws interest not only what we read or observe in art that deserves to be understood and questioned, but also how we read and observe the signs the poet and painter leave us.[348] Throughout his life he was concerned with uncovering truth, its representations, beauty, pain, and other notions related to art and aesthetics. More specifically, he was interested in the relationships among all the disciplines of art. Since he placed poesy in the center, all the other disciplines had to be approached by considering this one also. To this extent, Lessing may be said to have a theory of the beautiful. His claim is much smaller; he is not attempting to establish the rules of an all-encompassing theory of beauty. He is interested in what causes motion and action. The force for these he detects neither in beauty nor in anything ugly but in what might be perceived as slightly off, *uncomfortable* ("unangenehm"), or *unsuitable* ("unbequem").

According to Lessing in his work on drama, later the goal of *poesy* is to elevate the mind of the audience and to promote a cleansing of emotions (*catharsis*). In distinction to how Aristotle had formulated this term, Lessing does not present good or bad characters that clash. He leads us into the depth of conflicted characters with their potentials for both, good and bad, and a whole range of possibilities in between. In his works the action not so much a visible outer quality but rather an inner action portrayed by means of the character's language and actions. They speak indirectly via their emotions that motivate what they speak and do. These *inner actions* initiate potential future actions all of which will never be completely shown onstage. The outcome is never presented fully because Lessing insists that there must be room for emotions, speculation, and thought. Only if there is a sense of freedom will the audience, each member on their own and with multiple outcomes, engage with the theater play and what it means to them. His ultimate goal is to educate the public and to promote tolerance, respect, and love for one another. One of the ways this

346 Winckelmann, *Geschichte der Kunst* 150; Nisbet, *Lessing: Eine Biographie* 413; Gotthold Ephraim Lessing 313; and Richter, *Laocoon's Body* 56-57.

347 FA 5/2, 32; *Laocoön,* trans. McCormick 19.

348 See Baxmann et al., ed., *Das Laokoon-Paradigma* for a detailed debate on signs in Lessing's writings. The volume begins with the important sentence: "Lessings *Laokoon* weist über die Grenzen der Malerei und Poesie hinaus" (Lessing's *Laocoön* points far beyond the limits of painting and poetry), ix.

can happen, Lessing suggests, is through the evocation of "Mitleid" (*compassion*), an insight adopted in part from Aristotle's *Poetics.*[349]

Lessing's approach has several innovative features. Aristotle conceptualized compassion and fear as two polarized and equally important terms. Lessing places "Mitleid" in the primary position. He interprets fear as subordinate to compassion and only marginally as anything of relevance. Lessing combines poetics with ethics and at the same time tries to create a space for the imagination of the audience. He is careful not to press with imperatives but instead to leave conclusions open. He is careful to avoid labels, prescriptive terms, and prefers using of metaphors and metonymies. His writings reflect many differences with the dominant Enlightenment discourse.[350] Also, in distinction to Aristotelian poetics, Lessing was prepared to discuss the ugly in the arts. For him beauty was a matter of plurality conceptualized as *diversity in unity*: "Ein einziger unschicklicher Teil kann die übereinstimmende Wirkung vieler zur Schönheit stören" ("The harmonious interaction of many parts which produces beauty can be destroyed by a single unfitting part, without, however, making the object ugly").[351] He elaborates this idea and adds that if there were unsuitable parts that would make them not necessarily ugly. He allows for tension and nuances in this spectrum and he departs from Winckelmann's classist ideal yet while having ekphrastic hope and offering merely interesting amendments.

## 4. More shifting perspectives, questions, and consequences

Lessing approaches *poesy* in various ways throughout his life. It is possible to distinguish three separate yet related phases. The earliest is that found in his *Fabeln* (Fables), which appeared in 1759, the second is that of the *Laokoon* treatise of 1766, and the third is found in the parables that appeared separately in1778/79. In *Laokoon* Lessing draws attention to the relations between the visual arts, music, and "Poesie." He raises the problem of temporality in art by positioning on one side of the spectrum sculpture and painting, on the other side music, with poesy in between. Whereas sculpture and painting exist in space, music exists only in time and has the advantage of simultaneity, while poesy partakes of both the spatial and the temporal. Lessing tries to deal with the problem of temporality in his own interpretation of the Laokoon statue by proposing notions that have come to be characterized as a fruitful or poignant moment, and a nearly silent scream. These poetic concepts gained far-reaching theoretical

349 On this see Wilfried Barner, Gunter E. Grimm, Helmut Kiesel, Martin Kramer, *Lessing: Epoche–Werk–Wirkung*, 5th ed. (Munich: Beck, 1987), 196-197.

350 See, for example, many of the essays in Wolfram Mauser and Günter Sasse, ed., *Streitkultur: Strategien des Überzeugens im Werk Lessings* (Tübingen: Niemeyer, 1993), including Beate Allert, "Pluralisierung der Ringe," 113-120.

351 FA 5/2, 164; *Laocoön,* trans. McCormick 212. This insight initiates a discussion of the role of ugliness in poetry and painting in which Lessing modifies his Aristotelian approach. See Ulrike Zeuch, "Sensus communis, imaginatio und sensorium commune im 17. Jahrhundert," Adler and Zeuch, ed., *Synästhesie* 167-184.

consequences for later theorists, even those working with quite different media.[352] Lessing argues that since a painting can only depict one single moment in time, such a select moment must be chosen very carefully so that the implied potential of the entire action can be seen in a nutshell. The painter must think of the most pregnant moment without giving away too much and thereby restricting the imagination. Being an advocate of brevity, Lessing rejects the kind of Ekphrasis that would turn succinct images into detailed and all too ornamental descriptions and become tedious and boring in the end. For him vividness is key, both in the visual and verbal. It can only be achieved and maintained by constricting temporality.[353] He knows that the public has a limited time span in which to concentrate on an artwork or play. Yet on the other hand, one of the foremost principles of art is not to impose general meanings and to leave free reign to the imagination.

In the parables he wrote towards the end of his life, Lessing will open up specific avenues to infinite meanings and endless abstractions. While he had already liberated the poet from subordination to the painter, he then draws attention to new types of visuality as they exist in the realm of the verbal and to concrete tools such as metaphor and metonymy. In his 25th Paralipomenon he writes:

> Das bisherige erweiset, daß es der Poesie nicht ganz und gar an natürlichen Zeichen mangelt. Sie hat aber auch ein Mittel ihre willkürlichen Zeichen zu dem Werthe der natürlichen zu erheben, nemlich die Metapher.[354]
>
> [What is said now proves that poetry does not completely lack any natural signs. It still also has a means to elevate its arbitrary signs to the value of the natural, namely the metaphor].

He advocates metaphors as well as "Gleichnisse" (analogies and parables) in this context and sees a great strength in poetic imagery for that matter. Lessing is even then not an advocate of allegorical writing and insists on the immanent clues to the meanings as they are already suggested in any art work. Again he critically refers to "Allegoristerei" (mania for allegory) as something overdone and all too unpractical. Whereas the Enlightenment discourse to which Lessing's work mainly belongs is known for its encyclopedic efforts and a tireless quest to name all things in order to know them,[355] he prefers to give preference to letting go of pre-established norms. And this is where

352 Among them are the filmmaker Sergej Eisenstein and the art theorist Roland Barthes. See Allert, "Lessing im Kontext kunsttheoretischer Debatten," 371-387 and "Reconceptualizing a Pictorial Turn," esp. 195-200.

353 FA 5/2, 15.

354 FA 5/2, 310.

355 In the introduction to *Laokoon,* Lessing ironically comments on this approach: "An systematischen Büchern haben wir Deutschen überhaupt keinen Mangel. Aus ein paar angenommenen Worterklärungen in der schönsten Ordnung alles, was wir nur wollen, herzuleiten, darauf verstehen wir uns." (FA 5/2, 15): (We Germans suffer from no lack of systematic books. We know how to deduce anything we want in the most beautiful order from a few postulated definitions) (*Laocoön*, trans. McCormick 5). Furthermore, Lessing will not, as Baumgarten had done, take examples from a dictionary and then apply them regardless of context. Instead Lessing wants his examples, as he puts it, so that they taste more like their source "mehr nach der Quelle schmecken" (FA 5/2: 15) (McCormick translates "Smack more of the source," *Laocoön* 5).

in Lessing's *poesy* may also linger a critique of the tradition of mimesis. Lessing does not want any writer to imitate a painter. Each was free to reproduce reality in its own form. This is where Lessing's a new appreciation for silence has a place. Lessing was very much interested in "Anschaulichkeit" and vivid sense impressions that can be gained through poesy. He claims that a playwright must correlate the visual and the acoustic with the movements onstage. Lessing begins evaluating rhetorical strategies.[356] He favors performance over description. Even when he theorizes, he offers a performance citing various voices and eventually relying on readers able to draw their own conclusions. At the core of Lessing's approach to the visual is his notion that the more one sees, the more one should think about it. Lessing shares with many of his contemporaries the interest in the eyes, visual perception, but especially in his later works he turns to the power of writing and reading images, to the questions of how to process them in various processes of reflection and interpretation.[357]

Lessing did not accept the traditional hierarchy among the senses which favored the eye over the ear and further subordinated the other senses, nor did he idolize painting and sculpture as representing normative ideals, as did Winckelmann and to some extent Herder, although the latter shifted attention from the eye to the ear. Even though he focuses on "Poesie" (poetic writing), he places it on equal levels as painting and music. Even if it may be said that Lessing liberates the verbal from the visual, it is necessary to mention again that he does not dispense with images and visuality in general, but only with a certain tradition concerning them. In addition to being critical of allegorical excesses, he becomes aware that in poesy visual representations are not univocal. In fact they can mix arbitrary and natural signs and call

---

356 See Thomas Althaus, *Das Uneigentliche ist das Eigentliche: Metaphorische Darstellung in der Prosa bei Lessing und Lichtenberg,* Literatur als Sprache: Literaturtheorie–Interpretation–Sprachkritik 8 (Münster: Aschendorff Verlag, 1989); Allert, "Pluralisierung der Ringe" and Beate Allert, "Lessing, Novalis, Schiller: Romantisierung und Medienspiel," Richard Fisher, ed., *Ethik und Ästhetik: Werke und Werte in der Literatur vom 18. bis zum 20. Jahrhundert: Festschrift für Wolfgang Wittkowski,* Forschungen zur Literatur- und Kulturgeschichte 52 (Frankfurt am Main: Peter Lang, 1995), 223-245.

357 He was perhaps more conservative than Jean Paul, who literally transferred optical techniques (such as enlargement, displacement, dissection, etc.) into the poetic realm. At the beginning of his *Vorschule der Ästhetik* (Preschool of Aesthetics, 2nd ed., 1813), Jean Paul states a preference for "Bilderschrift" as he called it (the writing of images) over "Buchstabenschrift" (the writing of letters or fixed terminologies). He argued that images precede the language of fixed terminologies. It is via metaphor that those images that are not completely textualized enter the realm of poetic language. Such verbal images occur not only in the language that poets use but also that of children, who expand their worlds of experience by transposing and recombining known words for unknown things. This is how we learn and contribute to the growth of language. Expansion of human experience would not be possible without the poetic in language, and he asserted the idea "fictio supra naturam" (fiction over nature) (*Vorschule* 193), characterizing fiction as a way to better understand nature or to better approach reality. He acknowledged that he was very much inspired by Lessing, and praised him for his "geniale Freiheit und Besonnenheit" (the freedom and thoughtfulness of a genius). He found that Lessing's "allseitiger Scharfsinn," or all-around wit, had more of an ability to dissolve and to question things than his wisdom had to establish things and to affirm them (*Vorschule* 53). See also the essays in Claudia Albes and Christiane Frey, ed., *Darstellbarkeit: Zu einem ästhetisch-philosopischen Problem um 1800* (Würzburg: Königshausen & Neumann, 2003).

for an awareness of additional irregularities and nuances"[358] Goethe in his response to Lessing's *Laokoon* notices the departure Lessing had made from earlier positions and comments enthusiastically upon Lessing's innovations. In *Dichtung und Wahrheit* (Poetry and Truth) Goethe writes:

> Man muß Jüngling sein, um sich zu vergegenwärtigen, welche Wirkung Lessings *Laokoon* auf uns ausübte, indem dieses Werk uns aus der Region eines kümmerlichen Anschauens in die freien Gefilde des Gedankens hinriß. Das so lange mißverstandene: *ut pictura poesis*, war auf einmal beseitigt, der Unterschied der bildenden und der Redekünste klar, der Gipfel beider nun getrennt, wie nah ihre Basen auch zusammenstoßen mochten.[359]
>
> [One must be young in order to realize what impact Lessing's *Laokoon* had on us since this work swept us away from the region of a meager gaze into the free fields of creative thinking. The so long misunderstood *ut pictura poesis* was all of a sudden put aside, the difference between the visual and the verbal arts clear. The peaks of both were now separately outlined, no matter how closely their bases might have rubbed off each other].

Lessing had a great appeal for the young, a fresh approach to the visual and the verbal by distinguishing them clearly and this inspired a new intellectual activity. He provoked critical thinking and avoided simplistic equations or parallels between painting and poetry. His approach to the value and distribution of what he saw as the general rules governing the idea of beauty was welcomed and appreciated by some, but criticized by others who mistakenly paid little attention to his careful process-oriented approach that shifts importance to interactive features and to what Bennett succinctly characterizes as the poetics of reading or seeing.[360] In this context, Bennett also makes an argument that poetry is where "language differs significantly *from itself*, which makes an adequate terminology for literary criticism unattainable" and he states: "If we are not prepared to argue that a text operates to expand the limits of its language, to conquer new verbal territory, we are not treating that text as poetry".[361] By questioning what the limitations between the visual and the verbal are, and also by attempting to determine what exactly the distinction between poetry and poetics is, Lessing not only tried to draw dividing lines between them respectively but inserted new meanings into the discussion. He inserts differences not only between "natürliche Zeichen" (natural

358 "Die Malerei sagt man, bedienet sich natürlicher Zeichen. Dieses ist überhaupt zu reden wahr. Nur muß man sich nicht vorstellen, daß sie sich gar keiner willkürlichen Zeichen bediene" (*Laokoon, Paralipomena 23;* FA 5/2, 304) (One says painting uses natural signs. This is, generally speaking, true. However, one should not imagine that it [painting] were never to use any arbitrary signs). In other words, he hints at the fact that even painting cannot avoid arbitrary signs and that not all of the signs the visual arts use are "natural." He develops these nuances later. See also *Paralipomena 8.3.1,* FA 5/2, 262.

359 Johann Wolfgang Goethe, GMA 16 (1985), *Aus meinem Leben: Dichtung und Wahrheit,* ed. Peter Sprengel, 341. Also see Lessing, *Laokoon,* "Kommentar: Lessing 1778-1780." FA 5/2, 725-749 at 733-734; Bennett, *Beyond Theory* 119.

360 Some traces of Lessing's non-intrusive and open-ended poetics can also be found in Goethe's *Farbenlehre* as well as in Goethe's commentary on the Laokoon sculpture. See Beate Allert, "Hidden Aspects of Goethe's Writings on Color, Seeing, and Motion and Their Significance for a Feminist Visual Theory," Laura Doyle, ed., *Bodies of Resistance: New Phenomenologies of Politics, Agency, and Culture* (Evanston: Northwestern University Press, 2001), 144-191, 287-302.

361 Bennett, *Beyond Theory* 118.

signs) and "willkürliche Zeichen" (arbitrary signs) which he allocates either in the realm of the material visual arts (natural) or in the realm of the mental visual poetics but adds that these signs should have a "bequemes Verhältnis" (a suitable relationship) to the signified. Furthermore he still believes in intuitive cognition and the directness of immediate sense perception but he also gives importance to reflection as a key to an understanding and adds that there could always be exceptions to the culturally engrained rules.

The consequences of Lessing's discussion of the Laokoon statue are consistent with implications drawn from his fable of "Die eherne Bildsäule" where he indirectly asserts that there is no plagiarism in using the same material as others have used before which is very much in the spirit of Wolff's notion of the *Principium reductionis* as he defined it. In Lessing's discussion of the Laokoon statue, he is much indebted to others who wrote on the same monument as a springboard for developing their own ideas on the meaning of this ancient artifact and on art and beauty in general but he draws attention not only to content but also form and to the very different consequences he draws from the same thing. Lessing demonstrates how the process to establish meaning and the process of reception are inseparably intertwined and that the way the material is shaped, for example, the poetic features of a text are integral to its meaning. He suggests new readings of this artwork by drawing attention to potential expression, incomplete meanings, thus evoking imagination. Winckelmann had commented that the mouth of Laokoon–who is entwined in the coils of the dangerous serpents and has already been bitten –is only slightly ajar and not, as might be expected in real life, open and screaming.[362] Winckelmann explains this in terms of the attributes he associates with the character of the Laokoon, who for him had come to represent the Classical ideals of "edle Einfalt" (noble simplicity) and "stille Größe" (silent grandeur).[363]

As already indicated above, Lessing shifts attention away from the statue *per se* to its reception by the spectators. He argues that the artist must be aware of the medium being used, in this case, sculpture, and insists that it is the effect of what is being seen that matters. He invites his readers to sympathize with Laokoon in pain and to imagine the "silent scream." He reflects upon it but not in terms of the signified, the historical Laokoon, as Winckelmann had emphasized, but rather in terms of multiple possible signifiers, the attributes of the work of art, the medium of sculpture, and the process of reception: "Er mußte Schreien in Seufzen mildern; nicht weil das Schreien eine unedle Seele verrät, sondern weil es das Gesicht auf ekelhafte Weise verstellet" ("The scream had to be softened to a sigh, not because screaming betrays an ignoble soul, but because it distorts the features in a disgusting manner").[364]

362 "Die Öffnung des Mundes gestattet es [schrekliches Geschrei] nicht; es ist vielmehr ein ängstliches und beklemmtes Seufzen .... Der Schmerz des Körpers und die Größe der Seele sind durch den ganzen Bau der Figur mit gleicher Stärke ausgeteilet, und gleichsam abgewogen." ("The opening of his mouth does not permit it (a terrible scream); it is rather an anxious and troubled sighing .... The physical pain and nobility of soul are distributed with equal strength over the entire body and are, as it were, held in balance with one another.") *Gedanken* 32-35; "Gedanken" 43.

363 Winckelmann, *Gedanken* 36; "Gedanken" 45.

364 FA 5/2, 29; *Laocoön*, trans. McCormick 17.

For Lessing the only slightly opened mouth of the Laokoon figure in the statue reflects not a matter of stoicism as Winckelmann had thought. It is not a matter that has directly to do with on the level of the action represented; it is rather a matter of the medium and its restriction, the limitation of the visual art work with its dimension of space. In contrast to music where signs are tones that can be presented simultaneously, the sculptor had to select one single poignant moment in the action that is most effective. The sculpture has such a strong impact because the viewer is challenged to imagine more than what is already represented. Imposing any final image would have led to a much weaker or even opposite effect, such as disgust or abhorrence. Lessing finds an open mouth would work much less effectively in order to inspire sympathy and compassion with the suffering human attacked, together with his sons, by the serpents. Not only would it undermine the visuality that requires space for imagination, it would also not do justice to the transitory nature of art. Lessing recommends a mental experiment: "[M]an reiße dem Laokoon in Gedanken nur den Mund auf, und urteile. Man lasse ihn schreien und sehe" ("Simply imagine Laocoön's mouth forced wide open, and then judge! Imagine him screaming, and then look!")[365] The person represented in an artwork does not carry any predetermined meaning; what it is about comes rather from the interaction with the observer. It is therefore the need of the viewer to see the artwork before the climax of the action depicted. Lessing insists that the spectators' imagination have free range. If we were to imagine a screaming Laokoon with his mouth wide open the response would not be compassion but disgust. The artist would have overstepped the required boundary of the medium. A more subdued or visual representation of a nearly "silent scream" is more powerful than a distorted mouth.[366] An artwork should not force meaning but leave possibilities open. It should communicate by means of its own sign system to represent a truth through fiction. The observer must see more in the work of art than what is given in the fruitful or pregnant moment it presents. Lessing stresses in *Laokoon* that the process of production of meaning detaches itself from the intentions of the artist and becomes a matter of reception. Timing is crucial in these *pars pro toto* relations and requires the choice of the most "pregnant moment" for the scene the work of art represents. The painter and the sculptor can only choose one moment in time to depict. It should be able to spark imagination.[367]

Lessing points out that it takes time for the spectator to observe and to reflect upon an artwork with care and attention while at the same time having a sense-related interaction with it. The artist should not interfere with this future process nor cut cognition short. He asks how the most pregnant moment might be chosen and how the best effect might be achieved, mentioning ways of representation in painting and in

---

365 FA 5/2, 29; *Laocoön*, trans. McCormick 17. See also Reinhart Meyer-Kalkus, "Schreit Laokoon? Zur Diskussion pathetisch-erhabener Darstellungsformen im 18. Jahrhundert," Gérard Raulet, ed., *Von der Rhetorik zur Ästhetik: Studien zur Entstehung der modernen Ästhetik im 18. Jahrhunderts* (Rennes: Centre de Récherche PHILIA, Université de Rennes 2, 1992), 64-107.

366 This may not necessarily always be the case, as demonstrated by the counter-examples in Astrid Guderian-Driesen, *Die Stimme in der Kunst* (Bad Rappenau: Kulturhaus "Forum Fränkischer Hof," 1989), esp. "Der Schrei" 86-107.

367 FA 5/2, 32.

poetic writing that could promote the greatest openness for the sake of "freies Spiel" (free rein).[368] Lessing does not simply declare that there is polarity or an unbridgeable gap between painting and poetic writing.[369] He writes:

> Wenn es wahr ist, daß die Malerei zu ihren Nachahmungen ganz andere Mittel, oder Zeichen gebrauchet, als die Poesie; jene nemlich Figuren und Farben in dem Raume, diese aber artikulierte Töne in der Zeit; wenn unstreitig die Zeichen ein bequemes Verhältnis zu dem Bezeichneten haben müssen: So können neben einander geordnete Zeichen, auch nur Gegenstände, die neben einander, oder deren Teile neben einander existieren, auf einander folgende Zeichen aber, auch nur Gegenstände ausdrücken, die auf einander, oder deren Teile auf einander folgen.[370]

> [If it is true that painting in its mimetic process employs totally different means or signs than poetry, that painting uses figures and colors in space, yet poetry uses articulated sounds in time; if by definition the signs must have a comfortable relationship to the signified: So then the signs that are ordered horizontally (as sequences in space) can only signify objects next to each other horizontally, or whose parts exist sequentially, yet the signs that exist vertically (layered) can also express objects that exist in vertical order, that is simultaneously (in time)].

Lessing indicates that in poesy language can borrow its signs from music where the tones can occur at the same time and meanings be multiple and simultaneously valid. Their dimension is not primarily space but time. They use, as Lessing elaborates a bit further, metaphors that also consist of more than one designated meaning concurrently. Lessing sharply distinguishes between the means of the visual artist or painter whose signs are "Körper" or bodies and objects in space. They can use signs that are "figures and color in space" but only as they are arranged next to each other. The poet seems to have more freedom when using signs in time. Poetic language shares with music that its sigs are also "tones" (Töne") or "articulated sounds in time" that can occur on several levels simultaneously. Lessing then questions what he called before the "bequemes Verhältnis" (comfortable or suitable relations) between the signs and the signified. He adds that in the realm of poesy one may encounter uncomfortable, less predictable, and complex relations between the signs. Lessing consequently draws attention to a *gap* in the signification process and asserts that bodies exist in space *and* time: "Doch alle Körper existieren nicht allein in dem Raume, sondern auch in der

368 FA 5/2, 32; *Laocoön,* trans. McCormick 19.

369 Utz, *Das Auge und das Ohr.* In summarizing what he refers to as Lessing's aesthetics in chapter 3 (39–53), Utz draws upon the words of the Templar in *Nathan der Weise* as he addresses Nathan's daughter, Recha: "Wie ist doch meine Seele zwischen Auge / Und Ohr geteilt" (Act III, scene ii; FA 9, 545) (How my soul is so split between eye and ear). Utz connects this splitting of the senses with the historic division of labor in the nascent industrial age and also associates Lessing's *Laokoon* with a "Territorialisierung der Künste" (territorializing of the arts) and "eine Kolonialisierung des Körpers" (a colonizing of the body) (42).

370 FA 5/2: 116, my translation; ("[I]f it is true that in its imitations painting uses completely different means or signs than does poetry, namely figures and colors in space rather than articulated sounds in time, and if these signs must indisputably bear a suitable relation to the thing signified, then signs existing in space can express only objects whose wholes or parts coexist, while signs that follow one another can express only objects whose wholes or parts are consecutive") (*Laocoön,* trans. McCormick 78).

Zeit" (However, bodies do not exist in space only, but also in time).[371] Here Lessing seems to question his earlier argument that the temporal and the spatial belong each to a different order. He brings them together by using the word "bodies" in a figurative sense. He shifts the level of his own argument by drawing attention to the fact that language can go beyond its own limits and that meanings are never entirely given. Lessing goes even further beyond his earlier statements and raises questions including the basic ones of what is visible and what is invisible.[372] Since painting and the visual arts must be content with the visible, there is a problem, he argues, in that "Körper" or the figures in space continue to have meanings beyond that horizon, the temporal lid to all visibility:

> Sie dauern fort und können in jedem Augenblicke ihrer Dauer anders erscheinen, und in anderer Verbindung stehen. Jede dieser augenblicklichen Erscheinungen und Verbindungen ist die Wirkung einer vorhergehenden, und kann die Ursache einer folgenden, und sonach gleichsam das Centrum einer Handlung sein. Folglich kann die Malerei auch Handlungen nachahmen, aber nur andeutungsweise durch Körper [...] Die Malerei kann in ihren co-existierenden Compositionen nur einen einzigen Augenblick der Handlung nutzen, und muß daher den prägnantesten wählen, aus welchem das Vorhergehende und Folgende am begreiflichsten wird.[373]
>
> [They have an ongoing duration and in each moment can appear quite differently, and in another constellation. Each of these momentary appearances and constellations is the effect of a previous one, and can be the cause for a following one, and consequently function as the center of an action. Consequently, painting can also imitate actions, yet only metonymically via bodies or figures as signs [...] Painting can use in its co-existing

371 FA 5/2, 116; *Laocoön,* trans. McCormick 78.

372 This question was much later raised again and developed further by the painter Paul Klee in a piece first published in 1920: "In Lessings *Laokoon,* an dem wir einmal jugendliche Denkversuche verzettelten, wird viel Wesens aus dem Unterschied von räumlicher und zeitlicher Kunst gemacht. Und bei genauerem Hinsehen ist's doch nur gelehrter Wahn. Denn auch der Raum ist ein zeitlicher Begriff" (In Lessing's *Laokoon* on which we frittered away at one time youthful thought experiments, much fuss is made about the difference between spatial and temporal art. And on closer inspection, that is only a learned delusion. Even space is a temporal term). Paul Klee, "Schöpferische Konfession," Günther Regel, ed., *Kunst-Lehre. Aufsätze, Vorträge, Rezensionen und Beiträge zur bildnerischen Formlehre, 3$^{rd}$* ed. (Leipzig: Reclam, 1995), 60-66 at 62; see K. Porter Aichele, *Paul Klee's Pictorial Writing* (Cambridge: Cambridge University Press, 2002), 45-47; Beate Allert, "Reconceptualizing a Pictorial Turn," 211-212; K. Porter Aichele, *Paul Klee, Poet/Painter* (Rochester, NY: Camden House, 2006), 6-8.

373 FA 5/2, 116-17, my translation; "They persist in time, and in each moment of their duration they may assume a different appearance or stand in a different combination. Each of these momentary appearances and combinations is the result of the preceding one and can be the cause of the subsequent one, which means that it can be, as it were, the center of an action. Consequently, painting too can imitate actions [...] Painting can use only a single moment of an action in its coexisting compositions and must therefore choose the one that is most suggestive and from which the preceding and the succeeding actions are most easily comprehensible" (*Laocoön,* trans. McCormick 78). On the implications of "der prägnanteste Augenblick," see: Norbert Christian Wolf, "'Fruchtbarer Augenblick'—'prägnanter Moment': Zur medienspezifischen Funktion einer ästhetischen Kategorie in Aufklärung und Klassik," Alt et al., ed., *Prägnanter Moment* 373-404.

compositions only one single moment of an action, and therefore must select the most poignant one, from which the previous and the following becomes most sensible].

The continuation of movements is what changes meanings constantly. Since each appearance and each moment of an impression can become the center of a new action, the artist can only choose among all the possible coexisting compositions that may be implied. The most pregnant moment would suggest as many possibilities as possible. Since the choice of such an apparent frozen image out of the flux of time is not a way to control real time, it is only a way to use fiction in order to make sense of a much more complex and changing reality. Nevertheless, as Lessing is fully aware, meaning will always depend more on processes of reception than those of production. One must notice that in the amends to *Laokoon,* Lessing makes a concession to time, an attempt to allow temporality and simultaneity of meanings in metaphoric texts. Lessing appears to indicate that written approximations of such partial images (metaphors and metonymies) are also to some extent matters of simultaneous signs. Verbal signs can, just like the multiple tones of music, occur simultaneously, at the same time. Multiple meanings are not, as some critics have argued in the context of Lessing to be banned from the verbal.[374] I agree with Peter Burgard interpreting this as Lessing's move to combine the visual and the verbal and to allow aspects of temporality into verbalness, yet not as any sort of concession or meant against the visual but instead as the most articulate strength in Lessing's *Laokoon* and the related *Paralipomena.*[375] It is exactly this disobedience to his earlier rules which Lessing explains distinctly and which belong to his most astounding discoveries for Ekphrasis studies.

*Laokoon* is, however, most often debated as if Lessing were asserting a strict dividing line determining the boundaries between painting and literature, the visual and the verbal.[376] On the other hand, if understanding imagination and images means transposing them into a narrative, then visual art and metaphor must first be translated

374 See further Beate Allert, "Lessing im Kontext kunsttheoretischer Debatten," 378-379; Jeoraldean McClain, "Time in the Visual Arts: Lessing and Visual Criticism," *Journal of Aesthetics and Art Criticism* 44 (1985): 41-58; Michael Cohen, "Lessing on Time and Space in the Sister Arts: The Artist's Refutation," Ugrinsky, ed., *Lessing and the Enlightenment* 13-23.

375 Peter Burgard, "Schlangenbiß und Schrei," *Streitkultur* 194-202. Burgard's reading involves an equation, a textualizing of the visual, a complete and fluid Ekphrasis.

376 Interestingly, Nicholas Rennie in his article "Lessing's Lethotechnics: Memory and Perspective in *Laokoon,*" *Lessing Yearbook* 42 (2015): 103-124, argues: "If Chapter XVI of the *Laokoon* contains Lessing's most systematic attempt to distinguish the arts of time and the arts of space according to the logic of their signs, the chapter is also preoccupied with allowing forms of implication, or Andeutung, that complicate this core distinction." (103). It is at the core of my contribution to the *Laokoon* debate here also to show how Lessing writes not only about "bequemes Verhätnis" of signs to their objects but also takes into account that all bodies in space also exist in time and can in each moment of their duration appear differently and in different relations. Lessing makes the important additional statement which has often been falsely ignored: "In so fern nun diese Wesen Körper sind, oder als Köper betrachtet werden, schildert die Poesie auch Körper, aber nur andeutungsweise durch Handlungen" (FA 5/2, 116-117) ("Insofar as these beings or things are bodies, or are treated as such, poetry also describes bodies, but only through suggestion through actions") (*Laocoön*, trans. McCormick 78).

into discursive language before their meaning can be deciphered. However, Lessing does not necessarily propose a translation between media, a textualizing of the statue into narrative. Visualization of an artwork may be simulated by reading about it, yet there is no friction-free transfer of the visual into the verbal. In *Laokoon*, chapter 14, Lessing points out that a poetic picture is not necessarily something that can be converted into a material painting.[377] There is a residue, something that is not entirely translatable in the process. Metaphors, metonymies, and elements of ekphrasis remain unconverted. On the other hand, the poet makes the subject so concrete for us that we become more conscious of the subject referred to than of his words. Benjamin Bennett's reading of *Laokoon* as a poetics shows how Lessing goes "beyond theory" by initiating moments of reflection. These cannot simply be reduced to a comparison of painting and poetry, and instead they allow us an experience of multiple senses best achieved by poetry, including music, and dance.[378] Carol Jacobs has emphasized the significant "performative" features of Lessing's essay that depend primarily on the attentiveness of readers and spectators. In her interpretation, Lessing's *Laokoon* is not only an art-theoretical treatise; it also invites interaction and experience.[379] There are features of Lessing's text that seem to subvert or undercut his major argument about the borders between painting and poetry. Lessing inserts more subtleties of meaning to his arguments, drawing attention to the exceptional, and thus suggesting multiple sense perceptions and complex relations between painting and poetry.

In chapter 28 of *Laokoon,* Lessing offers his own interpretation of a statue known as the Borghese Gladiator or the Borghese Warrior,[380] agreeing in part with the interpretation of Johann Joachim Winckelmann in his *Geschichte der Kunst des Altertums,*[381] but going beyond it by interpreting the statue as a depiction of Chabrias (4th cent. BC.), the famous Athenian general practicing the defensive maneuver with which his name is associated, left knee forward, shield on the ground, and spear pointed at the enemy as described in the "Life of Chabrias" by Cornelius Nepos.[382] Because the statue appears to show the warrior with shield aloft, Lessing proposes an emendation to Nepos' text, reading "obnixo genu, scuto" (with braced knee, with shield) for "obnixo genu scuto" (with braced knee against the shield).[383] He is quite excited by his identification of the statue as a representation of Chabrias, because if he is right:

---

377 FA5/2, 112.

378 Bennett, *Beyond Theory* 128.

379 Carol Jacobs, "The Critical Performance in Lessing's *Laokoon,*" *Modern Language Notes* 102 (1987): 483-521, reprinted under the title *"Fictional Histories: Lessing's Laocoön," Telling Time: Lévi-Strauss, Ford, Lessing, Benjamin, de Man, Wordsworth, Rilke* (Baltimore: Johns Hopkins University Press, 1993), 95-127.

380 FA 5/2, 197-200. This 1st century BCE copy of a 3rd century BCE original now in the Louvre, was in Lessing's time stored in the Villa Borghese.

381 Winckelmann, *Geschichte der Kuns*t 366.

382 Cornelius Nepos, "Chabrias," *Cornelius Nepos*, trans. John C. Rolfe, Loeb Classical Library 467 (Cambridge: Harvard University Press, 1984), 130-137 at 132-33 also reports that the Athenians erected a statue of him in this pose in the Market square. Lessing identifies the Borghese Warrior with this statue.

383 The editions of Lessing's time interpreted this as if it read: "obnixo in scuto, obfirmato genu ad scutum" (with braced on to the shield, a firm knee against the shield) (FA 5/2,

> [S]o dürfte ich mich schmeicheln, ein besseres Exempel gegeben zu haben, wie glücklich sich die klassischen Schriftsteller durch die alten Künstwerk, und diese hinwiederum aus jenen aufklären lassen, als in dem ganzen Folianten des Spence zu finden ist.[384]

> [I should flatter myself that I have offered a better example, illustrating how successfully the classical writers may be explained by the ancient artworks and these vice versa to be illuminated by them, better than in the entire patchwork by Spence].[385]

Lessing obviously does not dismiss the potentials of helpful Ekphrasis and criticizes Spence for a lack of precision in this context. He insists that not only actions but intentions or gestures are already leading to actions. For example, Lessing suggests that a knee bent, braced in preparation for battle, must be already part of the interpretation process which involves a critique of images and movements as conceptualized by Spence. For Lessing, an artwork reflects not only on actions that actually happened or are shown onstage but it reflects moreover on ramifications, movements, emotions, and a variety of potentials involved.

In the 35th of his *Briefe, antiquarischen Inhalts* (Letters of Antiquarian Content),[386] Lessing defends his interpretation against the withering criticism of Christian Adolf Klotz, Professor of Philosophy and Rhetoric at the University of Halle. In his journal *Acta litteraria*[387] Klotz had accused Lessing of being ignorant of Latin. Lessing's comments are found in the collection of *Paralipomena* to the *Briefe, antiquarischen Inhalts*. In the first item, written probably in November 1768,[388] Lessing ruminates over why one is supposed to be able to say "obnixa frons" (a braced head),[389] but not "obnixum genu" (a braced knee). Such a description is appropriate and not the same as "genu flexum" (a bent knee) and it is entirely appropriate for the description of Chabrias. However:

> So vorteilhaft aber diese Stellung in der Schlacht gewesen wäre: so unschicklich würde sie zu einer Bildsäule gewesen sein; und so gern auch Chabrias seine Erfindung hätte aufzubehalten uns zu verewigen gewünscht, so würde er es doch lieber auf jede andere Weise gesucht haben, als durch eine Statue in der nemlichen Stellung, in der er eine sehr kleine und furchtsame Figur gemacht hätte, da er hingegen in der, wie ich ihn denke, eine sehr edle und kühne macht.[390]

---

199). The Loeb edition has the same text and translates "with buckler on knee" without comment (*Cornelius Nepos*, 131).

384 FA 5/2, 199-200. Joseph Spence, Polymetis: or, An Enquiry Concerning the Agreement between the Works of the Roman Poets, and the Remains of the Ancient Artists: Being an Attempt to Illustrate them Mutually from one Another in 10 Books (London: R. Dodsley, 1747). See Donald T. Siebert, Jr., "Laocoön and Polymetis: Lessing's Treatment of Joseph Spence," Lessing Yearbook 3 (1971): 71-84.

385 *Laocoön,* trans. McCormick 152.

386 FA 5/2, 467-469. This was the opening letter of the second volume published in 1769.

387 *Acta Literaria* 3.3 (1766): 283-320; 4.1 (1766): 92-98.

388 FA 5/2, 1186.

389 (Pseudo-)Ovid, "Halieutica" (Sea-Fishing), Ovid, *The Art of Love and Other Poems*, trans. J.H. Mozley, rev. G.P. Goold, 2nd ed., Loeb classical Library 232 (Cambridge: Harvard University Press, 1979), 310-321, line 12. The Loeb edition translates "obnixa frons" as "opposing forehead" (311).

390 FA 5/2, 586.

> [As advantageous as this position might have been, however, in a battle it would have been unsuitable for a sculpture; and as eagerly as Chabrias would have liked to preserve his invention to make it eternal for us, he would rather have done so otherwise than by means of a statue in this particular position, in which he would have made a rather small and scared figure, despite the way I think about him, namely as a very noble and courageous one].

It is a description of beauty, a human body that has dynamic qualities and represents energy and strength, a potential to win, perhaps even against all odds. To this extent then, according to Lessing's ekphrastic account, the actual statue is a disappointment. Lessing goes on to remind us that initially the figures on coins "gehören nicht zur Kunst, sondern zur Bildersprache" (belong not to the visual arts, but to a language of images").[391] Art, more specifically the visual and performing arts, were originally never to be understood as anything objectified, complete, static, or normatively fixed. Art was, as Lessing reminds us, a "Hülfsmittel der Religion" (a medium serving religion).[392] The earliest examples date from a time when "man nach der Bestimmung der Kunst erst noch tappte" (one was still groping for the definition of art).[393] Such "Bilder" were not replica of something which previously happened or existed in that shape and form; instead they were tied to something higher and ideal, something imagined more important and beautiful than anything one would grasp or make business with.[394] Such "Bildersprache" or language of images is linked to individual action with a meaning and hope for the community. It implies an unfinished quest. In short, it is not an "image" but rather a vision or a significant movement. It involves change in the society and an activity that is not yet completed. Yet it signifies a belief in a future resolution.

Lessing pursues his ekphrastic search by challenging both notions of image and of text and by linking them together with what throughout his work is developed as a rather coherent approach not only to aesthetics. He never completed his immense project of the *Laokoon* but his commentaries, notes, and letters about it give us a glimpse into how it might have proceeded. In part one of *Laokoon*, Lessing followed in

---

391 FA 5/2, 586. He also the comments on coins in *Laokoon*, chapter 2, footnote 8 (FA 5/2, 26-28; Laocoön, trans. McCormick, note b, 162-64, "Bildersprache" there translated as "the language of symbols") and chapter 9, footnote 3 (FA 5/2, 85-86; *Laocoön*, trans. McCormick, note c, 193-94, "Bildersprache" there translated as "symbolic language"). I would like to point out some further subtleties of the meanings of the visual here and draw attention to those "images" in Lessing's discourse that do not easily translate into words via ekphrasis because Lessing indicates in this context that something tends to get lost in such a transfer, something which seems to be associated with the danger of fetishism, lacking temporality.

392 On the connection between art and religion, see *Laokoon*, chap. 9 (FA 5/2, 83-90). Also in his late works Lessing promotes the Enlightenment ideals of freedom and effective communication and he offers numerous examples of characters that are truly in search for a better community and for societal change.

393 FA 5/2, 586.

394 On a fascinating article that explores related aspects, especially with focus on *Nathan der Weise* and Lessing's rhetorical use of images, coins, and money, see Fritz Breithaupt, "Wie ist Gesellschaft möglich? Geld und Medien bei Lessing und Simmel," Wolfgang Albrecht and Richard E. Schade, ed., *Mit Lessing zur Moderne: Soziokulturelle Wirkungen des Aufklärers um 1900: Beiträge zur Tagung des Lessing-Museums und der Lessing Society* (Kamenz: Lessing-Museum Kamenz, 2004), 67-77.

the footsteps of theorists such as Abbé Jean-Baptiste DuBos,[395] Le Comte de Caylus,[396] Joseph Spence,[397] and Johann Joachim Winckelmann[398] in challenging the previously existing *ut pictura poesis* tradition in literature and theory.[399] The relationship between images and texts was until then mainly defined or approached in terms of a comparison, so that the visual and the verbal arts were interpreted above all as "sister arts," on the basis of their similarity.

Initially Lessing sets out to establish boundaries between the visual and the verbal. Perhaps more precisely speaking, he raises for discussion issues that are involved in the difference and separation between painting and poetry. Then Lessing draws attention to the sign systems involved and he corrects his earlier notion that the signs of the visual being "bodies in space" are "natural signs" whereas the signs of poetic language are artificial if not arbitrary. They are most successful if they also appear to be natural, even if that is the creation of the artist. He begins to explore complex relations between images and texts by putting theater in the middle where both the visual and the verbal can come together for something new so that the illusion can be established that even signs that are arbitrary appear as if natural.[400] Lessing allocated to images and to visual artworks the dimension of space where only one single pregnant or poignant moment was to be depicted in the representation of any action. The dimension of time was considered integral to music with its simultaneity of signs,

395 See his *Réflexions critiques sur la poésie et sur la peinture*, 2 vols. (Paris: Jean Mariette, 1719; 4th ed., corr. and enl. 3 vols. Paris: Pierre-Jean Mariette, 1740).

396 Anne-Claude-Philippe de Tubières de Grimoard de Pestels de Levy. See his *Tableaux tirés de l'Iliade, et de l'Odyssée d'Homère, et de l'Eneide de Virgile, avec des observations générales sur le costume* (Paris: Tilliard, 1757).

397 Spence, *Polymetis (1747, 2nd* ed., 1755).

398 Particularly important are *Gedanken ueber die Nachahmung der griechischen Werke in der Malerey und Bildhauerkunst*, and *Geschichte der Kunst.*

399 "As painting so poetry." Horace "De arte poetica," line 361, *Satires, Epistles and Ars Poetica* 480. For a survey of the importance of the concept in the early modern period, see Rensselaer W. Lee, *Ut Pictura Poesis: The Humanistic Theory of Painting* (New York: Norton, 1967), and for the controversies it engendered see Niklaus Rudolf Schweizer, *The Ut Pictura Poesis Controversy in Eighteenth-Century England and Germany,* European University Papers, Series 18: Comparative Literature 2 (Bern: Herbert Lang, 1972); Hans Christoph Buch, *Ut Pictura Poesis;* Kohle, *Ut pictura poesis non erit;* Andreas Käuser, "Ut pictura poesis–ut musica poesis. Modifikation und Modalitäten von Anschaulichkeit um 1800," Helmut J. Schneider et al., ed., *Bildersturm und Bilderflut um 1800: Zur schwierigen Anschaulichkeit der Moderne* (Bielefeld: Aisthesis, 2001), 229-247.

400 The debate initiated by *Laokoon* was not restricted to the continent. Frederick Burwick, "Lessing's Laokoon and the Rise of Hermeneutics" describes the evolution and dissemination of textual hermeneutics that challenged and extended contemporary assumptions about the relationship between sign systems of verbal and visual arts from William Hogarth to Georg Christoph Lichtenberg who adapted and refined the arguments of Lessing's *Laokoon.* Burwick mentions among the English Romantics Charles Lamb, William Hazlitt, and especially Thomas De Quincey who published a translation of Lessing's *Laokoon* in Blackwood's *Edinburgh Magazine* 20, no. 119 (Nov. 1826): 728-744 and 21, no. 121 (Jan. 1827), 9-24. Burwick, "Laocoon and the Rise of Hermeneutics" (263-264, at 220) notes that De Quincey praises Lessing in in these terms: "What he did was to apply philosophy–by which I would be understood to mean, in a large sense, the science of grounds and principles–to literature and the fine arts; an idea which expresses accurately what the Grecians meant by criticism."

"Töne" (tones or sounds) in distinction from the visual arts with their consecutive signs. In the visual arts signs are "Körper" (bodies or figures) in space and they must be positioned sequentially or consecutively but not simultaneously. Hence the visual artist must select one single "prägnanter Augenblick" from the flux of time for the presentation, even if that moment represents or anticipates an entire action. Such cutting and selecting is at the core of effective visual art and it seems that Lessing also favors a style of condensing and minimalizing in his own approach to poetic language. As he suggests in his critical and art theoretical writings, this can achieve the most effective degree of visuality being least wordy or by having most understatement in its use of the verbal. By understatement I mean the ability to hint at something and being understood without much fanfare, with the least amount of pathos and emotional detail, and by the avoidance of a style of pictorial ornamentation that adds words without giving more substance to what has already been said.[401] Lessing's thesis seems to be: The more visual the less verbal.

But then the question is not only how the visual can be transformed into something completely verbal, but also how something verbal may become perfectly visualized. Furthermore, the dimension of time was not in the broader context of Lessing's visual-verbal experiments and theoretical deliberations reserved exclusively for the discipline of music. It cannot be completely bracketed, abstracted, or ignored. In order to enjoy an artwork fully one must forget time and be, as Michael Fried commented, as "absorbed" in the work of art as the figures depicted therein are absorbed by their own activities.[402] This is an issue, particularly in the context of Lessing's dramatic work where theatricality cannot only push the action to a climax but must also allow moments to reflect, to halt, to remember, to dream along, or to anticipate. Time is also an important although a less obvious constitutive feature in poetic language. "Dichtung" (the poetic) must navigate between the visual and its figurative signs and the musical with its acoustic signs. It can oscillate between the dimensions of space and time and it does so throughout Lessing's complex Ekphrasis theory. For this reason, Lessing's plan to explore "musical images" is in my view not in contradiction to what he says in Part 1 of *Laokoon*. Even there, Lessing problematizes the very boundaries he appears to establish, not at all in a categorical or imposing fashion, but rather in the context of the diagnosis of a problem with Ekphrasis and in his attempts to find productive answers to it. By experimenting with various rhetorical strategies, art theoretical ideas, and poetic case studies, Ralf Simon–who initially follows the standard line of reception history that interprets *Laokoon* in terms establishing the dividing lines between painting and poetry–describes Lessing's undertaking as an attempt to determine the specific forms of the aesthetic principles of exclusion, so that painting cannot do what poetry can, and *vice versa*: "den Versuch, die spezifischen formästhetischen und medialen Eigenlogiken beider Künste vor allem durch Wechselseitige Ausschlussverfahren so zu bestimmen, daß die Malerei das nicht sein kann, was die Poesie auszeichnet und umgekehrt" (what matters is the an experiment to determine the specific form-aesthet-

401 One of the two rules for *Poesie* identified by Lessing in *Laokoon* is: "Sparsamkeit in den Schilderungen körperlicher Gegenstände" (FA 5/2, 117): ("economy in the description of physical objects") (*Laocoön,* trans. McCormick 79).

402 Fried, *Absorption and Theatricality* 7-70 at 10.

ic and media-specific taxonomies of both arts above all through a mutual method of exclusion, so that painting cannot be what characterizes poetry and vice versa).[403]

Ralf Simon draws attention to rhetorics that must be taken into account in the context of a larger strategy, namely Lessing's educational project as a whole. It was not as if Lessing set out to advocate such a split. Lessing does not even polarize painting and poetry and if he appears to do so, he elaborates on certain amendments that are crucial for his approach to Ekphrasis and which may even be considered a reversed approach to it, since it actually involves the belief of a complete transfer of the verbal into the visual. This goes against or beyond the usual assumption that Ekphrasis means textualizing a painting or something visual that existed before. To Lessing, language itself is "visual" in a primary sense just as it is metaphorical. It allows the speaker, listener, or reader to expand one's horizon via experiencing the present as a part of something more. The use of words is not in contradistinction to using features of the visual arts; instead words can be, according to Lessing's proposal, "visual" in a metaphorical or metonymic sense that is contextually rooted. Both words and images are approached in relation to the effect of the illusion they can create and by considering certain additional criteria.

## 5. *Paralipomena* and Lessing's proposal suggesting "musical images"

In the 26th to 29th chapters of *Laokoon* Lessing explores the possibilities of developing a new sign system that breaks down the categories he had assumed were firmly established. There is a deconstructive move in the *Paralipomena* which led him to contemplate, for example, the notion of "musikalische Bilder" (musical images), an idea unthinkable in the context of his earlier writings, and obviously integrating not only more aspects of semiotics and synesthesia but also complexities of Ekphrasis. In a letter to Christoph Friedrich Nicolai of May 26, 1769, Lessing states that poetic writing should be able to transform "arbitrary signs" into "natural" ones based on a variety of rhetorical strategies and under certain conditions.[404] Such a transfer is based on what he calls a "doppelte Poesie" (two-fold poetic art) and it requires reflective

403 Ralf Simon, *Die Idee der Prosa,* 5. Simon in his chapter on Lessing (55–81) discusses not only Lessing's distinctions between painting and poetry in *Laokoon* but also the complicated history of Lessing's text production of this work by including in his analysis texts from Lessing's drafts and notes on the project which appeared in his posthumously published writings. "Lessings Nachlasskonvolut ist also keine spätere Korrektur des *Laokoon,* sondern vielmehr die komplexere Variante, auf die für die Drucklegung verzichtet wurde. Um die Komplexität wiederzugewinnen, wird es darum gehen müssen, die Nachlasstexte gegen den publizierten Text zur Geltung zu bringen" (Lessing's posthumous papers are therefore not a later correction of the *Laokoon* but rather a more complex version which was omitted in when it was published. In order to reconstruct that complexity, the task will consist of having to take into account the posthumous texts in dialogue with what was published).

404 FA 11/1, 608–11, #489; Vollhardt, *Laokoon* 269–272; Rudowski, *Lessing's Aesthetica in Nuce* 93–99.

imagination.[405] This is an important revision of his earlier theory in significant ways. Now he acknowledges that images not only can be translated into words but that also words can transform themselves into as-if images, appearing just as "natural." They are reflecting nature merely in another sense. Lessing appears to express hope in this context that ekphrastic transfers would work and that the difference between the sign systems could somehow be overcome. Vollhardt makes a remark that indicates that Lessing long before Goethe allows temporality back into the debate and into the dimension of visuality that had before been allocated to space alone.[406] If the visual realm could also adopt signs that work simultaneously, then visual and poetic strategies were no longer categorically divided from music and its dimension of time. Such moves and transformations had to rely on illusion. Therefore, if words are initially, at least as Lessing finds them in the opening chapters of *Laokoon,* "arbitrary signs," depending on conventions in the semiotic system of language, how could any "bildhafte Dichtung" (visual verbal representation) in the verbal realm be compared or understood for what it is in terms of its own right? Is it a question of rhetoric, semiotics, language philosophy, discourse analysis, media studies, or art theory? What difference does "poetic imagery" make in this context compared to the even more "arbitrary signs" of "begriffliche Sprache" (discursive language)? Can poetic images, as Lessing claimed, be equal to the images of the visual arts, or perhaps even supersede them in terms of vividness? How is the illusion accomplished? Lessing argues that sometimes poetic images can be more "colorful" and leave more intense and immediate sense impressions than any painted ones and this insight will be subsequently illustrated in more detail.

Lessing also argues that: "In so fern nun diese Wesen Körper sind, oder als Körper betrachtet werden, schildert die Poesie auch Körper, aber nur andeutungsweise durch Handlungen" ("insofar as these beings or things are bodies, or are treated as such; poetry also depicts bodies, but only by suggestion through actions").[407] To be able to make such suggestions or hints well depends on the rhetorical strength of poetic language. It can say things without saying them bluntly and it may be best to leave space to the recipient. The poet can make use of contiguities and mere possibilities. One can even suggest physicality without elaborating. Nothing should get lost in an overabundance of details. In contrast to the visual arts, the poet is also free to express "action in duration," events or contributing factors towards a plot over a longer period of time. Lessing adds: "Ich finde, Homer malet nichts als fortschreitende Handlungen, und alle Körper, alle einzelne Dinge malet er nur durch ihren Anteil an diesen Handlungen, gemeiniglich nur mit Einem Zuge" ("I find that Homer represents nothing but progressive actions. He depicts bodies and single objects only when they contribute towards these actions, and then only by a single trait").[408] Homer stands for Lessing as the ideal visual poet who is capable to present things vividly. Lessing

---

405 FA 11/1, 608; Vollhardt, *Laokoon* 270; Rudowski, *Lessing's Aesthetica in Nuce* 93.

406 Richter, *Laocoon's Body* 169 argues that it was Goethe who introduced the notion of the moment as "Übergang" (transition) but this is something which I think Lessing had already anticipated.

407 FA 5/2, 117; *Laocoön,* trans. McCormick 78.

408 FA 5/2, 117; *Laocoön,* trans. McCormick 79.

notes that it appears that Homer's success consists of not by following too closely any notion of linear plot development but by proceeding metonymically, selectively, and via an excellent choice of poignant moments in his poetic art. He does so, Lessing finds, because he was able to restrict his representation on the partial, the single "trait." One may add that Lessing discovers that it is a virtue of an effective poet to accept the metonymic. What happens is not only the result of a long linear narrative but rather due to contiguity of events that are grounded in character description. Events and their development cannot be recounted fully; a poetic text can portray pivotal moments only, clips or montage features of the action. What we get could be an entire spectrum of various instants. We could experience awe, beauty, surprise, fear, pity, compassion, or even pain. In any case, actions on stage should draw attention to the beautiful as it exists if we are willing to open our minds to it, and to aspects of possible change. There are numerous rhetorical strategies that may allow us to experience sense perceptions through poetic writing. In addition Lessing argues that in order for a text to be more visual it must necessarily be relatively brief, compact, and succinct. He is aware of a limited attention span and of the need not to exhaust the audience and spectatorship. But how to avoid too much abstraction will be the concern at the other side of the spectrum. Also of interest will be the aspect of *catharsis* or how possibly a cleansing of emotions in the sense Aristotle had suggested it, can come about. More about this will be discussed in the context of Lessing's dramatic works.

Lessing shifts new importance to the role of imagination in the interactive processes of production and reception.[409] According to Lessing's *Laokoon*, "Dichtung" (poetry) is only effective and art in a true sense if it is able to evoke the senses of "Mitleid" (sympathy) and "Mitleiden" (compassion). These and other human qualities are part and parcel of any media specific and semiotic structure and belong to an aesthetic which has a moral–albeit perhaps a hidden or almost "silent" ethical dimension–suggestive but not overpowering or coercive. Lessing gives attention to the need for a non-imposing mode of communication, one which may offer a free range of possibilities to the imagination of his readers and spectators. He is aware of possible power structures in the communication process and believes in the Enlightenment ideal that it takes courage to think and to let everyone think for themselves. Whereas it may well have been then a goal of the Enlightenment project in general to say everything, to conquer the world through words, to expand one's vocabulary and thereby one's horizons for the sake of an emancipated society, Lessing had a somewhat different approach. He was not interested in verbal expressions *per se*, nor did he try to describe everything in his works. He had to deal with censorship at times during his life and moved, for the sake of freedom of expression, from the pulpit to the stage. He found that truth could be best communicated via fiction and that messages could reach their addresses best if wit, humor, and irony could play a role and he experimented with various approaches to mimetic representation, testing the limitations of language. Lessing was concerned that thinking should not be detached from feeling and sense perceptions and he was keen in finding ways to make things evident, to document ideas via concrete examples and to follow an inductive rather than a

409 For examples, see Haßelbeck, *Illusion und Fiktion;* Richter, *Laocoon's Body;* Wellbery, *Lessing's Laocoon.*

deductive approach. He was interested in ways how to represent actions not only via description and teichoscopy, but also via an approach sensitive to intuitive cognition and a style of writing which he believed could have a strong potential to promote seeing and imagination and *Anschaulichkeit* (vividness). Lessing does not pitch the verbal against the visual as some critics have claimed. He does not erase images for words. Nor does he simply favor poetic writing over painting. He tries to establish ideas for a proposal of visual writing or verbal visualcy that should eventually result from a future emancipated public. He daringly probes the possibilities and boundaries of Ekphrasis with attention to language, rhetoric, imagination and tests them throughout his works from a variety of points of view. Performed and verbal images onstage as well as the so-called "musical images" Lessing refers to in his *Paralipomena* of to the incomplete Laokoon project seem to allow levels of visuality that can coexist without cancelling or absorbing each other.

# Chapter 5
# Drama Theory: Lessing's *Hamburg Dramaturgy* as *Fermenta cognitionis*

Abstract: With his project titled *Hamburgische Dramaturgie* (1767-1769) Lessing tried to establish a national theater at a time when in the German speaking provinces there was no unifying cultural center as it existed in London or Paris. Lessing knew of some excellent actors nationally and internationally but felt that a much more receptive and engaging audience was needed. He wanted to create an interactive public and turn readers and audiences into spectators. He had a vision of the Enlightenment that would expand what was written; it would have to be created through a shared imaginary and through performances onstage. These could exceed outdated or unrealistic theatrical norms. His enormous and often painstaking efforts in this regard are well documented in his *Hamburgische Dramaturgie,* a collection of essays and notes in the form of journals, periodical articles, reviews of foreign plays, and drafts of adaptations with annotated future production plans. These writings include many discourse theoretical and genre poetological reflections and Lessing's various responses to the profoundly changing landscape of the theater in Europe at the time. The *Lessing Yearbook* 14 (2014), edited by Monika Fick, was devoted exclusively to Lessing's *Hamburgische Dramaturgie.* It illustrates that there was a shift from "outer actions" or from visible events, to "inner actions," human character traits, emotions, and sense related motivations that are mainly the causes of real events. Incorrectly processed inner actions often culminate in apparently senseless and drastic happenings.[410] Their underlying, barely sensible yet powerful forces ultimately manifest themselves also in the visual realm as outer actions, albeit rather indirectly. It was Lessing's engagement to draw connecting links from that substructure of sense perceptions to thinking and action. His *Hamburg Dramaturgy* is an effort to present glimpses and poignant analyses of a previously uncharted territory. It sheds light on causes and promotes "Reize" (stimuli) beyond the usual or the merely spectacular.

## 1. From staged illusion to lived imagination

Lessing called his contributions to *Hamburgische Dramaturgie "Fermenta cognitionis,"* the yeast in the cognition process. They should serve as medium or as a chemical agent to energize something productive, emotional and critical responses in audiences. These published scholarly contributions and also the included casual remarks were initially published as a series of monthly journal numbers (*Stücke*). They were collected later under the title by which they are known today comprising a vast and multifaceted

410 *Lessing Yearbook* 14 (2014), ed. Monika Fick 1-305.

oeuvre.[411] It shows Lessing as a dramaturge, as a theoretical playwright and critic, as a stage producer, translator and commentator communicating with many artists and people.[412] If there was a gap between painting and poesy or between the works of the visual artist and the works of the literature writer, Lessing felt it could best be bridged by means of dialogue, play, and theater performances. Gestures and movements onstage are often those messages that not only parallel and underscore what is being said and heard; they may at times also reflect critically on the action onstage and provide additional levels of meanings, even counter-arguments. It was Lessing's goal to make performances into collaborations between the visual and the verbal. These collaborations could allow insights into sense perceptions and emotions that are in his view real forces leading to the actions as experienced in experienced real-life situations. Lessing drew attention to questions concerning what the best criteria may be for effective acting and for achieving the best performances. He favored moderation in expressing via body language, gestures, and mimes yet payed much attention to certain features of language, sound, and rhythm. He experimented in his plays as subsequently often discussed from a variety of perspectives with modes of representation that included images from non-congruent frames of temporality.

It may have been Lessing's most important contribution to European theater history and Enlightenment drama theory in general to have created what is known today as Lessing's staple "Illusionstheater" (theater of illusion). It differs both from the earlier

---

411 When preparing his contributions to the *Hamburgische Dramaturgie,* Lessing began to develop his own theory of drama. He first published his "Ankündigung" (Announcement) on April 22, 1767. On May 8, the first three Stücke (issues or numbers) were published as a single piece. From May 12-August 14 he published Stücke 4-31 and the numbers appeared biweekly. On August 21, 1767, the date the 32nd Stücke should have appeared, there was protest against unauthorized reprinting of the work, one of which had just appeared in Leipzig. There was a promise that the collected Stücke 1-32 would soon appear in a separate volume but that did not materialize. The warning against piracy was repeated on December 7 in response to an unauthorized Hamburg edition. Finally Stücke 32-35 were published on December 8, and four "omnibus issues," the last on January 5, 1768, concluded with Stücke 51. The serial publication of Stücke 52-82 continued at the rate of one or two per week until June 9, 1768. Stücke 1-82 and 83-104 were published in two volumes at the end of March, 1769. By this time the theater was in disarray and Lessing had parted company with it. The consortium had to give up production at the end of 1769. This year marks the end of Lessing's project for a *Deutsches Nationaltheater,* a project that nonetheless was significant in signaling a new beginning for German theater. See Robertson, *Lessing's Dramatic Theory* 123-132; FA 6, 877-879; Nisbet, *Lessing: Eine Biographie* 503; *Gotthold Ephraim Lessing* 383. Lessing's *Hamburgische Dramaturgie* has recently become available online in a complete English translation. See Wendy Aarons and Natalya Baldyga, "The Hamburg Dramaturgy in the Digital Age: A New Translation by Wendy Aarons and Sara Figal. Edited by Natalya Baldyga with Critical Introductory essays by Wendy Aarons, Natalya Baldyga, and Michael Chemers," *Lessing Yearbook* 41 (2014): 303-305 (http://mcpress.media-commons.org/hamburg.essay-1).

412 Robertson, *Lessing's Dramatic Theory,* describes the role of the "dramaturge" as follows: "Essential to the scheme of the Hamburg organisers was an official 'theater poet', a man of letters who could be depended upon to supply the theater with new pieces, provide translations or adaptations of desirable foreign works, lend a helping hand with prologues and epilogues on formal occasions and generally advise on the choice of the repertory" (116).

performances as known and from the later epic theater since it tries to find a middle path between the credible and the extraordinary events depicted. Lessing argues that a poet can make the "willkürliche Zeichen" (artificial signs) of language appear as if there were "natürliche Zeichen" (natural signs). He wanted to approximate something sublime and wonderful as usually attributed to the creations of fiction while basing it on what he perceived as the true colors of truth. He had a vision that everything onstage should be "mit wahren Farben geschildert" (presented with true colors).[413] What makes the stage the most perfect territory for experimenting with Ekphrasis is that theater involves visuality verbalness, and tactile sense perceptions. Whereas what we see is often commented upon by one or the other character onstage who is also a spectator and thus a model in providing ekphrastic narration, what we hear may not at all be how we would "read" the same scene as presented onstage. Processes of visual and verbal understanding are intertwined and are often not synchronized. This creates friction which Lessing actually welcomes for the intellectual stimuli it provides.[414]

Lessing did not abolish the fourth wall as Bertolt Brecht did later in the twentieth century. Brecht praised Lessing but dismantled his approach towards a "theater of illusion" for the sake of a new "epic theater." Brecht put the audience on the same level as the action of the play and abolished the podium.[415] He inserted more strategies and features that create a critical distance, even alienation from and between the characters and events onstage, again in order to make people think, yet from a pronouncedly very different point of view. Lessing opted for the goal of theater he called "Mitleiden" or compassion. One of his innovations was to work more with mixed characters, multiple perspectives, and to provide more questions than answers. He presented unexpected life situations that, as he decided, could not be fully resolved onstage in one way or another, especially not once and for all. What Lessing also seems to explore are, as he puts it in his *Hamburgische Dramaturgie*, "die Klippe der vollkommenen Charaktere" (the outer extremes, cliffs, or peripheries of perfect characters).[416] Lessing comments that Diderot did not offer any navigational chart to enable one to steer clear of such "cliffs" when his characters become sometimes extreme.[417] He tries to find his own

---

413 *Hamburgische Dramaturgie* XXIV (FA 6, 298). Lessing is discussing the character of Elizabeth in Thomas Corneille's play, *Le Comte d'Essex,* see John George Robertson, *Lessing's Dramatic Theory being an Introduction to and Commentary on his* Hamburgische Dramaturgie (Cambridge: Cambridge University Press, 1939; Rpt. New York: Benjamin Blom 1965), 79-80, 181-191.

414 Cf. Alexander Košenina, "Augenbühne versus Hörbuch. Was leisten die Sinne aus Lessings Theater?" Košenina and Stockhorst, ed. *Lessing und die Sinne* 213-230.

415 See Benjamin Bennett, *Modern Drama and German Classicism: Renaissance from Lessing to Brecht* (Ithaca: Cornell University Press, 1979); Mary Luckhurst, "Revolutionising Theatre: Brecht's Reinvention of the Dramaturg," Peter Thomson and Glendyr Sacks, ed., *The Cambridge Companion to Brecht,* 2nd ed. (Cambridge: Cambridge University Press, 2006), 193-208.

416 *Hamburgische Dramaturgie* LXXXVI (FA 6, 611). Cf. Robertson, *Lessing's Dramatic Theory* 411, where *Klippe* is translated "rock." It does not highlight the peripheral, the extreme as much as the word "Klippe" does, which in my reading is also well connected with Lessing's stance on clipping an image as suggested in *Laokoon.*

417 In *Hamburgische Dramaturgie* LXXXVI (FA 6, 611) Lessing writes "Die Klippe der vollkommenen Charaktere scheinet mir Diderot nicht genug erkundiget zu haben. In seinen Stücken steuert er ziemlich gerade darauf los: und in seinen kritischen Seekarten findet

work a way of staging those peripheral characters that have one or another perhaps even apparently "perfect" character trait but shows that this, when it is not balanced enough in the context of other features, turns out to become a dangerous flaw. He always left something unresolved about such exaggerated character traits and apparently thought that it was among the criteria of a successful artist to present something with specific significance in condensed form. He opts often for metaphors and metonymies, letting the part speak for the whole, and he presents everything as a cause for something else which it can set in motion, as fast and as vividly as possible, all depending on the mind of the observers.

It has been claimed that for Lessing the beautiful was more real than the ugly; at least he thought that art and the theater should promote *catharsis* and compassion. Despite his often criticized optimism, Lessing is not avoiding drawing attention to pain and suffering in the social conditions as they exist. As a true observer of reality, the poet allows reflections on problems in order to make people experience something important and relevant in the context of what he perceives as real life situations. He does so, however, by reminding the readers that "Dichtung" is literally an art of density. Contractions of narratives are necessary for successful presentations of poignant moments. He experiments with the question when it is best to cut any scene most effectively, that is for the most enduring and complex emotional impact. He explains that such performances would then best spark something of a deeper imagination, critical thinking, and reflection on problematic mechanisms that are intricately woven into the fabric and conditions of everyday society. Lessing's plays often end puzzling. This effect results from extrapolating not all of the numerous outcomes that were indicated as being possible. He is therefore not only an advocate of apparent naturalness onstage; he is also challenging the notion of "naturalness." He can be projecting something almost hyperreal, so exceptional that it can hardly be integrated into our understanding. He shows that dramatic events are natural when their multi-facetted sources have been previously ignored. His later works all have open endings. As in *Nathan the Wise* the curtain falls before any final resolution is presented onstage. He consciously wanted to allow a variety of interpretations of his plays and seems to suggest that he was true to his proposal in *Laokoon* that the more we see the more we must be able to imagine.[418]

Thomas Martinec has shown that Lessing is still indebted to the Aristotelian approach to drama, although Lessing made important innovations.[419] He bases the effect of a dramatic play no longer primarily on mimesis and questions of representation but rather on the sense perceptions of the recipients. He anchors subjectivity at the core of any successful drama interpretation and interprets it as the momentum for the

---

sich durchaus keine Warnung." (The cliff of the fully developed characters seems to me not sufficiently explored by Diderot. In his plays he navigates straight towards it, and in his critical ocean charts there is no warning whatsoever). In other words, Lessing wants to go one step further than Diderot in carefully exploring these dangerous borderline adjectives of human nature and those territories or cliffs under the water, the brink or abyss which may result, ironically sometimes from something mistakenly taken for "perfect."

418 *Laokoon* FA 5/2, 32.

419 Thomas Martinec, "Lessing und Aristoteles?" 82–100 and "Lessings Ästhetischer Sensualismus," Košenina and Stockhorst, ed., *Lessing und die Sinne* 141–160.

aesthetic process. Lessing actualizes the definition of tragedy from the sixth chapter of Aristotle's *Poetics,* according to which it is an imitation of actors and humans that causes sadness and horror. Lessing makes pity or compassion the only decisive passion (horror is no longer relevant) and promotes more complex sense perceptions. He introduces an epistemological and anthropological approach into the center of the aesthetic process. Only compassion by means of sensual experiences, much more than any reasoning, can according to Lessing allow for a true cleansing from troubling emotional states.[420] Further I would like to add that Lessing believes that a theater piece should allow the spectator to forget about time and to become absorbed in the action. This will promote the experience of sense perceptions, emotions, and thoughts that not only afflict the characters onstage, but make "real" sense to the spectators that will then have to make adjustments to their inner actions accordingly.

He sets a range of scenarios given a variety of conditions while probing the notion of any successful play. It is measured by the lasting impact its poesy has on the audience. The acoustic messages tend to entail more information than the presented visual ones and it will be the task of the public to connect such diverse messages and to engage them in their own cognition process. Best plays are usually relatively short, build on dialogue and multiple voices, avoid much narrative filtering and explicit moralizing. People should be able to sympathize with the various mixed characters, no matter whether they are to be ultimately condoned as "good characters" or not. The play has to be lively and avoid blatant artificiality. No plot should be mono-causal. Actions are a matter of conflicting social positions, associated multiple conflicting character traits, and numerous diverse interacting voices. No play, Lessing adds, should affirm or contribute to any of the stereotypes as they already exist in mundane society. It is among the tasks of the theater to expose prejudices critically. A play must be succinct, communicate well, and keep the audience engaged. Lessing is less interested in "äußere Handlungen" (outer actions) associated with the visible plot of the play, the historical events it represents, or the explicitly articulated happenings onstage but more interested in the development of "innere Handlungen" (innere actions). They are a "Folge von Empfindungen" (sequencing of sense perceptions and feelings) preceding actions onstage.[421] He appeals to the imagination and sees the "Ideal der Handlung" (the ideal of action) in an ideal but half hidden space. He suggests that among the features theatre should aim for are "Verkürzung der Zeit" (abbreviation of time), "Erhöhung der Triebfedern" (increasing the driving forces), and "Ausschließung des Zufalls" (avoiding the merely coincidental). He is also an advocate of mental stimulations by means of wit and humor. He finds that each should produce "Erregung der Leidenschaften" (arousal of passions). This will link the approach to théatre and aesthetics leads to ethical consequences. At the core is still the ancient

420 Aristotle says in the *Poetics*: "Tragedy, then, is mimesis of an action which is elevated, complete, and of magnitude [...] employing the made of enactment, not narrative; and through pity [eleos] and fear [phobos] accomplishing the catharsis of such emotions" (*Poetics*, ed. and trans. Halliwell, [6]1449b, 46-49). In my reading of Lessing I prefer to translate eleos, "Mitleid," as "compassion" rather than as "pity." All of Book II section 8 of Aristotle's *The Art of Rhetoric* is dedicated to an extended definition of eleos (ed. and trans. Freese. 224-231).

421 *Laokoon*, FA 5/2, 129; *Laocoön,* trans. McCormick 90.

concept of catharsis.[422] Lessing makes the spectators question what is happening. He gives only clues to the next questions of why and gives verbal hints of what the underlying driving forces might be. He finds: "Handlungen sind um so viel vollkommener, je mehrere, je verschiednere, und wider einander selbst streitende Triebfedern darin wirksam sind" (actions are all the more prefect the more frequent, the more diverse, and the more conflicting the driving forces are from within).[423] It is this inner complex and multiple sense-related energy of a packed action that needs to be unraveled by the recipients and which makes Lessing's approach so curious. He shifts attention to the links between language and sense perceptions thus providing a glimpse into the human soul. His notion of a universal sense perception and compassion as basic human character traits are of course utopian ideas. Lessing has been challenged in this regard over the years by many critics. Yet his work keeps attracting favorable attention not only by those interested in the dark human soul and the complexity of human passions but also by those who applaud Lessing for his socio-political engagement.[424]

## 2. Lessing's genre preferences and stage innovations

Lessing considers the drama the highest genre of *poesy* since it allows the writer not only to present abstract notions of the effects of certain character traits but also to show the inner-most mechanisms at work within the human mind. It makes us wonder at the genesis and development of character traits that are always not isolated features but embedded into societal structures, customs, and ethical codes as they impact human behavior. Whereas Molière and Plautus present actions but do not offer hints on how they are being formed within plausible circumstances, Lessing wants more: in-depth analysis into character development that is always situated in specific space and time If a play can only be understood rationally and in very general terms, then he finds it is lacking the appropriate dimensions required for a successful drama.[425] Moreover, Lessing is ambitious, not only in dealing with isolated character traits but especially with the "Vermischung verschiedener Leidenschaften" (mixture of various

422 *Laokoon Paralipomena* 8.2.8 (FA 5/2, 260).

423 *Laokoon Paralipomena* 3.9 (FA 5/2, 231).

424 See, the wide-reaching spectrum of critical commentaries in W. Daniel Wilson and Robert Holub, ed. *Impure Reason: Dialectic of Enlightenment in Germany* (Detroit: Wayne State University Press, 1993).

425 "Es muß aber alsdann diese Allgemeinheit sich nicht bis auf unseren Begriff von den *möglichen* Wirkungen des Charakters, im Abstracto betrachtet, erstrecken, sondern nur bis auf die *wirkliche* Äußerung seiner Kräfte, so wie sie von der Erfahrung gerechtfertigt werden, und im gemeinen Leben statt finden können. Hierin haben Molière und vor ihm Plautus gefehlt." *Hamburgische Dramaturgie* XCII (FA 6, 640), emphasis in original. (This generalization (i.e. that characters must be realistic) is not to be extrapolated all the way up to our concept of the *possible* effects of the character, considered *in abstract terms*, but only until its *real* enunciation of its forces, just as they are justified by the experience and how they can happen in common life. In this regard Molière failed and so did before him Plautus).

passions),[426] which, in his view, often complicate life and generate states of human ambivalence, confusion, and error that are at the core of most crime and human suffering For Lessing "Mitleid" (*eleos*) means sympathy and compassion with the characters.[427] He wants the spectators to consider the characters' all too often unfavorable circumstances which cause them to suffer. In the process, one should gain sympathy and self-awareness. What happens to these characters tends to precipitate crisis. But in order to achieve *catharsis*, or a cleansing of passions,[428] the characters have to be likable enough so that one is willing to become sufficiently engaged in their situation so as to imagine their pain. In Lessing's approach "Beauty" in a strict classical sense is not at all necessary and even those characters that break the law and act in ways we would not accept in real life have a right to exist. Lessing allows us through the characters he presents to widen our awareness for human suffering.

There is a wide spectrum of readings in the reception history of Lessing in this regard. On one hand interpreters have found that Lessing wrote plays belonging to neither tragedy nor comedy. They provide a context for human pain that is neither strictly a matter of external circumstances as often attributed to politics and society nor the result of something unavoidable, nor are they a matter of merely just a private struggle. Instead, his characters may well be engaged in the process of trying to find out where they stand in such a spectrum. They need to determine what such categories of "outer" and "inner action" mean for them in each case and how they can be dealt with personally and by extension dealt with by the public. Lessing made popular the new genre of the "Bürgerliche Trauerspiel" (bourgeois tragedy) that focuses on a rising middle class yet still caught by its own restrictive mindset.[429] Peter Szondi argues

---

426 *Hamburgische Dramaturgie* XCII (FA 6, 641).

427 Aristotle, *The Art of Rhetoric* II.8.2 (224-325): "Let pity (eleos) then be a kind of pain excited by the sight of evil, deadly or painful, which befalls one who does not deserve it"; II.8.13 (228-329): "For, in general, here also we may conclude that all that men fear in regard to themselves excites their pity when others are the victim."

428 According to Lessing, Aristotle does not clearly define catharsis since he leaves the level of discourse ambivalent. In his *Briefwechsel über das Trauerspiel* in a letter to Christoph Friedrich Nicolai dated 2 April. 1757, Lessing states: "Aristoteles würde bloß gesagt haben: *das Trauerspiel soll unsre Leidenschaften durch das Mitleiden reinigen,* wenn er nicht zugleich auch das Mittel hätte angeben wollen, wie diese Reinigung durch das Mitleiden möglich werde; und dieserwegen setzte er noch die Furcht hinzu, welche er für dieses Mittel hielt. Jenes hat seine Richtigkeit; dieses aber ist falsch. Das Mitleiden reiniget unsre Leidenschaften, aber nicht vermittelst der Furcht, auf welchen Einfall den Aristoteles sein falscher Begriff von dem Mitleiden gebracht hat" (FA 3, 716; emphasis in original; see also FA 11/1, 178-82) (Aristotle would merely have said that *Tragedy must cleanse our passions through compassion* if he had not at the same time wanted to name the means by which this cleansing would be possible through compassion, and therefore he also added fear which he considered as a means. The former is correct; but the latter is wrong. Compassion cleanses our passions but not by means of fear, a notion which Aristotle falsely associated with compassion). Throughout the *Hamburgische Dramaturgie* the "Reinigung der Leidenschaften" means *catharsis*: "diese Reinigung in nichts Anders beruhet, als in der Verwandlung der Leidenschaften in tugendhafte Fertigkeiten" (*Hamburgische Dramaturgie* LXXVIII, FA 6, 574) (this cleansing does not consist of anything but the transformation of passions into virtuous abilities). See further Robertson, *Lessing's Dramatic Theory* 369-380.

429 For background, see: Richard Daunicht, *Die Entstehung des Bürgerlichen Trauerspiels in Deutschland*, 2nd ed., Quellen und Forschungen zur Sprache- und Kulturgeschichte der

that Lessing gave a voice to those who used to be victims in the power structures of society.[430] Brigitte Prutti finds that the females suffer mostly in Lessing's plays,[431] while Susan Gustafson in her post-Lacanian reading in the footsteps of Julia Kristeva illustrates how females often get "abjected" or extracted from Lessing's plays.[432] Whereas some critics find fault with what they see as Lessing's silence in his plays, criticizing his work for not offering better solutions, others find him plausible exactly because he refuses to offer idealistic answers at a time in history when any solution would have been too far-fetched. Perhaps all he could do is to give expression to the rather deplorable social conditions and draw attention to pain that may in some cases be self-inflicted, whether it be by class or gender. He wants to emancipate the public yet he avoids simplistic answers.

Lessing provided a new kind of freedom to the actors in their process of acting onstage.[433] Ruth Emde finds from the point of view of an actress that Lessing almost expects too much from the players since his stage directions are often rather difficult to apply. They may be either too ambiguous or, as is all too often the case, completely lacking.[434] Everyone had to learn on their own how to use body language, mime, and physiology in order to communicate. Lessing learned from others on how to use body language, mime, and physiology in order to communicate.[435] He invented rather successful theatrical devices and techniques in his attempt to achieve an effect with which the spectators could best find empathy and aimed to have the audience identify themselves with the characters onstage, even to the degree that they could become completed absorbed in the show, cry, laugh, and experience a range of intense and varied emotions. Whereas he was committed to the notion of catharsis as it had come down to him from Aristotle, he also departed from his predecessors by writing his dramas in cumbersome Alexandrine verse and he replaced the Aristotelian notion of fear with what was for him the preferable emotion, "Mitleid" or empathy;

---

Germanischen Völker, N. F. 8 (132) (Berlin: Walter de Gruyter, 1965); Karl S. Guthke, *Das deutsche bürgerliche Trauerspiel,* 6th ed. (Stuttgart, Weimar: Metzler, 2006); Cornelia Mönch, *Abschrecken oder Mitleiden. Das deutsche bürgerliche Trauerspiel im 18. Jahrhundert. Versuch einer Typologie,* Studia Augustana 5 (Tübingen: Niemeyer, 1993).

430 Peter Szondi, *Die Theorie des bürgerlichen Trauerspiels im 18. Jahrhundert,* ed. Gert Mattenklott, 3rd ed., Studien Ausgabe der Vorlesungen 1 (Frankfurt am Main: Suhrkamp, 1977), 167. Also see Walter Benjamin, *Ursprung des deutschen Trauerspiels,* Rolf Tiedemann and Hermann Schweppenhäuser, ed., *Gesammelte Schriften,* 7 vols. in 14 (Frankfurt am Main: Suhrkamp, 1974–1989), vol. 1.1, 202–430.

431 Brigitte Prutti, *Bild und Körper. Weibliche Präsenz und Geschlechterbeziehungen in Lessings Dramen Emilia Galotti und Minna von Barnhelm* (Würzburg: Königshausen & Neumann, 1996).

432 Susan Gustafson, *Absent Mothers and Orphaned Fathers: Narcissism and Abjection in Lessing's Aesthetic and Dramatic Production* (Detroit: Wayne State University Press, 1995).

433 Not that the actors of Lessing's time acted favorably to his innovations. See Robertson, *Lessing's Dramatic Theory* 471.

434 Ruth B. Emde, "Die Schauspielerin im 'Kennerblick'," Erika Fischer-Lichte and Jörg Schönert, ed., *Theater im Kulturwandel des 18. Jahrhunderts. Inszenierung und Wahrnehmung von Körper–Musik–Sprache* (Göttingen: Wallstein, 1999), 449–462.

435 See Alexander Košenina, *Anthropologie und Schauspielkunst: Studien zur 'eloquentia corporis' im 18. Jahrhundert,* Theatron 11 (Tübingen: Niemeyer, 1995) and "Die anthropologische Neubegründung der eloquentia corporis," Markus Fauser, ed., *Gotthold Ephraim Lessing: Neue Wege der Forschung* (Darmstadt: Wissenschaftliche Buchgesellschaft, 2008), 95–105.

> Es ist unstreitig, daß Aristoteles überhaupt keine strenge logische Definition von der Tragödie geben wollen. Denn ohne sich auf die bloß wesentlichen Eigenschaften derselben einzuschränken, hat er verschiedene zufällige hineingezogen, weil sie der damalige Gebrauch notwendig gemacht hatte. Diese indes abgerechnet, und die übrigen Merkmale in einander reduzieret, bleibt eine vollkommen genaue Erklärung übrig: die nemlich, daß die Tragödie, mit einem Worte ein Gedicht ist, welches Mitleid erreget."[436]

> [It is a matter of agreement that Aristotle did not at all want to give any strict logical definition of tragedy. Because, without merely restricting it to the most essential attributes, he also considered various coincidental ones as they were being used at the time. But even after taking this into account and by reducing the remaining features into one another, there remains only one fully accurate explanation: namely that tragedy is, in one word, a poem that evokes compassion].

Lessing aimed, perhaps above all, at the spectator's most varied experiences for the sake of forgetting time–while enjoying the play, creating in the process a "colorful" theater in a sense to be subsequently discussed. What interests me here is how Lessing aimed at manipulating the sense perceptions and emotions of the audience and how he went out of his way to suggest that artificial and at times arbitrary signs were to be understood as if "natural." Nor is the effect of such perfect illusion achieved by means of the most colorful or emotional speech and Lessing admonishes his actors to use careful restraint and even minimalism in their gesticulations, mime, and language, in order to achieve the desired effect.

> Die Hände des Schauspielers waren bei weitem so geschwätzig nicht, als die Hände des Pantomimens. Bei diesem vertraten sie die Stelle der Sprache; bei jenem sollten sie nur den Nachdruck derselben vermehren, und durch ihre Bewegungen, als natürliche Zeichen der Dinge, den verabredeten Zeichen der Stimme Wahrheit und Leben verschaffen helfen. Bei dem Pantomimen waren die Bewegungen der Hände nicht bloß natürliche Zeichen; viele derselben hatten eine konventionelle Bedeutung, und dieser mußte sich der Schauspieler gänzlich enthalten.[437]

> [The hands of the actor were by far not as talkative as those of the pantomime. In the case of the pantomime the hands replace the speech; for the actor they should only increase its emphasis and help through their movements, as if natural signs of things, to give the generally agreed upon signs of the voice more truth and life. For the pantomime the movements of hands were not merely natural signs; many had a conventional meaning; but this is what the actor had to completely abstain from].

Lessing suggests to the actors onstage that they should be using moderation of hand movements and gestures. He puts more importance on their effective use of verbal language and the clear articulation of their moods. The performance should not be dazzling, or sensationalist. He distances himself from the popular style of pictorialism and opts for a style of minimalism. A theater play should induce thinking and critical reflection on the forces and feelings that underlie the often problematic social conditions being presented. In other words, theatricality would have to be subdued,

---

436 *Hamburgische Dramaturgie* LXXVII (FA 6, 566-567). On this passage see also Robertson, *Lessing's Dramatic Theory* 351-52; Thomas Martinec, "Lessing's Dramatic Theory," Robertson, ed., *Lessing and the German Enlightenment,* 119-137 at 130.

437 *Hamburgische Dramaturgie* IV (FA 6, 202). See Robertson, *Lessing's Dramatic Theory* 479-481.

understated at its best, and the actions onstage should allow a certain forgetfulness and absorption, draw the spectators into the mindsets of the characters, even if they turn out to be ridiculed, wrong, and needing to be corrected later.[438]

There is a great deal of discussion in the scholarship over the question of to what extent Lessing's drama was didactic or not, whether it was primarily to represent something for its own sake, or whether he wanted always to teach a lesson. I think it may well be a feature of his plays to cut down any explicit didactic stance in order to achieve emancipation of both the actors and the audiences. Lessing is concerned with liberating people–and this is a big part of his dramatic innovation. Actors should prefigure and illustrate the appropriate responses that they want the audience to experience, even if at first these responses appear contradictory. Lessing wanted the public to experience art without being told what it means and he experimented with various approaches in his search for the most effective interactions between the verbal and the visual onstage. He aimed at brilliant visibility, yet even more so he aimed at adequate language. He used elements such as setting, gestures, mime, tableaux vivants, and movements but equally important were those "poignant moments" that resulted from verbal interaction.

Lessing's special contribution to the history of the drama was assessed by the philosopher Georg Wilhelm Friedrich Hegel who later radically challenged Lessing's theater of illusion, demanding instead: "Der Schauspieler soll gleichsam das Instrument seyn, auf welchem der Autor spielt, ein Schwamm, der alle Farben aufnimmt, und unverändert wiedergiebt" (The actor should be like an instrument on which the author plays, a sponge, that absorbs all colors, and reproduces them unchanged).[439] Whereas Lessing focused on the individuality of each person onstage, Hegel and the dramatic theory of German Classicism demanded an aesthetic of distancing from the events being presented. Lessing called for empathic engagement with the play on the part of the audience, yet Hegel induced a rather passive and contemplative stance and aimed for stylized artificiality onstage, painterly tableaux, and the harmonic togetherness of the complete ensemble. Peter Heßelmann characterized the Classical or the Hegelian Theater as a theater of management and conscious directing that gave the writer or dramaturge the power to use their actors as almost passive and flexible objects. He writes about "ein die 'Concertierung' des Spiels garantierendes Regietheater" (a theater of direction which guarantees the concert-like togetherness of the play).[440] It was to create a sense of harmony and unity far from what Lessing had tried to achieve with his theater of illusion.

Lessing's theater that was designed to experiment with the "cliffs" faced both by actors who cannot be entirely manipulated and by the individuals in the audience

---

438 Lessing follows in that regard Diderot and his approach to painting as well commented by Fried, *Absorption and Theatricality.*

439 Georg Wilhelm Friedrich Hegel, *Vorlesungen über die Ästhetik,* ed. Heinrich Gustav Hotho, vol. 3, 3rd ed. vol. 14 of the *Sämtliche Werke: Jubiläumsausgabe,* ed. Hermann Glockner, 20 vols. (Stuttgart-Bad Cannstatt: Frommann-Holzboog, 1964), 519. Cited in Peter Heßelmann, *Gereinigtes Theater? Dramaturgie und Schaubühne im Spiegel deutschsprachiger Theaterperiodika (1750-1800),* Das Abendland, N.F. 31 (Frankfurt am Main: Vittorio Klostermann, 2002), 439.

440 Heßelmann, *Gereinigtes Theater* 439.

who will also be challenged to defend and assert their own critical thinking and in the process become aware of emotions that cannot be easily harmonized with any given *tableaux vivant*, or any elegant scenery, no matter how spectacular. Whereas Lessing as a playwright conceptualized his role as invisible and in a sense marginal, while shifting importance to the actors, the audience and the spectators, in the Hegelian approach to theater the so-called "Regisseur" was to produce meaning as something autonomous. The actors' role was then diminished severely and they were tuned into sponge-like receptors that had no more color or life of their own. They were to strictly obey the stage director's creative will ("Gestaltungswillen des Regisseurs"). Heßelmann in his account of this change in theater history comments that already soon after Lessing, Goethe prescribed in his "Regel für Schauspieler" (Rules for Actors, 1803) that: "Das Theater ist als ein figurloses Tableau anzusehen, worin der Schauspieler die Staffage macht" (The theater is to be considered a figureless tableau in which the actor is window-dressing").[441] The role of actors becomes severely regulated and they must move across the stage like the lifeless figures in a game. Actors then are at their best when least noticed as having personalities themselves. They must give up their own identity completely for the sake of perfect mimicry. At the same time the texts of the plays gained much more in importance and the so-called "Literaturtheater" (Literature Theater) gave the authors and poets complete power over the interpretation of the action:

> Die Durchsetzung des Literaturtheaters führte zu einer strikten Unterordnung der Schauspielkunst unter die poetischen Texte der Autoren. Der Kreativität des Schauspielers verblieb hier lediglich ein minimaler Entfaltungsraum.[442]

> [The execution of the literature theater led to a strict submission of the art of acting under the poetic texts of the authors. There was only a minimal space for development left to the creativity of the actors].

In the light of this development, Lessing's achievement was to be a modest playwright with the opposite intent, namely to emancipate the actors and hence ultimately the spectators. His poetic texts may not have been such high "literature" as those that followed in the wake of Goethe's Weimar Classicism, but I find Lessing's modesty as an author and the freedom he leaves to the actors attractive and in tune with contemporary sensibilities. It would be too reductionist to believe that Lessing was exclusively aiming for the perfect illusion onstage as has often been claimed, for his approach focuses attention on what was going on under the surface of mere "outer actions," shifting attention to the "innere Handlungen" determined by emotions, modes of thinking, and interpersonal relations. These factors which propel the events forward tend to be only partially shown, from a rather liminal perspective, or, in Lessing's words, with a propensity to highlight what happens at the outermost character features, the "Klippen" (cliffs).

Lessing draws attention to visual signs and to the transfer, interaction, and interference of messages onstage. He does not completely withdraw as an author or

---

441 Goethe, "Regeln für Schauspieler." See GFA I: 18 (1998), *Ästhetische Schriften 1771-1805*, ed. Friedmar Apel, 857-860 at 859.

442 Heßelmann, *Gereinigtes Theater* 439.

dramaturge. He finds that instead of a great deal of gesticulation and a flurry of movements it is best to let important messages speak as if they were framed, detached from temporality. In the "Ankündigung" (Announcement) to the *Hamburgische Dramaturgie,* Lessing proposes that his "Dramaturgie" will contain a register of all the plays that have been performed (in Hamburg) and he will be a guide to these performances in almost the same way as Diderot's curator in the Salons acted as a tour guide for the readers as if they were walking through the gallery:

> Diese Dramaturgie soll ein kritisches Register von allen aufzuführenden Stücken halten, und jeden Schritt begleiten, den die Kunst, sowohl des Dichters, als des Schauspielers, hier tun wird. Die Wahl der Stücke ist keine Kleinigkeit: aber Wahl setzt Menge voraus; und wenn nicht immer Meisterstücke aufgeführt werden sollten, so sieht man wohl woran die Schuld liegt.[443]
>
> [This dramaturgy shall contain a critical register of all the plays that have been performed, and will accompany each step which the art, both of the poet as well as the actor has accomplished. The choice of the pieces is not a minor thing: but choice presumes a mass of materials; and if not always masterpieces shall be performed, one may well see what to blame for it].

Lessing was consequently debating about what it would take to create successful plays. Even as a student in Leipzig when he was only seventeen he started writing about theater performances. The 81st of his *Briefe, die neueste Literatur betreffend* (Letters, Concerning the Newest Literature)dated February 7, 1760 contains a harsh evaluation of the state of theater in German speaking lands: "Wir haben kein Theater. Wir haben keine Schauspieler. Wir haben keine Zuhörer" (We have no theater. We have no actors. We have no audience).[444] To Lessing these constituents–theater, actors, audience–were necessary factors for a thriving theater scene. Without excellent actors even the best play is worthless. Lessing must be given credit for giving actors new recognition and more freedom onstage than his predecessors, although he still took language and precision of expression seriously. Without truly receptive and talented actors no play can engage the audience. And in order to make audiences into spectators one has to give them exactly the right amount of material, plus free range for their imagination. They can never be treated like puppets!

Lessing not only focused on the aspect of the need to be useful *(prodesse)* but equally so, or perhaps even primarily on the need to entertain (delectare). He wanted people to be able to enjoy and to experience something that would allow them to forget time. Yet they had to learn how to understand wit, irony, and satire as performed and feel sympathy and compassion for the characters. They also had to be able to experience pain and unfortunate social conditions with their characters. He wanted to spark ethical action and to show them something ultimately beautiful and thought provoking. Lessing highlights in his action-centered approach when using the notion of "Bewegung" (movement) and when stillness may have its place. Movement usually draws attention to the importance of the setting, the locale, where things come from and where they happen. They highlight the environment and the conditions for the

443 *Hamburgische Dramaturgie,* "Ankündigung" (FA 6, 185).
444 *Briefe, die neueste Literatur betreffend,* FA 5/1, 698-706 at 700.

action. Furthermore movement draws attention to the fact that events and things are "transitory" onstage. This mobility of signs is a key notion to the discourse on images onstage. Lessing draws attention to the kinesthetic, mobile, and temporary character of the art of acting ("Schauspielkunst") which, however, in some cases, may also borrow from the high art of painting where arresting an image, framing it and keeping it still, may also be a powerful technique:

> Die Kunst des Schauspielers stehet hier, zwischen den bildenden Künsten und der Poesie, mitten inne. Als sichtbare Malerei muß zwar die Schönheit ihr höchstes Gesetz sein; doch als transitorische Malerei braucht sie ihren Stellungen jene Ruhe nicht immer zu geben, welche die alten Kunstwerke so imponierend macht.[445]
>
> [The art of the actor stands here, between the visual and performing arts and poetry, in the middle. As a visible painting its highest law must be beauty; but as a transitory painting it does not have to give its positions always that kind of stillness which makes the old works of visual art so impressive].

## 3. Lessing on the transitory nature of dramatic art and consequences

Lessing develops his art of understatement for the stage. He finds that the success of a play depends in inseparable ways not only on any given script or written drama but equally upon the actors and upon the audiences. By shifting new importance to the body language and acting skills of the performers and by giving much attention to how the audience may feel and think about what they see and hear, he challenges the role of the playwright who becomes according to his approach disenfranchised. Lessing writes:

> Die Rechtfertigung des Dichters kann jederzeit angetreten werden; sein Werk bleibt da und kann uns immer wieder vor die Augen gelegt werden. Aber die Kunst des Schauspielers ist in ihren Werken transitorisch. Sein Gutes und Schlimmes rauschet gleich schnell vorbei; und nicht selten ist die heutige Laune des Zuschauers mehr Ursache, als er selbst, warum das eine oder das andere einen lebhafteren Eindruck auf jenen gemacht hat.[446]
>
> [The justification of the poet can be taken up at any time; his work remains there and can be placed before our eyes again and again. However, the art of the actor is in his works transitory. Whatever is bad or good flows by equally quickly; and not seldom it is the current mood of the audience rather than the actor which is more the reason why this or that may have left a more vivid impression].

---

445 *Hamburgische Dramaturgie* v (FA 6, 210).

446 *Hamburgische Dramaturgie,* "Ankündigung" (FA 6, 186). For an excellent essay addressing Lessing's so-called "transitorische Malerei" (transitory visualizing), the art between the painterly and the performative onstage while drawing distinctions between painting and drama, see Alexander Košenina, "Bühnen-Bilder. Von den Grenzen der Malerei und Dramaturgie bei Lessing," *Lessing Yearbook* 41 (2014): 161–174.

Lessing argues that for a play to be successful, passions should be not just "described" but instead "developed right before the eyes of the spectator" in a development that is consistent and plausible. He adds that one must let them grow with such illusory steadiness so that the spectator must sympathize, want it or not:

> Aber zu verhüten wissen, daß diese neue Verwickelungen weder das Interesse schwächen, noch der Wahrscheinlichkeit Eintrag tun; sich aus dem Gesichtspunkte des Erzählers in den wahren Standort einer jeden Person versetzen können; die Leidenschaften, nicht beschreiben, sondern vor den Augen des Zuschauers entstehen, und ohne Sprung, in einer so illusorischen Stetigkeit wachsen zu lassen, daß dieser sympathisieren muß, er mag wollen oder nicht: das ist es, was dazu nötig ist; was das Genie, ohne es zu wissen, ohne es sich langweilig zu erklären, tut, und was der bloß witzige Kopf nachzumachen, vergebens sich martert.[447]
>
> [To know, however, to prevent that these new entanglements neither weaken the interest, nor impact the probability; to be able to project oneself from the point of view of the narrator into the true distinct vantage point of each person onstage, not to describe passions but instead have them evolve in front of the spectator's eyes and without breaking the continuity, to have them grow in such an illusionary steadiness that this person must necessarily sympathize, no matter wanting it or not: this is exactly what is necessary, what a genius artist without knowing it does, without having it explained boringly, and that is what an only witty (but not truly talented) head will torture in vain to imitate].

Lessing rejects simplistic methodology for the sake of artistic freedom which he leaves not only to other writers and artists but also to his audience. He challenges overly detailed descriptiveness for the sake of a kind of performance that builds on passions and emotions that are hinted at and that will, given the course of action onstage, necessarily result from the sense impressions the spectator can intuitively understand. His approach exceeds merely deductive reasoning and takes real life experience, almost tacit understanding, into account. He wants to allow such a level of illusion that any additional auctorial voice would be superfluous. He has complete trust in performativity to the extent that the playwright and author must be almost forgotten and invisible behind the scenes of the emancipating spectacle with its authors at free range.

Lessing insists on a certain approach to temporality. In order to reach intensity of emotion, the action should never be interrupted, not at all during the duration of the entire play. Actions are, according to Lessing, completely "driven" or propelled by the character traits performed ("Triebfedern"). Their interactive functioning is a key feature for the interpretation of any plot. Lessing gives dramatic art a realist dimension and warns not to let language itself or the medium of acting interfere too much with the content of the play. It is only consistent then that he requests that actors should not to "overdo" or exaggerate their gestures and gesticulation. They should present themselves onstage in such a way that they literally "become" the person they are to personify. He draws their attention not only to the content of their words but also to tone and body language in order to correlate all the senses, a task which, as he realized later, was very hard to carry out sometimes. He draws elements of the visual from the imaginary repertoire of the artist, underpinnings of real artworks such as paintings or portraits, but he also includes dream or memory fragments into the dialogues. The

447 *Hamburgische Dramaturgie* II (FA 6, 187–188).

elements of ekphrastic transfer concern not only the translation of something visible (images) into something verbal (words), but sometimes also from the verbal back to the visual.

The audiences should become true "spectators" and this idea is what furthermore characterizes Lessing's specific synthetic sense-related yet rather abstract approach. What the spectators "get to see" are not merely set "images" (Lessing uses the term "Bild" in a rather basic and hence critical and outdated sense here because he associates it in this context with stasis and frozenness). Moreover, he asks for released transitory image-signs, or musical images, movements in the verbal realm. Lessing does so by already anticipating aspects of what Gilles Deleuze much later in the twentieth century theorized about in his postmodern and temporally fluid approach to theorizing the image process and especially the cinematic.[448]

Motions reflect passions and actions. These in turn provoke emotions and ultimately the spectators' imagined actions. The aesthetic becomes the political in a fluid way. Social criticism is to be mediated so that the audience should not get alienated but be taken in for the duration of the play. It should be spell-bound almost to its climax via illusion, enjoyment, and by drawn into the characters' fictional world. Lessing experiments with a reversed ekphrastic process in his various plays; a technique, which he realized later, has much to do with liberating the theater from an overflow of wordiness. It also means a departure from the restrictions of the Aristotelian unities. Lessing pays attention to determining the criteria for establishing the ideal length of a play, keeping the attention span of the audience as long as possible, by never showing too much. At the same time, he intends to help the audience to become spectator-like by stimulating their imagination and allowing them to sympathize or event to identify with the passions performed onstage.

However, given these rather innovative ideas, Lessing felt initially at a loss. He diagnosed a complete lack of these culturally necessary ingredients for a successful theater and was not shy (or even very tactful) in articulating his frustration in no uncertain terms. He had a rough start in the world of theater and it seems rather paradoxical that Lessing nonetheless tried to create a German stage that should be called a German National Theater.[449] In other words, Lessing was an incurable optimist who was not easily discouraged when it came to making a difference via ekphrastic efforts and his compassion for those who are suffering and deserve attention. At the same time he tried to use theater as a territory for play, for experimentation, and to have fun, not only to educate or to be didactic.[450] In the answer to his own question: "Was

---

448 See Deleuze *Cinema 1: The Movement-Image* (1986) and *Cinema 2: The Time-Image* (1989) and footnote 68 above.

449 See Robertson, *Lessing's Dramatic Theory* 116–126 and Klaus L. Berghahn. "Lessing the Critic: Polemics as Enlightenment," Fischer and Fox, ed., *Companion to the Works of Gotthold Ephraim Lessing* 67–87 at 70–72.

450 One could argue that Lessing as an avid player of cards (for money), used his plays as ways to test boundaries of speculation and to act out certain modalities and human responses. He applied eventualities drawn from real life but always with a twist towards fiction and sheer potentiality. By having a keen interest especially in mixed characters he was concerned with the human ability to be influenced, to have multiple sides or personality traits, and depending on their contexts, this could make them shine or make them look

ist Aufklärung" (What is the Enlightenment?) Immanuel Kant responded: "Aufklärung ist der Ausgang des Menschen aus seiner selbstverschuldeten Unmündigkeit."[451] (The enlightenment is the departure of human self-inflicted immaturity). It was felt that there was an urgent need for the German speaking people at the time to a "come of age," to grow up so to speak, to become adults responsible and self-aware in a larger society. A national theater would be indicative as a sign of new self-definition, the individuation of an entire culture. To create such a distinct theater was a goal Lessing fought for proactively and it seems that he was well recognized by his contemporaries. However, he was also very frustrated with what he had to work with, the less than ideal state of the arts and the attitudes of the people whose money in support of this enormous project he desperately needed.[452]

Lessing was less a critic who used strategies of polemics and social satire in his attempts to promote Enlightenment or to educate the public (prodesse) than an artist who emphasized, even before Friedrich Schiller, the importance of "Spiel" or play (delectare).[453] Lessing may not have found the audiences he wished for at the time. He tried to achieve his ekphrastic experiments by a variety of means that include presenting frozen images onstage, figures or bodies, as if they were statues framed, but moreover in such a way that they could have the Pygmalion effect on the spectator, bring the dead or merely bewitched or dormant again alive through loving care. The theater was an effort to move the audience and to bring emotions to the surface. Perhaps it could bring life, mobilize and invigorate a lazy, perhaps even all too set and lethargic crowd.

---

sinister, even criminal. At the core of his social depiction was not the reproduction of Aristotelian theater but the idea that all people share certain emotions and depend much on their environment. They all have, against all categorizing, the potential to change and are vulnerable as much as excitable.

451 Immanuel Kant, "Beantwortung der Frage: Was ist Aufklärung," Wilhelm Weischedel, ed., *Werke*, 6 vols. (Darmstadt: Wissenschaftliche Buchgesellschaft, 1966), vol 6: 53.

452 See further, Höyng, "Lessing's Drama Theory."

453 In the 14th and 15th Letters on Aesthetic Education of Schiller, "Über die Ästhetische Erziehung" (Briefe II 8/606-615), Schiller similarly describes a modality of interaction which qualitatively differs from that of the everyday common use of discursive language. Friedrich Schiller, *Über die Ästhetische Erziehung des Menschen*, FSA 8 (1992): *Theoretische Schriften*, ed. Rolf-Peter Janz et al., 556-676. In the 14th letter Schiller advances the notion of the "Spieltrieb" (play-instinct) as the origin of the plastic arts (FSA 8, 606-609) and in the 15th letter he comments: "[D]er Mensch spielt nur, wo er in voller Bedeutung des Wortes Mensch ist, und *er ist nur da ganz Mensch, wo er spielt*" (The human being plays only when existing in the full meaning of the word human being, and is only a complete human being when playing) (emphasis in original; FSA 8, 614). See Johan Huizinga, *Homo Ludens: A Study of the Play Element in Culture* (Boston: Beacon Press, 1955), 168-169. In the "Paralipomena" to his *Ästhetische Theorie* (1970), Theodor W. Adorno argues: "Feiert Schiller den Spieltrieb seiner Zweckfreiheit wegen als das eigentlich Humane, so erklärt er, loyaler Bürger, das Gegenteil von Freiheit zur Freiheit, einig mit der Philosophie seiner Epoche. Das Verhältnis des Spiels zur Praxis ist komplexer als in Schillers Ästhetischer Erziehung." (When Schiller celebrates the play instinct because of its lack of purpose as the essence of the human, then he declares, as a loyal citizen, the opposite of freedom as freedom, in agreement with the philosophy of his epoch. The relationship of art to practicing it is more complex than in Schiller's Aesthetic Education). Adorno, *Ästhetische Theorie*, GS 7: 389-479 at 470.

The gestures as shown in the play *The Matron of Ephesus* whose body language was intended to express grief, mourning, and complete introversion, were not at all readily understandable and evoked rather the ideas as if it were meant as the extraverted imitation of an ancient statue with Venus and Adonis. It draws attention to the spectator for the opposite effect than intended. She breaks her fast. Her bodily expressions did not seem to be immediately recognizable as "natural signs" but the visual signs prove to be as complicated to decipher as any verbal signs. *Miß Sara Sampson* on the other hand is a play that exhibits emotions and reflects drawing attention to problems with the verbal, with wordiness. It keeps the audience entranced and when initially performed it affected the public to such a degree that people were moving very slowly, almost unable to leave the theater after the end of the play. They seemed to get stuck in a mood of public arrest. The play stunned them as if done in by Midas. In the following plays, *D. Faust and Fatime,* Lessing experiments with shifting gender roles and metamorphoses and the problem how not only the mind controls the body but how acting may provoke certain emotions for real. Lessing's *Minna von Barnhelm* deals with a problem when the self, as in the case of a returning soldier after the war, is staged primarily for others. The play has a happy ending after what may be read as a series of misunderstandings and final catharsis. *Emilia Galotti* involves emotional ambivalence and insecurity. It begins with juxtaposing the portraits of two females that in the course of the play may be regarded as representing the sister arts, one being better in command with the visual and the other extremely verbose but unfortunately blind to her own dream images. They both end up getting violated in the end for different reasons and were unable to communicate among each other and to have made a rescuing make a bond. In other words, as these examples will variably show in detail while interactively juxtaposing characters, these plays critically mirror and reflect on each other. Lessing was an astute observer of human behavior and chose to present plots that were not only historic spectacles based on ancient traditions. He dealt with problems of current class and gender inequality, false stereotypes, and the impact of idols and problematic notions of the ideal and the real. Lessing succeeded in creating his own position in life and in defining ways to move others, although his efforts soon became tinged with a sense of disillusionment. He launched a project that was innovative and creative. If Lessing ultimately did not succeed in realizing his vision for the theater and his own professional goals as a dramaturge, it was not due to his personal failure. His vision of an enlightened audience with a German national theater is nevertheless important, especially considering his optimistic approach to find an art of understatement. Lessing was responding to literary currents from Italy, France, and England yet he had to deal with disagreeable conditions in many regards.

Hamburg was a *Hansestadt,* one of the wealthiest commercial cities in Europe.[454] Its population of around 100000 by the middle of the eighteenth century made it the third largest city in Europe after Vienna and Berlin and its citizens were more cosmopolitan than elsewhere in Germany and the local government there was known

---

454 Hamburg was a member of the Hanseatic League, a consortium of trading cities in Northern Europe, and a free imperial City within the Holy Roman Empire. See Donald J. Harreld, *A Companion to the Hanseatic League,* Brill's Companions to European History 8 (Leiden: Brill, 2015).

to be more democratic. Since 1678 it had a state-sponsored theater where mostly Italian Opera was performed. In 1765 the opera house was torn down and a new theater built on the site at the instigation of Konrad Ernst Ackermann[455] and opened with a performance by his troupe on July 31, 1765. But a year later the theater was in disarray, deeply in debt and subjected to the hostile attention of the press, in particular the critiques of Johann Friedrich Löwen who had initially been the candidate for dramaturge to the theater but who ultimately was rejected in favor of Ackermann. In an attempt to address the theater's problems, a Consortium of twelve Hamburg business men had been formed who had agreed to run the theater for ten years, although it was de facto under the control of the Swiss Abel Seyler. He had settled in Hamburg and the theater was the passion both of Seyler and his partner, the famous actress, Sophie Friederike Hensel. Seyler took over the management of the theater. Löwen became its director and it was at his instigation that the new enterprise was called a "Nationaltheater."[456] Towards the end of 1766, the Consortium approached Lessing with the offer to become the resident dramatist for the new theater. This he refused. He did accept, however, the next offer to become its dramaturge and in April 1767 he moved to Hamburg which would then be his home for the next three years.[457] The new National Theater in Hamburg opened with its first performance under his leadership on April 22, 1767.

As a dramaturge Lessing required an organ or venue in which to publish his remarks on the theater. Lessing wanted to create a text published as a bi-weekly journal engaging with both past and future performances and eventually to write a theory of "Schauspielkunst" ("the art of theater performance"). He had to build on the work by Johann Christoph Gottsched who had in *Versuch einer Critischen Dichtkunst* (Essay on Critical Poetics), first published in 1730, offered a normative drama theory. Lessing did not follow the same path Gottsched had taken, yet took some inspiration from him.[458] Lessing developed a theory which he coined "Fermenta cognitionis,"[459] that is, yeast for unfinished thinking. Hegel did not claim to provide a completed drama theory.

455 Producer of a famous acting company who in 1755 directed the first performance of Lessing's play. *Miß Sara Sampson,* in the theater in Frankfurt an der Oder.

456 Robertson, *Lessing's Dramatic Theory* 13-26.

457 Nisbet, *Lessing: Eine Biographie* 472-483; *Gotthold Ephraim Lessing* 359-367.

458 Höyng reflects on similarities and differences between Lessing and Gottsched ("Lessing's Drama Theory" 219). I doubt whether it was Lessing's first goal of the *Hamburgische Dramaturgie* to establish "a new canon of plays," and the 17th *Literaturbrief* of February 16, 1759 ought not be understood merely as a slippage into a kind of patriotism or as an attack on the French classicist style (FA 4, 499-501). Höyng tries to clarify the issue later in his essay in order to draw distinctions between Gottsched and Lessing but I doubt that Lessing "neglected the actors and the performative aspect of the plays" (221). For Lessing's place in the history of theater see Erika Fischer-Lichte, *Kurze Geschichte des deutschen Theaters* (Tübingen: Francke, 1993), especially 109-100 where she argues that Lessing is far and away from being chauvinistic or nationalistic. I agree that it is an all too popular misreading of Lessing to interpret his work as anti-French. See also Erika Fischer-Lichte, *The Show and the Gaze of Theatre: A European Perspective* (Iowa City: University of Iowa Press, 1997).

459 At the end of the *Hamburgische Dramaturgie* XCV (95) Lessing writes: "Ich erinnere hier meine Leser, daß diese Blätter nichts weniger als ein dramatisches System enthalten sollen. Ich bin also nicht verpflichtet, alle die Schwierigkeiten aufzulösen, die ich mache. Meine

His collection of writings that together comprise Lessing's *Hamburgische Dramaturgie* is an open-ended project, a theory in status nascendi, although it has more often been considered a historic document on European drama in the eighteenth century and as documenting the beginning of German theater.

## 4. Structure, summary, and problems with sequencing images

In my reading the *Hamburgische Dramaturgie* has five major themes: 1) Lessing's critique of overdone volume of voice and hyperactive pantomime and his approach to more appropriate body language onstage which should be encompass "Mäßigung" (restraint); 2) his critical discussion of Aristotelian theater; 3) his development of the central concept of compassion (including empathy and pity) which should replace the previously central Aristotelian concept of fear;[460] 4) his notion of "Handlung" (action), both outer and inner, as an alternative to sequencing "Bilder" (images) onstage; 5) his proposal for a minimalist aesthetics which consists of various cuttings, subtleties, discrete commentaries or sidelines, and elements of emphatic writing. Lessing suggested doing away with what he considered overdone voice volume and hyperactive pantomime with inappropriate gesticulations onstage for dramatic effects:

> Weg mit diesem unbedeutenden Portebras, vornehmlich bei moralischen Stellen weg mit ihm! Reiz im unechten Orte, ist Affektation und Grimasse; und ebenderselbe Reiz, zu oft hinter einander wiederholt, wird kalt und endlich ekel.[461]
>
> [Get rid of any such insignificant gesticulations, especially in moral plays away with it! Sensation at the wrong place is affectation and grimace; and the same sensation, repeated too often, becomes cold and in the end disgusting].

Lessing thinks that exaggerated pantomime and gestures are ineffective. He requests that actors should speak with less staged effort and in such a way that they could gain

---

Gedanken mögen immer weniger sich zu verbinden, ja wohl zu widersprechen scheinen: wenn es denn nur die Gedanken sind, bei welchen sie Stoff finden, selbst zu denken. Hier will ich nichts als *Fermenta cognitionis* geben" (FA 6, 655): (I remind my readers that these pages are supposed to be nothing less than a dramatic system. I am therefore not obliged to resolve all the difficulties I cause. My thoughts may appear to connect themselves less, yes even may appear to contradict themselves: if they are only thoughts in which they [the thoughts] find material to think on their own. Here I want to do nothing except distribute to the fermentation of cognition). Lessing disclaims providing a coherent theory and admits to develop thoughts that at times are disjointed and lack cohesion but he defends his efforts noting that they contain an energizing creative force, something like the yeast in dough.

460 Martinec, "Lessing's Dramatic Theory," finds Lessing's interpretation of Aristotle problematic as "[...] there appears to be no doubt that Aristotle did not intend to say that tragedy is all about evoking pity. After all, he introduces not only *eleos* but also *phobos;* moreover neither passion in its own right, but both are clearly related to the process of *catharsis* as the ultimate goal of *tragedy*" (130). Not that Lessing was unaware of the issues involved.

461 *Hamburgische Dramaturgie* IV (FA 6, 203).

the sympathy of the audience. He also suggested more appropriate body language because he realized that it does not only express emotions but can sometimes evoke them, and he was committed to an art of understatement or moderation.

He writes against the repetition of the same sentiments in a single play and advocates a wide spectrum of emotions and nuances of character traits onstage. He follows Shakespeare considering many aspects of performance considering the careful presentation of character traits and aims at presenting characters as natural as possible. He regards Shakespeare as an extremely talented dramatic poet, expert in acting and stage directing, and Lessing proposes Hamlet as a perfect model for the appropriate indication how voice modulation and gestures in a drama are to be best performed.

> Wenigstens ist jedes Wort, das er dem Hamlet [...] in den Mund legt, eine goldene Regel für alle Schauspieler, denen an einem vernünftigen Beifalle gelegen ist. "Ich bitte euch," läßt er ihn unter andern zu den Komödienten sagen, "sprecht die Rede so, wie ich sie euch vorsagte; die Zunge muß nur eben darüber hinlaufen. Aber wenn ihr sie mir so heraushalset, wie es manche von unseren Schauspielern tun: seht, so wäre mir es ebenso lieb gewesen, wenn der Stadtschreier meine Verse gesagt hätte. Auch durchsägt mir mit eurer Hand nicht so sehr die Luft, sondern macht alles hübsch artig; denn mitten in dem Strome, mitten in dem Sturme, mitten, so zu reden, in dem Wirbelwinde der Leidenschaften, müßt ihr noch einen Grad von Mäßigung beobachten, der ihnen das Glatte und Geschmeidige gibt."[462]

> [At least each word, which he puts in the mouth of Hamlet, is a golden rule for all actors who like to have reasonable approval. "Speak the speech," he makes him say to the other players. "I pray you, as I pronounced it to you–trippingly on the tongue; but if you mouth it, as some of our actors do: see, then I would have like it just as well of the town-crier had spoken my verses. Also do not saw through the air with your hand, but use it to speak; for in the very torrent, tempest, and as I may say the whirlwind of your passion, you must acquire and beget a temperance that may give it smoothness"].[463]

Lessing values to a certain extent the classicist approach aiming at the appearance of serene tranquility. However, Winckelmann established his norms "edle Einfalt" (noble simplicity) und "stille Größe" (quiet grandeur) with ideals of Stoicism in mind.[464] Lessing recommends restraint in the display of emotions onstage yet for medium-specific and not for extra-diegetic reasons. Also he wants the audience to gain enough varied opportunities to project their own diverse emotions. He shows in his own writing how overdone body language or excessive emotionality can lead to serious misunderstandings. Lessing explains the measured and self-aware roles he wants the actors to adopt in the following terms:

> Sie (die Kunst des Schauspielers) darf sich, sie muß sich das Wilde eines Tempesta, das Freche eines Bernini öfters erlauben; es hat bei ihr alle das Ausdrückende, welches ihm eigentümlich ist, ohne das Beleidigende zu haben, das es in den bildenden Künsten durch den permanenten Stand erhält. Nur muß sie nicht allzu lang darin verweilen.[465]

---

462 *Hamburgische Dramaturgie* v (FA 6, 209).

463 *Hamlet,* III.2.1-8. William Shakespeare, *The Complete Works*, ed. Stanley Wells and Gary Taylor (Oxford: Clarendon Press, 1986), 755.

464 Winckelmann, *Gedanken* 36; "Gedanken" 45.

465 *Hamburgische Dramaturgie* v (FA 6, 210-211). "Tempesta" is a reference to the Dutch painter Pieter Mulier whose violent seascapes earned him the nickname "tempesta" (storm); Lorenzo Giovanni Bernini, famous architect, sculptor and painter.

> [It (the art of the actor) can, yes it must allow itself more often the wildness of a Tempesta, the boldness of a Bernini. It contains everything explicable which is unique to acting without having the insulting elements which the visual arts obtain via their permanent position. Only one request: it cannot linger too long with it].

This request for brevity, for acting as a dynamic art form between the visual and the poetic, is what makes his art of understatement. It should include a wide emotional spectrum but a performance should never get stuck with one emotion, image, or one mood too long. It is Lessing's choice to call acting a "stumme Poesie" (silent poetry). For him acting should communicate its message as if it were "unmittelbar" (with immediacy), so that the spectators' senses are all activated in interpreting what is happening onstage.[466] Lessing wrote extensively about the use of the visual that should replace the verbal. He also requested a minimalist aesthetics in terms of visual language, which had to rely more on actions than images. Actions in drama should replace what images had been in painting and indeed mobilize the viewers to think about underlying causes and consequences of what they see.

## 5. Revising the Aristotelian theater–Lessing's ekphrastic turn

In his discussion of Aristotelian concepts Lessing proposes that the passions should not be verbalized extensively or being described in too much detail. Whatever is visually presented would be effective only when the most significant moments of actions were to be performed. One should avoid unnecessary complications of the plot. Commentaries should be kept at a minimum. Each person's perspective should be clearly imaginable to the spectators. Actions should follow an inner logic with respect to each character, make sense, and not appear to be arbitrary, contrived, or forced. The interactions among the characters should be cogent. Emotions are not simply a matter of description or to be regarded as ornament. They have the importance of structural essence for the entire plot. Emotions and passions have to speak for themselves via action, performance, and not via commentary. Actions should replace a mere sequence of images or *tableaux vivants.* What Lessing wrote about omitting the moral in the fable also applies to the stage. Meanings are not to be spelled out, especially not considering any actions outside of the time-frame of the play as presented onstage. The "Mauerschau" (teichoscopy, narration of absent events not to be seen onstage) must be fully comprehensive to the play here and now and make sense already through the immanent facts of the plot as shown. Following his own dictum that the more we see the more we must be able to imagine, Lessing avoids allegory and hidden meanings and suggests to use more tangible contiguities and *pars pro toto* relations, the metonymic. Plays should differ from narratives as meanings should not be told but derived completely from interactions that make the audience and spectator true participants in the construction of meaning. Lessing noticed in the opening number of the *Hamburgische Dramaturgie:*

466 *Hamburgische Dramaturgie* V (FA 6, 211).

> Eine kleine rührende Erzehlung in ein rührendes Drama umzuschaffen, ist so leicht nicht. Zwar kostet es wenig Mühe, neue Verwicklungen zu erdenken und einzelne Empfindungen in Szenen auszudehnen.[467]

> [It is not so simple to remodel a short sentimental narrative into a sentimental drama. Granted, it does not take much effort to think of new entanglements of the plot and to elaborate specific sentiments into scenes].

In order to gain such illusory continuity Lessing wants the medium to avoid interfering with the content of the message. His goal is to create the illusion of understated naturalness in the realm of art. He aims at undisturbed illusions and insists that the playwright should avoid any visual or rhetoric strategies that would lead to alienation and premature self-reflection, interfere with the flow of the action. He tries to keep the attention-span of the audience focused, for as long as can reasonably be expected. He warns his fellow playwrights not to prolong the scenes and suggests a frequent shift of mood to promote emotional catharsis. Lessing develops a number of important observations early on in the *Hamburgische Dramaturgie* which contain both a revision of the Aristotelian tradition and a new approach to compassion. For example, in his review of *Olint und Sophronia* by Johann Friedrich Cronegk, Lessing compares the play with the same episode in Book II of the *Gerusalemme liberata* of Torquato Tasso.[468] He uses the occasion to further develop his own ideas about the theater. He insists that a play must have a coherent plot, trimmed of any unnecessary details and entanglements. Most important is for him the projection of a strong sense of probability, plausible sensations suggested considering all the actions performed. Each character onstage should be important and the play itself should make each person's importance clearly understandable, without any additional commentaries by an authorial voice.

Lessing advocates a new approach to what any performance should ultimately attempt to accomplish. He was striving for a new sense of complete performativity, unity within action, all of which was to be presented through the engagement of the spectators' imagination. For example, Lessing favored the initial version of the narrative in *Gerusalemme liberata b*ecause he felt that it still had something like magic that went beyond the specific time frame and still spoke to people, even though they belong to a different culture: A magician (Ismeno) who is neither a Christian nor a Muslim but someone who developed from both religions his own syncretic approach, advises Aladine, the Muslim King of Jerusalem that he will save the city if he takes a miraculous statue of Mary from the Christian church and places it in the royal Mosque. Then Lessing asks: Why did Cronegk make the Ismeno figure an Islamic priest rather than a magician? The move is appropriate for the magician to make but not an imam since Islam does not tolerate any statues or images in any mosque. Nor is this the only place in his work that Cronegk demonstrates his ignorance of Islam. Lessing finds it crassest blunder to insist that the strictly monotheistic Islam were a religion of polytheists. Lessing points out that historical error and argues that cultural data should not be completely ignored by anyone writing drama. He criticizes any writer whose work unnecessarily tends to insult people and annoy or even anger

467 *Hamburgische Dramaturgie* I (FA 6, 187-188).
468 See Robertson, *Lessing's Dramatic Theory* 142-150.

audiences, whether in terms of their religion, their cultural identity, their profession, or their class. He argues in contrast to Cronegk that Tasso's narrative maintains an excellent balance between the main characters in this episode of Sophronia, a lovely, calm, "Schwärmerin" (naively sentimental girl) and Olindo, "einem hitzigen, begierigen Jünglinge" (an overreacting desiring young man).[469] Neither of them are intent on martyrdom, as Cronegk' s version suggests, nor are they presented as if their actions result from any overzealous practice of their personal religion.

Lessing challenges the contemporary fashion of sentimental plays driven by religious prejudice and based on ridiculing other people's heritage. He insists that it is to be understood in the context of history and cultural upbringing and to be understood as respectable and important. He returns to an Aristotelian notion of the completeness of form which demands cogency of all actions. Ethical action and personal integrity and tolerance for others are what counts. He argues for tact and thoughtful restraint, a minimalist use of words: "Wenn heldenmütige Gesinnungen Bewunderung erregen sollen: so muß der Dichter nicht zu verschwenderisch damit umgehen; denn was man öfters, was man an mehrern sieht, höret auf zu bewundern"[470] (If heroic thinking should ever evoke admiration, then the poet has to be not too lavish in handling those features, because whatever one sees often and repeatedly in various contexts stops then being admirable). He warns against redundancy and finds that religion is a private matter of personal integrity. It deserves respect rather than parody. Nobody should be unnecessarily insulted. Nor should there be any overdone praise. Lessing finds that the word "martyr" should be used most sparingly, if at all, and never blindly. He wants theater not to be propaganda of any kind, but something inspiring beyond cultural boundaries. It has to be open-minded.

Lessing also tells playwrights not just to go for special effects. For example the production of tears should have more reason than just an expression of melancholy.[471] In this light, it is interesting to reflect on his own *Miß Sara Sampson* which was his own concrete experiment in writing a play that was designed to provoke his audience to copious tears. But there he arranged it, so that the compassion was built up systematically throughout the play. He aimed at a momentary upset that would cause a sustained impact. Lessing was successful. It is reported on the first occasion when his play was staged that the audience remained sitting after the final curtain fell. Nobody left everyone had been–as an eyewitness proclaimed–turned into a crying statue.[472]

In the *Hamburgische Dramaturgie* Lessing uses contemporary plays and materials from all levels of performance in order to suggest revisions and improvements to the contemporary theater and with careful references to Aristotle's dramatic theory. Lessing made *eleos* "Mitleid" (compassion) instead of *phobos*, the most central emotion

469 *Hamburgische Dramaturgie* I (FA 6, 189).

470 *Hamburgische Dramaturgie* I (FA 6, 190). Also see Klaus Bohnen, "Von den Anfängen des 'Nationalsinns': Zur literarischen Patriotismusdebatte im Umfeld des Siebenjährigen Krieges," Helmut Scheurer, ed., *Dichter und ihre Nation* (Frankfurt am Main: Suhrkamp, 1993), 121-137.

471 Claudia Albert, *Der melancholische Bürger. Ausbildung bürgerlicher Deutungsmuster im Trauerspiel Diderots und Lessings* (Frankfurt am Main: Peter Lang, 1982).

472 Karl Wilhelm Ramler in a letter of July 25, 1755 to Johann Wilhelm Ludwig Gleim (FA 3, 1121).

for the stage. He translated phobos variously as "Furcht" (fear) or as "Schrecken" (horror).[473] In his seventy-seventh number of January 26, 1768, Lessing writes a treatise on compassion (Mitleid) engaging once more with the Aristotelian concept of fear before then dismissing it finally for the sake of all-inclusive compassion instead:

> Wenn Aristoteles diesen Begriff von dem Affekte des Mitleids hatte, daß er notwendig mit der Furcht für uns selbst verknüpft sein müsse: was war es nötig, der Furcht noch insbesondere zu erwähnen? Das Wort Mitleid schloß sie schon in sich, und es wäre genug gewesen, wenn er bloß gesagt hätte: die Tragödie soll durch Erregung des Mitleids die Reinigung unserer Leidenschaft bewirken. Denn der Zusatz Furcht sagt nichts mehr, und macht das, was er sagen soll, noch dazu schwankend und ungewiß.[474]

> [When Aristotle had this term (horror) associated with the affect of compassion, arguing that it would have to be necessarily tied up with fear for ourselves: was it then necessary still to mention fear in particular? The word compassion already implied it, and it would have been enough had he only said: the tragedy shall through the evocation of compassion produce a cleansing of the passions (catharsis). Therefore the addition of "fear" does not say substantially anything else, and furthermore makes, whatever he should say, even more volatile and uncertain].

The notion of "actions" that should increasingly replace of "images" is already contained in the "Ankündigung" (Announcement) to the *Hamburgische Dramaturgie* where Lessing makes a clear distinction between the art of the poet and the art of the actor. Lessing defines the work of a dramatic judge as someone who can correctly gain visualcy as required for any useful theater critic. He calls for impartial evaluation of poets and actors while drawing clear distinctions between them and he draws attention here to the discrepancies between images and words:

> Eine schöne Figur, eine bezaubernde Miene, ein sprechendes Auge, ein reizender Tritt, ein lieblicher Ton, eine melodische Stimme: sind Dinge, die sich nicht wohl mit Worten ausdrücken lassen.[475]

> [A beautiful figure, a magical facial expression, an eloquent eye, an attractive step, a lovely tone, a melodic voice: these are things that cannot be well expressed by words].

---

473 Lessing draws attention to nuances in the use of language (FA 3, 715-716): "Es sind doch wohl zwei verschiedne Dinge, Furcht und Schrecken? Und wie, wenn sich das ganze Schrecken, wovon man nach den falsch verstandenen aristotelischen Begriffen bisher so viel geschwatzt, auf weiter nichts, als auf diese schwankende Übersetzung gründete?" (Are they not after all, two different things, fear and horror? And how about if this entire horror, about which up to now one has prattled so much following the falsely understood Aristotelian concept, were nothing else as based upon this shaky translation?). While at this point he opts for "Furcht" (fear), in the first 73 *Stücke* of *Hamburgische Dramaturgie* he uses "Schrecken" (horror), reverting to "Furcht" in Stück LXXIV: "Und dieses–hätte man gar nicht Schrecken nennen sollen." (And this one should not at all have called horror.) He explains: "Das Wort, welches Aristoteles braucht, heißt Furcht: Mitleid und Furcht, sagt er, soll die Tragödie erregen; nicht, Mitleid und Schrecken. Es ist wahr, das Schrecken ist eine Gattung der Furcht; es ist eine plötzliche, überraschende Furcht." (The word, which Aristotle uses, is called fear. Compassion and fear, he says, should be evoked by tragedy, not compassion and horror. It is true, horror is a kind of fear; it is a sudden, unexpected fear).

474 *Hamburgische Dramaturgie* LXXVII (FA 6, 567).

475 *Hamburgische Dramaturgie* Ankündigung (FA 6, 186).

Lessing makes us aware of aspects that resist language thus drawing attention to ekphrastic failure which may sometimes be unavoidable. It is his passion to work with performance and not only the verbal translation of actions in order to get even those aspects of messages across that would normally elude the writer's skill. It is a matter of momentary stasis when words cannot get in synch with what we see. Whatever happens onstage must be transitory and interactive. Whereas vivid expressions cannot be experienced in the theater without good playwriting, Lessing does acknowledge that ultimately not only the meaning but also the brightness of effects depends on a range of factors that go far beyond the text of a play. Lessing was perhaps the first playwright to concern himself in print with the theoretical importance of acting and stage directing. He can be regarded as an advocate of modest playwriting, someone who cares for the talent of the actors and the creativity of the audience. His approach to sympathy and compassion is not only a matter of theoretical pronouncements but realized in those terms onstage. Whether or not Lessing's ideas including the need for cutting, streamlining the plot, redefining Aristotelian premises, and so on, can be considered as part and parcel of his art of understatement is questionable since Lessing's writing style in *Hamburgische Dramaturgie* is often convoluted and the argument not always easy to follow. He mixes the most specific observations with the most speculative assumptions and dispersed arguments. There is definitely a hiatus between Lessing's theory and praxis and this has not been unnoticed by his critics. While we have his foray into drama theory laid out in the *Hamburgische Dramaturgie,* the attempt to establish a Deutsches Nationaltheater in Hamburg was perhaps a failure from the start. Peter Höyng notes that a decade later a "Nationaltheater" was established in Vienna 1776, followed in Mannheim 1777, and in Munich 1778. These were organized under the patronage of the local aristocracy as a "Hoftheater" (courtly theater).[476] Lessing's legacy is having promoted in Hamburg the idea for a theater that was intended for the general (bourgeois) audience. Lessing was path-breaking in was trying to create a new approach to theater. His search for national identity in this context should no longer be held against him, nor need it be misappropriated for any nationalist agenda. There was barely anyone using the German language in the eighteenth century who was more eager to translate, understand, adopt, or even to transpose plays and to make them accessible for a wider public from other countries than Lessing. Part of the complexity of this undertaking is that Lessing did not always follow his own theoretical ideals and although he worked with a new approach toward drama, performance, and theater this project of the *Hamburgische Dramaturgie* remained as opposed to his plays most of which are completed successfully, an unfinished and perhaps even to some extent unearthed "work in progress."[477]

Lessing's investigations of the limits of language for the sake of visuality remain in my understanding consistent and ongoing from his early ideas on "Anschaulichkeit" (vividness) of the fable to his exchange of ideas with Diderot on sketches, through *Hamburgische Dramaturgie,* all the way to his late works. His minimalist approach to aesthetics runs through his entire drama theory and through all his related efforts as a creative fiction writer and playwright. His approach as exemplified in these reviews

---

476 Höyng, "Lessing's Drama Theory" 211.
477 Höyng, "Lessing's Drama Theory" 222.

and theoretical writings forms indeed the matrix of all of his ekphrastic experiments in the context of his creative work. Lessing's theatrical innovations have continued to be influential to the present. Playwrights and critics including Bertolt Brecht, Heiner Müller, and Botho Strauss accredited Lessing for his departure from Aristotelian strictures and for his attempt to shift attention from production to reception. He believed that in theater not only images but also forces matter. Energies and drives emerge with sense perceptions and emotions for catharsis. Lessing reflected with increasing disillusionment on the difficulties of overcoming culturally engrained boundaries in effectively applying such bright hopes for the visual to the verbal but gave new power to performative possibilities.

# PART II:
## EXPERIMENTS AND STAGING POIGNANT MOMENTS

# Chapter 6
# *The Matron of Ephesus* (1748–1771): Expressing Introversion

Abstract: Lessing suggests in *Die Matrone von Ephesus* that images are likely to be more powerful than words. He questions not only aspects of performance but already the so-called bodily "natural signs." Although they are associated with the visual arts, painting and sculpture, they can also be ambiguous. Lessing argues that it is the task of any successful poet to make the "willkürliche Zeichen" (arbitrary signs) of language appear as if they were actually "natürliche Zeichen" (natural signs). He assumes in *Laokoon* that the visual arts are characterized by "natural signs "or "Körper im Raum" (bodies in space) and seems to assert this notion as a valid assumption. However, as this chapter illustrates, complications arise when experimenting with it as a playwright. Each image can have multiple meanings and also an artwork requires a careful "reading" and contextualizing in time. Lessing challenges the effectiveness of gestures and of "Körpersprache" (body language). He makes his audiences reflect on multiple possible readings, not only of verbal but also of visual expressions, depending on the various contexts and interactive processes. He draws attention to the temporality of all actions in space and to the contingency of meaning, even on the most basic level where metaphors already cannot be avoided. Lessing engaged in an experiment with in his innovative adaptation of the ancient story on the *Matron of Ephesus* by Petronius, which was initially used as an exemplum illustrating for "the weakness" of women. Lessing turns the story around and transforms it into a tragi-comical case study illustrating the power of the body and the imagination, the complexity of visual signs, and an Ekphrasis that has consequences for a new interpretation while giving the female very different attributes than in the previous versions of the story. Lessing focuses much less on any Matron's inability to pursue her own intentions, her apparent "weakness," but rather her admirable ability to forget her grief and to change, something which could be interpreted as a strength instead.[478] Furthermore, it is not her fault if her messages get misunderstood. She would have been persistent in her fasting and in her mourning for her husband's death until her own. But the fact that she is persuaded to turn back to life from the brink of death does not automatically

---

478 Against earlier presentations of the Matron representing "female weakness" as in Petronius, Lessing presents a much more positive interpretation of the female. In his version of the play he brings the tableau-vivant of the Matron alive for good reasons. She may even illustrate the human potential for positive change, for being able to forget grief and to affirm compassion with the living. My reading on gender in Lessing contradicts in that regard the gendered interpretation of Lessing by W.J.T. Mitchell, "Space and Time: Lessing's Laocoön and his Politics of Genre," Mitchell, *Iconology* 95–115. I do not agree on the notion that in Lessing's work the images associated with the female are being erased or expelled by words, or on what he associates with masculinity. Instead, I argue for a wide spectrum of image-word relations in his works and examine his experiments with Ekphrasis and visual-verbal transformations.

mean that she is a moral failure as earlier interpretations of Petronius' version judged. I suggest that for Lessing Antiphilia illustrates a successful example of Ekphrasis. She comes to embody the ancient statue of Venus mourning her beloved dead husband Adonis in the eyes of Philokrates. Consequently she draws the love of her observer which then brings a vitalizing process into motion. She breaks her fast and returns to life and compassionate action.

## 1. Lessing's notes and his initial draft for his play *Die Matrone von Ephesus*

Lessing's draft for "Die Matrone von Ephesus" is among the most interesting of his unfinished plays. It is one of Lessing's earliest pieces dating back to his student years in Leipzig around 1748, although he continued to tinker with it at least until 1771. *Die Matrone von Ephesus* is a play that deserves to be regarded as an equal counter-piece to the surviving contemporaneous *Faust* fragment Karl Guthke has pointed out. The two works should be interpreted in dialogue with each other.[479] For example, Lessing's Faust twice asks the seventh spirit or ghost of hell: "Wie schnell bist du?" (How fast are you?) On the second occasion, the ghost answers: "Nicht mehr und nicht weniger als der Übergang vom Guten zum Bösen" (Not more and not less than the transition from good to evil). Faust replies: "Ha! du bist mein Teufel! So schnell als der Übergang vom Guten zum Bösen!–Ja, der ist schnell; schneller ist nichts als der!" (Ha! You are my devil! As fast as the transition from good to evil!–Yes, this one is fast: nothing is faster than him!).[480] The surprising transition from one state of being to another, once she snaps out of her pose and forgets her fast, is a prominent feature of Lessing's *Die Matrone.* His *Faust* is related to this idea of rapid change and unnoticeable metamorphosis. It is about an unsatisfiable hunger for knowledge, an extreme desire for speed to draw a finger through a flame and check out borderline sensations. This becomes a vice. Lessing's *Matron* is about love, the intensity of emotion, and desire to live, in contrast to the ancient version of the story where the female character is lacking not only morality but also any spark to live and to communicate beyond what is expected from her. Both *Faust* and *Die Matrone* show the human individual not as a stable entity but as vulnerable, under the influence of others, capable of changing directions from one moment to the next unexpected erratic and random ways. While Faust may be the proto-typical male, the Matrone could represent the proto-typical female, although Lessing warns against any simplistic formula and moves away from the topic as suggested in the previous sources. Whereas there the Matron may presented as an example of weakness according to most interpretations so far, in Lessing's version she is in my reading an agent, someone who proactively rescues another person. Ironically she is donating the already dead body of her deceased husband as a prop. As grotesque as this detail may be, it illustrates the artificiality of the play and calls for compassion,

479 Karl S. Guthke, "Nachwort," Gotthold Ephraim Lessing, *D. Faust, Die Matrone von Ephesus: Fragmente* (Stuttgart: Reclam, 1968).
480 FA 4, 63.

love for life, and a willingness to return to the living without being dogmatic about it. She forgets her grief through helping others. Further the play illustrates wit and makes people laugh.

Lessing has two alternative versions of the play. In each he addresses problematic human attributes and conditions as they are presented in the realm of the theater, visually and verbally. He asks theoretical questions about art and fiction. Important are not only ethical problems but also practical concerns of aesthetics. This project leads Lessing into experimenting with the possibilities and the limitations of verbal and visual expressions on stage while emphasizing aspects of the spatial and the paradox of expressing introversion. He is in the process of inventing skillful techniques of timing, abbreviation, verbal condensation, and the mastery of the so-called "pregnant moment" developed theoretically in *Laokoon*. He makes us ponder about techniques of condensation and how to turn images into actions. Here he provides critical meta-reflection and tests with a new strategy. He draws attention to the most action-packed, dense, open-ended, and potentially most significant moment, a pose or *tableau vivant*. By applying this, he draws on the contemporary genres of body art, the *Attitüden* (attitudes) and shifts emphasis to the spectators, so that they should actively participate in the construction of meaning.[481] The idea of personifying an image or acting it out may have unforeseen consequences as Lessing exemplifies while drawing both from the Pygmalion and the Midas myths which could either bring the statue to life through the loving gaze (*Matrone von Ephesus*), or that could possibly petrify the spectators, so that they appear lifeless, objectified, or shocked by the piercing eyes that are as dangerous as in the case of Emilia Galotti who is obsessed with whispers and words. She appears to be the powerful and vicious embodiment of the Prince's previously commissioned portrait, the picture of a rival of Emilia's repressed personality. Emilia then in turn gives agency back to her helpless father who then stabs her, as if blind, as to be elaborated later.

## 2. Sources Lessing critically engaged with

*The Matron of Ephesus* is originally a legend with its classical source in the "Eumolpus" section of Gaius Petronius Arbiter's first century proto-novel, *The Satyricon*.[482] Eumolpus is amusing his ship-board companions by telling a series of misogynistic stories to

481 Karin Wurst provides a detailed history of such performances in salons, private residences, and public meeting halls in European cities in the eighteenth century with Mme de Genlis in France, Lady Hamilton née Emma Hart in England and Italy, Henriette Hendel-Schütz and Elise Bürger in Germany. "Spellbinding: The Body as Art/Art as Body in the Cultural Practice of *Attitüden*," *Lessing Yearbook* 33 (2001): 151–181 at 151.

482 Petronius, *Satyricon*, ed. Michael Heseltine, rev. and corr. ed., Loeb Classical Library 15 (Cambridge: Harvard University Press, 1987. On the Matrone of Ephesus in literature and on the stage, see Gerlinde Huber, *Das Motiv der "Witwe von Ephesus" in lateinischen Texten der Antike und des Mittelalters*, Mannheimer Beiträge zur Sprach- und Literaturwissenschaft 18 (Tübingen: Gunter Narr, 1990) and Tiziana Ragno, *Il teatro nel racconto: Studi sulla fabula scenica della matrona di Efeso*, Tyche 3 (Bari: Palomar, 2009).

emphasize his point: "How no woman was so chaste that she could not be led away into utter madness by a passion for a stranger."[483] He tells a "true" story he had heard about "a married woman of Ephesus of such famous virtue that she drew women even from the neighboring states to gaze upon her."[484] When her husband dies, she accompanies the dead man into the tomb and stays fasting in the underground vault, weeping, and mourning. A devoted servant sits with her and fills the lamp from time to time. Everybody thinks of the Matron as a "true and brilliant example of chastity and love."[485] The narrator goes on to explain that about the same time, the governor of the province had ordered the crucifixion of three criminals. The sentence of each together is carried out in the vicinity of the cemetery. A soldier guarding the crosses with the corpses of the criminals on them notices a light in the tombs and hears someone sighing. He is curious and wants to see what is going on in the vault. He discovers the desolate woman in her grief, weeping and draping her hair over the dead man. When he sees the beautiful woman he "at first halted in confusion, as if he had seen a portent or some ghost from the world beneath."[486] His words cannot console her but he does not leave the women alone as he is asked to do. Instead, he offers the woman and her servant food and wine which he has luckily brought along.

In the *Satyricon* version, the servant, hungry after fasting for five days together with her female companion, starts to eat and drink. Finally, the reluctant woman "allowed her resolution to be broken down, and filled herself with food as greedily as the maid who had been the first to yield."[487] And the narrator goes on: "Well you know what temptation generally assails a man on a full stomach. The soldier used the same insinuating phrases which had persuaded the lady to consent to live, to conduct an assault upon her virtue [...] I need not hide the fact any longer. The woman did not hold back even this part, and the conquering hero won her over on both counts. So they passed not only their wedding night together, but the next and a third."[488] The appeal to be sympathetic to these characters is as if telling one to withhold any premature judgment. In the meantime a relative of one of the crucified thieves arrives and wants to take the body of his family member off the cross. When it is discovered that one body is missing, no longer hanging there, the soldier who was supposed to be guarding the execution site now has to fear punishment and is worried for own life. Then the "lady's heart was tender as well as pure."[489] She offers to hang the corpse of her dead

483 Petronius, *Satyricon* 268-69. [N]ullamque esse feminam tam pudicam, quae non peregrina libidine usque ad furorem averteretur.

484 Petronius, *Satyricon* 268-69. Matrona quaedam Ephesi tam notae erat pudicitiae, ut vicinarum quoque gentium feminas ad spectaculum sui evocaret.

485 Petronius, *Satyricon* 270-71. [A]ffulsisse verum pudicitiae amorisque exempum.

486 Petronius, *Satyricon* 270-71. [P]rimo quasi quodam monstro infernisque imaginibus turbatus substitit.

487 Petronius, *Satyricon* 272-73. [F]rangi pertinaciam suam, nec minus avide replevit se cibo quam ancilla, quae prior victa est.

488 Petronius, *Satyricon* 272-275. Ceterum scitis, quid plerumque soleat temptare humanam satietatatem. Quibus blanditiis impetraverat miles, ut matrona vellet vivere, isdem etiam pudicitiam eius aggressus est [...] quid diutius moror? ne hanc quidem partem [corporis] mulier abstinuit, victorque miles utrumque persuasit. Iacuerunt ergo una non tantum illa nocte, qua nuptias fecerunt, sed postero etiam ac tertio die.

489 Petronius, *Satyricon* 274-275. Mulier non minus misericors quam pudica.

husband there in order to replace the missing corpse of the criminal that had escaped and by doing so, rescue the guard. Everybody laughed about this surprising end of this story, except for one of the travelers named Liches who personifies a judge or *deus ex machina*. He responds with anger and says: "'Si iustus', inquit, 'imperator fuisset, debuit patris familiae corpus in monumentum referre, mulierem affigere cruci'" (If the governor of the province had been a just man, he should have put the dead husband back in the tomb, and hung the woman on the cross).[490]

Lessing comments on Petronius' narrative in the Section XXXVI of his *Hamburg Dramaturgy*. His commentary is part of a longer discussion of Charles Simon Favart's *Soliman* II.[491] He criticizes the presentation of the queen Roxelane because Favart's condemnation of her is so broad as to include all women. This reminds him of *Die Matrone von Ephesus*: "Man kennt dieses beißende Märchen, und es ist unstreitig die bitterste Satire, die jemals gegen den weiblichen Leichtsinn gemacht worden" (One knows this acerbic fairy tale, and it is indubitably the most bitter satire which was ever made against female frivolity).[492] Lessing makes a remark about the fluctuation between literary genres and how difficult it is to categorize this work. At the same time Lessing criticizes the drama based on a story written by Houdar de la Motte.[493] He also offers a critique of aversion by his friend Christian Felix Weiße.[494] Lessing had helped Weiße in revising this piece between 1745 and 1748.[495] He comments: "Houdar de la Motte und andere, machten den Versuch; aber ich berufe mich auf jedes feinere Gefühl, wie dieser Versuch ausgefallen" (Houdar de la Motte and others made this experiment, but I appeal to each of the finer sense perceptions so as to evaluate these versions).[496] These previous versions of the story fail, according to Lessing, because they make the Matron "ekel und häßlich" (disgusting and ugly). They do not consider her as a human individual with multiple attributes, nor do they probe deeply enough into the motivations behind her behavior. Because of her extreme devotion to the one she loved she became vulnerable. Lessing quotes in Latin the condemnation by Lichas, but adds:

> Und diese Strafe scheinet sei uns um so viel mehr zu verdienen, je weniger Kunst der Dichter bei ihrer Verführung angewendet; denn wir verdammen sodann in ihr nicht das schwache Weib überhaupt, sondern ein vorzüglich leichtsinniges, lüderliches Weibsstück insbesondere.[497]
>
> [And this punishment she seems to deserve all the more, the less art the poet has used towards her seduction; since we condemn in her consequently not any weak femaleness in general, but rather an extremely frivolous, corruptible female in particular].

490 Petronius, *Satyricon* 276-277.
491 *Hamburgische Dramaturgie* XXXVI (FA 6, 357-362 at 358-59). See Ragno, *Il teatro nel racconto* 367-375. For Soliman II, see Robertson, *Lessing's Dramatic Theory* 235-239.
492 FA 6, 358.
493 Houdar de la Motte, "La Matrone d' Ephèse," *Œuvres*, 11 volumes (Paris: Chez Prault L'ainé, 1754) 5: 469-510.
494 Christian Felix Weiße, *Die Matrone von Ephesus: Ein Lustspiel, in einem Akte* (Leipzig Weidmann, 1767).
495 Fick, *Handbuch* 341.
496 FA 6, 358.
497 FA 6, 359.

Lessing points out in other words that art should not serve to condemn in general any female. It is the task of the artist to illustrate a specific individual. What appears to some as a particularly weak female may to others be the strongest person they cannot think of. He appeals to empathy given her intensity of emotions and her willingness to help the poor devil who would have been hanged otherwise. He moves to action, unexpectedly so. Lessing's interest is not to present a general biting satire but to show the complexity of what happens to a person in such a condensed context. In doing so, he speculates that the artist would have to highlight specific character traits in the story and not just tell a story that ends up with any "false" or unmotivated generalizations.

Lessing had by this time already read a draft of his dramatic version of the story. It was his idea, as he puts it, "den bittern Spott des Herrn Weiße über das schönere Geschlecht zu mildern (to soften Mr. Weiße's bitter scorn for the more beautiful gender). [498] Whereas Weiße's play had ridiculed women who are presented as if they are essentially lacking in strength of character, Lessing took a completely different approach in writing his version. He is in my reading illustrating very opposite attributes of the female character here. Following the desiderata outlined for such a drama in the *Hamburg Dramaturgy* he is interested in allowing the audience to see this woman as a person with multiple character traits which can then lead to rather different interpretations in judging the outcome of the action. He adds that in order to bring this play onstage effectively, one would have to use the same ending "but not the same ending." What this riddle means has so far not been deciphered but obviously it was Lessing's interest to reverse the plot somehow to shift the meaning:

> Kurz, die petronische Fabel glücklich auf das Theater zu bringen, müßte sie den nämlichen Ausgang behalten, und auch nicht behalten; müßte die Matrone so weit gehen, und auch nicht so weit gehen. –Die Erklärung hierüber anderwärts![499]
>
> [In short, in order to bring the Petronian fable happily onstage, it would have to keep the same ending, and also not keep it; the Matron would have to go as far, but not as far.–The explanation about that somewhere else!].

Lessing makes clear that he is concerned with exploring the subtlety of emotions and conflicting motivations for the action. He makes an interesting argument in support of the Matron's behavior. Can she possibly be excused? He makes room for language-critical moments and allows for certain gaps in the play, pauses that may be incriminating the expectations of the audience and observers, instead calling for pity and sympathy. Whereas in earlier versions of the story, cynicism was been most dominant feature of the story, Lessing opts for a degree of minimalism. He is turning the sharpest and most biting satire into a dramatic dialogue that presents a case of something intriguing and funny but not necessarily abhorrent. He illustrates what could perhaps happen to a character transformation in extreme circumstances and sets

498 Cited by Theodorus C. Van Stockum, "Lessings Dramenentwurf 'Die Matrone von Ephesus'," *Neophilologus* 46 (1962), 125–134 at 128.

499 FA 6, 359. Lessing does not provide further clarification of this point in his surviving writings.

the stage for critical thinking based on his own version of the play which gives the female a more favorable position.[500]

## 3. Close Reading of Lessing's surviving fragment *Szenar*

Two fragments of Lessing's play on this *Matron of Ephesus* material have survived. The first appears under the heading "Szenar" with an outline of five "Auftritte" (scenes) summarizing the action of the play in condensed form. The second appeared under the heading "Ausführung" (Execution). Here first a close reading of Lessing's *Szenar*. Whereas in in Eumolpus' version of the story the characters are all anonymous, Lessing gives them individual names. The widow is Antiphila, the maid Mysis, and instead of one soldier there are two in Lessing's version, the foot soldier Domos and his officer Philokrates. The husband is named Telamon and the officer claiming to be his friend is Cassander. This "Szenar" ends with the words spoken by the maid Mysis. The question whether or not there is a seduction scene in Lessing's version depends on the question what the word means. Was the mourning lady "seduced" into accepting food and turning back to the world of the living, or what exactly happened? It is left open to any specific performance and to the imagination of the audience. Another important change is that the replacement of the missing corpse with the husband's body remains only an idea and is not acted out onstage. And it is the servant's idea, not that of the Matron. This shift makes the Matron appear much more likeable. We learn very little about the Matron herself–Lessing places new emphasis on the female servant. Not only is she the first person we see onstage at the beginning of the play, she is the one who sets an excellent example in standing up for her life and for human rights. She finds that there is no need to continue to mourn with fasting. She is not willing to follow her lady to death and takes responsibility for her own life. She refuses to starve herself to death just for so-called loyalty or obedience. There is a limit to suffering and to dependency. Mysis' actions may well express personal integrity.

Lessing's second more substantial fragment is the remnant of comments he wrote later. It is a more advanced piece consisting of eight almost complete scenes beginning with the maid Mysis waking up confused and wondering where she is. She realizes that she is underground, inside a vault near a grave, together with her lady, Antiphila, "das Täubchen von einem Weibchen" (the little dove of a female).[501] Outside it is windy and rainy. She begins to worry that her lady could catch a cold in this weather. Then Mysis consoles herself remembering that Antiphila said she wanted to die for sorrow. In contrast she realizes, speaking for her own self and soon for others that she wants life more than death. She adds to this comment that to be a slave is to be unfortunate, to say the least.

---

500 For editions of *Die Matrone von Ephesus* see: FA 6, 147-77, 872-875. Lessing, *D. Faust, Die Matrone von Ephesus: Fragmente*, ed. Guthke; G. E. Lessing, *Die Matrone von Ephesus–Eine Komödie*, ed. Gerhard Kirchhoff (Munich: Max Hueber, 1969).

501 FA 6, 149.

Then she hears a sound. The second scene is without any text, only this comment: "Dromo draußen" (Dromo outside).[502] The third scene has Antiphila speaking in her dream. She asks whether the table is set and the wine is there. Mysis tells her to sit up and to realize that this is just dreaming. Antiphila falls back into sleep. Mysis puts oil in the lamp and attempts to sleep also. Then one hears sounds again. In the fourth scene Dromo enters: "Hier bin ich schon wieder" (Here I am again!)[503] This time he brings along his master, Philokrates, who then approaches Antiphila looking at her with much admiration. She seems to be beautiful, devoted, and compassionate. The admirer orders Dromo to bring wine, food, a table and some chairs from their tent outside.

The fifth scene begins with asking: "Wie? Sie wollen Ihre Wohnung hier aufschlagen?" (What? You are about to make this place your abode?)[504] Philokrates begs her to have pity on him and tells her that is too cold outside. She responds: "Sie wollen mich unglücklich machen? Was wird man von mir denken, wenn die Stadt hört, daß ich Sie eine ganze Nacht bei mir geduldet?" (You want to make me unhappy? What will people think of me when the city hears that I had tolerated you here with me all night?) He teases her reminding her of the notion that she wanted to die anyway and says: "Wer kein Mitleid mit sich selbst haben will, muß darum nicht aufhören, es mit andern zu haben" (Whoever does not want to have pity for him or herself must therefore not stop to have compassion for others).[505]

The sixth scene begins with Philokrates bringing crisp bread, dates, figs, and wine. He says he just remembered an oracle. It had told him that he would find the best woman among the dead. He always thought the oracle was fooling him yet now he could see it in the process to fulfill itself. Dromo comments that his master is very skillful in lying. In turn, Dromo is sent out. He should take a look and see whether the prisoner, a pocket thief, is still hanging there.

The seventh scene has only the enigmatic note: "Fortsetzung. Antiphila anfangen zu wanken" (Continuation, Antiphila appears to begin to oscillate).[506] What is interesting here is that Antiphila instantly externalizes her problem pondering over the question whether or not she should let Philokrates stay with her or not. She sees herself through the eyes of others and interprets her situation from an outside position rather than for her own self regardless of what others may think. Philokrates' earlier comment that in a sense she is already dead When she gives in to break her fast and to accept food, she may have made a decision to return to life, or, as some might read it, she has succumbed to the will of others. In the eighth scene Dromo comes back with the news that the dead criminal outside is no longer there.

What follows is the laconic sentence "Erklärung der Witwe" (Explanation of the widow), without any explicit details. We as readers of Lessing's play can imagine what she might have said, perhaps presumably that she gives consent for the substitution of the bodies, her husband's corpse to replace the living man who would be about to

502 FA 6, 149.
503 FA 6, 150.
504 FA 6, 151.
505 FA 6, 151.
506 FA 6, 152.

be killed senselessly otherwise. But then Dromo tells them that the dead man is still in his place and that there is nothing to worry about. Philokrates responds with anger and wants to punish his servant "unter dem Schwerte" (under the sword) for lying and teasing him like this. Dromo responds that this could hardly be appropriate since it was thanks to his finesse that the beautiful widow had to make her "Erklärung" (explanation). Philokrates drops the idea of punishing Dromo and asks Antiphila to forgive him too. She, in response, shouts: "Ihr Götter, welche Beschimpfung?–Wozu bin ich gebracht worden?–" (You Gods, what an insult!–What have I been made to do?–).[507] Dromo in his joking way suggests that she should marry him. It would be best to leave this place "wo sich ein Beispiel der ehelichen Liebe ereignet hat" (where an example of married love as occurred Mysis replies: "Ist es nicht genug, daß ihr uns verführt, müßt ihr uns auch noch verspotten?" (Isn't it enough that you have seduced us, do you then also have to mock us?)[508] This is the first time that in Lessing's texts the word "seduced" is mentioned. What it means in the context remains vague and this is where the play of this version ends.

There is, however, an alternate seventh scene by Lessing containing a dialogue between Philokrates and Antiphila. Philokrates asks why the dead man should be annoyed with him for taking his property. He asks: "Mit mehrem Rechte könnte ich zürnen, daß er mir Zuvor gekommen" (I could have more reason to be annoyed with him for having been there before me). Antiphila responds that this is correct only if love is limited to this life: "Aber werden wir nicht auch jenseits dem Grabe lieben?" (But shall we not love beyond the grave?) Philokrates assures her: "Ah, liebe Frau, wer hat Nachricht von dort her?– Der Genuß des gegenwärtigen Augenblickes ist für uns alles–" (Ah, dear woman, who has news from there?–The pleasure of the moment of the presence is everything for us–).[509] This scene contains two further brief fragments, first a quotation by the widow reflecting on her recent sickness. When she was on the verge of death, she ordered a coffin made. Then she recovered and found that her husband in the meanwhile had ordered a coffin for himself. Both coffins have been placed in their tomb. This fragment ends with the sentence: "Ah! wer hätte glauben sollen, daß er den seinigen zuerst füllen würde!" (Ah, who would have thought that he would fill his coffin first!)[510] Lessing was meditating on the fact that death can happen in unexpected ways and he tried to stage numerous perspectives between body and soul, the visible and the imaginable.

## 4. On Lessing's second version of the dramatic fragment, *Die Matrone von Ephesus* called *Ausführung* (Execution)

The second fragment begins with a prologue on whether or not Philokrates is similar in appearance to her dead husband suggesting that the problem of betrayal may be

507 FA 6, 152.
508 FA 6, 153.
509 FA 6, 153.
510 FA 6, 154.

one of varied shades of interpretation which can lead to deception. Was Antiphila fooled to such an extent that she thought her dead husband had come back to life? Was she mad and therefore must she be excused for her mistake? The longest surviving version of *Die Matrone von Ephesus* is the so-called "Ausführung" (Execution) with eight scenes. The setting underground is an almost dark vault. There are two coffins, one open, one closed. There is a lamp in the middle yet its light is dim. Antiphila and Mysis are both sleeping. Very precise stage directions are given about their positions. The first scene is the same as in the traditional version: The maid Mysis is waking up first and asserting the fact that she does not want to die in this sinister place.

The second Act has Dromo entering the vault. He acts as if he has just seen a ghost. He appears to be afraid of Mysis. He appears surprised to have found someone down in this cave and signals to greet her. He raises her curiosity and they start up a conversation. Mysis must respond to his slightly funny remarks. Yet she is thinking that when he first saw her, he must have been convinced that she is perhaps a ghost. This evokes fear of the underworld, fear of error in his memory, and fear of the unrecognizable. Her anxiety sparks uncanny imagination. She becomes aware of her own limitations in playing the role of the faithful servant accompanying her lady in mourning. She now worries this could cost her own life. He comments that the wind has just extinguished the lamp. Now it is even darker than before. We know that someone is there but cannot see. Mysis lights a lamp for the intruder in the cave and walks around. She finds Antiphila sleeping. She gesticulates that he can come over to inspect her, to find out that she is not really "a ghost." Mysis tells Dromo that her lady was very much loved by her husband who passed away. Since his death she has not eaten anything. Dromo says he is amazed that the lady is not looking for a second husband instead: "Nun? Warum nicht? Einen zweiten, einen dritten, einen vierten–nur nicht alle auf einmal!" (Well? why not? a second, a third, a fourth–just not only once in all).[511] He is talking in provocative ways and trying to make her realize that she is not dead yet and that life goes on Mysis sends Dromo out reprimanding him that he shall never again enter such a sacred place and talking like this. Then there is a hint that this is a location "wo sich nun bald ein Beispiel der ehelichen Liebe eräugen wird, dergleichen die Welt noch nie gesehen" (where soon an example of married love will take place, one of a kind the world has never seen before).[512] This sentence can be understood in numerous ways, depending on the perspectives.

One may ask whether for example the widow will die for love being faithful to the man she mourns, or whether she will die in a sense by giving in to a the man who entered the cave. Will he abuse her weakness or will he rescue her, perhaps become her second husband? Will he be able to "seduce" her from fatal mourning and bring her back to life? Or will he violate the privacy of the vault and impose himself thus making the widow a victim of his own erotic desire? The scene may foreshadow that the newcomer will be able to win her attention. Then they hear someone outside calling. Dromo leaves. He commands Mysis not to die.

The third Act contains a dialogue between Mysis and Antiphila who is talking to her husband in her sleep (no food and wine this time). She cannot believe that her

511 FA 6, 158.
512 FA 6, 159.

husband is dead and is delirious. Mysis is trying to console her. She informs her that there must be troops in the area. She says a soldier had been here to light his lamp and he said he will return with his commander soon. Antiphila requests that Mysis should block the entrance and firmly demands not to let anyone in. She does not want to see anybody nor be seen by anybody. She orders Mysis to tell any possible interloper from now on that she is already dead. But Mysis replies that they would become even more curious, out of pity. These words won't do. Instead, Mysis has another idea for her lady that will demonstrate her unwillingness to communicate. She gives what are in effect stage directions to Antiphila, telling her what to do when they hear someone approach: "Gehen Sie geschwind, werfen Sie sich auf Ihren Sarg; tun Sie, als ob Sie noch schliefen–So dürfen Sie doch nicht mit ihnen sprechen" (Go hurry up, throw yourself onto his coffin, pretend as if you were still sleeping–you need not then speak to them).[513]

By telling her to throw herself over the coffin in order to demonstrate her intense introversion and mourning, the maid does not realize that this gesture or body presentation might lead to very different assumptions on the part of the spectator. The audience is drawn into the mind of these characters who speak about what they think they could or should do. This opens up a realm of eventual possibilities about the scenes to follow yet there are gaps. The spectators must be participating in the scene as the actresses prepare a *tableau vivant* for the unwelcome visitors who, as we already suspect, are not inclined to understand or interpret the message as it was originally intended. When Philokrates enters the underground vault, he is told that Antiphila is asleep: "Desto besser! So kann ich erst sehen, ob sie des Tröstens werth ist" (Even better! Then I can see first of all whether or not she is worthy of being consoled). But when he catches a glimpse of her, he is struck by her beauty: "Götter! Was erblicke ich!" (Gods! What do I see!)[514] He orders Dromo to bring the torch closer so that he can observe her better. When he gets a careful look his amazement knows no limits: "Venus, als sie ihren Adonis beweinte, war nicht rührender" (Venus as when she was crying over her Adonis, was not more heartrending).[515] He identifies the *tableau vivant* before him with paintings of a scene frequently appearing in works of visual art: "Venus Mourning over her Dead Adonis."

This was a popular motif in Renaissance art and afterwards. Antiphila had thrown herself over the coffin of her husband, just as her maid had suggested, before the two men entered the vault. She is found involuntarily playing the role of Venus. Or she becomes Venus so to speak in this perfect spectacle. It is as if she were turned in an act of Ekphrasis into the famous statue. So she cannot help but evoke the powerful Pygmalion myth: The statue, Venus mourning her dead Adonis, comes to life through the loving gaze of the Matron's spectator, Philokrates. He is now her loving admirer, he interprets her posture in terms of this the image, and he falls in love with her or her ideal spirit of devotion. In his own private way he now motivates erotic desire, yet that is now merely the result of the projections by the audience unto him.

513 FA 6, 164.
514 FA 6, 165.
515 FA 6, 166.

Mysis asks the men to leave, but Philokrates makes enthusiastic comments about the beautiful picture he sees and thinks to recognize somehow. Antiphila appears to wake up, seems not only acting but really being confused when she is asking: "Mysis, wo bist du?–Wer war das?–Wer sprach hier?–Wer faßt mich bei der Hand? Warst du es?–Oder träumte ich?–Was ist das für licht?–Wer is hier, Mysis?" (Mysis where are you?–What was that?–Who has just spoken?–Who held my hand? Was it you?–Or did I dream it?–What kind of a light is this?–Who is here, Mysis?)[516] She first mixes up her dead husband, Mysis, with whoever else might be there; their roles in her waking or her dreaming get blurred. In her confusion and dream-like bedazzlement she speaks to Philokrates and asks him to no longer interrupt the silence of this sacred place. Philokrates asks for shelter during the cold night and gives a report on the political struggles in the outside world. He explains what danger he is in and begs the widow not to stop having compassion for others. She responds politely then and, as if she had forgotten the situation suddenly, she strangely apologizes for the dark and uncomfortable place and acts as friendly hostess. Philokrates sends Dromo out to get more lights, chairs, and a table from the tent. In the fifth scene, Philokrates complements Antiphila for her name and for her beauty and then goes off to help Dromo.

The next scene finds Antiphila blaming Mysis for the odd situation they find themselves in. They prepare to leave the sheltered space of the vault in order to flee the expected visitors whom they expect to return. The scene illustrates an uncomfortable coincidence. It ends abruptly with Antiphila on the stairs on her way to the exit. She exclaims: "Götter, es ist zu spät!–Er kömmt schon" (Gods, it is too late!–He is coming already).[517] Again, there is more than one possible meaning of this brief enigmatic statement in the context. In the seventh scene Philokrates returns and employs several persuasive rhetorical strategies. First he indicates that he actually knew Antiphila's husband and that everyone in Ephesus always praised his outstanding hospitality. He claims to have shared many adventures in the war with her dead husband to have been his close friend ever since youth. Mysis remarks that he probably read his name on the epitaph on reentering the vault and is reluctant to believe him. Philokrates bribes her to keep quiet: "Aber liebe Mysis, wette was du willt; du sollst alles gewinnen: nur sei mir nicht zu wider–Unterstütze mich–" (But dear Mysis wager whatever you want; you shall win everything; only don't be against me–Support me–).[518]

Philokrates is able to entangle Antiphila in conflicting emotions. But is she true to the love for her husband when paying attention to hospitality for his friend? Or does she follow the will of her dead husband by being friendly and helping a mutual friend? Is her reluctance to do so only because she is concerned with the conventions of polite society? What does she really feel? Can she decipher what her innermost truth is? Apparently she wants to share her mourning with the intruder who claims to mourn for her husband being his friend also. But this may just as well be an arbitrary move of an instant. Philokrates treats her as a Goddess, as personified spirit of beauty, hope, and life. This in turn appears strangely reciprocated by Antiphila who then plays her role so well that she forgets herself. She becomes what she acts perfectly. The

516 FA 6, 167.
517 FA 6, 172.
518 FA 6, 174.

*mise-en-abîme* in the play is unprecedented. The projected figure of Venus has Mysis under a spell. She literally becomes the image which she was going to resemble only. The mimicry is perfect. She may have been "seduced" back to life. She decides to live and to help another person. She has in effect become Venus, the symbol of love.[519] As the play progresses, she appears to accept her new role. She embraces life again. Act VIII continues this transformation from fasting to hosting, yet only to the point where the food is brought into the vault. Here the fragment breaks off. Again multiple readings are plausible.

While the play is not completely finished it is seems possible that she will take Philokrates as her second husband. The use of the word "seduction" in these fragments stands in contrast to the same motif in *Emilia Galotti*. But here the result is not murder, not suicide, but rather a situation which makes us think about the conflicting messages of the visual and the verbal. The Matron is restored back to life. The signs of expressed introversion and rejection of her visitor were read in a twisted meaning, but what happens in the end does not present her as example of female weakness as earlier accounts of the story had it, but rather as an individual of strength able to find her new place in a struggle between loyalty, love, death, and life. Lessing sheds a critical light on hierarchies, roles as they are commonly associated with class and gender, and with social conventions.

## 5. Interpreting Lessing's transitory visual signs

Diverse types of visuality play a role in Lessing's works, including statues, paintings, scenes, or *tableaux vivants*.[520] They all form the background for much of Lessing's contribution to Ekphrasis studies and constitute a repertoire for the images and the imagination by readers and spectators. Whereas in the Pygmalion myth a statue becomes alive through the loving gaze of the observer, in this play the main protagonist is close to death mourning her husband. In the vault where she has thrown her body over a coffin as a gesture of uttermost pain and despair she tries to signal her unwillingness to speak to anyone. She is in the process of fasting and close to death.

---

519 Lessing detects a process of transference as only much later much commented in psychology from Sigmund Freud to Melanie Klein and others.

520 On the *tableaux vivants* in the eighteenth century, see: Kirsten Gram Holmström, *Monodrama, Attitudes, Tableaux Vivants: Studies on some trends of theatrical fashion 1770-1815,* Stockholm Studies in Theatrical History 1 (Stockholm: Almquist and Wiksell, 1967); Dagmar von Hoff, Dagmar and Helga Meise, "Tableaux vivants–Die Kunst und das Leben: Kultform der Attitüden und lebenden Bilder," Renate Berger and Inge Stephan, ed., *Weiblichkeit und Tod in der Literatur* (Cologne: Böhlau, 69-86); Liselotte Hermes De Fonseca, "Wachsfigur–Mensch–Plastinat: Über die Mitteilbarkeit von Sehen, Nennen und Wissen," *Deutsche Vierteljahrsschrift für Literaturwissenschaft und Geistesgeschichte* 73.1 (1999): 43-68; Birgit Jooss, *Lebende Bilder: Körperliche Nachahmung in der Goethezeit* (Berlin: Reimer, 1999); Bettina Baumgärtel, "Die Attitüde und die Malerei. Paradox der stillen Bewegtheit in Synthese von Erfindung und Nachahmung," *Zeitschrift des deutschen Vereins für Kunstwissenschaft* 46 (1992): 21-42. Also see Inka Mülder-Bach, *Im Zeichen Pygmalions. Das Modell der Statue und die Entdeckung der Darstellung im 18. Jahrhundert* (Munich: Fink, 1989).

In the course of the story, which takes numerous twists and turns, she is visited by intruders who have their own problems. One of them is smitten by the image of the beautiful figure which he seems to recognize from an ancient painting and through his intervention the Matron eventually comes to life again, even though the attention of the observer completely ignored her own intended body language, expressing nothing but withdrawal and introversion. Perhaps she had become the objectified image of misplaced erotic desire, or perhaps her mimicking of the ancient statue was so perfect that she actually personified the artwork and the difference between art and life was then no longer traceable. For whatever reasons, her visitor Domo and her friend Mysis are able to break her fast and rescue her from joining her dead husband. They win her back, perhaps even against her will, into a more communicative state of mind. She ultimately eats and drinks, and moves to action. She decides that she must now save the life of another person. She can only do that by donating the corpse of her dead husband so that he could hang instead of the pocket thief whose guard is now delighted. Despite this grotesque twist of events, the question is how to evaluate such behavior and what it may mean for the poetic constellation experiment.

Lessing not only probes a border of visuality here, he also tests the taste of the public, as well as the notion of personal freedom. He is negotiating private versus public spheres and he seems to present the Matron in a more friendly light than the narrators of the story before. The Matron is misunderstood for her own conscious gestures, body language, and actions in a mood of mourning and compassion for her deceased spouse. Yet her expressions of emotion have a counter-productive effect. She has in an act of introversion, that becomes seen by one spectator as one of extroversion instead, thrown herself on the coffin. She is lying there for the longest time while refusing to speak, to eat, and to interact with anyone, except momentarily her maid or female companion Mysis who must shield her from the outside world. Is she at fault? He avoids giving any answer.

In this play Lessing is dealing with the transitory nature of visuality and with the question of timing images best before the intended climax of the major events in the plot. As he argued, in order to be clear and visually effective, a scene must allow the viewer to concentrate on the selected most action-packed and condensed moment of the entire play. Lessing claimed in his *Laokoon* that images belong to the dimension of space and their signs, bodies or figures shown, are best presented in a contracted sequence, yet not all at once or concurrently. The visual should be restricted to the carefully selected, most poignant moment as if held still or clipped from the flux of time. The realm of "Dichtung" or poetic language navigates in a tension between the visual and the verbal and their associated dimensions, space versus time. It is it the prerogative of drama not only to be restricted to the visual but to include dialogue and simultaneous movements. It can moreover articulate acoustic and kinetic features intertwined. Lessing pays much attention to body language, pantomime, and gestures. He approaches the issue how to deal with time, even in the visual. He uses the story as a specific dramatic experiment.

Lessing's remake of *Die Matrone von Ephesus* is one of his case studies exploring the limits of communicability. It reflects on actions surrounding the visual and presents a body onstage while probing potentials and boundaries of layered meanings and related actions. This play explores how the dramatic art of acting a successful performance onstage differs from showing just a painting or a sculpture. It also challenges the notion of ekphrastic translatability of the shown setting into a verbal account. The figures onstage normally interact, move, and the words are meant only to be suitable to their actions.

The play Lessing worked on here is one that has the visual and the verbal in tension dispersing. A lying body over a coffin is not only a "natural sign" that means one thing onstage such as sadness and mourning; it has, as Lessing well illustrates, a range of possible meanings and implications beyond that which are unpredictable. The art of "Schauspielkunst" (acting) involves a conscious and careful approach to visual signs, bodies in space that evoke certain emotional associations and thoughts. They may not be presented completely within the narrative time frame. It is my thesis that with this play Lessing illustrates that not only the signs of language are artificial but also the visual signs. They are multivalent and metaphorical and defy any simplistic categorization.

In making this point, Lessing challenges the prevalent notion of his time that gestures were to express universal meanings and easily understood according to a classicist rhetorical tradition. As Alexander Košenina pointed out there was a "Wendung der Schauspielkunst" (paradigm shift or turn of the art of acting) in the eighteenth century, so that not only scientific efforts were made to empirically reconstruct certain gestures and bodily expressions with an associated catalogue of related mental dispositions. Dietrich Christoph Rommel, professor of eloquence and rhetoric in Marburg, argued in his writings that a theory of drama does not precede the art of performing, but rather the other way around.[521] According to the body's ability not only to simulate certain emotions but to induce them, art has a primary position in the study of the human. It is at the core of anthropology, a new science that places the human in the center of interest.

John Zammito has associated the beginning of anthropology with Kant, Herder, and their circles, but one should not exclude Lessing from among the pioneers of this emerging discipline.[522] How to perform the most rhetorically apt gestures is therefore not simply a matter of applying a previously existing set of art-theoretical and rhetorical rules. Instead, the questions include how to describe what the artist actually does:

> Auch die Theorie der Declamir- und Gebehrdenkunst geht nicht der Kunst vor, sondern nach, macht nicht den Künstler, sondern beschreibt ihn; [...] Sie bezeichnet die Grenzen der Kunst, giebt Regeln und Beurteilungen an die Hand, lehrt das ungebundene Genie Ordnung und Plan, und ist ein Ausfluß der Poetik.[523]

---

521 Košenina, "Die anthropologische Neubegründung" 95–105.

522 On the beginning of anthropology in the German tradition John Zammito, *Kant, Herder, and the Birth of Anthropology* (Chicago: Chicago University Press, 2002). H. Baran and A.W. Halsall in their article in the *Princeton Encyclopedia of Poetry and Poetics*, 4th ed. (2012, 55–56) find that "the greatest practical utility for the various studies grouped under the big top of anthropology came during the period 1860–1925, when literature was understood as a continuation of an ancient social practice of human culture practically from its beginnings" (55). The *Anthropological Review* began in 1863 and the *Magazine of Anthropology* in 1866.

523 Dietrich Christoph Rommel in his *Theorie der Kunst überhaupt*, as cited in Košenina, *Anthropologie und Schauspielkunst* 26.

> [Also the theory of declamation and gesticulation does not precede the art, does not make it an artist but it follows it; it does not make the artist but describes him or her [...] It designates the boundaries of art; gives rules and criteria at hand, teaches the unlimited genius order and plan, and is a tributary of poetics].

Ambiguities cannot be avoided and the most immediate emotional expression may be much more misguided than any reflected, more understated expression would be. From Lessing's perspective the *tableaux vivants,* as well as all images can hardly be conceptualized in terms of any mono-causal logic. Nor can they be subsumed under the main current of dominant Enlightenment discourse. While Lessing may have been an advocate for the Enlightenment, he was simultaneously one of its harshest critics by probing rationality and what he critically called in his *Laokoon* a mode of representation that draws its meaning from hidden contexts and culturally assumed sources. To Lessing the abundant use of allegories leads to "Allegoristerei," which he equates with a lack of "Anschaulichkeit" (vividness) in the context of the given artwork.

*Die Matrone von Ephesus* illustrates that visuality is not transparent. It is difficult to read. Even a *tableau vivant* cannot be deciphered according to any static codes or given "natural signs." Although there are certain codes in body language which dramaturgy uses in the eighteenth century and also Lessing adopts, matters get complicated considering various disciplines, such as medicine, science, and anthropology. Accordingly, also the relations among signs and the codes playwrights are working with include complex relations that are not always "bequem" (comfortable). The same gesture may express more than one kind of emotion and the reading of a sign cannot be simply deduced from a set formula or simply guessed. Visible facial and bodily expressions are prone to the art of "Verstellungskunst" (acting in disguise), a topic which might be regarded as a rich territory of explorations in the eighteenth century drawing interest from the liberal arts as well from other disciplines.[524] Conventions cannot always be used as reliable keys to decipher physical interactions and movements onstage, and the image-word correlation does not always does suffice for any reader to be able to decipher what is really seen. In *Die Matrone von Ephesus* Lessing reflects on the difficulties encountered in expressing emotions accurately, especially those involving aspects of introversion, such as mourning, sadness, depression, and melancholy.[525]

Moods, emotions, and sense perceptions are fragile and transient. They tend to change in the process of being expressed. It is not only a discovery of our own century, as recently James Elkins wrote, that "images stare back."[526] Already in the eighteenth century there was a public debate on the possibility of inflicting real sensations by pretending them. Since there is a psycho-physical connection, real emotions and even sickness or happiness can possibly be produced by pretending or projecting oneself via attaining their attributes. Lessing is well aware of some early studies on psychosomatic

---

524 Ursula Geitner, *Die Sprache der Verstellung: Studien zum rhetorischen und anthropologischen Wissen im 17. und 18. Jahrhundert,* Communicatio 1 (Tübingen: Niemeyer, 1992).

525 See Christian von Zimmermann, "Verinnerlichung der Trauer. Publizität des Leides," Achim Aurnhammer et al., ed., *Gefühlskultur in der bürgerlichen Aufklärung,* Frühe Neuzeit 98 (Tübingen: Niemeyer, 2004), 47-74.

526 James Elkins, *The Object Stares Back: On the Nature of Seeing* (San Diego: Harcourt Brace, 1996).

symptoms that may well exist widely in society. This has relevance also for Lessing who participated in debates on strategies how to best present and decipher onstage visuality. He also gave advice to the actors on how to create most impact while searching for the most capable actors. Even if they were quite talented, how could they produce performances that were fool-proof, plausible, and regarded as authentic? Should one offer a sense of naturalness in the realm of art, rely on earlier productions and conventional settings, or be daring something strikingly new? Lessing chose to reflect on knowing the artificiality of signs, to use a dose of wit, irony, and self-reflection, in order to appeal to those in the audience who may have courage to think a step ahead? Lessing considers various options within a range of possible scenarios while measuring some limitations, including the context of this play.

By incorporating moments that highlight the difference between words and images into the writing of his play, Lessing challenges the dominant theatrical assumptions of his time. He questions simplistic categorical notions of what "the moral" of the story and its natural outcome may be. He raises philosophical questions about the dividing line between what is outside and inside, what belongs to the mind, what to the body, and where the plot happens. In the case of *Die Matrone von Ephesus*, he adapts a text from antiquity and transposes it onto the German stage by leaving much of the stage directions to the interpretation by the actresses and actors. He also shifts importance to the audience. He takes a risk by investigating through writing his own version of this ancient story whether readers may find it repulsive, or whether they could possibly be drawn into questioning how effective gestures or body language can be. He ponders about what changes could be invented to the story that could ideally rescue the previously condemned female from the discontent of the public. He shows that although visuality is important, its signs are not always reliable. He inserts a philosophical dimension and critical self-reflection. Lessing finds that the worst sin is "Trägheit" (inertia). This story also challenges ocularcentrism of the mainstream Enlightenment discourse and demonstrates that looking is not everything. What we see is a complicated process that has sense perceptions and memory images, life and art, impact each other. How the outcome is to be evaluated depends on each life situation.

Similarly a question will be whether Faust must be punished or not and Lessing leaves that open as well. If the Matron deserves to be severely punished with death as Lychis demanded in anger, another position was formulated through the subsequent retelling of the story in Lessing's drama that instead make us reflect on issues of human error, basic human needs, and the shortcomings of intentionality. Lessing makes us reflect on the possibly powerful transformation of images into texts, or of characters into images. Antiphila was identified with the statue of Venus, so she gets rescued back to life. Lessing's version of the play illustrates that role-playing and art can change reality. Emotions shift in the process of their staging. And what is even more radical an observation is the fact that everything we do may be a staging of one kind or another. The stage has become an invasive phenomenon. Theatrical performance happens more often than we think. But Lessing warns the public that whenever emotions are expressed in an all too extroverted a manner, then expressing them is overdone and communications derail.

In another fragment from around this time, a similar reversal is suggested. It also plays on sudden changes in behavior, poking fun at clichés. Lessing's fragment "Der

Schlaftrunk" (The Sleeping Potion) of 1767 describes a scene with a man in crisis. He refuses to die and is well aware of the intense desire of his surrounding family members to take over his possessions. This stands in stark contrast with Lessing's version of the Matron. The man in "Schlaftrunk" lacks any spark for true rescue but the Matron changes from extreme sorrow towards happiness. Lessing's "Schlaftrunk" ends not with resignation but with a refusal to give into melacholy and depression. At the same time it emphasizes temporality. Samuel Richard asks: "Aber Bruder, hast du gelesen von einem Maler, der mit einem einzigen Pinselstriche ein lachendes Gesicht in ein weinendes verwandeln konnte? Ich bin so ein Maler" (But brother, have you ever read about a painter who could with one single brushstroke turn a laughing face into a crying one? I am indeed such a painter).[527] What one sees in a picture depends, as Lessing inserts more than any conventions on the freedom of the artist to let his or her figures act and on their abilities to bring old myths alive and to engage the public. Images and scenes can open up to a variety of interpretations beyond what was written in any traditional context before. In other words, Lessing stands here on the side of the painter and advocates images that are not stable but moments of action, instants of a move, and the freedom of such an actress.

## 6. Unsettling effects and open questions

Lessing's versions of *Die Matrone von Ephesus* have a variety of unsettling effects. He addresses a gap in measurable time, a change so abrupt, that what happens has to be shown only through abbreviated or partial images, momentary gestures. Philokrates has compared Antiphila to Venus mourning over her dead Adonis. He is in awe over her "unendliche Reize" (endless charms) and he could easily spend an entire year in contemplation: her hair, her neck, her bosom, her hips, her feet, and her arms. He comments: "Diese ganze Stellung, so malerisch hingeworfen" (The entire pose so picturesquely sketched).[528] Then he takes her hand and kisses it. She seems to wake up from her trance. What is the function of this staged picture or this ekphrastic text in Lessing's account of the story? Perhaps it is the so-called "poignant moment" in this play, the underlying subtext for the entire action. In the moment Antiphila becomes aware that she is seen as a picture of Venus, that she is, as Philokrates says many times, a Goddess, she also becomes aware that her mourning, fasting, and silence. She is elevated to another level of existence. Prior to this interpretation, she was not conscious of her role-playing and thought of her actions as expressions that simply belong to the realm of nature. Now that her actions are reflected as artificial, or as resembling the sublime, things could change for her. The paradox of such the attempt to express withdrawal spatially or emotionally, or an unwillingness to communicate, becomes counter-productive. What comes across is an entirely different message. Philokrates interprets this pose as unnatural reminding him of the scene from the life of Venus, the Goddess of Love. He acts out in a sense the myth of Pygmalion trying to bring the

527 FA 6, 124-125.
528 FA 6, 167.

statue to life. Now Antiphila is apparently compelled by the logic of the interpreted fiction to act out this projected role. She now becomes a victim of her staging, or perhaps she accepts her new agency?

One may argue that Philokrates had a compelling visualization and to that extent then she is indeed "seduced" by Philokrates. She gets drawn into his interpretation of her figure and violated in that sense. Instead of understanding her reality as involving a choice of roles, she cannot distance herself from the *simulacra*. Before she was just acting out an emotion, her mourning for her husband who had just died, but the staged "reality" of it now has its own momentum. The world of the visual media has consumed her; her identity has vanished to a point of no return. She now lives out the fiction that Philokrates has constructed upon viewing her. Had she realized that what seemed natural is already artificial, then she could have distanced herself in different ways. However, she internalizes completely becoming the embodiment of Venus. The scene in which Antiphila poses in order to express a state of mourning and which Philokrates interprets in his own interest as an image of Venus mourning her dead Adonis is then the subtext for the action of the entire play. It addresses the difficulties of conflicting messages that are associated with the visual versus the verbal. And how does playing not only repeat but possibly also change reality? How does the expression of emotion affect those very emotions to be expressed in the process?

It is possible to compare this poignant moment in Lessing's *Matron* who appears to undergo a complete personality change through mimicry and projection with another constellation in Heinrich von Kleist's *Marionettentheater*. There a very talented and most able dancer has lost his balance and his ability to dance gracefully and effortlessly once and for all after one single moment of self-reflection. His all-changing mirror experience happened when he became aware of himself in terms of another. An observer compared his gesture for a moment with the precise pose as depicted in an artwork thus also dangerously conflating art and life.[529] This moment of mirroring self-reflection strikes a conflation between reality and art which then leads to a non-reversible process of stagnation. The dancer has from that moment on lost his marvelous talent and he must train to repeat consciously what he well was able to perform intuitively with so much elegance before. The request to repeat the very same movement was an impossible command and made the dancer fall out of his naïveté, the human state of harmony with nature. Now the dancer has lost his "natural" state of being. The text becomes a cultural document, turns the value hierarchy of the classical discourse upside down. It reverses mimetic expectations so that the image in art precedes and undermines what is seen in reality. Attention is being drawn to instable conditions in an act of performance. It can absorb the actor into something or someone else irretrievably, even to a loss of self. Helmut Schneider writes that Heinrich von Kleist "questions the priority of the interior over the exterior, the spiritual over the corporeal, and the meaningful over the accidental." He adds that this results to the notion of "metaphor over literal, signified over the signifier, the soul, or the mind, over

529 Heinrich von Kleist, "Über das Marionettentheater," *Sämtliche Werke und Briefe,* ed. Ilse-Marie Barth et al., 4 vols. (Frankfurt am Main: Deutscher Klassiker Verlag, 1987-1997), vol. 3 (1990): 555-563 at 561.

the body."[530] I would like to say that in Lessing's case considering this story the body seems to win over the mind and perhaps this speaks in contrast to Kleist for materialism in his approach. To conclude there is a stark difference between such moments of reflecting on the artificiality of the natural in Lessing or in Kleist. Antiphila does not have the problem of repeating a motion that she can no longer perform as is the case with the dancer in Kleist. Instead, she has identified herself with the image that is projected onto her by her admiring observer. What she poses is actually what she is or rather, what other people think she is. Her inside is absorbed into her apparent outside. Her naïveté makes her ironically speaking (and also in the vocabulary of Kleist), a Goddess. What she is seen to pose is actually what she becomes. In other words, the collision between boundaries and then their quick dissolving–albeit presented in a more abstract fashion than in the case of Petronius' story–makes Lessing's version not any "milder" or less critical of the female protagonist. He does not spell out any "seduction scene" in words other than that she eats again and returns to life but whether or not she makes her body the object of the male gaze is an open question. It is contextualized in a way that is just as suggestive, open-ended, powerful, or perhaps even violent as in the version by Petronius. Whether or not Lessing's retelling is close or similar to that of Petronius remains to be debated. Lessing shows on one hand how this woman can turn from sadness and depression to be a vital member of a helpful society again He shows on another hand that women do not have a space of their own and that they have to fit given images and imposed expectations. Antiphila has her soul emptied to such a degree that she has nothing to lose when she undertakes the *tableau vivant*. Body and soul are not entirely separate, they interact. In this play, the body appears to have won over the soul (hunger matters) and the outside over the inside. The disruptive force and the provocative effect of the play result from a staged logic that permeates all levels of the plot and, at moments, confounds even the roles of gender.

Did not Antiphila also mistake Mysis for her dead husband at a moment before she noticed that the man who had entered the vault was neither her husband nor Mysis? And we remember that in one version, Lessing insisted that there was a similarity between Cassander and Philokrates. What to do with the similarities between the first and what may be the second husband? Lessing avoids a value judgment and leaves the matter open. While solutions are not given and endings not final, they stand in brisk contrast to other seduction scenes in Lessing's "Bürgerlichen Trauerspielen" where death or suicide follow. Can turning into an image or identifying with a *tableau vivant* offer yet another alternative? Antiphila could process the image of herself as Venus perhaps by understanding humor, by operating on more than one level of logic, and by learning how to interpret metaphor. Did she distance herself from the one image she had come to identify with? Is she the victim of mimicry or a perfect actress? We do not know what ending Lessing would have liked best. What matters, is the stern scrutiny of his cultural criticism and the assumed visual literacy, a prerequisite for much of European literature at that time and a key to Lessing today.

---

530 Helmut J. Schneider, "Deconstruction of the Hermeneutical Body: Kleist and the Discourse of Classical Aesthetics," Veronica Kelly and Dorothea von Mücke, ed., *Body and Text in the Eighteenth Century* (Stanford: Stanford University Press, 1994), 209-226 at 221.

Barbara Stafford has shown that the radical advances in optics in the eighteenth century triggered a series of major changes in contextualizing and defining the visualization of knowledge. Microscopes made visible what was hidden before and what did not seem to exist; at the same time seeing changed the world itself.[531] What was seen was no longer easily linked with touch and intuition. It was no longer based on earlier concrete sense perception. It became so abstract that it did not affirm truth but made it even more questionable. Christopher Collins demonstrated that these changes affected also writing and textualizing as he calls it, the "nature of the supernatural image."[532] Lessing was intrigued by seeing but he also reflects critically on the gaze and what it may imply. He seems to have a sense of sympathy for the extreme character that has difficulties of seeing herself other than through the eyes of others. He seems to take pleasure in the fact that eventually Antiphilia accepts the food and, according to his version gets eventually "seduced" back into life, even if only using the word as a way of speaking, not literally. Lessing's version of the Matron gets liberated from her state of melancholy and depression through an image that inspired the observer. She gains her life back through the interest and dialogue with another person. She accepts rescue from the stone vault, together with her friend Mysis whom she had wronged by pulling her into her own misery. She realizes that she must decide quickly to rescue yet another person who would otherwise be hung and killed. It is therefore not only her apparent weakness that characterizes Antiphilia's character. Lessing draws attention to a needed sense of justice for catharsis, the cleansing of lethargic emotions, and compassionate action.

The need to decipher the intended meanings of the figures on display does not stop for Lessing where it did for others who dealt with the same material before. He succeeds to energize the reception and gives the example of an artwork that gains epistemological relevance. *Die Matrone von Ephesus* is intricately connected with theoretical approaches to showing, staging, and the depth of the so-called "real." It illustrates a loss of identity, a ghost-like existence, and the rescue through an image of love.[533] What begins as a commentary on the strange reversibility of Ekphrasis ends

---

531 Stafford, *Body Criticism* 341-398.

532 Christopher Collins, "Writing and the Nature of the Supernatural Image," Allert, ed., *Languages of Visuality* 242-261.

533 I am aware of the dominant interpretation of this text so far as documented in the essay by Hugh Barr Nisbet, "Lessing and Misogyny: *Die Matrone von Ephesus*" in John L. Hibberd and H. B. Nisbet, ed, *Texte, Motive und Gestalten der Goethezeit. Festschrift für Hans Reiss* (Tübingen: Niemeyer 1989), 13-31. Although I agree that the Matron is set on the surface as a rather ridiculous example of a female weakness all the way from Petronius to Lessing, I would like to suggest that this piece by Lessing may actually be part of his corpus of "rescues" or "Rettungen" thus turning to the audience and spectatorship for innovative alternative readings. I think it could also exemplify an aspect of necessary enlightenment and be interpreted quite differently. See Michael Multhammer, *Lessings 'Rettungen'. Geschichte und Genese eines Denkstils*, Frühe Neuzeit 183 (Berlin: De Gruyter, 2013). On similarly provocative moves and open possibilities in Lessing's work, see Horst Steinmetz, "Die Sache, die Person, und die Verselbständigung des kritischen Diskurses. Offene und Verdeckte Antriebe in Lessings Streitschriften," Mauser and Saße 483-493. Compare Jürgen Stenzel and Roman Lach, ed. *Lessings Skandale* (Tübingen: Niemeyer, 2005).

as a play challenging the presumed "naturalness" of all signs, including the opaque visual. Lessing's proposes that art has power over reality and the body over the mind. The Matron truly becomes a statue and luckily outlives her misery via art in an act of trickery. In his story, her pose resembles that of the well-known ancient artwork, the statue of Venus as she is brought back to life by Adonis. This image and the Pygmalion myth are stronger than all earlier intended messages. The spectators cannot "read" accurately or decipher natural signs of what they see; nor can the characters avoid a spark of humor and empathy in Lessing's play despite the grotesque setting. The plot remains open and Lessing is obviously at odds with stereotypical class and gender implications.

He dramatizes a story for a test case on performance and visuality in an era of almost fatal repression and lets the female protagonist emerge vitalized, against all odds. Lessing's female character is allowed to experience qualitative change through an awareness of her own sensuality, asserting physical needs such as food, and through compassionate human interaction. She gets rescued by truly becoming the image of love. Although she attempted to express her extreme feelings of introversion and otherworldly desire, her messages had to bounce back. Lessing draws attention to the Here and Now and his play demonstrates that her intuitive move just to stretch herself laying and resting on the coffin in a state of introversion cannot be acceptable for any observer. Lessing's reading of this image leads to opposite effects. But how to evaluate this perhaps fruitful conflation of art and life remains up to the spectators or dreamers for centuries to come.

# Chapter 7
# *Miß Sara Sampson* (1755): Exhibiting Emotions and Problems with Wordiness

Abstract: This play was written after a bet Lessing had made with his friend Mendelssohn that he could write a play that would bring the audience to tears. The play exposes certain socio-political conditions arising out of issues of class and gender at a time when the middle class was on the rise. The quest for identity not only involves dealing with aspects of a generational divide, falling in love, and at least the idea of marriage between members of different classes. It also involves internalized behavior patterns and thoughts that are culturally conditioned and very difficult to overcome, even for the sake of personal freedom. Some critics have interpreted this play as being derived from Samuel Richardson's epistolary novel *Clarissa* (1748). But Lessing is following less the footsteps of Richardson than those Diderot. Carl Niekerk convincingly argues that Lessing is negotiating an approach to a "Radial Enlightenment" as defined by Jonathan Israel.[534] Lessing shares with Diderot a sharp and uncompromising social criticism and the notion that the body ultimately wins over the mind. Both authors take a materialist stance in their position that the existing problems of inequality in terms of class and gender must be addressed by concrete reforms. They are not something to be simply erased, avoided, or compensated by art.

## 1. Lessing's bet with Mendelssohn and his play

During the years following 1748 after he had moved to Berlin, Lessing had become familiar with the sentimental style of so-called *"Empfindsamkeit,"* a movement associated with the age of sensibility and new attention to sense perceptions and feelings. This style challenged logocentric reasoning and emphasized sensations and physical stimuli

534 Carl Niekerk, "Lessings Körperlichkeits-Entwürfe zwischen Richardson und Diderot," Košenina and Stockhorst, ed., *Lessing und die Sinne,* 99–121 and Jonathan I. Israel, *Radical Enlightenment. Philosophy and the Making of Modernity 1650-1750* (Oxford: Oxford University Press, 2001). Baruch de Spinoza is interpreted as a key figure for what Israel calls "Radical Enlightenment," especially because he privileges the body over the mind in his monotheistic theory of human subjectivity, something which had important critical and political implications in seventeenth century Europe. Both Diderot and Lessing take Spinoza's ideas further and contribute to a dense bundle of arguments that are in a sense anti-Kantian and question the superior role of reason. According to Niekerk Lessing tends to give in his bourgeois plays the body and the senses more of an agency than the mind, no matter how well intended and for whatever unsettling outcome. I would like to add that Lessing shares with Herder the acknowledgement of the power of the unconscious and of images that often precede articulated language. See Allert, "Herder's Mental Imprinting: Cognition and 'Gestalt' Formation" Allert, ed., *J. G. Herder* 105–119.

("Reize"). which This movement had become increasingly popular in European theater and was mainly associated with comedy.[535] It was led to performances in a style called the "comédie larmoyante" (tearful or sentimental comedy) in France and it was the rage of a new generation that had a more liberal attitude towards the expression of emotions, sexual desire, and physicality. Lessing was not against expressing emotions but he was skeptical about the separation of body and mind as suggested by Cartesian Enlightenment logic. He tried to make sense of emotions in the context of cognition processes that cannot be separated from logic. Lessing's innovation was to apply the principles of "Empfindsamkeit," careful sense perception, to plays of a different genre. He put center-stage the "Bürgerliche Trauerspiel," (bourgeois tragedy), plays set in the present dealing with issues of concern to the rising middle class. Lessing expressed in letters to his friends Mendelssohn and Nicolai that he wanted to create something new, something other than the "larmoyante" comedies of the French. He was planning a theater piece that would place less emphasis on showing "Tränen des Mitleids" (tears of pity), but would actually induce such tears in the audience.[536] His new play would evoke an entire range of human emotions.[537] It should distill empathy and compassion and make people really cry. It should indicate a process in which a person is becoming self-aware but at the same time illustrate that this self-awareness is the end-result of a challenging and difficult process. Lessing experiments with tensions between images and words and draws attention to the power of materiality. His play appears to illustrate how what we see may impact us more than what we hear. The visible and tangible of the here and now tend to be stronger than any dream or memory to be soon only vaguely remembered.

*Miß Sara Sampson* was the first in the series of sentimental plays with tragic endings. The play is a pioneering work in experimenting with the disparity between the physical and mental realms and the clashes that result. There are matters not simply to be decoded one at a time as outlined in his theoretical works; rather they depend on multiple meanings resulting from ekphrastic presentation as expressed verbally and by body language onstage. Lessing draws attention to the dimension of space, or what we see onstage. He also evokes the ominous dimension of time which exceeds visibility and holds hidden meanings in realms of simultaneous yet shifting sign systems. The immediate impetus for Lessing's writing *Miß Sara Sampson* is said to have been "eine Wette" (a wager) between Lessing and his friend Mendelssohn after they had attended together one of the French "larmoyant" plays in Berlin in May 1755. Mendelssohn,

535 See Gerhard Sauder, *Empfindsamkeit.* Vol. 1: *Voraussetzungen und Elemente;* Vol. 3: *Quellen und Dokumente* (Stuttgart: Metzler, 1974-1980–no more published) and Richard Daunicht, "Die Definitionen des Dramas und die Comédie larmoyante," *Die Enstehung der Bürgerlichen Trauerspiels* 6-18.

536 Letter to Moses Mendelssohn, Nov, 13, 1756 (FA 11/1, 122-124 at 123). Steve Martinson argues that Lessing's interest in gambling, playing games, and betting influences his writing style. Steven D. Martinson, *Projects of Enlightenment. The Work of Gotthold Ephraim Lessing: Cultural, Intercultural, and Transcultural Perspectives,* Hermeia 11 (Heidelberg: Synchron, 2013).

537 Wilfried Barner, "Zu viel Thränen - nur Keime von Thränen." Über *Miß Sara Sampson* und *Emilia Galotti* beim zeitgenössischen Publikum," Rainer Gruenter, ed., *Das weinende Saeculum,* Beiträge zur Geschichte der Literatur und Kunst des 18. Jahrhunderts 7 (Heidelberg: Winter, 1983), 89-105.

like numerous people in the audience, was in tears, being emotionally struck by the sentimental play. Lessing teased him, saying how easy it was to make old ladies cry! Mendelssohn replied that this is easier said than done. Lessing responded: "Was gilt die Wette? In sechs Wochen bringe ich Ihnen ein solches Stück!"[538] (How about this for a bet? In six weeks I'll bring you such a play!)[539] The next morning Lessing vanished for six weeks, left Berlin for an isolated location, a "Dachstube" (garret) in Potsdam.[540]

When he returned to see Mendelssohn again, he brought with him the finished play, *Miß Sara Sampson: Ein Bürgerliches Trauerspiel in fünf Aufzügen* (*Miß Sara Sampson: A Bourgeois Tragedy in Five Acts*). This is the first German larmoyant or sentimental play and with it Lessing initiated a series of similar "Bürgerliche Trauerspiele" (bourgeois plays), moving attention away from the nobility and upper class and focusing on the rising middle class and their private sphere. What was considered "inner action" consisting of feelings, emotions, and sensations, was given new importance against the backdrop of "outer action." Inner actions were discovered as actually fueling the historical or political events although they arise from the private sphere, the family and the individual person and their interacting character traits.

Lessing's play was first published in July 1755 as part six of Lessing's *Schriften*, together with his comedy *Der Misogyne.*[541] It had its stage première on July 10, 1755 in Frankfurt an der Oder, performed by the famous Ackermann troupe and it was a great success. Lessing was present for the première and must have enjoyed being a member in the audience. There was a second improved edition of the play published by Voss in 1772, but without the name of the author and without any mention of the work being either "bürgerlich" (bourgeois) or a "Trauerspiel" (tragedy). While Lessing did not invent this dramatic genre,[542] he did make it respectable, and his making the concerns of the rising bourgeoisie the center of attention in his plays has been much commented on, as have been his use of the concepts pity and fear.[543] Lessing's later

538 Lessing's Leipzig friend Ewald Christian von Kleist noted in a letter to Johann Wilhelm Ludwig Gleim dated March 2, 1755 that Lessing had spent seven weeks in Potsdam writing a play (FA 3, 1206).

539 This anecdote was recorded much later in 1792 by Friedrich Wilhelm Basilius von Ramdohr (1757-1822). See FA 3, 1204.

540 Richard Daunicht, *Lessing im Gespräch: Berichte und Urteile von Freunden und Zeitgenossen* (Munich: Fink, 1971), 82.

541 Completed in 1748. see FA 1, 303-339.

542 The earliest "bourgeois tragedy" is considered to be by Paul Landois, *Silvie, Tragédie en prose* (Paris: Chez Perrault fils, 1742).

543 See Karl Guthke, *Das deutsche bürgerliche Trauerspiel*, 6th ed. (Stuttgart: Metzler, 2006, first 1972). There has been a long and intricate scholarly discussion in response to Guthke's interpretation (see the studies listed in Fick, *Handbuch* 147) and his path-breaking study on pity and empathy in Lessing was challenged head on by Claudia Mönch in her comprehensive study based on an analysis of 242 plays, *Abschrecken oder Mitleiden. Das deutsche bürgerliche Trauerspiel im 18. Jahrhundert Versuch einer Typologie*, Studia Augustana 5 (Tübingen: Niemeyer, 1993). Mönch claims that the primary goal of this genre is not empathy as in Lessing but rather the concept of the bourgeois tragedy "wird von der Doktrin der poetischen Gerechtigkeit vorgegeben, folgt der Abschreckungsdidaktik" (350) (is prescribed by the doctrine of poetic justice, followed by the didactic of fear). Guthke responds to Mönch's position throughout the sixth edition of his *Das deutsche bürgerliche Trauerspiel* and in detail in his essay, "Rührstück oder 'Schreckspiel'? Die Rezeption des deutschen bür-

correction and deletion of the word "bourgeois" may indicate that he wanted to focus less on class struggle than, as one could well argue in the context of putting it together with *Der Misogyne,* on gender implications. Moreover there are epistemological and language-philosophical issues at the core of this play, and Lessing experiments with varying poetic strategies including going well beyond any one single poignant moment for it does not end until we have seen the outcome of a crime and a death onstage.

When *Miß Sara Sampson* first appeared, it received rave reviews. It was also severely criticized in some quarters, especially with respect to the ending with Sara dying onstage and talking to the very end. This seems to have been an Ekphrastic move which does not resolve itself harmoniously. It has the actress describe her own last thoughts in the process of dying and literally frame that pitiful image. It stunned people and broke a long-standing *taboo* in the theater. There has been much speculation over the revisions in the second edition of the play. It seems plausible that Lessing was no longer comfortable with version of the play as he had first written it. He changed his thinking about it, as well as his approach to rhetoric. It still seems an odd and rather verbose play. Even so, Lessing was not interested in undertaking major revisions and kept the play mainly as it was, including the horribly slow and gruesome death of Sara. She keeps talking and interacting, even though she is in agony. The poison she swallowed runs through every vein in her body.

## 2. Approaches to pity and compassion

Lessing distinguishes various approaches to pity that can range from sympathy to compassion as documented in a letter to Christoph Friedrich Nicolai of November 29, 1756. This notion changes, Lessing comments, since it is not necessarily associated with anger or fear. It can be, however also result from being faced with violence or shock.[544] The first degree of pity he calls "Rührung" (being touched emotionally). It can also be associated with "Beklemmung," a sense of being saddened, melancholic, or depressed. It can, given certain further conditions, produce tears. Lessing explains that such a corresponding feeling one may get when, for example, seeing a beggar, or when becoming not only aware of this person but also familiar with the disaster and misery that has struck the poor fellow. The more elaborate the circumstances, the more unbearable the emotion with the result perhaps of more tears. He shows how

gerlichen Trauerspiels im achtzehnten Jahrhundert," *Jahrbuch des Freien Deutschen Hochstifts* (2008): 1-80. See also Peter Szondi, *Die Theorie des bürgerlichen Trauerspiels* (Frankfurt am Main: Suhrkamp, 1973).

544 FA 11/1. 134-136. All quotations of this text are from this version but the letter was first published in which was published in 1789 in the *Gelehrter Briefwechsel zwischen Johann Jacob Reiske. Moses Mendelssohn, und Gotthold Ephraim Lessing* (FA 3. 683-686). For helpful commentaries see Robert Petsch, ed. *Lessings Briefwechsel mit Mendelssohn und Nicolai über das Trauerspiel. Nebst verwandten Schriften Nicolais und Mendelssohn* (Darmstadt: Wissenschaftliche Buchgesellschaft, 1967).

emotions can be mixed. Laughter and tears may no longer be adequate sometimes and the body language is almost at a loss when sensations are complicated.[545]

Lessing explains in this letter that tears are provoked only if one gets familiar to a certain degree with the individual's good qualities and the nature of their misfortune ("*Tränen* erweckt er nur dann in mir, wenn er mich mit seinen guten Eigenschaften so wohl, als mit seinen Unfällen bekannter macht") (Tears are evoked in me only if he makes me more familiar with his good qualities, as well as his mishaps). Moral judgments cannot be ignored when cognitively processing perceptions. Emotions are dependent on what we see and know.[546] Lessing adds that tears can only flow when both of these criteria were met simultaneously "und zwar mit beiden *zugleich*." As long as we as spectators like the person, we can sympathize with the individual or sometimes even be induced to cry. But this is only one side of the coin. If we were to see this person in a rage, then our sympathy would cease. If someone kills his wife, his children, and himself, the spectators' tears stop flowing. Actions matter more than words. "Weinen Sie noch?–Hier erstickt der Schmerz die Tränen, aber nicht das Mitleid, wie es die Berwundrung tut. Es ist–" (Do you still cry?–Here the pain suffocates the tears, but not the pity, as admiration would do. It is–). But even if we still have pity, it is no longer just emotional, but requires critical thought to sustain it. Lessing ends his comment here without completing his thought. The dash indicates a gap, a moment of silence. It stands for pain, for intensity of emotion, for something not to be captured in words. He adds: "Ich verzweifelter Schwätzer! Nicht ein Wort mehr." (Me, such a despairing gossiper! Not one word more). Silence in this context indicates the power of the factual, something which freezes out and cancels wordiness and any auctorial voice.[547]

Whereas tears in these comments of Lessing to Nicolai still have positive and liberating connotations, their abrupt ending has to do with the impact of violence and the limits of language. *Miß Sara Samson* is such a play exploring the boundaries of what is presentable and explicable. It investigates how images and words can be correlated given certain extreme constellations of conflicting emotions and the effect of shock. Lessing realized that an overabundance of words is sometimes the unintended consequence of attempting to display emotions onstage. It might be better to let the events themselves take over, that is, to cut words to a minimum and frame the action into a powerful montage of images. Some critics were puzzled by the fact that during the performance the audience was frequently in tears, yet at the end of the play there

545 See Bernhard Greiner, *Streitkultur des Als Ob: Die Komödie als transzendentale Bedingung des Streitens in* Minna von Barnhelm (Tübingen: Niemeyer, 1983).

546 In fact this distinction in eighteenth century discourse and related tensions is at the core of the reading of this play in Peter Michelsen, *Der unruhige Bürger. Studien zu Lessing und zur Literatur des 18. Jahrhunderts* (Würzburg: Königshausen & Neumann, 1990), esp. 107-136.

547 Silence results in this context from the tears. On tears and crying in eighteenth century literary works, see Wilfried Barner, "'Zu viel Thränen-nur Keime von Thränen.' Über Miß Sara Sampson und Emilia Galotti beim zeitgenössischen Publikum." On tears in literature and art, see Rainer Gruenter, ed., *Das weinende Saeculum* (Heidelberg: Winter, 1993) and on modes of representation and communication about and with tears in literary texts across the centuries see Beate Söntgen, and Geraldine Spiekermann, ed., *Tränen* (Munich: Fink, 2008).

were no tears at all. The audience was stunned instead, as if hypnotized, having the feeling they had been turned into statues.[548] August Wilhelm Iffland described his experience after having seen *Miß Sara Sampson* as follows:

> Ich bin in Tränen zerflossen während dieser Vorstellung. Das Gute, das Edle wurde so warm und herzlich gegeben - die Tugend erschien so ehrwürdig! Die Leiden der Menschen kannte ich bis daher nur durch Hübners biblischen Geschichten oder von armen Leuten, welche Almosen empfingen: von einer solchen Leidensgeschichte, von einer solchen Sprache hatte ich keinen Begriff
>
> [I melted in tears during this performance. The good, the noble was given so warmly and from the heart - virtue appeared so worthy of honor! The human sufferings I knew until then only through Hübner's Biblical stories or from poor people, who collected alms. I had no notion until then of such an account of suffering, of such a language].

Lessing clearly won his bet with Mendelssohn. The question for Lessing the playwright had been how to write such a play that would cause strong visibly obvious emotional impact. Lessing wanted to test the boundaries of the visual and the verbal and their intricate dynamic relation onstage. He wanted to find such a "language" that does not only produce thoughts but that is capable of turning audiences into spectators, metaphorically speaking at least, into catharsis, so that they can experience important aspects of life and be moved by theater and art.

In the revised version of the play the language is interspersed with more gaps and pauses of the speech. In Section XIV of his *Hamburgische Dramaturgie* Lessing defends his play. He argues that the characters have flaws that are necessary and fully intended. He compares his play with one by Voltaire and cites Voltaire's defense of his play *L'Enfant prodigue* (1736) against the criticism of a friend: "Man kann nicht immer alles ausführen, was uns unsere Freunde raten. Es giebt auch notwendige Fehler. Einem Bucklichten, den man von seinem Buckel heilen wollte, müßte man das Leben nehmen. Mein Kind ist bucklicht; aber es befindet sich sonst ganz gut."[549] (One cannot always proceed as our friends tell us to do. There are also necessary incongruences. One has to deprive a hunchback of life if one wants to cure them of their hump. My child is a hunchback, but is, nevertheless, perfectly alright). Lessing defends the exposure of disability in this play, his illustration of uncomfortable communications and the limits of verbal sign systems in the given culture. His characters are odd or disabled because the playwright wanted them to be that way for important reasons. What may be mistaken as their s0-called flaws (the hump) is exactly what may define their most important character strength. Lessing stands up for Sara who may have been "handicapped" in one way or another but yet deserves our sympathy even more so. Lessing wants us to have compassion with his characters even if or because they appear odd. He demands sympathy for his characters rather than what most critics

---

548 The poet Karl Wilhelm Ramler in a letter to Ludwig Gleim, July 25, 1755 reported: "Herr Leßing hat seine Tragödie in Frankfurt spielen sehen und die Zuschauer haben drey und eine halbe Stunde zugehört, stille gesessen wie Statuen und geweint" (Mr. Lessing saw his tragedy play in Frankfurt and the spectators listened to it for three and a half hours, sat as statues, and wept). FA 3, 1221.

549 *Hamburgische Dramaturgie* XIV (FA 6, 252). Voltaire's "friend" was the art collector François Berger (1684-1747).

tend to do, that is to categorize, dismiss, idolize, or stereotype them. He warns against judging them by physical appearance and instead draws our attention to the correlations between what we see and hear, the visual and the verbal, sense perceptions and ethical features.

*Miß Sara Sampson* draws its inspiration from the work of the English novelist Samuel Richardson, the playwright George Lillo, a sentimental play by Edward Moore, Louis-Sébastien Mercier, and the political drama of Johann Jakob Bodmer.[550] Also Voltaire and Rousseau had written *larmes,* plays making people cry. But there are important differences. Lessing made allusions to the conventions of these writers, as well as to those of Classical tragedy yet he established a new genre situated in between.[551] All of Lessing's early plays written before 1750 had imitated the fashions of his time and were in line with the principles of Johann Christoph Gottsched who had the say in Germany concerning all matters of the theater. But Lessing's retreat into seclusion in 1755 to write *Miß Sara Sampson* signaled a departure from the dictates of Gottsched and his own earlier style and is decisive for Lessing's development as an original playwright.

Lessing distanced himself from Gottsched and that of the mainstream French tradition of the "comédie larmoyante" by incorporating new ideas and influences from England, the country of Shakespeare.[552] Considering aspects of gender and sexuality, Carl Niekerk finds that although Lessing's *Miß Sara Sampson* (1755) was influenced by Richardson's novel to some extent as already documented in scholarship, in this play he is closer to Diderot's *La Religieuse.*[553] It is noteworthy that Sara articulates her own sensuality when she says:

> Es sei Liebe oder Verführung, es sei Glück oder Unglück, das mich ihnen in die Arme geworfen hat; ich bin in meinem Herzen die Ihrige, und werde es ewig sein. Aber noch bin ich es nicht vor den Augen jenes Richters.[554]
>
> [Be it love or seduction, be it happiness or misfortune that have thrown me into your arms; I am in my heart yours, and will forever be that. But yet I am not so in front of the eyes of that judge].

Although we may find ambivalence and an internalized voice of her father in her words, she expresses her own feelings and stands up for them freely, no matter what the consequences may be. The fact that they are fatal could make this play appear at first glance as a strange exotic camel, rather than a locally well-known donkey. Lessing felt that this play perfectly suited his approach as he entered into the new and uncharted territory of the bourgeois tragedy and we may find that the female

550 Gisbert Ter-Nedden, *Lessings Trauerspiele: Der Ursprung des modernen Dramas aus dem Geist der Kritik,* Germanistische Abhandlungen 57 (Stuttgart: Metzler, 1986), 1.

551 Peter Pütz, *Die Leistung der Form: Lessings Dramen* (Frankfurt am Main: Suhrkamp, 1986), 118.

552 In his 17th *Literaturbrief* of February 16, 1759 Lessing distanced himself explicitly from Gottsched and a certain French tradition that continued to be prevalent in Germany (FA 4, 499–501).

553 Carl Niekerk, "Lessings Körperlichkeits-Entwürfe" 103.

554 FA 3, 442.

characters are not short of courage. Lessing set the stage for many plays to follow and his influence continues down to the present.[555]

## 3. Lessing's play *Miß Sara Sampson* reviewed

The plot of the play seems simple. Sara gets killed for having made a wrong decision that sets her inner conflict in motion as she gets stuck between Mellefont, her lover (and his past), and her father (and his renewed presence). By running away with her lover she had flouted the moral conventions of the time. Instead of the expected punishment and scolding for her transgression, she is put off kilter by her father's amazing forgiving and his understanding response. She has difficulty in comprehending this behavior instead of accepting it in her favor.[556] For example, a psychoanalytical reading could suggest that Sara had internalized her father's position and expected his disapproval of her new relationship as if he was her alter ego.[557] Theological readings have associated her father's forgiveness with something she cannot accept because of her own stubbornness. Despite her move to pursue the love interest with Mellefont she is tied up with exaggerated obedience to some imaginary ideal and ultimately unable to change. She is confused when her own projected image of herself and the image she has of her father, the firm judge, who now strangely accepts her as she is, do not match. His unexpected forgiveness and his offer for reconciliation with her find her dumbfounded and confused. She also becomes conflicted when she becomes aware of a rival in her own new life, her lover's previous mistress Marwood. She appears in disguise as Lady Solmes but does not get recognized by Sara for a long time into the action which will then have its own uncontrollable dynamics. Marwood was introduced to Sara as a distant relative of Mellefont and as it turns out has a daughter. She did not come initially for revenge but becomes the decisive protagonist in this plot.

It has been much debated whether or not Marwood is the sole driving force determining the action of the play, or whether it is ultimately an inner drama with multiple agents. Even Sara's own mistakes may end up killing her.[558] Must she die as

555 Hans-Peter Bayerdörfer, "Markante Signale: Zur Bühnengeschichte von Lessings Dramen seit 2000." *Lessing Yearbook* 37 (2006/2007): 67-78.

556 For a theological interpretation of this, see Leonard P. Wessell, *G. E. Lessing's Theology. A Reinterpretation. A Study in the Problematic Nature of the Enlightenment* (The Hague: Mouton, 1977), 220-233.

557 Among the psychoanalytic readings, see Peter Horst Neumann, *Der Preis der Mündigkeit. Über Lessings Dramen. Anhang: Über Fanny Hill* (Stuttgart: Klett Cotta, 1977).

558 Karl Eibl, *Gotthold Ephraim Lessing: Miss Sara Sampson–Ein bürgerliches Trauerspiel,* Commentatio 2 (Frankfurt am Main: Athenäum, 1971), 156, suggests that Sara's telling Marwood of her dream in 1.7 suggests to the latter the means of getting rid of her rival. "Hätte Lessing deutlicher als gerade durch den Verweis auf den Traum zeigen können, daß Saras Tod einer Kausalität folgt die nicht zum 'realen' Nexus allein gehört? Sara veranlaßt Marwood durch ihre Worte dazu, ein Urteil zu vollstrecken, das bereits am Anfang gesprochen ist" (Could Lessing have shown more clearly than through the reference to this dream that Sara's death results from a causality that does not alone belong to the 'reality' Nexus? Sara through her words makes Marwood execute a judgment which is articulated right at the

a result of the poison placed in her drink by Marwood, her jealous rival, or could Sara have prevented this?[559] Had Sara not ignored her dream warning her of events to come and if she had not been talking about her private dream in public, mindless of whom she was talking to, perhaps everything would have turned out much differently or could have been resolved in peace. The play ends violently and presents a victory of stark images over words. Moreover, in my reading it demonstrates that wordiness is harmful and inefficient. Lessing seems to show that spoken words are easier to forget that what we see or read. Just at the moment when Sara had said too much, a letter that arrives from Marwood makes Mellefont turn around in his own choice between the women. He remembers the past and is less interested in the present. The play reflects not only on personal destinies or character traits but also on complicated roles in society.[560] Moreover the play draws attention to the visual over the verbal. Images and written words seem to be more powerful than words spoken all too abundantly. Marwood seems to win over Sara after all.

Although we know that some of the emotional responses to the early staging of the play are culture-specific and that it would be very unlikely that a performance today would elicit such a response, it is worthwhile to study how emotions and rhetoric are inter-connected. What rhetorical and visual strategies did Lessing use in his play and through his stage directions in order to have such an effect? How is Lessing's approach related to his drama theory? What consequences can we draw from the implications of these early performances? Lessing explores to what extent the visual can be expressed by the verbal and investigates what the potentials and shortcomings of language are. He also experiments with imaging and with reading bodily expressions. How should the agonizing death-throes of a character be presented onstage to an audience? How to present action visually when the visual is a medium rather of

---

beginning). I am not convinced of this reading but agree that Sara's fear contributes to her own death. She had intuition in her dream that she was going to be pushed into an abyss but could not process these sensations adequately or respond effectively. In other words, she did not take her senses and her dream seriously enough. She did not trust them sufficiently to understand their hidden message and possible consequences if she did not withdraw from both Marwood and Mellefont. Another interesting reading of this scene has been offered by Ter-Nedden: "Meine Gegen-These lautet: der Traum wie das, was er antizipiert, also der Mord, folgt aus einer ganz natürlichen Interaktions- und Psycho-Logik; und eben diese Verwandlung des Mirakulösen ins Natürliche ist die Lessing am Motif des Orakels reizt" (My counter-thesis is this: the dream as much as what it anticipates, namely the murder, follows from a completely natural interaction and psycho-logic; and it is this metamorphosis of the miraculous into the natural that Lessing finds attractive in dealing with the oracle motif) (*Lessings Trauerspiele* 45).

559 According to Ter-Nedden, Lessing takes the paradoxical notion of a "mörderische Retterin" (murderous rescuer) (Act IV, scene viii) from one of the Medea epigrams in the *Anthologia Graeca* (*Lessings Trauerspiele* 45). See also Isabelle Wenzlaff-Mauderer, *Wenn statt des Mundes Augen reden. Sprachlosigkeit und nonverbale Kommunikation in* Miss Sara Sampson *(1755),* Düvall und Charmille *(1788),* Kabale und Liebe *(1784) und* Penthesilea *(1808)* (Munich: Iudicium, 2001).

560 See Inge Stephan, "So ist die Tugend ein Gespenst: Frauenbild und Tugendbegriff im bürgerlichen Trauerspiel," *Lessing Yearbook* 17 (1985): 1-20; Reprinted in Peter Freimark, Franklin Kopitzsch, and Helga Slessarev, ed., *Lessing und die Toleranz, Sonderband zum Lessing Yearbook* (Detroit: Wayne State University Press, 1986), 357-374.

space but not of time? Lessing is innovative in the way he seems to suggest through his script facial expressions, body language and gestures onstage, not only to complement the emotions that correspond with the written text of the play or the words that accompany the action, but also in order for the visual to precede the verbal. In the fourth and fifth acts especially we can find responses by characters anticipating later actions in the play.

Although Lessing's later plays were considered successful in terms of sparking intellectual debates and initiating more elaborate written reviews, one could well argue that *Miß Sara Sampson* was Lessing's most influential and powerful dramatic work, affecting those people who viewed it with the most surprising and sensational reactions.[561] It suggests that Lessing was a very perceptive playwright capable of invoking the most emotional and sympathetic response from an audience. Part of his success is a direct result of his innovative correlation of visual and verbal communication. The words and gestures of his characters draw attention to visible signs that cannot be captured completely or paralleled by verbal ones. Body moves, facial expressions, looks, and gestures gain importance of their own.[562] They are signs that are contextualized from both sides of the ekphrastic spectrum: the visual and the verbal. Furthermore, this play draws attention to notions of acting in real life while blurring the boundaries between staged and real events. It heightens the dramatic effect by drawing people into the action. Apparently Lessing questions the "natural signs" of the visual by showing that all language, including body language is performed. Decoding is required in each context and it is the task of everyone in the audience to pay attention to such context-specific nuances of meaning with attention to minute details.

Lessing uses new dramatic strategies to show, not only to tell, what really matters in the play. He makes an analogy between the performance and the sculpting of plastic art and links drama with visuality in such a way that the spectators become aware on one hand of acting as a daily human activity, not something just confined to the stage. On the other hand he attempts to emancipate the audience by giving them the same right as sculptors would have in using the material provided for the best possible outcomes. The audiences become spectators and also participate in the production of meaning of what they see. In addition, as any close reading reveals, *Miß Sara Sampson* can be understood as offering multiple possible endings and thus offers a variety of perspectives that each makes sense. Together they appear to be incompatible or cancelling out each other. I would like to argue that the play projects

561 And yet in 1758, the Altona gymnasium director, Johann Jakob Dusch (1725-1787), criticized *Miß Sara Sampson* in the following terms: "Ich wollte ihnen also zeigen, daß die Handlung kaltsinnig, langsam, ohne Bewegung gerade fortgeht" (I thus wished to show you that the action moves straight ahead coldly, slowly, without any movement ). These comments appear in two letters published by Dusch, *Vermischte, kritische und Satyrische Schriften nebst einigen Oden auf gegenwärtige Zeiten* (Altona: David Iversen, 1758), 46-100. Reprinted in Eibl, ed., *Miß Sara Sampson*, 217-242 at 229. A little earlier on the same page, Dusch had called the action "kalt, eiskalt" (cold, ice-cold). See also a similar sentiment, 230. Lessing rejects this harsh criticism by Dusch in his *Literaturbriefe*, especially numbers 41 (May 24-June 14, 1759) and 77 (Jan. 3, 1760) (FA 4, 561-81, 683-697).

562 Lessing contributes in this way to a new semiotics of *eloquentia corporis* in the context of 18th century discourses. See Košenina,"Die anthropologische Neubegründung," *Anthropologie und Schauspielkunst* 95-105.

three possible endings and that the final one is almost arbitrarily the one which comes last. The actual last scene of the play that presents Sara's death under very specific and drawn-out circumstances is therefore not necessarily the only consequence of the previous actions. It baffled audiences to such a degree that people were not able to get up and leave. The spectators remained sitting in the theater, caught, speechless and puzzled. Lessing wrote the play in "reimfreier Jambus" (rhyme-less prose), departing from the traditional Alexandrine verse scheme that was considered appropriate for serious drama. While still conforming to the reigning Aristotelian norms of the unities of time and space, Lessing created a fresh approach to theater and made "Mitleid" (compassion) the driving force. By stirring empathy in the audience and leaving enough spaces for the imagination, this play allowed the audience to project emotions, to emphasize. The play was in tune with a certain cultural-specific mood of the time. Whereas Lessing had a spark of irony, as his "Wette" (bet, wager) suggests, he was able to strike a chord with the public, which deserves to be linked with Lessing's theorizing about Ekphrasis.

## 4. Lessing's probing visual and verbal boundaries

Lessing's works experiment the boundaries between the visual and the verbal. Lessing seems to probe the notion of a transfer from one medium to another. It is not only an application of whatever philosophical, theological, or other preconceived ideas Lessing may have had at the time when he wrote this play; it is rather a test case in an attempt to capture the ambivalent and subtle emotions in the context of rather different sign systems. Whereas Marwood represents seeing and presence (the body), Sara represents words and ideas (the mind), albeit not at the best measure. Lessing's play illustrates how language not only mimetically reflects what is out there physically or what is also visible in space. He makes us reflect on how language can destabilize what is "real." Characters in the play are bodies that move; make gestures, and articulate verbal signs. They speak and interact in such a way that what they express can have multiple meanings or reflect on the use of language interactively, depending on the specific recipient in the context. One interesting scene is in act two, scene three when Marwood exclaims not only to Mellefont but to all members in the audience: "So wie ich jetzt bin, bin ich ihr Geschöpf, tun Sie also, was einem Schöpfer zukommt; er darf die Hand von seinem Werke nicht eher abziehn, als bis er es gänzlich vernichten will" (So as I am now I am at the same time your creation; therefore go ahead and do what is needed for any creator to do. Do not withdraw your hand until you want to completely destroy your creation).[563] She is enraged about being used as a plaything and a projection of Mellefont's fantasies.

Here she already resembles a living statue. Her own suggestion that any creator would destroy what he has created in the end is provocative, as if it did not matter at all what the statue really was. It seems counter-intuitive to make the audience think of destruction in the same vein as creation. While it draws us, almost as if we were

563 FA 3, 456.

sculptors, into the process of this dramatic performance, in such a way that we are not only mere spectators but taking an active part in the action onstage, we are told already that the artwork is transient and what we do with it matters. She makes us to a large extent responsible for what we think we are seeing and what will happen onstage. While she predicts that we shall probably destroy her, the implicit plea is to let her go, to set her free.

As seems most plausible to her former lover Mellefont who is apparently no longer interested in her, we can still "save" her for future action and thus empower her to develop an agency of her own. The words that are being expressed, such as Marwood requesting Mellefont to withdraw his hand, are actually displaced. He already has withdrawn from her completely. It is she who cannot let go of their relationship. She expresses the opposite of what appears to be actually intended, namely her own plan to take the action from now on into her own hands. In the context of this play this means for Sara to welcome her death freely and for Marwood to plot revenge. She will, as the end of the play suggests, not be molded by others, but will turn out to be the driving force, trying to create her own destiny while challenging those around her. She blames those who have immobilized her and turned her into an arrested "statue."

Already the beginning in the first scene extends the action via teichoscopy or "Mauerschau." We are told what happened and see it only through the narrative of the characters onstage. We are seeing the room of an inn: Sir William Sampson, Sara Sampson's father, enters. Waitwell, his old servant, is talking about what has happened Sara: "das beste, schönste, unschuldigste Kind, das unter der Sonne gelebt hat [...] verführt" (the best, most beautiful and most innocent child that ever lived under the sun [...] seduced).[564] Sir William asks Waitwell not to talk about it since, as he points out; words bring him even more pain than silence: "O schweig! Zerfleischt nicht das Gegenwärtige mein Herz schon genug? Willst du die Martern durch die Erinnerung an vergangene Glückseligkeit noch höllischer machen?" (O silence! Doesn't the present already tear up my heart enough? Do you want to make the torture even more hellish through the memory of past happiness?).[565] Since silencing Waitwell does not work, Sir William requests that Waitwell must change, as he put it, "deine Sprache" (your language), since otherwise he would not listen at all:

> Ändre deine Sprache, wenn du mir einen Dienst tun willst. Tadle mich; mache mir aus meiner Zärtlichkeit ein Verbrechen; vergrößre das Verbrechen meiner Tochter, erfülle mich, wenn du kannst, mit Abscheu gegen sie; entflamme aufs neue meine Rache gegen ihren verfluchten Verführer; sage daß Sara nie tugendhaft gewesen, weil sie es so leicht aufgehört zu sein; sage, daß sie mich nie geliebt, weil sie mich heimlich verlassen.[566]
>
> [Change your language if you want to do me a favor. Don't scold me; make me because of my tenderness a criminal; magnify the transgression of my daughter; fill me, if you can, with horror against her; enflame again my revenge against her damned seducer; tell me that Sara never really was virtuous because she so simply stopped being so; say that she never loved me because she secretly left me].

564 FA 3, 433.
565 FA 3, 433
566 FA 3, 433-434.

Sir William requests that in order to calm his emotions and to spare him from additional pain after what already happened, one must, if silence is not possible, at least talk about the so-called "Verbrechen" (crime) of his daughter (ignoring her father's will by loving a man who then became her seducer) only in terms of an exaggeration. Silence, distortion, or exaggeration are what the old man suggests in order to deal with losing his daughter or questioning her virtue, what at first seems to be the same to him. He is afraid to believe that it was her own fault that she was seduced and this he wants to hear Waitwell tell him. Words of blame and admonition, anger and disappointment must override his fatherly love for Sara. We are reminded of the New Testament father who willingly welcomed back his prodigal son.[567] Sir Samson apparently wants to resist his initial conciliatory emotions by requesting that Waitwell magnify in his words whatever may be Sara's misbehavior. Her mistakes should be blown up into huge proportions in an unforgiving language in order to soothe his pain and turn pity into anger. Words should cancel out the emotion of missing his daughter and his inclination to remain connected and friendly to her. Sir William finds it too hard, against the norm of expected behavior, to remain attached to his daughter whom he may still love but whom he now intends to scorn and reject. Words should silence and absorb his feelings which he wants to forget.

This ambivalence of his emotions is so unbearable that he attempts to distance himself further from it by giving stage directions to Waitwell: Sir William wants to become the angry father as he thinks he should be. His own reflection on the role he is playing draws the spectators immediately into the production of meaning, to engage the ability of words to change feelings, and the correlation of thinking, mental dispositions, and words. Whereas Sir William is at first free of anger, his role becomes so destabilized that he masquerades as another persona. Waitwell can no longer really talk with him in his "normal" manner and must change the tone of his language from one pitch to another, so that his master can better distance himself from his own sympathy towards Sara and really get angry.

Waitwell, on the other hand, does not obey his master. Instead of reproaching Sara and articulating her obvious character flaws, he responds honestly: "Sagte ich das, so würde ich eine Lüge sagen, eine unverschämte, böse Lüge" (If I were to say as you demand, then I would tell you a lie, an infamous wicked lie).[568] He simply cannot speak up against Sara in order to inflame her father's anger. Sir William gives in, saying that he would rather be loved by an unvirtuous daughter than by none at all ("Ich würde doch lieber von einer lasterhaften Tochter, als von keiner, geliebt werden"). Then Sir Sampson shifts responsibility for what has happened to someone else instead, namely the "Wirt" (innkeeper) who has apparently housed everyone without discrimination, Sara and her suitor Mellefont included. The innkeeper appears in the next scene and says that he wants very little to do with Sara's father and his obnoxious demands, similarly rejecting any involvement or responsibility on his part for whatever has happened or for whatever guests in his house may or may not do. He is not interested in the secrets of his clients or any gossip. "Sie würden mein Haus in einen üblen Ruf bringen, und gewisse Leute würden sich scheuen, bei mir abzutreten. Unser

567 Luke 15: 1–30.
568 FA 3, 434.

einer muss von allen Sorten Menschen leben" (You would give my establishment a bad reputation and certain people would be reluctant to come here. Someone like me must live from all sorts of people).[569]

The innkeeper's approach is one of tolerance and respect for everyone's private sphere (as well as his self-interest in protecting his business). He cannot and does not want to control people who stay in his inn, not even when requested to do so by Sir William Sampson. He acts not as a moral guardian but, as he admits, rationally. He has people stay in his inn regardless of whom they are or who they may be in the eyes of others. He is not interested in the alleged seduction of Sara Sampson either. His assertive response seems to humble Sir William. The innkeeper then notices this silence and makes a comment saying that now he realizes that there must be a certain emotional bond among the various parties of his current house guests. He then allows Sara's father to follow him. The audience is in part excluded from dialogues which apparently follow. It is a scene illustrating moments of compassion without being wordy about it, almost exemplary.

The third scene shows apparently Sara's seducer Mellefont in dialogue with his servant Norton commending him on his "Schweigen" (silence). Mellefont makes a confession saying that in the past he was more often seduced than wanting to seduce others. He presents himself as harmless and human, even vulnerable, appearing not at all as the libertine others will soon make him out to be. This discrepancy between inner and outer perspectives seems to be typical in this play. For example, Mellefont says that he regrets his previous behavior and the actions of his past and is ready to enter a new engagement with great energy and hopes for the future. The audience thinks of Sara. He adds: "Ich hatte noch keine Unschuld in ein unabsehliches Unglück gestürzt. Ich hatte noch keine Sara aus dem Hause eines geliebten Vaters entwendet und sie gezwungen einem Nichtswürdigen zu folgen, der auf keine Weise mehr sein eigen war" (I would not have brought an immense disaster upon any innocent person. I would not have taken any Sara from the house of her beloved father and forced her to follow someone good for nothing no longer in control of himself).[570] It is at this point that Mellefont is very close to what appears to be an honest and self-critical reflection. He could, given his introspection and honesty for a moment, become a worthy partner and deserving future husband for Sara. This cheerful notion seems to point to a happy ending, and everything appears to be arranged. But there is, of course, a twist of events.

His words entail only a momentary vision, a moment of thinking how to make peace with Sara and how to distract attention from his past. He must feel compassion both for Sara and her father and obviously cares. He says that he did not want to hurt any of them. For a split moment he may even think he is ready for commitment and marriage. The audience soon finds out however, that this moment was a matter of illusion, empty words, or a missed opportunity. As soon as other elements come into the picture and more people enter the room, Mellefont switches off this reflective stance and begins to play a completely different role. He appears to be increasingly losing control over his feelings, including his deepening estrangement from Sara and

569 FA 3, 435.
570 FA 3, 437.

her father, and becoming disconnected from his previous statements for the sake of a new, self-assertive persona. He has, as becomes clear, other business to deal with.

In scenes four to nine of the first act, Mellefont is visited by Betty, Sara's maid, who reports how bad the night had been for her lady. In a state of tears she was sorely lamenting her situation. Apparently she has been torturing herself all night with doubts, longing, and desire to make peace, to love, and to be loved. On the one hand, she wants to unite with Mellefont, the man whom she loves and apparently is engaged to. On the other hand she wants to be reconciled with her father whom she misses dearly and regrets having ignored him for some time. She knows that these two desires are hardly compatible but hangs on to her wish to have them all magically reconciled. But the notion of powerful happy dreams is immediately undermined as Betty reports a dream Sara had during the night and in doing so, she also describes what Sara looked like when she reported it. In the middle of the night, Sara burst into Betty's room full of fear: "Plötzlich fuhr sie in die Höhe, sprang auf und fiel mir als eine Unglueckliche in die Arme, die von einem Mörder verfolgt wird" (Suddenly she leaped into the air, ran towards me and fell into my arms, as someone unhappy running away from a murderer).[571] Sara was shaking in cold sweat; her face had turned pale, and all of Betty's efforts to calm her failed. Finally in the morning, "nur mit stillen Tränen" (only with silent tears) did Sara request to see Mellefont. After Betty's report Mellefont tells Betty that he will go see her, yet only to learn that Sara is already on her way to his room. Betty's vivid narration has an alarming effect. It certainly does make Sara's arrival onstage less attractive. Her dream as just narrated prefigures the entire plot of the play. Sara and Mellefont are no longer in harmony.

While Norton exclaims: "Gott, die arme Miß!" (God, the poor Miss!), Mellefont resists responding sentimentally: "Wessen Gefühl willst du durch deine Ausrufung rege machen?" (Whose emotions do you want to mobilize with your exclamation?), adding, perhaps cynically: "Sieh jetzt wird die erste Träne, die ich seit meiner Kindheit geweinet, die Wange herunterlaufen!" (See there the first tear since I have ever cried since my childhood runs down my cheek!).[572] He reflects on his situation as if from the outside and as if he is only marginally concerned. He seems to realize that the situation has turned out to be complicated. Mellefont tries to control himself by saying: "Eine schlechte Vorbereitung, eine trostsuchende Betrübte zu empfangen" (A poor preparation for receiving someone who wants to be consoled). He asks Norton for advice on how to act now, while anticipating the possible scene he wants to avoid: "Nun wird sie kommen und wird unwiderstehliche Tränen weinen. Verwirrt, beschämt, werde ich vor ihr stehen. Rate mir doch, was soll ich tun? was soll ich sagen?" (Now she will come and cry irresistible tears. Confused, humbled I shall stand in front of her. Advise me then, what I should do? What I should say?)[573] Norton wants to see peace and reconciliation and tells Mellefont to do whatever Sara wants him to do. Mellefont get cynical and plots "kleine Grausamkeiten" (small cruelties) but does not overlook the scheme of his agents. He will try to postpone the wedding day, find excuses to withdraw. He acts according to his own dictum in his role as a cool,

571 FA 3, 438.
572 FA 3, 438.
573 FA 3, 439.

calculating chauvinist. He has no regrets having seduced Sara and says he is ready to drop the affair.

The Act ends with Sara's verbose, overly wordy commenting of her private emotions. Mellefont simply ignores what she says. Her attempt to persuade Mellefont to return to her and to fix the date for their wedding becomes in this context ridiculous and absurd. This twist of events may illustrate that images are stronger than words and what we see counts more than what we hear at this point in the play. Without any critical self-reflection she continues her speech revealing her heart. In a last resort, Sara begins narrating her dream. The nightmare Betty had already mentioned, its redundancy, must not only bore the audience now but Mellefont too. She is exhibiting herself and her language tries to evoke pity in vain. Her words take on a momentum of their own. Their rhythmic cadences and descriptiveness exemplify what Lessing scolded in his Laokoon essay as "Schilderungssucht", or a mania to describe everything. Sara's eloquence has no effect on Mellefont. He is more drawn to seeing Marwood than to listening to Sara. It was Marwood's looks that seduced him in the first place and a certain image of her still holds him captive.

Some critics have praised Lessing for giving abandoned women such a powerful voice onstage, others have scolded him for letting this abandoning happen. I am more inclined to say that he highlights communicative mistakes in this context. He challenges simplistic notions of Ekphrasis that would assume that translating the visual into the verbal comes without loss. Lessing raises attention to the power of images over words. This may not always be a good thing as illustrated here.[574] Sara's dream contained, as she recalls her memory of it in her dialogue with Mellefont,

574 Beate Sturges, *Lessing als Wegbereiter der Emanzipation der Frau,* The Enlightenment: German and Interdisciplinary Studies 1 (New York: Peter Lang, 1989) writes: "Mit Sara Sampson ist es Lessing gelungen, eine entschlossenere weibliche Gestalt dem Publikum vorzustellen. Sara ist die erste Heldin Lessings, die sich von einem Mann verführen läßt, mit ihm 'in Sünde' lebt und tapfer genug ist, sich über die öffentliche Meinung hinwegzusetzen. Sie bekennt sich freimütig zu ihrer 'unglücklichen Leidenschaft'" (133) (With Sara Sampson Lessing succeeded to introduce to his public a more decisive female character. Sara is Lessing's first heroine who lets herself be seduced by a man, lives with him 'in sin, and is brave enough to ignore public opinion. She admits liberally to her unhappy passion'"). Sara is nevertheless an example of blindness and error. Such a reading would pursue a line of thinking already suggested by Otto Mann in his book *Lessing. Sein und Leistung*, 2nd ed. (Berlin: de Gruyter, 1961), 233-234. He interprets the play as "eine aus der Antike geschöpfte große Tragödie" (a tragedy extracted from antiquity) and writes: "Der große tragische Grundmangel des Menschen ist eine Blindheit. [...] Mellefont ist schon blind, wenn er die gesetzlosen Beziehungen aufnimmt zu der Witwe Marwood. Hätte er sehen können, so hätte er schon hier die letzte Konsequenz sehen müssen, den Tod der Sara. Der alte Sampson ist unwissend, wenn er diesen Mann in sein Haus einführt; Sara täuscht sich, wenn sie glaubt, diesem Mann vertrauen zu können." (The great deficiency of the human is his or her tragic condition of a basic blindness. [...] Mellefont is already blind when he enters the lawless relations with the widow Marwood. If he were able to see then he would have already also seen the last consequence, the death of Sara. The old Sampson is ignorant when he has this man enter his house. Sara makes an error when she believes still to be able to trust this man). I think that Sara is particularly oblivious when she ignores the content of her dream. She talks about it without gaining any self-awareness that would have rescued her from her own blindness her. See also Ann Schmiesing, "Remembering and Forgetting in *Miß Sara Sampson*." *Lessing Yearbook* 27 (1995): 19-37.

"schreckliche Bilder" (horrible images).[575] Mellefont scolds her for clinging to her own self-inflicted pain. Why does she allow her all too vivid imagination to torture herself: "Wie meine vernünftige Sara sollte sie für etwas mehr halten? Träume, liebste Miß, Träume!-Wie unglücklich ist der Mensch! Fand sein Schöpfer in dem Reiche der Wirklichkeit nicht Qualen für ihn genug? Mußte er, sie zu vermehren, auch ein noch weiteres Reich von Einbildungen in ihm schaffen?"(What, my unhappy Sara should think of them as something more ? Dreams, dearest Miss!-How unhappy is the human! Did his or her creator not find enough tortures in the realm of reality? Did he, in order to increase them, have to create yet another realm of imaginations?)[576] Sara lacks self-respect and critical attention to her own dream images. In addition she falls prey to the games of the mind while being almost blind to what happens before her eyes.

## 5. "Horrible images"–Forgotten?

An ekphrastic scene is when Sara describes her dream, these "schreckliche[n] Bilder" (horrible images) "als ich mich auf einmal an dem schroffsten Teile des schrecklichsten Felsen sahe" (when I saw myself on the brink of a frightening cliff).[577] She was following Mellefont in her dream and hears behind her father calling. She stops and turns around to see him, but she slips and almost falls from the rock into the abyss. To her pleasant surprise she notices that she is held back that very moment by a person amazingly resembling herself ("von einer mir ähnlichen Person").[578] Her narrative continues: "Schon wollte ich ihr den feurigsten Dank abstatten, als sie einen Dolch aus dem Busen zog. Ich rettete dich, schrie sie, um dich zu verderben! Sie holte mit der bewaffneten Hand aus–und ach! ich erwachte mit dem Stiche." (Already I wanted to express my fiery thanks when she pulled a dagger from her chest. I saved you, this person screamed, in order to destroy you! She raised her arm with the weapon in her hand –and oh! I woke up from the stab).[579] The dream contains a surprising turn of events, it is a *non sequitur*. The person who comes to help is like a sister or friend, someone close to her yet turns out to be a murderer in disguise. Despite of this realization, Sara is not done with her descriptions. She strangely continues talking, almost while silencing any real insight here. She keeps commenting the surface of a strange mixture of emotions: "Wachend fühlte ich noch alles, was ein tödlicher Stich Schmerzhaftes haben kann; ohne das zu empfinden, was er Angenehmes haben muß: das Ende der Pein in dem Ende des Lebens hoffen zu dürfen" (As I awoke I felt everything, how much pain a fatal stab could have; without sensing what it must have in terms of relief: that the end of pain could hopefully be the end of life).[580]

575 FA 3, 441.
576 FA 3, 441.
577 FA 3, 441.
578 According to some interpretations this person has been identified with Marwood although one could also see it as an alter ego, a part of her own identity trying to hold her back.
579 FA 3, 441.
580 FA 3, 442.

Her thoughtless comment saying that death would perhaps be more preferable to her rather than being rescued expresses very negative feelings that are the beginning of another downward spiral for her. There is momentary despair, melancholy, and self-denial. She may in an act of manipulative speech, a form of blackmail attempting to force Mellefont to say exactly what she wants to hear from him. He does so for an instant, but immediately back-peddles. He tells her to forget the dream and that it is all just a fabrication of her mind, of her britttle nerves: "Ach, liebste Sara, ich verspreche ihnen das Ende Ihrer Pein ohne das Ende Ihres Lebens, welches gewiß auch das Ende des meinigen sein würde. Vergessen Sie das schreckliche Gewebe eines sinnlosen Traumes" (Ah, dearest Sara, I promise you the end of your pain without the end of your life, which would certainly be the end of mine as well. Forget the terrible web of a senseless dream).[581] The fibers of sense perceptions seem to be at fault yet Sara insists that she does not have the power to forget or to ignore them. She requests action on his part in order to accept the situation as it is. Why cannot she take responsibility for her own wish to live? Why does she make herself so dependent on him?

Mellefont apparently tries to console her: "Der erste Augenblick Ihres Zweifels müsse der letzte meines Lebens sein" (The first moment of your doubt must be the last one of my life).[582] But he does certainly not set any wedding date with Sara. He acknowledges now his persistent entanglements with Marwood, his previous lover who may return. As the following scene with Morton, Mellefont, and Sara then illustrates, it is impossible not to dwell on complications once they are articulated. Words have emotional consequences that are hard to be erased once expressed. The plot seems to stagnate. Despite all of the emotional turmoil no outcome is in sight. The end of act one is marked by the arrival of a letter from Marwood mediated by Norton who now insists that Mellefont should read it. Since he is shivering and cannot do so, Mellefont requests that Norton read it for him. He begins: "Es wird so gut sein, als ob ich Ihnen den längsten Brief geschrieben hätte, Mellefont, wenn Sie den Namen, den Sie am Ende der Seite finden werden, nur einer kleinen Betrachtung würdigen wollen–") (It will be just as as if I had written you the longest letter, Mellefont, if you were to honor the name at the end of the page with a small consideration–).[583] Mellefont laments that he wishes he had never met Marwood and that this letter had never arrived. Yet his body language, his shivering, tells more. He is tired of words and shifts his attention to the visual: "Sage nichts! - Laß sehen [...] ob sie ihre Wohnung angezeigt hat. Hier ist sie" (Say nothing!–Let me see [...] if she has indicated where she is staying. Here it is!)[584] Marwood is obviously not only someone from his past. Her physical appearance still has an emotional impact on him although he claims otherwise. She is lucky enough to use the written medium, a letter just when he is tired of too many words spoken. This letter reached him at the moment just when he had enough of the spoken words from Sara. Her style of communication turned him off and in turn it motivates him now to open up again communication with Marwood, perhaps even in protest. Despite the fact he does not read the letter to the end, it has the effect of

581 FA 3, 442.
582 FA 3, 446.
583 FA 3, 447.
584 FA 3, 449.

capturing his attention more than any spoken words could have done. When Mellefont meets Marwood the situation becomes even more complicated, especially when Arabella also enters, Marwood's daughter. The child is lovable and delightful to see.

The second act opens with Marwood in her room in another inn, wearing a negligée and preparing herself for the impending visit of Mellefont. Hannah her maid is trying to soothe her anxieties, saying: "Fassen Sie sich ja. Er kann vielleicht jeden Augenblick kommen" (Calm down. He could possibly arrive any moment).[585] Marwood talks about her strategy to win Mellefont back by also bringing along her daughter Arabella, whom Mellefont loves dearly. She seems bitterly reproachful of herself and expresses her worry that she might be rejected. She blames the unavoidable impact of the "Hand der Zeit" (hand of time).[586] We soon learn in the next act when Marwood actually meets Mellefont that she does not only act as a lady but has a sharp wit, and is a master of rhetoric devices. She reveals herself, as Mellefont succinctly puts it randomly, as a "snake" which one would best to avoid: "Was für eine Schlange! Hier wird das beste sein zu fliehen."[587] Ironically he does not flee and is drawn to the monstrous.[588]

He asks multiple questions: "Sagen Sie es nur kurz, Marwood, warum Sie mir nachgekommen sind? was Sie noch von mir verlangen? Aber sagen Sie es nur ohne dieses Lächeln, ohne diesen Blick, aus welchem mich eine ganze Hölle von Verführung schreckt" (Tell me quickly, Marwood, why you have come after me? What do you still want from me? But tell me this without such a smile, without this gaze, from which an entire hell of seduction frightens me).[589] Marwood explains that she thinks Mellefont is being tyrannized by his own desires. She reminds him that she has been his confidante for a long time and promises to give him free range for a month to do as he likes so that he may find out what it is he really likes about his new flame, the "Landmädchen".[590] She frames Sara as ideal yet with irony. She requests that he must not vanish completely but to stay in contact with her. She makes fun of his new "Gebieterin" (Lady) who seems to be so virtuous:

> Du wirst an deine schöne Heilige die Reihe Zeit genug kommen lassen. Soll ich wohl einen kleinen Überschlag machen? Jetzo bist du im heftigsten Paroxysmo mit ihr; und diesem geb ich noch zwei, aufs längste drei Tage. Hierauf wird eine ziemlich geruhige Lieb folgen; der geb' ich acht Tage. Die andern acht Tage wirst du mir gelegentlich an diese Liebe denken. Die dritten wirst du dich erinnern lassen; und wann du dieses Erinnern satt bist, so wirst du dich zu der äußersten Gleichgültigkeit so schnell gebracht sehen, daß ich kaum

585 FA 3, 449.
586 FA 3, 450.
587 FA 3, 452.
588 This is a perfect example of one kind of misunderstanding where psychological insights are needed and the usual logic fails. Hans Helmut Hiebel, "Mißverstehen und Sprachlosigkeit im 'Bürgerlichen Trauerspiel.' Zum historischen Wandel dramatischer Motivationsformen." *Jahrbuch der deutschen Schillergesellschaft* 27 (1983), 124–153. On the importance of the snake motif, also as a poetological device, see Susan Gustafson, "Windungen und Wendungen in Lessings *Laokoon*," Wolfgang Albrecht, Dieter Fratzke, and Richard Schade, ed., *Mit Lessing zur Moderne: Soziokulturelle Wirkungen der Aufklärers um 1900*, Erbepflege in Kamenz 24 (Kamenz: Lessing-Museum 2004), 21-36.
589 FA 3, 452.
590 FA 3, 453.

die vierten acht Tage auf diese letzte Veränderung rechnen darf.-Das wäre nun ungefähr ein Monat.[591]

[You will give your beautiful Saint time according to the sequence of expected timing. Should I make a small calculation? Now you are in the most ardent feverish paroxysm with her; and for this I shall give yet two or at most three days. Then there will a somewhat calmer love follow; I will give it eight days. The next eight days you will only think occasionally of this love. By the third eight days you will have to be reminded; and when you have had enough of this reminding, then you will have brought yourself to the uttermost state of boredom so soon that it is hardly necessary for me to tally up the fourth eight days of this last stage.-This would be roughly a month].

Although this proposal seems tempting, Mellefont rejects this supposition "Vergebens, Marwood, suchen Sie alle Waffen hervor" (Marwood, you are searching in vain to apply all your weapons).[592] Marwood responds by saying she will return to him all the visible and tangible objects he has ever given her. She knows this will remind him of the happy moments they spent together which she characterizes as a time when silences were meaningful. Everything said or unspoken then was easily understood ("das beredte Stillschweigen").[593] Then she makes an analogy between herself and a statue while again reminding him that any artist ought not to dispense with his artwork before having finished its creation. Arabella, her daughter, enters the room and runs to embrace Mellefont affectionately. Marwood asks Mellefont to forgive everything and to be reunited again with them both as a new family based on their existing bonds. Marwood stands, in other words, for the motto: "Seeing is believing." Her eyes have become those of a basilisk that stun Mellefont and he is not her only prey. She embodies the power of the image, the body, and visuality.

## 6. Being caught between the returning visual Marwood and the all too verbal Sara?

Marwood demands that Mellefont must choose. Either Marwood or Sara: "Nun sind wir allein. Nun sagen Sie es noch einmal, ob Sie fest entschlossen sind, mich einer jungen Närrin aufzuopfern?" (Now we are alone. Now tell me once again whether you have firmly decided to make me a victim for the sake of a young fool?).[594] Marwood reminds him of an inheritance which Mellefont can only receive, as he once told her some time ago, under certain conditions which still have not been met. She argues this is something he should not ignore now. Mellefont tells her that it is no longer any of her business and that he will enjoy whatever he will have with "einer würdigern Gattin" (a more deserving wife).[595] But the snake has already bitten so to speak. At this point he seems to be anticipating that Sara will be his wife, a notion he has denied

591 FA 3, 454.
592 FA 3, 454.
593 FA 3, 456.
594 FA 3, 462.
595 FA 3, 463.

until now. This sentence comes as a surprise to say the least and it causes more pain for Marwood. At this point she shouts; "Sieh in mir eine neue Medea!" (See in me a new Medea!).[596] She threatens poison and a dagger and exclaims she will kill even the child Arabella. Mellefont appears shocked but the best response he can come up with is: "Sie rasen" (You are out of your mind).[597] Then he moves to a strategy of playful acting which would allow him to buy time in this impasse between the past, the present, and the future. Options have become incompatible. Mellefont does not take his words very seriously. In the following scene he agrees with Marwood that she could arrange to meet Sara under the pretext of being his distant relative who has come on a visit. Maywood's purpose for such a meeting is, according to her words, so that she can read in her glances her entire future fate: "Lassen Sie mich Ihre Sara wenigstens einmal sehen. [...] Um in ihren Blicken mein ganzes künftiges Schicksal zu lesen" (Let me see your Sara at least once. [...] So that I can read in her eyes my complete future fate).[598]

Act three begins with Sir William Sampson and Waitwell talking together. In the meantime Sir William has written a letter to his beloved daughter Sara and asks Waitwell to deliver it to her, a task Waitwell gladly accepts. In this letter Sara's father forgives her for disobeying him. He wishes her happiness with her fiancé and says he wants to make peace with his beloved daughter after all. Another letter is mentioned in the following scene which is quite the opposite, namely, Marwood's letter to Mellefont which the latter uses to excuse himself for his delay in seeing Sara. He announces the content of this letter which the audience knows comes from Marwood, and which announces the arrival of a relative who had learnt about his whereabouts and who wants to see him and Sara as well.

As soon as Mellefont leaves the room, Sara expresses her wish that it may not be one of these arrogant ladies who are full of their own virtues, who can with a scornful glance and a single deprecating shrug of shoulders make a devastating judgment, singling out the other person as someone who deserves nothing but pity. These words are something of a premonition for what is to following the subsequent scenes. Attention shifts from verbal eloquence to body language, facial expressions, gestures, and moves. There are hints that not only accompany words but give them their poignancy. It is an exquisite example of Lessing's art of Ekphrasis using both sign systems but without dissolving the discrepancy and tension between images and words. Sara and her maid receive a visit from Waitwell. Sara is afraid there might be bad news and even worries that it might be her father's death, but quite the opposite. Waitwell delivers Sir William's letter which contains his "aufrichtiges Bedauern" (sincere regrets).[599] Although he apologizes only for his "harsh words" he wishes above all his daughter's affection. He cannot be angry any longer. He is sympathetic with her and no longer charges her for having fallen into the power of this upper class seducer. Now the father who may also be an authorial voice on a higher plane is asking his daughter for peace. Waitwell stays to see her response.

596 FA 3, 464.
597 FA 3, 464.
598 FA 3, 466.
599 FA 3, 472.

Instead of being relieved and happy at this news, Sara gives a rhapsody of a monologue. She reveals her state of mental anguish, faced with the need to write a response to her father's letter. She expresses thoughts based on her feelings of what happened and analyzes her emotions. This scene illustrates the complications involved in trying to express in writing anything so private. A language crisis has set in. "Ich darf mich nicht fürchten, in Übertreibungen zu geraten, wenn ich auch schon die gräßlichsten Züge anwende.–Ach warum muß ich nun gestört werden?" (I should not be afraid to slip into any exaggerations, even if I make use of the most horrible expressions.–O why do I have to be disturbed now?).[600] It is interesting to compare this disturbed ekphrastic scene with the earlier moments in this play. Whereas then she was indeed all too wordy and did not worry at all about spontaneously exhibiting her emotions, now she had apparently learnt something and acts as a language critic of her own. But it is, as we shall see soon, too late. She gets more than punished.

Mellefont introduces Marwood to Sara as Lady Solmes who first flatters the new "Miß." She expresses regret over the news that Sara has apparently lost her dear father over her new relationship. It comes as a surprise to Marwood to learn about the content of the letter Sara had just received. Now that it seems that all the obstacles at least as far as the couple Sara and Mellefont are concerned are removed, she seems to have lost her case. Yet nobody appears to take such news at face value. Lady Solmes alias Marwood argues rejects this news and argues that this could all be a trick, a matter of "Verstellung" (pretense) on the part of Sara's father. She leaves the room abruptly saying she is not feeling well.[601] The following scenes reflect on the probability of a happy reunion between Sir William and Sara. There are devoted servants acting as loyal friends illustrating the importance of reliable mediators in conflict while shifting attention to what up to now had been marginal characters.

Act four consists of nine scenes ranging from a meeting between Mellefont and Sara, a lovely encounter, in which they express their affection and love for each other and surprisingly at this point appear to confirm their wedding plans. Then there is a monologue by Mellefont starting out with the exclamation: "Was für ein Rätsel bin ich mir selbst" (What a puzzle I am to myself).[602] Although he admits a feeling of happiness in planning to marry Sara he immediately takes it back by saying that he loves "this angel" yet feels already like her "prisoner." He prefers the notion of "Sara Sampson my lover" compared to the notion of "Sara Sampson my wife."[603] His monologue ends with the idea of affirming that he wants to get rid of her, although he makes sophisticated distinctions between "Gesinnungen" (feelings as associated with morality) and "Einbildungen" (fantasies as associated with images only). He opts for the latter. Marwood, the world of seeing, has won over Sara, the world of spoken words.

In the following scene Marwood becomes Medea. Mellefont tells Norton that he has seized a dagger from Marwood when she tried to kill him in the company of Arabella: "Sieh, dieses Mördereisen riß ich ihr aus der Hand, *er zeigt ihm den Dolch, den er*

600 FA 3, 479.
601 FA 3, 482.
602 FA 3, 489.
603 FA 3, 489.

*Marwood genommen:* als sie mir in der schrecklichsten Wut das Herz damit durchstoßen wollte" (See, this murder weapon I tore out of her hand [*he shows him the dagger which he had taken from Marwood*), when she in the most horrible anger wanted to pierce my heart). Here the stage direction becomes more important than any spoken words and it shifts importance again to the verbal to the visual. Mellefont tells Norton that Marwood had insisted on seeing her rival. He admits her due to his leniency. He is curious to see her humbled in this meeting. He refers to Marwood as a wasp which has lost its sting by pointing to the dagger. We find out in the next scene that Marwood has again all of Mellefont's attention. He tries to make peace and wants to live with her and her daughter Arabella. Marwood in her monologue reflects on her own "Verstellung" which means both disguise and misplacement locally. Unfortunately, similar to Sara in this play, she does not act according to her own words (otherwise she would have left).

The most dramatic scene in the play is when the two women confront each other. Whereas Sara expects to be congratulated by this so-called relative Lady Solmes for her engagement to Mellefont, her visitor indicates by her frequent use of "aber" (but) and by thoughtfully pausing often that she is reluctant to offer her congratulations. She is having second thoughts, as she puts it, about this liaison. Sara then becomes a little too eager in wanting to find out more about the possible reasons for her visitor's holding back. She thinks it is a distant relative of her fiancé. She falls into the trap set by her rival. Lady Solmes reveals that she is Marwood and Sara learns that her relationship with Mellefont which she thought was a matter of the past is still ongoing. "Aber Miß, kennen Sie denn diese Marwood, welche Sie so getrost eine Lasterhafte nennen?" (But Miss, do you really know this Marwood, whom you call so confidently a lady without virtues?)[604] She tortures Sara giving her own interpretation of who Marwood actually is. She defends herself by making that monster much more friendly and human than any simplistic character description could have ever done. It is again an illustration of empty words. Actions matter.

## 7. Why wordiness cannot win

Marwood's use of language is eloquent but to the point. She is capable of drawing Sara into the story about why she came to visit with interest and sympathy. Lady Solmes also reports to Sara that Marwood had received a letter from the father of her child whom she still loves but who had left her for a younger woman. Sara, who was ignorant of this past of her fiancé, is now utterly uncomfortable in her own role and sighs. What can she say? When she is told that Mellefont still loves this Marwood, Sara replies, "Sie töten mich, Lady" (You kill me, Lady).[605] She finds these words literally mortifying and has the function in her response to parallel the kind of sympathy which the audience should then also feel with respect to the various figures onstage that have such conflicting points of view. What follows is a series of interruptions and common misunderstandings that further prolong the actual solution of any kind

604 FA 3, 501.
605 FA 3, 505.

between the main characters. For example, the maid rushes in requesting that Mellefont should come at once announcing the arrival of a stranger: "Der Fremde, mein Herr –Er will Sie nur auf ein Wort sprechen. Er sagt, er habe keinen Augenblick zu versäumen–"(The stranger, my Lord –He just wants to speak a word with you. He says he does not have a second to waste–).[606] Timing is of essence here.

Mellefont acts delighted proposing that this arrival has to do with good news concerning his financial situation, the inheritance from his aunt he had anticipated and earlier given as a reason to Sara that it would be better to wait with the marriage for family complications. Mellefont requests that the two ladies entertain each other while he goes to take care of this, just for a moment. Sara politely asks Marwood to please sit down. During the ensuing conversation it is revealed that Lady Solmes is in fact Marwood, the mother of Mellefont's child. Sara apparently cannot accept the offer of her friendship and flees in horror. Marwood, in a moment of monologue, mentions that the poison she was saving for herself could be put to another use. The fifth act consists of eleven scenes illustrating the slow process of her poisoning Sara and Sara's slow and torturous death. While it is one level a result of Marwood's poisoning Sara, there are other factors in the play that contribute to her demise, including her own inability to contain her fear, to keep her dream to herself and to understand its visual message for her own best use, and to communicate effectively, especially with those whom she loves.

The first scene of the fourth act opens with the *tableau vivant* in which Sara is sitting in an armchair, not feeling well. Betty is waiting with her for the return of Mellefont who is out with Norton. Betty makes some critical remarks about Mellefont's absence. Sara defends him: "Nicht wahr Betty, du hältst ihn auch für unschuldig?" (Betty, you also think of him as not guilty, right?) Sara blames herself for having encouraged Mellefont to take care of the inheritance business, which is, she thinks, the reason for his absence now. Betty asks Sara: "Fühlen Sie nicht Miß, daß Ihnen ein wenig besser wird?" (Don't you feel becoming a bit better, Miss?) Sara responds: "Nichts Betty.–Ein Stich, tausend feurige Stiche in einem!–Sei nur ruhig; es ist vorbei." (Nothing Betty.–A stabbing pain, thousand fiery stabbing pains in one! –Stay calm, it is over).[607] Here the play could have ended if Lessing had applied the critical standard of brevity that he has worked out in the *Fabeln*. Strangely, the play continues.

In the second scene Norton arrives and reports that Mellefont will arrive soon and that the stranger was a swindler. Sara wants to know whether Norton told Mellefont what happened and he answers: "Alles" (Everything). He explains that of course he can imagine what fear Sara must have had for him in the meantime (thus indicating that he has no idea what actually has happened to her). Sara defends Mellefont and Norton shouts: "Warum soll Mellefont niemals Unrecht haben!" (Why should Mellefont never be wrong?)[608] He walks away excusing Sara's unsuitable comments. Her love, as foolish as it may have been in the circumstances, has already excused her for saying what she did ("Die Liebe hat sie bereits entschuldigt").

606 FA 3, 498.
607 FA 3, 511.
608 FA 3, 512.

Mellefont arrives and reports how Marwood tricked him into an intrigue that was "plumpe List ohne Zweifel" (a bold trick without any doubt) while still not noticing anything concerning Sara's fragile state of health. Sara asks for Marwood to return but then contradicts herself: "Lassen Sie doch einen abgematteten Feind, der den letzten fruchtlosen Sturm gewagt hat, ruhig abziehen" (Why not let an exhausted enemy quietly go, someone who has dared the last fruitless storm).[609] He notices however that without her she would not know things she now realizes ("Ich würde ohne Marwood vieles nicht wissen"). This comment should indicate that he becomes aware of his wrongdoing yet remains strangely without real consequences in this play. Mellefont is curious about what she is referring to and adds that he hopes that it was nothing to his disadvantage. Then Sara wants know why Mellefont did not come to her first after almost being killed by Marwood with the dagger, adding that she is afraid that she may have been the reason for this dangerous attack: "Warum aber lassen Sie es nicht das erste sein, mir von der Gefahr zu sagen, in der sich Ihr kostbares Leben befunden hat? Ich, Mellefont, würde den Stahl geschliffen haben, mit dem Sie Marwood durchstoßen hätte?" (Why didn't you let me to be the first to be told about this danger in which your precious life found itself? I, Mellefont would have sharpened the blade with which Marwood would have stabbed you).[610] This is not what Mellefont was expecting and he asks Betty: "Betty was ist ihr geschehen?–Das sind nicht bloße Folgen der Ohnmacht" (Betty what has happened to her? These are not just the consequences of a swoon).[611] Sara has been poisoned by Marwood and she endures a long and painful process of dying. Her father arrives and she makes peace with him, Betty is falsely accused having given Sara the medicine from Marwood's hand after Sara had fainted. It becomes clear Marwood is responsible for the fact that Sara is dying of poison. She has fled taking Arabella with her, but is taken into custody by Sara's father. Mellefont takes his own life with Marwood's dagger so that he may die with Sara. This final scene seems to visually prolong the agonies Sara has to endure. It provides a meta-perspective from which all the pain seems to be lifted away. Sir William comments on the death of Mellefont: "Er stirbt! Ach, er war mehr unglücklich als lasterhaft" (He dies! O, he was more unlucky than immoral).[612] He suggests a reconciliation. When the doctors arrive to take care of the sick patient, it is too late. But the last sentence to be spoken points to the security of Arabella who now has found a new home. What makes *Miß Sara Sampson* innovative is in how Lessing experiments with the articulation of emotions and how he uses wordiness in an attempt to tap into the ambivalences and complexities of an individual's private struggles. He questions not only what language articulates but also what it alludes to, even at the margins. The articulations of emotions and thoughts clash. The description of what can be seen onstage does not match and ultimately fails. Had Sara not pushed Mellefont (and the audience) to listen to a torrent of words when she described her dream, her emotions, and her subtle fears then he would perhaps have not withdrawn. He was distracted by Marwood's letter and Sara did not even listen to her own dream and innermost feelings.

609 FA 3, 513.
610 FA 3, 513.
611 FA 3, 516.
612 FA 3, 526.

Marwood is brief and assertive. Mellefont falls under Marwood's spell. Seeing her disarms him. But there are several poignant moments and premature endings in this play. The final ending seems to be somewhat arbitrary. Perhaps there was the clash between emotions associated with the middle class characters that Sara represents in contrast to the reasoning associated with the interests of the male political sphere represented by Mellefont. His image is viewed critically and most critics link him with corruption, coldness, and other character flaws.

The bourgeois family, Sara Sampson's world, seems more virtuous and honorable than that that of the nobility or the courtly sphere as represented.[613] Yet it would also be short-sighted to see in Mellefont as stereotypical libertine. There are intricate reasons for why they ultimately do not marry. Most readers find that there existed a possibility that a marriage between them could have happened under slightly better circumstances. The complications reflect on real historical and social conditions of Lessing's time. The denial of a happy ending may well express authenticity. Lothar Pikulik argues for the subversive power of the bourgeois, which in the person Sara Sampson stands on the verge of entrance into the nobility through marriage.[614] He considers it a sign of progress that classes seem to be ready to mingle and to merge. In his assessment it is "only" due to Mellefont's previous lover, Lady Marwood, and to her active intervention from outside that the union of Sara and Mellefont cannot succeed. The bourgeois Sara encounters difficulties and ultimately violence. He finds that Sara's dream is just a nightmare. It seems to me that such an interpretation focusing on the tension between the bourgeois and nobility ignores many more aspects of this play especially the tension between the visual and the verbal media as represented by these conflicting female characters.

The question remains why Sara must die. There are several interesting perspectives and interpretations focusing on her death.[615] Why is Mellefont so reluctant to marry Sara, even after the reconciliation between Sir William and his daughter, and even after all obstacles seem to be dealt with to the satisfaction of all those concerned? The father has consented to this union and in doing so he may well represent a higher order. Nevertheless Mellefont is still unable to make up his mind and to choose once and for all between past, present, and future and so is actually his daughter Sara. They are stuck in ambivalence. Various interpretations can be summarized under the rubrics of Biblical, Classical, and philosophical-theological readings. More recent studies link it with psychology and anthropology.[616] Michelsen questioned the notion of obedience for the sake of emotions as exemplified in this play. There seems to be a replacement of obedience by affection, tenderness, and love. These emotions tend to be still fragile

---

613 See for example, Katrin A. Wurst, *Familiale Liebe ist die wahre Gewalt. Die Repräsentation der Familie in G. E. Lessings dramatischem Werk*, Amsterdamer Publikationen zur Sprache und Literatur 75 (Amsterdam: Rodopi, 1988), 102–123.

614 Lothar Pikulik, *"Bürgerliche Trauerspiele" und Empfindsamkeit* (Cologne: Böhlau, 1966).

615 An excellent example is Gloria Flaherty, "The Art of Dying on Stage." *Lessing Yearbook* 21 (1989): 103–121.

616 Peter Michelsen, *Der unruhige Bürger* and Peter-André Alt, *Tragödie der Aufklärung* (Tübingen: Francke, 1994), both address aspects in Lessing's writing that are to be associated with the persistent importance of myth, religion, law, legal aspects, and other influential cultural codes.

and marked by ambivalence. Such tentative love across social class barriers cannot yet quite invalidate or make obsolete what Michelsen correctly considers the prevailing patriarchal structures that were dominant at that time in German and European history.

Some critics have seen Emilia and Marwood as Virgina and Medea in bourgeois dress interpreting how Christian and Classical elements are combined and interwoven with other aspects of the play.[617] Ter-Nedden's interpretation is most interesting. He finds the disappointed marriage expectation between the bourgeois Sara and the noble Mellefont a matter of Lessing's conscious staging of human error. Instead of showing the process of the Enlightenment only via successful reasoning Lessing consciously employs a more subtle strategy in showing *ex negativo* what shortcomings exist. They are not only, as previous critics of Lessing have shown, in the society where certain class struggles are obstructing emancipation and enlightenment. As Lessing illustrates that shortcomings or errors of communication are moreover lingering in the habitual daily spontaneous but dangerously non-reflected use of language. This may be especially the case when expressing a mixture of sense perceptions and resulting emotions. Even gestures which one assumes are basic natural signs can harbor flagrant misunderstandings.

Ter-Nedden points out that it was already Conrad Wiedemann's discovery that Lessing's play *Philotas* was not a patriotic drama as often thought but rather a sophisticated play about the mistakes of faulty patriotism in a very specific case study. He finds that both in *Miß Sara Sampson* and in *Emilia Galotti* old myths get evoked and reinterpreted for powerful challenges towards critical thinking towards something new. In *Miß Sara Sampson* it may well be the myth of vengeful Medea that comes to life in the figure of Marwood. I would like to add to Ter-Nedden's take on this that there is also the myth of Medusa whose eyes gaze has a paralyzing effect, especially if not noticed and acknowledged for what they represent, potential danger as in a staring basilisk. As for the play *Emilia Galotti* Ter-Nedden observes that it must not be understood as a faulty actualizing of the moralistic Virginia ethos but instead as its moral-critical problematization ("nicht als fehlerhafte Aktualisierung des moralischen Virginia-Ethos, sondern als dessen moralkritische Problematisierung verstanden werden muß").[618] Lessing uses "Versatzstücke der Tradition" (fragments of tradition). He does his own thing with these through interesting rhetorical strategies, adaptations, and

617 Lydia Butt, "Mitleid ex machina. Die Disproportion der Affekte in Sophokles' *Philoktet* im Spiegel von Lessings Theorie der Tragödienwirkung," Katja Battenfeld et al. ed., *Gefühllose Aufklärung. Anaisthesis oder die Unempfindlichkeit im Zeitalter der Aufklärung* (Bielefeld: Aisthesis 2012), 117-139. On the other hand, see Natalie Binczek. *Kontakt: Der Tastsinn in Texten der Aufklärung,* Studien zur deutschen Literatur 182 (Tübingen: Niemeyer, 2007) and her essay: "Das veränderliche Gewebe. Zur Empfindungstheorie in Lessings *Laokoon*," *Zeitschrift für Ästhetik und Allgemeine Kunstwissenschaft* 49.2 (2004): 219-235.

618 Gisbert Ter-Nedden, *Lessings Trauerspiele,* 3; Conrad Wiedemann, "Ein schönes Ungeheuer. Zur Deutung von Lessings Einakter 'Philotas'," *Germanisch-Romanische-Monatsschrift,* N.F. 17 (1967): 381-397. Also see Robert Holub, "The Enlightenment of Dialectic: Jürgen Habermas' Critique of the Frankfurt School" in Wilson and Holub, *Impure Reason* 34-47. He explains that "failure" plays a key role in the much larger context of "Strukturwandel und Öffentlichkeit" (structural change and publicity), key terms in Habermas' critique of the Enlightenment project.

various co-existing levels of montage.[619] Elements or supposedly familiar features are then taken out of the expectation of their previous genre, out of their prescribed world view and their normative credibility. Instead they now reveal blind spots in a new arrangement and contribute to the end of the *tragedy classique* for the sake of what Ter-Nedden calls "Historismus avant la lettre."[620] I agree with Ter-Nedden that Lessing consciously leaves space in his use of imagery and language to promote critical thinking and imagination by the spectator, reader, and audience of the play. He depicts ambivalence of emotions often observed as resulting from such interactions.

I want to add that as far as I can see no interpretations so far have paid any attention to Sara's mania to describe everything in detail, her "Schilderungssucht," something Lessing rejected explicitly in his poetic theory. Her overabundance of wordiness and her stubborn attempts to inappropriately absorb all images and feelings into verbal expression while at the same time ignoring the more subtle images and faint emotions covered up in her own dream are among the factors which contribute to the tragic ending of the play. Lessing's artistic approach to testing the limits of understanding and his plea understatement are at the core of this play. He gives most power to the character who is struggling most with finding succinct words and to be minimalist in expression. There is a problem of unresolved Ekphrasis since what we see cannot always be told. One would have never expected that Sara even in the moment of dying would be able to unite with Mellefont and her father in the way she did. Lessing is, after all, an idealist who believes not only in visible but also invisible dimensions of life. Sara is poisoned, but the question remains to what extent she may have provoked her own demise. By telling her frightful dream in which she was killed by "a person similar to herself" she actually suggested to Marwood to make her, Sara, the victim of this triangle relationship.

Had she not shown her fear and projected feelings of jealousy and rivalry perhaps the two females in the play could have actually been like sisters in bringing Mellefont to face his actions and make a choice for truth and harmony. If one wants to read this destructive sister relationship as an allusion to the paragon conflict between the first lady, Marwood as the visual and the second, Sara as the verbal, it is obvious that if visuality prevails verbalness must give in. In other words, Lessing anticipates a critique of Enlightenment discourse that tends to replace images by words and he asserts the semiotic firstness of sense-related modes of expression Verbalness is still restricted or gets, as in this symbolic case, victimized. Sara has not found her own voice yet. If so, it is too late. Unfortunately she dies for the sake of Marwood who represents Medea. In any case, her daughter Arabella gets saved in Lessing's plot of this tragic play.

One may ask whether Lessing was striking out in a new direction with this play or merely following the fashion of the time. Was he just riding the wave of "Empfindsamkeit" in the era of sensibility and did he achieve the praise he did only because he wrote something that happened to be fashionable, and in France at least already *en vogue*? Did he adapt George Lillo's *The London Merchant* (1731) and Edward Moore's *The Gamester* (1753) which had recently been translated from English into German and performed on the German stage? Both plays involve the motif of seduction of a

619 Ter-Nedden, *Lessings Trauerspiele* 4.
620 Ter-Nedden, *Lessings Trauerspiele* 4.

virtuous girl from a middle class family by a gambler and misogynist who belongs to a higher class but is morally corrupt or at least unstable, a theme which is found in Lessing's play. But such an interpretation would not capture the play's essence. Richard Daunicht reports that according to a much cited comment by Eduard Devrients the play *Miß Sara Sampson* had an effect on Lessing's contemporaries "like an egg of Columbus ("wie ein Ei des Kolumbus").[621] It opened an entirely new world to dramatic art and its characters such as Mellefont, Marwood, and Sara have meanwhile become staples and belong to the repertoire of the classical German theater. More than creating a dramatic synthesis between the French sentimental plays and the English tragedies of the time, Lessing had his own agenda. I must agree with Otto Mann that it is actually a play on blindness. Mann interprets the play as a tragedy adopted from antiquity. He comments on *Miß Sara Sampson*:

> Der große tragische Grundmangel des Menschen ist seine Blindheit. Wenn Aristoteles vom tragischen Helden fordert, er solle ein mittlerer Charakter, ein Mensch mit einem Fehler, mit einer Harmatia sein, so ist dies vorwiegend ein Fehler, eine Schranke im Erkenntnisvermögen. Der Mensch ist eben da am bedingtesten, wo er den Göttern am nächsten steht, in seiner Vernunft, Ödipus ist blind, wenn er den Vater tötet, die Mutter heiratet. Und mehr noch, er ist der Blinde, der glaubt, sehend zu sein, der dem körperlich blinden, aber geistig sehenden Tiresias verspottet, er sei der Blinde, und der hören muß, daß er nur mit dem äußeren, nicht mit dem inneren Auge sieht. Mellefont ist schon blind, wenn er die gesetzlosen Beziehungen aufnimmt zu der Witwe Marwood. Hätte er sehen können, so hätte er hier schon die letzte Konsequenz sehen müssen, den Tod der Sara. Der alte Sampson ist unwissend, wenn er diesen Mann in sein Haus einführt; Sara täuscht sich, wenn sie glaubt, diesem Manne vertrauen zu können; Mellefont täuscht sich, wenn er glaubt durch Sara sich noch retten zu können. Die Marwood weiß nicht, daß sie durch den Schritt, durch den sie den Geliebten für sich retten will, ihn endgültig verliert. Mellefont weiß nicht, daß er durch die Schritte, durch die er ein größeres Unglück verhindern will, das größte herbeiführt, Auch der alte Sampson kann nicht sehen, daß er durch sein Kommen, durch das er seine Tochter retten will, ihren Untergang bewirkt. Und Sara weiß nicht, wen sie in der Gestalt der Lady Solmes vor sich hat; so reizt sie unwissend die Marwood bis zum Giftmord.[622]
>
> [The great tragic basic flaw of humans is their blindness. When Aristotle demands from the tragic hero that he should be a mediocre character, a human with a flaw, with a Hamartia, than this is dominantly a mistake, a limit in the cognition ability. Humans are erroneous most of all where they stand closest to the divine in their reasoning. Oedipus is blind when he kills his father, marries his mother. And more so, he is the blind person who believes to be seeing, who mocks the physically blind but spiritually seeing Tiresias, saying that he is the blind one when in fact he only does not see with his outer but with his inner eye. Mellefont is already blind when he makes illegal contact with the widow Marwood. Had he seen, then he would then already have seen the last consequence, the death of Sara. Old Sampson is ignorant when he leads this man into his house. Sara is deceived believing to be able to trust this man. Mellefont is mistaken when he believes to be able to rescue himself through Sara. Marwood does not know that through her move trying to regain her lover she will lose him completely. Mellefont does not know that through the steps he takes in order to prevent a disaster, he brings about an even greater one. Also old Sampson cannot see that through his arrival, by which he wants to rescue his daughter he promotes her

---

621 Daunicht, *Die Entstehung 299. The expression means to be the latest sensation, something truly innovative or spectacular.*

622 Otto Mann, *Lessing. Sein und Leistung*, 2nd rev. ed. (Hamburg: Von Schroeder, 1961), 233–234.

downfall. And Sara does not know whom she has in front of her as Lady Solmes; so she provokes Marwood unknowingly up to her killing her by poison].

One can well argue that Lessing's innovations have much to do with his own development in defining an approach to poetics, to visual representation, and to his search for an answer to the underlying Laokoon problem having to mediate between the sister-arts painting and poetry or between the visual and the verbal. There are intricate moments in this play involving the construction of identity, along with the correlation between visual, haptic, and verbal aspects. The play brings to awareness that knowledge is not identical with seeing and that even in the visual realm there are no simple comfortable signs. Staging is an activity that is a matter of mutual interaction between playwright, actors, and audiences. Lessing shifts agency in numerous ways. *Miß Sara Sampson* marks a juncture of two lines of development, Lessing's move from French to English ideals and also his search for something new of his own.[623] The play therefore documents not only the coming of age of the bourgeois play. It also indicates the tentative beginnings for the foundation of an approach to representation in the arts and a new literary genre. Lessing challenges a tradition of mimesis, or what it means to imitate nature in art or life in theater. By having Marwood be the main protagonist next to Sara, Lessing raises the marginalized ex-lover to a position of prominence and has her express her anger, not just as if she were a modern Medea but also as someone worthy of pity and compassion. Sara does not know who Marwood is when she first speaks with her. In the end she is willing to adopt the child Arabella and exemplifies forgiveness. The play was successful in illustrating the tensions between images and bringing a new awareness to difficulties with the process of Ekphrasis. The play leaves the characters speechless and is a spectacle unseen before. The dying image of Miß Sara is frozen in time. Lessing framed it in order to express powerfully the consequences of mistakes that stem from the power of the gaze or unrelated seeing and being seen and a lack of understatement and critical self-reflection when using words. Had Marwood been understood as an embodiment of Medusa things would have turned out to be quite different.[624] The tragic ending could have been avoided. Such possible and indirectly suggested interventions did not take place. Had Sara been understood as an example of empty words she would not have been taken so seriously in her own suggesting as if she were willing to die.

Frederick Burwick in his essay on Ekphrasis makes a reference here without mentioning Lessing to two poles of a dynamic. One leads to the animation of an artwork by looking at it as in the *Pygmalion* myth. The other leads to a frozen state or to death as marked in *Medea*.[625] These determine of what is later characterized as ekphrastic

623 Although the play became a sensation for propegating English influences, it has been mostly ignored in English reception history.

624 Winfried Woesler makes this connection in his essay "Lessings *Miß Sara Sampson* und Senecas *Medea*." *Lessing Yearbook* 10 (1978): 75-93. For an excellent survey on Lessing and the drama of antiquity see Uta Korzeniewski, *"Sophokles! Die Alten! Philoktet!" Lessing und die antiken Dramatiker* (Constance: Universitätsverlag Konstanz, 2003).

625 Frederick Burwick in his introductory chapter "Visual and Verbal Modes," Frederick Burwick and Jürgen Klein, ed., *The Romantic Imagination. Literature and Art in England and Germany*, Studies in Comparative Literature 6 (Amsterdam: Rodopi, 1996), 1-16, gives an excellent glimpse into the Ekphrasis discourse. Burwick has since been one of

hope, a belief in making the visual effectively verbal, or ekphrastic fear, an anticipation of dangerous or harmful images that can stare back. Lessing addresses both in case studies he proposes for our own critical interpretation. Whereas there continue to be debates over what really constitutes an image in the first place this huge question can be approached from a variety of angles. These include iconology, semiotics, phenomenology, and hermeneutics. Through an Interart perspective Lessing provides basic premises for these theorists. He explores ekphrastic processes taking into considering both sides of this spectrum, on one side "ekphrastic hope" with the belief in transformation from one mode of representation into another, on the other side "ekphrastic fear" dealing with iconophobia and the problem of lost images in the verbal. Lessing gives us an example of a statue coming alive, the Pygmalion effect, in *Die Matrone von Ephesus* and an example of the Medea effect in a temporal freezing in *Miß Sara Sampson.* Lessing's ability to create something of a public "arrest," immobilizing the audience in an emotional state of inactivity, confusion, and inertia was, I think, part and parcel of his Enlightenment educational project of trying to emancipate and to empower onstage those who were normally deprived of speech and to cause irritation and puzzlement to those who were all too comfortable within their outdated and perhaps all too self-indulgent mind sets.

The scholarship of this play continues to be riddled with the question why Lessing decided to present the slow and painful process of a dying female on stage. The play calls for empathy and compassion. In my reading this play also raises the question why Sara forgot her helpful dream as soon as she had she talked about it. Had she remembered it, she could have perhaps prevented he tragic death. Also, had she not talked about it at the wrong time and described what she saw in her dream she would also possibly been rescued. Lessing ends his play with a magically frozen image. It is the grotesque and statue-like image of Sara's body in pain onstage. Her process of dying with poison apparently does not silence her when that may have been expected. She keeps talking and commenting her own represented image in a strangely detached process of Ekphrasis. The play continues much longer than expected and becomes almost unbearable. It had a stunning effect, the stagnating of an entire audience. Its members felt shock or as if they had become frozen into statues themselves. Lessing avoided any false and all too superficial reconciliation, whether it be between daughter and father as seems already indicated earlier in the plot, or between the females who may interact no more as rivals but as compassionate sisters. The end does not allow for any couple to arise happily thereafter. The play avoids with this untimely death of the protagonist the idea of any detached idealism, along the lines of Diderot. Both Lessing and Diderot agreed that that physicality deserves undivided attention. Also physicality and images persist, despite or regardless of words. It is a play on problems with the timing of images that can barely be verbalized. If so, they may well be out of synch, either overdue, or just like Sara's corpse onstage, way too early.

*Miß Sara Sampson* is a play full of messages that get stupidly or unintentionally expressed publicly when they should have been better kept private. Images of a dream

---

the foremost specialists on this topic in comparative Literature and the interart debate. Also important in this context is Sabine Gross, "Image and Text: Recent Research in Intermediality," *Monatshefte* 93.3 (2001): 355-366.

are being ignored but the action indicated within such a mise-en-abîme energizes the action. A moment of insight and reflection gets extrapolated with enormous consequences. Lessing shifts attention to sensual awareness and from the mind to the body. His play is an eye-opener calling for more attention to visual messages before they become verbal and the danger of spoiling images by words. This play established Lessing as a successful playwright and had a major impact. It explores the limits of culturally engrained misconceptions. It stages a predictable, foreshadowed, yet consistently ignored dynamics between powerful images and week words. It underscores mixed messages before staging a gruesome death, resulting as far as outer actions are concerned from the poisoning of Sara Sampson by Lady Marwood, her jealous rival.[626] The death is also resulting from Sara's error ignoring her own dream, emotions, and subtle intuitions. Attention is drawn to such inner actions that manifest themselves poignantly in moments and decisive events before they become evident and ultimately causing violence. This play is Lessing's case study illustrating what can happen when adequate processing of any such significant glimpses into the unconscious, into dreams, into what we see, hear, and sense gets ignored. He makes a link from aesthetics to ethics because not only important physical sense perceptions get ignored but also possible ethical interventions as needed.

626 See Helga Kraft, "Gotthold E. Lessings Marwood in *Miss Sara Sampson*," Helga Kraft and Elke Liebs, ed., *Mütter, Töchter, Frauen. Weiblichkeitsbilder in der Literatur* (Stuttgart: Metzler, 1993), 35-36. One may also read this struggle between the females as a psychological drama between conscious and unconscious parts of one psyche, depending on temporality.

# Chapter 8
# *Faust* and *Fatime* (1758-1759): Time Split and the Speed of the Real

Abstract: This chapter illustrates how Lessing probes boundaries between thoughts and actions. It also deals with the visualization of character traits that are marginal, often unnoticed, but extreme and consequential. Lessing highlights subtle thresholds between the good and the bad, the visual and the textual. How to distinguish between the realms of the mind and those of objectifyable reality? Intentions and desire become in his discourse already *in nuce* actions. His Faust experiment provides a glimpse into the current religious and philosophical debates. In this play perfect character traits may be regarded from another perspective as dubious or as flaws. One thing could turn out to become its opposite, thus challenging any binaries. A development from idea to action is fluid and barely distinguishable for the spectators. They have to rely on their imagination when their usual deductive logic fails. In other words: neither what we see, nor what we expect is what we get onstage. Lessing's *Faust* draws attention to a setting that emphasizes speed, temporality, and the much overlooked dimension of time in the process of seeing. It sheds light on human capabilities that allow unpredictable turns of the events. He challenges the Aristotelian notion of providence for the sake of shared individual responsibility. He draws attention to the dark side where humans or devils are agents of forces they cannot control. Things happen so fast that they escape our field of vision. Lessing deals with examples of crime and human transgression. His first Faust fragment entails a mental experiment with one of the devils drawing a finger through a flame without feeling any pain. The question is: How long would this test symptom-free last? How long to wait? Even the beginning of the play highlights an ambiguity of having heard or merely imagined the tolling of a bell. Similarly in Lessing's play *Fatime* timing is extremely important, a matter of life and death. The question is: How long could any actress feign serene happiness? What if circumstances threaten her personal integrity? She must find her own way.

## 1. Scholarship and thesis: *Faust* as a personally charged and timely experiment

In October 1755 just half a year after Lessing had withdrawn for six weeks into a Potsdam garret to write *Miß Sara Sampson* he returned to Leipzig. While he had enjoyed the unprecedented success of his break-through drama, he was ready to start something new. He had set out to defend "pathetic tragedy"–albeit in a somewhat subdued mode–against the backdrop of the heroic drama. He engaged critically with the Aristotelian tradition trying to turn the tables on it for the sake of brisk character changes. Instead of "Furcht" (*phobos*) which was explicated as the prime emotion for *catharsis* in the Aristotelian tradition, Lessing suggested, as already mentioned above, that catharsis should be provoked through Mitleid (compassion). [627] He argued that no fear is completely altruistic. According to his dictum: "Der mitleidigste Mensch ist der beste Mensch" (The most compassionate person is the best person) Lessing promoted empathy and compassion among people and suggested that whatever causes pain to one person can also bring pain to others. He proposed that the theater should address "moralische Betrachtungen" (moral considerations).[628] It should lead to a personal *catharsis* during the performance and thus also contribute to the necessary struggle for better social conditions. He elaborated on the idea that a "Nationaltheater" was desperately needed.[629] It should play a vital role in learning from other cultures through adaptations, engage with numerous languages, and it should help to establish a national identity.

When Lessing began in 1755 to work on his *Faust* he was well aware of the popular Faust books and legends.[630] As the story developed in its retellings Faust had become no longer a tragic figure but rather the vehicle for boisterous and popular comedy such as in the English play *The Life and Death of Doctor Faustus, Made into a Farce* (1684) by William Mountfort,[631] or the Vienna farce, *Leben und Tod Fausts* (1715) by Josef Anton Stranitzky. Through the *Hanswurstiaden* featuring the comic buffoon, Hans Wurst being a kind of clown or fool, also numerous Faust legends had become already in certain aspects popularized.[632] There was a wide range of *Volksbücher* (chapbooks) in circulation dealing with and purporting to be written by "Faust." He was supposedly a legendary mystic, astrologer, magician, fool, and womanizer.[633] Lessing was interested in reclaiming the story for a more serious drama. Experimenting with this material allowed him to engage in questions of philosophical, theological, and poetic

627 *Hamburgische Dramaturgie* LXXVII (FA 6, 567). See also Aristotle, *Poetics,* ed. and trans. Halliwell, (6)1449b-1450b, 46-55 at 46-49.

628 *Hamburgische Dramaturgie* III (FA 6, 199).

629 Lessing introduced this concept in the last piece he wrote under the title *Hamburgische Dramaturgie dated April 19, 1768, when it was clear that his attempt to establish such an institution in Hamburg had failed. Hamburgische Dramaturgie* CI-CIV (FA 6, 679-94 at 684 and 690).

630 The saga of Faust was first printed in Germany in 1587 as the *Historia von D. Johann Fausten dem weitbeschreyten Zauberer und Schwarzkünstler* by the printer Johann Spies in Frankfurt am Main in 1587 and was subsequently frequently republished and retold. In Lessing's early play *Der junge Gelehrte* (1748) (The Young Scholar), there are two references to the Faust story (FA 1, 139-237 at 142 and 160). His working on a version of a Faust play is first documented in a letter from Moses Mendelssohn to Lessing on November 19, 1755 (FA 11/1, 69-72 at 69). For further background information see FA 4, 823-827.

631 First performed perhaps as early as 1684 but not published until 1697. See William Mountfort, *The Life and Death of Doctor Faustus* (1697), Augustan Reprint Society 157 (Los Angeles: William Andrews Clark Memorial Library, 1973), viii. Also see Elizabeth M. Butler, *The Fortunes of Faust, Magic in History* (College Station: Pennsylvania State University Press, 1998), 57-59.

632 See also Gunther Mahal, "Lessings Faust: Planen, Ringen und Scheitern," *Faust-Blätter* 11 (1972), 525-551 at 526-527.

633 On the German grimoires supposedly written by Faust, see Owen Davies, *Grimoires: A History of Magic Books* (Oxford: Oxford University Press, 2009), 118-23 and Adolf Jacoby, "Höllenzwang," Hanns Bächtold-Stäubli and Eduard Hoffmann-Krayer, ed., *Handwörterbuch des deutschen Aberglaubens, 3rd* ed., 10 vols. (Berlin: de Gruyter, 2000), 4: cols. 258-261.

dimensions. He wanted to actualize some ancient sources in using elements of magic and surprise. Moreover, he set out to explore how to visualize something onstage that was beyond the horizon of the visible and also way out of the norm. His surviving fragments of the play suggest that it would have been a play about performing something nearly impossible to explain. It should have had an outcome that is not predictable and would have allowed the spectators to empathize and to draw their own conclusions.

Monika Fick finds that the theme of Faust appears not at all suitable for Lessing, at least not at first glance. He is an author well-known for striving towards ultimate truth and understanding. Lessing expressed appreciation for "für den höchsten Trieb im Menschen" (the highest of all human drives), that is for the search towards knowledge and wisdom.[634] Fick reminds us that Lessing is known for asking what is reasonable but Faust wants more. She points out that Lessing was a Deist and that he considered the historical so-called "positive religions" however as something transitory.[635] He is described as a rationalist and "als einen nüchternen Aufklärer" (down-to-earth contributor to the Enlightenment).[636] But there is another side to him that is less well-known. Lessing was a writer and a gambler. He dealt with extremes of emotion and passion. He had an interest in Freemasonry and in social utopia. Whenever Lessing uses Gothic motifs such as devils, ghosts, other-worldly dreams they are usually matters to be overcome for the sake of contentment and reason. In his essay from 1773 "Leibniz von den ewigen Strafen" (Leibniz on the eternal punishments) Lessing challenges the notion of "ewige Verdammnis" (eternal damnation).[637] The idea of eternity was not anything he claimed to understand. The question is open whether in the end Lessing finally succumbed to the overpowering weight of logical reasoning or the Leibnizian tradition when he gave up his attempts to complete his Faust play. It seems that punishing Faust was something expected in the narrative, at least in the versions circulating up until then. Lessing was outspoken on how he resented the melancholic imaginative power ("melancholische Einbildungskraft") as he found it associated with certain Faust plays. He wrote passionately about this in a letter to Georg August von Breitenbauch on December 12, 1755.[638] Inevitably Lessing had to deal with the Faust materials as they were known to him and to the public of his time. There had to be the character of an unhappy scholar, an educated person, wanting more knowledge and experience than was humanly available to him. He therefore makes a pact with a "devil" or some otherworldly creature, in order to gain access to new abilities and to change his fate. Unfortunately Lessing's complete sketch of his *Faust* does not survive and how the play was to end is merely a guess. But given Lessing's opposition to the

634 Fick, *Handbuch* 191.

635 Also see Toshimasa Yasukata, *Lessing's Philosophy of Religion and the German Enlightenment: Lessing on Christianity and Reason* (New York: Oxford University Press and The American Academy of Religion, 2002), especially chapter 6 "Lessing's Basic Thought in The Education of the Human Race," 89-117.

636 FA 4, 783.

637 Fick, *Handbuch* 191. See FA 7, 472-501. Monika Fick refers to Lessing's rejection of "ewige Verdammung." The word Lessing uses is "ewige Verdammnis" in "Leibnitz von den ewigen Strafen" (FA 7, 472-501 at 484, 491, and 492).

638 FA 11/1, 79-80 at 79.

notion of "eternal damnation" and his enthusiasm for open-ended learning, it is very likely that he anticipated Goethe in some ways by finding a miracle, or a strategic poetic surprise to exculpate Faust before the end of the play.[639] Monika Fick asks: "[W]as konnte Lessing an einem Stoff finden, der den Interessen des Aufklärers geradezu entgegengesetzt zu sein scheint?" (What could Lessing find in material that seems to be squarely opposite to the interests of the Enlightenment writer?)[640]

An answer to this question can be found in Lessing's experiments with narratives and poetic features, his attempt to explore temporality in the realm of the visual. Lessing's Faust fragments can best be understood in the context of his search to approximate sense perception and thinking, cognition processes and articulate expression. He sets out to illustrate how actions are consistent results of character traits and specific circumstances. Not only what we do matters. What we think and feel matters equally. Ideas and thoughts are already actions, although that transition tends to be subtle and probably barely traceable in the common use of language.[641] Alexander Košenina noted in *Anthropologie und Schauspielkunst* that during the years 1747/1748 and 1751/52 Lessing was a student of medicine at the University of Wittenberg and in the year 1751 he published a review of Samuel Schaarschmidt's *Physiologie.* It had appeared posthumously in 1751, edited by Ernst Anton Nicolai, a professor of medicine in Halle.[642] Nicolai challenged the Cartesian division between body and mind. He rejected the Leibnizian model with its notion of a pre-established harmony between the two, as it was then popularly interpreted. Body and mind were thought of being controlled externally, as if by a clock maker or a *Deus ex machina.* Nicolai rejected the hypothesis of *Occasionalismus* (occasionalism) in the sense of Nicolas Malebranche (1638-1715) who had conceptualized all activities and interactions as resulting solely through remote stimuli from a Divine source.[643] As Richard A. Watson points out:

> Malebranche's occasionalism seems to result from his abandoning an inexplicable doctrine of Cartesian secondary causes, both between minds and bodies and among bodies. He offers instead the primary cause of everything. He appeals to God's direct causal action.[644]

639 Christian Felix Weiße reports in a letter to Johann Peter Uz (1720-1796), after having meet Lessing in 1755, that Lessing was aware Goethe wanted to produce something on Doctor Faust. See Robert Petsch, ed. *Lessings Faustdichtung mit erläuternden Beigaben,* Germanische Bibliothek II: Untersuchungen und Texte 4 (Heidelberg: Winter, 1911), 44.

640 Fick, *Handbuch* 191.

641 Lessing anticipates to some extent Wassily Kandinsky, *Punkt und Linie zu Fläche: Über das Geistige in der Kunst,* 10th ed., intro. Max Brill (Bern: Benteli Verlag, 1952). Already Lessings draws attention to the poignant moment of an artwork or the narrative. The artist or writer must almost artificially isolate, select, or cut one distinct instant from the flux of time.

642 Košenina, *Anthropologie und Schauspielkunst* 5. The review appeared in Berlinische Privilegierte Zeitung 106.4.9 (1751), (FA 2, 200-201).

643 See Steven Nadler, "Introduction, *Causation in Early Modern Philosophy: Cartesianism, Occasionalism, and Preestablished Harmony* (University Park: Pennsylvania State University Press, 1993), 1-8 at 4-5 and Richard A. Watson, "Malebranche, Models, and Causation," Nadler, *Causation* 75-91.

644 "Malebranche, Models, and Causation," 83, "There is therefore only one single true God and one single cause that is truly a cause, and one should not imagine that what precedes an effect is its true cause." Nicolas Malebranche, *The Search after Truth, trans. and ed. Tho-*

Lessing distanced himself from Malebranche and his occasionalism. Instead he was much interested in the errors of the senses and problems with their readability.[645] Further Lessing did not agree with the notion that the senses were more prone to error than any deductive thinking would. To him thinking was based on sense perceptions and hence such a dualistic credo was obsolete. Lessing knew the work by Ernst Platner, professor of medicine and philosophy in Leipzig, a dominant voice in the group *Philosophische Ärzte* (philosophical doctors). In 1772 Platner wrote *Anthropologie für Ärzte und Weltweise* (Anthropology for Doctors and Cosmopolitans) and became the co-founder of a new discipline, thus contributing, along with their mutual friend Johann Gottfried Herder, to the rise of anthropology.[646] This discipline was established as a new approach to epistemological, physiological, and philosophical questions with the concept of *influxus physicus (the influence of the body on the soul) at its core.*[647] Lessing paid attention to the connection of body and soul and to their interrelated components. These are sense perceptions, knowledge formation, cognition, and thinking. These ideas were already in the process of being formulated in certain circles during the early 1750s to which also Lessing belonged and form the matrix for his *Faust.* Only fragments of Lessing's Faust play as he outlined it exist today. Robert Petsch reported that most of the documents, including the main version of Lessing's *D. Faust* from 1755, must have existed once upon a time. They are documented in the context of numerous letters to and from Lessing. It is reported that in 1775 this material was lost in in a chest which disappeared apparently in transit from Dresden to Leipzig (to be forwarded to Wolfenbüttel) and was never retrieved.[648]

But we still have some materials that are not to be ignored. Regardless of the long history of incubation of this work, it marks a period of transition in Lessing's life and in his approach. He accepts referring to magical and strange esoteric elements for his own reasoning while experimenting with scientific methods of empirical testing and probing the threshold of physically noticeable or even measurable pain. He shifts importance from the dimension of space to time and he begins to more challenging the directly visible in order to detect what may be underneath.[649] The Faust theme continued to haunt him and there are reports written between the years 1768-1775

---

*mas M. Lennon and Paul J. Olscamp* (Cambridge: Cambridge University Press, 1997), 451. The postulation of the ancient philosophers such as Aristotle that there might be other sources of causation is "[t]he most dangerous error of [their] philosophy," *The Search after Truth* 446. It is noteworthy that Lessing's Faust investigates this Aristotelian concept while making the human characters more responsible for their own actions.

645 See, for example, *The Search after Truth, Book One: The Senses,* 1-86, on "occasional errors of the senses" in detail.

646 See Zammito, *Kant, Herder* 250-253 and Alexander Košenina, *Ernst Platners Anthropologie und Philosophie: Der 'philosophische Arzt' und seine Wirkung auf Johann Karl Wezel und Jean Paul,* Epistemata: Reihe Literaturwissenschaft 35 (Würzburg: Königshausen & Neumann, 1989), 25-31.

647 See Eileen O'Neill, "Influxus Physicus," *Causation,* ed. Nadler, 27-55 and Košenina, *Ernst Platners Anthropologie* 27-28 and 107-129.

648 For details on the origins and state of this work, see Petsch, *Lessings Faustdichtung* 11-25. On the missing chest, see: FA 4, 825-826, 836-837; Nisbet, *Lessing: Eine Biographie* 531-535; *Gotthold Ephraim Lessing* 405-409.

649 FA 4, 781-788, 827-832.

indicating that Lessing was working on a new version of his *Faust* play. According to these notes he was ultimately to exclude supernatural elements from the plot. But since no further documents of this plan only this plan survive, it will not be further discussed here[650] Lessing's surviving fragments are, this much I would like to assert poetic experiments with new anthropological implications. They involve an interactive *influxus physicus* and illustrating the dynamics between the visual and the other senses. Lessing was testing boundaries of Ekphrasis in trying to conceptualize the limits of perception. The ability to pass one's finger through the flame of a candle without experiencing any burning sensation is a matter of speed. He thought about the threshold of error and pain and ways to imagine something that was neither visual, nor tactile, but still a possible and strangely measurable matter of fact. He was curious about modes of representation. He wanted to draw attention to things that one cannot present onstage and cannot be cogently explained. He used dialogue of the characters and omitted any superior or external commentator.

## 2. Political history and Lessing's circumstances

In 1755 Lessing left Berlin where he had been since1752. He returned to Leipzig. Soon he accepted to work for a rich Leipzig merchant by accompanying his son Johann Gottfried Winkler on a long educational tour across Europe. They were in Amsterdam on May 10, 1756 preparing to go to England just when Friedrich of Prussia invaded Saxony precipitating the Seven Years' War (1756-1763).[651] After Lessing returned with Winkler to Leipzig he met again some of his former acquaintances from his earlier Berlin days. To his surprise some were now on the side of the Prussians in their bid to take over the region. Among them was Ewald Christian von Kleist, a high ranking Prussian officer. He was a poet popular among literary circles including those frequented by Lessing. Kleist's landlady invited Prussians and Saxons to have lunch

650 See the recollections of Christian Friedrich von Blankenburg (1744-1796), "Schreiben über Lessings verloren gegangenen Faust," written in Leipzig on May 14, 1784 (FA 4, 64-65). In 1786 the recollections of Johann Jakob Engel (1741-1802) were published. He recreates from memory a dialogue between Satan and four devils who confess their misdeeds (Petsch, *Lessings Faustdichtung* 48-50; FA 4, 66-69). This looks like a rewriting of the scene between Beelzebub and the devils from the Prelude of the earlier text published in the same volume as Engel's recollections but based on the manuscript fragments Lessing had.

651 Nisbet, *Lessing: Eine Biographie* 295-298; *Gotthold Ephraim Lessing* 222-224. Friedrich Wilhelm II (the Great) of Prussia had conquered the Austrian province of Silesia in two wars 1741-1745. In an attempt to regain this lost territory, the Austrian Empress, Maria Theresa (whose ascension to the throne in 1740 had provided Friedrich with the excuse to invade Silesia), set about to form an alliance with France, Russia, Sweden and Saxony with the aim of curbing the power of Prussia (who was supported in this struggle by England). When Friedrich learned of this alliance, he decided to strike first and invaded Saxony. When peace was made in 1763 there was little to show for the tremendous loss of human life in central Europe as the borders remained the same as they had been in 1756. The country that gained the most from the struggle was England which deprived France of its colonial possessions in Canada and India.

together. Lessing's own fellow Saxons did not like that. Their protest and dislike made Lessing eventually feel uncomfortable. He was trapped both politically and professionally. When Winkler could not pay the money that had been agreed upon in order for Lessing to continue traveling with his son Lessing's debts grew quickly.

In 1758 he returned to Berlin in the hope of finding a new position. This was, however, not to be realized. Lessing participated in a lively coffee house culture, had regular encounters with friends that included Karl Wilhelm Ramler, Christoph Friedrich Nicolai, and Moses Mendelssohn. Lessing joined writers and critics in both a "Montagsklub" (Monday Club) and a "Freitagsklub" (Friday Club) and frequented meetings in the "Baumannshöhle" (Builder's Cave) often for a glass of wine chatting with interesting company. He was writing productively, although not at the level he found exemplary in Lope de Vega and some others he admired, particularly Shakespeare."[652]

Conflicting loyalties during the war were also dividing Lessing's friends. He tried to stay out of politics and rejected any idea of going to war. Lessing had reviewed Johann Wilhelm Ludwig Gleim's fables favorably, although he had privately admitted that he never liked them completely as they did not leave enough space for imagination.[653] When Gleim became a fervent patriot and supporter of Frederick the Great his writings of chauvinistic songs and poetry for propaganda were no longer acceptable to Lessing's taste and we can see from Lessing's correspondence that he struggled to distance himself from Gleim. He tried to dissociate himself for political reasons which he felt must also be traceable in writing styles and various approaches to poetics. Lessing was perplexed and really puzzled with Gleim's almost seamless transition from being an intellectual partner and friend devoted to the world of *poesy* and then corrupted into becoming an alienating advocate of war.

The almost unnoticeable juncture between the good and the bad is an underlying problem in Lessing's *Faust.* Gleim wanted to influence Lessing to turn to his war advocacy but Lessing really wanted to keep his distance. He wrote in a letter to Gleim on December 16, 1758 that he would prefer being a "Weltbürger" (a cosmopolitan), much rather than being a "Patriot."[654] Lessing used a bit of sarcasm and was a fervent defender of peace. He rejected the style of advertisement and tried to endorse rhetoric that allowed the addressee a sense of freedom. He tried to stand up for cultural production anywhere in the German language, not just that in particularized Prussia. He had a vision to be culturally inclusive and to give free range of the imagination to multiple audiences and spectatorships. To some extent, however, Lessing could not avoid to get entangled with politics- He writes in his letters that what happened

652 See Lessing's letter to Gleim, July 8, 1758: "Ich schreibe Tag und Nacht und mein kleinster Vorsatz ist jetzo, wenigstens noch dreimal so viele Schauspiele zu machen, als Lope de Vega. Erstens werde ich meinen *Doctor Faust* hier spielen lassen" (I am writing day and night and my smallest intention is now to compose at least three times as many plays, just like Lope de Vega. First I would have my *Doctor Faust* performed here) (FA 11/1, 292-293 at 293). Felix Lope de Vega Carpio is said to have written about 1800 plays. The titles of more than 600 plays are recorded and of these about 458 scripts are documented.

653 FA 4, 117-129.

654 FA 11/1, 305-306 at 305.

then was against his will.[655] All of a sudden, Lessing left Berlin on November 7, 1760 without letting anybody know. He had accepted a new post in Breslau in Silesia, now Wrocław, Poland, as the secretary of the Prussian General Friedrich Bogislaw von Tauentzien. He felt uneasy and conflicted by this move and his own shifting loyalties. He felt forced by the overwhelming need to make a living. In a letter to his friend Mendelssohn Lessing tried to explain and to excuse himself for apparently having switched sides of the political spectrum and for his sudden and unexpected departure.[656] He felt caught between financial needs, incompatible surroundings, and the urgent need for a job.

Beginning in 1759 Lessing had been involved in a new project, a weekly journal, *Briefe, die neueste Literatur betreffend.* These he published together with Christoph Friedrich Nicolai and Mendelssohn. The journal ran until 1765. For several years Lessing seemed to become more of a literary critic than an author of original works of literature although his articles were usually written from a fictional perspective. He liked the auctorial voice of a narrator addressing somebody who had just returned from the war, wounded, being curious to learn what had been going on in German literature and culture in the meantime. Of the 332 letters which ultimately appeared, Lessing was responsible for 55.[657] The most significant is the 17th *Literaturbrief* of February 16, 1759. In it Lessing muses that only a Shakespeare could do justice to the story of "Doctor Faust," but nevertheless says that one of his friends (i.e. Lessing himself incognito) had in fact made such an attempt.[658] He then teases his readers with a snippet, scene three of the second act of a play called "Faust und die sieben Geister" (Faust and the seven spirits). This is the only fragment from his writing on Faust that was published during his lifetime.[659]

## 3. The first version of Lessing's *Faust*

Lessing draws attention to idiosyncrasies that exist and he wants to collect productive energies turning to what might be called a "produktive Kritik." He got involved in studying remote scripts, philosophical and theoretical treatises. He gained new ideas through the translations of little known foreign works including esoteric scripts. He

655 See, for example, his letter to Ramler, December 6, 1760, FA 11/1, 353-355, esp. 354.

656 FA 11/1, 356-357.

657 FA 4, 783.

658 Lessing's championing of the Faust theme is part of his continuing quarrel with Gottsched who rejected this theme as being inappropriate for a revitalized German theater. He argued it should take the subject matter of the French classical tragedians as its model: "Das Mährchen von D. Fausten hat lange genug den Pöbel belustiget: und man hat ziemlicher maßen aufgehört solche Alfanzereyen gern anzusehen" (The fairy-tale of Doctor Faust has amused the riffraff long enough; and one has pretty much ceased liking to watch such phantasmagoria) in *Versuch einer Critischen Dichtkunst,* fourth edition (1751), 185-186.

659 For the 17th *Literaturbrief* of February 16, 1759, see FA 4, 499-501. The scene from the Faust play which should appear beginning on the bottom of FA 4, 501 is found on FA 4, 61-63.

wanted to switch from the mundane experiences which characterized the sentimental material in *Miß Sara Sampson* to something more philosophical, testing boundaries and dynamics between the visual and the verbal. His previous work was successful in having made a spectacle. It had forced the public in the theater to stare, to find themselves watching innocent people die, and to feel rather upset and puzzled with this imposed voyeurism. He had dared to address the problem of false escapism through death and he was now to turn his attention to modes of expression that could perhaps change predictable fatality. At the core of *Faust* is the idea that something can change in one single significant instant, or that time matters a great deal. He also makes the recipients question what is uncontrollable "Schicksal" (fate) and make us ponder about any meta-perspectives that could further explain the notion of the poignant moment. It is identified as containing more than one potential action in the ongoing flux of time. The protagonist had to deal with forces that are uncanny and apparently uncontrollable. Yet the play also draws attention to the ability of humans to change for a good cause. Lessing challenges the notion of "ewige Verdammnis" (eternal damnation) and questions what "eternal" could really possibly mean, a concept so far removed from any imaginable thinking. Lessing had been familiar with the Faust motif since his school years at the University of Leipzig. He already referred to it in his comedy *Der junge Gelehrte* (*The Young Scholar*, 1748) where Anton, a servant to the young scholar, Damis, says to his master in the opening scene:

> Aber sagen Sie mir nur, was lesen Sie denn da für ein Buch? Potz Stern, was das für Zeug ist! Das verstehen Sie? Solche Krakelfüße, solche fürchterliche Zickzacke, die kann ein Mensch lesen? Wenn das nicht wenigstens Fausts Höllenzwang[660] ist–. Ach, man weiß es ja wohl, wies den Leuten geht, die alles lernen wollen.[661]
>
> [But just tell me, what kind of book are you reading here? Goodness gracious, what kind of stuff this is. Do you understand it? Such funny characters, such horrible zig-zags, how can anybody read this? I bet you: this is Faust's *Höllenzwang* [Infernal Command].–O, one knows very well what happens to those people who want to learn everything].

Here Faust is identified as a master magician who through his spells and incantations, sometimes expressed in terms of fantastical magic figures or "runes" ("Krakelfüße" and "fürchterliche Zickzacke"). Apparently they gave him power to make demons submit to his will. His story is also the prime example of what happens to people whose intense desire for learning and knowledge motivates them to venture beyond the boundaries of what is good for them. No matter how much Faust acted under the influence of circumstances, he was to be responsible for his own actions. Lessing expresses his criticism by means of developing poetic writing that offers only dialogue. It clearly projects an urgent a need for change. Although it may have been a reaction to the impeding war mentality around him, Lessing's *Faust* fragments have been seen as

660 This is a reference to any number of early chapbooks with *Höllenzwang* (Infernal Command) in the title and supposedly written by Faust, such as *Doktor Johannes Faust's Dreifacher Höllenzwang* re-edited from the edition of J. Scheible (1849) (Graz: Geheimes Wissen, 2008), or from the numerous printings of a volume, variously assigned to the Jesuit College in Prague or Rome and usually dated early in the 16th century, republished as: *Doctor Fausts großer und gewaltiger Höllenzwang* (Graz: Geheimes Wissen, 2009).

661 FA 1, 142.

a work indicative of Lessing's unbroken optimism and as his efforts with rationalizing theology. Some commentators see in it a sign of Lessing's cosmopolitan scholarship and curious experimenting anticipating elements of Goethe's *Faust.* Others have seen the play as a response to various contemporaries, especially a critique of Gottsched who seemed to be "der Inbegriff des pedantischen and phantasielosen Gelehrten" (the ultimate pedantic scholar without any imagination).[662] Yet Lessing's Faust fragment draws attention not only to a scholar at fault. It allows for the possibility of a passionate individual who seeks liberation from the mundane passing through the fire as unscathed as a finger quickly traversing a candle's flame. Can the senses be trusted?

## 4. Contextualizing Lessing's *Faust* and its innovations

Lessing's initial impulse to compose his own drama on Faust may have resulted from his attending a popular Faust play on June 14, 1754.[663] Faust scholarship, particularly in German, mostly focused on Goethe in the context of the Faust motif, so that any other versions of *Faust,* including Lessing's, tend to be read only through the lens of Goethe's version. When these other *Faust* versions are taken into consideration it is mostly in terms of finding thematic continuity with Goethe's text. This would certainly not do justice to Lessing nor to Heinrich Heine who in his version of *Faust* then actually returned to some aspects of Lessing's version but in the end does not allow for any reconciliation. Heine presents a character who has transgressed the boundaries of this and the other world in acts of hubris and who in the end is being punished by being snatched away from the earth and drawn down into the ground into infernal realms below.[664]

As has already been noted, in *Der junge Gelehrte,* a servant named Damis had accused his master of reading "Fausts Höllenzwang," a grimoire supposedly written by Faust and full of fantastically drawn magic figures and seals. While this may refer to one of a number of popular chapbooks, there is a good likelihood that Damis is referring to an early published version of *Dr. Faust's großer und gewaltiger Höllenzwang.* An argument can be made that Lessing either owned a copy, or at least had access to

---

662 FA 4, 784.

663 Petsch, *Lessings Faustdichtung* 11; Nisbet, *Lessing: Eine Biographie* 204; *Gotthold Ephraim Lessing* 274-275. The play was put on by Franz Schuch's company, and according to Mahal, "Lessings Faust" 528, the play was: *Unglückselige Gelehrsamkeit des Welt-berufenen Ertz-Zauberers Johannis Fausti Doctor Wittenbergensis* (Unlucky erudition of the world-renowned arch-magician, Johannes Faustus Doctor Wittenbergensis), a well-known play known to have been in various forms in the repertoire of numerous acting companies whichever used the German language.

664 Fore more on Heine's Faust details see Beate Allert, "Heine's *Dr. Faust: A Ballet Poem" in Faust Adaptations from Marlowe to Aboudoma and Markland,* ed. Lorna Fitzsimmons (West Lafayette: Purdue University Press, 2016), 67-77. This juxtaposes Heine's Faust version against Goethe's where Faust appears to be rescued from above. The fact that Heine presents his version in form of a dance ballet ows some inspiration from Lessing who already paid much attention to timing, steps, and consistent moves from inner to outer actions.

one.[665] The book contains a brief narrative which serves a preface to the spells and incantations which make up most of the book. Faust has gained mastery over a powerful spirit, Asteroth, who produces another demon, Mochiel, as a potential servant. Faust asks how fast he is and when he is told as fast as the wind, dismisses him. The same thing happens to the second demon, Anigiel, who says he is as fast as a bird in flight. Only Aziel, who is as swift as human thought, proves fast enough and goes on to serve Faust for a long time.[666] A version of this "Trial by Speed" is the subject of the third scene in act two of the *Faust* play which Lessing inserted into the 17th *Literaturbrief* of 1759.[667] The scene features Faust and seven spirits or devils.[668] It opens with Faust asking the assembled company if they are the fastest spirits of Hell. But they are not all equally fast.

> FAUST Und welcher von euch ist der Schnelleste?
> DIE GEISTER ALLE Der bin ich!
> FAUST Ein Wunder! daß unter sieben Teufel nur sechs Lügner sind.–Ich muß euch näher kennen lernen.[669]
>
> [FAUST And who among you is the fastest?
> ALL THE SPIRITS It is me!
> FAUST What a surprise! That among seven devils there are only six liars.–I must get to know you better].

The first spirit when questioned about how fast he is replies: "Du könnest eher eine Probe, als eine Antwort haben" (You can rather make a test of it instead of getting an answer). Faust then asks what he is doing: "Du fährst mit deinem Finger schnell durch die Flamme des Lichts–FAUST–Und verbrenne mich nicht" (You are passing your finger

665 In 1767 when Lessing was working on his second version of *Faus*t, he was trying to get hold of a copy of the "Clavicula Solomonis." See his letter to his brother, Karl, September 21, 1767 (FA 11/1, 476-477 at 477). Note that Goethe's *Faust* has a copy: "Für solche halbe Höllenbrut / Ist Salomonis Schüsssel gut" (For such a half-baked hell-spawn, the *Clavicula Salominis* is good). See Goethe, *Faust*, "Studierzimmer [I]," 1257-1258 (GFA 7/1, Texte, ed. Albrecht Schöne, 61). For Latin and German editions, see Adolf Jacoby, "Clavicula Salomonis," *Handwörterbuch des deutschen Aberglaubens* 2: cols. 88-93 at 88-89. For an English version, see *The Key of Solomon the King (Clavicula Salomonis)*, ed. S. H. MacGregor Mathers (Cambridge: Cambridge University Press, 2012), first published 1889.

666 Doctor Fausts großer und gewaltiger Höllenzwang (2009), 53-54, translated by Robert Blanchard as The Black Book of Doctor Faust: Doctor Johannes Faust's Miracle and Magic Book, or The Black Raven, or also named The Three-Fold Coercion of Hell, 2nd ed. (Palm Springs, CA: International Guild of Esoteric Sciences, 1992), 44-45.

667 There is an English translation of this scene in Butler, *The Fortunes of Faust* 116-117. On the "trial by speed" which dates back to the earliest Faust narratives, see Elizabeth M. Butler, *Ritual Magic* (Cambridge: Cambridge University Press, 1949), 184-185; The Fortunes of Faust, 114-117.

668 These seven spirits may be based on the "sieben Großfürsten" (seven dukes) of the "höllische Reich" (infernal empire) listed in the *gewaltiger Höllenzwang* (55-56): Aziel, Mephistophilis, Marbuel, Ariel, Aniguel, Anisel, and Barfael. Blanchard in *The Black Book* (56) makes the following substitutions: for Aniguel–Aziahel, and for Barfael–Barbuel. The names Lessing gives to three of his demons, Chil, Dilla and Jutta, have to my knowledge no connections to any earlier Faust materials (FA 4, 838-839).

669 FA 4, 62.

quickly through the flame of a candle—FAUST And not burning myself).[670] He then sets the devil the task and asks him if he is fast enough, to fly through the flames of hell and not be burned. But the devil does not move indicating that he is not capable of accomplishing this. Faust pours scorn upon him before turning to the second spirit who calls himself Chil, that is, "Pfeil der Pest" (arrow of the plague).[671] He is not fast enough, nor Dilla, carried on the wings of the wind,[672] nor Jutta who travels on beams of light,[673] nor the fifth spirit who in the traditional story is always the winner being: "So schnell als die Gedanken des Menschen" (as quick as human thoughts). Faust finds this promising, but then recollects how sluggish some peoples' thoughts are. The sixth spirit is: "So schnell als die Rache des Rächers" (As quick as the revenge of the revenger). This oblique reference to ultimate truth rattles Faust. He also rejects this spirit, because the revenger cannot be all that swift if he, Faust, sinful as he may be, is still alive. His choice will be the seventh devil claiming to be the fastest of them all. Lessing's Faust votes the most transient and the most rapidly changeable of these devils. How fast is he? "Nicht mehr und nicht weniger [schnell] als der Übergang vom Guten zum Bösen" (No more and no less [fast] than the transition from the good to the bad). "Ja, der ist schnell, schneller ist nichts als der" (Yes, that one is fast, nothing is faster than that one).[674] Faust has finally found a spirit suitable to be selected as one to serve him. The other devils are dismissed and the scene ends. The seventh devil stands as a test case for exploring temporality. Lessing was a critic of the notion of providence yet may have felt a bit compromised about his new position. He became aware in the context of his experiences with a changing political climate how hard it was to resist external needs and to remain focused on the good in one's own path through life. He makes us think of extreme speed and how to resist the impact of time, perhaps also the power of imposed necessity. Under scrutiny are also the questions concerning the ability, potential, and boundaries of human change and what it means to be loyal and true to one's character. Among Lessing's concerns in the play is the observation that extreme positive characteristics can turn into an extreme with rather negative consequences, no matter how positive the same features or character traits are if they were correctly balanced within proportionate measure. He makes us wonder about the transition from good to bad and how contextually dependent all characteristics ultimately are. There are additional questions concerning dramaturgy, such as the tensions between thinking and acting onstage, seeing versus hearing. His play can spark the spectators' imagination. But can it do so without departing too much from the relevant here and now? Lessing makes us wonder about the abilities and limits

---

670 FA 4, 62.

671 Possibly related to Hebrew *shelach* (spear). See "The New Strong's Expanded Dictionary of the Words of the Hebrew Bible" in James Strong, *The New Strong's Expanded Exhaustive Concordance of the Bible* (Nashville, TN: Thomas Nelson, 2010), i-iv, 1-303 (separate pagination), Hebrew word #7973 (281).

672 Possibly related to Hebrew *dâlâh* (dangle). Strong, *New Strong's,* Hebrew word #1802 (63).

673 Possibly related to Hebrew *yâthar* (excel). Strong, *New Strong's,* Hebrew word #3498 (124-125). For a different explanation, see FA 4, 838-839. It seems odd to me that if two of the names given to the spirits have Hebrew roots why the third name should not have one also and suggest that all three names Lessing uses have Hebrew origin.

674 FA 4, 63.

of human metamorphosis, the noticeability of human change, and problems with visibility and hearing. How to notice any subtle appearances and sounds and how to notice the transition from the good to the dangerous? Will such movement later cause pain? The question that I see implicit is also: How can language describe things that fluctuate and that change their meaning qualitatively in the process of describing them? How to detect the turning points? Can the change from the good to the bad happen so quickly that it escapes our seeing and sensing completely? How fool-proof are the senses of sight and of sound, once so celebrated and taken for granted in the philosophical debates of the Enlightenment?

The key problem is how to differentiate between the multiple sense perceptions, memories, and expectations. The mind seems to project. Sense perceptions become dubious at times. It is possible that there is merging or false splitting of inner and outer realities. Attention is drawn to non-linear time experiences that may us realize the difficulties to perceive and to represent "truth" adequately although is consist always of a conglomeration of multiple facets. There are issues of identity. How can one evaluate a character when the person keeps changing? Karl Guthke finds Lessing's interest in Faust "paradoxical" from the start but then correctly points out that Lessing may have been very creative when in his very final version Faust was probably to be rescued.[675] Lessing's description of the transgression of human boundaries in his *Faust* differs greatly from Goethe's *Faust.* There Faust turns to magic when making a deal with Mephistopheles. Lessing's Faust turns to sources, popular legends, literature, and poetic theory. Faust will elect the fastest spirit as his "servant" as he wants to become a master of temporality. Since that master really cannot be seen, this may also indicate that in fact Lessing opts for abolishing any "servant." Any poor "devil" will no longer be needed.

## 5. Lessing's second version of *Faust*

The second *Faust* fragment first published in 1786 presents the opening of the play. The scene is an old cathedral and opens with a prelude ("Vorspiel") involving a verger and his son: "In einem alten Dome–Der Küster und sein Sohn, welche eben zu Mitternacht geläutet oder läuten wollen" (In an old cathedral–The verger and his son who have either just tolled the midnight bell, or wanted to toll it).[676] The main concern here is precise timing. The audience (and perhaps even the verger) are not sure whether or not the midnight bell has been tolled. Not knowing the difference between wanting to or having already tolled the bell confuses intention with action. This raises questions about how not to conflate outer and inner notions of time, or how to get them in harmony despite not knowing the difference really. The problem

675 Karl S. Guthke,"Lessings Faust-Dichtung," *Wege zur Literatur: Studien zur deutschen Dichtungs- und Geistesgeschichte* (Bern: Francke, 1967), 247-255 at 249-251. First published as: "Problem und Problematik von Lessings Faust-Dichtung," *Zeitschrift für Deutsche Philologie* 79 (1960): 141-149.

676 FA 4, 59.

of finding out whether it has actually been rung or whether it is being rung was only a matter of imagination placed as it is at the beginning of the play. This suggests that the search for the correct moment is something that will prove pivotal for the entire action of the scene. Words are taken back or corrected as soon as they are spoken. The audience and the readers of this text are faced with the question whether they may also have missed the crucial moment. Did they hear the bell toll, or did it ring only in their mind? Are the actors playing for real, or are they only rehearsing the act before the actual play begins? Whether the signal of the bell is reliable is a question that remains unresolved. The audience of the play is to participate in the action and must sympathize with the insecurity of verger and son.

Goethe begins his *Faust* with a dialogue between the master of heaven and earth and Mephistopheles. Mephistopheles accepts the challenge and the deal with the master to tempt and win over Faust. Lessing also has a similar scene in his prelude. But instead of a beginning setting in heaven or in a study room, Lessing's play gives his play the setting of an old cathedral among ruins outdoors. There are devils sitting invisible on the altars, their presence revealed by their conversations. Beelzebub is present and various devils, ghosts, or simply spirits "erscheinen" (appear—presumably visibly) before him. They each report on the result of their missions. One has put a city to fire. A second has sunk an entire fleet in a storm. A third devil belittles the accomplishments of these others as "Armseligkeiten" (paltriness). He has seduced a virtuous man from the good to the bad by getting him so drunk that he later committed adultery and murder. The conversation then turns to Faust who might not prove so easy to change. The third devil accepts the challenge to deliver Faust to hell in twenty-four hours. At this moment, says another devil, he is sitting by his nocturnal lamp and studying the "Tiefen der Wahrheit" (depths of truth). "Zu viel Wißbegierde ist ein Fehler; und aus einem Fehler können alle Laster entspringen, wenn man ihm zu sehr nachhänget" (Too much thirst for knowledge is a mistake; and from a mistake all vices may spring if one becomes too much lost in it).[677] At this point the third devil sets about making his plans. The location is, to be more precise, outside a cathedral, old and perhaps dilapidated. It is a sacred place but already destroyed. We are not sure what to expect. The opening words have suggested that outer time stands still for those that may have entered the cathedral in reflection, meditation, and quiet prayer. Attention is drawn from "theatricality" as Michael Fried would call it, to "absorption."[678] One is made aware of the act of seeing while participating in it. This leads from a state of a dreamlike reverie and silence to contemplation and devotion.

It seems to be a timeless location or one to dismiss time. The setting suggests that the figures onstage do well to forget about themselves for a while and to focus on something beyond their daily activities with undivided attention. This shift from an outer to an inner existence in such place around the midnight becomes uncanny only when we hear about a group of "devils" that are, as we are told, gathered invisibly on the altars. They can only be heard. The split between hearing and seeing, the separa-

677 FA 4, 59.
678 Fried, *Absorption and Theatricality* 10.

tion of the senses, is a theme that occupied Lessing.[679] From this first moment on we are presented with the problem of splitting moments, causing confusion between the senses, and resulting puzzlement. There may be a difference between sign and signifier, tolling the bell and experiencing midnight. Not to be able to differentiate between wanting to ring the bell and having done so in reality means not to be in control of one's action, to be forgetful or lack attention to one's own deeds. It raises the problem of responsibility and reliability. Lessing further seems to ask is what actually "the real" is and whether or not it can ever be universally experienced? Could it be restricted to individual consciousness? The problem with intentionality is that interruptions are always possible. There are discrepancies between outer and inner realities.

The first scene in act one opens with the stage directions: "Dauer des Stücks von Mitternacht zu Mitternacht" (The piece runs from midnight to midnight). It is to span of time the third devil assumed was all he would need to deliver Faust to hell. Faust is reading by his lamp occupied with various doubts from scholastic philosophy ("aus der scholastischen Weltweisheit"). He recalls that a scholar had supposedly once been able to summon the devil by using Aristotle's word *entelechy, as legendary for calling up a vital force or even a spirit.*[680] He himself has tried this several times without success. He decides to try it one more time. The hour is right (is it midnight he wonders?) and he reads an incantation. Scene two opens with a "Geist" (spirit or devil) who appears with a long beard and wrapped in a cloak rising up through the floor. Faust is startled, asking who disturbs him, where is he and: "Ist das nicht Licht was ich empfinde?" (Is it not light that I feel?) [681] The question we may ask is why it comes from below and not from above.[682] He steadies himself and begins to question the spirit asking who summoned him. The spirit replies that he had been dozing and dreamed that he was not well. Then he heard a voice cry "Bahall." [683] The third time the name was uttered he appears. Faust wants to know who the spirit is. It is not sure: "Ich bin–ich bin nur erst kürzlich was ich bin" (I am–I am only quite recently what I am). Then Faust wants to know: "Aber wer warst du?" (But who were you?) The question confuses the spirit. Pressed to recollect some memories of a previous state it triggers something vague. Faust tries to help by asking the spirit its name: "Ich hieß–Aristoteles. Ja, so hieß ich. Wie ist mir?" (I am called–Aristotle. Yes, that what I am called. What am I like?). [684] The spirit who is in fact the one who has undertaken to draw Faust or to

679 Utz, *Das Auge und das Ohr* interprets Lessing's innovation as newly drawing attention to the splitting between sense perceptions that all of a sudden can no longer be synchronized. See his chapter "Wie ist doch meine Seele zwischen Auge und Ohr geteilt" (How my soul is divided between eye and ear), 39-57. Utz does not mention Lessing's *Faust* in this regard.

680 Aristotle, *On the Soul. Parva naturalia. On Breath,* trans. W. S. Hett, Rev. ed., Loeb Classical Library 288 (Cambridge: Harvard University Press, 1957), (413b) II.ii, 76-77, line 18.

681 FA 4, 60.

682 It was Heine's Faust ballet that then picked up on this notion as found in Lessing with the light coming from the ground instead of from above. In Heine's Faust version there will be a monstrous hand in the end that pulls Faust into the ground for punishment in contrast to Goethe's version where Faust gets lifted into the air above.

683 Hebrew *ba'al* (master, the name of a deity frequently mentioned on the Old Testament). See Strong, *New Strong's,* #1165 (42).

684 FA 4, 61.

seduce him from the good to the bad, now begins to respond in detail to all of Faust's difficult questions. The scene ends with the spirit protesting saying it is exhausted and no longer capable to answer any of Faust's questions, neither as human nor as a spirit.

In scene three the spirit disappears. Faust, elated with his success as a sorcerer of a kind, decides to use the incantation again to summon yet another spirit. Scene four has a devil appearing while raising the question: "Wer ist der Mächtige, dessen Rufe ich gehorchen muß! Du? Ein Sterblicher? Wer lehrte dich diese gewaltigen Worte?" (Who is the powerful one whose commands I must obey? You? A mortal being? Who taught you these powerful words?)[685] At this point the fragment breaks off. Lessing's *Faust* was to pursue the idea that what appears to be a virtue or a character strength may then turn out to be a danger, a vice, or even a fatal flaw. when it has become something extreme and all too dominant. Being able to call up the spirits of those that belong to another time may not be in the interest of the here and how. There may have been a logical need to end the fragment here.

## 6. Aspects of language: Comparing Lessing's *Faust* with that by Goethe

For both Lessing and Goethe timing is important. What has to be taken into account is not only the word but also the "Geist" (spirit).[686] Both are concerned with issues of meaning that often hinge upon the most adequate translation. They search precision in language that cannot do without paying careful attention to the context. For Goethe, Faust has this problem:

> Geschrieben steht: "Im Anfang war das Wort!"[687]
> Hier stock' ich schon! Wer hilft mir weiter fort?
> Ich kann das Wort so hoch unmöglich schätzen,
> Ich muß es anders übersetzen.
> Wenn ich vom Geiste recht erleuchtet bin.
> Geschrieben steht: im Anfang war der Sinn.
> Bedenke wohl die erste Zeile,
> Daß deine Feder sich nicht übereile!
> Ist es der Sinn, der alles wirkt und schafft?
> Es sollte stehn: im Anfang war die Kraft!
> Doch auch indem ich dieses niederschreibe,
> Schon warnt mich was, daß ich dabei nicht bleibe.
> Mir hilft der Geist! Auf einmal seh' ich Rat
> Und schreibe getrost: im Anfang war die Tat.[688]
>
> [It stands written: "In the beginning was the Word!"
> Here I already stop! Who helps me further?

685 FA 4, 61.
686 2nd Cor 3, 6: "Denn der Buchstabe tötet, aber der Geist machtet lebendig." "For the letter killeth, but the spirit giveth life."
687 John 1, 1. "Im Anfang war das Wort." "In the beginning was the Word."
688 Goethe, *Faust*, "Studierzimmer [I]," 1224-1237 (GFA 7/1, 61).

It is impossible for me to appreciate the word that highly,
I have to translate it differently
Whenever I am really enlightened by the spirit.
It stands written: In the beginning was the force.
Think well through this first line
So that your pen does not get too much into a hurry.
Is it the mind that effects and creates everything?
It should stand there: In the beginning was the deed!
Yet also while I am writing this down
Something already warns me, that I will not stick with it.
I am helped by the spirit! At once I see a suggestion
And write confidently: In the beginning was the Deed].

Lessing similar to Goethe interrogates the various sign systems, words, and images and he also refers to the Biblical difference between the letter and the spirit of words. In Goethe's *Faust* here is a pact which Faust makes with Mephistopheles and it concerns the ability to obtain an "Augenblick" (moment) that could be so decisive that whatever happens afterword's can be ignored for the time being. Time would the potentially have been allowed to stand still. If that state of ideal being, such bliss, could be experienced and if Faust would ever have admitted to being so happy saying that the moment did stand still, then Mephistopheles would rightfully have won. Then he could claim his soul. This does not really happen as we know from a close reading of Goethe and the related scholarship. Goethe uses sophisticated language, the subjunctive referring to such moment. It is only to be imagined yet never fully realized at the ultimate climax of the play. Since Faust avoids the indicative form in saying that the moment stood still he gets apparently saved. However there are sounds and forces from above that come to rescue him and it was his luck having used his words carefully.[689]

Lessing's Faust is also a complex poet work and it is related to the other fragment, *Fatime.* Again, an individual has to be described either as good or evil as in the case of Faust. A character has to be staged as looking happy despite her tears in the eyes just at the moment before. Questions considering both cases include: How to distinguish natural from artificial signs, pretense from truth acting from honest expression of real emotions? How to be able to gauge the essence, integrity, or authenticity of a character? Can one do that just by looking? The answer must be given regarding one an instant only. Whatever qualities these characters feature signify there will be an art in capturing them correctly. The surviving Faust fragments give readers a glimpse into Lessing's conscious efforts to condense time, to highlight rapid actions.[690] He

689 When Faust makes his pact with Mephistopheles he gives him an instance of when his life would be immediately forfeit: "Werd' ich zum Augenblicke sagen: / Verweile doch! du bist so schön!" (If I were to say to a moment: Stop! you are so beautiful!) See Goethe, *Faust,* "Studierzimmer [II]," 1699-1700 (GFA 7/1. 76). But the verb *werden* is carefully couched in the subjunctive mood, giving Mephistopheles false hope that this is what will happen, whereas Faust is making clear that it is only something that might possibly happen.

690 J.M. Van der Laan, "Lessing's 'Lost" Faust' and Faustus Socinus," *Lessing Yearbook* 38 (2008-2009): 53-65 refers to scholars such as Arthur Henkel, Hans Henning, and Karl-Heinz Hucke who doubt that the legendary "nearly complete manuscript ever even existed" (53). But Van der Laan argues that "Lessing's Faust remains especially significant"

experiments with significant compacted moments of "Dichtung" while shifting attention to the acoustic with simultaneous signs or tones. The Faust fragments illustrate Lessing's conscious approach to art in terms of understatement. The short scenes end up questioning the processes of seeing and staging. Lessing had already worked with acoustic versus visual experiments attempting to present images or scenes that contain the most poignant, delightful, and consequential moments extracted from the flux of time. Nevertheless he wants to leave space for the absorption in the temporal.

In both his *Faust* and *Fatime* plays Lessing works on historical material of literature which he reinterpreted and revived in his own language and style. He creates dialogues that have particular significance for the specific actions of these plays and considering a language-critical semiotic dimension. Lessing seems to indicate meanings that are not obvious and shifts attention to whatever may have appeared marginal before. Lessing's *Faust* makes a reasonable deal with a character, an insignificant poor devil whose claim is that he is able to master time, be in control of speed, and able to change so quickly that nobody can see it. Lessing makes an allusion also as a playwright hinting at to what happens behind the curtain onstage where, almost as if by magic, the same actors have to play sometimes various roles and are forced to switch clothing and outfits in rapid succession. His elected "devil" says he is as quick as the change from good to evil and presumably back again. But what really happens is that he relies on the bad perceptual skills of his audience. He anticipates film images that are actually distinct sequences of pictures at first but are perceived as actions thanks to the flaw of human cognition making them blurred. He makes use of disability in a productive way, thus showing that blindness is only another degree of the usual way of seeing. His swift flexibility and ungraspable movement with great speed make him the best among his peers. Lessing celebrates a Faustian servant. He is drawn to such a figure and is also a co-actor. And Lessing affirms that Faust is allowed to change. In response to the use of stable, framed tableaux he opts for movements onstage that mobilize imagination.

The challenge of correct seeing is that metamorphosis occurs so rapidly that it eludes visibility. Actions happen that cannot be observed. One can see only what has happened by looking at visual effects. But these are rarely informative about how things have developed. Lessing had relied, like many Enlightenment thinkers of his time, on concrete sense perceptions, on the eyes, on language, and on the ability to formulate truth. Lessing now reflects critically on the use of certain epistemological assumptions. They were to be come contested by philosophers but by his own experience. Lessing processes in his playwriting certain ideas on how to evaluate actions. He

---

and links Lessing's Faust manuscript with that by Fausto Sozzini (known in Latin as Socius) which disappeared. He points out that Christopher Marlowe's *Tragicall History of D. Faustus* was first published the same year of Sozzini's death, in 1604. Van der Laan raises interesting research questions in associating Faust's urge to know with Lessing's late statements in the "Duplik" (1778), according to which it is the honest search and not necessarily the possession of truth which may ultimately count. Although the chest containing Lessing's Faust manuscript according to Van der Laan "truly went missing" (63), he suggests that "there is still an occasion to discover," as he puts it, "lost works by Bach, Mozart, and Beethoven today, not to mention the 'lost' manuscript of the sixteenth century Faust-book in the very library Lessing himself once supervised" (63). That book, he claims, should still be located.

brings to attention that the spectators normally do not know what the sequences of actions and the chronologies of such complex choreography are. How can we say this is a good or a bad person based on certain actions if we cannot trace these actions back to the complete development in their social history from beginning to end? How can one run a finger through a flame and not burn it? How fast does one have to move to pretend that time has no consequences? If change comes about so suddenly it cannot be detected. Our moral judgment may at times be superficial and purely speculative. Lessing works with a fictional device to challenge not only poetics but also ethics. He is critical of categorical language that excludes the invisible. He rejects an all too simplistic notion of clarity based more on probability than truth. The need of cutting time and of editing texts into distinct segments appears to be an act of "Willkür" or often arbitrary. Lessing illustrates that time includes not only action but also inaction, states in between, such as dreaming or waiting. Lessing's dramatic fragments *Faust* and *Fatime* both articulate something less obvious than what is being presented onstage or said on a mundane level. These plays draw attention to multiple perspectives considering the unfathomable impact of temporality both unto what we see and what we don't see. They indicate equally stark consequences of actions and of inactions. And he gives attention to the invisible and grapples with accepting rapid change.

## 7. Lessing's *Fatime* (1759)

This play exists in two versions. There is the outline for a play in 15 scenes called initially *Phatime* and apparently to be set in Arabia.[691] A second version called Fatime on which I shall focus on here, exists in a manuscript dated July 5, 1759. This version is set in the Ottoman Empire.[692] While the first two complete scenes are in prose Lessing switches to verse for the remainder of the fragment.[693] The verse section has been highly esteemed by some Lessing scholars. The early twentieth-century Germanist Waldemar Oehlke praised its "dialogische Feinheit" (sophisticated dialogues). It reminded him of the verse in *Nathan der Weise* (1779) often considered to be Lessing's

691 FA 4, 70-72. Lessing's brother Karl explains in the introduction to his edition (1786) that from this plan one can well deduce the entire action of the play and figure from the essence of the plot that Lessing intended to show only "ohngefehr wie aus dem Skelet der ganze Körper" (approximately, like from a skeleton the entire body"). It is, in other words, a perfect example of Lessing's experimenting with understatement. It may well be that instead of not being finished as the result of external influences, which is the usual interpretation, the play is complete, a minimalist play reflecting not only on content but on the process of acting and engaging the imagination of the spectators by non-verbal gestures and actions.

692 This is not the only one of Lessing's dramatic fragments to be set in this region. See my essay "Gotthold Ephraim Lessing, Giangir, or the Rejected Throne (1748)," Yermolenko, ed., *Roxalana* 239-242 and Allert "Roxalana in German Baroque and Enlightenment Dramas: Lohenstein, Haugwitz, Lessing, and Weisse," 89-108, esp. 100-103.

693 FA 4, 73-79.

best work.[694] He notes that perhaps it was the death of Ewald Christian von Kleist at the end of August that robbed Lessing of the desire to continue working on the play.[695] Yet there may also be intrinsic reasons for its abrupt ending. Not much scholarship has ever focused on this interesting fragment yet its complexity is engaging.

Like the first *Faust* fragment, *Fatime* is also about timing. It also raises questions in the realm of metaphor, such as the ability to create images that are convincingly real or act as mirror-like reflections in the realm of art. The *Fatime* fragment may well be a meaningful contribution to the philosophical debate on mimesis and the discussion about "natural" signs in visual art. In this work the danger comes from being seen or from being analyzed too closely. Fatime's problem is how to maintain a happy appearance that does not give any of her real emotions away. She struggles onstage since she says she cannot mask her feelings and lacks control over her appearance. Her circumstances require a certain mind set and appearance. What matters above all is that she performs, hides her ambivalence, acts wife when she is welcoming her husband. The Sultan returns home after a long journey and a military campaign overseas. How can she possibly please this emperor and his people? How can she prevent any suspicion about her possibly having betrayed him albeit if only in her thoughts or desires? He is known as a tyrant and it is impossible for her to love him, yet Fatime must smile and quickly do away with a few inevitable tears as soon as Abdullah's arrival is announced. Her dilemma is how to control her feelings and in doing so, to gain control over her body language and facial expressions. What are the powers of the mind over the body when it comes to preserving one's integrity and ensuring one's safety? In a conversation with the Sultan's servant and her guardian and companion during her husband's absence, she gets instructions how to look, to project cheerfulness, what to say, and what not to say. She sighs.

Scene three opens with her friend's desperate plea: "Fatime! Fatime!—Noch ist es Zeit; noch kannst du uns retten! Hemme diese Tränen; ersticke diese Seufzer; und rufe die Heuterkeit, wo nicht in deine Seele, wenigstens auf dein Gesicht zurück. Verstelle dich!—Ach! was muß ich dir raten, ich Unglücklicher!"(Fatime! Fatime!—There is still time; you can still rescue us! Stop those tears; hold these sighs; and call back cheerfulness, if not in your soul, then at least on your face. Mask yourself!—Ah, what do I have to give you advice for, unhappy me!) The stage directions reflect on performance not only onstage but possibly also in daily life.

Spatial and the temporal dimensions require different signs There is a disparity between images and actions. Sculpture and painting are, as elaborated in *Laokoon,* the arts of space and must present actions in one single poignant moment. Such an instant is decisive for everything to happen in the progression of the figures in space. Music presents its signs through simultaneity of tones that have multiple levels of progression and layered meanings. "Dichtung" must hold the tension between the

694 The phrase is attributed to Oehlke yet the commentary does not indicate from which of his works it comes (FA 4, 840).

695 FA 4, 840. Ewald Christian von Kleist, who had been severely wounded in the Prussian defeat at Kunersdorf (now Kunovice, Poland) on August 12, 1759, died of his wounds on August 24 in Frankfurt an der Oder, a short distance to the west of the battlefield. See Lessing's anguished letter to Gleim, September 6, 1759, announcing Kleist's death (FA 11/1, 332-333).

realm of space (the visual) and time (music). It has to navigate in between. These dramatic fragments explore theoretical issues raised in *Laokoon* and are examples of Lessing's realization that the spatial and the temporal, what is seen and what is heard, tend to clash. In Lessing's *Faust* we are reminded of this by the choice of devil number seven in the first fragment and the sound (or the absence ) of a bell in the opening prelude to the second fragment. Fatime must avoid suspicion on the part of the Sultan, avoiding giving any grounds for bringing punishment upon herself. She may be forced live for the moment. The arrival of the Sultan has been announced and she must pretend to be cheerful despite the fact that this is not at all her true emotional state. *Fatime* illustrates that here is no safe meta-perspective. Everything depends upon specific temporality. Lessing's own stage directions make us realize that gestures are as important as words. In these fragments the temporal dominates the spatial in such a way that opaque multiple, sometimes anonymous voices suggest conflicting ideas. The figures onstage interact dynamically with hidden inner voices that are not seen but can also not be ignored. This requires active imagination from everyone in the audience.

Faust is a character living a life completely devoted to learning and scholarship. He seems in danger of being changed and, as one of the so-called "devils" already triumphantly proclaims from the start, he is setting himself up for trouble because he does not allow distractions. He is completely absorbed into what he does. Whereas *Faust* offers a critique of seeing by staging invisible protagonists that are plotting against the scholar Faust in the dark, *Fatime* stages the danger of being seen. She gives a marvelously poignant example for a rhetorical device such as ellipsis which speaks through abbreviation and silence. Things are expressed being not saying them. Allusions and shorthand messages are also used and there is the image of the basilisk, a creature whose glances are as dangerous as if they were boiling poison.[696] Seeing has negative undertones in this context. Being seen by such a creature means intrusion, probably death.

> Eifersucht kocht Gift
> Im eitervollen Herzen; erstickter Neid
> Preßt Gall und Fluch auf die verbißne Zunge,
> Und soll doch Honig von den Lippen fließen,
> Und Schmerz und Freundschaft aus den Augen lachen,
> Die gern des Basilisken Vorrecht übten,
> Und gern mit jedem Strahl mich töteten?[697]

> [Envy brews poison
> In the festering heart; suffocated envy
> Presses gall and curse on the bitter tongue
> And yet honey is supposed to flow from the lips,
> And pain and friendship to laugh from the eyes,
> Which would rather practice the privilege of the basilisk
> And eagerly kill me with each ray?].

696 On this fabulous creature see: Hermann Güntert, "Basilisk," *Handwörterbuch des deutschen Aberglaubens* 1: col. 935–937.
697 FA 4, 76.

Fatime is afraid. She refers to her husband as "tyrannischen / Kurzsichtigen Gebieter!" (tyrannical / short-sighted ruler).[698] She addresses the other ladies in the harem who have all gathered to offer their welcoming obsequies to this tyrant. With irony she refers to herself as the one chosen by his "Eigensinn" (stubbornness). She is envied by the other women who are her co-competitors for the master's heightened and jealous attention. They call her ironically "Glücklichste" (the happiest).[699] She is expected to call back her "Heuterkeit" (in today's spelling "Heiterkeit" or cheerfulness).[700] This is a term that has also often been associated with art in general. Fatime makes the laconic statement: "Man ist noch sehr glücklich, wenn man nicht bloß glücklich ist".[701] (One is still very happy, even if one is not always happy).[702] What makes us wonder here are what the degrees of happiness are. Words appear porous and do not capture the necessary details. Her language criticism is aimed at the inadequate expression of sensations, feelings, states of mind. She seems to be hinting at the fact that language is most often used without precision, disconnected from true emotions and not at all in tune with the speakers. Language is coded and consists usually of exaggerations. Even if one is happy at times one claims to be happy in general. One usually avoids addressing the complexities that come with an awareness of transient emotions depending on temporality. By saying that she can still be called "happy" even though, as we know from the context, she cried a minute ago, she is "not only happy." In other words, she excludes her unhappy moments for the sake of rhetoric and to master the situation at the moment. She says what is appropriate or expected in the situation and thus falls into lying. She draws attention to a deficit of language that omits more than one perspective at a given time. She indicates succinctly that there are degrees and levels of expression in language that all too often tend to be ignored. Fatime distinguishes between the general "man" (one) and her own particular self, between universal and individual truth opting for a rough equation in favor of the individual. Lessing seems to show that dangers can perhaps best be dealt with humor as the poem at the end of the fragment illustrates. This play advocates a kind of seeing which is enunciated by means of numerous voices. Without indicating who the speakers are, "Auftritt II" consists of commands, questions, statements, and poetic images. It begins: "Bleib hier! Du lachst, / Du bist leicht noch die Redlichste" (Stay here! You are laughing, / you may well be the most honest one"). The response is ambivalent: "Das bin ich auch!" (That is what I also am!)[703] The following sentences advocate laughter and compare yawning and catching one's breath while indicating that an open mouth is not at all a "natural sign." It can result from various circumstances or off-chance reasons:

> Bleib hier! Und warum lachst du?
> Weil?
> Ich leichtlich lach, und Lachen mir bekömmt.

698 FA 4, 76.
699 FA 4, 76.
700 FA 4, 75.
701 "Glücklich" which is here translated "happy" has also connotations of being fortunate and lucky.
702 FA 4, 74.
703 FA 4, 78.

Doch lachst du doch wohl nicht so wie du gähnst
o wie du Atem holst? /Ohn äußern Anlaß-
Was brachte dich zum Lachen?
Darnach fragst du?
Das Lächerliche glaub ich; denn das macht
Zu lachen -
Und wo war das Lächerliche?
An euch? an mir?
Laß sehn![704]

[Stay here! And why are you laughing?
Because?
I happen to laugh easily, and laughing becomes me.
But don't you laugh just like you yawn,
Just like catching a deep breath? Without any external reason? -
What made you laugh?
Do you ask for that?
I think it is because of the ridiculous
Which makes one laugh –?
And where was anything ridiculous?
Something about you? About me?
Let's see!].

Lessing experiments with language, inserts questions, pauses, riddles, and overtones. This illustrates the dilemmas involved in expressing outer and inner actions succinctly, events and emotions, something one may attempt to express through short-cutting expected communications. Can one avoid trouble by speeding up complicated answers for the sake of short, eloquent and precise formulations? The dialogue has voices that are not allocated to specific characters but seem to questions Fatime and playfully give answers indirectly or anonymously while reallocating focus and frame. There is the suggestion of an analogy between Fatime and the image of a bird, shifting its attributes from one species to another. It is mixing characteristics in what may seem "unnatural" ways. She seems to identify herself with a strange fantasy creature, a bird that has attributes of rather diverse kinds of birds combined, so that one cannot say whether it is a dove, an owl, an eagle. It is a creature hybrid creature wildly conjured up by a painter or poet. If such a creature were real in nature, it would be an "Unding" (something impossible), something nonsensical, merely to be laughed at:

Wär nicht ein kleines, schwaches, weißes Täubchen
Mit großen schaften Uhusklauen, mit
Gekrümmtem spitzen Adlerschnabel, wär
So ein Geschöpf der wilden Phantasie
Des Malers, in der weiseren Natur
Ein Unding, wohl nicht ein Geschöpf zum Lachen?[705]

[Wouldn't a small, weak, white little dove
With large sharp claws of an owl, with
Bent pointed beak of an eagle,

704 FA 4, 78.
705 FA 4, 79.

> Would such a creature of the wild fantasy
> Of the painter, be in the wiser Nature
> Something impossible, not merely a creature to laugh at?].

In other words, Fatime's visualization as this fabulous bird is a way to metaphorically express her own artificial existence, her sense of being misunderstood in her life situation. She cannot make her eyes, hands, and mouth correlate, or get in synch with the movement and rhythm of this odd staccato poem. She expresses a state of unease as an actress. In doing so she highlights the problem many actresses onstage may have when compelled to perform something they cannot personify. She may also indicate the dilemma of a female character in the eighteenth century that has now found its rightful corporeal place in society. Had Lessing completed the play it would have ended up a tragic one. Erich Schmidt comments on Lessing's *Fatime*:

> Gewiß wollte Lessing ursprünglich in Prosa eine lakonische, durch die drei Einheiten gebundene Katastrophe geben, reich an spitzen Epigrammen ('Man ist noch sehr glücklich, wenn man nicht bloß glücklich ist'). Er legte sie bald etwas breiter an, um dann eine ganz neue, volle Exposition in Jamben zu dichten [...] Diese beiden Szenen gehören zu den interessantesten Leistungen einer fortschreitenden Charakteristik. [706]

> [Indeed. Lessing originally wanted to give a laconic catastrophe in prose, bound up with the three main characters, enriched by pointed epigrams ('One is still very happy even if one is not always happy,' etc.). He then structured it somewhat more broadly in order to work out a completely new, full exposition in iambus verse [...] These two scenes belong to the most interesting achievements considering a consistently progressing character description].

Fatime is one of Lessing's poetic experiments with visual-verbal dynamics and with the problems of staging an impossible image. In this case the phantom bird has the body of a dove, the claws of an owl, and the beak of an eagle. It is an icon of dissimulated femininity, the transformation of a person who happens to be torn between incompatible sense perceptions. Lessing highlights the challenge to serve as a projection screen for others while trying to find an appearance and expression of one's own. He calls for our compassion although nobody can understand this creature of another world. It is certainly something original.

706 Erich Schmidt, *Lessing: Geschichte seines Lebens und seiner Schriften,* 4th ed. 2 vols. (Berlin: Weidmann, 1923), 1: 346 quoted in FA 4, 841.

# Chapter 9
# *Minna von Barnhelm* (1767): Unemployment and Staging the Self for Other(s)

Abstract: *Minna von Barnhelm* has been considered Lessing's best comedy. It was first published by Voss (Berlin, 1767) and has ever since been the most frequently performed of Lessing's plays. It is often interpreted as a play on gender roles and contemporary social conditions in Germany. Unfortunately the play was misused during the Nazi era as a celebration of militarism since it seems to celebrate a soldier and the military mentality. It should instead be interpreted as a play promoting pacifism as it shows a soldier suffering from post-war traumatic stress which has led to the breakdown of his personal identity as the result of the war. I argue that this play is on one level a historical document showing what demotion, unemployment, and disability can do to people, especially after a war. On another level it is one of Lessing's experiments with poetic language and word-image relations. It shows that language can under specific circumstances communicate, even at a time when, psychologically speaking, images of self and other are broken and need to be restored. Minna is able to reconnect her communication with Tellheim, perhaps through her ability to link the visual and the verbal and to use language carefully and succinctly. The play is not only a comedy as may seem upon first glance but it also deals with serious questions about human dignity and ethical values, such as honor, equality, independence, and loyalty. It addresses questions of identity that involve inner and outer "gestalts" (images) of self and other and the reconstruction of ideals after they have been shattered. Characters who love each other are puzzled and out of harmony with each other. Communication breaks down, not only because people are not always saying the truth or because they are not nice to each other, on the contrary what causes these wounds according to this play are a combination of false politenesses and an overdone sense of protection.

## 1. Genre: A Comedy?

This play belongs to a genre of post-war literature and suggests that one should come to terms with one's own imaginaries of the world, others, and oneself. It is a play first about loss and mourning since it turns out that all the characters are somehow wounded. Issues of gender are at the core of the play.[707] The impact of catastrophic circumstances and personal losses are problematic and constructive for the plot. Less-

707 For interpretations focused on women in the eighteenth century and the importance of gender roles in *Minna von Barnhelm* see Brigitte Prutti, *Bild und Körper;* Beatrice Wehrli, *Kommunikative Wahrheitsfindung. Zur Funktion der Sprache in Lessings Dramen,* Hermaea, N.F. 46 (Tübingen: Niemeyer, 1983); Barbara Becker-Cantarino, *Der lange Weg zur Mündigkeit: Frauen und Literatur in Deutschland von 1500-1800* (Munich: Deutscher Taschenbuch Verlag

ing not only pokes fun at contemporary traditional notions of what male means in opposition to female; he also challenges any clear boundary between the professional versus the family spheres and again shifts attention to sense perceptions and emotions.[708] The war is in the past and a process of healing characterizes the plot with Minna and Franziska being the rescuing forces, so that the play actually comes to a happy ending with apparently all the couples in harmony and the prospect of life in peace restored. Is language adequate to resolve conflict? What is the power of laughing, playfulness, and teasing which they are able to use to turn things around?[709] It seems that the rediscovery of an engagement ring, a visible and tangible symbol, albeit sold and misplaced, brings ultimately rescue here. Scholarship so far has mainly glossed over the intricacies of Lessing's language criticism as articulated in this play. It is a philosophical but also witty and ironic commentary on the importance of images, the complicated construction of self and others, and on the difficulties communicating.

The main characters of the play depend on idols they have created of each other and for themselves. They have trouble understanding what really happens among them. Their expected roles no longer function as expected. The play illustrates the decisive impact of temporality, both on the visual and the verbal levels of communication. Certain postwar events have destabilized the character's sense of self and belonging, so that he withdraws completely. While one can argue that this play presents the breakdown of a relationship, one can equally make the case that it is about successfully reestablishing communication. The play begins with the reference to an engagement ring sold for the purpose of financial survival. By sheer coincidence and constructed through funny metonymies, the ring is recovered and a healing of

---

1989), and Gail Hart, *Tragedy in Paradise: Family and Gender Politics in German Bourgeois Tragedy 1750-1850* (Columbia, SC: Camden House, 1996).

708 Günter Saße, *Liebe und Ehe. Oder: Wie sich die Spontaneität des Herzens zu den Normen der Gesellschaft verhält. Lessings* Minna von Barnhelm, Studien und Texte zur Sozialgeschichte 40 (Tübingen: Niemeyer, 1993) and *Die Ordnung der Gefühle: Das Drama der Liebesheirat im 18. Jahrhundert* (Darmstadt: Wissenschaftliche Buchgesellschaft, 1996). For a summary of the most popular interpretations see Fick, *Handbuch* 269-292.

709 Stefan Busch. in his "Blasphemisches Lachen in Klopstocks *Messias* und Lessings *Minna von Barnhelm*. Zur Herausbildung eines literarischen Leitmotivs der Moderne." *Lessing Yearbook* 33 (2001): 27-54. Lessing's *Minna von Barnhelm* is a "Lustspiel" or a comedy but Busch emphasizes Tellheim's horrifying laughing ("furchtbares Lachen") (42). Such a laughing may be ironic, or even cynical. It is here, as Busch explains, indicative of melancholy. Nevertheless, in the last scene of this play, Minna is able to spark Tellheim's liberating kind of laughter. Tellheim's laughing begins with a "fürchterliches Gelächter" (horrible laughter) first expressing upset or even anger, if not only mockery. Then this laughing seems to express mixed emotions before it becomes a laughing of comic relief ("zu befreiendem Lachen") (49). Such laughing can possibly dissolve tension. It can be indicative of new emotions and thoughts. It is a poetic strategy of Lessing's play that moods can quickly be turned around. Lessing associates laughter with an entire range of possible meanings. This is something later to be echoed in Friedrich Maximilian Klinger, *Die Zwillinge* (The Twins, 1776), Karl Philipp Moritz, *Anton Reiser* (1785-1790) and in the works by Ludwig Tieck and Georg Büchner. Also see Antje Arnold, *Rhetorik der Empfindsamkeit. Unterhaltungskunst im 17. und 18. Jahrhundert*, Quellen und Forschungen zur Literatur- und Kulturgeschichte 73 (Berlin: De Gruyter, 2012).

psychological wounds seems to take place in the course of the twisted action. The ring's belonging gets restored and the owner redeemed.

One could argue for Lessing's modernity in writing this play, since this play illustrates unstable human relationships. It reflects critically upon preoccupied notions of self and others and upon the fixation on outdated yet self-destructively framed concepts of reality. This must counter-acted via fiction, humor, and wit. Lessing shows that this may be done through a new art of dramaturgy. A successful visual-verbal link must be e reestablished. The play invents renewed communication between the characters. Despite delayed endings and numerous twists of the plot it performs reconciliation. There is the prospect of marriage between the four main characters: Tellheim and Minna will reunite and Werner and Franziska will depart for Persia together. A turning point from confusion to communication in this play is brought about through verbalizing images and through reflecting on false representations of the self. The performance of this play must liberate Tellheim from his harmful projections of what others may think of him. There are several curious poignant moments where turning against such products of a wounded mindset occurs and where after disaster and sorrow a new hope for the future arises. It can surface in the changing protagonist's imaginary when he learns that there is not only strength in giving but also in receiving.

Lessing has been criticized for not offering more of a satisfactory solution to the problems he articulated through the characters in the play and that the happy ending with the prospect of a double marriage among best friends in peace falls flat. Yet this play gains another dimension through Lessing's theoretical contributions on Ekphrasis. Lessing offers a critical, open-ended reflection challenging the old mimetic notion that images reproduce only what is already there. Instead, this play apparently tries to instill the notion of new imaginaries via poetic intervention so that words can produce visible change despite persisting icons and stereotypes.

The play is set during the Seven Years' War (1756-1763), a fierce and escalating battle that involved nearly all of Europe. Prussia invaded Saxony in order to frustrate an anti-Prussian alliance headed by Austria and including Saxony. Later in the war Prussia and England on the one side faced off against an alliance consisting of Austria, Russia, France, and Sweden. The war ravaged not only Prussia, Saxony, Thuringia, Silesia, Bohemia, and Moravia, but also involved the French colonial territories in Canada and India. After the death of more than half a million people the war finally ended on February 15, 1763. A peace treaty was signed in Castle Hubertusburg in Saxony, a pact between Prussia and Austria, reestablishing the borders as they had existed in 1756. Austria failed to regain Silesia which Prussia had seized from it in the two wars of 1741 and 1745. The Seven Years' War caused immense destruction and suffering, even after the cessation of violent hostilities.

*Minna von Barnhelm* is an important historical document reflecting on this war and on post war conditions. Above all it reveals mentalities. Lessing had become very familiar with the military and social situation during his times in Berlin, Leipzig and Breslau. In 1760 Lessing became secretary of the Prussian General, Friedrich Bogislaw von Tauentzien. When von Tauentzien was put in charge of Prussian forces at the

Siege of Schweidnitz (now Świdnica, Poland) he was accompanied by Lessing.[710] Afterwards in 1763, Lessing went with the general to Potsdam where they met with the king and von Tauentzien was appointed as Governor of Silesia.[711] During this time Lessing had many opportunities to see the horrible destruction of the war and its aftermath. It was no longer on the battlefield where victory and defeat had to be decided. The territory to be conquered was now internal and the ensuing struggles took place in the human soul. Military values continued to haunt the former military personnel of all ranks and made them often feel and act as outsiders. The rest of society found it hard to understand these ex-combatants.

In the "Bürgerliche Trauerspiel" *Minna von Barnhelm* the principal character Major von Tellheim has been entrusted with collecting the "Kontribution" (levy) imposed upon the populace of Saxony by the Prussian military. He had to raise the money in cash and this was expected to be carried out with perfect accuracy. The demands for payment enforced "mit der äußersten Strenge" (with the utmost severity).[712] When it came to collecting the levy in the district in which Minna von Barnhelm lived, Tellheim was faced with a situation that eventually made him choose to avoid oppressing the people of the region by giving in advance a sum out of his own pocket, equivalent to the minimum amount demanded. [713] He received a promissory note from the government of Saxony, but his claim was disputed after the armistice. The promissory note is interpreted as a bribe for not extracting as much money as possible from the region. Further, the revelation of this temporary breech of regulations is grounds for Tellheim to be dismissed. He had behaved with the best of intentions and not for selfish reasons. He is charged with having made a deal with the enemy. He did not act as a traitor as his superior claimed. His selfless actions under the circumstances were completely misunderstood and misconstrued. He was instantly demoted. For him honor had always been the highest of all values. When he lost his position and rank he became disoriented and doubted all contact with people, even his closest friends who were trying to help him. He could not tolerate the shame and was unable to find the right words to defend his case. He simply did not have any adequate language for how to present the case. The result is that he comes off as being stiff, moralistic, and lacking eloquence. His language crisis reflects Lessing's own realization that words

---

710 The siege was the last major military operation of the Seven Years' War and lasted from July to October 1762.

711 Nisbet, *Lessing: Eine Biographie* 383-88; *Gotthold Ephraim Lessing* 291-294.

712 FA 6, 83. Tellheim is said to be based on Lessing's good friend, the Prussia Major, Ewald Christian von Kleist, who died of wounds received at the Prussian defeat at Kunersdorf in 1759. "Wachtmeister Werner" owes his name to the Generalleutnant Johann Paul von Werner, who in 1757 took command of Hussar-Regiment H 6 (the so-called "Brown Hussars") with the rank of Oberst (Colonel). He became famous for his relief of the Prussian city of Kolberg (now Kołobrzeg, Poland) in 1760.

713 This is based on an incident which took place in 1761. Friederich II had demanded a sum of 20,000 Thalers from what was then the Saxon city of Lübben to be paid in three days. A "Dragonermajor" (Major of Dragoons) in the invading army, Anton Rudolf Marschall von Bieberstein, paid the sum out of his own pocket to prevent damage to the city buildings. Marschall von Bieberstein also was given the nickname "Tell" by his troops because of his prowess with the pistol. See Nisbet, *Lessing: Eine Biography* 446; *Gotthold Ephraim Lessing* 339.

are sometimes in vain. Images or imaginaries are so powerful than one is not able to approximate them by speaking. Images in this context are tainted with prejudice and a matter of dangerous projection and fixation.

## 2. The socio-political dimension

Even though the events of the Seven Years' War happened long ago, the play's being set in the aftermath of war is what gives it persuasiveness and authenticity. This play was horribly misinterpreted by the National Socialist regime and Nazi readers who used it for their own propagandistic purposes at a time when territorial expansion was a hot and contested topic. The play's message was distorted as if it was actually celebrating Prussian-German history and militarism during the Seven Years' War. Yet the play actually rejects the Prussian mentality as symbolized by the poodle running after someone who happens to be named Just (Tellheim's adjutant).The National Socialists repressed this motif and emphasized what they interpreted as the idolizing of military life, something they imposed on the dominant meaning of the play. A film based on Lessing's text titled *Das Fräulein von Barnhelm* directed by Hans Schweikart appeared in 1940. It changes the narrative and the essence of the play drastically.[714] In an essay "Lessing and the Third Reich" (2005), Ann Schmiesing provides important insights into Lessing's work with respect to Enlightenment thought and multiculturalism. She critically analyzes Schweikart's film which, as she astutely points out, does not do justice to Lessing's play. She notes in particular the opening scene in the film. Prussian soldiers are shown marching past a hill on which a windmill stands which "sails suggestive of an enormous swastika."[715] Schmiesing finds that this kind of Nazi symbolism in the film is not only inconsistent with Lessing's work; it has done severe damage to his reception for absolutely no sensible cause. Whoever knows Lessing's works including *Die Juden* (The Jews, 1754), *Nathan the Wise* (1779) and his letters must then be aware that Lessing unwaveringly promoted multiculturalism.[716] Lessing's "philosemitism" has also been well documented by Barbara Fischer in her work on Lessing reception.[717] Willi Goetschel's helpful essay "Lessing and the Jews" points out that all of Lessing's work can be characterized as being very sympathetic to Jews and Judaism, even if at times this "cost him the respect of those preoccupied with

714 See Karsten Witte, "How Nazi Cinema Mobilizes the Classics: Schweikart's "Das Fräulein von Barnhelm," Eric Rentschler, ed., *German Film and Literature: Adaptations and Transformations* (New York: Methuen, 1986), 103-115; Jo-Jacqueline Eckardt, "Das Lessingbild im Dritten Reich," *Lessing Yearbook* 23 (1991): 69-78.

715 Ann Schmiesing, "Lessing and the Third Reich," Fischer and Fox, ed., *Companion to the Works of Gotthold Ephraim Lessing*, 261-280 at 261.

716 Schmiesing, "Lessing and the Third Reich" 261.

717 Barbara Fischer, "Lösungsansatz 'Raum' versus 'Zeit': Jüdische Reaktionen auf Lessings *Nathan der Weise* im Vor-Shoah Deutschland," *Lessing Yearbook* 32 (2000): 324-339 and *Nathans Ende? Von Lessing bis Tabori: Zur deutsch-jüdischen Rezeption von* Nathan der Weise (Göttingen: Wallstein, 2000).

the myth-building of German nationalism in the nineteenth century."[718] After Hitler's fall and Germany's "Entnazifizierung" (denazification) Lessing's play gained a new interest and attracted sociological and political readings. They mostly focused on its representations of class struggle. The play's lasting appeal may have to do with the fact that it involves a courageous protest on the part of those who lost their jobs when their employers, be it the State or any public or private agency, decides to let them go, even for no plausible reason except merely financial profit. No consideration is given to the severe consequences for those who are suddenly unemployed.[719] Lessing's play has scenes dealing with finances, debt, borrowing, issues of trust and friendship. And there is the economic struggle and the wish for freedom, loyalty, and lasting peace. What I find curious is how images and words are being juxtaposed and negotiated interactively.

## 3. Rampant images

Lessing's characters do not seem to exert control over telling and describing images onstage. Lessing demonstrates a desire to emancipate his readers and his audiences in order for them to think and draw conclusions on their own. The strength of his play is that it allows for a variety of readings. One may claim that the play is not only a comedy; but it is also under the guise of humor, an anti-war play, containing pacifist manifesto through its poking fun at certain aspects of Prussian mentality, being stubbornness, pride, punctual adherence to norms, and extremely rigid social etiquette. The characters exhibit likeable aspects in their respect for others, their self-esteem, and their generosity. The ending of the play defends peace over war and it calls for respecting the private sphere. The female characters from Saxony seem to win with their humor and optimism over the Prussian male characters winning them to their side against all odds in the end. It seems that Minna's and Franziska's rhetorics offer not only better logic but use charms and humor to intervene. Minna's whimsical scheme is nothing but a way to offer her compassionate intervention. Also she is able to forget her own emotional wounds in the process. The regaining of Minna's ring is something that takes courage and imagination with both love and self-respect. Although this ending does not offer reconciliation on all levels, its strength has to be linking the characters' emotional entanglements with real social problems. These have

718 Willi Goetschel, "Lessing and the Jews," Fischer and Fox, ed., *Companion to the Works of Gotthold Ephraim Lessing,* 185-208 at 186. See also; Jonathan M. Hess, "Lessing and German-Jewish Culture: A Reappraisal," Robertson, ed., *Lessing and the German Enlightenment* 179-204; Monika Fick, "Lessing und die jüdische Aufklärung," *Handbuch* 490-518.

719 It is this outspoken critique on behalf of the unemployed, the poor, and the middle class worker that saw Lessing interpreted as a socialist fighter in Marxist and post-Marxist reception. These interpretations resisted the nationalistic appropriation of Lessing in the nineteenth century. Among the Marxist critics is Franz Mehring who saw in Lessing a representative of a broad political enlightenment opposed to the national conservative movement. See his *Die Lessing-Legende. Eine Rettung* (1893. Rpt. Frankfurt am Main: Ullstein, 1972). 317-322.

credibility and outweigh the sweet or merely superficial answers. The issues addressed are deep-seated and culturally engrained, such as more than ridiculous gender roles, socio-political issues of class difference, and issues with group identity. The play addressed is the importance of ethical decisions even if these decisions appear absurd. In the end the play advocates Tellheim's decision to live and to let go of his trauma for a new beginning in peace. Although this is a sharp comedy, it has depth of conflict, is a love story after the war, and ends with a shared celebration of Tellheim's healing. He has regained his consistent identity.

The question remains whether Lessing imposes a happy ending despite some irresolvable complexities. Do these simply get pushed aside as Peter Michelsen argued?[720] Or is the happy ending not any failure on the part of Lessing, not merely a superficial poetic trick? The answer depends also on Lessing's theoretical approaches to his art of understatement. There is an elaborate use of metaphor and symbolism in this play which makes the use of language, especially in the scenes with Minna, effective. Her witty and poignant talk is challenging the outdated set of fixed ideas and falsely engrained images Tellheim has forced upon himself and hence also upon her. Lessing gives examples of beauty and ethical behavior not as something to be described but shown by specific examples in the action. The play reflects a generosity expressing hope. It offers an undogmatic message about compassion. The inspiration comes from the vivacious female characters onstage.

> Ich nenne das schönste Lustspiel nicht dasjenige, welches am wahrscheinlichsten und regelmäßigsten ist, nicht das, welches die sinnreichsten Gedanken, die artigsten Einfälle, die angenehmsten Scherze, die künstlichsten Verwicklungen, und die natürlichsten Auflösungen hat: sondern das schönste Lustspiel nenne ich dasjenige, welches seiner Absicht am nächsten kömmt, zumal wenn es die angeführten Schönheiten größtenteils auch besitzt.[721]
>
> [I call the most beautiful play not that which has most probability and regularity, not that which has the most sensible thoughts, the most courageous ideas, the most pleasant jokes, and the most natural solutions: but I shall call the most beautiful comedy that which approximates its intentions the closest, especially if it already possesses (that it has) the already mentioned beauties].

What makes beauty alive onstage has for Lessing to do with positive attributes of some consistent characters. Through their actions they are able to evoke a vision towards a better reality. Regardless of adverse circumstances they live unscathed and uncompromisingly for this vision.

## 4. Lessing on the play and readings

As Lessing had already elaborated in his *Hamburgische Dramaturgie* a play does not simply contain what is talked about in it. It is better to give concrete examples linking

720 Peter Michelsen, "Die Verbergung der Kunst," 192–252.

721 Lessing, "Beschluss der Critik über die Gefangenen des Plautus" [1750], FA 1, 865–878 at 876–877.

abstract ideas with specific sense perceptions. The play is not to tell but to show and to make imaginations vivid. *Minna von Barnhelm* is such an experiment in which the performance is more than anything that could be succinctly summarized. Images may be detached from words and sometimes verbalizing them puts them in a new perspective. Lessing gave the play the subtitle "das Soldatenglück" (the soldiers' luck), thus drawing attention to soldiers and their circumstances. The play shows Tellheim as a character who thinks that it is necessary to stage his self for another after he has been injured and hurt by the war. He must compensate for what he lost. He is injured to the point so that he rejects emotions, even love and compassion. He is afraid to hurt others. What happens in the duration of the plot of the play allows him to let go of his depression and inertia. What distinguishes this play from earlier plays is that there seems to be no real villain. We encounter onstage no personified evil or malicious character. We learn indirectly of cruel behavior yet are not shown any of it directly onstage. Differences of thinking and diverse states of mind create all of the conflict we get in this play and its successful performance.

Attention is drawn to the circumstances that lead to these differences. We are to reflect on personal and private backgrounds that are culture-specific and integral to these individual histories in their real life situations. Although there is some ridiculing and poking fun at people, this play reflects optimistically on the all the ultimately sympathetic characters who are closely enmeshed in absurd situations. Minna and Tellheim each suffer extreme disappointment, but they succeed in getting rescued. Their obstacles are temporary. Problems can be solved and social demotion can be reversed. But the process of reversing one's bad luck in this play takes effort. Five acts are packed with wonderfully surprising scenes. The male characters are Prussians who lack eloquence and communicative skills. They express fossilized opinions and repeat stereotypical errors. The female characters, mainly from Saxony which had recently been overrun by Prussia, insist on their own reasoning. They end up being persuasive and their rhetorical skills deserve applause. Their good humor makes things happen as they energize the entire action onstage. Minna von Barnhelm and her maid Franziska possess wit and rhetorical skills and, as the final scene of the play illustrates, obtain victory over the stiff but honest and well-meaning Prussian Major Tellheim and his loyal friend Paul Werner. Minna and Franziska can best articulate their thoughts, develop a clever plan to cope with misunderstanding due to the events of the war. They are able to turn things around and energize the action of the plot. We may also notice a loyal friendship between Tellheim and Werner despite their differences and diverse mentalities. These friends trust each other. Whereas Tellheim will in the end settle down with Minna and never be a soldier again, Werner leaves to Persia and gets engaged with Franziska, Minna's friend. This play belongs to Lessing's so-called "Toleranzstücke" advocating generosity and friendship against the background of adverse political events and circumstances beyond individual control.

## 5. The marginal and the essential

Minna von Barnhelm presents the reconciliation between Saxony and Prussia, brought together primarily through a decree of the Prussian cabinet. Lessing was able to study elements for this play directly in the office where he worked under von Tauentzien. According to early commentators, Lessing's most important influences on this work came from Diderot. However, the Frenchman in the play, Riccault de la Marlinière, is not one of the main characters and has been criticized by some reviewers as nonessential and superfluous. Yet he has a function in being light-hearted, upbeat, and cheerful and succeeds in making people laugh and sympathize with him. He is the one who brings good news. He earns Franziska's trust. She gives him coins to gamble on her behalf. This is another poignant moment in the play drawing attention not only to character traits but to materiality. When Lessing moved from Berlin to Breslau he translated and published an edition of Diderot's Theatre. He said he wanted to bring nature and truth back to the stage. He was, as is well known, fed up with the lack of a national theater in Germany and tried to create one. Minna von Barnhelm is a decisive step in this direction. It belongs neither to the genre of high tragedy, nor to the bourgeois "Trauerspiel." It differs from the well-known European comedies that usually avoided politics and history altogether. Lessing was inspired by Diderot's Ecole des amis (1737). In it happens to be the character Nivelle de la Chaussée, a discharged wounded soldier stricken with poverty. He feels that he has lost his honor and is fixated on an ideal, an image he had of himself, a victorious solder. In his current circumstances he feels terribly inadequate, even to the extent that he insists he must reject his fiancé despite his love for her. He is not only hurt by others but also by his own self-inflicted image of himself, an obsession. He is unfortunately for almost the entire duration of the action onstage unable to forget and to let go.

Lessing must have been inspired by this psychological dilemma as presented by Diderot and he used such material to work with.[722] When *Minna von Barnhelm* was staged in the Hamburg Theater on September 30, 1767, Lessing had won a battle with censorship in Berlin. The play had been banned at first because of its political content. Lessing then made a formal public request, a Promemoria ("Bittschrift"), in order to persuade the government to reverse the ban. He was then allowed to direct and to schedule the performance of his new play. Not only did he win this administrative battle with censorship. The play became a huge success. It was repeatedly performed until May 19, 1768 and attracted large audiences. Goethe praised Lessing's play very highly saying it was true to the historical facts. He commented on it in his *Dichtung und Wahrheit* (Poetry and Truth):[723]

---

722 Richard Critchfield, "Lessing, Diderot, and Theatre." *Eighteenth Century German Authors and their Aesthetic Theories,* ed. Richard Critchfield and Wulf Koepke (Columbia, SC: Camden House, 1988), 11-28.

723 See FA 6, 812-831 for extracts from contemporary reactions to the play. Goethe further comments in the seventh book of his *Dichtung und Wahrheit:* "Die gehässige Spannung, in welcher Preußen und Sachsen sich während des Krieges gegeneinander befanden, konnte durch die Beendigung desselben nicht aufgehoben werden. Der Sachse fühlte nun erst recht schmerzlich die Wunden, die ihm der überstolz gewordene Preuße geschlagen hatte.

> Eines Werkes aber, der wahrsten Ausgeburt des Siebenjährigen Krieges, von vollkommen norddeutschem Nationalgehalt, muß ich hier vor allem ehrenvoll erwähnen; es ist die erste aus dem bedeutenden Leben gegriffene Theaterproduktion, von spezifisch temporärem Gehalt, die deswegen auch eine nie zu berechnende Wirkung tat: *Minna von Barnhelm*.[724]

> [One work, the most honest creation of the Seven Years' War, of perfectly Northern German national content, I must mention above all as deserving praise; it is the first theater production taken from meaningful live events, of specific historically accurate content, which therefore also had also an uncountable effect: *Minna von Barnhelm*].

We may want to reflect upon Goethe's line of questioning. What makes this play by Lessing so realistic? What makes it also almost timeless and relevant to the present? Its impact comes from focusing on concrete specifics and making everything plausible without imposing any general credo or opinion. It is an experiment investigating a human situation in which there seems to be no satisfactory way out. The characters are entangled in such a way that freedom or free choice in their lives appears to be illusory to them, even to such a degree that the only possible way out seems to be turning into one's own self, into an as-if-mode, trying to construct a new identity.

Such an imaginary transfer leads to a staging of selves within the play as if of another "reality," something neither given, nor merely dreamt, yet something which can only exist in the creative mind, in positive thinking, and in the realm of poetic language. It is able to perform "comedy" under the most adverse circumstances. Given such comic relief and such an ability to distract from one's own situation for the sake of another, whatever that may be, the play introduces a new comical dimension to the theater genre in Germany. Lessing expressed in poesy ("Dichtung") what political freedom could look like. Tellheim anticipates such freedom in the end. Finally his love for Minna defends art that is autonomous but more than escapism. Therefore it has an indirect political function by letting go of an immediate response to politics. It draws attention to language and mentalities injured by war and social conditions. The play advocates indirectly a decisive step towards creating a new national theater. It appeals to change from the inside of the human mind, the imaginaries, and to allow

---

Durch den politischen Frieden konnte der Friede zwischen den Gemütern nicht sogleich hergestellt werden. Dieses aber sollte gedachtes Schauspiel im Bilde bewirken. Die Anmut und Liebenswürdigkeit der Sächsinnen überwindet den Wert, die Würde, den Starrsinn der Preußen, und sowohl an den Hauptpersonen als den Subalternen wird eine glückliche Vereinigung bizarrer und widerstrebender Elemente kunstgemäß dargestellt" (GMA 16, 305). (The nasty mood in which Prussia and Saxony were against each other during the war could not be mended through ending it. Even more so the Saxon felt painfully the wounds which had been inflicted to him by the Prussian who had become excessively proud. Through a political peace treaty the peace between the conflicted minds could not be immediately regained. This should be attained actually through the play as presented. The poverty and the friendliness of the female characters from Saxony win over the stubbornness of the Prussians, and via the main protagonists as well as the subaltern characters a happy reconciliation of bizarre and contradictory elements is created via art). In other words Goethe accredits Lessing with using art to provide an imaginary and suggestive harmony in anticipation of something alternative to reality after the destruction of the Seven Years' War. This play is political by showing that the wounds that were historically resulting from the war could be healed in a spirit of freedom.

724 GMA 16, 304-305.

new human bonds to arise. It is a play in which the characters project for themselves alternative constructions of identity more in tune with the present time. This play is not only a historically and locally specific one but also philosophically relevant.

In the first scene Major von Tellheim's servant named Just is sitting in the corner of a room.[725] The location is an inn where he has spent the night and is mumbling in his sleep. He is awaking angry, upset, and mad with the "Wirt" (innkeeper) for having thrown out someone whom Just is now about to look for. The innkeeper walks in, wishes Just a good morning and mentions that the Major, Just's master, did not come home. The innkeeper says that he did not simply throw him out but that he had to clear the room for a new guest, a lady who could actually pay for her stay right away. He adds, excusing himself, that he found another room for the Major. He offers servant Just a drink but cannot calm him down. Just remains angry on behalf of the missing Major, defending his master with a stubborn and devoted anger:

> Und was hilfts Ihn, Herr Wirt? bis auf den letzten Tropfen in der Flasche würde ich bei meiner Rede bleiben. Pfui, Herr Wirt, so guten Danziger zu haben, und so schlechte Mores!–Einen Mann, wie meinen Herrn, der Jahr und Tag bei Ihm gewohnt, von dem Er schon so manchen schönen Taler gezogen, der in seinem Leben keinen Heller schuldig geblieben ist; weil er ein paar Monate her nicht prompt bezahlt, weil er nicht mehr so viel aufgehen läßt, – in der Abwesenheit das Zimmer auszuräumen!

> [And what good is that to him, Mr. Innkeeper? I stand by what I said until the last drop of this bottle. Shame on you, Mr. Innkeeper; to have such good Danzig schnapps in the house and such bad manners!– To clear out a gentleman's room in his absence, a man such as my own master, who had lived here for a long time, from whom you have taken many good coins, who never remained to anyone in debt during his entire life, because for a couple of months here he has not paid promptly, because he did not spend so much anymore].

The innkeeper tries to defend the eviction. He has rented this room to another house-guest saying that all inns in the neighborhood are occupied at the time and that such a "junge, schöne, liebenswürdige Dame" (young, beautiful, amiable lady) could not be left out on the street. He thinks that Just's master, the Major, as a gentleman would have freely offered her his own room had he been here to meet her in person. He adds that he has found another room even if it may not be such a nice one as the previous one. Tellheim, the Major, arrives and finds them quarreling. The innkeeper apologizes for the inconvenience. He mentions a pouch containing 500 thalers he is taking good care of. This makes for a welcome after all: "Mein ganzes Haus ist zu ihren Diensten" (My entire house is at your service).[726]

It soon becomes clear that the Major has been dismissed from his military service, that he has no money and no job. Nevertheless he acts like a gentleman in speaking to the innkeeper. This opening scene illustrates Just's loyalty to his master Major Tellheim but also gives insight's to Tellheim's character, even in his time of need. He is generous. The innkeeper's actions are plausible, d neither cruel, nor odd. The audience may well understand his need to make some money. We may observe the style of the Major

725 Just will turn out to be as his name taken from English suggests, "gerecht," (fair and honest, i.e. just).

726 FA 6, 13, 16.

who is now not to be talked into taking his room back but acts firm in accepting the situation. This means that the space he was given and already had occupied has now been given away for reasons that remain open. They may well have to do, as becomes clear later, with his tardiness paying his bills and the innkeeper's insistence to get paid immediately. The new person in that room is Minna and she has more cash to offer.

Tellheim informs Just that he has no more money, nor does he know how to get any. It is as if Tellheim gives stage directions regarding what he thinks should be done and in doing so draws attention to mimes, body language, and conflicting emotions as represented by the characters' actions onstage. It is as if Lessing critically reflects on his own role as the one being in charge of the meaning of the play. He is illustrating a gap between so-called "natural signs" (for example Just's emotional expressions of anger, stamping and spitting) and those that would be much more appropriate (dropping a bag of money with a scornful mien into the landlord's hands). He pokes fun of useless anger and makes the audience think of what else could be done in such a situation. When reference is made again to the bag with the 500 thalers already mentioned Tellheim explains that in this bag is not his money but only what he was entrusted to keep for someone else, Paul Werner.

## 6. Metonymic *pars pro toto* relations

In this play many events happen offstage and what we see is only a fragment of what matters. In the next scene a lady in mourning arrives and introduces herself as the widow of a former "Stabsrittmeister" (Cavalry Officer) of Tellheim's. He is suffering the pain of having lost her husband. She is on her way to the countryside where a friend has offered her a place to stay. Tellheim encourages her to speak freely, not to be ashamed of her misfortune: When she addresses him "Mein Herr Major" this reminds everyone present that her husband was his friend. Tellheim recalls his friend Marloff and asks the lady how he could help her. She says: "Ich darf nicht abreisen, ohne seinen letzten Willen zu vollziehen. Er erinnerte sich kurz vor seinem Ende, daß er als Ihr Schuldner sterbe, und beschwor mich, diese Schuld mit der ersten Barschaft zu tilgen. Ich habe seine Equipage verkauft und komme seine Handschrift einzulösen" (I cannot depart for my travels without acting according to his last wish. He remembered shortly before his death that he would die in your debt and beseeched me to take care of this debt with the first ready cash available. I have sold his carriage and horses and come to take care of this).[727] She offers the money to Tellheim as a given, yet he refuses to accept it. He claims that he was the one who owes Marloff and that it had always bothered him that during six years of shared happiness, misfortune, honor and danger he was never able to express his gratitude to him. He recalls that Marloff had left behind a son and is about to admit his own momentary state of "Verwirrung" (confusion) when the lady, understanding what he is about to say, interrupts him, and thanks him for his generosity, while still refusing to take the money back. Tellheim is not interested in this money. He says taking it would be like stealing from his best friend

727 FA 6, 18-19.

or his orphan son. He freely insists that Lady Marloff should take it. She does accept it in the end, her motherly instincts overriding her own pride and sincere generosity.

The seventh scene is devoted to Tellheim. It begins with a brief dialogue during which he is tearing up Marloff's document transferring the money to him. He says he does not want to be tempted by this. He wants to be protective of the widow and her son: "Armes, braves Weib! Ich muß nicht vergessen, den Bettel zu vernichten [...] Wer steht mir dafür, dass eigner Mangel mich nicht einmal verleiten könnte, Gebrauch davon zu machen?" (Dear brave woman! I must not forget to destroy this poor paper [...] Whoever can guarantee me that my own need may not someday seduce me into making use of it [the money] myself?)[728] At this point his servant named Just returns with tears in his eyes. He was supposed to have written down the amount as due as to him by his master. But he is simply not able to do so, saying he would rather be dead than have to take his leave. Tellheim responds: "Ich kann dich nicht länger brauchen; ich muß mich ohne Bedienten behelfen lernen" (I have no more use for you. I must learn to take care of myself without anyone's assistance). Tellheim appears to dismiss his servant. Just must still get three and a half months' salary paid back, the amount he used to receive in order to pay for the household expenses. Yet he feels that he still owes his master Major Tellheim a substantial sum. He acts as a loyal friend rather than as an employee. Just behaves in a way identical to how Tellheim had done previously with respect to Lady Marloff. He mimics the most recently repressed generosity of his master whom he obviously doesn't want to leave despite the unfortunate circumstances. Similar character traits are reflected and further ridiculed in an anecdote about a poodle, introduced into the discourse by Just who says:

> Machen Sie mich so schlimm, wie Sie wollen; ich will darum doch nicht schlechter von mir denken, als von meinem Hunde. Vorigen Winter ging ich in der Dämmerung an dem Kanale, und hörte etwas winseln. Ich stieg herab, und griff nach der Stimme, und glaubte ein Kind zu retten, und zog einen Budel aus dem Wasser. Auch gut; dachte ich. Der Budel kam mir nach; aber ich bin kein Liebhaber von Budeln. Ich jagte ihn fort, umsonst; ich prügelte ihn von mir, umsonst. Ich ließ ihn des Nachts nicht in meine Kammer; er blieb vor der Tür auf der Schwelle. Wo er mir zu nahe kam, stieß ich ihn mit dem Fuße; er schrie, sahe mich an, und wedelte mit dem Schwanze. Noch hat er keinen Bissen Brot aus meiner Hand bekommen; und doch bin ich der Einzige, dem er hört, und der ihn anrühren darf. Er springt vor mir her, und macht mir seine Künste unbefohlen vor. Er ist ein hässlicher Budel, aber ein gar zu guter Hund. Wenn er es länger so treibt, so höre ich endlich auf, den Budeln gram zu sein (I.9, 16-17).[729]

> [Make me as bad as you like; I will not think any worse of myself than of my dog. One evening last winter at sunset I walked along the canal and heard something whining. I climbed down, groped in the direction of the voice, and thought to be rescuing a child, and pulled a poodle out of the water. Also OK, I thought. The poodle came running after me; but I am not a fan of poodles. I chased him away, in vain; I smacked him away from me, in vain. I did not let him into my room at night; he remained outside on the doorstep. Whenever he got too close to me, I shoved him away with my foot; he yelped, looked at me, and wagged his tail. Never has he received even a bite of bread out of my hand; and yet I am the only one whom he listens to, who is allowed to touch him. He runs along in front of me, and shows me his artistic performances without being requested to do so. He

728 FA 6, 20.
729 FA 6, 22.

> is an ugly poodle, but it is a rather good dog. If he continues to behave like this, then I shall finally stop being annoyed by poodles].

Tellheim sees a parallel and sympathizes with Just who simply cannot be angry at his dog for following him everywhere. He just comes to tolerate him. He says: "Nein, es gibt keine völlige Unmenschen" (No, there are no completely inhuman humans).[730] He allows Just to stay with him and accepts his unwavering loyalty. He realizes that he actually depends on his servant now that he has lost an arm in combat:

> Ganz gewiss!–Sie wollen sich ohne Bedienten behelfen? Sie vergessen Ihrer Blessuren, und daß Sie nur eines Armes mächtig sind. Sie können sich ja nicht allein ankleiden. Ich bin Ihnen unentbehrlich; und bin–ohne mich selbst zu rühmen, Herr Major–und bin ein Bedienter, der–wenn das Schlimmste zum Schlimmen kömmt,–für seinen Herrn betteln und stehlen kann.[731]
>
> [Most certainly!–You want to take care of yourself without servants? You forget your wounds and that you are only able to use one of your arms. You cannot even dress yourself on your own. I am indispensable; and I am–without praising myself, Mr. Major–an employee who–if the worst comes to the worst–can beg and steal for his master].

Just makes the Major uncomfortable for offering help to an invalid. Full of pride, Tellheim rejects this offer: "Just, wir bleiben nicht beisammen" (Just, we will not stay together). However, the servant knows his master well enough to avoid further tirades and mumbles simply: "Schon gut" (Alright then).[732] He pretends in a sense not to have heard it, just like he would like to have Tellheim also ignore his earlier (in retrospect rather stupid) statements. The forgetting of memory and the erasure of words are contextualized in this scene. It indicates increasing insight and compassion.

## 7. Close readings that exemplify misunderstandings

Tellheim and Just are then joined by a "Bedienter" (a servant). He brings a message requesting that Major Tellheim should move back in his own room again. The messenger was sent by a lady whose name Tellheim tries to find out. The messenger begins to tell him the lady's circumstances and surrounding gossip. Tellheim brusquely interrupts by asking him to focus on what the question was and then to leave. This scene again shows that saying too much can have counter-productive consequences. Tellheim abhors superfluous language and makes the audience reflect on what it takes to communicate effectively. Tellheim commands Just quickly to leave and admits his sense of feeling uncomfortable: "Mache Just, mache, daß wir aus diesem Hause kommen! Die Höflichkeit der fremden Dame ist mir empfindlicher, als die Grobheit des Wirts" (Hurry up, Just, hurry up, so that we get out of this house! The politeness of this strange lady is more irritating to me than the rudeness of the innkeeper).[733] Feel-

730 FA 6, 23.
731 FA 6, 23.
732 FA 6, 23.
733 FA 6, 24.

ing under pressure from various quarters, he chooses to sell a ring, the only valuable object he has and he says to Just: "Hier nimm diesen Ring; die einzige Kostbarkeit, die mir übrig ist; von der ich nie geglaubt hätte, einen solchen Gebrauch zu machen!–Versetze ihn, laß dir achtzig Friedrichdor darauf geben"[734] (Here take this ring, the only precious thing which I have left; I would not have believed that I should make such a use of it!–Pawn it and have them give you eighty gold Friedrichs for it).[735] Just is to use this money to have the innkeeper paid off. He must clear all of his belongings out of this inn and take them to the next available place. Then a meeting is set in the nearby coffee house. Just is ready to take care of these tasks. They are about to leave when on the way out Tellheim reminds Just not to forget the pistols that are still hanging behind his bed and also not to forget the poodle. Just decides to pawn the ring with the innkeeper. Before he does this Paul Werner enters, a former comrade and friend. He brings "frisches Geld" (fresh money) for Tellheim. He says that normally he would have come earlier but he had heard about a certain Persian Prince Heraclius offering new positions for soldiers to fight against the Ottomans and he wants to go for that.[736] Just refuses to accept any money but he does admit that he and Tellheim are living on credit and when they run out of credit they have to move on.

The second Act takes us to a private space, the room of the ladies, Minna von Barnhelm and her servant and best friend young Franziska. They occupy the room which Major Tellheim and Just had vacated. It is early morning and they are expecting a response from the Major having written him a note the day before indicating that he could take his room back. Major Tellheim would have already replied had it been him, Minna thinks. She expresses the hope that she will find her fiancé perhaps through this officer. Therefore she sends him a note and thanks him for having left his room to her.[737] Minna feels optimistic saying: "Franziska, mein Herz sagt es mir, daß meine Reise glücklich sein wird, daß ich ihn finden werde" (Franziska, my heart tells me that my journey will be happy, that I shall find him). Franziska replies: "Man traue doch ja seinem Herzen nicht zuviel" (One should not trust one's heart too much).[738] Later they converse about people often talking about virtues they don't have. Minna claims that Tellheim is the most courageous person of the world while pointing out the differences between his actions and words. She lets his actions speak and asks about his muteness now: "Freund und Feind sagen, daß er der tapferste Mann von der Welt ist. Aber wer hat ihn von Tapferkeit jemals reden hören? Er hat das rechtschaffenste Herz, aber Rechtschaffenheit und Edelmut sind Worte, die er nie auf die Zunge bringt"

734 The gold currency circulating at the time had the same value whether it was issued by France ("Louisdor"), Prussia ("Friedrichsdor"), or Spain ("Pistolen") and the plays uses all three terms at random. Each gold coin was valued at five thalers.

735 FA 6, 24.

736 The reference is to Heraclius II, as King in Eastern Georgia, not Persia. After having established an independent kingdom and defeating the Persians at the Battle of Kirkhbulakh in 1752, Heraclius tried unsuccessfully to get Russian support to raise an army of mercenaries for an invasion of Persia.

737 FA 6, 29: "Die Wahrheit zu sagen, ich ließ ihm das Kompliment auch bloß machen, um Gelegenheit zu haben, mich nach diesem bei ihm zu erkundigen" (To tell you the truth, I had made him my compliment merely to have the opportunity to ask him about this).

738 FA 6, 29.

(Friend and foe say that he is the most courageous person in the world. But who has ever heard him talk about courage? He has the most honest heart, but honesty and generosity are words which he would never bring to his tongue).[739] This comment by Minna draws attention to Lessing's theoretical statements about the writing of "Dichtung" or the need to condense language and to focus on verbal restriction when talking about the most important truths.

The fact that Tellheim is characterized by Minna as almost wordless does not take away the possibility that he has much to say. He deserves a second look. His lack of communication does not take anything away from Minna's strong belief in his excellent character. Yet the women are concerned about Tellheim's whereabouts since he has only written once since peace was declared. He sent only the note saying that he is approaching the fulfillment of his wishes. Franziska worries more than Minna. Tellheim may be dead or may rest in the arms of another woman. Minna responds not to torture her, no more chit-chatting away: "Du Quälgeist! [...] Doch schwatze nur!" (You pest! [...] But chatter away).[740] Minna insists that she must hurry towards him. Her optimism is based on her being grounded in what she feels. Her positive attitude is further illustrated in a scene where she gives a present to Franziska so that she may join her in her hopes and fully sympathize with her situation.

Minna is not unaware of the problems Tellheim may have. She says: "Sein Regiment wird nach dem Frieden zerrissen. [...] Wer weiß, welche Umstände–" (His regiment was demobilized after the Peace Treaty. [...]Who knows what circumstances–)?[741] At this moment someone knocks at the door. The innkeeper enters and requests information. He claims he needs to fill out forms required by the police concerning their names, where they come from, and why they are here. The young ladies first give general answers such as coming from Saxony, but then he wants more specific information. Minna adds that she is from Thuringia.[742] As the questions become more personal and invasive, the women's responses become catty and tongue-in-cheek. The innkeeper finds himself at an impasse trying to continue his investigation. There is a brief exchange about whether the title Miss or Mrs. would be more appropriate. Then the innkeeper becomes aware of the similarity between Minna's ring, the one she is wearing and the one he had just purchased in a deal made with Just. He says:

> –Ich muß Ihnen einen Ring zeigen, einen kostbaren Ring. Zwar gnädiges Fräulein haben da auch einen sehr schönen am Finger, und je mehr ich ihn betrachte, je mehr muß ich mich wundern, daß er dem meinigen so ähnlich ist.–O! sehen Sie doch! [...] Welch ein Feuer! der mittelste Brillant allein, wiegt über fünf Karat.[743]
>
> [I must show you a ring, a valuable ring. Dear Miss you also have a very beautiful one on your finger. The more I see it the more I wonder how similar it is to mine.–O look, look! [...] What fire! The middle diamond alone weighs over five carats].

739 FA 6, 29.
740 FA 6, 30.
741 FA 6, 30-31.
742 The western part of the Electorate of Saxony.
743 FA 6, 35-36.

Minna recognizes it as the engagement ring she gave to Tellheim. She asks the innkeeper where he got it from and refers to its engraving of her name inside. The innkeeper breaks out in a frenzy of apologies. He is now afraid that his own actions make him a criminal. Claiming that he got this ring in the most honest way of the world ("auf die ehrlichste Weise von der Welt"), he proclaims:

> Sie werden mich nicht in Schaden und Unglück bringen wollen? Was weiß ich, wo sich der Ring eigentlich herschreibt? Währendes Krieges hat manches seinen Herrn, sehr oft mit und ohne Vorbewußt des Herrn, verändert. Und Krieg war Krieg.[744]
>
> [You will not want to cause me harm and misfortune? What do I know about where the ring actually comes from? During the war, many things have changed their owners, very often with and without advance knowledge of the owner. And war was war].

Minna insists that the innkeeper must bring her the man from whom he got it. When she hears that he did indeed get it from Tellheim and that Tellheim owes money to the innkeeper, she pays him this amount from her own "Schatulle" (cash box) and retrieves the ring. Franziska pushes the innkeeper out of the door. Minna is so happy to have found Tellheim that she makes gifts to Franziska, wanting her to join her cheerful mood. Tellheim arrives. The moment he sees Minna he runs towards her with an embrace: "Ach! meine Minna.–" (Oh! my Minna.–). She responds: "Ach! mein Tellheim–" (O! My Tellheim! –).[745] His body language overrules his previous doubtful words.

But despite this spontaneous gesture which may reflect the truth at this time, the resolution of their difficulties is far from being in sight. Minna says that she has found what she was looking for. Tellheim makes a statement diametrically opposed to it: "Sie suchten einen glücklichen, einen Ihrer Liebe würdigen Mann; und finden–einen Elenden" (You were looking for a happy man, one deserving of your love, and you find–a miserable wretch).[746] He further elaborates on this explaining why such an unhappy person must not love anything or anyone. Such a miserable person deserves to be unhappy. Since he cannot claim victory over himself he would drag those whom he loves down into in his own misery. This would not be fair. He explains the necessity on his part to withdraw in order not to draw her into his suffering. He uses the third person singular throughout in order. He distances himself from his own persona speaking. He is alienated from his innermost feelings and talking will not mend anything.

The dialogue contains sentences that reflect on Tellheim as stubborn. Above all he is shown to be a selfless individual strictly following the moral standards he believes in. He has obviously internalized a certain image of personal perfection or an ethical stance so rarefied that Minna cannot reach him. She requests that he should answer her without equivocation and without evasion ("ohne Wendungen, ohne Winkelzug").[747] Instead he should simply and honestly answer the question whether he still loves her or not. Yet he responds evasively. He says he will give her an answer if and when he possibly would be able to. He indicates he cannot say and deconstructs

744 FA 6, 36.
745 FA 6, 42.
746 FA 6, 43.
747 FA 6, 44.

his own words leaving things unsaid. He draws awareness to innermost complexities, to an experienced language crisis. Minna ends up having to cut through this entangled exchange. She interrupts Tellheim's barely coherent mutterings to claim that she has heard exactly what she wanted to hear. She reads his words against the grain:

> DAS FRÄULEIN Wollen Sie mir die einzige Frage beantworten?
> TELLHEIM Jede, mein Fräulein–
> DAS FRÄULEIN Wollen Sie mir auch ohne Wendung, ohne Winkelzug antworten? Mit nichts, als einem trockenen Ja, oder Nein?
> TELLHEIM Ich will es,–wenn ich kann.
> DAS FRÄULEIN Sie können es.–Gut: ohngeachtet der Mühe, die Sie angewendet, mich zu vergessen,–lieben Sie mich noch, Tellheim?
> TELLHEIM Mein Fräulein, diese Frage–
> DAS FRÄULEIN Sie haben versprochen, mit nichts, als Ja oder Nein zu antworten.
> TELLHEIM Und hinzugesetzt: wenn ich kann.
> DAS FRÄULEIN Sie können; Sie müssen wissen, was in Ihrem Herzen vorgeht.–Lieben Sie mich noch, Tellheim?–Ja, oder nein.
> TELLHEIM Wenn mein Herz–
> DAS FRÄULEIN Ja oder nein!
> TELLHEIM Nun ja!
> DAS FRÄULEIN Ja?
> TELLHEIM Ja, ja!–Allein–[748]

> [MINNA Will you answer me just one question?
> TELLHEIM Each, my Lady–
> MINNA Will you answer me without equivocation, without evasion? With nothing other than a dry: Yes, or No?
> TELLHEIM I shall–if I can.
> MINNA You can.–Good: Ignoring the effort you have made to forget me, –Do you still love me, Tellheim?
> TELLHEIM My lady, this question–
> MINNA You have promised not to answer except with a yes or a no.
> TELLHEIM And added, if I can.
> MINNA You can; you must know what happens in your heart.–Do you still love me, Tellheim? Yes, or No.
> TELLHEIM If my heart–
> MINNA Yes or no.
> TELLHEIM Then, yes.
> MINNA Yes?
> TELLHEIM Yes, yes!–Except–].

## 8. Complications with words that cannot change images

Tellheim has given his answer but again things are not settled. He repeatedly wants to qualify, take back or change words and keeps editing what he said. This draws attention to the shortcoming of language. It stagnates meanings coercively. Tellheim tries to explain that even though he is still called Tellheim he is now actually someone quite

748 FA 6, 44.

different, not at all the Tellheim she once may have known. He draws attention to the impact of time. It makes language outdated at the moment of its articulation. It already anticipates to some extent the language crisis as it was to be later articulated at the turn of the nineteenth to the early twentieth century by Hugo von Hofmannsthal. In his fictional yet highly philosophical text "Ein Brief" (1902) it is then paradoxically well described in a letter supposedly by Philipp, Lord Chandos to Francis Bacon. In a similar vein Lessing's Tellheim insists that in his experience the name of a person and that person's identity no longer match.[749] Because people change and names tend to remain fixed words tend to be quickly outdated. He stands for an example of someone nobody knows. Minna should not claim to recognize him. He feels that he is not the person she may have known in the past:

> Sie nennen mich Tellheim; der Name trifft ein.–Aber Sie meinen, ich sei Tellheim, den Sie in Ihrem Vaterlande gekannt haben; der blühende Mann, voller Ansprüche, voller Ruhmbegierde; der seines ganzen Körpers, seiner ganzen Seele mächtig war; vor dem die Schranken der Ehre und des Glückes eröffnet standen; der Ihres Herzens und Ihrer Hand, wann er schon ihrer noch nicht würdig war, täglich würdiger zu hoffen durfte.–Dieser Tellheim bin ich ehe so wenig,–als ich mein Vater bin. Beide sind gewesen.–Ich bin Tellheim,

---

749 "Kaum weiß ich, ob ich noch derselbe bin, an den Ihr kostbarer Brief sich wendet; bin denn ich's, der nun Sechundzwanzigjährige, der mit neunzehn jenen "Neuen Paris" [...] hinschrieb." Hugo von Hofmannsthal, "Ein Brief," *Brief des Lord Chandos. Poetologische Schriften, Reden und erfundene Gespräche,* ed. Hansgeorg Schmidt-Bergmann (Frankfurt am Main: Insel, 2000), 127-138 at 127. "I hardly know if I am still the same person your precious letter is addressing. I am now twenty-six. Am I the same person as the nineteen-year-old who writes *The New Paris*?" "A Letter," Hugo von Hofmannsthal, *The Lord Chandos Letter and other Writings,* trans. Joel Rotenberg (New York: New York Review Books, 2005), 117-128 at 117. The author of this letter has become immobilized because of the realization that words are incapable of correctly ever describing reality or the truth. He gives a description of the stages of his experienced inability: "Zuerst wurde es mir allmählich unmöglich, ein höheres oder allgemeines Thema zu besprechen und dabei jene Worte in den Mund zu nehmen, deren sich doch alle Menschen ohne Bedenken geläufig zu bedienen haben" (von Hofmannsthal, "Ein Brief" 131-132): (First I gradually lost the ability, when discussing relatively elevated or general topics, to utter words normally, used by everyone with unhesitating fluency) (von Hofmannsthal, "A Letter" 121). Lessing draws attention to the trouble involved in condensing any complicated action into an artwork or into a narrative so that it can capture the most poignant moment, but Chandos seems to find all moments fleeting and disjointed, even though they are all that we get. For him there seems to be no connecting line that would link them cohesively into any representation. No description, no language would be fully adequate. He adds: "nämlich weil die Sprache, in welcher nicht nur zu schreiben, sondern auch zu denken mir vielleicht gegeben wäre, weder die lateinische noch die englische noch die italienische und spanische ist, sondern eine Sprache, von deren Worten mir auch nicht eines bekannt ist, eine Sprache, in welcher die stummen Dinge zur mir sprechen, und in welcher ich vielleicht einst im Grabe vor einem unbekannten Richter mich verantworten werde" (von Hofmannsthal, "Ein Brief" 138): ("It is that the language in which I might have been granted the opportunity not only to write but also to think is not Latin or English, or Italian, or Spanish, but a language of which I know not one word, a language in which mute things speak to me and in which I will perhaps have something to say for myself someday when I am dead and standing before an unknown judge") (von Hofmannsthal, "A Letter" 127-128).

der verabschiedete, der an seiner Ehre gekränkte, der Krüppel, der Bettler.–Jenem, mein Fräulein, versprachen Sie sich; wollen Sie diesem Wort halten?[750]

[You call me Tellheim; the name is accurate.–But you think that I am that Tellheim whom you knew in your homeland, the glowing man, full of expectations, full of desire to gain honor; who was in command of his complete body, his complete soul; for whom the barriers to honor and happiness stood wide open; who was allowed to be, or to become daily more so if he was not already, deserving of your heart and your hand.– I am as far removed from this Tellheim – as I am from my father. Both are in the past. – I am Tellheim, the discharged soldier, wounded in his honor, the cripple, the beggar.–To that one, dear Miss, you promised yourself, do you want to keep your word?]

Tellheim is suffering from a serious identity crisis due to his professional demotion, his physical and psychological injuries. He is emotionally handicapped and feels no longer to be the person he was. In an identity split, a disassociation from the self, he does not recognize the personal bond he had made earlier with Minna. Tellheim in his new and alienated state of being must give Minna her freedom back. It is a matter of integrity to him. He is caught up in a double-bind because the more he loves her the less he feels worthy of being associated with her. Whatever she will say does not reach him in his self-inflicted pain. Tellheim has construed such a powerful negative image of himself that it makes him a prisoner of his own imagination. He is caught in a snare of his own making.

## 9. From the oral to the written

Would the play have ended here, it would have been a tragedy. Lessing chose to carry the plot to a happier ending, albeit only tentatively. He does so ironically again through images rather than through merely words. Having drawn attention to the conflict between names and identities, the gap between people who can master language and are capable of expressing their feelings and thoughts in an instant and those for whom language is deficient, incapable of expressing truth and their emotions, Lessing now makes use of a notion suggested earlier by Minna. Language can be twisted, equivocated, and thus be used by splitting it into its own complexities for multiple meanings at the same time. Tellheim decides to write a letter to Minna. He has not given up completely using verbal language. He shifts from the oral to the written medium. He wants to explain his withdrawal. She refuses to read the letter but instead makes an appointment for another meeting in person. This gives her an opportunity not just to hear the letter read, but to observe his gestures and facial expressions as well. Just brings Tellheim's letter to the ladies' quarters. Franziska asks about Tellheim's other servants whom she remembers from before the war: Wilhelm, Philip, Martin, and Fritz. Just tells her that they have all left the Major under dubious circumstances and Franziska realizes that indeed Tellheim has only one servant and that is Just. She admits: "Ich verdiene den Biß.–Ich bedanke mich Just. Ich setzte die Ehrlichkeit zu tief herab. Ich will die Lehre nicht vergessen" (I earned that reprimand.

750 FA 6, 45-46.

Thank you Just. I valued honesty not highly enough. I will not forget this lesson).[751] Franziska feels surprised and finds that she is learning that honesty is what apparently rescued Just compared to all others who took off on their own with whatever they could steal from Tellheim. It is perhaps no coincidence that the entire next scene is all about problems of honesty as they affect the image and evaluation of Tellheim. The innkeeper enters the room and tells Franziska what he observed during a brief encounter of Tellheim's with Minna. This is a scene involving gesticulations and complicated body language. He reports:

> Ich war nicht lange hier, so prellte auf einmal die Türe bei dem gnädigen Fräulein auf. Der Major stürzte heraus; das Fräulein ihm nach; beide in einer Bewegung, mit Blicken in einer Stellung–so was läßt sich nur sehen. Sie ergriff ihn! er riß sich los; sie ergriff ihn wieder. Tellheim!–Fräulein! lassen Sie mich!–Wohin? So zog er sie bis an die Treppe. Mir war schon bange, er würde sie mit herabreißen. Aber er wand sich noch los. Das Fräulein blieb an der obersten Schwelle stehn; sah ihm nach; rief ihm nach; rang die Hände. Auf einmal wandte sie sich um, lief nach dem Fenster, vor dem Fenster wieder zur Treppe, von der Treppe in dem Saale hin und wider. Hier stand ich; sie ging dreimal bei mir vorbei, ohne mich zu sehen. Endlich war es, als ob sie mich sähe; aber, Gott sein bei uns! ich glaube, das Fräulein sahe mich für Sie an, mein Kind. "Franziska" rief sie, die Augen auf mich gerichtet, "bin ich nun glücklich?" Darauf wischte sie sich Tränen aus dem Auge, und lächelte, und fragte mich wiederum "Franziska, bin ich nun glücklich?"–Wahrhaftig, ich wußte nicht, wie mir war. Bis sie nach ihrer Tür lief; da kehrte sie sich nochmals nach mir um: "So kommt doch, Franziska; wer jammert dich nun?"–Und damit hinein.[752]

> [I was not here for long when the door of the dear Lady's room flew open suddenly. The Major stormed out, the Lady behind him; both in a movement, with gazes in such a position–something like that one can only see and not describe. She grasped him; he tore himself free; she gripped him again. Tellheim!–Miß! Let go of me!–Where are you going?–So he pulled her to the top of the stairs. I was already afraid that he would tumble down with her. But he escaped her embrace. The Miß kept standing at the top-most stair; looked after him; called him wrung her hands. Suddenly she turned around, ran to the window, from the window back to the stairs, from the stairs to the hallway back and forth. Here I stood; she passed me three times without seeing me. Finally it was as if she saw me, but, God be with us! I think the Miss saw me thinking it was you, dear child. "Franziska" she cried, fixing the eyes upon me, "am I happy now?" At that she wiped the tears from her eyes and laughed and asked me once again, "Franziska am I now happy?"–Honestly, I did not know what was going on. Until she went to her door; then she returned back again to me: "So come now, Franziska, whom do you pity now?"–And with that said she went in].

There is no brute force in this episode; the movements appear airy, liquid, and as if in a sleeplike trance. Franziska is surprised to hear this account of events and says to the innkeeper "das hat Ihnen geträumt" (You must have dreamt it). He denies that this could have been a dream, insists that these events must have occurred but adds that he would give a great deal to have any key to understand what happened. [753]

751 FA 6, 51.
752 FA 6, 51-52.
753 FA 6, 52.

## 10. The Key Within

Franziska responds: "Den Schlüssel? zu unsrer Türe. Herr Wirt, der steckt innerhalb; wir haben ihn zur Nacht hereingezogen; wir sind furchtsam" (The key? to our door. Herr Innkeeper, it is inside, we have taken it with us inside; we are fearful). He replies that he does not mean that key, switches levels of language from the literal to the metaphoric meaning of the word and insists: "Nicht so einen Schlüssel; ich will sagen, mein schönes Kind, den Schlüssel; die Auslegung gleichsam; so den eigentlichen Zusammenhang von dem, was ich gesehen" (Not such a key; I want to say, my dear child, the key; the interpretation so to speak; the actual context of that which I have seen).[754]

The question remains hanging unresolved. Franziska changes the subject and asks when dinner is. The innkeeper almost forgets what he wanted to say but does add in leaving that he wants Minna to know that she can keep the ring which he had pawned from the Major, that it is hers and that he will charge her account the hundred gold coins ("Pistolen") he spent for it.[755] Paul Werner returns with ninety gold coins which he gives Franziska. In the following exchange he finds out how much both ladies respect Tellheim, his own friend, who is now in trouble and to whom he wants to bring help and good news. When he hears that Tellheim had pawned the ring he had from Minna, he first tries to brush it off by saying that the Major could have had ten rings on each hand during the war in Saxony and that he probably just wanted to get rid of it when he pawned it. He thinks that the Major probably wanted to forget the person of whom the ring reminds him. Franziska continues her conversation with him probing him for his opinions on Tellheim's loyalty. She is relieved when she becomes aware that Werner is a loyal friend of Tellheim and happy to see that Werner too would want Tellheim to be reunited with Minna. In the process she finds herself increasingly attracted to Werner. Werner runs into Tellheim and reports that he met the widow Marloff whose husband owed Tellheim a great deal of money and gave her a sum to deliver to Tellheim, while announcing that the rest would come later. Tellheim is not interested in any of this money and tells Werner that this is a lie and that he had already told Lady Marlow that all of the money is to be used for her son.

Again gestures, staring, eye contacts, and physical expressions are important elements of this scene and supplement the written text so that a summary can barely do justice to the intricacies of visual-verbal dynamics. Werner continues to try to get Tellheim to accept money from him and makes the strong argument that borrowing and accepting help from a friend is much more a sign of loyalty and friendship than rejecting any help. He asks whether Tellheim is willing to acknowledge that he is already his creditor by reminding him that it was he, Werner, who twice before this saved his life.

> Sie wollen mein Schuldner nicht sein? Ja, das ist was anders *etwas ärgerlich:* Sie wollen mein Schuldner nicht sein? Wenn Sie es aber schon wären, Herr Major? Oder sind Sie dem Manne nichts schuldig, der einmal den Hieb auffing, der Ihnen den Kopf spalten wollte,

---

754 FA 6, 52.

755 That is, he is charging her 20 *Pistolen* (100 thalers) more than he had given Tellheim for the ring.

und ein andermal den Arm vom Rumpfe hieb, der eben losdrücken und Ihnen die Kugel durch die Brust jagen wollte?–Was können Sie diesem Manne mehr schuldig werden? Oder hat es mit meinem Halse weniger zu sagen als mit meinem Beutel?–Wenn das vornehm gedacht ist, bei meiner armen Seele, so ist es auch sehr abgeschmackt gedacht.[756]

[You don't want to be my creditor? Well, that is something else. *Somewhat annoyed:* You don't want to be my creditor? What if you were so already, Mr. Major? Or don't you owe anything to the man who once intercepted a blow that would have split your head apart, and on another time struck the arm from the torso, which was about to pull the trigger and send a bullet through your chest?–What can you be more indebted to this man? Or does my neck have less to say in this matter than my wallet?–If this is the purpose intended, by my poor soul, so is it also a very tastelessly intention.

Tellheim defends himself in his stubbornness, claiming he would have acted the same way and protected his friend in a similar situation. He indirectly confesses that he did something similar. Tellheim confirms that he does not want to be in debt. He gets teased by Werner who says that a man like him cannot always be in need. Werner has no doubt that Tellheim will get a great deal of money in the future and simply won't accept Tellheim's arguments. When Werner acts as if hurt and disappointed by Tellheim for having his offer rejected things turn around. They shake hands. Tellheim accepts help from Werner having finally understood that being in need means no shame but the opportunity to accept help from a friend. The time of the appointment for Tellheim to meet Minna is set. Minna, after her reading Tellheim's letter full of arguments about why he had to withdraw from their engagement is now certain of his love. She thinks he simply wanted to spare her the trouble he is in and lacks self-confidence given his handicap. She pretends not to have read the letter. She knows that it will be much harder for him to communicate the same message in person. As she tells Franziska she has a critical perspective on Tellheim's exaggerated pride but is not giving up her engagement to him:

DAS FRÄULEIN Sein Bief! O, sein Brief! Jede Zeile sprach den ehrlichen, edlen Mann. Jede Weigerung, mich zu besitzen, beteuerte mir seine Liebe. [...].Bloß ein wenig zu viel Stolz, Franziska, scheint mir in seiner Aufführung zu sein. Denn auch seiner Geliebten sein Glück nicht wollen zu danken haben, ist Stolz, unverzeihlicher Stolz! Wenn er mir diesen zu stark merken lässt, Franziska–
FRANZISKA Sie wollen seiner entsagen?
DAS FRÄULEIN Ei, sieh doch! Jammert er dich schon wieder? Nein, liebe Närrin, Eines Fehlers wegen entsagt man keinem Manne. Nein: aber ein Streich ist mir beigefallen, ihn wegen dieses Stolzes mit ähnlichem Stolze ein wenig zu martern.[757]

[MINNA His letter! O, his letter! Each line spoke the honest, noble man. Each refusal to accept me confirmed his love to me. [...] However, a little bit too much pride, Franziska, seems to me to be in his conduct. Because, not wanting to give thanks to one's lover for one's happiness is pride, unforgivable pride! If I allow myself to notice this too strongly, Franziska–
FRANZISKA You will let go of him?
MINNA Ah, see now! You have pity on him again already? No, dear silly girl, One does not let go of a man on account of one flaw. No, but a scheme has come to my mind, to torment him a bit because of this pride with a similar pride].

756 FA 6, 60.
757 FA 6, 68.

The play draws attention to the materiality of written words that allow insights into the psyche of the author. It is Minna's advantage that she is able to take the face value of Tellheim's letter in her own attempts to tease out Tellheim's changed perspective in her dialogue partner soon later.

## 11. A Möbius strip ending

Minna has concocted an intrigue according to which she will demonstrate to Tellheim what it means to be treated with too much pride. She announces her uncle's arrival and claims that he has disinherited her due to her liaison with Tellheim. Before this happens, another person is introduced, Riccault de la Marlinière.[758] He wants to find Tellheim and goes to his room but discovers that it is now occupied already by Minna and her maid. His language switches between French and broken German as he explains that he is a poor gambler who has lost everything. Minna has pity on him and gives him money with the result that she is scolded by Franziska. Subsequently de la Marlinière will become central to the action of the play. He is a good messenger who comes to announce that Tellheim has been rehabilitated by the military staff. He will be rewarded for his services after all and paid handsomely by the King. Finally Tellheim's honor is reaffirmed and his situation completely reversed. He has a new position in life. It is Tellheim now who must according to social codes help Minna. For tactical reasons she claims to have lost everything given the intervention of her uncle. The scheme works. Tellheim wants to help and happily agrees to marry her. In the end their bond of love is confirmed and their marriage will soon take place. Minna's pretense was used to mend indirectly what had gone wrong. It shows that fiction and art can sometimes cure what was miscommunicated in real life. Peace between Tellheim and the world appears paralleled with the relationship Tellheim and Minna. This constellation is reinforced by a new bond that gets established between Tellheim's friend Werner and Minna's friend Franziska. Against the despair and miscommunication of the earlier scenes, the play ends in reestablished communication and relief.

And as far as the visual-verbal constellations are concerned, the play poses a challenge to the readers. A series of actions that are cumbersome to unravel verbally get captured visually in symbolic motifs that undergo deals in the interaction of the characters and gain newly assigned meanings. Examples are the reassignment of the hotel rooms to shifting parties, the selling and repurchasing of Tellheim's wedding ring, the turning around of the story about the inheritance, etc. These retellings and playful schemes are part and parcel of a metaphorical strategy to recontextualize words for new meanings. The continuous repositioning of the main characters' attributes has the effect that their evaluations change interactively. This makes this play interesting

758 This character may have been introduced in homage to Diderot. For the impact of Diderot's works see Claudia Albert, *Der melancholische Bürger;* Crowther, *Diderot and Lessing as Exemplars of a Post-Spinozist Mentality;* Johannes Friedrich Lehmann, *Der Blick durch die Wand. Zur Geschichte des Theaterzuschauers und des Visuellen bei Diderot und Lessing* (Freiburg im Breisgau: Rombach, 2000); Worvill *'Seeing Speech': Illusion and the Transformation of Dramatic Writing in Diderot and Lessing.*

and gives us a playful sense of auto-poetic revisions. The play also draws attention to difficulties that arise from the traditional attempt of people to stage themselves for others in order to please. People tend to anticipate presuming what others would think. They do not wait to see but tend to act upon all too quickly for misconstrued assumptions. This play mocks fixed notions of self and other and the social conditions that apparently made Minna's intervention via fiction necessary. The crisis of the plot gets resolved through metonymic language, metaphors, and a play within the play. It reflects on contiguities and momentary constellations and meanings, on the temporality of images. Lessing refers to his plays via equivocations and evasions which ultimately bring it end in a Möbius strip. What was upside is now turned down and what was below has gotten the upper hand. Minna has proven to be not only to be the most resourceful, inventive, and enlightened figure of the play. She wins Tellheim back through the use of fiction, some acting which is funny but has the effect that he must accept his own more humble self, accept his actions that were previously misunderstood. Minna represents a new type of language, the language of the heart. Tellheim was detached from his true feelings but can consequently through the game by his friends reconnect with them and heal. With a good dose of humor this play reflects on inadequacies of fixated images of the self in a time of change. It shows a gap between private and public spheres and turns hierarchies around. It projects a vision of ekphrastic hope that will adequately allow a correlating images and words, and also emotions and actions. One more observation: The good messenger Riccault de la Marlinière may in fact be in homage to Lessing's friend Diderot who at times similarly acted as a *deus ex machina* offering good news from afar. This scene may encapsulate a positive experience of recovery, a promise to communicate better, and a viable hope that one can change reality through fiction.

# Chapter 10
# *Emilia Galotti* (1772): Portraits and Displacements

Abstract: *Emilia Galotti* is another of Lessing's "Bürgerliche Trauerspiele," a play which ends with a gruesome murder. A father turns his dagger against his own beloved daughter, apparently to rescue her from a dangerous aristocratic suitor, but also to preserve her "virtue"– perhaps even with her own consent. Lessing omits the ending of the Roman Virginia fable in which the daughter's killing is followed by a popular uprising against the tyrannical behavior of the court. Emilia on her wedding day has fallen irretrievably in love with the wrong man, an aristocrat. Given the circumstances and the timing there is no hope in sight of any satisfactory resolution. Lessing's ending focuses on the private sphere and an "honor killing." While some critics have considered the play "tragic," others have rejected this term.[759] The play begins with a highly symbolic and foreshadowing opening, a dialogue between Conti, the painter of two portraits, and his aristocratic client, the Prince who is no longer satisfied with the picture he painted of the Duchess Orsina and dismisses it. The Prince is fascinated with the second portrait. It depicts his new object of desire, the bourgeois Emilia Galotti. The Prince buys it and we are left reflecting on false mimetic relations between ideas and images, images and persons, and on dangerous projections that lead to fatal error. The play also draws attention to Emilia's dilemma being caught between the voice of her father, the moral ideals engrained unto her through her cultural upbringing, and her impulse now to define her own desire and to pursue a struggle for personal freedom. While it is the portrait of Emilia that captures the attention of the Prince, it is in the end the language of the Countess Orsina, his previous lover and the object of Conti's first portrait who seems to get heard rather. Her command of language, her amazing verbal expressions, and her returning from the past is what ends

759 The word "tragic" has been questioned from a variety of points of view. Franz Mehring, *Die Lessing-Legende* 350: "Tragisch läßt sich der Ausgang der *Emilia* nicht begründen, und zwar deshalb nicht, weil er sich historisch allzu gut begründen läßt" (The end of *Emilia* is not tragic because it can all too well be explained historically). He rejects the eighteenth- and early nineteenth-century readings of the play as "künstliche Übertragung einer rauhen Römertugend in moderne Zustände" (artificial imitation of a harsh Roman ethical system into modern socio-political conditions). Mehring claims that Lessing's play ended not with the motif of a father killing his daughter in order to save her from rape or any the transgression of a tyrant, a theme to be found in book III of Livy's *Ab urbe condidata.* Rather Lessing exposes conflicts that could not be reconciled even without any external threat given the particular time in history. Also see the chapter "Emilia Galotti als Revision des republikanischen Trauerspiels" by Gisbert Ter-Nedden, *Lessings Trauerspiele* 164–177. Further P.M. Lützeler, "Die marxistische Lessing-Rezeption. Darstellung und Kritik am Beispiel der *Emilia Galotti*-Interpretation in der DDR" in *Lessing Yearbook* 8 (1976): 42-60. Also Lützeler, *Geschichte in der Literatur. Studien zu Werken von Lessing bis Hebbel* (Munich, Zürich: Piper, 1987), 15-39.

up controlling the action.[760] The play reads like a parable and has moments of introspection offering poetic comments both from inside and outside the representatives of the visual and the verbal. Even when moments of reflection are hinted at, these are intrinsic to the plot. They reflect on what is happening as if from afar. These dramatic strategies extrapolate complicated interactions and impasses between the visual and the verbal. They make disjuncture noticeable thus momentarily breaking the illusion, and drawing the spectators into the empathy for both competing representatives of the sister arts.

## 1. Theoretical premises

It is one thing to express something via an understatement in a minimalist and clever suggestive manner so that the addressed person in the dialogue is intellectually challenged but has a fair chance of understanding the message correctly. It is another thing to use an understatement out of context or at the wrong time so that it cannot be understood and leads to a lack of communication. Consequences may be detrimental in either case. It all depends on an awareness of what can be said and understood in a specific context at a specific time. An illustration of this is Lessing's play *Emilia Galotti* which was first performed in 1772. It teaches ex negativo how to use better, more effective understatements than the various fictional speakers who tend to fail to communicate through what they say. The rhythm of their words, gestures and body language draw attention to communicative errors and off-synch actions. There are falsely timed images, proverbs, epigrams, or brief messages that make the spectator pause and think about possible deeper or alternative meanings than those presented on the surface level of the plot. There are numerous dialogues that derail.[761] Reference is made to animals, furies, lions, and sheep and we, the audience in the theater, or the readers of Lessing's play, may wonder what the underlying fables of this eloquent and complex plot of the play may be. We are offered a spectacle that in the end seems very absurd and violent. However, the action is builds momentum towards that ending step by step with a certain consistency.

Lessing seems to be experimenting in *Emilia Galotti* with having us gage why visual-verbal communication goes so wrong in this play. He makes the audiences see and think about what it would take to achieve the ability to use language more

760 Brigitte Prutti, *Bild und Körper. Weibliche Präsenz und Geschlechterbeziehungen in Lessings Dramen* Emilia Galotti *und* Minna von Barnhelm (Würzburg: Königshausen & Neumann, 1996), 10-63, especially the opening chapter "Das Bild des Weiblichen und die Phantasie der Künstler/Väter: Emilia Galotti." Prutti bases her study on Silvia Bovenschen, *Die Imaginierte Weiblichkeit: Exemplarische Untersuchungen zu kulturgeschichtlichen und literarischen Präsentationsformen des Weiblichen* (Frankfurt am Main: Suhrkamp, 1979). Very perceptive is also Barbara Becker-Cantarino, "Patriarchy and German Enlightenment Discourse: From Goethe's *Wilhelm Meister* to Horkheimer and Adorno's *Dialectic of Enlightenment* in Germany," in Wilson and Holub, *Impure Reason* 48-64.

761 On the use of the epigram in *Emilia Galotti,* see Jürgen Schröder, *Gotthold Ephraim Lessing: Sprache und Drama* (Munich: Fink, 1972), esp. the chapter, "*Emilia Galotti*: Die Kunst des Dialogs," 189-222.

effectively. The play makes use of contiguities or metonymic *pars pro toto* relations but also involves many indirect messages that only attentive dialogue partners would have been able to process to a better outcome. As elaborated in the *Hamburgische Dramaturgie* successful understatements take timing into careful consideration and correlate language and gestures. Context and framing matter. These concerns are essential for the production of this play and for Lessing's script. There are metaphors, words, or sentences that derive meanings from specific contexts that are being used but often only hinted at marginally.[762] What makes Lessing's play not only interesting but also a contribution to visual-verbal theory is the precise shifting of the focus within a given metaphorical frame, so that multiple windows of speculative opportunities appear.[763] Much of the action in Lessing's dramas remains a matter of teichoscopy or *Mauerschau* (referring to happenings in a play that are merely reported but not acted out visually onstage). Most of the plot actually takes place behind the fourth wall in the theater performance, while what we see and hear are causes and effects of the action, mental processes that are decisive and suggestive for what may have happened on another level of the action. Hints and allusions are key components. Lessing seems to favor a playful mode of communication but makes the action in the end all the more provocative. He draws the entire audience to become detectives or insiders comparable to what had previously done with his play *Miß Sara Sampson* when almost everyone in the audience was finally stunned and crying. Again he wants to do away with the audience's usual boredom and complacency and have performances that could promote pity, empathy, and compassion.[764] Ideally such a play could liberate people from stereotypes. Yet any such educational goal would have to be reached via something playful or "Spiel" as subsequently theorized by Friedrich Schiller.[765] Since art or poetic language is considered a kind of play, almost returning to a pre-civilized state of being and closer to empathic affect, it can well anticipate or magically present a sense of shared freedom that is lacking in current society. But it can well be experienced at any

762 For a definition of metaphor in the context of "focus" and "frame" of a sentence, see Max Black, *Models and Metaphor, Studies in Language and Philosophy* (Ithaca, NY: Cornell University Press, 1962), 25–47 at 28.

763 An example would be the metaphor of a dance in which each step should be a matter of precision. In Act IV, scene i (FA 7, 342) Marinelli tells the Prince that his going to the church that morning to see Emilia was a step whichdoes not really belong to the dance ("ein Schritt, der dennoch nicht in den Tanz gehört." He adds, reponding to the Prince's question what impact it had, that it provided the rhythm for everything to follow ("doch voritzo den Takt"). Later (FA 7, 356) Countess Orsina exclaims to Emilia's father that she is the Prince's rejected lover and shouts in addition that in due course his own daughter will be one like that, his rejected lover, also. Perhaps one day all the rejected women will like furies tear the Prince's limbs one by one apart and rip from his body the heart that he had he promised to all of them: "Ha! das sollte ein Tanz werden! das sollte" (Ha! That should become a dance! that should). The play *Emilia Galotti* has a complex publication history as it appeared in four editions during Lessing's lifetime. The FA text is that of the first edition with Lessing's manuscript corrections (FA 7, 829). For a full scholarly edition with all the variants see Gotthold Ephraim Lessing, *Emilia Galotti: Ein Trauerspiel in fünf Aufzügen. Historisch-Kritische Ausgabe*, ed. Elke Monika Bauer (Tübingen: Niemeyer, 2004).

764 On Lessing's unique position in the tradition advocating pity, see Hans-Jürgen Schings, *Der mitleidigste Mensch ist der beste Mensch.*

765 Schiller, *Über die Ästhetische Erziehung des Menschen. Theoretische Schriften.* Ed. Rolf-Peter Janz et al. FSA 8 (1992): 556–676.

specifically fortunate time, if in fact art can succeed in making such a mode plausible to our senses. To some extent the ultimate project of the Enlightenment may have failed.[766] However, it did successfully bring the awareness for the need to communicate to the whole person, to link body and mind, physicality and thinking, feeling and being, and Lessing did not underestimate the importance of sense perceptions.[767]

Although autonomy is ideally approximated in the realm of art as fragile as it may be, it is pursued in this context with rather destructive consequences. The performed lack of ethics in this play has drawn harshest critics. It provides along with Lessing's plea for understatement, an aesthetic tool to counteract any simplistic model of mimetic representation in art. Michael Fried's concept of "absorption" in the process of observing images and Wolfgang Kemp's adaptation of a quote by John Ruskin as "Der Betrachter ist im Bild" (The artist is in the image) may help to reflect on Lessing's use of imagery and his allusions to art, especially with respect to this play's important opening scene.[768] Lessing seems to draw attention to what will be the final "poignant moment." But here it does not highlight beauty but rather vulnerability and pain.[769] The myth of Pygmalion is evoked in the first scene of *Emilia Galotti* but it is then applied hypostatically when the Prince misreads Conti's paintings which to him are objects in the same way he actually treats the women they represent. He buys the pictures and insists on his right to dismiss any of them any time as he pleases.[770] In that sense "the image" here is associated with two portraits. The females they picture that are not at all brought to life through the love of the observer but rather mortified in each distinct case through his possessive gaze. This evokes the Midas effect, death by touch. The painter or the narrator has completely lost control over the artworks that are now appropriated by the self-indulgent spectator or powerful owner of such reinvented paintings.

## 2. Lessing's play *Emilia Galotti* in context

Lessing was not in the audience when *Emilia Galotti* was presented onstage for the first time. It was performed by the Döbbelinsche Troupe in Braunschweig on March 13,

766 Peter-André Alt, *Tragödie der Aufklärung: Eine Einführung* (Tübingen: Francke, 1994).

767 See, for example, the essays in the first and second sections of: Hans-Jürgen Schings, ed., *Der Ganze Mensch. Anthropologie und Literatur im 18. Jahrhundert,* DFG-Symposion 1992 (Stuttgart: Metzler, 1994), 7-334.

768 Fried, *Absorption and Theatricality* 10; Wolfgang Kemp, ed. *Der Betrachter ist im Bild. Kunstwissenschaft und Rezeptionsästhetik.* The title is an adaptation of John Ruskin: "Then FINE ART is that in which the hand, the head, and the heart of a man go together. "Lecture 2: The Unity of Art," *The Two Paths: The Works of John Ruskin*, new. ed., vol. 10 (Sunnyside, Orpington: George Allen, 1884), § 54, pg. 49.

769 On pain in Lessing's work, see the interesting essay by Christine Ivanović, "Schmerz als Provokation der Visual Culture" in Schmitz-Emans and Lehnert, ed., *Visual Culture* 83-95, linking Lessing's work in that regard with texts by Franz Kafka and Peter Weiss.

770 This is also what Roland Barthes refers to as "the perfect instance: This crucial instant, totally concrete and totally abstract is what Lessing subsequently calls (in the Laocoön) the *pregnant moment.*" Roland Barthes, *Image. Music. Text*, trans. Stephen Heath (New York: Noonday Press, 1977), 73.

1772. Lessing unfortunately had a toothache that day. This play had been a long time in the writing. Lessing was not able to finish it until he moved to Wolfenbüttel in 1770 to become a librarian at the Herzog August Bibliothek. The final changes also had to do with the fact that Lessing had to finish it for a special occasion ("Gelegenheitsdichtung"), namely the birthday of the Herzogin von Braunschweig-Wolfenbüttel, Philippine Charlotte of Prussia, a sister of Friederich II.[771] The text was published in Berlin the same year. Lessing had been working on the plot of the play since the seventeen-fifties. He had translated and reviewed the writings of others dealing with the famous Virginia materials from Antiquity especially after Samuel Crisp had successfully premiered *Virginia* in London in 1754.[772] Lessing was motivated to write such a tragedy also and it intended it as a critical response to Crisp. He first titled it *Das befreite Rom* (Liberated Rome), yet when revising it Lessing abandoned such a political orientation and apparently, as documented in his correspondence with his brother Karl later, Lessing thought he had to limit his work and make it both less pompous and less ambiguous. He decided to focus exclusively on one instead of two topics: Instead of dealing with a personal murder on one hand and a public revolt on the other, he wrote that he chose to focus on the personal theme, a family crime with a father killing his daughter for the sake of honor. Lessing highlights the private sphere but I think it would be short-sighted to assume that therefore his play has no political dimension. Lessing submitted a truncated version of this play for a literary competition organized by Christoph Friedrich Nicolai in 1758. Lessing had first commented on his ideas about such a play in a letter to Moses Mendelssohn of October 22, 1757.[773] After some correspondence back and forth he then, according to a letter to Nicolai on January 21, 1758, titled it *Emilia Galotti.*[774] He considered it enough of a tragedy to see a daughter getting killed by her father for whom morality was more important than his daughter as a living person. He focused on the family interaction onstage in his revised version of the play and was ready to omit the political upheaval and the public revolt, motifs that had in the original source concluded the narrative. Lessing's reputation may have suffered subsequently as a result of this choice.[775] For example, Friedrich Kittler read the play as if it were "die Geburt der Familie im bürgerlichen Drama und durch das bürgerliche Drama" (the birth of the family in the bourgeois drama and through the bourgeois drama).[776] It may also been instead rather strategic and in line with his theoretical approach for Lessing to leave out the specific political

771 On this see Nisbet, *Lessing: Eine Biographie* 637-638; *Gotthold Ephraim Lessing* 485-486; Fick, *Handbuch* 345-346; Klaus Bohnen, "Lessing zu Feier: Über den 'Nachruf' auf einen unbequemen Autor in Geschichte und Gegenwart," Klaus Bohnen, ed. *Lessing: Nachruf auf einen Aufklärer. Sein Bild in der Presse der Jahre 1781, 1881 und 1981* (Munich: Fink,1982), 175-182.

772 See also his review of the *Virginia* of Augustin Montiano y Luyando in *Hamburgische Dramaturgie* LXVIII, FA 6, 521-526.

773 FA 11/1. 255-256.

774 FA 11/1, 266-268 at 267.

775 For a summary of the long and complicated history of reception and interpretation of *Emilia Galotti* see Fick, *Handbuch* 347-372; FA 7, 857-927; Lessing, *Emilia Galotti*, ed. Bauer 181-285; Edward Dvoretzky, *The Enigma of Emilia Galotti* (The Hague: Martinus Nijhoff, 1963).

776 Friedrich A. Kittler, "'Erziehung ist Offenbarung': Zur Struktur der Familie in Lessings Dramen," *Jahrbuch der Deutschen Schillergesellschaft* 21 (1977): 111-137.

implications of the play in order to give space to the spectators' imagination and to avoid explicit or overdone didacticism.

Lessing based his drama on concrete observations given his own social environment and his own life circumstances. His frame of reference is more interesting than any narrow mimetic reading. Lessing's situation did not allow him to use language in a completely censor-free environment. His strategy of cutting had a thoughtful, philosophical, and language-theoretically reason. One may even go as far as to argue that it also involved his own personal integrity. He felt it was none of his business to become involved in political interventions through his art. He wanted to curtail the narrative and make compact what he had to say through his use of "Dichtung." The theater allowed both verbal and visual signs and through them he explored the boundaries of communication.

For example, Lessing presents a scene with a young woman who is talked to. Her seduction is only potential but does not happen. Her father fears for her honor (and his own?) and her killing is prophylactic, nonsensical, and absurd. The father stabs his daughter not because he is angry with her but ostensibly in the name of love, freedom, morality, and justice. Numerous psychoanalytic interpretations exist. Brigitte Prutti argues for the killing as "inzestuöse Opferhandlung" (incestuous act of sacrifice).[777] The father Odoardo becomes furious when thinking about his daughter not only leaving him for a marriage he had not condoned, but worse for a marriage she had decided upon without his consent and with someone he considered his political adversary, someone from the court. He is angry at the rejection of his authority and upset about the awkward timing of her decision also. Emilia finally submits to her father Odoardo. She does so perhaps because she wants his love more than anything else. She admits that she would have to truly follow her own desire if she gave up obeying her father. Horst-Peter Neumann has pointed out that Emilia had an encounter with her Freudian "Es" when she listened to the whispers in church that morning earlier. Then she is caught by her superego ("Über-Ich") since the father's voice is something she has internalized.[778] Susan Gustafson in her Lacanian reading and by applying ideas from Julia Kristeva's psychoanalytic theory, emphasizes the "abjection of the female" throughout the play.[779] In any case, I think that the metaphor is telling that Emilia is soon going to be compared to a rose whose petals have been ripped off before it was time. This rose was picked not by winds of fate or as seasonal but by through untimely violence.[780] But that notion shows that she is made to let go and that this means neither a voluntary return to the father, nor an act of suicide, as some critics have claimed.

In the father's perspective there seems to be no doubt that Emilia was doomed to fall after what happened. Her fiancé is dead and he wants to "rescue" her not only from punishment if she was part of an intrigue which he must suspect now, but also

---

777 Brigitte Prutti, *Bild und Körper* 10-145 at 127.

778 Horst Peter Neumann, *Der Preis der Mündigkeit. Über Lessings Dramen* (Stuttgart: Klett Cotta, 1977).

779 Gustafson, *Absent Mothers and Orphaned Fathers* 170-216 and Martha Kaarsberg Wallach, "Emilia und ihre Schwestern: Das seltsame Verschwinden der Mutter und die geopferte Tochter," Kraft and Liebs 53-72.

780 See "Eine Rose gebrochen, eh der Sturm sie entblättert," Bonn, *Vom Schönen* 80-92.

from the power and influence of a rich and influential politician whose sexually motivated advances apparently did not frighten her into running away. The father denies his own responsibility for her death even though he actually kills her. Some readings have linked that idea with religious connotations, sacrifice, martyrdom, existential doubt and fears about *Theodizee.*[781] It seems that Lessing presented complex characters whose true identity cannot completely be disentangled from the powerful images others have created for them and control them even after glimpses of true insight at moments, in fleeting self-reflection. This contradiction and stark tension throughout this play illustrates how difficult the process of Enlightenment is.

Emilia lingers when in that surprise meeting with the Prince who sits behind her in church whispering compliments in her ear exactly on her scheduled wedding day with Appiani. She cannot help but be listening to the Prince's flirtatious words from behind her. She is flustered by the Prince's advances but nevertheless proud and stupidly happy. She tells her mother about this exciting private encounter and then her words prove to have a life of their own. Her mother Claudia realizes that her daughter might have really fallen in love with the Prince and although she knows that it is her daughter's wedding day with someone else, she senses ambivalence, is keen to have her climb the social ladder upwards, and tends to support her daughter against the strong intervention by Odoardo later. Everything seems slightly out of synch. The Prince has his servants try to prevent Emilia's wedding to happen that day. In the process to put a halt on that events escalate and spin out of control. Without the Prince's complete knowing, Marinelli acts as his agent and as the mastermind of the crime together with those he hires to execute everything involved with the kidnapping of Emilia and her parents on the way to the planned wedding. Emilia's fiancé Appiani gets brutally murdered in the process yet attempts are made to stage this as an accident. Emilia and her parents are kidnapped to the Prince's pleasure castle (Lustschloß).

Emilia, not knowing what happened, finds herself in the Prince's Castle where she meets him again, actually to her pleasant surprise, since she believes to be in love with him. She also meets the intriguing and self-imposing former mistress of the Prince, Countess Orsina, who is determined to win him back or exert her revenge but comes in disguise as a Lady Solmes. Whereas Emila has difficulties in articulating her thoughts and emotions, Orsina is perfectly in control of her words and she is most eloquent in her protest against what has happened to her. It is a powerful speech and numerous critics have commented Orsina as the strongest and most forceful female on stage in German ever. She interacts cleverly also with Emilia's father Odoardo and wins his compassion. This makes the plot even more intricate and dense. Under the pretense of being a relative of the Prince and as if she had come about an inheritance matter to resolve, she gets to speak to Emilia. The dialogue between these rivals builds up to the periphery in the play with a dagger handed over from Orsina which will eventually be in the hands of Odoardo.

The play ends violently in the moment Emilia understands who Orsina really is. She admits that she has feelings of her own which she may not be able control, implying that she loves the Prince, against her will. Her father, who is trying to rescue

781 Hermann J. Weigand, "Warum stirbt Emilia Galotti?" *Fährten und Funde: Aufsätze zur deutschen Dichtung* (1967): 40–50 and G.A. Wells, "What is wrong with Emilia Galotti?" *German Life and Letters* 37.3 (1984): 163–173.

her virtue and to prevent her from following her instincts and erotic desires, in the end after some additional wrinkles in the interaction kills her with the dagger, handed to him by Orsina, Emilia's rival. It seems to be an act of parodied sacrifice, or twisted love and self-defense. It has been noted that Emilia in the end talks less about her love for the Prince than about her own sensuality and eroticism which she experiences with fear of her own unknown self. It is about the depth of a person gaining a glimpse into her psyche which to her has always been externally controlled territory. She is far from being emancipated. Her father seems to be shocked with her own spiraling fear and acts without reason. What leads to the murder are falsely timed images and words throughout the play, moments of consciousness that are tragically missed. What the audience sees are moves that come too slowly or too quickly and which then lead to mishaps. It is the untimely temporality of the visual that precipitates the violence in this play.

Much has been written about Lessing's use of the notion of catharsis as well as other aspects of the Aristotelian theater, including his reception of Seneca's plays.[782] If watching a play can produce a cleansing of the soul, a clearance of the mind through emotions that may imply beauty and pity, then that may suggest Lessing may have reached his goal with his version of the story of the virgin martyr, Virginia. What matters for Lessing are the scenes of failed and often much abbreviated, hyphenated communication, even among people of the same social class and cultural background. These involve failed calculations of what can and what cannot be said in context and the lack of correlations between textual and nonverbal elements in language, features which all imply and illustrate throughout the play a wide spectrum of untimely and thus misplaced uses of words.

It is ironic that the play is not overly wordy, by far not as much as *Miß Sara Sampson,* but that the formulaic proverbial, often truncated sentences that are being used here also derail. This failure or communicative misuse of understatement is tragic I think. We should not ignore that Lessing was a critic of language. He is critical when it is being used by speakers regardless of whom their communication partners might be and regardless of context. It seems that at times Lessing did not have much faith in human communication, especially when class differences, cultural divides such as court and country life, gender polarizing, and naïve assumptions are taken into account. It was Lessing's achievement in the eighteenth century to have already experimented with signs that do not match their signifieds. Words have a plurality of meanings, always depending upon the specific timing in the contexts in which they are being used. Language is often not effective in communicating for reasons Lessing found puzzling but at least to a large extent avoidable.

---

782 On catharsis see Eun-Ae Kim, *Lessings Tragödientheorie im Licht der neuen Aristotelesforschung* (Würzburg: Königshausen & Neumann, 2002), 54-56, 71-76; and on Seneca, Wilfried Barner, *Produktive Rezeption. Lessing und die Tragödien Senecas* (Munich, 1973).

## 3. The power of whispers

It is possible to censor speech to avoid necessary repercussions and Lessing once made the shift from pulpit to stage in order to communicate more freely and more efficiently with a select group. But one runs the risk, as Lessing also realized, to truncate the message so severely that even the most intimate or presumably smartest dialogue partner cannot understand its meaning. It matters whether messages are whispered, spoken audibly, or even shouted. Why does Emilia whisper in her mother's ears telling her only in a subdued voice whom she has met? What was whispered to Emilia that morning in church where she met the Prince? Did the Prince through his whispering draw more attention to his words than he could have done had he spoken more loudly? Would Emilia have involved her mother so intimately into this had she not whispered herself in recounting about the meeting with the Prince? Did she, in whispering, admit the emotional impact which the flattering words of her new admirer had on her, despite the fact that this was indeed the morning of her wedding day to someone else? Her whispers, it seems, intrigued her mother more than any normal speech would have done and she was quickly drawn into the plot.

Lessing experiments with such modalities of voice. Further he tests the temporality of sounds, visual, and verbal impressions and introduces a number of criteria to experiment and to show how language onstage can in the worst case scenario completely derail.t. He not only advocates understatement but makes us reflect on volume of voice, the length or brevity of sentences, the syntax, and various features and potentials of language, its time-specific metaphoricity, and layered or multi-dimensional "Winkelzüge" (evasions, diagonal moves).[783] Lessing probes the boundaries of language while drawing close attention to the temporality of messages in the play, thus making this drama one of missed occasions and false understatements. While the main problem in the *Faust*-fragment was to deal with time, to work against the nuisance of missing the tolling of the bell, to find the devil who can master speed the best, and to counter-act the fear of what may come later. *Emilia Galotti* deals with misplaced and miscalculated coincidences, gaps in communication, and secrets drawn out of proportion. These accelerate the action towards the bad ending. The major events are initially motivated by boredom and impatience. The play builds momentum on problems resulting from inaccurate timing of actions and inactions. It requires double attention with respect to the plot which was to induce pity and compassion and with respect to the complexities of seeing and listening carefully to visual and verbal communication. The failure to listen carefully leads to an erosion and breakdown within

783 Ter-Nedden, *Lessing's Trauerspiele* 1–12, claims that "Fehler" (mistakes) are what actually holds the plot of Emilia Galotti together and what makes this play so interesting. His reading is in my view one of the best interpretations of the play. However, he does not follow through with any close analysis of the use of language in this play. Ralf Simon develops this approach further and then links the first Act of the play with a reflection on "Formen des Nichtwissens" (forms of not-knowing) in eighteenth century philosophical and epistemological discourses: "Ein falsches Bild. Oder: Was passiert, wenn Katharsis Form wird? Zu Lessings *Emilia Galotti*," Hans Adler and Rainer Godel, ed., *Formen des Nichtwissens in der Aufklärung* (Munich: Fink, 2010), 249–262.

the family dynamics and undermines personal understanding. The play exposes fatal human errors in even the most mundane interactions.

It is unfortunate that the play has been read as if it were anti-political by many who argue that change for Lessing is a matter that does not come from the outside but inside. The play may well be about the integrity of the bourgeois family and its attempt to live according to a moral code which is however not at all binding to those who are their social superiors and who govern them. It seems as if Lessing insists in this play on establishing the dominance of the private over the public sphere, a reading which deserves to be questioned. One could very well argue that the play has an indirect political dimension. In question are truth, justice, law, and order.

The opening scene of *Emilia Galotti* with the painter Conti sets the stage for the entire play. The setting is the study of the Prince of Guastalla, Hettore Gonzaga, sitting at his desk piled high with letters and administrative forms. These require his timely response and each demands his undivided attention. He looks at the pile and sighs: "wenn wir allen helfen könnten: dann wären wir zu beneiden" (if we could help everyone: then we were to be envied).[784] Being able to help everyone would do much more good than helping only a few who would then attract the envy of those whose petitions remain unanswered or rejected. And since envy is not desirable but helping people really is, the statement in the context creates an unnecessary ambivalence. It serves almost by implication as an excuse for the Prince here not to help anyone. Nevertheless, this statement still sounds perfectly reasonable taken out of context since the idea wanting to help people here in this first scene reflects positively on the character of the Prince. But this chance of making him appear as well-meaning is immediately undermined when he approves a petition involving considerable expense merely because the name of the petitioner happens to be coincidentally "Emilia:" "Aber eine Emilia Bruneschi–nicht Galotti, Nicht Emilia Galotti (But a certain Emilia Bruneschi–not Galotti. Not Emilia Galotti).[785] He cannot be objective in the matter and imposes his own personal likes or dislikes on matters requiring fairness. His administrative responsibilities somewhat do not interest him and wear him out. He summons his Chamberlain Marinelli to accompany him on a drive outdoors for a break.

When Marinelli arrives, he brings the unwelcome news that the Countess Orsina has arrived in the city. The Prince has already received a letter from her but seems wanting to avoid any meeting. His inattentive approach to his responsibilities of government is further emphasized in the final scene of the first act. The Prince is willing to sign a death-sentence without thinking twice about it. He has a position of power at court but is treating a matter of such immense importance completely irresponsibly. He exemplifies a lack of care, professionalism. He has no sincere interest in the people for whom he is responsible. Private and public spheres clash.

784 FA 7, 293.

785 FA 7, 293: This Emilia Bruneschi has: "Viel gefordert; sehr viel" (Demanded a great deal; a very great deal). Subsequently, the Prince seems to have second thoughts when handing the petition over to one of his councilors, Camillo Rota: "Noch ist hier eine Bittschrift einer Emilia Galotti–Bruneschi will ich sagen.–Ich habe meine Bewilligung zwar schon beigeschrieben. Aber, doch–die Sache ist keine Kleinigkeit" (So here is a petition from Emilia Galotti–Bruneschi I meant to say.–I have already affixed my approval. But, yet–the matter is not a trivial one) (FA 7, 293). He abandons his responsibility by letting Camillo Rota decide if the petition is to be approved or not.

DER PRINZ Was ist sonst? Etwas zu unterschreiben?
CAMILLA ROTA Ein Todesurteil wäre zu unterschreiben.
DER PRINZ Recht gern.–Nur her! geschwind.
CAMILLA ROTA *stutzig und den Prinzen starr ansehend*: Ein Todesurteil –sagt' ich.
DER PRINZ Ich höre ja wohl. Es könnte schon geschehen sein. Ich bin eilig.
CAMILLA ROTA *seine Schriften nachsehend*: Nun hab ich es doch wohl nicht mitgenommen!– Verzeihen Sie, gnädiger Herr.–Es kann Anstand damit haben bis morgen.[786]

[THE PRINCE What else? Something to sign?
CAMILLA ROTA A death sentence should be signed.
THE PRINCE With great pleasure.–Here with it! Quickly.
CAMILLA ROTA *pausing with puzzlement and looking at the Prince with a firm gaze:* A death sentence–I said.
THE PRINCE Of course I hear you. It may already have happened. I am in a hurry.
CAMILLA ROTA *shuffling through his papers:* Now I may have not brought with me after all!– Excuse me, dear Lord.–It can be postponed until tomorrow].

This scene draws attention to the importance of listening carefully to words. The Prince does not pay attention to what Rota is saying. His response is surprising to say the least. If he did hear what was said, then he is cruel or making a very bad joke. But the Prince appears to be just a bit distracted to those in the audience who may have missed the point. The scene shifts importance to a person of lesser status in the social ladder, Rota, his secretary, who has a sense of administrative responsibility. He does not obey blindly. He fortunately finds an excuse to postpone the matter on this occasion. This prevarication, which could in fact save a person's life, is therefore justified at this pivotal moment. Rota thinks on his own, acts in favor of a necessary delay in order to avoid the Prince giving his signature in a hurry. Rota's intervention gives the person in question who is not otherwise mentioned another chance to live. A little conversation like this decides a person's life or death, and it is Lessing's way to say: Words matter. What has happened in this one single moment is indeed significant. We may later notice in retrospect that this was a poignant moment for the action of this play.[787]

786 FA 7, 293.

787 Schröder also notices this about *Emilia Galotti* and sees in the play something modern in this style. He writes: "So pendelt es sich, im Grunde schon seit der Exposition, zwischen einer Vielzahl von möglichen Schlüssen auf den tatsächlichen ein. Dieser selbst enthält dadurch ein Moment des Zufälligen, Fragwürdigen und Unschlüssigen. Man hat die Fragwürdigkeit dieses Schlusses mit Vorliebe negativ, d.h. als psychologische Schwäche gesehen. Den Zeitgenossen eines Pirandello, Brecht, Frisch u.a., die das psychologische Drama durch eine neue Ästhetik des Spiels abgelöst haben, sollte es jedoch nicht schwerfallen, auch das Anregende darin zu entdecken. Was er dem Zuschauer an psychologischer Gewalt schuldig bleibt, vergütet er ihm, vor allem im Schlußauftritt, durch seinen geistigen Spielraum: Es könnte auch anders sein…". (So already, in fact, it oscillates, from the opening scenes with a multitude of possible conclusions until the actual conclusion. This ending is, considered by itself, thus often interpreted as a moment of arbitrariness, questionable and inconclusive. One has preferably interpreted this questionability of the ending as something negative that is as a psychological weakness. However, contemporaries of Pirandello, Brecht, Frisch and others who replaced the psychological drama with a new aesthetics of the drama, would then have no difficulties at all to find something inspiring in it. What Lessing owes the spectators in terms of psychological power, he repays them, especially in the final scene, through his mental space: It could also have been

There is a wide spectrum of the Prince's behavior traits shown between the opening and the final scenes. Each contains understatements. Not only is he willing to sign a form "recht gern" (with pleasure) although it may involve a death sentence. He is also ready to give consent to criminal action through other agents. On the surface his truncated sentences sound normal–or even trivial–but given the context they are horrendous. The Prince's mercurial changes of mood and his demonstration of self-inflated narcissism are reflected in his nonchalant use of language thus revealing serious flaws in communication. Lessing's strategy in this play is to present a series of scenes that highlight how split seconds and only miniature comments may have enormous consequences with ethical impact. By misaligning images and words he shows also in later scenes several missed opportunities, ignored or failed messages illustrating the importance of temporality while raising an awareness of the problems associated with truncations and verbal short-cuts.

The first piece of paper the Prince picks up at random is the petition of a certain "Emilia Bruneschi." This triggers a mental image. It reminds him of a young lady named Emilia Galotti whom he met briefly and who left a strong impression on him. In the midst of reverie over this image, the new object of his desire, he receives the letter from Countess Orsina, his previous projection of desire. She announces her visit. This is something that does not exactly please him at this time but he cannot help to stumble over his words that give away his ambivalence: "Desto schlimmer–besser wollt' ich sagen" (Even worse–better I wanted to say).[788] This apparently contradictory and abbreviated statement packs an entire mood swing and radical change of meaning into one single sentence, thus revealing the discrepancy between the spontaneous "no" and the expected or perhaps strangely still lingering "yes" answer. The *non sequitur* in the meaning is bridged on the surface visually by an m-dash. The Prince corrects himself in order to sound polite, when in fact he feels his fantasy interrupted and disturbed by the unwelcome reminder of a previous liaison. He reacts spontaneously, but then catches himself, because his class and his position require that he be always polite. Being "nice" on the surface is what lies at the heart of his later becoming criminal. But at this point the audience is not sure what is going on. It has yet to be explained who the Countess Orsina is. In what way is it "even worse" or "even better" that she is in town? Is Orsina's arrival frankly just another unpleasant additional interruption which comes at an inopportune time? Or does the Prince have other perhaps almost unconscious reasons to act so inconsistently? Having said something more positive, "even better," his words have an anticipatory, suggestive power with respect to his own actions. It is already as if he actually did welcome her against this previous logic. This turns out to be personal failure, indecision, and false politeness. His interactions reveal in subtle ways something involuntarily, especially by the slippages in his use of language. He has repressed emotions regarding his former relationship with Orsina, himself, and his erratic behavior gives the listeners an insight into a gap of integrity.

---

otherwise...) (*Gotthold Ephraim Lessing* 210-211). Lessing is already toying with implicit and possible hidden actions resulting from the same pivotal moments. This is not due to a weakness of rhetorical consistency. I agree with Schröder that Lessing is innovative here and wish to add that he experiments with an art of understatement that requires an intensified mode of seeing and reading.

788 FA 7, 293.

## 4. Written words dismissed

The tension of the play is not primarily based on a shocking and horrible crime of a tyrant, but on the consequences that result from a character's lack of consistency and from the dangers inherent in giving credence to superficial talk and ambivalent emotions. These result in a murder that might have been clearly avoided. The Prince pays little attention to the words he says. He cuts important messages short that require careful consideration for their implications. Instead of giving an honest reply to Orsina's messenger (he could have said that he has no time for such a response which seems implicit in his gestures and words), the messenger is told to leave, empty handed. The Prince now reveals what has been his relationship with the Countess.

> Meine teure Gräfin! *bitter, indem er den Brief in die Hand nimmt:* So gut, als gelesen! *und ihn wieder wegwirft.*:–Nun ja; ich habe sie zu lieben geglaubt! Was glaubt man nicht alles? Kann sein, ich habe sie auch wirklich geliebt. Aber–ich habe![789]

> [My dear Countess! *bitter, as he takes the letter in his hand:* As good as if I had read it *(and throws it down again)*–O well; I believed that I loved her. What aren't all the things one believes in? It may be that I have also really loved her. But–I have!].

The words the Prince speaks and the gestures he makes also imply information onstage for opening up trains of speculation on the part of the audience. So even the last sentence in the past tense: "I did [love her]" may, or may not be convincing given his earlier reluctance to see her. What happens at this already poignant moment in the play? It shows us by means of bracketed allusions to gestures, the life of the Prince beyond this statement. We know already that by giving the letter another look, he probably cannot completely suppress its message in the long run. It will come back to haunt him later along with all of the other unfinished official business cluttering up his desk. But the prince's train of thought is interrupted by the announcement of the arrival of Conti, a painter and portrait artist.

The following scene sees Lessing engaging with Ekphrasis, describing paintings through words and involving a visual-verbal dynamic.[790] Conti brings the Prince the portrait of a lady he had requested a while ago, but which now apparently comes too late. When it was ordered the object was much of interest to the Prince, but now it is something he has no desire for. The timing for the completion of this delayed project turns out to be most awkward since the portrait happens to be a painting of

789 FA 7, 294.

790 According to Alexander Košenina, this play is the first German drama in which a painter presents his reflections on the aesthetic process of visual representation onstage: "Lessing nutzt nun seine Überlegungen zur Ästhetik, um das für die tragische Verwicklung ausschlaggebende unbedingte Verlangen des Prinzen nach Emilia Galotti und seine gleichzeitig erkaltende Zuneigung für Osina anschaulich zu machen. Dies geschieht nun vor den Augen der Zuschauer, indem zum ersten Mal in einem deutschen Drama ein Maler auf der Bühne seine Kunst präsentiert" (Lessing makes use of his reflections on aesthetics in order to show in detail what is decisive for the tragic entanglement, the Prince's immediate desire for Emilia Galotti and his simultaneously cooling affection for Orsina. This happens in front of the eyes of the audience while for the first time in a German play, a painter presents his art onstage). *Anthropologie und Schauspielkunst* 203.

the Countess Orsina.[791] The Prince's mood which is one of trying to dissociate himself from that past relationship overshadows his reception of the painting. He cannot comprehend it properly as art and sees in it, as he admits to Conti, rather an object of possession, a commodity:

> DER PRINZ *nach einer kurzen Betrachtung:* Vortrefflich, Conti–ganz vortrefflich!–Das gilt Ihrer Kunst, Ihrem Pinsel.–Aber geschmeichelt, Conti; ganz unendlich geschmeichelt!
>
> CONTI Das Original schien dieser Meinung nicht zu sein. Auch ist es in der Tat nicht mehr geschmeichelt als die Kunst schmeicheln muß. Die Kunst muß malen, wie sich die plastische Natur,[792]–wenn es eine gibt–das Bild dachte: ohne den Abfall, welchen der widerstrebende Stoff unvermeidlich macht; ohne das Verderb, mit welchem die Zeit dagegen ankämpfet.[793]

> [THE PRINCE *after briefly reflecting:* Excellent, Conti–simply excellent!–I mean your art, your brush.–But it is flattering, Conti; completely and infinitely flattering!
>
> CONTI The original did not seem to have this opinion. But indeed it is not any more flattering than art must flatter. The artist must paint just like plastic nature–if such a thing exists–the picture imagined; without the residue that the resisting material makes inevitable, without the decay with which time fights against it].

According Conti's statement, art does not merely mimetically represent nature, even if that were possible, for it has to have its own imagination. As a result it would be a mistake to search for the original figure in the artwork. Unfortunately, the Prince has a hang-up with the woman whose portrait he now sees and to whom he has now an aversion, even though he once may have loved her. He is therefore unable to fully appreciate the artwork. What it represents may well be more beautiful than what nature offers. The Prince is particularly unhappy with the way her mouth is painted and argues:

> DER PRINZ Ich leugne nicht, daß ein schöner Mund, der sich ein wenig spöttisch verziehet, nicht selten um so viel schöner ist. Aber, wohl gemerkt, ein wenig: die Verziehung muß nicht bis zur Grimasse gehen, wie bei dieser Gräfin. Und Augen müssen über den wollüstigen Spötter die Aufsicht führen–Augen, wie sie die gute Gräfin nun gerade gar nicht hat. Auch nicht einmal hier im Bilde hat.
>
> CONTI Gnädiger Herr, ich bin äußerst betroffen–
>
> DER PRINZ Und worüber? Alles was die Kunst aus den großen, hervorragenden, stieren, starren Medusenaugen der Gräfin Gutes machen kann, das haben Sie, Conti, redlich daraus gemacht.–Redlich, sag' ich? Nicht so redlich wäre redlicher. Denn sagen Sie selbst, Conti, lässt sich aus diesem Bilde wohl der Charakter der Person schließen? Und das sollte doch. Stolz haben Sie in Würde, Hohn in Lächeln, Ansatz zu trübsinniger Schwärmerei in sanfte Schwermut verwandelt.[794]

> [THE PRINCE ... I do not deny that a beautiful mouth that is a little bit contorted in a mocking fashion is not seldom even more beautiful. But, one should pay attention, a little bit: the contortion should not go over to a grimace, just like it does with this Countess. And the eyes must keep in check the lascivious mocker–eyes, like those the good Duchess now really does not have. Not even here in the picture.

791 See Bonn, *Vom Schönen* 47-56.

792 "Idealbild einer der Natur entsprechenden Form" (ideal representation of form equivalent to nature). FA 7, 930.

793 FA 7, 295-296.

794 FA 7, 296.

CONTI Dear Lord, I am extremely mortified–.

THE PRINCE And for what reason? Everything which art was able to make out of those large, protruding, glowering, staring Medusa eyes of the Countess, that you, Conti, have honestly been able to make out with them.–Honestly, I say? Not so honestly would be more honest. Then say for yourself say, Conti, is one to deduce from this image the character of this person? And one can do so. Pride you represented as dignity, scorn as smiling, a tendency for sad dreaming into a mild lethargy].

The Prince is attempting to read features and character traits expressed in the painting in line with his current appreciation or lack of it, in this case rather of the Countess Orsina. Details which are supposed to show off her winsomeness, such as her seductive smile, he willfully misinterprets, turning the smile into a grimace. Yet then he seems to correct himself indirectly, acknowledging that in real life her smile is also rather exaggerated, a superior or perhaps even cynical one and that by implication she has not mastered the art of understatement herself. He rejects her as an image because she resists it. Conti is alarmed and, as he puts it, "mortified" that he could have suggested any such thing in a portrait he painted for him. The Prince continues by scolding Conti for the presentation of the eyes of the Countess, but his description of them is gratuitously unflattering. Her eyes he compares to the eyes of the Medusa whose gaze turned living objects to stone. He is afraid of her looking at him because the image he made of her now stares back. Prince nevertheless praises Conti has having done well, too well perhaps: "Nicht so redlich wäre redlicher" (Not so honestly would be more honest). Conti has in the Prince's view represented pride as dignity and scorn as smiling. Had he been less "honest" in wanting to paint a portrait that would have gained the approval of both sitter and patron, he would have been more honest because he would have identified the flaws in the Orsina character. Unfortunately the Prince is not able to see the artwork for what it actually is but only in terms of what he expects from it. He projects his memory and wishes onto it. He is not able to read the visual, lacks visualcy, and imposes his own personal opinions and feelings about the person depicted in the artwork.

The painter Conti drew attention to the Medusa eyes he associated perhaps for very telling reasons, perhaps without knowing fully but rather unconsciously but correctly. It is the character of Orsina as he, the artist and sensible observer, perceives her in the context with his own eyes. She will stare back to haunt the Prince who has violated her rights. She also represents, as the action of the play soon reveals, an outspoken female voice expressing her stark protest. The Prince does the same thing when he sees the second portrait, that of Emilia Galotti. He reifies the drawing, turns it into an object as if it were his. He commodifies and appropriates the artwork conflating signification with the thing itself, here the persona of his own imaginary. In doing so, he takes claim of this woman whom he now aspires to "possess:"

DER PRINZ Soviel er will! *gegen das Bild:* Dich hab' ich für jeden Preis noch zu wohlfeil.– Ah! schönes Werk der Kunst, ist es wahr, daß ich dich besitze?–Wer dich auch besäße, schönres Meisterwerk der Natur! was Sie dafür wollen, ehrliche Mutter! Was du willst, alter Murrkopf! Fordre nur! Fordert nur!–Am liebsten kauf't ich dich, Zauberin, von dir selbst!–Dieses Auge voll Liebreiz und Bescheidenheit! Dieser Mund! und wenn er sich zum Reden öffnet! wenn er lächelt! Dieser Mund!–Ich höre kommen.–[795]

795 FA 7, 299-300.

> [THE PRINCE As much as he wants! *toward the picture:* At any price I have you yet too cheaply–Ah! beautiful work of Art, is it true that I own you? –If only I were to own you also, even more beautiful masterpiece of Nature! Whatever you want, honest Mother! Whatever you want, old grouchy-head! Go ahead and demand! Just demand!–Ideally, I would buy you, enchantress, from yourself!–This eye full of charm and modesty! This mouth! and when it opens itself to speak! When it smiles! This mouth!–I hear some one coming–].

He is obviously obsessed with wanting to own the image and its content. He is fixated on the portrait of Emilia which he treats as if it were her surrogate or his literally.[796] He also finds it not completely as expected, since he has his own projections of her imagined perfections. He is fixated on the figure of Emilia he has constructed in his mind.[797] In addition to not respecting the painter's artwork for what it is, he treats it as a commodity and measures its value in terms of the price he is willing to pay for it Emilia herself. This conflation of sign and signifier, his ignorance of metaphoricity and of levels of signification draw attention to a problem in the use of language. We can notice this earlier when Conti asked by the Prince how he or how his art were doing. His answer was "Prinz, die Kunst geht nach Brot" (Prince, the art follows bread), thus highlighting the dilemma of his own financial dependency. He challenges the notion of autonomous art since both the artist and the recipient are contingent upon market issues and socio-political structures they cannot avoid.

Again it is the mouth and the eyes in the portrait that the Prince analyzes. When he admits that he loves her mouth just when it opens a bit to speak, this statement stands in stark contrast to what he said about the previous portrait of Orsina (who will speak all the more in real life). This constellation reminds us as well of Sara Sampson's admirer Mellefont who had difficulties coping with Sara's abundant wordiness. We shall see that Emilia is, as here mentioned with respect to her eyes, the more "modest." Her picture seems more likeable since when she opens her mouth there is not the same kind of threat that the Prince in contrast feels by the Medusa-like gaze of Orsina who will prove to be the most eloquent and verbose character in the play. Emilia, on the other hand, is drawn to the man who whispers, one who comes to meet her unannounced in church, has a foible for understatement, and enjoys her eyes even when shielded a bit. She is drawn to the man who promises her enhanced social status and she flirts with the unknown. She becomes enamored of someone belonging to another world and being drawn to her own sense of insecurity. As the play ultimately shows social classes impact all the characters. However, there are instabilities on both sides of the spectrum. The many pauses in the Prince's utterances indicate not only an instability as already mentioned but also his inability to use and to comprehend language on art.

---

796 See Bonn, *Vom Schönen* 57-63.

797 Ralf Simon, "Ein falsches Bild" 249-262, uses the word "Bildidolatrie" (idolization of images) to characterize the Prince's being captured by the idol he has made up in his mind. When seeing the portraits by Conti he has no understanding of art since the Prince is unable to appreciate paintings for what they are and makes a double error: He projects his inner image on the painted one, as well as ignoring the artificiality of the artwork, its medium-specific features.

## 5. Frenetic moves

The scene shifts to the Galotti household. There are comings and goings that create a hectic, nervous atmosphere. Everyone appears busy doing their thing but waiting at the same time. It is the morning of Emilia's planned wedding to Appiani. Emilia's father Odoardo is out riding and his wife Claudia surprised by his untimely return. Whereas the notion of "Haarspalterei" (hairsplitting) is commonly used in German as a way to refer to the danger of getting lost in the nitty-gritty of language; it is here actually used here in referring to a lack of attention to details that sparks trouble. By using understatements Lessing seems to draw attention to the danger that may lie in ignoring one minute detail in communication and also by being overwhelmed by a mass of details. The playing with words, often in unusual ways, is loaded with significance considering what follows.

The scene had opened with Emilia's mother Claudia outside the house being greeted by their servant Pirro who announces the arrival of his master, her husband Odoardo: Claudia exclaims: "Mein Gemahl? Ist es möglich?" (My husband? Is that possible?) Pirro answers: "Er folgt mir auf dem Fuße" (He' following me hard on my heels). Claudia replies: "So unvermutet?–*ihm entgegen eilend:* Ach! Mein Bester!–" (So unexpectedly? *Hurrying towards him:* Ah! My dearest!–).[798] Although these gestures appear marginal at this point in the play, they have symbolic meaning from a meta-perspective since they almost summarize what the plot will be: Odoardo will not only physically ride behind Pirro. He will literally be one step behind him. He will also follow him metaphorically on the path of the action, into the crime scene. And Claudia's question whether that is possible referring to her husband's arrival will be the ultimate question in the play after he has killed his daughter. But such insight into redundant formulas is not given, although this meaning-packed use of little phrases and subtle allusions will later serve as an easy index reflecting on missed opportunities considering all the characters interactions. When Odoardo wants to know where Emilia is, just at the moment of his return to the house in order to give her his best wishes for her wedding day, he is told by Claudia that she is not here since she had decided to go to mass, that she left everything, taken her veil, and hurried to church. Odoardo, surprised, seems a little bit concerned, asking whether she went all by herself. Claudia responds: "Die wenigen Schritte– –" (Those few steps– –), Odoardo replies with proverbial utterance which in retrospect can be seen as fateful understatement: "Einer ist genug zu einem Fehltritt!–" (One step is enough for a stumble).[799]

The third scene reveals that their servant Pirro supplements his income with highway robbery. He is shown meeting with his accomplice, Angelo, whom he greets with the question: "Und du wagst es, wieder ans Licht zu kommen?" (And you dare again to come out into light again?)[800] He reminds Angelo that after his last murder he was declared an outlaw with a price on his head. Angelo has come to pay Pirro his share from the sale of a ring seized in an earlier robbery. Then Angelo wants to know why the old Galotti was riding by himself and what he wanted:

798 FA 7, 308.
799 FA 7, 309.
800 FA 7, 309.

ANGELO: Eins muß ich doch fragen.–Da kam ja der alte Galotti so ganz allein in die Stadt gesprengt. Was will er?

PIRRO Nichts will er; ein bloßer Spazierritt. Seine Tochter wird heut abend auf dem Gute, von dem er herkömmt, dem Grafen Appiani angetrauet. Er kann die Zeit nicht erwarten–[801]

[ANGELO: Yet one thing I must ask.–Wasn't it old Galotti who galloped all alone into town. What does he want?

PIRRO: He doesn't want anything, a simple ride. His daughter will be married this evening at the estate from where he came to the Count Appiani. He cannot patiently wait until then–].

As the conversation continues, it becomes clear that Angelo is particularly interested in drawing information out of Pirro concerning the disposition and route of the bridal party. Too late Pirro realizes what he is being drawn into: "Ha! Laß dich den Teufel bei einem Haare fassen und du bist sein auf ewig!" (Ha! Let the devil catch you by one hair and you are his forever!). We will later find out that Pirro and Angelo are working for the Prince and his Chamberlain Marinelli. Their scheme is to prevent the marriage, get rid of the Appiani and thereby clear the field for the Prince to pursue his interest in Emilia. Odoardo is unhappy that Emilia is taking so long. He has an urgent errant with Count Appiani who will be returning to his distant estates after the marriage. This turns out to be a sore spot for Emilia's mother. But her father wants her away from the temptations of the city and the court which he hates for its lack of virtue and honorable conduct, typified by the self-serving conduct of court officials like Marinelli. Furthermore Appiani has ruined his chances at court by marrying Emilia because Odoardo is convinced that the Prince hates him. His wife protests and says at a recent event the Prince spent a considerable time with Emilia and that he: "Schien von ihrer Munterkeit und ihrem Witze so bezaubert" (Appeared so enchanted by her cheerfulness and wit).[802] He had spoken words of praise concerning her beauty. This Odoardo does not want to hear: "Lobeserhebungen? Und das alles erzählst du mir in einem tone der Entzückung?" (Phrases s of praise? And all this you recount to me in a tone of delight?)[803] But he forces himself not to say too much to his wife about this matter or to scold her. He represses his uneasy feelings and reflects in a brief outburst on his false politeness: "Du hättest mir das sogleich sollen gemeldet haben.–Doch ich möchte dir heute nicht gern etwas Unangenehmes sagen. Und ich würde, *indem sie ihn bei der Hand ergreift:* wenn ich länger bliebe.–" (You should have reported this to me right away.–But I would like not to say anything unpleasant to you today. And I would [*As she takes him by the hand*] if I stayed longer). Again because he is so much of a hurry that he does not want to take the time to explain his concerns, and not wanting to bring up anything that could spoil the mood on this presumably happy wedding day, there will be a price to be paid for cutting his conversation short. After Odoardo's departure his wife shrewdly reflects on his character, his extreme and unbending sense of propriety that filters everything though his own particular heightened sense of virtue: Even more revealing is her analysis of the relationship between the Prince and

801 FA 7, 310.
802 FA 7, 313.
803 FA 7, 313.

Odoardo which she sees in homosocial terms.[804] But here the occluded female instead of cementing the relationship between two men will serve to intensify their enmity.

> Welch ein Mann!–O, der rauhen Tugend! –wenn anders sie diesen Namen verdienet–Alles scheint ihr verdächtig, alles strafbar!–Oder, wenn das die Menschen kennen heißt.–wer sollte sich wünschen sie zu kennen? –Wo bleibt aber auch Emilia?–Er ist der Vaters Feind, folglich–folglich, wenn er ein Auge für die Tochter hat, so ist es einzig; um ihn zu beschimpfen?–[805]

> [What a man!–Oh, raw virtue!–if indeed it has earned this name–everything appears suspicious to it, everything liable to punishment!–Or if that is called knowing people. –Who would want to know them? –But where is now Emilia?–He [the Prince] is the enemy of the father: therefore–therefore, when he has an eye for the daughter, so is that for the sole reason in order to insult him?–].

At his point Emilia rushes in and reveals what actually happened during a brief encounter she had while in church. She unexpectedly heard whispers behind her and heard a series of flattering comments which the Prince presented in the most intense but subtle way. He gains her attention by means of softly spoken truncated sentences and his words have urgency since it is her wedding day. Yet this new admirer claims he is serious in his declaration of love. His words seem of particular importance since they are so completely unexpected and out of context and they are expressed to the audience only by means of Emilia's emotional report to her mother. When she arrives home from church, she throws herself in her mother's arms. Not surprisingly, her mother is startled: "Was ist dir meine Tochter? Was ist dir?" (What's the matter with you, my daughter, what's the matter with you? Emilia relies: "Nichts, gar nichts." (Nothing, nothing at all).[806] Her understatement makes her mother even more curious and she notices that Emilia is obviously flustered. The mother reads her daughter's body signs and takes them more seriously than her words. She knows that something important must have happened and when Emilia, asked again, gives additional information, she does so in staccato sentences riddled with hesitations and pauses so that her mother gets the sense that much more happened than what she is being told. Emilia, on the other hand, takes everything that happened in church, as if it were either sacred or blasphemic, as if the location determined what had happened. It is as if she were making confession when she finally recounts that when she was kneeling down in church, she heard a voice behind her whispering very close to her ear and it

---

804 "'Homosocial' is a word occasionally used in history and the social sciences, where it describes social bonds between persons of the same sex." Eve Kosofsky Sedgwick, *Between Men: English Literature and Male Homosocial Desire* (New York: Columbia University Press, 1985), 1. Sedgwick follows René Girard who "traced a calculus of power that was structured by the relation of rivalry between the two active [male] members of an erotic triangle" (*Between Men* 21). The occluded or hidden apex of the triangle is occupied by the female. In a traditional marriage arrangement the agreement was made between two men and the woman was "trafficked" to cement a male-male relationship. See Gayle Rubin, "The Traffic in Women: Notes on the 'Political Economy' of Sex," Rayna R. Reiter, ed., *Toward an Anthropology of Women* (New York: *Monthly Review Press*, 1975): 157-210, 396-416.

805 FA 7, 314.

806 FA 7, 314.

was, as she stutters towards the end of her explanation, the Prince himself who left such a strong impression on her with his words.

> EMILIA [...] Aber es währte nicht lange, so hört' ich, ganz nah' an meinem Ohre,–nach einem tiefen Seufzer,– nicht den Namen einer Heiligen,–den Namen,–zürnen Sie nicht, meine Mutter–den Namen Ihrer Tochter!–Meinen Namen!–O daß laute Donner mich verhindert hätten, mehr zu hören!–Es sprach von Schönheit, von Liebe– Es klagte, daß dieser Tag, welcher mein Glück mache,–wenn er es anders mache,–sein Unglück auf immer entscheide–Es beschwor mich–hören mußt' ich dies alles. Aber ich blickte nicht um; ich wollte tun, als, ob ich es nicht hörte.–Was konnt' ich sonst?–Meinen guten Engel bitten, mich mit Taubheit zu schlagen; und wann auch, wann auch auf immer!–Das bat ich; das war das einzige, was ich beten konnte.– Endlich ward es Zeit, mich wieder zu erheben. Das heilige Amt ging zu Ende. Ich zitterte, mich umzukehren. Ich zitterte, ihn zu erblicken, der sich den Frevel erlauben dürfen. Und da ich mich umwandte, da ich ihn erblickte–
> CLAUDIA Wen, meine Tochter?
> EMILIA Raten Sie, meine Mutter; raten Sie–Ich glaubte in die Erde zu sinken–Ihn selbst.
> CLAUDIA Wen, ihn selbst?
> EMILIA Den Prinzen.[807]
>
> [EMILIA [...] But it was not long before I heard very close to my ear–after a deep sigh–not the name of a Saint–the name–don't be angry, my mother–the name of your daughter–my name!–O I wish that loud thunder would have prevented me from hearing more!–The voice spoke of beauty, of love–The voice complained that this day, which will make my happiness–it will make it that–will decide its misfortune forever.–The voice implored me – I had to hear all of this. But I did not turn around to look, I wanted to act as if I did not hear–But what else could I do–Pray to my Guardian Angel to strike me with deafness and even if, even if forever!–That's what I prayed; that was the only thing which I was able to pray for.–Finally, it was time to stand up again. The Holy Service came to an end. I shivered at having to turn around. I shivered to look on that which had allowed itself such blasphemy. And when I turned around, when I glanced at him–
> CLAUDIA At whom my daughter?
> EMILIA Guess, my mother, guess–I thought I would sink into the earth.–He himself.
> CLAUDIA Who himself:
> EMILIA The Prince].

What makes this dialogue so very important to the mother is its suggested emotionality of her daughter and the coded, almost non-decipherable sentence elements. The if-clause ("wenn er es anders mache") suggests an alternative train of events so that this day instead of making her happy and him unhappy, might end up making them both happy. Mother and daughter seem to be aware of the significance of this statement and are to some extent alarmed. On the surface however, Emilia has been flattered by the Prince's advances and she feels that whatever she heard she heard against her will.[808] It is also remarkable that she says she avoided looking at him and when she did, she felt unable to respond, neither verbally nor visually. Her inability to communicate has consequences also in the eyes of her mother who senses this failure and is now trying

807 FA 7, 115-116.

808 This also suggests that she is entering into her marriage with Count Appiani because that is what her father wants. He has made it clear the Count is a very suitable husband for his daughter and he cannot wait until he is officially his son-in-law. We do not get to hear what Emilia thinks.

to protect her daughter from a scolding from her father, commanding her to keep all this a secret. Claudia does not really seem to think about the implications of what the Prince has said, but is more than anything concerned about how her father will react: "Gott! Gott! wenn dein Vater das wüßte!" (God, God! If your father knew about this!) and when Emilia, who is certain that she did nothing wrong suggests telling him about this encounter, her mother silences her explicitly and also begs her not to say a word to her fiancé Appiani about it: "Sag' ihm nichts. Laß ihn nichts merken!" (Tell him nothing. Let him suspect nothing!)[809] By cutting off Emilia's ability to express herself, to consult with other family members and her own fiancé, she almost criminalizes her, draws down false suspicion upon her and leaves her lacking self-respect, thus fueling the action of the plot unconsciously yet complicity.

Marinelli and Appiani meet. Their conversation leads to a verbal confrontation that almost becomes a physical fight between them. Marinelli had come to request that Appiani serve the Prince by leaving home immediately and taking care of a task that will require the postponing of his wedding with Emilia. Obviously the Prince has his own plans and is using his authority to make Appiani obey. Although Appiani is characterized has having an air of melancholy about him and a touch of reluctance or ambivalence about his immanent wedding with Emilia, he adamantly refuses to carry out this order of the Prince. He insists on his right to protest since he is not one of the servants of the Prince. Otherwise he suspects nothing, and brushes away any worries, intuitions and any possible concerns he might have had about the consequences of his having said no to a person in power. He insists that his wedding will take place that same day regardless despite Marinelli's ominous statement: "Nur Geduld Graf, nur Geduld" (Only patience Count, only patience).[810] What appears here as a friendly response can be understood as an understatement for it is in fact a dangerous threat. The following events bear witness. The threatening undertones should have been recognized and taken more seriously by Appiani if he was to have any hope of thwarting the fate that was being prepared for him. The actual crime, the kidnapping of Emilia and the murder of Appiani are revealed to the audience as piecemeal only through hints and comments. These rhetorical strategies underscore the visual-verbal tension and suggest that the action is more frightening and scandalous than can be talked about.

## 6. The heinous crime

The Prince and Marinelli meet and work on the details of their intrigue which is often couched in coded formulas and subversive hints only. This conversation stands out as

809 FA 7, 117.

810 FA 7, 325. Marinelli's threatening use of "Geduld" (patience) contrasts with the way in which the word has recently been used: Emilia says to Appiani she will soon be ready in her wedding finery: "Eine kleine Geduld, und ich stehe so vor Ihnen da!" (A little patience, and I will stand like this before you) (FA 7, 320); Count Appiani says to Claudia: "Perlen bedeuten Tränen!–Eine kleine Geduld!–Ja, wenn die Zeit nur außer uns wäre!" (Pearls stand for tears.–A little patience–Yes, if only time was outside of us), (FA 7, 331).

being significant in terms of the meta-perspectives on the entire play's main plot, at least if one has an inkling of what might happen next. Marinelli reports that Appiani did not accept the honor as offered ("angetragene Ehre"). This notion which frames the suggestion to postpone Appiani's wedding for the sake of an unexpected call to duty in the most harmless manner possible.[811] The Prince is disappointed that Appiani did not act according to their plan and he uses a proverbial expression to scold Marinelli: "Ich versprach mir von Ihrem Einfalle so viel!–Wer weiß, wie albern Sie sich dabei genommen. Wenn der Rat eines Toren einmal gut ist, so muß ihn ein gescheiter Mann ausführen. Das hätt ich bedenken sollen" (I promised myself so much through your idea–Who knows how silly you behaved in carrying it out. If the advice of a fool is sometimes a good one, then one must have a clever man carry it out. I should have thought of that).[812] (By insulting Marinelli for his supposed stupidity, the Prince pushes him to find another solution to bring their scheme to a successful conclusion. I should have thought about that). Marinelli takes a hint: "... entweder er mich oder ich ihn. Ich ihn: so ist das Feld ganz unser. Oder er mich, wenn auch: so muß er fliehen und der Prinz gewinnt wenigstens Zeit" (... either he me or I him. I him: then the field is completely ours. Or he me: if so, then so must he flee and the Prince gains time at least).[813] He then uses common expressions to sanitize his language and hides the specific content of what he is talking about in order to make his scheme more palatable to the Prince.

When the Prince asks if he would be indeed prepared to die on his behalf, Marinelli responds: "Ha! man sollt' es voraus wissen, wenn man so töricht bereit ist, sich für die Großen aufzuopfern–man sollt' es voraus wissen, wie erkenntlich sie sein würden" (Ha! one should know beforehand, when one is so foolishly ready, to make oneself a victim for the Powerful–one should know in advance, how grateful they will be).[814] Yet it becomes implicit that he is talking about a possible assassination. Marinelli tries to play things down and uses another proverbial sentence while indicating that the use of "Gewalt" (force, power, violence) may not be avoidable: "Es ist eher ein Mädchen mit Gewalt entführt worden, ohne daß es einer gewaltsamen Entführung ähnlich gesehen" (It has happened before that a girl was abducted with force without having this look as if it were a violent abduction).[815] By saying that, he is actually requesting obliquely to get the Prince's authorization for the use of weaponry and force. The Prince seems aware of that but gives a guarded, almost coded response: "Wenn Sie das zu machen wüßten, so würden Sie nicht erst lange davon schwatzen" (If you knew how to do that, you would not first chatter about it at length).[816] He silences his agent and hence avoids giving his explicit consent which could rebound to his detriment. His command is to speak less and to pursue towards more action as already self-understood.

By shutting those around him up, urging them not to say anything, and by being nearly mute about it, he pushes Marinelli to take action and to go ahead with the plan

811 FA 7, 326.
812 FA 7, 326.
813 FA 7, 326.
814 FA 7, 326.
815 FA 7, 327.
816 FA 7, 328.

as alluded to. Nothing is said explicitly about what needs to be done and what needs to be avoided. No ethical boundaries are set. While the Prince appears to brush aside the import of so-called "Unglücksfälle" (accidents) that Marinelli mentions *en passant* being as vague as he can possibly be, he is saying nothing. He seems to be giving his silent approval to such a plan, defers responsibility, and is hiding behind his agents. Marinelli has the say more or less on his own now, gaining responsibility he does not have to vouch for. Perhaps he would not have kept his rank of chamberlain for very long if he were not able to read the import of such apparent disinterestedness. In response to Marinelli's attempts to discuss the plan and its possible deadly outcome, the Prince just rushes to add that it is not his style to punish his people for things beyond their control. Whatever happens, he alludes, should not be traceable:

> MARINELLI Aber für den Ausgang müßte man nicht stehen sollen.–Es könnten sich Unglücksfälle dabei ereignen.
> DER PRINZ Und es meine Art, daß ich Leute Dinge verantworten lasse, wofür sie nicht können![817]

> [MARINELLI But one would not have to be responsible for the outcome.–There might be accidents that happen in the process.
> THE PRINCE And it is my way to let people be answerable for things for which they cannot be responsible].

At this moment they hear a gun shot. Marinelli quickly adds to his sentence that he just wanted to confirm what he assumed anyway, thus making the Prince completely responsible for the action he approved–at the very time it was being carried out. When Marinelli and Angelo meet, the latter first takes off his mask and reports losses on both sides. One of Angelo's accomplices, Nicolo, has been killed which upsets him and he demands his pay. Also he indicates vaguely that Appiani was severely injured and may even be dead but he claims that he could not see exactly what happened. Marinelli replies: "Und wie er sich vielleicht nun martern muß, der arme Graf!" (And how he may perhaps have to suffer now himself, just like a martyr, the poor Count!).[818] He frames Appiani as a martyr which implicitly may serve him and his agents to sanctify the cause of Appiani's immanent death. This and serves by implication as quasi alibi for the murderers. Such framing is of course totally inappropriate but makes the audience aware of fine differences in metaphoricity and fields of association which shed interpretation on things that may well have to be further investigated.

The next step for Marinelli is to direct the blame onto someone else: "Pfui, Angelo. Das heißt sein Handwerk sehr grausam treiben–und verpfuschen" (Shame on you, Angelo. This means you carried out your trade very cruelly–and messed it up). He orders Angelo not to let the Prince know anything about this and to keep quiet about it: "Aber davon muß der Prinz noch nichts wissen" (But the Prince must not yet know anything about this). The uncertainty about Count Appiani's death in fact bothers Marinelli. Although he clearly appears as one of the most heinous characters in the play, Lessing avoids giving him only negative features. A hint of pity seems noticeable when Marinelli adds: "Dieser Tod. Was gäb ich um die Gewißheit?" (This

817 FA 7, 328.
818 FA 7, 330.

death. What would I give for knowing with certainty?)[819] Somehow the scheme has derailed and lets everyone assume the worst.

Although Marinelli has abducted Emilia, the Prince now has a problem. What to do next? Marinelli recalls that the essence of successful rhetoric is the art of pleasing and convincing, something the Prince may have forgotten, yet something which is "das Vornehmste" (the most elegant of all). He counted on his master's forgetfulness, so that he had free hand to pursue his own intrigues. His comments serve as the rhetorical device of a *Paralipsis* (Greek "leaving-aside").[820] It is a speech act by this speaker Marinelli to draw attention to a topic by claiming not to mention it. It is the method of an argument that involves denial on his part (since he does not speak about Appiani's murder and his responsibility), or the explicit refusal to tell the Prince what he actually did and that he did it in his behalf. How to tell others, including Emilia, what happened? And how to present the actual events? He reminds the Prince that she or anyone should not be unnecessarily alarmed and that once needs to be careful about what to say. It is a clever mode of wrapping not only the Prince, but also the audience into Marinelli's selfish logic.

It is a kind of reasoning that reminds us of the fable with a fox clothed as a lamb. He is trying to finesse the impression that he is innocent. Similarly, the Prince feels he has every reason to be content with the execution of his will as long as nobody knows who did it. Nobody can track him down. The fact that it is Marinelli who actually provides a metaperspective here symbolically elevates the servant over the master. It is another unexpected twist of communication that keeps the audience on toes. In his eloquence, Marinelli points out, that there is "an equation" between art and love and that what he just did was a piece of "art." Although he actually refers to a murder and abduction he makes these (not only in the fictional plane) appear as if they were in this context "just done for love." He tries to package the intrigue about the kidnapping of Emilia and her parents and the murder of Appiani as nothing but a minor wrinkle of developments as planned. He presents his scheme in an understatement that serves here as a trick to gloss over what really happened and to avoid speaking about the consequences. Reference is made always only to the very next "Schritt" (step) in the sequence of events, drawing attention to language and the medium and away from the facticity of anything that happened. He is ridiculing any reductive methodology and will not stick, as he comments in his self-assertive mode, to anyone's "mere" deductions.[821] Marinelli resists any long term perspective and a philosophical perspective. He offers the performance of a metaphorical "dance" obsessed with what is next only. Marinelli calls what he did a "game" (Spiel) and it serves the goal of art in general. He refers to the urgent need now to please and to convince all the person(s) involved even after they feel that their rights have been violated. He acts as if he was a dramaturge and giving stage direction to his players. Pleasing or making people at ease is now "das Vornehmste," which in this context means the most important thing of all.[822] Marinelli evokes such an "art" of ignorance–as the case

819 FA 7, 330.
820 D. Veraldi and S. Cushman, "Paralipsis," *The Princeton Encyclopedia of Poetry and Poetics*, ed. R. Greene et al. (Princeton: Princeton University Press, 2012), 997.
821 See FA 7, 331 (Act III, scene iii) and FA 7, 342 (twice, Act IV, scene i).
822 FA 7, 331.

would have to be here–as if winning Emilia to his side would be something to which the Prince could still aspire, no matter what has happened. The reference to "Kunst" (art) in this context is slightly ironic and it further suggests that there could be a parallel between Emilia and everyone in the audience. Emilia has been abducted and now has to be won over by the Prince. But we know that there are many horrible things that have meanwhile happened offstage. Whereas it now seems that the one remaining, difficult task of the Prince is to win Emilia against all odds, this is set against a backdrop of politics, intrigue, and corruption in society. Nobody can say that this play is not also a political one.

Yet there is one more poignant moment of reflection and puzzlement in the play, yet only if it had resulted in real insights. The Prince is reluctant to proceed and has some scruples after hearing the latest news. There is just a miniature hint of remorse on his part. Yet he skipped this occasion and proceeds nevertheless to follow the course of events he has already set in motion. He knows that it proceeds without his control or complete knowledge but given his reluctance he will not turn any wheel. He has not only to win Emilia over to his side now, but the entire audience as well. What a task! "Seeing" is hard to achieve under these circumstances and we are reminded that when the Prince asked Marinelli earlier in the play for "Licht" (light) he certainly only got a very dim one.[823] Emilia was told to be quiet earlier when the "accident" happened and when she was taken from her carriage. She is now, after her "rescuers" have brought her to the Prince's residence Dosalo, his Lustschloß" (castle of pleasures), speechless. She feels a void and is dazzled between the relief still to be alive, even after the attack by some thieves, and her affection for the Prince whom she barely knows. She is thinking that the Prince's agents have rescued her but fears that indeed something horrible must have happened. There is something uncanny about this unexpected encounter. She incorporates a state of inertia, an as-if existence, as if she were a playing someone else, nearly turning into a statue, unable to move and to overcome intense and conflicting emotions.

> Stumm und niedergeschlagen und zitternd stand sie da; wie eine Verbrecherin, die ihr Todesurteil höret. Ihre Angst steckte mich an, ich zitterte mit und schloß mit einer Bitte der Vergebung. Kaum getrau' ich mir, sie wieder anzureden.[824]

> [Silent, depressed, and shivering, she stands there; like a criminal who listens to her death sentence. Her fear was contagious to me. I shivered with her and closed with a prayer for forgiveness. I have barely the courage to talk to her again].

If Emilia ever had a wisp of affection and perhaps even an erotic attraction for the voice she heard in the morning whispering seductive words into her ear, and if in fact she was for a split moment enchanted with the Prince as a new admirer of hers, she is now frightened to death. Perhaps it is a moment of catharsis for her. It comes too late. At this point, it looks like the Prince has a moment of insight into her situation and even compassion for Emilia. He feels sorry for having set Marinelli's dangerous scheme in motion and sees Emilia as a victim who, he now thinks, must be spared

823 See FA 7, 339 (Act IV, scene i).
824 FA 7, 331.

further humiliation. But this moment of momentary insight has no consequences. Facts matter more than feelings and thoughts at this point.

## 7. The postponed ending

Had Lessing carried out this moment of the play to its logical consequences, the ending would have been different. The one victim would have been Appiani but there would have been no further deaths. Emilia would have learnt to reflect on and to respond to words more proactively. Yet since the play still has only reached midpoint. There will not only be many more twists and turns in the plot, but also more demonstration of speech acts that involve understatements. Speakers' pretend that whatever is said is not anything that really matters a great deal. Words seem to be less important than moves. Interactions are just like further steps in a dance, with a rhythm that drives the action of the play towards the catastrophe, the additional stabbing in the end.

After the report of the death, Marinelli receives a request from Emilia's mother wanting to see him. He ponders what to do about her, since he is aware that Emilia is hidden in this very same room which Claudia now wants to enter. But he really cannot deny her entry. He admits: "Freilich, sie wird Augen machen, wenn sie den Wolf bei dem Schäfchen sieht" (Certainly she will look surprised when she sees the wolf with the little lamb).[825] This calls to mind one of Lessing's own fables ("Das beschützte Lamm") adapted from the fables of Aesop.[826] Instead of a fox and a dog, Lessing's imitation features a wolf-like dog, Hylax who is protecting a "frommes Lamm" (innocent lamb).[827] He is accosted by Lykodes, another wolf-like dog who demands that Hylax hand the lamb over to him for protection.[828] Hylax refuses and Lykodes attempts to take the lamb by force: "Hylax will es mit Gewalt behaupten, und das arme Lamm—Trefflicher Beschützer!—wird darüber zerissen" (Hylax wishes to hold on to it by force, and the poor lamb—splendid protectors!—was as a result torn to pieces). Emilia is in a sense fought over by two wolf-like dogs, her father and the Prince, both of whom will be standing unharmed at the end of the play. Emilia will be, metaphorically speaking, torn into pieces. She will be stabbed by her own father's hand.

Claudia can do not much more than watch this sequence of events take place irrevocably. She is one of the most torn, problematic. She wants the best for her daughter but is under control of her husband Odoardo. She does not seem to have the horror of courtly life that her husband has. She may even sympathize with her daughter's desire and sense her newly awakened interest in autonomy and freedom

825 FA 7, 336.

826 *Fabeln,* Book II, number xi (FA 4, 320. This fable is loosely based on number 157, "Vulpes et Canis," in Hauptmann, *Fabularum Aesopicarum collectio* 118–119. See now Perry, *Aesopica* #41, 337-338, Chambry #36; *Fables,* trans. Gibbs, #373, 175–176. Lessing's "Nachahmung" (imitation) of Hauptmann's Fable 157 is in "Über den Aesopus" (FA 4, 419)

827 The name of a dog in Virgil's 8th "Eclogue" line 107. Virgil, *Eclogues, Georgics, Aeneid IV,* ed. H. Rushton Fairclough. rev. G. P. Goold. Loeb Classical Library 68 (Cambridge: Harvard University Press, 1999), 82–83.

828 Meaning "wolf-like."

which she associates with a higher social position Claudia is a compromised character entrapped in power structures wanting to win attention from those whom she would be better off avoiding. Emilia is like a "frommes Lamm" to be awaken from child-like naiveté as soon as she will literally "see" what has happened–and then scream–. Then her mother Claudia wakes up and no longer cares about offending the nobility. Yet her understanding is not processed fully although she has a glimpse of part of the truth.

Claudia lifts the veil for the audience as in a poetic strategy of *Parabasis*, a term that Lessing may have known from Aristophanes, one of the ancient comedians, who through this poetic strategy of vision in the play "punctures the curtain of fantasy" to speak about here and now.[829] She breaks the illusion of the action for a moment and paradoxically "makes the spectators part of the spectacle" by giving them such a glimpse. [830] The mother not only fights for her lamb metaphorically speaking, she is in a dream-like state, hysterical so to speak. She ignores any other levels of reality and her anger is expressed and framed as a good thing at this point. She not only feels that bad things already have happened but also appears to have a premonition that things will end tragically. She does not dare to lift that curtain any more yet it is her lasting contribution that she is a witness of sorts. She negates partially what she knows, even at this advanced point of the plot and although she may be clairvoyant. Claudia recognizes Marinelli from her brief encounter with him that morning in her house where he had spoken with Appiani. Upon her demand to see her daughter, Marinelli replies with a trite formula: "Mit vielem Vergnügen, gnädige Frau" (With much pleasure, dear lady).[831] Then she remembers that there had been a dispute between Marinelli and Appiani. Marinelli tries to sweep such memory under the carpet: "Streit?–Was ich nicht wüßte: ein unbedeutender Wortwechsel in herrschaftlichen Angelegenheiten" (Dispute?–I don't know anything about that, a meaningless verbal exchange about affairs of governance).

He minimizes the importance of the dispute which ended with Appiani's rejection of Marinelli's request to accept the untimely commission by the Prince to leave the country at short notice on government business. This refusal later cost him his life, Marinelli tries to distract Claudia from what was really going on then, that is, men's business. But she remembers that the refusal of this "earnest request" was met with a shouting match and then a fist fight. This recollection is not anything "meaningless." Instead, as it turns out, it is an intuitive clue that will help Claudia to link pieces of the action almost to the point where she understands what was going on. She also remembers that the last word she heard Appiani say before his death was the name of "Marinelli." For a moment she thinks that this was in fact an accusation, a hint who murdered him. But then insecure, she takes her sentence back, acknowledging that this could be her own private interpretation only. She then remembers the tone in which it was said but realizes that tones cannot be interpreted except by the person who hears them. She found the utterance revealing and her interpretation of it makes

829 Gregory Jusdanis defines the term "Parabasis" in *The Princeton Encyclopedia of Poetry and Poetics*, 4th ed., ed. Roland Greene et al. (Princeton: Princeton University Press, 2012), 995-996 at 996 based on the Athenian ancient work of Aristophanes where the "curtain" of fantasy gets "punctured."

830 Jusdanis "Parabasis" 996.

831 FA 7, 337.

sense to her. She knows that Marinelli is in fact the person responsible for Appiani's death but, being insecure in this knowledge and only partially in touch with her own feelings she gets distracted again.

Marinelli, through the art of cunning persuasion attempts to calm Claudia by indicating that the Prince does have an interest in her daughter. But this makes things worse. She knows her husband's opinion of the Prince and what this will led to. She accuses Marinelli as "feiger, elender Mörder" (coward, contemptuous murderer) and "Kuppler" (procurer).[832]When she is told to consider where she is and to keep her voice down, she shouts: "Wo ich bin? Bedenken wo ich bin?–Was kümmert es die Löwin, der man die Jungen geraubt, in wessen Walde sie brüllet? (Where I am? Think about where I am?–Does the lioness care whom was has robbed her cubs in whose forest she is roaring?).[833] This sentence resonates with the earlier animal imagery and helps Claudia to affirm her shouting in the Prince's castle. Claudia literally turns into a lioness. She realizes that her daughter has been robbed, to say the least and she is angry now.

Her story within the story also offers a meta-perspective on language. It can frame key events. Words like her shouting the accusation of murder fall out of the expected narrative sequence. Language becomes fragmented here for the sake of truth that cannot be held back, toned down, or balanced. Attention is drawn to pain that can barely be expressed textually. She points to an image or a fable within the dialogue that condenses the visual-verbal dynamic. In response to Claudia's "roaring," Marinelli laughs. He apparently does not "understand" that the mother's behaving like a lioness is more than a matter of speech. It indicates a serious turn of events. Emilia in the next room has recognized her mother's voice and Claudia goes to her. The Prince when coming from the room with Emilia, on the way also meets Marinelli with whom he has this dialogue:

> DER PRINZ *als aus dem Zimmer von Emilien kommend*: Kommen Sie, Marinelli! Ich muß mich erholen–und muß Licht von Ihnen haben.
> MARINELLI O der mütterlichen Wut! Ha! ha!ha!ha!
> DER PRINZ Sie lachen?
> MARINELLI Wenn Sie gesehen hätten, Prinz, wie toll sie sich hier, im Saale gebärdete–Sie hörten sie ja wohl schreien! Und wie zahm sie auf einmal ward, bei dem ersten Anblicke von Ihnen–Ha! ha!–Das weiß ich ja wohl, daß keine Mutter einem Prinzen die Augen auskratzt, weil er ihre Tochter schön findet.[834]

> [THE PRINCE *as he is coming from Emilia's room:* Come Marinelli! I have to recoup myself–and must get illumination from you.
> MARINELLI O motherly anger! Ha! ha! ha! ha!
> THE PRINCE You are laughing?
> MARINELLI If you had seen Prince how wildly she behaved here, in the hall–You probably heard her scream! And how she became tame at the first glance of you–ha! Ha!–I know quite well that no mother will scratch out the eyes of a prince only because he finds her daughter beautiful].

832 FA 7, 338.
833 FA 7, 339.
834 FA 7, 339.

Again the image of the lioness protecting her cub is evoked, but here by Marinelli. He does not draw a parallel to Emilia's mother and her screaming but points out two things: There was an abrupt pause in Claudia's screaming, a human pause. He interprets it as a shift in her perception and emotion, as a sign of her malleability. He sees it as a sign of her opportunism to consent to forgive the Prince who comes as potential son-in-law. He thinks of an opportunistic chance for her daughter to raise her social status. Yet this is rather arbitrary and in fact a self-serving interpretation on the part of Marinelli. The Prince on the other hand has another perspective:

> Sie sind ein schlechter Beobachter–Die Tochter stürzte der Mutter ohnmächtig in die Arme. Darüber vergaß die Mutter ihre Wut, nicht über mir. Ihre Tochter schonte sie, nicht mich, wenn sie es nicht lauter, nicht deutlicher sagte–was ich lieber selbst nicht gehört, nicht verstanden haben will.[835]

> [You are a bad observer–The daughter fainting fell into the arms of the mother. Therefore the mother forgot her anger, not because of me. She was protective of her daughter, not of me, whenever she said expressed what she said not more loudly, not more clearly–things which I would have rather not have heard or understood].

Claudia takes Emilia into consideration by lowering her voice. The words are also directed to the audience: "You too are a bad observer." Although the Prince acts in a superior manner, he is not someone who Marinelli or any members of the audience can expect clarification from. Marinelli tries to ingrate himself with the Prince and adds: "Doch gnädiger Herr–ehe Sie es mir mit dem trockenen Worte sagen, wofür Sie mich halten–eine einzige Vorstellung! Der Tod des Grafen ist mir nichts weniger als gleichgültig" (And yet, Sir, before you tell me in plain language what you take me to be–just a phantom of your imagination! The death of the Count is for me nothing less than irrelevant).[836] He interprets his interaction with Appiani as having constituted an affront to his "honor" because he had demanded satisfaction for Appiani's insults, yet not received. Therefore the Count's death was a kind of retribution. Besides, he seems to suggest that accidents merely "happen." The Prince is prepared to accept this explanation: "Ich verstehe, nun gut, nun gut. Sein Tod war Zufall, bloßer Zufall" (I understand, well then, well then. His death was coincidence, sheer coincidence).[837] He follows Marinelli, albeit with a stutter, in his line of reasoning. He knows well enough that there are other interpretations of the event that will not come to the same conclusion: "Ich, ich glaub es.–Aber wer mehr? Auch die Mutter? Auch Emilia?–Auch die Welt?" (I, I believe it,–But who else? Also the mother? Also Emilia?–Also the world?)[838] The Prince's awareness of the awkwardness of this version trying to discover and immediately to repress the truth does not prevent him from further agreement with and ethical concession to Marinelli, when he says: "–auch ich erschrecke vor einem kleinen Verbrechen nicht. Nur, guter Freund, muß es ein kleines stilles, heilsames Verbrechen sein"(–also I am not scared of a little crime. Only, good friend, it must be a little, small, useful crime).[839] This is how language is truncated to

835 FA 7, 339-340.
836 FA 7, 340-341.
837 FA 7, 341.
838 FA 7, 341.
839 FA 7, 341-342.

minimize something that is so horrid that it must be silenced. The play explains notions of "little crimes" that involve omissions of logic and acts of cowardice, refusals in things for what they are.

At this point the Countess Orsina arrives. She interprets the failure of the Prince to respond to her letter that morning as a confirmation of their appointment, not as a rejection. She had found out about his departure to Castle Dosalo and taken that as a positive response to her own request to meet him there. When she heard the screaming and was then not allowed to enter the room, she drew her own conclusions of what was going on especially since she had been alarmed by the accident on the way and rumors about a crime. She does not want to face the fact that the Prince is no longer interested in communicating with her and that she has been replaced by another woman in his life. She shouts to Marinelli to tell him: "Soviel Worte soviel Lügen!" (As many words as many lies!) This is perhaps the most cynical statement in the entire play and it summarizes a kind of language crisis that is attributed to a lack of "seeing." She adds: "Ich werd es ja wohl sehen" (I will just as well see for myself).[840] She has the strength, in contrast to the other female characters in the play, to initiate and follow through conflict, to accept confrontation as needed, and to talk openly. She has been able to liberate herself from some of the gender restrictions imposed by her society. Once the center of attention, she found herself rejected, an object of indifference, yet now she is committed to turn into Medusa herself. She will, can stare back and address the crime:

> Gleichgültigkeit! Gleichgültigkeit an die Stelle der Liebe?–Das heißt, Nichts an die Stelle von etwas. Denn lernen Sie, nachplauderndes Hofmännchen, lernen Sie von einem Weibe, daß Gleichgültigkeit ein leeres Wort, ein bloßer Schall ist, dem nichts, gar nichts entspricht. Gleichgültig ist die Seele nur gegen das, woran sie nicht denkt; nur gegen ein Ding, das für sie kein Ding ist. Und nur gleichgültig für ein Ding, das kein Ding ist–das ist so viel als gar nicht gleichgültig.–Ist dir das zu hoch, Mensch?[841]
>
> [Indifference! Indifference instead of love?–This means nothing instead of something. Then you, you parroting court-dwarf, learn something from a woman, namely that indifference is an empty word, just a mere sound, which corresponds to nothing, to absolutely nothing. The soul is indifferent only to whichever it is not thinking about, only to a thing which for it is nothing–that is as much as not at all indifferent.–Is this too lofty for you, fellow?].

The Prince tries to disengage himself from this company and turns to conversation with Marinelli, Orsina learns that she had been displaced in the Prince's mind for Emilia Galotti. She accuses the Prince of being a murderer. She already knew through her informants that the Prince and Emilia had had an encounter in the church that morning. To her the conspiracy is obvious. She threatens to announce her suspicions in the town square the next day, just at the moment when Odoardo enters. The spheres divide again.

840 FA 7, 345.
841 FA 7, 346.

# 8. Meta-perspectives?

The Countess Claudia is outspoken. Marinelli says to her that she is a philosopher although he is hardly a reliable witness.[842] Yet Orsina's reflections in fact offer a profound insight into the state of mind of a woman who finds herself rejected. Through this meta-perspective Lessing twists the events surrounding the Galotti family in such a manner that the previous understatements are highlighted as a process of false equations and replacements that lead to indifference, the most heinous of all human vices. Indifference is the actual anonymous force which manipulates the actions and the apparent understatements of the play. It is indifference that stands in contrast to what is needed to counter-act the crime. What seems to be the essence of Orsina's speech and what makes sense in her words, is what she ultimately lacks awareness of herself when she gives the dagger to Odoardo who, in an act of self-punishment and despair stabs his own daughter whom he apparently wants to spare more embarrassment.

It is so ironic that Marinelli seems to be the one who gives an insight into the play's rhetorical strategy when he remarks to the Prince: "Wozu dieser traurige Seitenblick? Vorwärts! denkt der Sieger, es falle neben ihm Feind oder Freund" (What about this mournfulglance to the side? Straight ahead! Thinks the victorious fighter, no matter whether or not next to him enemy and friend are falling).[843] This plea disrupts the usual progression of events. It suggests in fact the opposite: One should look not only forward linearly but take into consideration the many possibilities of the side. By drawing attention to marginal figures and minor understatements this drama exhibits a variety of poetic constellations that foreground discrepancies between images and words. One must see to it not only to be fixated on one's own personal goals but be aware of dimensions of time and space, actualized myths and fables, voices and intricacies of language, however subtle and multiple they may be.

The language in *Miß Sara Sampson* was packed with wordiness and with elaborate descriptions of emotions and inner actions, especially when Sara speaks. *Emilia Galotti* in contrast is a masterpiece of abbreviated language and in the expression of emotions in the context of minimalist verbalness. It is symbolic that the instrument that causes Emilia's death is a cutting instrument, a dagger. The play is also full of epigrammatic proverb-like utterances and whereas proverbs are usually meant to express truths that are always valid, the use of such sentences here is slightly different. A gap is revealed between inner and outer images and worlds that only meet metonymically. The play shows the shortcomings of any mono-causal or simplistic logic.[844] When the process of learning, of finding out what happens in *Miß Sara Sampson* leads from crisis to clarity and ultimately reconciliation with the father, all information that Emilia's father gets leads instead to more confusion and anxiety. Logic seems to twist meanings into their opposites. The mother plays a particularly problematic role since she knows more than what she is willing to admit, even to herself. The play makes Emilia not only

---

842 FA 7, 346.
843 FA 7, 356.
844 For very perceptive comments in this context see Alexander Košenina, "Bühnen-Bilder. Von den Grenzen der Malerei und Dramaturgie bei Lessing," *Lessing Yearbook* 41 (2014): 175–190.

appear as the victim of a crime as was Sara, but she is also complicit in it through her own lack of care, her own inability to look with visualcy, and her failure in the use of communicative articulation.[845] The image of a dance which runs through the play seems to harmonize things only on the surface. It acts as a coding of sorts. It captures only one level of the discourse, the superficial sequential one. It is interspersed with images and gaps in the dialog. Interruptions and pauses may reveal that whatever appears on the surface of language could be a matter of pretense. It may hide or gloss over the rough material. The fact that Emilia is in the end killed by a dagger in her father's hand, given to him by Orsina, seems upon first glance arbitrary. She is monstrous not only in her verbose rebellion against the treatment she experienced by the Prince. She is also monstrous when she acted as if she were something of a sister or fellow female friend, pretending to be polite while being intensely competitive, jealous, and in fact her fatal adversary.[846] The question remains about the real culprits of the play.[847] The multiple voices will always be coextensive without final metaperspective of any and much will be left to the interpretation of each performance of the play with its marvelous roles to act.[848] As spectators and listeners or as readers and critics

---

845 Lessing has long been critiqued for the inconclusive ending of this play from a variety of perspectives, whether they are in terms of aesthetic theory and the use of language, or in socio-political terms, from a feminist perspective, or by just presenting a glimpse into what seems rather individualized madness: For examples see John Poynter, "The Pearls of Emilia Galotti." *Lessing Yearbook* 9 (1977): 81-96, Albert M. Reh, "Emilia Galotti–'großes Beispiel der dramatischen Algebra' oder 'Algebra der Ambivalenz'?" *Lessing Yearbook* 28 (1997): 83-104 and Brigitte Prutti, "Coup de Theatre–Coup de Femme or: What is Lessing's Emilia Galotti dying from?" *Lessing Yearbook* 26 (1994): 1-27. Also see Martin Schenkel,"Wer über gewisse Dinge den Verstand nicht verliert, der hat keinen zu verlieren. Zur Dialektik der bürgerlichen Aufklärung in Lessings *Emilia Galotti*." *Zeitschrift für deutsche Philologie* 195 (1986): 181-186. On the inconclusive ending, see also Georg-Michael Schulz, "Das 'Lust- und Trauerspiel' oder Die Dramaturgie des doppelten Schlusses. Zu einigen Dramen des ausgehenden 18. Jahrhunderts." *Lessing Yearbook* 23 (1991): 111-126 and G.A. Wells, "What is wrong with Emilia Galotti?" *German Life and Letters* 37.3 (1984): 163-173.

846 Karen J. Kenkel, "Monstrous Women, Sublime Pleasure, and the Perils of Reception in Lessing's Aesthetics," *PMLA* 116.3 (May 2001): 545-561. Also see Heidi M. Schlipphacke, "The Dialectic of Female Desire in G.E. Lessing's *Emilia Galotti*." *Lessing Yearbook* 33 (2001): 55-78. One may also take into account aspects of agency and personal freedom, in the context of tradition and changing perspectives: Martin Bollacher, "Tradition und Selbstbestimmung. Lessings *Emilia Galotti* in geistesgeschichtlicher Perspektive," *Literatur und Geistesgeschichte. Festschrift für Richard Brinkmann*, ed. von einem Red.-Kollegium (Tübingen: Niemeyer, 1981), 99-118.

847 See, for example Georg-Michael Schulz, "Das 'Lust-und Trauerspiel' oder Die Dramaturgie des doppelten Schlusses. Zu einigen Dramen des ausgehenden 18. Jahrhunderts." *Lessing Yearbook* 23 (1991): 111-126 and Wolfgang Wittkowski,"Bürgerfreiheit oder -feigheit? Die Metapher des 'langen Weges' als Schlüssel zum Koordinatensystem in Lessings politischem Trauerspiel *Emilia Galotti*." *Lessing Yearbook* 17 (1985): 65-87.

848 See J.J. Lamport, "The Death of Emilia Galotti: A Reconsideration," *German Life and Letters* 44 (1990): 25-33. Also see Johann Friedrich Lehmann, *Der Blick durch die Wand. Zur Geschichte des Theaterzuschauers und des Visuellen bei Diderot und Lessing on the multiplicity of possible interpretations.* For interesting comments on the performance history of this play from the start, see Wolfram Mauser, "'Ich stehe für nichts.' Zur Uraufführung von G.E. Lessings *Emilia Galotti* im Hoftheater zu Braunschweig." Gerd Biegel, ed., *Lessing in Braunschweig und Wolfenbüttel* (Braunschweig: Braunschweigisches Landesmuseum, 1997), 111-123.

we must draw our own lines between those that are at fault and those who may have just been negligent.[849] It is a bourgeois play in that it shows a lack of attention to the implications of aristocratic power structures and the dangerous desire to gain status in society riddled with so many hurdles and communicative errors.

849 For an excellent performance and interpretation, see the CD Andrea Breth (Director, Inszenierung), *Emilia Galotti von Gotthold Ephraim Lessing, Aufführung des Wiener Burgtheaters.* The Theater Edition by BelAir Edition GmbH & Friedrich (Berlin Verlagsgesellschaft GmbH, ZDFE 2005). (ISBN 7000000621925). For another fascinating performance of *Emilia Galotti* drawing attention to the staccato of movements, steps by the actors and steps in the logical development from inner to outer actions see Michael Thalheimer, Director and Wolfgang Bergmann, ed. Deutsches Theater Berlin.*Gotthold Ephraim Lessing. Emilia Galotti.* ZDfB Enterprises GmbH, DvD ZDFE 2008 (*www.theateredition.de*) (ISBN 4 280000101129).

# PART III:
## Visual-Verbal Dynamics in Lessing's Late Works

# Chapter 11
# *Ernst and Falk* (1778): Lessing's Metaphor "Wolfsmilchraupe"

Abstract: Various scholars have demonstrated that Lessing's *Ernst und Falk: Gespräche für Freimäurer* (*Ernst and Falk: Conversations for Freemasons*) is tightly interwoven with his own biography. According to Monika Fick, this work has basically two leitmotifs ("Leitmotife"): First Lessing's quest to trace Freemasonry back to its origin and second Lessing's personal experience with Freemasonry. [850] These are rather complex historical matters. We may read Lessing's fictional work in the context of ongoing historical debates concerning the search for original sources of this movement, his efforts to find something of a collective identity, a sense of belonging, and striving collectively to realize a great shared vision. Fick emphasizes in her interpretation that Lessing experienced a major disappointment with Freemasonry and the Lodge he had joined. As soon as he finally got accepted and initiated into the Order, he did not find the expected sense of shared values and belonging. What I am interested in mainly is how Lessing then proceeded after he realized that there is a gap between the ideal and the real and how in *Ernst und Falk* he actually writes about his newly discovered visual-verbal dissonance. Lessing's disappointment is in my reading related to another third leitmotif in this text that has so far been mainly ignored in scholarship. It concerns a critique, not directly of the ideal for the sake of asserting the real, but of institutionalized worldviews, grandiose visions that aim at unity, and generalizing images. Lessing's *Ernst and Falk: Conversations for Freemasons* is to be interpreted as a rhetorically fascinating effort trying to in articulate and to come to terms with the perceived dissonance between images and words and, as I would argue, the dangerous shortcomings of any all too prescriptive or presumptuous use of language. It is written with a header subtitled "Conversations for Freemasons" hinting at the fact there is no detached or neutral meta-perspective. We, the readers of these dialogues, are left with multiple voices and various points of view.

## 1. Lessing and Freemasonry: Scholarship so far and thesis

Scholarship on *Ernst und Falk* mainly has so far been concerned with Lessing's search to locate and to identify the origin of Freemasonry. Lessing admired its great vision, the ideal of a hierarchy-free discourse, and of sharing ethical criteria for human behavior to further the commitment to the Enlightenment goals: loyal solidarity and free intellectual exchange, a bonding among all members, even across national and local borders. This movement has been the subject of numerous theories and competing

850 See Fick, *Handbuch* 403–426.

narratives that have long been debated among Freemasons and their commentators.[851] According to Rolf Keil, it is a common belief that the origins of Freemasonry lie in the British Isles and that Freemasonry is an offspring of the Enlightenment ("ein Kind der Aufklärung"). It was intended as a platform where hierarchy-free dialogue could be practiced ("der herrschaftsfreie Dialog geübt werden konnte"). It spread throughout Europe by means of thinkers, poets, often representatives of the nobility. They had an abstract idea of brotherhood under the symbols of wisdom, strength, and beauty ("abstrakte Idee einer Verbrüderung von Weisheit, Stärke und Schönheit"). [852]

However soon in Germany, France, and Austria the nobility among the Freemasons were no longer satisfied with these three ideals. In 1737 Andrew Michael Ramsay, a Scottish exile living in France, argued in the Great Lodge in Paris that Freemasons were descendants of the crusading military orders of the early Middle Ages, such as the Knights Hospitalier. Rolf Kiel, then master of the "Lessing Loge № 759" in Frankfurt am Main, tied the origin of Freemasonry with the Knight Templars.[853] The notion that the Freemasons had apparently medieval sources was disseminated by Karl Gotthelf von Hunt who spread Ramsay's ideas in Germany. These ideas culminated in his order called "Strikte Observanz" of 1764, a manifesto that made the order hierarchically regulated and exclusive.[854] The British system was based on the constitution of 1723 by James Andersen. It continued but then excluded for the most part members from Germany and France in which sometimes Freemasonry was forbidden by their governments. Lessing had been in contact with numerous Freemasons.[855] Among them were actors he had met at the theater, the poet Christoph Friedrich Nicolai, Lessing's publisher Christian Friedrich Voß, and Lessing's friend and business partner Johann

851 See the overview in Rolf Keil, Master of the Lodge "Lessing Nr. 759" in Frankfurt am Main, "Vorwort," Gotthold Ephraim Lessing, *Ernst und Falk: Gespräche für Freimaurer 1-5. Modernisierte Sprachfassung mit zwei bisher verschollenen Gesprächen für Freimaurer,* ed. Evert Kornmeyer (Frankfurt am Main: Edition Königliche Kunst, 2011), 8-15.

852 Keil, "Vorwort" 10.

853 See Albert Chodowiecki, *Vom Reißbrett der Loge 'Lessing' Or. Valparaiso. Auswahl von Reden und Vorträgen von Johanni 1870 bis 1882, Zusammengestellt vom Schriftführer der Lessing Loge* (Leipzig: Findel, 1883) and Vortrag gehalten in der Trauerloge am 15. Februar 1881 zum Andenken an G. E. Lessing (Bern: Francke, 1981). The Knights Templar was a military monastic order, founded in 1120 with headquarters on the Temple Mount in Jerusalem. They rapidly became one of the most important military orders, both as an effective fighting forces and an organization heavily involved in European finance. Their influence began to diminish and in 1307. King Phillip IV of France, who was heavily in debt to the order, had its leaders arrested, tortured and burned at the stake for heresy. The order was disbanded in 1312 and their assets confiscated. But the lurid details of the trials and the accusations of secret rituals and occult powers meant that their memory was kept alive in succeeding centuries.

854 This effort ran counter to the efforts by Lessing in trying to do away with hierarchical structures for the sake of more inclusiveness of the audience in line with his entire Enlightenment project. On this broader topic, see Jonathan I. Israel, *Democratic Enlightenment. Philosophy, Revolution, and Human Rights 1750-1790* (Oxford: Oxford University Press, 2011). Also see Klaus Bohnen. "Nathan der Weise. Über das Gegenbild einer Gesellschaft bei Lessing," *Deutsche Vierteljahrsschrift für Literaturwissenschaft und Geistesgeschichte* 53 (1979): 394-416.

855 Richard van Dülmen, ed., *Der Geheimbund der Illuminaten.* (Stuttgart-Bad Cannstatt: Frommann-Holzboog, 1975).

Joachim Christoph Bode, master of the Lodge Absalom on the three Nettles ("Absalom zu den drei Nesseln"). It was next to the Order St. George on the green Spruce ("St. Georg zur grünen Fichte") one of two lodges in Hamburg at Lessing's time. Both lodges apparently still exist. In 1767 Lessing applied for admission but Bode turned him down arguing that because the Lodge had acceded to "Strikte Observanz" there was no longer any "regular" Lodge.[856] After having met with his friend Johann Gottfried Herder (poet and theologian and also a Freemason), Lessing again requested to join a Hamburg Lodge.

Finally in August 1771 the Master of the Clandestine Lodge "Winkelloge named "Zu den drei goldenen Rosen" (To the three golden Roses) accepted his application.[857] Georg Johann Freiherr von Rosenberg admitted G.E. Lessing to become an officially registered Freemason with the registration number 56. He was initiated into the first three grades of Freemasonry. However, the experience turned out to be a terrible disappointment for Lessing. No visit there is documented after his initiation. He apparently never visited his Lodge again.[858] The second leitmotif, Lessing's well documented disappointment with the Lodge once he was its member has also been commented upon by numerous historians and critics of *Ernst and Falk.* Lessing was disenchanted with institutionalized Freemasonry as practiced during his time. He found it greatly at odds with what he expected. All of this is especially well documented and explained in the secondary literature on *Ernst und Falk*, especially in the scholarship by Roman Dziergwa, Peter Michelsen, and Paul Müller.[859]

I find that there is here is a third leitmotif or rather an intricate issue in *Ernst and Falk* which has so far been overlooked, Lessing's quest to understand Ekphrasis, a problem with visions that as soon as they are being verbalized dissolve and have lost their appeal and vitality. There is a problem with the transfer of visions into words. Lessing makes us notice that the visual does not readily transform into the verbal. Lessing is dealing with a loss that is apparently doomed to occur not only in the context of Freemasonry but also frequently in the process of articulating, formalizing, and institutionalizing ideals. Lessing seams to realize that the greater the ideal vision, the greater the disappointment with the real. Lessing deals with this more than sobering realization and questions how not to spoil secrets in using language metaphorically and metonymically. It appears that Falk turns to strategies using words that are less prone to be loaded with false expectations. In its beginning stage, considering children and early cultures, languages seem to have plenty of creative metaphors. Then metaphors are increasingly replaced by catachreses and terminologies. Language becomes fixed and images stagnant. Just like a "Wolfsmilchraupe" which plays an ex-

---

856 Keil, "Vorwort" 12.

857 Rosenberg's lodge was affiliated with the Swedish system of freemasonry, not the mainline Scottish "Strikte Observanz," which was also dominant in Germany.

858 Keil, "Vorwort" 13.

859 Roman Dziergwa, *Lessing und die Freimaurerei: Untersuchung zur Rezeption von G.E. Lessings Spätwerk* Ernst und Falk. Gespräche für Freymäurer *in den freimäurerischen und antifreimäurerischen Schriften des 19. und 20. Jahrhunderts (bis 1933)*, Europäische Hochschulschriften I: Deutsche Sprache und Literatur 1332 (Frankfurt am Main: Peter Lang, 1992); Peter Michelsen, "Die 'wahren Taten' der Freimaurer. Lessings *Ernst und Falk,*" *Der unruhige Bürger* 221-280; Paul Müller, *Untersuchungen zum Problem der Freimaurerei bei Lessing, Herder und Fichte*, Sprache und Dichtung, N.F. 12 (Bern: Paul Haupt, 1965).

emplary role in Lessing's *Ernst and Falk,* a metaphor sheds into an empty "Worthülse" (word-husk), something without meaning, merely a term, a catachresis, a word that is nothing but an empty shell having lost its essence. This third leitmotif is at the core of Lessing's *Ernst und Falk*, a text written as an open-ended dialogue. It does in my reading not erase the lasting belief in human liberation but contains much skepticism about formulating and asserting a great vision.

## 2. Lessing's text and context

Lessing initially sent the first three of these *Conversations* to several friends before they were published anonymously in Göttingen 1778. The word "Wolfenbüttel" appeared on the title-page which gave a hint as to who the author may have been.[860] *Gespräche* 4-5 were written by Lessing about the same time. Because of the intervention of Herzog Charles William Ferdinand, Duke of Braunschweig-Lüneburg, they were not part of the initial publication but appeared anonymously in Frankfurt 1780. All five *Gespräche* were published together as a single work in Göttingen in 1787.[861] This edition contained a description of the Masonic vision, the beautiful dream of an enlightened society promoted by those who vow to do whatever they can to help others, to do the good ("gute Taten") and to promote happiness on earth. This was a vision that had attracted Lessing. Those belonging together in such a commitment do not want to limit their ideals to only speculative realms but achieve concrete results in society. Or at least this is what Lessing hoped for. He was eager to begin engaging with them on such activities by joining for active membership.

Falk articulates in *Gespräch* 4 that there should be an end to all "Schema, Hülle, Einkleidung" (schemata, shell, wrapping, clothing).[862] The readers get a hint that one should not be restricted to one religious dogma or any hierarchical institution, be it denominational, cultural, national, or international. Instead one's commitment should transcend such boundaries. If members had such ties, then this was their private matter and they should not interfere with their larger goals. Additional affiliations by members were irrelevant in the context of their Freemasonry, as long as they were not to contradict the order's ideal principles. As members they were given certain guidelines but left free to pursue their humanitarian work in any other affiliation as personally suitable. They all belong, this was the idea, to the free realm of an interreligious, global society.[863]

---

860 Lessing sent the manuscript text of *Gespräche* 1-3 to his friends Herder, Bode, Joachim Heinrich Campe, Matthias Claudius, Goethe, Johann Georg Hamann, Friedrich Heinrich Jacobi, and Georg Christoph Lichtenberg before it was published anonymously.

861 There is a sixth *Gespräch,* referred to at the end of the fifth, which has been reconstructed from Lessing's notes. These remained long unpublished and are not included in the analysis here. See Karl S. Guthke, "Lessings *Sechstes Freimaurergespräch,*" *Literarisches Leben im achtzehnten Jahrhundert in Deutschland und in der Schweiz* (Bern: Francke, 1975), 315-332, first published in *Zeitschrift für deutsche Philologie* 85 (1966): 576-597.

862 FA 10, 54.

863 An interesting question has been raised by Hans-Georg Richert, "Die *Declaration of Independence* und Lessings *Ernst und Falk*: Eine bare Koinzidenz?" Uwe Faulhaber et al.,

As soon as it is experienced in terms of social privileges and written about, this vision appears to have drawn unwelcome attention from people, including those in power, and it faced unwarranted criticism from ignorant others following. Members were perceived as being arrogant or all too grandiose. Such an organized vision was then apparently regarded as a threat to existing organizations and institutions and aroused unnecessary suspicion as being itself a powerful political force which lead unavoidably to destructive misunderstandings. It could even raise suspicion as soon as it became itself discovered and abused as a political force leading to the spreading of misunderstandings.[864]

To keep such a marvelous vision safe demands a certain degree of confidentiality, secrecy, and anonymity all three of which were integral to the traditional aura surrounding the Freemasons. They nevertheless defined and formulated themselves, historically speaking, by means of their own symbols and group identity markers. Their images or codes were strictly private and not a matter of public record. This in addition to their vision for a better future made Lessing curious and he ventured to find out not only about their ideals but also about their mechanisms of interacting as a live community in the "real" world. He could only do so by becoming an insider but that was to prove not at all straightforward.

However, once initiated, disillusionment set in immediately. The Lodge in Hamburg that accepted him had been founded by Georg Johann Freiherr von Rosenberg and it was rumored that he lived off the proceeds. Lessing was initiated for free.[865] But Lessing does not seem to have had contact with the other members. His initiation took place in von Rosenberg's home into the 2nd and 3rd levels of the order. It "erfolgte vom Standpunkt des allgemeinen Logenrechts völlig ungesetzlich und entsprach nicht den gültigen freimaurerischen Formen" (occurred completely illegally from the point of view of the general by-laws of the Lodge and did not conform to the usually applied Freemasonry forms).[866] This experience almost spoiled Freemasonry for him altogether, but it led to his writing *Ernst und Falk* with its questioning of certain institutional practices. However, it did not diminish Lessing's enthusiasm for the Masonic ideals. Although Lessing had a negative experience during his initiation, his subsequent writings had a positive influence resulting in Lessing being regarded as an important and highly influential member of the order. The conundrum of wanting to verbalize a vision yet at the same time experiencing loss of precision in the process highlights a philosophical, existential, ekphrastic problem, the workings of which Lessing attempted to understand and to counteract with much effort and skill. He is fully aware of the fact that a vision, as soon as it is formulated, runs the risk to become a flat theory. If a theoretical goal were reachable by means of actions–then talking

---

ed. *Exile und Enlightenment. Studies in Comparative Literature in honor of Guy Stern* (Detroit: Wayne State University Press, 1987), 77-86.

864 It has been argued that a certain strand of Freemasonry, the so-called Illuminati, were responsible for the French Revolution with its ideals of a classless society, which ended in violence and horrible bloodshed. For a more accurate assessment, see Hans-Jürgen Schings, *Die Brüder des Marquis Posa: Schiller und der Geheimbund der Illuminaten* (Tübingen: Niemeyer, 1996).

865 Dziergwa, *Lessing und die Freimaurerei* 104-107.

866 Dziergwa, *Lessing und die Freimaurerei* 107. See also Nisbet, *Lessing, Eine Biographie* 765-766; *Gotthold Ephraim Lessing* 586-587.

about it would hopefully also become increasingly superfluous. In other words, the more one were to talk about goals, the further away they yet appear to be. Not to mention that these goals might also be signs of disorientation and lack of focus.

## 3. Textual analysis of Lessing's *Ernst und Falk*

In the first dialogue or *Gespräche*, Falk is enjoying the morning and Ernst finds his silence an indication that he is thinking deeply about something. As soon as Falk is interrogated with the banal question what he is thinking about his marvelous insights, dream-like observations, and vaguely associated thoughts are gone.[867] Even if he does not feel consciously disturbed and is willing to respond with an open mind in a friendly, polite manner, his replies seem all too short or elusive to Ernst. He apparently expects an answer expressed in more categorical definite language. He wants "Begriffe" (terminologies"), yes or no answers, expressions of clarity and firm decision. Falk on the other hand seems to be rather tenuous, speculative, evasive, and brief. He is more introspective and reluctant to have his thoughtful enjoyable morning interrupted by any talking.

Nevertheless Ernst succeeds in drawing him further into the conversation. Ernst must recognize that talking about the most important existential things can be such a private and difficult matter that much patience is needed and that one has to listen for the meaning between the words. He is a good sport and also treasures friendship. The notion that "[n]ichts geht über das *laut denken* mit einem Freunde" (nothing is more important than *thinking aloud* with a friend),[868] is being evoked as an ongoing process that then spans all five of Lessing's *Gespräche.* Asked whether he is a Freemason, Falk does not give any straight or simple answer but uses understatements, images, and merely hints in response. The shared process of "thinking together in private with a friend" takes place not by means of the announcing any preconceived ideas.

Falk is obviously trying to engage Ernst in finding answers to big questions. The first thing I find important to note is that, although this is a dialogue and apparently one of the participants is a Freemason and the other not, it would be all too simplistic to identify Falk with Lessing.[869] He uses his characters, Ernst and Falk, as voices to

---

867 This is the kind of looking Michael Fried writes about in *Absorption and Theatricality.*

868 FA 10, 14. See also, Wilfried Barner, "'Laut denken mit einem Freunde.' Anmerkungen zu Lessings *Ernst und Falk,"* Ortrud Gutjahr et al., ed., *Gesellige Vernuft: Zur Kultur der literarischen Aufklärung. Festschrift für Wolfram Mauser* (Würzburg: Königshausen & Neumann, 1993), 1-12.

869 See for example, Fick, *Handbuch* 422: "Indem sie das 'Geheimnis' bewahren, werden die Dialoge somit selbst zu einer freimauererischen Tat, da Falk (bzw Lessing) eben diese Empfindungsweise in Ernst (bzw. in den Adressaten den Teilnehmern an der Wolfenbüttler Versammlung [...]'veranlasst' und ihr 'Aufkeimen' begünstigt." (By keeping the 'secret' these dialogues themselves become a deed of Freemasonry, since Falk [i.e. Lessing] 'causes' just this mode of sensation in Ernst [i.e. the participants in the Wolfenbüttel Congregation] [...] and thus promotes its 'flourishing'). I find Monika Fick's interpretation helpful in some regards but do not think that either Falk or Ernst can be identified with the person Lessing. They are both his fictional voices offering the various sides of a complex argument. Although the reader may find the cheerful Falk more attractive than

express an inner dialogue that does not fit into the notion of an insider versus an outsider. Rather, these dialogues dissolve any temptation to talk in binaries and to suggest lines of reasoning that do not cancel or merely contradict each other; but instead are complementary in a mutually productive way. Conversely, when talking about what we see, we may actually change, as James Elkins notes, "the object" of seeing and the objectifying no longer works as expected.[870]

This deconstructs the notion of what we actually did see. Whatever it may have been at some poignant moment that prompted us to speak about it, we tend to lose that same impetus in the process of looking while recording what we see verbally. The process of textualizing verbally has an impact on what is being seen or has been seen to such an extent that seeing and speaking about it become almost mutually exclusive. It is similar to Falk having to talk about his feelings of enjoying the beautiful morning since one reason why he liked it so much was its silence and that feeling vanishes in talking to Ernst. Not only that, he expresses difficulties in even recalling it. Additionally, if what we see is really a problem in society, then talking about it is also far less effective than ethical action would be. In order to change things for those that are in need or even in pain, discussions can even be a waste of valuable time as Lessing vividly recounts in his parable of the burning palace.[871] Verbalizing images changes them to such an extent that a person may well have lost the imaginative ability to produce further similar and consecutive images in the process of reflecting and speaking. Such depletion is a real problem for Enlightenment thinkers, something Lessing was acutely aware of. He associates Freemasonry with Enlightenment ideals. Moreover, in his *Conversations t*he question is raised how long it would take people to do "the good" without talking about it, merely because it "is" the good? Then people would no longer be interrupting and deconstructing the process of doing so and finally become authentic. Falk's comments seem to suggest that it might even be best to forget about the formula to do good deeds and to go ahead with doing then while forgetting any proclamations. The question: "Wie lange dauert deine Brunnenkur noch?" (How long will your spa treatment last?) is a justified expression of impatience and perhaps even a plea to act in the Here and Now. To compare the instructions by Freemasonry with "Brunnenkuren" (spa treatments) is of course ironic.[872] One can only wish for things one does not have, for as soon as they are obtained or achieved, they become as fragile as the enjoyable morning which opens the first of *Gespräche:*

the somber Ernst, they both have valid points of reasoning. Lessing was occupied with many questions he raised in *Ernst and Falk* until the end of his life.

870 Elkins, *The Object Stares Back,* esp., Ch. 2, 46–85.

871 Beate Allert, "About a Burning Building in Eco and Lessing, or: How to Process Messages." *Lessing Yearbook* 29 (1997): 57–86.

872 FA 10, 41. Also in *Gespräche* number four: "Ich habe meine Brunnen-Cur längst beschlossen" (I have decided upon my spa-treatment a long time ago) (FA 10, 45).

ERNST Woran denkst du, Freund?
FALK An nichts.
ERNST Aber du bist so still.
FALK Eben darum. Wer denkt, wenn er genießt? Und ich genieße des erquickenden Morgens.
ERNST Du hast recht; und du hättest mir meine Frage auch nur zurückgeben dürfen.
FALK Wenn ich an etwas dächte, würde ich darüber sprechen. Nichts geht über laut Denken mit einem Freund.
ERNST Gewiß.
FALK Hast du den schönen Morgen schon genug genossen, fällt dir etwas ein; so sprich du.–Mir fällt nichts ein.
ERNST Gut das!–Mir fällt ein, daß ich dich schon längst um etwas fragen wollte.
FALK So frage doch.
ERNST Ist es wahr, Freund, daß du ein Freimäurer bist?
FALK Die Frage verrät mir, dass du keiner bist.
ERNST Freilich!–Aber antworte mir geradezu.–Bist du ein Freimäurer?
FALK Ich glaube es zu sein.[873]

[ERNST What are you thinking about?
FALK About nothing.
ERNST But you are so quiet!
FALK Exactly. Who thinks when he is enjoying himself? And I am enjoying the refreshing morning.
ERNST You are right; and you should have just returned my question.
FALK If I were thinking of something I would rather speak about it. Nothing is more important than thinking aloud with a friend.
ERNST Certainly.
FALK Have you enjoyed the beautiful morning long enough, does something come into your mind; then you speak–nothing comes to my mind.
ERNST Good! It comes to my mind that I have wanted to ask you something for a long time.
FALK Do ask then.
ERNST Is it true, friend, that you are a Freemason?
FALK The question tells me that you are not one.
ERNST Certainly! But answer me straight away. Are you a Freemason?
FALK I believe that I am].

Falk recognizes that Ernst should not ask him whether or not he is a Freemason if he were one himself. Apparently he would just know it intuitively. Anyway, such questions will become obsolete. At the same time, Ernst finds that Falk's answer saying that he would believe so implies either some uncertainty or a hint of denial. He thus frames, willingly or not, Falk's answer as ambivalent. Falk replies: "Oh doch! Ich bin mir meiner Sache so ziemlich gewiß."[874] (Oh yes! I am rather certain of this matter of mine). Although he gives a positive answer again, he is suggesting that this matter is his (thus vaguely marking a personal boundary, or indicating that probing further would mean an invasion perhaps). He is also using the qualifier "rather certain" and not "certain," thus leaving a little bit of space or questioning open, perhaps expressing even a hint of doubt himself.

---

873 FA 10, 14–15.
874 FA 10, 15.

Ernst replies: "Dann wirst du ja wohl wissen, ob und wann und wo und von wem du aufgenommen worden bist."[875] (Then you will probably know whether and when and where and by whom you have been admitted). He takes the answer clearly for a yes and then wants to know the facts, the date of Falk's membership to Freemasonry and the documented data of his initiation. Falk responds: "Das weiß ich allerdings, aber das hat nichts zu bedeuten."[876] (Certainly I know that but this is insignificant). His answer appears like a paradox; it confirms knowledge of these significant or even legal facts but then denies or challenges their significance. Ernst is puzzled and asks: "Nicht?" (No?) Falk raises a very general counter question, an exclamation rather: "Wer nimmt auf, und wer wird nicht aufgenommen!"[877] (Who does not accept, and who does not get accepted!) Although its meaning indicates a question it is expressed as a statement with an exclamation mark. He is making it sound like a critical comment drawing attention to what is customary, to what is usually done. In so doing he is challenging the hierarchy between the person who gives and the person who accepts such membership. He is perhaps implying that this entire action of initiation is a matter of minor importance, something merely custodial, or he is making Ernst comprehend that it is not the external factors that are so important but the understanding from the inside. Ernst requests that Falk should explain this and Falk gives his answer:

> Ich glaube ein Freimaurer zu sein; nicht weil ich von älteren Maurern in einer gesetzlichen Loge aufgenommen worden bin, sondern weil ich einsehe und erkenne, wofür und warum die Freimauererei da ist, wann und wo sie gewesen ist, wie und wodurch sie gefördert oder gehindert wird.[878]
>
> [I believe to be a Freemason; not because I have been accepted by older masons into a Lodge that is legally constituted, but because I have insight and recognize what for and why Freemasonry exists, when and where it existed, and how and by what it is being promoted and hindered].

Falk gives his own criteria for considering himself a Freemason whether or not he was initiated formally into a Lodge that is legally recognized, for more important to him is his personal insight into what Freemasonry stands for, its existence, and what it means to him to promote its goals. The dialogue continues and Falk affirms Ernst's question whether it would also be possible to get accepted without knowing what he knows and Falk responds: "Leider nicht" (Unfortunately not). Then Ernst wants to know: "Und könntest du wissen was du weißt ohne aufgenommen zu sein"[879] (And could you possibly know what you know without being accepted?). Falk gives this answer:

> Warum nicht? Die Freimäurerei ist nichts willkürliches, nichts entbehrliches: sondern etwas notwendiges, das in dem Wesen des Menschen und der bürgerlichen Gesellschaft gegründet ist. Folglich muß man auch durch eignes Nachdenken eben so wohl darauf verfallen können, als man durch Anleitung darauf geführt wird.

875 FA 10, 15.
876 FA 10, 15.
877 FA 10, 15.
878 FA 10, 15.
879 FA 10, 15.

> [Why not? Freemasonry is nothing arbitrary, nothing indispensable: rather something necessary based on the essence of the human and on bourgeois society. Consequently, one must be able to get there just as well through thinking on one's own than being led to it by instruction].

He establishes Freemasonry affirmatively as something integral to humanity and at the core of bourgeois society. At the same time he disconnects it from its historically-given institutional foundations, claiming that one could get to it just as well individually rather than through official membership. This daring and controversial idea, which could be read as heterodoxical if one were to insist on the required legal procedures and formulations, is perhaps Lessing's attempt to avoid the usual textualizing of his vision. By raising the possibility that Freemasonry could after all be a metaphor does not mean at the same time that it is any less important. In fact he defends it as indispensable, necessary, and unavoidable. This idea is further backed up by additional comments that indicate that the same attributes that one could expect from any good person or any "rechtschaffnen Bürger"[880] (decent citizen) could also be expected from a Freemason. What inspires a person to do the good does not need to have anything to do with any attribute to Freemasonry. Ernst asks: "Wer hat, dieses zu sein, nicht außer der Freimäurerei, Antrieb und Gelegenheit genug?" (Who does not have sufficient motivation and opportunity outside of Freemasonry to gain these qualifications?) Ernst insists: "Aber doch entsteht in ihr und durch sie ein zusätzlicher Antrieb"[881] (But within it and through it arises an additional stimulus). The role of the institution becomes rather fragile in this dialogue.

Ernst is critical of the notion of "Antrieb" (stimulus) making fun of such a weak thing and compares it to the spokes of a wheel. Does a wheel go faster only because it has one more spoke ("Antrieb")? Falk says he cannot contradict him ("Da kann ich dir nicht widersprechen?") and responds: "Mein Freund, sei billig! Hyperbel, Quidproquo jener schalen Reden und Lieder! Anfängerwerk! Jüngerarbeit!"[882] (My friend, be fair! An exaggeration, misunderstanding, as if shallow speeches and songs! Initial effort! Work of youngsters!). Falk explicitly rejects hyperbolic flowery language and attributes it to the work of less experienced people. Again he is hinting to the need for understatement *ex negativo.* Ernst apparently wants to paraphrase this in his own words by adding: "Das will sagen: Bruder Redner ist ein Schwätzer!"[883] (That suggests: Brother Orator is a gossiper!) Falk acts surprised as if this comment was a *non sequitur* and gives his answer again–now from another angle–by shifting from the notion of talking as a wasting of empty words to the notion of acting, a metaphorical "speaking" of actual deeds, actions that can, as he claims "speak" on their own. There is yet another level of language alluded to and Lessing seems to suggest a semiotics of signs that exceeds the linguistic or semantic level:

> FALK Ja, nun merke ich worauf du zielest. Wie konnten sie mir nicht gleich einfallen, diese Taten, diese sprechenden Taten. Fast möchte ich sie schreiende nennen. Nicht genug, daß

880 FA 10, 18.
881 FA 10, 18.
882 FA 10, 18.
883 FA 10, 18. In Germany, Orator is the third highest official of a lodge after the Master and the Senior Warden.

sich die Freimäurer einer den andern unterstützen, au das kräftigste unterstützen: denn das wäre nur die notwendige Eigenschaft einer jeden Bande. Was tun sie nicht für die gesamte Bevölkerung eines jeden Staats, dessen Glieder sie sind?[884]

[FALK Oh, now I see what you are getting at. How could they not come to my mind immediately, those deeds, those speaking deeds? I almost want to call them screaming ones. Not enough that the Freemasons support each other, even in the most forceful manner: since this would only be the necessary attribute of any association. What could they not do for the entire population of each state, of which they are members?].

He indicates that helping each other within the group does not qualify as the essential typical trait of a Freemason. The help must go way beyond that and make a difference to the entire population of that state of which they are member. It remains open whether the notion of the state is to be taken literally, such as referring to a country, nationality, or whether it is meant rather metaphorically as a broader frame of reference, similar to the beginning of the first *Gespräch* where Ernst talked to Falk and interrupted his state of mind in the early morning.

Another connotation may also set the tone if the reader remembers Lessing's *Laokoon.* The notion of "screaming deeds" could be interpreted as rather ironic since it echoes the notion of the screaming Laokoon who must be shown in such a way that his mouth is only a bit open as if it were a sigh. In the artwork of the statue an almost silent scream seems expresses the pain best. The minimally opened mouth means the sculptor has respected the limits of the visual representation. Minimalist style has to do, according to Lessing, with media specific boundaries and captures a "poignant moment" of the action visually drawing compassion best. For Lessing it was important not to exceed the boundaries of the artwork in order to leave space for the audience to interpret, freedom for the imagination, and ultimately to enable the public to emancipate itself by not imposing too much. Here similarly, the notions of "screaming actions" or "loud deeds" that advertise themselves are not considered favorably.

Falk gives a number of positive examples: Freemasons in Stockholm that have created an orphanage, Freemasons in Dresden that have provided jobs for poor young women who can now knit and quilt, and Freemasons in Braunschweig that have given poor talented boys the opportunity to learn drawing. When Ernst mentions that he read in the news about Freemasons in Berlin that support Basedow's Philanthropic Educational Institute,[885] Falk responds by saying first he needs to see a receipt written in Basedow's own hand and wonders if the support came not just from Freemasons in Berlin but Freemasons in general. According to Falk it is absurd to raise the question of ownership in reference to good deeds. When it comes to money and authority the question of who it was behind it may be a distraction, since there may well be others involved. Falk indicates that whatever Freemasons do in terms of good deeds, they may well have done the same had they not been Freemasons. He adds: "Vielleicht!–Vielleicht, daß alle die guten Taten, die du mir da genannt hast, um mich eines scholastischen Ausdruckes, der Kürze wegen zu bedienen, nur ihre Taten *ad extra*

884 FA 10, 19.

885 The educational reformer, Johann Bernhard Basedow, established his "Philanthropium" in Berlin in 1774.

sind"[886] (Perhaps!–Perhaps all the good deeds which you have enumerated here, in order to use a scholastic term for its brevity, their deeds are only *ad extra*). But these deeds may have been done only to catch the public's eye, to be framed in such a way as to draw attention. Then they would only be mere gesticulations one should not take too seriously. Falk adds: "Ihre wahre Taten sind ihr Geheimnis"[887] (Their true deeds are their secret). These deeds are so big, so wide, he explains, that complete centuries must pass before one can ever say that they did it. "Nicht wohl!–Nur so viel kann und darf ich dir sagen: die wahren Taten der Freimäurer sind so groß, so weit aussehend, daß ganze Jahrhunderte vergehen können, ehe man sagen kann: das haben sie getan!"[888] (Not so simple. Only this much I can and may tell you: The true deeds of the Freemasons are so enormous, so extensive, that entire centuries may pass before one can say: this is what they have done!) The notion of "seeing" has now been elevated into that of a meta-perspective and is associated with a kind of vision that overlooks time. Lessing requested in his theoretical works when he affiliated the visual with the dimension of space and music with the dimension of time that the signs of visuality remain focused on signs as bodies in space and on a sequential order, whereas the signs of music, tones, have signs in time but these signs, tones, exist at the same time together, simultaneously. Lessing now introduces a third dimension beyond time and space in the context of *Ernst und Falk* where the ultimate look is a kind of seeing that has its own temporality absorbed in itself.

## 4. Boundaries of the philosophical discourse

Also in this context, the speaker admits to have reached a border when commenting: "Gleichwohl haben sie alles Gute getan, was noch in der Welt ist,–merke wohl: in der *Welt*!–Und fahren fort, an alle dem Guten zu arbeiten, was noch in der Welt werden sind,–merke wohl: in der *Welt*!" (Anyhow, they have done all the good things that are yet in the world–mark well, in the *world*!–And to go further, they are working on all the good things which yet will be in the world mark well, in the world!) The perspective presented here has its eye on the future containing the conviction that all the good things to come will be associated with the Freemasons. Ernst protests: "O geh! Du hältst mich zum besten"[889] (Go on! You are making a fool of me).

Falk at the end of this first *Gespräch* points to a butterfly identifying it as one whose caterpillar feeds on cypress spurge or Wolfsmilk (*Wolfsmilchraupe*).[890] This curi-

886 FA 10, 20; "nur ihre Taten *ad extra* sind": that is, their deeds are only external, official, and visible deeds as opposed to inner ethical-moral convictions.
887 FA 10, 21.
888 FA 10, 21.
889 FA 10, 21.
890 The cypress spurge (*Euphorbia cyparissias*) is one of the shrubs known as Wolfsmilk, so called because of the "bite" of its poisonous sap. The "Wolfsmilchraupe" is the caterpillar of the "Wolfsmilch Ringelspinner" or Ground Lackey Moth (*Malacosoma castrensis*). Though called a butterfly (*Schmetterling*) it is technically a moth or *Nachtfalter*. Lessing's point of the argument is how transient are not only images but also words and their meanings.

ous little creature he then parallels with the so-called "wahre Taten" (real deeds) of the Freemasons. They could not very well be called "great deeds" because such is just an exotic name for something that changes its name with its mode of existence over time. The concept of "good deeds" in general has the potential to become superfluous. In the same way that caterpillars cease to exist the moment they turn into butterflies, so-called "good deeds" too may cease to exist or become completely normal and unremarkable when a better state of being is achieved. Whereas there could perhaps not be any better word at the moment to give a name to what these so-called "good deeds" are, there is still the possibility that they may become, as is here indicated, ultimately dispensable or obsolete. The two friends Ernst and Falk leave each other with this riddle about the *Wolfsmilchraupe* resonating until the next conversation. They run behind the butterfly Falk has seen, but they are unable to catch it. The conversation ends with a gap, an uncompleted ending in which image and object escape. This can be seen as a form of understatement in this context which highlights the ability of language to shift focus and frame metaphorically and actually to add levels of frame within metaphoricity so that not only change or diaphoric progress can be alluded to, such as from one creature (caterpillar) to the next (butterfly) in time. Moreover the names suggest a leveling not only from one aspect to the next but a layering of meanings simultaneously. In German the butterfly is named after the plant Wolfsmilk which its caterpillar eats and the name of the plant is itself borrowed from an animal, since its juice "bites" like a wolf and has not only a bitter flavor but also the ability to be dangerous in terms of its sap which is known to cause allergic reactions to those who touch it. All these images are interconnected in such a way that multiple frames of reference inspire the imagination in the pursuit not only of the question of who the Freemasons are, but also how their achievements may be hard to name. Names are as arbitrary as words tend to be, yet their significance is a matter of point of view which depends on time. There are linkages between different species and creatures in nature showing us that the actual most essential changes in meaning, the shedding of forms, can barely be seen or detected with the individual's eye.

The second *Gespräch* begins with Ernst asking: "Nun? wo bleibst du denn? Und hast den Schmetterling doch nicht?"[891] (Now? Where are you? And haven't you yet caught the butterfly?) Ernst has not forgotten what they were talking about in the first conversation and returns to the notion of trying to catch the butterfly they had seen. Falk replies again with an understatement drawing attention to "another side" which cannot be accessed at the moment: "Er lockte mich vom Strauch zu Strauch, bis an den Bach.–Auf einmal flog er auf die andere Seite.") (It lured me from bush to bush, right to the stream.–All of a sudden it flew to the other side.) By means of an interesting metaphoric twist, the focus and the frame of the metaphor are reversed here, Ernst responds: "Ja, ja. Es gibt solche Locker!"[892] (Yes, yes. There are such lurers). It is not the catcher (observer) who is now luring the butterfly, rather it is the butterfly which has itself become the agent of the action by drawing the pursuer away (and astray?) in the process. Reference is made again to the riddle that arises from the opening

891 FA 10, 22.

892 FA 10, 22. The noun "Locker" which Lessing uses here is associated with the verb *"locken"* meaning luring, hunting, or catching animals.

discussion of the first *Gespräch:* Is Falk is a Freemason or not, who are the Freemasons, and what does it all mean.

From this moment on in the conversation, the roles of Ernst and Falk are no longer those of one asking and the other one replying, but rather they appear to both to have the same role. Falk begins: "Hast du nachgedacht?" (Have you thought about it?) Ernst responds that yes he has been thinking about the riddles that Falk raised: "Über was? Über deine Rätsel?– Ich werde ihn auch nicht fangen, den schönen Schmetterling! Darum soll er mir aber auch weiter keine Mühe machen.–Einmal von den Freimäurerei mit dir gesprochen, und nie wieder. Denn ich sehe ja wohl; du bist, wie sie alle"[893] (About what? About your riddle?–I would not catch it either, the beautiful butterfly! Therefore he should not give me any further trouble.–Once I spoke with you about Freemasonry but never again. Because I see all too well: You are just like they all are). Falk protests: "Wie sie alle? Das sagen diese alle nicht." (Like all of them? All of them do not say that). Then Ernst says:

> Nicht? So giebt es ja wohl auch Kätzer unter den Freimäurern? Und du wärest einer?–Doch alle Kätzer haben mit den Rechtgläubigen immer noch etwas gemein. Und davon sprach ich.[894]
>
> [No? So then there are still heretics among the Freemasons? And would you be one of them?–But all heretics always still have something in common with the orthodox. And this is what I spoke about].

The riddle about the beautiful butterfly may suggest that perhaps the notion of Freemasonry may at some point be obsolete and take on another form of existence via metamorphosis. It is not a matter of saying it was wrong or not necessary, but it would be a mistake to hang on to outdated forms that may longer be adequate when the content has changed. The idea of transformed truth is something at the core of this image but spelling it out in judgmental services would also not do justice to the delicacy of the matter. Lessing proposes that this butterfly cannot and should not be "caught" but left freely. In that sense he also undermines the clear distinction between the heterodox and the orthodox for the sake of mutability and timing.

## 5. Fragile binaries

Ernst introduces again another fragile binary in contrasting the heterodox and the orthodox on an abstract plane which he soon deconstructs. Based on this conversation he points out similarities between them, thus rhetorically bridging the gap when he states: "Rechtgläubige oder kätzerische Freimäurer–sie alle spielen mit Worten und lassen sich fragen und antworten, ohne zu antworten".[895] (Orthodox or heretical Freemasons–they all play with words and let themselves be asked and answer without answering). At this point being caught in paradox Falk deflects the conversation from

893 FA 10, 22.
894 FA 10, 22.
895 FA 10, 23.

this line of argument: "Meinst du?–Nun wohl, so laß uns von etwas anderem reden. Denn einmal hast du mich aus dem behaglichen Zustande des stummen Staunens gerissen–".[896] (Is that what you think?–Well then, let us talk about something else. Since you have once before torn me out of the comfortable state of silent admiration–). He thus reminds him of the very beginning of the first conversation when he was quietly admiring that beautiful morning until being interrupted in his meditative state by Ernst's questioning. The response is swift: "Nichts ist leichter, als dich in diesen Zustand wieder zu versetzen–Laß dich nur hier bei mir, und sieh!"[897] (Nothing is easier, than to put you again into that state. Only sit next to me and see!)

Ernst shows Falk an anthill and draws attention to how busy the ants are and what order they have. Everyone seems to carry something and do something and nobody seems to stand in the way or hinder the others: "Sie helfen einander sogar"[898] (They even help each other). Ernst and Falk move from talking about ants to the question what ways of knowing may govern these actions. And what kind of human government would be similar to be able to be so marvelously well organized? Is the State something necessary for the happiness of the individual? A hint is made that in some cases this could be just like a "Bemäntelung der Tyrannei" (disguise of tyranny). Falk responds with more questions: "Glaubst du, daß die Menschen für die Staaten geschaffen werden? Oder daß die Staaten für die Menschen sind?"[899]) (Do you believe that people are made for the states? Or that the states are there for the people?) Again they are facing first an apparent binary which then they are trying to disentangle. Ernst agrees that some people may insist on one version, whereas others may see the truth quite differently. It is Ernst's insight in this context to see that "a truth" can be something else when evaluated by a different person according to each specific situation. However, he quickly adds that he thinks that this strategy of reasoning by focusing so much on the context each time might easily become misused: "Eine Wahrheit, die jeder nach seiner eigenen Lage beurteilet, kann leicht gemißbraucht werden"[900] (A truth which everyone evaluates according to one's own situation can easily be misused). At this point Falk finds that Ernst has already become "ein halber Freimaurer" (half a Freemason).[901]

Ernst is surprised and wants to know what criteria he is using. Falk explains: "Du. Denn du erkennst ja schon Wahrheiten, die man besser verschweigt" (You. Because you already recognize those truths which one would better not talk about). Ernst adds: "Aber doch sagen *könnte*" (But yet *could* say). Falk explains further with a paraphrase it as if it were a proverb: "Der Weise *kann* nicht sagen, was er besser verschweigt".[902] (The wise person *is* not able to say what would better not be said). The fact that there is an option to leave blanks, to choose carefully what to express and when to keep silent, is highlighted in this conversation as something Falk draws attention to.

896 FA 10, 23.
897 FA 10, 23.
898 FA 10, 23.
899 FA 10, 24.
900 FA 10, 24.
901 FA 10, 24.
902 FA 10, 24.

Next Ernst and Falk explore a difference between goals and means. When asked to talk about means that are normally excellent, they recognize that these can nonetheless lead to their opposite. This idea is expressed by Ernst. In response, Falk mentions ships that are excellent means to travel into remote countries. However, they can nevertheless in some cases become the cause for numerous people never to arrive since shipwrecks can happen. One does not claim there is a problem with the system of navigation if by accident a ship does not to arrive at its destination. One must be similarly careful in assessing blame on means that are intended well but sometimes fail to achieve their goals. Falk wonders in response why so many people do not seem to gain happiness through the rules governing a state ("Staatsverfassungen"). Falk defends the existence of constitutions and asks Ernst to imagine what would happen if there were no states. Would people then still meet each other simply as one human being meets another? Or would these encounters be like the present that is when a German meets a Frenchman, an Englishman, etc. they frame each other anxiously. He thus draws attention to the negative impact of national boundaries and to the ideal possibility that people belonging to different states could nonetheless meet regardless of those distinctions:

> FALK Das ist: wenn itzt ein Deutscher einem Franzosen, ein Franzose einem Engländer oder umgekehrt begegnet, so begegnet nicht mehr ein *bloßer* Mensch einem *bloßen* Menschen, die vermöge ihrer gleichen Natur gegen einander angezogen werden, sondern ein *solcher* Mensch begegnet einem *solchen* Menschen, die ihrer verschiedenen Tendenz sich bewußt sind, welches sie gegen einander kalt, zurückhaltend, mißtrauisch macht, noch ehe sie für ihre einzelne Person das geringste mit einander zu schaffen und zu teilen haben.[903]

> [FALK This means: If today a German meets a Frenchman, a Frenchman an Englishman, or vice versa, then it is no longer just one *mere* human meeting another mere human, who are due to their identical nature being attracted to one another; instead such a person meets another such person conscious of their different tendencies, which then makes them cold, reticent, mistrusting, even before they have the slightest thing in common, or before they want to share anything, no matter how minimal].

## 6. Who or what creates meaning? A vision

What is being expressed here is that even the most minor thing can be a matter of conflict if the conditions are adverse, or if people don't understand each other because of national, cultural, and personal differences. This expresses stark social criticism in terms of what national boundaries have done to people and how narrow-minded they become. States that are there to help to unite people can also lead to separating them instead. Instead of gaining freedom through their countries and constitutions there is sometimes a negative impact. Individuals may feel restricted by the same boundaries that were established initially to protect them and to promote their happiness. Ernst and Falk agree that there is a basic bond between people, that humans are alike and have a natural attraction to one another, and it is their implicit wish to increase shared interaction and communication among themselves. It seems that one has to overcome

903 FA 10, 28.

distinct customs, languages, and religions that often stand unnecessarily in the way of such communication. Falk recognizes that bourgeois society may, completely against its good intentions, also do much harm:

> Nun sieh dort das zweite Unheil, welches die bürgerliche Gesellschaft, ganz ihrer Absicht entgegen, verursacht. Sie kann die Menschen nicht vereinigen, ohne sie zu trennen; nicht trennen, ohne Klüfte zwischen ihnen zu befestigen, ohne Scheidemauern, durch sie hin zu ziehen.[904]
>
> [Now see the second disaster which the bourgeois society causes completely against its intention. It cannot unite the people without separating them, nor separate them without stabilizing the abyss between them, without raising walls of demarcation through them].

They speak about an additional dilemma which leads to the building of walls splitting people apart. It involves class differences and by implication notions of property that manifest themselves in the unfortunate division between rich and poor. Falk indicates that it is within the boundaries of each State to change its conditions from within and that one is required to respect the bourgeois laws as given.

> FALK Aber geboten kann es doch auch nicht sein; durch bürgerliche Gesetze nicht geboten!–Denn bürgerliche Gesetze erstrecken sich nie über die Grenzen ihres Staats. Und dieses würde nun gerade außer der Grenzen aller und jeder Staaten liegen.–Folglich kann es nur ein Opus supererogatum sein: und es wäre bloß zu wünschen, daß sich die Weisesten und Besten eines jeden Staats diesem *Operi superogato* freiwillig unterzögen.[905]
>
> [FALK But it cannot be required; cannot be required by bourgeois laws!–For the bourgeois laws never extend themselves beyond the borders of its State. And this would precisely lie outside of the borders of all and of each State.–Consequently it can only be an *Opus supererogatum;*[906] and it would have to be wished that the wisest and the best of each State would undertake voluntarily such an *Opus supererogatum.*]

This seems the vision of the future as it can be approximated conceptually at this point. It would not mean tearing down laws and constitutions that exist for good reasons but erecting a still higher order, a legal system that would have validity beyond the boundaries of the States. At the beginning of the third *Gespräch,* Ernst paraphrases what they were talking about: "Wende dich itzt, wie du willst.–Genug, ich denke mir nun aus deinen Reden die Freimäurer als Leute, die es freiwillig über sich genommen haben, den unvermeidlichen Übeln des Staats entgegen zu arbeiten"[907] (Turn yourself whichever way you want to.–Enough, I understand now from your conversations Freemasons are people who have voluntarily taken the task upon themselves to work against the inevitable troubles of the state). Although Falk seems to agree partly to this sentence and confirms: "Bleib dabei!" (Stick to it!), he also insists on editing or cutting it some: "Menge nichts hinein, was nicht hinein gehöret.–Die unvermeidlichen Übel des Staats!" (Do not mix into it anything that does not belong in there.–The unavoid-

904 FA 10, 30
905 FA 10, 32.
906 The *Opus supererogatum* is a work going beyond ordinary expectations. On this principle the ideal, optimal, state of the future should be built. See Marianne Willems, "Der 'herrschaftsfreie Diskurs' als 'opus supererogatum.' Überlegungen zum Interaktionsethos des 'bloß Menschlichen'," Mauser and Saße, ed., *Streitkultur* 540-551.
907 FA 10, 32.

able weaknesses or defects of the State!) He specifies further that he is not referring to any specific unavoidable flaws affecting this or any state or its constitution. Those are never anything a Freemason would get to deal with, at least not "as Freemason." They are rather to be handled by those citizens who according to their insight and courage dare to tackle them yet at their own risk: "Nicht den unvermeidlichen Übeln, welche, eine gewisse Staatsverfassung einmal angenommen, aus dieser angenommenen Staatsverfassung nun notwendig folgen. Mit diesen gibt sich der Freimäurer niemals ab; wenigstens nicht als Freimäurer"[908] (Not the unavoidable flaws which, once accepted by a certain constitution of a State has will then consequently follow from it. With those a Freemason does not get bothered, at least not as a Freemason). Instead, what Freemasons are concerned with is, as Falk mentions, are "Übel ganz andrer Art" (flaws of a completely different nature). Is it then the task of the Freemasons, Ernst wonders, to correct: "Nicht Übel, welche den mißvergnügten Bürger machen, sondern Übel, ohne welche auch der glücklichste Bürger nicht sein kann" (Not the flaws that make a malcontented citizen, but those which even the happiest citizen cannot avoid). There are flaws a Freemason wants to counteract. Falk verifies this: "Richtig! Diesen entgegen–wie sagtest du?–entgegen zu arbeiten?"[909] (Correct! Against these–how did you put it?–to work against?) Asked further what then defines the specific actions of the Freemasons, Falk gives a completely satisfying answer to Ernst. At least it seems so on the surface level of the conversation. He points out that Freemasons have never made a secret of their policy to take any suitable man into their Brotherhood, especially if this person has favorable talents, regardless of nationality, religion, class, or status in bourgeois society. He adds that there is an the analogy between artist who can very well make silver but can also deal with materials of a lesser quality or expense, so that not everyone would have to consider him to be a silversmith: ("Warum sollte der Künstler, der Silber *machen* kann, nicht mit altem Bruchsilber handeln, damit man so weniger argwohne, daß er es machen kann?")[910] The *Gespräch* comes to an end, but the epilog announces that Ernst becomes a Freemason. What he discovered is a topic reserved for the fourth and fifth Gespräche which were at the time unpublished. Falk pleads for understatement and suggests not to announce such findings too loudly. It would be better to let actions in time prove the point, to let facts stand for themselves, uncommented. Such modest behavior speaks more reliably than any mode of advertising or predicting. This makes us reflect on the art of naming things wisely, poignantly.

The fourth *Gespräch* begins just at the point when apparently both Falk and Ernst have completed a "Brunnenkur," the visit to a spa, thus indicating joint activity now as brothers in a Lodge. Ernst asks: "Und befindest Dich wohl darauf? Ich freue mich" (And you are doing well? I am glad). Falk replies: "Was ist das? Man hat nie ein 'ich freue mich' ärgerlicher ausgesprochen" (What is this? I have never heard anyone say 'I am glad' in a more angry way). He notices a discrepancy between Ernst's words and the tone, the semantic content of what he heard and the gestures and mimes that accompanied them. Ernst admits that he is an angry mood and says "Ich bin es auch, und es fehlt wenig, daß ich es nicht über Dich bin"[911] (So I am [angry] and it

908 FA 10, 36.
909 FA 10, 37.
910 FA 10, 45.
911 FA 10, 40.

it's a close thing that I am not angry with you). He explains further: "Du hast mich zu einem albernen Schritt verleitet"[912] (You have induced me to take a silly step). Falk reminds him that apparently it was his choice to do so. By suggesting that each member is responsible for becoming a member in the society, he rejects Ernst's insinuation that the blame is his (Falk's). Falk may have won him over through his rhetoric, but he refuses to be reproached for this. The reader is given no specific information on precisely what this wrong "step" may have been, but the context clearly suggests that it was Ernst's decision to become a member of the Freemasons.

FALK Und soll doch Schuld gehabt haben?
ERNST Der Mann Gottes spricht dem Volk von einem Lande, da Milch und Honig fließt, und das Volk soll sich danach nicht sehnen? Und es soll über den Mann Gottes nicht murren, wenn er es, anstatt in dieses gelobte Land, in dürre Wüsten führt.[913]
FALK Nun, nun! Der Schaden kann ja doch so groß nicht sein.–Dazu sehe ich ja, daß du schon *bei den Gräbern unserer Vorfahren* gearbeitet hast.
ERNST Aber sie waren nicht mit *Flammen*, sondern mit Rauch umgeben.
FALK So warte, bis der Rauch sich verzieht, und die Flamme wird leuchten und wärmen.[914]
ERNST Der Rauch wird mich ersticken, ehe mir die Flamme leuchtet und mich wärmen, sehe Ich wohl, werden Andere an ihr, die den Rauch besser vertragen können.
FALK Du sprichst doch nicht von Leuten, die den Rauch gern beißen lassen, wenn es nur der Rauch einer fremden fetten Küche ist?[915]
ERNST Du kennst sie also doch?
FALK Ich habe von ihr gehört.[916]

[FALK And I should have bear the responsibility for this?
ERNST The man of God spoke to the people of a land in which milk and honey flow, and should not the people desire that? And should the people not grumble about the man of God, when he, instead of into this Promised Land, leads them into barren deserts?
FALK Now, now! The damage cannot be all that bad. And in addition I see that you have already worked near *the graves of our ancestors.*
ERNST But they were surrounded not by *flames but by smoke.*
FALK Then wait until the smoke dissipates itself and the flame will shine and spread warmth.
ERNST The smoke will suffocate me, before the flame shines and spreads warmth, I see very well, others will be warmed by it who can tolerate the smoke better.
ERNST You're not speaking about people who willingly let the smoke sting them only because it is the smoke of a strange juicy kitchen?
FALK So you know them too?
ERNST I've heard of them].

912 FA 10, 45. That some scholars identify Falk with Lessing has already mentioned but at this point, if so inclined, one can make a strong case that Ernst speaks in Lessing's voice expressing his frustration attendant on his initiation into von Rosenberg's Lodge. See Müller, *Untersuchungen zum Problem der Freimaurerei bei Lessing* 16–19.
913 Speaking from the Burning Bush, God promised to lead Moses' people to a land of "milk and honey" (Exodus 4) but they would wander many years in the desert before they reached it. In some Masonic accounts Moses is considered a Grand Master.
914 The "graves of our ancestors" and "flames" (fire) are Masonic symbols appropriate to the very junior third grade or degree (Master Mason) which was the highest ever achieved by Lessing. In the Scottish Rite, the highest degree is the thirty-third.
915 The reference here is to the kitchen in which was prepared the food for the meal at the end of the Lodge's activities.
916 FA 10, 45-46.

Ernst processes his disappointment by referring to Moses. His people were angry with him as he let them wander in the desert instead of bringing them to the Promised Land, so why should he not be angry with Falk who promised access to the high ideals of the Freemasons. Falk does not think the matter is that serious, it is just a matter of perspective. After all there was the flame or symbolic fire that was there to provide light and warmth. But the reality is otherwise, for the fire appears not well prepared and heavily smoking. The smoke is suffocating Ernst and he does not have the patience to wait like those who endure the smoke because they are already anticipating the meal that is going to follow. Falk reminds Ernst to continue his own path. In the following passages of this dialogue the parable of the fire and the flame is developed further so that the actual smoke prevention device, the chimney, stands for the Freemasons on the way to insight. But it would also be possible to experience the warmth and light of the flame without this company: "Ich sollte Dir nicht gesagt haben, daß man die höchsten Pflichten der Mäurerei erfüllen könne, ohne Freimäurer zu heißen?"[917] (Shouldn't I have told you, that one can fulfill the highest duties of Freemasonry without being called Freemason?)

Ernst now explains why he actually made the decision he did and indirectly withdraws his previous reproach of Falk saying he has ultimately nothing to do with himself deciding to become a Freemason. Ernst says: "Vielmehr erinnere ich mich dessen–Aber Du weißt ja wohl, wenn meine Fantasie einmal die Fittig ausbreitet, einen Schlag damit tut–kann ich sie halten?–Ich werfe Dir nichts vor, als daß Du ihr eine solche Lockspeise zeigtest.–"[918] (Much the more I remember this–But you know that if once my fantasy spreads its pinions and beats then once–can I stop it?–I do not reproach you anything except that you showed it such a bait). Ernst became officially a Freemason without the presence or concrete knowledge of Falk who asks him: "Und warum sagtest Du mir nicht ein Wort von Deinem Vorsatze?"[919] (And why did you not say one word of your plan to me?) Ernst acts surprised at first and wonders whether Falk would not have advised him against becoming a Freemason. Falk confirms that this is exactly what he would have done, but "rasche Knaben" (impetuous boys) cannot be talked into taking up the "Gängelwagen" (baby-walker, restrainer) again just because they are unsteady on their feet. He was on a path everyone has to follow. Ernst defends his decision to take the path he did since he was tired of any further "Vertröstungen" (postponements) and so made the move.[920] He is now aware of his own decision but is warned that more patience will be needed.

Falk reminds him that not everyone who claims to be able to make gold is able to perform such a trick. At the end of the fourth *Gespräch* mention is made of the Knights Templar who were said to be alchemists and Freemasons. What follows is a debate not only about equality among Freemasons but also about the need for all to be accepted and treated "freely" beyond all existing restrictions of religious or ethnic alliances. Ernst gives an example of discrimination in his Freemasonry circle. Falk seems to understand and to agree with his objection but then tries to console him by pointing to a future goal. He speaks up for the idea of accepting everyone, including a

---

917 FA 10, 46.
918 FA 10, 47.
919 FA 10, 47.
920 FA 10, 47.

cobbler, a postman, a merchant, a prince, an artist, no matter what their trade, profession, or work. Ernst adds that modern Freemasonry seems to be too preoccupied with its material status and in cozying up to authority. This leads to a discussion about more conflict:

> FALK Zwar!–ja wohl!–nichts dauert ewig–Vielleicht soll dies eben der Weg sein, den die Vorsehung ausersehen, dem ganzen jetzigen Schema der Freimäurerei ein Ende zu machen–
> ERNST Schema der Freimäurerei? Was nennst Du so? Schema?
> FALK Nun! Schema, Hülle, Einkleidung.
> ERNST Ich weiß noch nicht–
> FALK Du wirst doch nicht glauben, daß die Freimäurerei immer Freimäurerei gespielt?
> ERNST Was ist nun das? Die Freimäurerei nicht immer Freimäurerei gespielt?
> FALK: Mit anderen Worten! Meinst Du denn, daß das, was die Freimäurerei ist, immer Freimäuerei geheißen?[921]
>
> [FALK True!–indeed!–nothing lasts forever–Perhaps this should be just the way which destiny decided, to make an end to all of the present schema of Freemasonry.
> ERNST Schema of Freemasonry? What do you mean? Schema?
> FALK Well, schema, wrapping, accoutrements.
> ERNST I do not yet understand–
> FALK You surely do not believe it that the Freemasonry has always played at Freemasonry?
> ERNST What is this? Freemasonry not always played at Freemasonry?
> FALK In other words! Do you think that this, what is Freemasonry is, has always been called Freemasonry?].

The concept of a "past future" or a possibility that existed once upon a time but got never materialized in terms of any recorded history seems the topic here. Ernst and Falk are equal voices in Lessing's theoretical discourse, and although fictional, they are his way of articulating an urgent reality. Freemasonry itself has become not only a matter of historical investigation concerning its beginnings but, equally important, a test case for visuality that will in the process of its verbalizing possibly undermine its foundations. The dissolution of Freemasonry could, as Falk seems to suggest, be a goal promoted by its own architecture in ways that can be barely logical from any fixed given point of view. The notion of "play" is meant by Falk not only as a way to tease or to fool Ernst as he first suspected; it is a necessary way to operate language, so that it allows freedom at a time when such freedom cannot be practiced as announced. Nor can it be imagined in any permanent and stable or permanent way.

## 7. Words as empty shells and the search for meaning

Lessing's *Gespräche* in *Ernst und Falk* suggest that words are like wrappings, packages, or empty shells.[922] Once the caterpillar has outgrown its phase, it may turn into a butter-

921 FA 10, 54.

922 On Lessing against wordiness see Klaus L Berghahn, "Lessing the Critic: Polemics as Enlightenment," Fischer and Fox, *A Companion to the Works of Gotthold Ephraim Lessing* 67-87 and "Zermalmende Beredsamkeit." Lessings Literaturkritik als Polemik. Ein Essay," *Lessing Yearbook* 24 (1992): 25-44.

fly. It also may not feed literally on the milk of a wolf, but on the plant that bears only this name with white milky-colored juice. Levels of metaphoricity shift and need to be understood through each of their contexts. When metaphors turn into catachreses, one may add, they are no longer innovative and do no longer describe something new. They are sheer formulas that do not give any incentive to think further. Then it is time to let go of them. Lessing uses wit and metaphor himself to touch upon very sensitive matters concerning problems with institutionalized "truth" or any established form thereof. He challenges the validity of institutions if they claim to monopolize whatever their truth may be although it may not be comprehended or even documented as agreeable for others. In the context of his religious and philosophical debates, Lessing formulates in his *Eine Duplik* (1788) the following:

> Nicht die Wahrheit, in deren Besitz irgend ein Mensch ist, oder zu sein vermeinet, sondern die aufrichtiges Mühe, die er angewandt hat, hinter die Wahrheit zu kommen, macht den Wert des Menschen. Denn nicht durch deren Besitz, sondern durch die Nachforschung der Wahrheit erweitern sich seine Kräfte, worin allein seine immer wachsende Vollkommenheit besteht. Der Besitz macht ruhig, träge, stolz –
> Wenn Gott in seiner Rechten alle Wahrheit, und in seiner Linken den einzigen immer regen Trieb nach Wahrheit, obschon mit dem Zusatze, mich immer und ewig zu irren, verschlossen hielte, und spräche zu mir: wähle! Ich fiele ihm mit Demut in seine Linke, und sagte: Vater gieb! die reine Wahrheit ist ja doch nur für dich allein![923]
>
> [Not the truth in whose possession any human being is or believes to be, but rather the sincere efforts applied to find truth establish human value. Because not the possession of truth but the efforts to find it form human abilities and creative forces expand. This is exactly what growing human perfection consists of. The possession makes people stale, sluggish, and proud.–
> If God held in his right hand all the truth, and in his left held enclosed the singular always active drive to find truth, albeit with the codicil that I would always eternally be erroneous, and if he said to me: Choose! I would grasp modestly his left and would say: Father give! the pure truth is only for you alone!].

He emphasizes that what matters is the honest desire and passion to find truth and that the process matters. The results cannot just be claimed verbally; they have to be made plausible so that everyone can see them. The temporality of any vision should be kept in mind. He acknowledges that the dimension of time cannot be avoided, even though the dimension of space seems to be dominant when it comes to painting and all things visual. Despite the parameters Lessing gave in his *Laokoon* of 1766, he now seems to make further amends to his theoretical approach, hinting at the fact that poets should borrow strategies from musicians. Time cannot be bracketed or excluded, not even for visuality.

Lessing had once a beautiful vision of finding a hierarchy-free, enlightened discourse, shared among all the Freemasons and then everyone. But what he encountered was a sense of emptiness and loss. he realized how presumptuous and way too ambitious such a claim was. He turned apparently to an anti-visual and anti-theoretical stance. Like never before in his life, Lessing's fictional dialogues in *Ernst und Falk* stages the construction and institutionalizing of this idea as nothing but "empty shells." This deconstructive move in Lessing's late work is not only of biographical relevance;

923 FA 8, 510.

it is at the core of Lessing's deep theoretical contributions to Ekphrasis, visual-verbal dynamics, and his ongoing attempts to replace symbols and unifying concepts and generalizations with more differentiating expressions. Lessing offers through this open-ended dialogue between Ernst and Falk insights into the temporality of vision. He illustrates through multiple voices how hard it is to build consensus without any invasion of privacy. In beautifully contextualizing the word "Wolfsmilchraupe," he illustrates how context and timing matter. Temporality of vision makes all the difference in a consideration of caterpillars or butterflies, plants or animals, oppressed or liberated humans. It is the essence of art that it is more complex than linear discursive reasoning.

Visuality cannot do without metaphor, metonymy, and special moments of staged coincidence. Images still remain as unfinished thoughts and metaphors are fertile ground from which seeds and grand prospects can arise. Vividness or "Anschaulichkeit" is basic to "Dichtung" and art. This is Lessing's philosophical credo. He draws attention to the problem that insights can get spoiled by talking about them. Emotions, moods, and sensibilities matter. Lessing warns of the negative when images undergo institutionalization. He questions how visions and images could be transferred into texts or discursive language without a serious loss. Questions about Freemasonry appear to be at the core of these Gespräche. Nevertheless, there is a theoretical discussion about the potentials and limitations of Ekphrasis. It is a text that is not only historically informative provocative for the belief in visual-verbal transfer. Lessing is not only advocating Ekphrasis but also a harsh critic. As an artist he did not leave us blind to shortcomings of the discourses he experienced as being practiced. He acknowledges through the conflicting voices of those speaking for "truth." The dream, vision, or ideal of a hierarchy-free forum is unquestioned and it would allow anyone to speak and interact without personal defense. He adheres to the notion of a shared interest in world peace and global wisdom. It may transcend religious and cultural differences and go far beyond any given formula. But both Freemasonry and Enlightenment are grandiose notions and concepts that will eventually become obsolete. Actions and visible truths will make talking about these superfluous. Lessing's Gespräche between the fictional characters Ernst and Falk suggest that images persist, even when they cannot be verbalized. The voices articulate differences of perspective. These are symptomatic for an increasingly pluralistic society. Lessing nevertheless calls for more ethical action than for speculative talking.

# Chapter 12
# *A Parable of the Burning Palace* (1778): Lessing and Eco

Abstract: At the core of *Eine Parabel vom brennenden Palast* (1778) are miscommunications about its unique architecture, a lost blueprint, and the need to rescue the essence of the building. It contains theoretical reflections and remarks about the futility of just looking when intervention is needed. One needs to act before the building burns down and rescue what one still can be rescued. Everyone should help extinguish the fire instead of scurrying around after the ground plans. Seeing cannot be isolated from the other senses. Ekphrasis is being contextualized in the context of this parable. The text is indicative of specific problems with language and exposes what happens when focus and frame get mixed up, and when distinct levels of metaphoricity are being ignored. Lessing's parable can well be compared to that by Umberto Eco who uses it to draw attention to the so-called "extensions" that are all too often ignored in the approach of semiotics. Both Lessing and Eco consider language as a building which has its own beauty and integrity.

## 1. Parables on a building on fire in the works by G.E. Lessing and by Umberto Eco

Lessing's *Eine Parabel vom brennenden Palast* is on one level an epistemological experiment exploring the perception of a fire and the actions of the bystanders in response.[924] If we see a fire it may not be enough just to think about it. What is needed a physical response, an action which is more than being a mere spectator. The semiotician Umberto Eco in his *Theory of Semiotics* gives a similar example of a message concerning a burning house. He refers to Lessing implicitly and he uses his own story to illustrate a communication process that can neither be adequately explained by semantics nor by a code theory, if it were to exclude all questions about what he calls "extensions."[925] He draws attention to the fact that the extensions (elements that exceed verbalness) have to be taken into account.[926]

---

924 Lessing's full title of this work is *Eine Parabel nebst einer kleinen Bitte, und einem eventualen Absagungsschreiben an Herrn Pastor Goeze, in Hamburg* (FA 9, 41-44): (A parable next to a small request and an eventual regret letter to Mr. Pastor Goeze in Hamburg) will be cited from FA 9, 41-44 without further page numbers. I shall abbreviate it as *Eine Parabel.*

925 Umberto Eco, *A Theory of Semiotics* (Bloomington: Indiana University Press, 1976). This is Eco's revision and rewriting in English of *La struttura assente* (Milan: Bompiani, 1968), of which the German *Einführung in die Semiotik*, German version by Jürgen Trabant (Munich: Fink, 1972) is a revised translation.

926 Eco explains: "The *referential fallacy* consists of assuming that the 'meaning' of a sign vehicle has something to do with its corresponding object." But by the same reasoning it

> Whoever receives the message / your house has burned down / probably thinks of his house and if he is wise checks as to whether the statement is true or false, even if he is a code theorist who distrusts extensions.[927] But these two facts are not pertinent to a theory of codes, which should only study the conditions under which the message may be communicated and comprehended. The reasons why a message acquires sense are independent of the fact that the addressee may have a house which is *actually burning*. The 'pragmatic' response to the signals which produce behavior (the addressee running home) is independent of the truth or falsity of the assertion, as are all possible translations of the message (the addressee drawing a house for an illiterate friend).[928]

By means of the message "your house has burned down" Eco sets out to challenge simple semiotic relations. He illustrates that such simple a sentence as "your house has burnt" could still have multiple levels of referentiality. It would be an understandable, pragmatic response if anyone upon hearing this sentence were to go home and quickly check whether or not the statement applies to one's own house or whether such a claim is true and personally of consequences or not. Eco indicates that such a response, moving to action, is not usually of any concern to code theorists. They are only interested in the causality strictly on the verbal plane but usually ignore the extensions of semantic meanings. He, on the other hand, similar to Lessing, uses such a message in order to probe the visual and call attention to tactile and other sense-related aspects as well. What connects these texts, this narrative episode in Eco's *Theory of Semiotics* and Lessing's *Eine Parabel* is that in both cases a parable of a burning building is used to challenge certain assumptions about the poetic constellations between the visual and the verbal. There are theoretical reflections about problems with communications.[929] It is not only the isolated motif of a fire which matters here since the motif of a fire could easily be found in numerous other places of Lessing's work.[930] Lessing uses the narrative *Eine Parabel* here specifically in order to contribute to a theoretical debate and to discuss philosophical and epistemological issues.

It is my thesis that Lessing in this context offers valuable insights into the substructures of thinking, into the realm where images and metaphors precede the discourse of fixed terminologies.[931] It is the imaginary space where language participates in its

---

is also a fallacy to assume that "sentences correspond to an actual state in the world" and can only be considered true if that is in fact the case. "Since the theory of codes is only interested in sign functions and the rules of their possible combination, sentences should only be a matter of sign production. Nevertheless, there is a way in which the extensional approach may disturb a theory of codes–thus producing an *extensional fallacy*" (Eco, *A Theory of Semiotics* 62-63, emphasis his). His anecdote about the message "your house has burned down" illustrates that there are sentences to which we assign truth value given our experience of the real world. Even if to do so is to engage in an "extensional fallacy," a problem that can be addressed by introducing pragmatics into language theory.

927 The German version of this passage has a "Professor der Semiotik" instead of a "code theorist." Umberto Eco, *Einführung in die Semiotik* 72.

928 Eco, *Theory of Semiotics* 65.

929 FA 9, 39-52.

930 For studies on the motif of fire in Lessing's work, see Ehrhard Bahr, "Die Bild- und Sinnbereiche von Feuer und Wasser in Lessings Nathan der Weise." *Lessing Yearbook* 6 (1974): 83-96 and Helmut Göbel, *Bild und Sprache bei Lessing* (Munich: Fink, 1971).

931 Hans Blumenberg makes such an important distinction between metaphors and terminologies and places metaphors at the roots of thought. He argues: "Die Metaphorologie sucht an die Substruktur des Denkens heranzukommen, an den Untergrund, die Nahrlö-

own theoretical tool-making and where meanings are not yet fully to be extrapolated. While in the twentieth century the auto- referential dimension of language has been commented upon in terms of what Fredric Jameson termed "the prison-house of language,"[932] Lessing's narrative seems a bit more optimistic about the effectiveness of communication. He associates language not with a prison but with a palace. It has multiple entrances and oddly shaped windows. One must enter it in order to understand its purpose. Nevertheless, there are problems also associated by Lessing with such a palace. There is an apparent fire and people have trouble speaking or doing something helpful about it. Similar to Lessing, Umberto Eco links his fictional text on a fire also with a theoretical reflection. Semiotics is what links these two authors intertextually and moreover there is a search for the something more than the visible, the essence or the message of the building which may be hidden in the smoke.

Lessing's *Eine Parabel* is a self- or auto-referential narrative about various kinds of misunderstanding. What Eco approaches as a problem of multiple thresholds in the process of sense-making, Lessing describes in terms of multiple entrances into the palace symbolic for language. Once inside, everything seems to make sense. For anybody looking at it from the outside, is there any clarity whatsoever. For both authors, language cannot be isolated from real life situations and time in space. Language cannot be conceptualized as if it were a closed system removed from the humans who make daily use of it. Lessing describes the search for meaning not only in terms of a search for the blueprints of the palace, its ground plans. This would be an undertaking that he demonstrates could be obsolete although culturally still operative. Both authors shift attention from the question about the origin and the intentions of the builder(s) to specific situations communicating about it, words, signs, and actions related to its structure. They make sense only to readers and listeners who are participating interactively. Lessing's architecture of language is characterized by a preference for doors over windows. Eco's theory may have opened yet another theoretical window to his narrative building by framing the "extensional fallacies" themselves as interesting territories for further exploration. In both cases theory and praxis are intertwined and metaphors have become basic.

## 2. The Background to Lessing's *Eine Parabel*

In 1769 Karl Wilhelm Ferdinand, heir to the dukedom of Braunschweig-Wolfenbüttel arranged for Lessing to be offered the position of librarian of the Bibliotheca Augusta

sung der systematischen Kristallisationen, aber sie will auch faßbar machen, mit welchem 'Mut' sich der Geist in seinen Bildern selbst voraus ist und wie sich im Mut zur Vermutung seine Geschichte entwirft," (*Paradigmen* 13); "metaphorology seeks to burrow down to the substructure of thought, the underground, the nutrient solution of systematic crystallizations; but it also aims to show with what 'courage' the mind preempts itself in its images, and how its history is projected in the courage of its conjectures" (*Paradigms* 5).

932 Fredric Jameson, *The Prison-House of Language: A Critical Account of Structuralism and Russian Formalism* (Princeton: Princeton University Press, 1972).

in Wolfenbüttel, a post he took the following year.[933] Between the years 1773-1777 Lessing as a Ducal Librarian edited six volumes under the imprint of the Library: *Zur Geschichte und Literatur aus den Schätzen der Herzoglichen Bibliothek zu Wolfenbüttel.*[934] In two of these volumes he printed fragments from a manuscript with a brief commentary and claimed it was found in the Ducal Library. These fragments would eventually prove to be selections from an unpublished work of the German Deist philosopher and scholar Hermann Samuel Reimarus, his *Apologie oder Schutzschrift für die vernünftigen Verehrer Gottes.*[935] The first fragment appeared in volume three (1774). Five further selections were printed in volume four (1777), followed by the "Gegensätze des Herausgebers."[936] The appearance of these fragments from Reimarus triggered a series of attacks on them and on their editor by anti-deist and conservative thinkers. Among them was Johann Melchior Goeze, Hauptpastor of Hamburg.[937] Goeze's first attack (on Lessing's "Gegensätze des Herausgebers") appeared in *Freywillige Beyt*räge zu

933 Nisbet, *Lessing: Eine Biographie* 509; *Gotthold Ephraim Lessing* 388. Founded in Wolfenbüttel in 1572, the Herzog-August-Bibliothek (Bibliotheca Augusta) came into prominence with the addition of the collection of rare books and manuscripts amassed by August der Jüngere (1635-1666), Herzog von Braunschweig-Wolfenbüttel. Leibniz served as librarian from 1690-1716, and from his time it has had the reputation as one of the finest research libraries in Europe. For Lessing's term as librarian see: Nisbet, *Lessing: Eine Biographie* 600-627; *Gotthold Ephraim Lessing* 457-477.

934 For selections see: *Zur Geschichte und Literatur* I-II (FA 7, 377-581; III-IV (FA 8, 55-134, 171-350); V-VI (FA 10, 103-159).

935 FA 8, 173-250. Lessing must have obtained the manuscript during his time in Hamburg (1767-1770) from Reimarus' children, probably from the daughter Elise. See Gerhard Alexander, "Wie kam Lessing zur Handschrift der Wolfenbütteler Fragmente?" *Philobiblon* 16 (1972): 160-173 at 162-163. There appears to have existed an earlier version of the text unpublished until 1972. See Hermann Samuel Reimarus, *Apologie oder Schutzschrift für die vernünftigen Verehrer Gottes,* ed. Gerhard Alexander, 2 vols. (Frankfurt am Main: Insel, 1972). Although the manuscript was Lessing's private property, the fact that he had claimed that the manuscript was part of the library holdings allowed it to be seized by Karl I, Herzog von Braunschweig-Wolfenbüttel, in July 1778. It has since disappeared (Reimarus, *Apologie* 1, 14-17). For the significance of Reimarus see William Boehart, *Politik und Religion: Studien zum Fragmentestreit Reimarus, Goeze, Lessing* (Schwarzenbeck: Rüdiger Martienss, 1988), 31-123 and the commentary in FA 8, 841-852.

936 "Von Duldung der Deisten: Fragment eines Ungenannten" (FA 8, 115-134); "Ein Mehreres aus den Papieren des Ungenannten, die Offenbarung betreffend" (FA 8, 173-311). The "Gegensätze" also includes the first 53 §§ of *Erziehung des Menschengeschlechts* (1778). For complete text see FA 10, 73-99.

937 On Goeze see Boehart, *Politik und Religion* 124-261 and the essays in Heimo Reinitzer and Walter Sparn, ed., *Verspätete Orthodoxie: Über D. Johann Melchior Goeze (1717-1786),* Wolfenbütteler Forschungen 45 (Wiesbaden: Harrassowitz, 1989). The bibliography on "Der Fragmentenstreit" is extensive. For further details see Wilfried Barner et al. *Lessing: Epoche–Werk–Wirkung.* 5th ed., 282-307; Boehart, *Politik und Religion* 373-472; FA 8, 723-741, 960ff.; FA 9, 725-749, 753-780, 821ff, and with respect to "Eine Parabel," Arno Schilson, "Glanz der Wahrheit oder blendender Stil? Überlegungen zu Gegenstand und Methode in Lessings Streit mit Goeze," Mauser and Saße, ed., *Streitkultur* 56-77. As a result of this controversy Karl I, Herzog von Braunschweig-Wolfenbüttel suspended Lessing's privilege of freedom from censorship, placed restrictions on the topics on which he could publish and in July 1778 confiscated the manuscript of Reimarus (Reimarus, *Apologie* 1: 15-16; FA 9, 711). See Nisbet, *Lessing: Eine Biographie* 701-744; *Gotthold Ephraim Lessing* 537-70 and Fick, *Handbuch* 372-402.

den Hamburgischen Nachrichten aus dem Reiche der Gelehrsamkeit, numbers 55-56 (December 12, 1777), followed by a second in the same periodical numbers 61-63 (January 30, 1778).[938] Lessing's first response to the attacks by Goeze was "Eine Parabel nebst einer kleinen Bitte, und einem eventualen Absagungsschreiben an Herrn Pastor Goeze, in Hamburg" which first appeared anonymously in March 1778.[939] Although *Eine Parabel* appears together with these two other items, it will here be considered as a separate narrative.[940] It is a fictionalized reply to a dogmatic attack which Lessing did not articulate in legal or theological language but by shifting discourses into the realm of metaphor. Lessing's text is a parable and one of the characteristics of such texts is their openness. Generally speaking, there are two schools of interpretation regarding *Eine Parabel*. The first one is concerned with historical details, the relationship of the text to Lessing's biography, the *Fragmentestreit*, and Lessing's stance vis-à-vis orthodox Protestantism and other Enlightenment thinkers. The second school is concerned with broad ontological, existential, or philosophical concepts in making links between *Eine Parabel* and other related literature.[941]

My focus here is neither biographical, nor one of influence study. It is not about the direct adaptation of one author's text into the text of another. The parable by Lessing has so far mainly been identified with "Das Haus der Theologie" (the house of theology).[942] But the building, or rather the palace, can also be interpreted as the "house of language." I am expanding upon an earlier observation I made when I wrote in an essay that this palace in Lessing's "Parabel" is "über den Palast, der für die Architektur der Sprache steht."[943] But I must correct something: It is not only "the architecture of language" for which the palace "stands," as if it were "there" in a visual space projected by Lessing's text. It is an imaginary that has be yet created by the readers, us, and this can possibly be resulting from the effects of this particular architecture to be considered. The palace is not only a static object to be interpreted, but something to be conceptualized in interaction with other *referents* and *interpretants* in the vocabulary by Umberto Eco or the concept of signs "Zeichen" that Lessing

938 FA 9, 804-820.

939 FA 9, 39-52, 821-837.

940 "[S]o daß Lessings 'Parabel' als ziemlich eigenständiges poetisches Gebilde zu betrachten ist" (FA 9, 823). See Göbel, *Bild und Sprache* 107-119.

941 For example, Theodor W. Adorno, "Prismen," *Kulturkritik und Gesellschaft,* GS 10, 2 vols., 1: 9-287; Heinz Politzer, "Lessings Parabel von den drei Ringen," *German Quarterly* 31 (1958): 161-177; Reprint: Gerhard Bauer and Sibylle Bauer, ed., *Gotthold Ephraim Lessing Wege der Forschung* 211 (Darmstadt: Wissenschaftliche Buchgeschellschaft, 1968), 343-361; Revised version: *Das Schweigen der Sirenen: Studien zur deutschen und österreichischen Literatur* (Stuttgart: Metzler, 1968. 339-372 and 425-428), and Karol Sauerland, "Lessings Palast-Parabel–ein literarisches Kleinod, das über das Streitobjekt hinauswuchs," Mauser and Saße, ed., *Streitkultur* 457-461.

942 Johannes von Lupke, *Wege der Weisheit: Studien zu Lessings Theologiekritik,* Göttinger theologische Arbeiten 41 (Göttingen: Vandenhoeck & Ruprecht, 1989) passim, in particular 54, 72-75, 180 and FA 9, 827-831. In his "Eine Duplik" (FA 8, 505-586), published early in 1778 (FA 9, 1025), a response to an attack on Lessing by Johann Heinrich Reß (1732-1803), minister in Wolfenbüttel (FA 8, 475-503), Lessing used the image of a building whose presence belied the efforts of fools who would dig into its foundations to make sure the building was well constructed. (FA 8, 16- 17). See also Göbel, *Bild und Sprache* 196-219.

943 Allert, "Pluralisierung der Ringe" 120.

used in his *Laokoon* and *Paralipomena*. From this vantage point it is possible to explore the language-theoretical and visual-verbal aspects of Lessing's parable and to correlate them with Eco's semiotics.

## 3. Lessing and Metaphor

Hans Blumenberg and consequently Barbara Stafford have elaborated the plausible idea that it is through the metaphoricity of language that readers gain insights into the substructure of language, into the realm where images precede fixed concepts and definite endings, and where the construction of meaning is an unfinished process.[944] But in order to understand the metaphoricity of Lessing's parable, metaphor cannot be approached in terms of the traditional substitution model, as if it were a secondary language structure, a shortened simile, or derived from a previously fixed meaning. Instead, the approach used will be an interaction model of metaphor in which the meanings of metaphors depend entirely upon the context in which they are used. Furthermore, such metaphors resist paraphrasing because they do not just replace literal meanings.[945] While they depend on the specific situation in which they are used, their meaning is defined in terms of tradition, culture, and habit, even though any context may itself be metaphoric–which is the reason why any meaningful communication must take into account a variety of interacting elements and various framing devices.[946]

In *Eine Parabel* Lessing uses language not only as a fictionalized response to refute the real accusations by Goeze and as a way to defend himself in the religious and political battles at hand, but he also uses it as a commentary on language and communication itself. *Eine Parabel* addresses language itself by means of its own metaphoricity–as a way of checking itself by its own rhetorical underpinnings–or, to put

---

944 Blumenberg, *Paradigmen* 13 and *Paradigms* 5. Also see Stafford, *Body Criticism* 4-9.

945 On interaction models see the seminal essays by Max Black, "Metaphor," *Proceedings of the Aristotelian Society* 55 (1954-1955): 273-294 (Reprinted in Johnson, *Philosophical Perspectives on Metaphor*, 63-87) and "More about Metaphor," *Dialectica* 31 (1977): 431-457 (Rev. rpt.: Andrew Ortony, ed., *Metaphor and Thought*, 2nd ed. [Cambridge: Cambridge University Press, 1993], 19-41) and his book, *Models and Metaphors*. See the discussion of this work in Carl R. Hausman, *Metaphor and Art: Interactionism and Reference in the Verbal and Nonverbal Arts* (Cambridge: Cambridge University Press, 1989), especially the chapters on "Interactionism" (30-40) and "Max Black's Defense of Creative, Cognitive Insight" (83-88). Further, with reference to Black, *Models and Metaphors*, see Floyd Merrell, *Semiotic Theory of Texts*, Approaches to Semiotics 70 (Berlin: Mouton de Gruyter, 1985), Appendix II "Metaphor and Metonymy" 193-200.

946 Jonathan Culler warns against a simplistic use of the notion context by explaining "context is not given but produced; what belongs to a context is determined by interpretive strategies; contexts are just as much in need of elucidation as events; and the meaning of a context is determined by events. Yet when we use the term context we slip back into the simple model it proposes. Since the phenomena criticism deals with are signs, forms with socially-constituted meanings, one might try to think not of context but of the framing of signs: how are signs constituted (framed) by various discursive practices, institutional arrangements, systems of value, semiotic mechanisms?" *Framing the Sign: Criticism and its Institutions*, Oklahoma Project for Discussion and Theory 3 (Norman: University of Oklahoma Press, 1988), xiv.

it in Eco's terms as "a self-clarificatory system" of its own mechanisms.[947] Such related implicit processes work to construct Lessing's architecture, the palace to which his text refers, and consequently the levels of language that escape linearity. My investigation is limited to Lessing's model of language and communication as implicit in his narrative text. Since I approach *Eine Parabel* as a text about communication and miscommunication, it will be crucial to find out how to relate to the palace, what actions are needed to do so, and how to avoid misunderstandings which occur surrounding it. Indirect messages may be inductively gained from the narrator who indicates that in order to understand the architecture of the palace, one must enter it and that there is no outside meta-perspective.

The task is a paradoxical one: how can we enter the palace of language if we are already implicated in it the moment we use language? *Eine Parabel* is a text about a building with an unexpected architecture. It is a story about a palace that symbolizes the architecture of language in relation to the people who interact with it. It is a commentary about language from an inside perspective, a narrative on communication while being itself a part of communication. It is also about miscommunication and reflecting problems with multiple meanings and effects. Towards the end of the text we shall find out that the same words (such as "here" or "there") are being used almost arbitrarily while accompanied by gestures that are, however, pointed towards different locations. There are multiple voices that seem to repeat the same words but each time with a different meaning and never clearly understood. The problem of language in time and space is articulated from several points of view that reveal discrepancies between the verbal and the haptic and between literal meanings and metaphoric ones.

*Eine Parabel* begins: "Ein weiser tätiger König eines großen, großen Reiches, hatte in seiner Hauptstadt einen Pallast von ganz unermeßlichem Umfange, von ganz besonderer Architektur" (A wise active king in a large, large kingdom, had in his capital a palace of immeasurable size, of a very special architecture). This fairy-tale like narration is not about the subject of the king, but it is a story about a palace, its architecture, and people's responses to it. We know very little about the king, hardly anything, but the attributes "weise" and "tätig" characterize him as taking part in the activities related to the palace. The architecture is not only the grammatical object of the first sentence here, but most importantly the "object" of the narration and described with respect to the people that inter act with it. Attention is drawn to the specifics of its architecture: "Unermeßlich war der Umfang, weil er in selbern alle um sich versammelt hatte, die er als Gehülfen oder Werkzeuge seiner Regierung brauchte" (The size was immeasurable because in the same he had gathered everyone whom he needed as helpers or tools of his government). What characterizes this building is that its circumference is not measurable in any quantitative terms. It is located in a large realm ("großen, großen Reiche") in the indefinite space or a world of a detached fairy tale. The building does not easily lend itself to calculations. It cannot be estimated or understood immediately. The actual size of the palace or its greatness cannot be described in numbers or by any countable formula. It must be deduced rather in terms of "Gehülfen oder Werkzeuge" (helpers and tools) who are needed ("er ... brauchte"). The fire may destroy it if nobody comes to rescue. The building is not outside of

947 *Theory of Semiotics* 68–69.

society, not apart from daily business, not autonomous or free from necessity. It requires care-takers, perhaps such as us, the readers, to maintain it. There is a correlation between the power of the palace and what it is people do in it, a relationship that is interactive and dynamic. The palace is not a usual building: "Sonderbar war die Architektur: denn sie stritt so ziemlich mit allen angenommenen Regeln; aber sie gefiel doch, und entsprach doch" (Strange was the architecture because it fought pretty much with all accepted rules; but nevertheless it was likeable and appropriate). The specific features of this architecture, about which so far we know very little, are described indirectly, by mentioning the effect they have on the observer, astonishment, perhaps even bewilderment. The explanation links the palace and its understanding with cultural codes, habits, and expectations. If people find the architecture of the palace provoking or insulting, it is because the palace does not fit in its culture, its time. It conflicts with certain dominant norms while yet at the same time conforming to such classical ideals, simplicity and grandeur. The debate among the bystanders can be viewed as an interpretation of the palace that does not match the given context. It can furthermore be read as a much too narrow response by those who have adopted certain assumptions without ever questioning their arbitrariness. Lessing may indicate that such criticism of the architecture of the palace has to do with a lack of tolerance. We may wonder why people are not interested in something new they are not accustomed to. The implied narrator immediately shifts towards those who nevertheless find the architecture of the palace agreeable.

He explains: "Sie gefiel: vornehmlich durch die Bewunderung, welche Einfalt und Größe erregen, wenn sie Reichtum und Schmuck mehr zu verachten, als zu entbehren scheinen" (It was pleasing mainly through the admiration which simplicity and greatness can spark when one tends to despise richness and decoration more than to find it lacking). There is something cohesive or consistent about it, especially if one was inclined to despise pomp and overdone decoration rather than to miss such features. There are hints about an unusual logic of this architecture and about the fact that it resists—albeit for good reasons—the superficial glance. It is a building with its own non-habitual beauty ("aber sie gefiel doch, und entsprach doch"). The pleasure they experience with it, has—as the narrator adds—to do with its permanence and its comfort ("Dauer und Bequemlichkeit"). It is not a general stability which is associated with the duration and long-lasting existence of the palace itself, but it has to do with those being involved in the ongoing daily business, an interactive quality. "Sie entsprach: durch Dauer und Bequemlichkeit. Der ganze Pallast stand nach vielen vielen Jahren noch in eben der Reinlichkeit und Vollständigkeit da, mit welcher die Baumeister die letzte Hand angelegt hatten: von außen wenig unverständlich; von innen überall Licht und Zusammenhang" (It was adequate through persistence and comfort. The entire palace stood there after many, many years exactly with the same cleanliness and completeness as the building masters had given it with their final touches: from outside not very well understandable; from the inside everywhere light and connectivity). From the inside the building looks neat, attractive, and intact despite its long existence. Its "Baumeister" (architect or architects) or literally building master(s) must have put final touches on it.

Since the word "Baumeister" in German could be either singular or plural, we do not know how many builders contributed to the construction. There seems to be a certain understatement, something modest which does not need to be said that makes the palace apparently all the more convincing to the few at least. Its architecture speaks for itself, has a message that may not need translation. It may have to be understood in terms of its own medium, in the realm of the architecture, space. Something may not have to be said but rather seen. This difference is kept clear in the process of narration. The narrator seems to challenge notions of persuasion, advertisement, or ostensible messages. "Wealth" is located not in things we see but is documented when things go without saying, without announcement, when they please the observer. One may speculate that the narrator indicates in such a way that the palace due to its own beauty and logic needs no explanation. At the same time, it is paradoxically inferred that the palace will remain puzzling to those who do not enter. Clearly, seeing alone will also not be enough. While some observers find it "ein wenig unverständlich" (a bit incomprehensible) there is, as the narrator claims, "von innen überall Licht und Zusammenhang." This promise seems to draw the readers of this text, into its architecture, into an interaction with it, while "the object" (in Eco's sense), the palace, has turned into a "sign" for further interpretation.

Now we learn about the arguments of the critics as fictionalized already by Lessing in the parable itself: "Was Kenner von Architektur sein wollte, ward besonders durch die Außenseiten beleidiget, welche mit wenig hin und her zerstreuten, großen und kleinen, runden und viereckigen Fenstern unterbrochen waren; dafür aber desto mehr Türen und Tore von mancherlei Form und Gestalt" (Whoever wanted to be an expert in architecture was especially taken back by the outer sides which were interrupted by somewhat not very well distributed large and little, round and square windows; but there were all the more doors and entrances of all kinds of shape). Those who considered themselves as the authoritative experts were most offended by the facades, by the outsides which did not have as many windows as expected, but just a few, scattered here and there. While this apparent lack of windows seems to be compensated very well by the overabundance of doors. This seems to provoke even more criticism by those who find the various sizes of the few windows intolerable. This seems to go against established norms. We are told that there is enough light in the palace, although this might be surprising: "Man begriff nicht, wozu so viele und vielerlei Eingänge nötig wären, da ein großes Portal auf jeder Seite ja wohl schicklicher wäre, und eben die Dienste tun würde. Denn daß durch die mehrern kleinen Eingänge ein jeder, der in den Pallast gerufen würde, auf dem kürzesten und unfehlbarsten Wege, gerade dahin gelangen solle, wo man seiner bedürfe, wollte den wenigsten zu Sinne" (One did not comprehend why so many and so many kinds of entrances would be necessary since a large portal on each side certainly would have been more appropriate and would have served the same purpose).

The opening sentences contain presuppositions, information that is given by implication whether it is understood by these fictional observers or not.[948] The text thereby invites us, the readers, to be insiders who know more than most spectators

948 For the distinction between "ordinary" and "technical" usages of the word "presuppositions," see Eco, *The Limits of Interpretation* (Bloomington: Indiana University Press, 1990), 222-223 and his entire chapter titled "Presuppositions," 222-262. For example: "John met the man with the red hat" presupposes that there is a man with a red hat. Among the many presuppositions in Lessing's narrative are that enough light gets into the chambers,

of the palace. We are then among the minority to whom it makes sense that there is light inside. According to the narrator's own point of view, no further attention need be paid to the facades, to the outside of the palace, where the odd and funny-shaped windows may cause disapproval or unease to the traditional observers. The multiple chambers in the palace indicate that there are private spaces, that even from the inside not everything can be observed or grasped.[949] Considering the religious quarrels Lessing had with Goeze, this part of the parable could be linked with Lessing's insistence on personal beliefs, with freedom of the individual, and with a plea for tolerance and harmony that comes only from peaceful coexistence of those who differ, but who may nevertheless share insights and experiences. It is noteworthy that nobody in the palace can observe each room at once. Everything depends on a specific perspective and there is never any metaperspective described. There will always remain something out of sight. A more intimate knowledge of this building is required in order to comprehend its beauty and it is indicated as one of the main features of the palace that one must enter it, more than once, to learn how to understand its integrity.

## 4. Multiple entrances

While some critics of the building keep arguing that two portals would have served the same function as these many little entrances and been much more reasonable, the proposition of the sentence indicates that the architecture has its unique cohesive-

that there are enough windows, that the many entrances make sense, and that the architecture of the palace is reasonable although under attack by many critics.

949 This is an interesting counter-model compared with Jeremy Bentham's "Panopticon" which the English philosopher first published in 1791 in the form of 21 letters written from Russia in 1787 (*The Panopticon Writings*, ed. and intro. Miran Božovič, *Wo es War* (London: Verso, 1995), 29-95. As Jeffrey Garrett comments in his essay "Teichoscopy in the Wall Novels of Peter Schneider and Uri Orlev," Allert, ed., *Languages of Visuality* 215-225 at 220: "The Panopticon was a rotunda-shaped building offering an unobstructed view from a central tower into hundreds of rooms or cells arranged radically around it. Bentham lavished special attention on the creation of protected, mono-directional lines of sight." It has been commented upon not only as an apparatus of control as in the sense of Bentham, but also in terms of the principle of "panopticism" by Michel Foucault who used the expression as a form of domination which functions "as a pure architectural and optical system." See *Discipline and Punish: The Birth of the Prison*, trans. Alan Sheridan, 2nd Vintage ed. (New York: Vintage, 1995), at 205. Foucault applies the term also to notions of manipulative language that one could characterize as anti-metaphorical, anti-figurative, and monocausal. Garrett has strongly connected the control mechanism of the Panopticon as described by Bentham with an especially perverse aspect of Nazi language use, "the rejection of the figurative and, accompanying this, the revindication of the literal meaning of certain usually–very violent–idiomatic expressions" ("Teichoscopy" 221). Garrett refers to Karl Kraus who spoke of Nazi use of language as "Absage ans Bildliche and Revindication des Phraseninhalts." See Karl Kraus, *Die dritte Walpurgisnacht*, 2nd ed. (Munich: Kösel, 1955), 122. In a footnote Garrett adds: "It is clear that the Nazi's rejection of the figurative closely parallels their attitude towards abstract painting and other forms of non-representational art" ("Teichoscopy" 225). With respect to these relevant observations, Lessing's architecture of the palace in *Eine Parabel* is characterized by multi dimensionality and features that structurally counteract control and supervision.

ness. Each entrance has a specific meaning with respect to each person entering and working inside. Those who enter the building will each be able to reach their specific goal inside the building as quickly as possible. The multiple different entrances make, as the comment implies, perfect sense. Such sense-making is established in this narration as counter-logic to the expectations of the authorities on architecture. These authorities could be interpreted, aside from the context of the theological debate with Goeze, as the practitioners of the dominant discourse of the Enlightenment based on such expectations as linearity, immediate functionality which assumes analogies between purpose and means, goals and process.[950] They argue that one portal would have been sufficient for all and that these multiple entrances are inefficient. It does not seem economical or "reasonable" to the critics that the palace has "extra" entrances and offers each person a different way to go. At the same time, these features give the palace Lessing has in mind a special kind of efficiency focusing on the individuals and their distinct tasks that must be taken care of.[951] What is challenged here, are simplistic generalizations, the notion of binaries, and a thinking that characterizes symmetries and reductionist equations. These are features associated with dogmatism and perhaps even with the dominant Enlightenment discourse. Lessing's parable, however, opens a venue for with respect to multiple senses, shows that they are interrelated dynamically, even while they are quite different from each other.[952]

## 5. The dispute and the call for the blue prints

"Und so entstand unter den vermeinten Kennern mancherlei Streit, den gemeiniglich diejenigen am hitzigsten führten, die von dem Innern des Pallastes nie gesehen, die wenigste Gelegenheit gehabt hatten" (And thus among all the presumptuous experts much dispute came about, which was led most feverishly by those who had never

950 For the argument that Lessing's multi-directional use of language, his preference for metaphoric over linear discursive language, and his tendency towards open-endedness reveal a subversion of the dominant discourse of his time and that this makes it possible for Lessing to be regarded as one of the harshest critics of the Enlightenment while at the same time being one of its defining figures, see Allert, "Pluralisierung der Ringe" 115-116.

951 This observation reminds us perhaps of Lessing's statement in §91 of *Die Erziehung des Menschengeschlechts* "Es ist nicht wahr, daß die kürzeste Linie immer die gerade ist" (FA 10, 98). This clearly indicates Lessing's stance pro figurative language and criticizes the simplistic idea–which has often and generally too quickly been attributed to the Enlightenment discourse–that the principle of linearity could lend itself to an all-pervasive model of understanding.

952 This observation is related to Claudia Brodsky-Lacour's comment which has important semiotic implications that also apply to *Eine Parabel*: "Lessing's *Laokoon* seeks to defend the identity of the arts by questioning the equation of verb and image which, seeming to bestow riches, threatens to usurp the very ground of reception. Maintaining that ground may well prove critical to our understanding of current interpretive tendencies [...] More specifically, the non-mimetic understanding of language advanced in *Laokoon* contradicts a view of the conception of language in Lessing's entire century most widely promoted in our time by the schematic historicism of Foucault." See "Is that Helen? Contemporary Pictorialism, Lessing, and Kant," *Comparative Literature* 45.3 (Summer 1993): 230-57 at 234-235.

seen the palace from the inside or had least of an opportunity to experience it). The quarrels were fought most heatedly by those who lacked opportunities to actually see much of the inside of the palace. Although they cannot experience its core, this does not hinder them apparently from having much to say about the palace, establishing themselves in the process as the authorities about it. They have arrived at their truncated conclusions despite lack any personal verification of their ready-made opinions. The main issue here is not an individualizing perspective that would blame only these short-sided experts (or readers of Lessing's text themselves) but an understanding of more general or objective factors, such as the power of cultural codes, the impact of habits and circumstances, and the larger dynamics of how language carries ingrained thought-patterns. The text suggests that the judgment of these experts or self-made authorities would be better postponed and that these mechanisms and power structures should be brought to the surface.

There is yet another challenge to usual expectations noted: "Auch war da Etwas, wovon man bei dem ersten Anblicke geglaubt hätte, daß es den Streit notwendig sehr leicht und kurz machen müsse; was ihn aber gerade am meisten verwickelte, was ihm gerade zur hartnackigsten Fortsetzung die reichste Nahrung verschaffte. (Also there was something about which one would have thought upon first glance that it would make the dispute necessarily very simple and short; what had however entangled him most, what currently provided him richest fueling for its obnoxious continuation) . The parable continues: "Man glaubte nemlich verschiedne alte Grundrisse zu haben, die sich von den ersten Baumeistern des Pallastes herschreiben sollten; und diese Grundrisse fanden sich mit Worten und Zeichen bemerkt, deren Sprache und Charakteristik so gut als verloren war" (One believed to have various old blueprints which traditionally stemmed from the first building masters of the palace; and on these blueprints words and signs had been imprinted whose codes and characteristic meanings was practically lost).

None of the ground plans that these people possess is the original ground plan for the palace. There may have never been only a single most irrevocable one and if so it is now impossible to reconstruct once and for all, especially not in these circumstances when the building is burning.[953] The ground plans are diverse ("verschieden") as to origin and by any standards of demonstrable authenticity. They are inaccessible or obsolete.

As Walter Benjamin has reminded us: "Das Hier und Jetzt des Originals macht den Begriff seiner Echtheit aus" (The Here and Now of the original determines its authenticity).[954] The presumed ground plans are at best copies competing for authenticity. Their owners defend a believed authenticity. The desperation and intensity with which they fight for their position indicates insecurity on their part over the exact relationship of their particular ground plan to their imagined original. These owners fall victim to a phenomenon that Benjamin was subsequently to elucidate:

953 FA 9. 559:"—Möglich daß der Vater nun / Die Tyrannei des einen Rings nicht länger / In seinem Hause dulden wollen!—" (—It is possible that now the father did no longer wanted to tolerate the tyranny of one ring in his house—) (*Nathan der Weise* Act III, scene vii).

954 Walter Benjamin, "Das Kunstwerk im Zeitalter seiner technischen Reproduzierbarkeit," *Gesammelte Schriften,* ed. Rolf Tiedemann and Hermann Schweppenhäuser, 7 vols. in 14 (Frankfurt am Main: Suhrkamp, 1974-89), 1.2/3, 431-508, 983-1063 at 476.

> Die Echtheit einer Sache ist der Inbegriff alles von Ursprung her an ihr Tradierbaren, von ihrer materiellen Dauer bis zu ihrer geschichtlichen Zeugenschaft.[955]

> [The authenticity of something is the essence of everything traceable from its origin, from its material duration up to its historic accountability].

Those who claim to own these ground plans are faced with the dilemma of being unable to interpret the words and signs marked upon them. They cannot prove their originality. The inability to understand these words and signs make these ground plans rather obsolete or useless. They have no meaning divorced from the reality of the actual building. The intentions of the master builders, as legitimate as they may have been, cannot be applied retrospectively to the present. They are no longer applicable since the language of the words and signs that were marked on them are lost, extinct, at least as the present tense of the narration is concerned. These signs and words have become meaningless for an understanding of the palace today Lessing differentiates between the words and the signs found on the ground plans.[956] He emphasizes the fact that languages change, that words become outdated, and that the meanings of the same word are not always the same. Nor are the ways predictable or known so that one could access them from outside perspective.

## 6. Readings of Lessing's *Eine Parabel*

Heinz Politzer has drawn an analogy between Lessing and Kafka which has to do with the miscommunication about these ground plans.[957] While he bases his argument primarily on Lessing's "Ringparabel" in *Nathan der Weise*, I suggest that it nevertheless also applies to the passage at hand. I find that the "Ringparabel" and *Eine Parabel* are connected with respect to the loss of the original ring and the loss of the original ground plans. Politzer comments: "Schon Lessings Parabel ist ebenso bedeutsam durch das, was sie aussagt, wie das, worüber sie sich ausschweigt" (Lessing's *Eine Parabel* is already as meaningful through what it expresses as it is through what it keeps silent).[958] He finds that the importance of silence in Lessing's parables is what links Lessing and Kafka. In addition, he points out that the father in Lessing's parable of the ring does not know, as the father in Boccaccio's version of the parable (*Decameron* 1.3) still did, where the original ring disappeared when he had the copies made for his sons. It has been argued that with Lessing it is the use of the ring and not the ring itself which determines its meaning.[959] Likewise in *Eine Parabel* one might argue that the "original"

955 Benjamin, "Das Kunstwerk" 477.

956 Words are signs in the context in which they are used, but there are also wordless signs or signs of nonverbal characteristics that influence the reading of words. Since the language is gone, how can words be deciphered and how does Lessing's text here circumvent such a decoding by referring to a palace that has, in a way, replaced the ground plans not in any sense of substitution but rather in terms of a qualitative change, a leap from one space of signification to another?

957 References are to Politzer, "Lessings Parabel von den drei Ringen" (1958) as reprinted.

958 Politzer "Lessings Parabel" 347.

959 Allert, "Pluralisierung der Ringe" 114.

ground plan is lost and that there exist only copies, the meanings of which are not pre-given. We can no longer resort to lexically prescribed meanings of words, but must take each situation in which they are being used into account.

Karol Sauerland has made an interesting comparison also between Lessing and Kafka and refers in this context to Theodor Adorno's statement that it would have required only "der geringsten Akzentverschiebung" (the most minute shift of accents) in order to turn the parable by Lessing into one by Kafka.[960] Sauerland argues that in Lessing's *Eine Parabel* the palace represents rationality that has become so strong and powerful that it makes no sense any more trying to explore the ground plans which underlie its construction and functioning. And she adds: "Bei Lessing findet sich naturlich keine 'kleine Partei', die meint, daß es die Grundrisse überhaupt nicht gebe. Auf diesen Einfall kommt erst Kafka in bezug auf die Gesetze" (In Lessing one finds of course no 'small party 'that argues that there really don't exist any blue prints. This idea comes only with Kafka regarding such laws).[961] This seems to be contradicted by the text: "Nur wenige sagten: 'was gehen uns eure Grundrisse an?'" (Only a few said: 'How do your blue prints at all matter to us?) Sauerland writes that it makes no sense to be inquisitive and to search for the ground plans because rationality (represented by the palace) has become so "übermächtig" (overly powerful) "daß es sich nicht verlohnt, die Prinzipien, welche seinem Bau und Funktionieren zugrunde liegen, zu erforschen, aber die Draußenstehenden können es nicht lassen, immer wieder über sie nachzugrübeln" (that it is not worth it to explore the principles which underlie the building's architecture and functioning, but those standing outside it cannot let go of constantly pondering about it).[962] According to Lessing the original ground plans are presently lost and the search for them is fruitless and unnecessary. Now there is more than one copy and all of the existing versions seem equally right or wrong. What needs to be found or recreated through ethical action are rather the attributes or the qualities the ring, not the objects themselves. If everyone in the palace were to respond to the current emergency, a vital feature of the palace would be rescued as well.

## 7. An alternative account

There is a metaphorization process indicated in both parables. In the case of the "Ringparabel," it is the magic, the love by the people, and the peaceful understanding that would qualify a new emperor. Who it is will depend on the person wearing the ring and qualifications that will be documented by actions rather than the image of the ring itself.[963] In the case of *Eine Parabel* it is the insight, the cohesiveness, and especially

960 Sauerland, "Lessings Palast-Parabel" 458; Adorno,"Prismen," *Kulturkritik und Gesellschaft,* GS 10, vol. 1, 282. Adorno's discussion of the "Goezestreit" and response to Lessing's *Eine Parabel* can be found in §8 of "Aufzeichnungen zu Kafka", "Prismen," GS 10, 1: 254-287 at 278-283.

961 Sauerland, "Lessings Palast-Parabel" 459.

962 Sauerland, "Lessings Palast-Parabel" 459.

963 This metaphoric shift implies in the context of the "Ringparable" a multiplicity of co-existent meanings (more than one ring) and the problem of open-endedness. Recha, who symbolizes the incommensurable and the return of the repressed, indicates that the

the involvement with the actual palace that matters, not the search for the lost original ground plan(s), of which many diverse and arbitrary copies and reconstructions are circulating. There is clearly a shift from the importance of the flat paper of the initial ground plan towards that of a figurative three-dimensional building with people in a real life situation. This supersedes any diagrams, words, and one-to one significations; in fact, it makes them outdated and superfluous. As in the "Ringparabel" there is a shift or metaphoric move "von Zeichen und Bezeichnetem" (from sign and signified) to the use of those that carry the ring and to their ethical behavior. As I wrote in an earlier essay: "Der Ring besitzt seine Wunderkraft nicht von vornherein, sondern hängt ab vom Gebrauch des Trägers, vom Diskurs, in dem er eine interpretationsbedürftige Rolle spielt, die ihrerseits für die implizite Sprachtheorie Lessings ausschlaggebend ist. Verschoben wird die Aufmerksamkeit vom Was zum Wie, vom Sprecher zum Hörer, von der lexikalischen Bedeutung des Wortes zur metaphorischen" (The ring possesses its magical power not in a pre-given way, it rather depends on the use of its carrier, on the discourse in which it plays a role that needs to be interpreted and which itself is decisive for Lessing's language theory. Attention is shifted from what to how, from speaker to listener, from the lexical meaning of the word to the metaphoric).[964]

A similar shift of attention is expressed, I think, in Lessing's *Eine Parabel* where the dilemma of the quarrel about the palace is not only a problem of the apparent loss of an object. What also matters is the context of a given "language" and the narration continues with the remark that the quarrel is reinforced by those who pretend and claim "to own" these ground plans, those who act as if they alone possessed whatever truth may be. While bystanders and spectators of the fire want to put an end to the uncomfortable debate by imposing their appropriated answers, they actually prolong the battle, thus undermining the peace. They are making the palace into an object of contention. They insist that everyone else should adopt their own private logic or answer to where the ground plans may be. In doing so words are nothing but contributing factors for the intensifying lack of communication and the continued destruction of the palace. They ignore the need to do something about the fire. It is ironic to read in these abstract terms about a problem with false generalizations and with ideas of what may be private, separate rooms that all belong to the palace. The quarrels of the bystanders distort the matter at hand and have irritating effects leading to nothing but the postponement of desperately needed ethical action.

---

overlooked queen in the chess game has consequences for Saladin. He does not win the game this time but his sister Sittah does. Similarly the exclusion of the female in Nathan's *Ringparabel* (there seem to be only three sons) may lead to a metaphoric resurfacing of such a key figure on another level of signification. Rüdiger Zymner interprets Lessing's Ringparabel as "Kunst-Apotheose," or as a celebration and a defense of art. See on a related argument Rüdiger Zymner, "'Der Stein war ein Opal ...' Eine versteckte Kunst-Apotheose in Lessings morgenländischer Ringparabel?" *Lessing Yearbook* 24 (1992): 77-96.

964 See my earlier essay "Pluralisierung der Ringe" 114. Not only does Lessing emphasize the importance of the usage of words (or "rings"), his three-dimensional model draws attention to numerous users of language or the *interpretants* (in the sense of semiotics according to Eco). Compare Eco, *Theory of Semiotics* 14-16, Floyd Merrell, *Semiotic Theory of Texts* 114-120, *Semiosis in the Postmodern Age* (West Lafayette: Purdue University Press, 1995), 176-210, and Peirce's *Semiotics Now: A Primer* (Toronto: Canadian Scholar's Press, 1995), 3-14. These offer interesting ramifications concerning related processes of verbal signification.

The next step in the narration is to illustrate the various attempts to explain words and signs: "Ein jeder erklärte sich daher diese Worte und Zeichen nach eignem Gefallen. Ein jeder setzte sich daher aus diesen alten Grundrissen einen beliebigen Neuen zusammen." (Everyone thus explained these words and signs according to their own pleasure. One of them composed from these old blue prints a new arbitrary one). Words and signs have been taken out of their context, their extensions have been ignored. The owners who are not only fooled into ignoring extensions act as theorists, but also into assigning meaning arbitrarily to the signs on their own individual whim. The people have repressed and forgotten that the constructed ground plans they came up with reflect nothing but self-invented versions of a much larger puzzle. Instead of acknowledging their own framing devices, they take the plans falsely for the object signified, not just as a sign and they therefore commodify the result.[965] Such arbitrary notions of truth are then forced upon others which then would lead to an invasion of privacy, of space, and as the misuse of certain codes or keys that were picked up by the wrong users. This is apparently how the majority of people claim to be right about the palace: by insisting on the ownership of ground plans the authenticity of which cannot be verified. Attention is drawn to mechanisms of turning words and texts into commodities.[966]

Then perspective is shifted again from a majority to a minority, a few who question the relevance of these inaccurate or arbitrarily invented and superimposed ground plans: "Nur wenige sagten: was gehen uns eure Grundrisse an? Dieser oder ein andrer: sie sind uns alle gleich. Genug, daß wir jeden Augenblick erfahren, daß die gütigste Weisheit den ganzen Pallast erfüllet, und daß sich aus ihm nichts, als Schönheit und Ordnung und Wohlstand auf das ganze Land verbreitet" (Only a few said: what do your blue prints matter to us? One or another, they are all the same to us. It is enough that we experience in each moment that the most generous wisdom fills the entire palace and that nothing but beauty and order and wellbeing radiates from it across the entire region). A few understand the arbitrarily and historically changing meanings of the ground plans and realize that such blueprints are in a way all the same. They have more important things to do than getting preoccupied with them. Each moment they work in the palace, they actually experience something beautiful and agreeable ("die gütigste Weisheit den ganzen Pallast erfüllet"). Action offers insights to them, even though they were not liked by those who had little actual knowledge of

---

965 What the parable challenges here is the positivist equation of words and facts.

966 See Drucilla Cornell's chapter on Charles S. Peirce's analysis of semiotics in: *Transformations: Recollective Imagination and Sexual Desire* (New York: Routledge, 1993), 23–44. It addresses the institutionalization and internalization of meaning as habitual structures of thought that are often taken for granted as representational schema. She characterizes Peirce's description of the self in this context as anti-individualist. One might point out with respect to Lessing that also the most appropriate rationality in *Eine Parabel* is not represented by any totality, but also not just by any one person alone, it is rather a minority. Otherness plays a decisive role. And Cornell's closing statement of her chapter is: "Charles Peirce's pragmatism, which I defend, does precisely that: it stops circumscribing the *nomos* and invites us to new worlds" (*Transformations* 44). Or, to quote Eco: "To choose Nomos against Physis meant to disregard all the cases of onomatopoeia, not to speak of syntactic iconism. To choose Physis against Nomos meant to disregard all the cases of blatant arbitrariness, that is, the majority of linguistic terms." Umberto Eco, *Limits of Interpretation* 219.

the palace. This split is expressed by the narrator in the following terms: "Sie kamen oft schlecht an, diese Wenigen! Denn wenn sie lachenden Muts manchmal einen von den besondern Grundrissen em wenig näher beleuchteten, so wurden sie von denen, welche auf diesen Grundriß geschworen hatten, für Mordbrenner des Pallastes selbst ausgeschrien." (Those few were often not at all welcomed by the others! Whenever they with a bold courage illuminated one those these so-called blueprints a little more closely they were considered by those why had sworn that these were true as if they were accused to be the arsonist). The conflict apparently escalates among the spectators, the mob. Those who actually shed light on one or the other ground plan get shouted down by those who had sworn on their own ground plan and act as if setting fire on the palace.

It is clear that such false accusations have nothing to do with the reality of the context but also that both sides in this quarrel made mistakes. The narrator of Lessing's parable actually takes side with those what apparently have done nothing and whose work has been misunderstood.[967] The text goes on with the comment that the few were not affected by this and became most skillful in doing their work in correlation with the palace and the tasks at hand: "sie kehrten sich daran nicht, und wurden gerade dadurch am geschicktesten, denjenigen zu gesellet zu werden, die innerhalb des Pallastes arbeiteten, und weder Zeit noch Lust hatten, sich in Streitigkeiten zu mengen, die für sie keine waren" (they were not affected by this and became the most skillful, exactly because they were among those working within the palace and had no time or any inclination to mingle with quibbles, which for them were nothing). The common misunderstanding which is revealed in this part of the parable concerns a need for realizing the so-called fire, the erosive or self-illuminating power of language. It works most destructively if ignored or levels of referentiality are not clearly distinguished. In a sense, what Lessing calls for, is awareness for what Eco describes in terms of "extensions." These link aesthetics with ethics and require attention to non-verbal aspects that are also integral to speech acts. But as we shall see in Lessing's parable, most people respond to this message about the fire in ways that are not appropriate in the context. This requests careful attention and further analysis.

967 There are two interesting different accounts of the fire in Lessing's work. Peter Heller in his "Postscript: Fire" to *Dialectics and Nihilism: Essays on Lessing, Nietzsche, Mann and Kafka* (Amherst: University of Massachusetts Press, 1966), 59-68 juxtaposes "with due allowance for the simplification and exaggeration," the fire-worshiper Lessing with Goethe, "the Neptunist ... not sympathetic to fire"(59) and links Lessing with Heraclitus and with the Nietzsche of the "Ecce Homo" poem (#62) in *Die Fröhliche Wissenschaft*, "Flamme bin ich sicherlich!" (Friedrich Nietzsche, *Die Fröhliche Wissenschaft*, *Werke*, ed. Schlechta 2: 7-274 at 232. Ehrhard Bahr, "Die Bild- und Sinnbereiche von Feuer," comments that this positive symbolism of fire may be correct with respect to *Eine Parabel* but that it is contradicted by *Nathan der Weise* where the symbolism of water is treated much more favorably than that of fire.

## 8. On how to process the message "Feuer! Feuer in dem Pallaste!"

In the last part of *Eine Parabel*, we read more about the responses to the fire alarm in the palace: "Einstmals, als der Streit über die Grundrisse nicht so wohl beigelegt, als eingeschlummert war,–einstmals um Mitternacht erscholl plötzlich die Stimme der Wächter: Feuer! Feuer in dem Pallaste!" (Once upon a time, when the struggle about the blueprints was put aside or dormant–once at midnight all of a sudden the sound of the guard shouted 'fire', 'fire in the palace'). And the narrator tells us the effect this alarm had: "Und was geschah? Da fuhr jeder von seinem Lager auf; und jeder, als wäre das Feuer nicht in dem Pallaste, sondern in seinem eignen Hause, lief nach dem Kostbarsten, was er zu haben glaubte,–nach seinem Grundrisse. Laßt uns den nur retten! dachte jeder. Der Pallast kann dort nicht eigentlicher verbrennen als er hier stehet!'" (And what happened? Then everybody jumped up from their resting place and everyone, as if the fire was not in the palace, but in their own house, ran for the most valuable things they believed they had,–everyone for their own blueprint. Let us only save that! everyone thought. The palace cannot burn more literally anywhere else than here). In German the distinction between literal and metaphoric has often been associated with "eigentlich" as the literal sense and "uneigentlich" as the derived or metaphoric one.[968] This terminology is now reversed since, first of all, the palace is not only to be understood in its literal meaning, as an object one should look at. It is a symbol itself which needs further elucidation. Second, if the ground plans were to be taken as indices pointing towards the palace, they would have to represent the original ground plans for the palace. But as we have already learned in the parable, this assumption is taken as false or fragmentary to say the least. There is no directly visible similarity between these ground plans and the palace. The fact that people run home to rescue their ground plans from the fire instead of running to the palace where the actual fire seems to be, mocks any simplistic common assumption about mimetic relations between the visual and the real, or between the verbal and the credible. The visual image (ground plans) and the text (about the palace and the fire) have gone separate ways and their logic has become disjointed. The expectation of mimetic representation is linked in this text with a problem of fixation: when people believe to own meanings (ground plans), to possess originals, they are preoccupied with their own small notion of text and cannot take part in reality where fire alarm means, even if this is part of a text itself, that one should best run where the fire is more likely to be. By making false equations between their visual diagrams and the actual object of narration, those who misunderstand the fire alarm in Lessing's narration have forgotten the pragmatic dimension that Eco so succinctly emphasizes. When confronted with the communication your house has burned down, Eco considers those people to be wise

968 What happens here in Lessing's parable as a response to the fire alarm cannot be adequately interpreted in terms of the substitution model of metaphor or in terms of the early semiology that drew the line between signs and signifiers. What we need is the notion of a third point of reference that would help us make the connection not only between index and symbol, but also the interpretants implied. It is not enough to argue that the misunderstanding in Lessing's parable comes from the reversal between the "eigentlich" (literal) and the "uneigentlich" (metaphoric) or reality (palace) and text (ground plans).

who actually check whether or not the statement is true. They must go home and see whether it concerns them personally or not. The pragmatic response is to run home regardless of whether or not one is falling into what he calls "the extensional fallacy." But in Lessing's parable this is not what happens. Those who receive the message "Fire in the palace" run not to the palace, but to their homes–which are not in danger–each to consult their individual (and different) ground plan in order to speculate on where it might be that the palace burns. Those who think they have to run to find their ground plans when the palace is burning are wasting valuable time. They are stuck with a distorted logic of causality having made the ground plans into fixed formulas and commodities, clinging to the notion that somehow they are more real than the actual palace. Instead they should understand the logic of effects, of multiple senses, and respond in a way that is more "eigentlich."[969]

Seeing is not enough. When a building is burning, looking alone will not help. And when there is smoke there must not always be fire. Numerous options are possible. What is lacking here is a translation (in the sense Eco uses this term) from one sense to another. The alarm they hear does not get processed beyond verbalness, beyond a fixation on logocentricity (or pure code) as long as "extensions" in the sense of Eco are not taken into account. Lessing makes us read the parable already against the grain and shows that not only the distinctions between categories can get reversed. Yet Eco adds that the hypostatization of indexes into semiotic objects has potentially fatal results. Since the dynamic of the communication process is blocked by the arbitrary objectification as shown, words that are now treated as objects, are mistakenly protected at all costs. It seems to me that the palace embodies the metaphoric, the three-dimensional, the interactional, whereas the ground plans the literal, two-dimensional, and static. One must forget about the ground plans for the moment when rescuing the palace from the fire is the first matter of urgency.

According to a substitution model of metaphor–which is here challenged by Lessing's implied interaction model–it is not even enough to think that the ground plans represent mimetically the intentions of the master builders. The original ground plans are lost and the made up copies are misunderstood to represent the reality of the palace itself. It cannot be emphasized enough that, according to Lessing, the ground plans have actually very little to do with the palace and are only falsely linked with it by the miscommunicating interpreters in his narration. The metaphoric with respect to the palace cannot be relegated to any concept of analogy, substitution, replacement, or abbreviated simile. The meaning we are looking for as readers of Lessing's parable cannot get more real, more actual, or more eigentlich, (essential) than the building of the palace; the ground plans on the other hand indicate assumptions, prejudices, and can well be forgotten. Lessing's narrative continues:

> Und so lief ein jeder mit seinem Grundrisse auf die Straße wo, anstatt dem Pallaste zu Hilfe zu eilen, weil einer dem andern es vorher in seinem Grundrisse zeigen wollte, wo der Pallast

969 The word *eigentlich* in German has been associated with language in the sense of the literal, whereas *uneigentlich* has been connected with the metaphoric. On the problematics of these terms in the context of Lessing, who advances the metaphoric to a position of Firstness, and the debate between Goeze and Lessing, which also has to do with a Naturalist on one side and a Fabulist on the other, see especially Althaus, *Das Uneigentliche ist das Eigentliche* 48–117.

> vermutlich brenne. Sieh, Nachbar! hier brennt er! Hier ist dem Feuer am besten beizukommen.–Oder hier vielmehr, Nachbar; hier!–Wo denkt ihr beide hin? Er brennt hier!–Was hat es für Not, wenn er da brennte? Aber er brennt gewiß hier!–Lösch ihn hier, wer da will. Ich lösch ihn hier nicht!–Und ich hier nicht.–Und ich hier nicht!–
>
> [And so everyone ran with their blueprint into the street instead of coming to help the palace, because everyone wanted to be first to show the others first where in their own plan the palace might be burning. Look neighbor! Here it burns! One could best get to the fire this way.–Or rather, here, neighbor here!–What do you both think? It burns here! I cannot distinguish it here!–And I not here!–And I not here!–].

This passage indicates numerous dialogue partners coming from different directions. It cites various voices. Their words are identical ("Er brennt hier!") (It burns here!) but they are all pointing at something else. This constellation make us reflect upon the fact that even such a simple word as "hier" (here) refers to different locations each time with respect to each speaker's perspective. These spectators in the parable seem to ignore the reality of the addressee. Nobody seems to respond in action to the emergency of the palace on fire. Lessing illustrates how "here" is already a sign with meanings that are completely contextual. The same sentence can point to different directions. "Here" could be anywhere on anyone's speculative or mental map. The protest by those who say: "Und ich hier nicht!" (And I am not here) adds little clarification since "here" could be anywhere, including somewhere we cannot see. All we know is that the "here" of one voice is not the "here" of another. The voices seem strangely removed from the scene and lack true compassion to help extinguish the fire. The inactivity of these bystanders seems to illustrate the ignorant readers who do not realize that they must actively participate in the construction of meaning. Lessing's text may also express a certain helplessness considering the vast scale of possible readings when it comes to truly decipher so-called visuality. He now calls for more than a disinterested neutral gaze.

## 9. Optical illusion? Critical reflections

The final sentences in Lessing's *Eine Parabel* reverses expectations by readers that may now have been provoked: "Über diese geschäftigen Zänker hätte er denn auch wirklich abbrennen können, der Pallast; wenn er gebrannt hätte.–Aber die erschrocknen Wächter hatten ein Nordlicht für eine Feuersbrunst gehalten" (Because of these busy bickerers the palace could have really burnt down.–However, the frightened guards had erroneously taken the northern lights for a burning fire). The parable which had begun in a fairy tale idiom now ends with *Eucatastrophe*.[970]

It turns out that the palace is actually not on fire. It was perhaps a false alarm, an optical illusion. The potentially tragic consequences of peoples' inactions have been

970 "But the 'consolation' of fairy-tales has another aspect than the imaginative satisfaction of ancient desires. Far more important is the Consolation of the Happy Ending. Since we do not appear to possess a word that expresses this.–I will call it *Eucatastrophe*" (J. R. R. Tolkien, *On Fairy-stories. Expanded Edition*, ed. Verlyn Flieger and Douglas A. Anderson (London: HarperCollins, 2008), 75.

voided for once. Yet relying on false readings of what they have seen is nevertheless a risk that remains. Lessing seems to have turned the outcome of the plot in his parable around for a less threatening ending yet he gives us a problematic view about what the current condition of communication via language may be like. An answer to the question of whether or not there was a fire has not been completely circumvented.[971] The main issue at hand is the problem of communication when even seeing correctly is nothing at all given. Lessing's parable about the palace, its architecture, the fire alarm, and the effects of each one of these elements in his narration on people examines what could happen if *extensions* were being ignored, if ground plans were not understood as indices but as fixed objects or commodities. Lessing uses this parable to defend metaphoric language. These he detaches from traditional notions of mimetic representation. His parable offers multiple interpretations but it strongly argues against the conflation of the senses and against determinacy, stasis, and linearity. Lessing insisted: "Ich kenne keinen blendenden Stil, der seinen Glanz nicht von der Wahrheit mehr oder weniger entlehnet. Wahrheit allein giebt echten Glanz; und muß auch bei Spötterei und Posse, wenigstens als Folie, unterliegen" (I do not know any brilliant style that does not borrow its brilliance more or less from truth itself. Only truth gives it a real brilliance and it must, even when used in mockery and for fun, form the basic matrix).[972] Lessing consistently draws attention to stylistic matters, to rhetorics, and to metaphoricity in language, the context here and now. Physicality matters more than any mindsets. Yet nevertheless not every truth is visible. Content and form, message, and the specific situation in which it is being used, are not separable. The use of words as metaphors and the use of Lessing's parable itself are not simply attempts to escape a notion of positivistic facticity in language and to bring to awareness the limitations of prescriptive use of words when what he sees requires more immediate attention.

971 The extent to which Lessing's parable was misunderstood, willfully or otherwise, can be seen in the "counter-parable," "Fragment eines Gesprächs" by Johann Salomo Semler (1725-1791), Professor of Theology in Halle, and published in 1779 (FA 9, 1346-1350). Lessing had published *Eine Parabel* to answer Goeze's attack on him for editing the fragments from Reimarus. Semler attacks Lessing for the same reason and also in the language of a parable involving a building and a fire. Sir John Bowling denies to the Lord Mayor of London that he is an arsonist. According to this story, Sir John had by chance one afternoon discovered a candle in a house left carelessly burning and worried that it could be dangerous if left unattended. He thinks to avoid the danger of having a fire break out at night by throwing the candle into a pile of straw at that very moment, thus relying upon the excellent London fire brigade to extinguish the fire immediately. The fire department proves successful. The Lord Mayor orders that Sir John be committed to Bedlam, the insane asylum. Semler says that Lessing in publishing this material has acted the same way as Sir John and that he too should be committed to an asylum. Lessing jotted down a response to Semler first published posthumously in 1784. It includes the following: "Nun bin ich mit dem großen Tollhause, in welchem wir alle, mein Herr Doktor, leben, zu wohl bekannt, als daß es mich besonders schmerzen sollte, wenn die Tollhäusler der mehrern Zahl mich gern in ein eigenes Tollhäuschen sperren mochten" (Now I am with the great mad-house, in which we all live, my dear doctor; too well known that it would particularly hurt me if the greater part of the asylum inhabitants would really like to lock me up in their little madhouse ("Gegen Johann Salomo Semler" FA 9, 719). See further Joachim Bark, "Brandstifter Reimarus," Mauser and Saße, ed., *Streitkultur* 147-156 at 149 and Althaus, *Das Uneigentliche* 50.

972 "Anti Goeze 2," FA 9, 149-154 at 150-151.

It makes us consciously participate in the actions and possibly precarious events concerning the palace of language.[973]

Does Lessing impose a harmonizing ending by interpreting the fire as an optical illusion? Is he returning to ancient sources according to which the smoke rescued people from being seen by those who want to harm them? [974] Or does he challenge the dominant discourse of the Enlightenment that made that what is observed into that which is the most real? Does this text anticipate a critique of logo-centricity and imago-centricity, concepts which are perhaps presupposed by the majority of people in his narrative? I think that this ending offers a rhizomic causality, a multilinear logic.[975] While the palace could have burned and the point is made clear how inappropriate the search for the ground plans would have been, the palace itself seems to be a phantom, a sign for something else, and so it is the fire which in the end can do no harm. What is at stake, however, is the problem of referentiality and attention is shifted again to the observers, the readers, and the actions in the construction of meaning. *Eine Parabel* is similar to Eco's about processing the message "your house has burned down" in that it too is concerned with effects and responses rather than with a chain of arguments in terms of mono-causality. There are multiple effects and applications rather than the search of lost ground plans. Both narratives are commentaries on miscommunications that result from false assumptions, ignored extensions, or reversed dynamics. They address the problem of the socially ingrained norms that underlie language, sense perception, or behavioral patterns. Those who did not run home to the meanings they believed to own, may be seen as the same

---

973 On Lessing's style see Jürgen Schröder, *Gotthold Ephraim Lessing* 73–105. Peter Michelsen, "Lessing, mit den Augen Goezes gesehen," Mauser and Sasse, ed. *Streitkultur* 378–391 at 380. Lessing's responded to Goeze's criticism of the inappropriate metaphoricity of his language with statements such as: "Also von der, von der Wahrheit lassen Sie uns sprechen, und nicht vom Stil" (Also let us speak about it, about the truth, and not about style). "Anti-Goeze 2," FA 9, 151.

974 Deena E. Grant, "Fire and the Body of Yahweh." *Journal for the Study of the Old Testament vol* 40.2 (2015): 139–161. In the *Old Testament* of the Hebrew Bible "Yahweh's holy of holiest houses" is "not a cult image of the deity but rather an arc and two cherubim (Exod 99.1; 132.7). Yahweh himself is represented aniconically in the empty space between the cherubim and above the arc (Exod 25.22). The aversion to iconism evident in the Bible is implied in Israel's archeological record as well." (139–140). Lessing was probably familiar with this important source my graduate student Ryan Buss has brought in a recent class discussion to my attention. Lessing may have used the smoke to draw attention to the invisible but nonetheless powerful interactions between and beyond the humans. As Deena E. Grant put it: "Yahweh nourishes, protects amd guides his people. Similarly, to get too close to Yaheweh is not only prohibited, but potentially lethal" (161).

975 Gilles Deleuze and Felix Guattari, *A Thousand Plateaus: Capitalism and Schizophrenia,* trans. Brian Massumi (Minneapolis: University of Minnesota Press, 1987), esp. 3–25, introduced the term rhizomic into current critical discourse. Merrell explains the semiotic relevance of the rhizome metaphor compared to the semiological metaphor of bifurcating tree branches: "Within a rhizome, connectedness is nonlinear. Everything is connected to everything else in converging, diverging, involuted, convoluted curves and tangles incessantly doubling back on themselves in a finite but unbounded sphere of self-reference" He adds: "Tree structures are branching and *bi*-nary; rhizome structures are *n*-ary. At each juncture of the former there is a choice between *this* or *that*; each point in the latter is connected to all other points by lines in all directions and where the next move will take one nobody knows."

as those wise ones in Eco's narrative who check whether the message received is true or false. There exist for both, Eco and Lessing, limits of interpretation and it makes no sense trying to resort to a model of pre-given ground plans when we are dealing with life situations and multilinear, rhizomic causalities. At the same time, both Eco and Lessing emphasize the active role of the reader and the importance of the Here and Now. Lessing's parable warns us not to be fooled and makes us realize that the construction of truth is an ongoing process, requiring immediate and careful action, and that communication involves a process not any less intricate than the unlimited semiosis that Eco defines as the distinguishing characteristic of a semiotic theory of signs. In the context of Lessing, the search for a correct reading of signs, be they visual and verbal, is a challenging and never completely ending task. It requires careful attention to the possible contexts and the exact but often elusive timing of suggested images and words.

# Chapter 13
# *Nathan the Wise* (1779): The Search for the Ring and the Missing Queen in the Chess Game

Abstract: Lessing's final play *Nathan der Weise* was published 1779 only three years before the author's death. It has remained immensely popular ever since and remains obligatory on almost all standard reading lists in German and European literary studies. There are many interpretations and a vast scholarly literature associated with it. What interests me in the context of this study on visual-verbal dynamics is merely how Lessing uses a word or an object such as the ring to highlight meanings that are associated with by means of metaphor and metonymy. It is all about the timeliness of meaning. Although we may have reasons to know what a word means, whether or not we have found that meaning depends on the specific context in which it is being used. Lessing provides as a key to understanding this entire drama by offering a *Parabasis*, an intertext that summarizes and mirrors in a way the entire action of the play. It is about finding a ring which is lost for now but has symbolic meaning. He provides a brief *Märchen* or fairy tale within the drama which appears to offer a solution or remedy in the long run. It makes us reflect on methodology and on the entire action of the play. Whereas the play appears to have an open ending because of the unfinished search for the ring, this parable reflects on the ring not as an object but rather as something that could be recreated for its associated attributes that then in turn might lead to recovery of the meaningful quest. Although all of three sons of the late emperor demonstrate by their actions and because of the lack of peace, love, and human compassion in the world that none of them have the genuine ring, there seems to be only one remedy, namely the active reconstruction of the ring's initial attributes. If these were practiced in real life, then that would indicate that anyone who could exercise the power of the ring's attributes, namely peace and love and other ideal characteristics that the father was once said to have had, must be the legitimate heir. The idea of searching for an actual ring shifts in the course of events to a search for the attributes associated with it. This has consequences for Lessing's approach to the loss attributed also to the process of Ekphrasis, and it will be our task as readers and, at least metaphorically speaking, spectators of this text, to reconstruct the meaning of the vision even if only indirectly.

## 1. The play and what matters here

*Nathan der Weise* (1779) is Lessing's most famous work.[976] The play is subtitled "ein dramatisches Gedicht" (a dramatic poem), turning attention from the major presenta-

976 Its reception history has well been documented by Hans-Friedrich Wessels, *Lessings* Nathan der Weise (Königstein im Taunus: Athenäum, 1979). See the first part of the book on

tion of actions and realized events onstage to the less obvious incidents presented via poetic images on the side. Some of the most important elements of the play are shown metonymically, through moments of introspection and outside commentaries that offer a meta-perspective to everything told. There are interesting textures of interconnected underlying mentalities that activate the plot for a variety of readings. What matters are in Lessing's own words, the "Sprungfedern" (coiled springs) of the senses that are located in emotions, beliefs, and forces. These motivate and drive all the passions. What characterizes the play further are an extended beginning and an extended ending. There are additional components of the action to imagine that exceed the horizon as shown onstage.

Between these flexible boundaries of beginning and ending the play presents a cohesive plot. It points to the essence of historical yet untimely events, the pogrom against the Jewish people which killed Nathan's wife and his children. Such tragic events are hidden from the view of the spectators yet referred to and then left to the spectators own historic memory. Nathan seems to have dealt with his trauma proactively since he then adopted his step daughter Recha. It is she, however, who also in the opening scene is said to have been almost burnt alive in a fire when Nathan's house almost burnt down while he was away on business. Recha is saved but the play is not only about Nathan's private sphere. It has a broad socio-political dimension and has often been cited as a document for Lessing's multi-culturalism since the final scenes of the play make us project the possibility of harmony among various cultures. It is up to the public to think about yet so far unrealized future consequences of the play's conclusion. What is needed is peaceful action symbolized by the "Ringparable." This intertext is based on Boccaccio's *Decameron*. A ring has been lost in the process of being passed down through numerous generations. Because a father loved his three sons equally, he had copies of the ring made for them. But in the meantime, the original has been lost. The original ring bestows peace and harmony, so its loss is highly symbolic. The original ring must be found again in the future despite the odds and despite the behavior of political leaders who fight against each other senselessly.

The play begins in the aftermath of a fire that has burnt down Nathan's house in his absence. What has happened during his business trip depends on who is talking, their experiences, memories, and ways of thinking and how they process these events cognitively. Nathan is relieved to find out through the maid Daja that his Recha has

"Verbreitung, Aufnahme und Wirkung (1779-1781)," 8-87, followed by "Von Lessings Tod bis Friedrich Schlegel" (88-149), and chapter 6 on the reception after Friedrich Schlegel plus the excursions into the reception history and historical contexts that establish Lessing's play as canonical in the context of critical discourses that made tolerance into a desirable virtue and stipulated ideals of humanity. Also see Thomas Dreßler, *Dramaturgie der Menschheit–Lessing* (Stuttgart: Metzler, 1996); Jonathan M. Hess, *Germans, Jews and the Claims of Modernity* (New Haven: Yale University Press, 2002); Angelika Overath, Navid Kermani, Robert Schindel. *Toleranz: Drei Lesarten zu Lessings Märchen vom Ring* (Göttingen: Wallstein, 2003); Karl-Josef Kuschel, *"Jud, Christ und Muselmann vereinigt"? Lessings* Nathan der Weise (Düsseldorf: Patmos, 2004) and Monika Fick, *Lessings* Nathan der Weise *und das Bild vom Orient und Islam in Theatertexten aus der zweiten Hälfte des 18. Jahrhunderts*, Wolfenbüttler Vortragsmanuskript 29 (Wolfenbüttel: Lessing Akademie, 2016).

survived the fire.[977] His grief at his losses is relieved by the news that she lives allowing him to embrace life again in the shadow of his own earlier traumatic experiences in which he lost his own wife and children in an anti-Jewish pogrom, information that is revealed through *teichoscopy*, in dialogue and retrospection and through narration and report. Recha been saved; she is now well and can relax. But she has to learn how to let go of her trauma. It is not enough to thank angels and otherworldly forces but, as Nathan insists, she must acknowledge the person who helped her because that person deserves acknowledgement and reward for his brave actions. The problem is that she only remembers having seen "the wings of an angel" carrying her from the flames of the fire to safety. But this experience makes sense only when she lets go of her fantasy that what she thought were angelic wings were actually the sleeves of the white tunic worn by the person, a Knights Templar, who rescued her. But it is not only Recha who has difficulties letting go of an image for the sake of concrete action. Her rescuer as well, the Templar, has difficulties acknowledging what he did and accepting any communication with Nathan who in his eyes is a non-person belonging to another culture and religion. The Templar is Christian, Nathan is Jewish. There are significant barriers that have to be overcome before effective communication is possible.

Hans Mayer presented Lessing less as a cultural hero than a figure in whose work it became possible to imagine diverse cultural identities.[978] Jonathan Hess puts it succinctly in arguing that this play is about how, "to decipher the 'antinomies of Jewish emancipation'."[979] We may trace ambiguities of tolerance in Lessing's work. Some critics have argued that it is after all too lofty and too malleable a defense of Jews since it merely promotes the idea of a noble wise Jew, who is, after all human. His Jewishness, as has later been much debated, seems to be of an assimilated kind, perhaps compromised in favor of an abstract vision of humanity, despite the fact that the main character in the play, Nathan the Wise, seems modeled after Lessing's Jewish friend Moses Mendelssohn. Such a vision and possible shortcomings are also discussed in Ritchie Robertson's book *The "Jewish Question" in German Literature, 1749-1939.* He furthermore illustrates that there are new interesting interventions by Jewish intellectuals in response to Lessing's trajectory and I agree with him that it would not be adequate to just call the play *Nathan the Wise* "too malleable" or "lofty" as Adam Sutcliffe put it.[980]

---

977 Daniel Müller Nieleba, "'Die arme Recha, die indes verbrannte!' Zur Kombustibilität der Bedeutung in Lessings Nathan der Weise," Eva J. Engel and Claus Ritterhoff, ed. *Neues zur Lessing-Forschung. Ingrid Strohschneider-Kohrs zu Ehren* (Tübingen: Niemeyer, 1998), 105-125.

978 Hans Mayer, "Lessings poetische Ausdrucksform." *Lessing und die Zeit der Aufklärung* (Göttingen: Vandenhoeck & Ruprecht, 1968), 130-147.

979 Jonathan M. Hess, "Lessing and German Jewish Culture" 183.

980 Adam Sutcliffe, "Lessing and Toleration," Robertson, ed., *Lessing and the German Enlightenment* 205-225 at 220: "The irresolvable ambiguities that adhered to Spinoza's Jewish status, hollowed of any philosophical significance and yet never fully erased and forgotten, are reproduced in Lessing's characterization of Nathan. His Jewish universalism appears at first sight to overcome the oppositions between ethnic particularity and philosophical universalism, and between private partisanships and unrestricted humanist compassion. On closer examination, however, this mirage dissolves. Just as the philosophical wisdom modeled by Nathan is elevated above the level of ordinary religions and denuded of consoling rituals and convenient codifications they provide, Nathan's relationships are so pure and lofty as to place him in a category apart from the complex emotions and vicissitudes that characterize lived intimacies between humans."

The play is not out of line in comparison to Marlowe's *The Jew of Malta* and Shakespeare's *The Merchant of Venice.*[981]

At the core of the play is the "Märchen" (fairy-tale), the "Ringparabel" that actualizes the quest for "truth" in reference to the "People of the Book" and their diverse religions. Apparently the three rings are indicative of Judaism, Christianity, and Islam. Lessing Already Lessing had earlier, when he switched from the pulpit to the stage and from discursive language to metaphor, learned to switch from philosophical discourse to fiction in order to deal with abstract thoughts. Here again, the move to poetic language is a strategy to avoid direct political confrontation or even censorship. He tries to textualize a vision of major proportions. As grandiose as it may be, it simply advocates ideas such as that all humans are physically "related" regardless of their religion, that "intuitive cognition" matters even when, for example, this may mean having to question tradition. As it turns out in the course of the play, Sultan Saladin had on an earlier occasion rescued the Templar. He thought he recognized the features of a relative. Yet he too is about to learn that it is not biological birth but friendship and mutual respect beyond cultural alliances that truly connects people. These rather vague statements as expressed in this play have been much celebrated and scolded over the years.[982] It is my specific interest here to pursue the question of how the visual becomes verbal so that it is recognized as being "authentic" and what poetic strategies are employed in the process.

The play ends with suggesting a vision according to which a peaceful society could still happen perhaps one day in the distant future. This would signify that the attributes of the original ring, the brilliance of its opal, will be recreated imaginatively by those who can realize appropriate human actions. Finding the original ring is complicated since the ring was supposed to have been bestowed by the father only on the one of the three sons whom he loved the most. This one would then consequently become his rightful heir. But since he loved all of his sons and could not decide whom he loved most all of the sons have possibly received equally valid or invalid copies of the ring. Perhaps none of them has the genuine ring, at least as far as Lessing's

981 Jonathan M. Hess, "Lessing and German-Jewish Culture" documents carefully how this play came about, how it was forbidden in Nazi Germany, and what reception it has received ever since. He points out that Lessing's source for the Ringparabel was not primarily Boccaccio's *Decameron* but "a Jewish source, in Solomon ibn Verga's *Shevet Yehudah,* a late medieval text Wiener had translated and published in 1856" (Hess 195).When Lessing was still elaborating principles of aesthetic representation an in response to the Göttingen professor of oriental studies Johann David Michaelis who had complained that Lessing's Jew in his earlier play *Die Juden* was not plausible enough, Lessing moved from the main criterion of internal consistency of a play to its verisimilitude and built his writing on observations he had as the son of a Protestant theologian with any Jewish people, mainly scholars and friends he worked with. On the Jewish reception see Barbara Fischer, *Nathans Ende? Von Lessing bis Tabori: zur deutsch-jüdischen Rezeption von* Nathan der Weise (Göttingen: Wallstein, 2000) and more critically Hans Mayer, *Außenseiter* (Frankfurt am Main: Suhrkamp, 1975) and "Der weise Nathan und der Räuber Spiegelberg. Antinomien der jüdischen Emanzipation in Deutschland," *Jahrbuch der Deutschen Schillergesellschaft* 17 (1973): 253-272 and Hess, "Lessing and German-Jewish Culture," 183. For the broader context, cultural studies at Lessing's time, and the Jewish emancipation, see Hess, *Germans, Jews and the Claims of Modernity* (New Haven: Yale University Press, 2002).

982 See Fick, *Handbuch* 449-471.

narrative in the present is concerned. None of the heirs in question can convincingly demonstrate in their behavior and the radiance of their inner beauty the necessary attributes associated with the criteria of the genuine ring. It seems clearly lost. Its absence marked by the fact that peace, tolerance, and generosity do not exist in the society as is.

Yet there is a chance that the ring's power may nevertheless be retrieved at some distant time in the future, if it could be possible to reconstitute the attributes associated with the original ring. It was carried by a person loved by God and the people, someone who brought peace and tolerance and who was exemplary in ethical actions. Lessing makes us question what it would take to reconstitute such attributes convincingly. Who among all the members of all audience that have seen or will see the play would be able to convince a judge at some time in the future, that they by, as shown by their action and demeanor, are indeed the true deserving heir? Only then would the ring with its opal no longer be "lost." In other words the physical ring may no longer be available to be seen, but it may still exist, metaphorically speaking, through its related attributes. In this Lessing projects ekphrastic hope. The ring may be intangible but yet it may be visible and its continued existence may still be a matter of great consequence. Someone may in effect now, or well into a distant future, demonstrate through their ethical conduct and exemplary character and their peaceful and benevolent actions that the transformation of the visual into the verbal is possible. If such a carrier could once again make "anschaulich" (visible) to everyone the qualities that were attributed to the power of the ring, "Sanftmut, Verträglichkeit, Wohltun, Ergebenheit in Gott" (gentleness, tolerance, ethical actions, and divine devotion), then that could be a sign that the ring was also one again visible having been "found." Whereas the drama cannot avoid temporality for the sake of images, Lessing takes advantage of the poetic intertext to create an image, or rather a tableau vivant that is timeless.[983] It transcends the boundaries of the drama onto a whole other level, projecting as it does an enlightened, tolerant society, promoting respect for various religions and cultural backgrounds, and making a plea for diversity and multiculturalism.

## 2. Teichoscopy

The play opens with a scene presenting first of all the servant Daja. She is reporting to Nathan, her employer, the events which took place during his absence as he returns home after a journey. A fire almost destroyed his house and his adopted daughter Recha almost lost her life. The events reported are what Daja recalls remembering Recha's own description of what she experienced during her traumatic experience. It is therefore something of an ekphrastic narrative. Memory images surface to consciousness and are being narrated indirectly in the process of this recasting of the events. These have an impact now and are reflected in Daja's physicality, her countenance,

983 Neil Flax, "From Portrait to Tableau Vivant: The Pictures of *Emilia Galotti*." *Eighteenth-Century Studies* 19.1 (1985): 39–55.

her gestures, and her body language. Daja's vivid narrative translates what she heard into what she now imagines. She gives her visual account of the events verbally to Nathan. There are multiple degrees of Ekphrasis involved in this transmission. The scene we, the spectators and listeners, are being presented with, is of a peculiar visual-verbal nature. It is an imaginative account of what may have happened, but also a rather odd double-ekphrastic scene with various sign systems at play interactively.

NATHAN
[...]—Weiß sie es denn,
Daß ich gekommen bin?
DAJA
Das frag ich Euch!
Noch zittert ihr der Schreck durch jede Nerve.
Noch malet Feuer ihre Phantasie.
Zu allem, was sie malt. Im Schlafe wacht,
Im Wachen schläft ihre Geist: bald weniger
Als Tier, bald mehr als Engel
NATHAN
Armes Kind!
Was sind wir Menschen!
DAJA
Diesen Morgen lag
Sie lange mit verschloßnem Aug', und war
Wie tot. Schnell fuhr sie auf, und rief: "Horch! Horch!
Da kommen die Kamele meines Vaters!
Horch! seine sanfte Stimme selbst!" Indem
Brach sich ihr Auge wieder: und ihr Haupt,
Dem seines Armes Stütze sich entzog,
Stürzt auf das Küssen. – Ich, zur Pfort hinaus!
Und sieh: da kommt Ihr Wahrlich! Kommt Ihr Wahrlich!
Was Wunder! Ihre ganze Seele war
Die Zeit her nur bei Euch – und ihm. –
NATHAN
Bei ihm?
Bei welchem Ihm?
DAJA
Bei ihm, der aus dem Feuer
Sie rettete.
NATHAN
Wer wer das? wer?—Wo ist er?
Wer rettete mir meine Recha? wer?[984]

[NATHAN:
[...] Does she know at all
That I have come?
DAJA
This is what I am asking you!
Still the horror shivers through each nerve.
Still her phantasy paints fire.
In everything else what it paints. Awake in sleep.
While awake sleeps her mind: sometimes less

984 FA 9, 487-488.

Than an animal, sometimes more than an angel.
NATHAN
Poor child!
What are we human beings!
DAJA
This morning she was lying
For a long time with her eyes closed, and was
Like dead. Quickly she got up and screamed: "Listen! Listen!
There the camels of my father come!
Listen! Even his gentle voice itself!"–In the meantime
Her eyes shut again: and her head
Lacking the support of her arm
Fell on the pillow!–I, out of the entrance!
And see; there you are really coming! You are really coming!
What a miracle! Her soul was
The entire time only with you–and him.–
NATHAN
With him?
With what him?
DAJA
With the one who saved her
From the fire.
NATHAN
Who is that? who?–Where is he?
Who rescued my Recha? who?].

This dialogue draws attention to a mixture of sense perceptions that are in part based on the factual events of what happened during Nathan's absence from home and in part based on the inner and subtle perceptions, the mental processing of the events as they belong to the psychological conglomerations of Recha's experience of the trauma. Memory images are mixed with ideas that frame the chaotic moments into cognitive snippets of visual and other sensory data. Daja reconstructs vividly what Recha remembered in surviving the fire. She must have experienced fear and horror and her rescue now appears as a miracle. In Daja's narrative account there is a merging of factual data and distinct personal moments in this context. Her story blurs their visions of both. She projects on Recha's experience her own point of view. Perspectives get entangled. This simulates a teichoscopy from an inter-personal perspective which, as we soon learn, is not quite identical either with Recha's account, nor the information that Nathan has garnered from others. The audience hears what had happens through Daja's emotionally packed description. Recha's memory images are still torturing her. The textualizing of her visual experience will to some extent deconstruct the imagery as initially projected by Daja, yet it will not make it absurd or obsolete. Multiple perspectives coexist but do not cancel each other out. The speed of the events during the fire seems to have been so extreme that Daja empathizes with Recha and also cannot distinguish in her account exactly what happened at each moment. And by looking at Recha, she cannot distinguish in her dream-like state whether it was fear, trauma of the fire, or happiness to be rescued that have had the most overwhelming impact on her emotions. Whatever Recha may have experienced remains hidden from the public however and gets communicated to the audience only through Daja's staccato account of the events. Nathan offers reasonably calm responses.

In the following dialogues with Recha, Nathan tries to have her forget and let go of her delirious notion of what happened. She imagines that an angel with white wings carried her out of the fire. He says that she must now soon properly thank the person who deserves acknowledgement for his compassionate action. They find out it was the Templar who rescued Recha from the fire and carried her out, his cloak flapping over the flames. This intense memory image apparently created the illusion that he had wings. The message is that instead of a projected vision of another worldly miracle, not only Recha but also Daja and the spectators in the audience need to process the events differently. They must understand the events in such a way that apparently artificial signs are not processed as natural or even supernatural. It is reality and not fantasy which should have the last word. When Nathan meets Recha she confirms:

RECHA
[...] ich, ich bin ja nicht
Verbrannt. Wir wollen wir uns freun, und Gott,
Gott loben! Er, er trug Euch und den Nachen
Auf Flügeln seiner *unsichtbaren* Engel
Die ungetreuen Ström' hinüber. Er,
Er winkte meinem Engel, daß er *sichtbar*
Auf seinem weißen Fittiche, mich durch
Das Feuer trüge–[985]

[RECHA
[...] I, I did not
burn. Let us be glad and God,
God Praise! He, he carried you and your boat
On the wings of his *invisible* angels
Across the treacherous currents.[986] He,
he summoned my angel so that he *visibly*
On his white pinions carry me
Through the fire–].

In the process of attempting to understand what really happened Nathan gives Recha hints so that she realizes that she is not yet fully aware of herself and of what surrounds her. There are not only visible but also invisible things that have contributes to her naïve conjectures. These ideas are plausible in the process. Yet they are avoidable since she is only describing things as closely as possible to her own emotions and understanding. Despite Nathan's attempts to rationalize the events, her notion of the angel makes no sense to him. The story reflects personal ways of processing the dangerous fire she lived through and her resulting mental state. The visual narrative almost "paints" colors of the events that happened. Nathan's return marks a new starting point in Recha's life. Lessing offers the visual description of absent things as a strategy to describe her projected imagery in dealing with her trauma and suggests that she should let go of her personal conjectures. Whereas Daja may take Recha's reference to angels, feathers, and wings all too literally, Recha's ability to present her experience visually in those images serves as a surrogate for having shown the actual

985 FA 9, 491. Emphasis mine.

986 The reference is to the fact that Nathan on his business trip had to cross major rivers like the Euphrates, the Tigris and the Jordan.

events onstage. What is being reported are examples of verbal responses that have been subsumed into a visual account, yet on another level of the discourse. These vivid sentences are for Nathan also not only a matter of rational reflection but stir other personal experiences, memories, images, and emotions. They remind Nathan of his own earlier trauma when he lost his wife and entire family in a fire due to a violent pogrom. It is as if more than two "poignant moments," two horrible fires, have already occurred before the action of the play begins. They frame the actual drama in ways that make it indeed allegorical in ways Lessing would not have considered when he first set out to write his drama theory. The textualizing of such an image does to some extent deconstruct the imagery as presented by Daja and Recha. Yet it does not make it absurd or irrelevant. Recha's story is, as she is fully aware of herself, not only about visible but also about invisible things that in her conjecture are plausible. Despite Nathan's attempts to rationalize these fantasies and to transform images into reasonable ways of language, the play does not contradict the notion of "Wunder." It presents other miracles along the way. The visual narrative "paints" the event that happened through verbalized images.

## 3. What does "seeing" mean?

Recha's mind seems to slip from a state of being aware to an almost catatonic state of sleepwalking and back. She finds it difficult to be fully awake or deeply asleep since her images are so intense that they overrule her thoughts. She must learn to accept "the truth" which is her fortunate rescue from the dangerous fire. She must also learn in the course of several dialogues that the individual who rescued her was actually not "an angel" but an individual who, as Nathan insists, must now be explicitly thanked. Daja's account of Recha's narrative echoes the same imagery in which she had summarized what she saw. This provokes Nathan later to correct her point of view. She had taken the person with the cloak who rescued Recha for "an angel" as Recha told her. She did not question this notion any further. Nathan does critically reflect on this image as also the audience should. He argues that it could well be a "Wunder" or miracle that she was saved but that is just a matter of speech. What happened is much more "natural" than what she may want to believe. Even if as it appears to be, a *Tempelherr* in his white cloak saved her, this is no less "miraculous" he insists, since the Sultan Saladin saved the Templar twenty years ago as we learn later. This was done perhaps because the Templar reminded Saladin of his beloved brother whom he believed dead but who we learn in the very end of the play is in fact alive and identical with the Templar, Curd von Stauffen. When the Templar is revealed as a human this means for Recha the loss of her angel. Her concerns are dismissed by Nathan in a proverb: "Der Topf / Von Eisen will mit einer silbern Zange / Gern aus der Glut gehoben sein, um selbst / ein Topf von Silber sich zu dünken–!"[987] ("The iron pot readily wishes to be lifted with silver tongs from the glowing fire in order to appear as a pot of silver–!) And Nathan asks whether she would not want to do good

987 FA 9, 494–495.

things in return to the being who rescued her, whether it may be an angel or a human being. He tries to get her to distinguish dream and from reality and favor the latter. Such temporalizing of events by means of the use of ekphrastic imagery is a deviation from Lessing's earlier idea that a playwright should focus on what is present in space and onstage only. He is no longer trying to limit the action of the play to that extent. The invisible has become as important as the visible and the temporal dimension gains importance compared to the spatial. The drama involves a conglomeration of various genres of the visual and verbal, including poems, epigrams, stichomythia, fairy tales, fables, and a parable. All of these add to the progression of one single action which is presented as a clip from the aftermath of major catastrophes and a projected vision. This play was written at a time when Lessing had financial troubles. He had to borrow money in order to finance the publication of the play. His writings in support of it appeared in various journals in Berlin, Hamburg, Gotha, and Leipzig. Through this he was able to get subscription fees and subsidies before it was staged in 1779. In December 1778 Lessing also received a loan by his friend Moses Wessely. Fortunately, the play was a huge success from the time of its publication in 1779 and Lessing was able to pay off his debts.[988]

While the play has been successful ever since, it is not an easy work to perform. In this regard it received adverse criticism, even from Goethe.[989] He commented that Lessing left a great deal to the discretion of the producer, to the creative talents by the actors, and to the interpretation of the public. The play is a marvelous sketch and ends with a framed image. Some critics felt it was a bit too contrived, too framed, and as a still life too hard to perform well. In any case, it was this work which made Lessing in the eyes Friedrich Schlegel and many after him, a German playwright to be compared to Shakespeare.[990] Many details that normally were expected to be fleshed out by the author, Lessing left consciously open. He wanted to give free range not only to the imagination of the spectators but also to the actors. This was not just a matter of pedagogy. He did not want to teach under the cloak of fiction. The presentation of the Tempelherr is a puzzling challenge. While he may be considered a hero for having rescued Recha from a fire, he happens to be a mixed and rather complicated character, not at all an angel, as Recha and perhaps others falsely assumed.

988 Fick, *Handbuch* 445.

989 "Nicht weniger werden die Schauspieler sich alle Mühe geben, was an Ausarbeitung ihrer Rollen noch fehlte nachzubringen, so daß das Stück jährlich mit Zufriedenheit des Publikums wieder erscheinen könne" (Not any less will the actors put every effort into it to fulfill themselves creatively whatever may have been missing in the execution n of their roles). Goethe, "Weimarisches Hoftheater," GFA I: 18 (1998), *Ästhetische Schriften 1771-1805*, 842-849 at 845.

990 The Romantic, Friedrich Schlegel had a great appreciation for Lessing and was instrumental in shaping the Lessing reception for his contemporaries and also for following generations. In his *Vorlesungen über dramatische Kunst und Literatur: kritische Ausgabe,* ed. Giovanni Vittorio Amoretti, 2 vols. (Bonn: Kurt Schröder, 1923), 2: 292, he comments on *Nathan der Weise:* "Die Form ist freyer und umfassender als in den übrigen Stücken Lessing's, sie ist beynahe die eines Shakespeareschen Schauspiels" (The form is freer and more inclusive than in the other plays by Lessing; it is almost that of a Shakespearean play).

# 4. Lessing's late "language of images" and evocative language gaps

Lessing admitted that the fiction was not something in which to conceal a message. Whatever cover was needed to present "the truth," it was only provisional and had to remain sketchy. There are several innovations here. There are also complications which Lessing admitted in dealing with the intricacies of verbalizing images and making language vivid. It seems that Lessing could no longer believe in the efficiency of language as much. Story telling was a last resort only in response to a financial need but not a medium with which to share wisdom. It is surprising that the story Nathan tells in response to Saladin who comes for money is one that talks about coins that are flat, imageless, but still carrying a potential value.

There is one image especially that deserves attention, the stone in the ring which is an opal with its symbolic brilliance. Its value cannot be determined per se; that will always depend on each specific circumstance and the human transactions involved. The play summarizes *in nuce* Lessing's careful stance on the frictions and boundaries between the visual and the verbal. He proposes a notion of restrictive Ekphrasis, on delayed processes in the transformation from one to another medium. He suggests multiple levels of discourse that cannot be condensed any more to the frame of five acts or the space of one play. These levels of discourse require temporality and so much of it that it would take generations of audiences and spectators to complete the plot. It seems that Lessing still advocates the persistence of the image against the gaps in verbalness. And he is trying to counter the ultimate understatement, silence. He seems to have revoked his *Laokoon* idea that the temporal should be ignored for the spatial in the realm of the visual and that allegories were to be avoided. Immanence of the artwork is no longer a viable option. It seems ironic that Lessing may have become a Romantic *avant la lettre* and that Goethe's Classical reservation about *Nathan der Weise* that one must completely "round it up" in order to finish it was to the point.[991]

In his *Paralipomena zu Nathan der Weise* Lessing documents the changes and revisions he had made to the play.[992] Among its innovations was the use of "Blankvers" instead of the expected Alexandrines. *Nathan der Weise* has most often been interpreted as Lessing's plea for tolerance and for the peaceful coexistence of people from vari-

---

991 "Was das Stück durch Abkürzung allenfalls gelitten hat, ward nun durch eine gedrängtere Darstellung ersetzt, und man wird für die Folge sorgen, es poetisch so viel wie möglich zu restaurieren und zu runden" (What the play may have suffered through abbreviations was then substituted with a more condensed mode of presentation, and one will take care of the consequence by restoring it poetically and thus as a whole, as well as possible at least). Goethe, "Weimarisches Hoftheater," GFA I: 18, 845.

992 Fick comments that Lessing had been drawn into a religious debate and that during the writing of this work he shifted issues concerning such vast and abstract concepts as "truth" and "judgment" increasingly away from religion and philosophy and instead turned for poetic images to develop heuristic approaches. He also linked poetic writing with ethics and what she calls "Subjektivierung der Glaubensinhalte" (subjectively applying the contents of faith) (*Handbuch* 449). I would add that by shifting attention to the individual in each context, Lessing returns to his earlier theoretical approach in wanting to teach through the stories themselves and not though additional imposed moral interpretation.

ous religions and cultures and as such has not lost its appeal.[993] Lessing shifted away from showing violence and death onstage as he did with his bourgeois plays. This last play is highly metaphoric. Instead of showing everything in detail this play uses the strategy of teichoscopy. The important events have already happened before the play begins and we are left with consequences, the resolutions of which are a matter ultimately to be determined by the members of the audience themselves. There are subplot entanglements in scenes and in dialogues, intricacies, numerous perspectives and suggested ideas but questions are more abundant than giving any answers.

Friedrich Schlegel made insightful comments about *Nathan der Weise* when calling this play the "*beste Prosa*, welche Lessing geschrieben hat" (*best prose* which Lessing has written).[994] Lessing was successful in making his presentation appear "natural." Nevertheless, there are paradoxes to be observed in the context of the play which Lessing calls "ein dramatisches Gedicht" (a dramatic poem). He draws attention to signs in language that may appear "natural" although they are built upon "willkürliche Zeichen" (arbitrary signs) as explained in *Laokoon*. It seems that the mixing of genres and the layering of multiple frames of reference reveals the stagedness of the play. The play is does not hide the fact that it is a performance. It makes the public realize that what appears on stage may be artificial yet it aims at the real. Whatever has the effect of the supernatural is actually human-made. Moreover, whatever seems now far-fetched is still relevant here and now.[995] The play draws attention to margins of discourse, to the philosophical and political implications of the dialogues, to diverse characters representing distinct cultures, and it speaks to the audience. The debate about the play's unique and mixed genre is long and complex. It seems that Lessing turned to a mode of writing that involves multiple levels of time frame in the action and contains "Zufälle" (coincidences) that bring these timings of actions ideally together. This is the effect of more than one "Kunstgriff" (artistic device), forceful poetic intervention.

Whether or not we accept the events as plausible is up to the presentation of the performance, the skill of the actors, and the receptivity and creativity of the audience. What matters is that element of freedom and liberating "Spiel" that allows thinking not only about facticity but also in terms of contingency. It becomes a kind of gambling in the realm of fiction.[996] Numerous temporal levels coexist without erasing or negating each other. Volker Nölle in his interpretation of *Nathan* notices a "Metaphernregie" (directing through metaphors). He argues that there are various "Metaphernströme" (streams of metaphors) and "Metaphernketten" (chains of metaphors) at work in this play. Words do not only follow a method of "Veranschaulichung" (making something visible) but in the context of this play they imply shifts from one

---

993 See Allert, "Pluralisierung der Ringe."

994 K.W. Friedrich Schlegel, "Über Lessing," *Charakteristiken und Kritiken I (1796-1801)*, ed. Hans Eichner, KFSA 2 (1967): 100-125 at 121. This work first appeared in the Lyceum der schönen Künste 1.2 (Berlin 1797) and then in Lessings *Gedanken und Meinungen aus dessen Schriften zusammengestellt und erläutert von Friedrich Schlegel*, 2 parts (Leipzig: Junius, 1804). By emphasizing the statement "*die beste Prosa*," Schlegel is saying that even though the play is in verse, this verse is so natural and unobtrusive that it has an impact similar to prose.

995 On related observations see Susan Gustafson, "Windungen und Wendungen in Lessings *Laokoon*," Albrecht, Fratzke and Schade, ed., *Aufklärung nach Lessing* 21-36.

996 Martinson, *Projects of Enlightenment*.

level of discourse to another ("Sinnverschiebungen, Akzentverschiebungen").[997] Schlegel accurately commented upon Lessing's mix between "hohe Philosophische Würde" (high philosophical dimension) and the lack of any expected theatrical effects, such as pathos. Instead this play offers a spicy combination of tones and flavors, including very enthusiastic and very cool and calming elements.[998]

This odd mixture had also interesting consequences for gender studies in the reception history. Susan Gustafson draws from the psychological approach of Julia Kristeva arguing that the abjection of the female in numerous works by Lessing, especially *Nathan der Weise*, is a serious matter involving negation and repression.[999] Jill Kowalik on the other hand links this work directly with Lessing and his biography and points out that it was written from the point of view of a mourning male.[1000] Similar to Nathan who mourns his wife and children who were tragically killed, Lessing also at the time was mourning the death of his wife and child. There are no women mentioned in the "Ringparabel". This may be a point to introduce the question of whether Lessing's work contributes to anti-or proto-feminist way of thinking? Gayatri Chakravorty Spivak makes clear: "The discourse of men is in the metaphor of women".[1001] Drawing from Silvia Bovenschen's *Imaginierte Weiblichkeit,* Inge Stephan on the other side of the spectrum places *Nathan der Weise* in the context of regression and diagnoses a reduction of the earlier much broader, perhaps "more enlightened," images of females.[1002] She sees a shift from the cosmopolitan, world-clever woman of the earlier plays back to the more restricted concept of the sheltered female, such as the daughter Recha, who lives at home.[1003] She claims that in contrast to Gottsched, Lessing followed Rousseau who reactivated an outdated image of the female as inferior, passive, and uneducated.

Helga Slessarev makes helpful differentiations. She cites a letter Lessing wrote to his brother Karl on February 1, 1772: "Ich kenne an einem unverheirateten Mädchen keine höheren Tugenden als Frömmigkeit und Gehorsam" (I know in an unmarried

---

997 Volker Nölle, *Subjektivität und Wirklichkeit in Lessings dramatischem und theologischem Werk,* Philologische Studien und Quellen 87 (Berlin: Erich Schmidt, 1977).

998 Schlegel, "Über Lessing" 121: "Die hohe Philosophische Würde des Stücks hat Lessing selbst ungemein schön mit der theatralischen Effektlosigkeit oder Effektwidrigkeit desselben kontrastiert; mit dem seinem Ton eigenen pikanten Gemisch von ruhiger inniger tiefer Begeisterung und naiver Kälte." (Lessing himself contrasted the high philosophical dignity of this play with the lack of theatrical effects, or the inappropriateness of its effects; with a piquant mixture of calm, intimate, deep enthusiasm and naïve coldness).

999 Gustafson, *Absent Mothers* 217-266.

1000 Jill Ann Kowalik, "*Nathan* as a Work of Mourning." *Lessing Yearbook* 21 (1989): 1-18.

1001 Gayatri Chakravorty Spivak, "Displacement and the Discourse of Women," Mark Krupnick, ed., *Displacement: Derrida and After* (Bloomington: Indiana University Press, 1983) 169-195. See also by Teresa de Lauretis in her chapter "The Violence of Rhetoric," *Technologies of Gender: Essays on Theory, Film, and Fiction* (Bloomington: Indiana University Press, 1987), 31-50.

1002 Silvia Bovenschen, *Die imaginierte Weiblichkeit: Exemplarische Untersuchungen zu kulturgeschichtlichen und literarischen Präsentationsformen des Weiblichen* (Frankfurt am Main: Suhrkamp, 1979). For a critique of Bovenschen position, see Susan Cocalis, "Der Vormund will Vormund sein: Zur Problematik der weiblichen Unmündigkeit im 18. Jahrhundert," Marianne Burkhard, ed., *Gestaltet und Gestaltend: Frauen in der deutschen Literatur*, Amsterdamer Beiträge zur neueren Germanistik 10 (Amsterdam: Rodopi, 1980), 33-55 at 55.

1003 Inge Stephan, "So ist die Tugend ein Gespenst" 9; *Lessing und die Toleranz* 363.

woman no better virtues than piety and obedience).[1004] Then she notices that Lessing's writings are sometimes paradoxical and finds that they reveal, perhaps against the intentions of the author or at least of the dialogue partner, elements of female emancipation, a proto-feminist reading I find attractive. Recha remains however, a marginal figure in the play although this figure has, perhaps a critical function. I would like to add to the debate that the search for the missing queen in the chess game is indicative that there is a gap in the logic of this entire play. The search for the ring is paralleled by the search for the missing queen in the chess game between Saladin and his sister Sittah. Just like the parable of the ring this provides the context for a search. The search for the ring depends not only upon finding the original son of the father but the determination of the legitimate heir depends on his living and incorporating in his ethical actions the attributes of the original ring. The search for the queen in the chess game also calls for the participation of new but forgotten figures and encourage new participants in the search. The father's dilemma over which son he should give his ring (his love and power) was restricted to his sons and so far has not included any daughters. But the end of the parable remains open and leaves space for that possibility. The solution the father has found can only be temporary. None of the three sons–as long as they fight–can have the credibility as the legitimate successor of the father or be the emperor.

The search for the ring must continue obviously not in a linear way, not the same way as before. We may have to look at the framing of the questions themselves and the positioning of the speakers as they relate to each other Nathan is approached as a possible donor for money when the war for the crusades has depleted the resources of the Sultan as well as Al Hafi. What is the loss of one is no longer contextualized as the gain of another. The lack of the queen in the chess game does not make Sittah really a winner of the first kind. We may look for indirect messages of the "Ring parable" and follow up on these hints that help us read it from a different perspective. We can approach it intertextually, explore taxonomies and narrative strategies that fulfill (or do not fulfill) specific tasks in the discourse in which they are used.

## 5. Queen missing in the chess game

For example, in the context of the chess game, second act first scene, Sittah makes a remark to Saladin that he has overlooked (übersehen") his queen. He seems a bit distracted in this game and responds with a comment about the "Steine" (stones or chess figures) which seem all much too similar, too smooth. He asks: "Wer giebt uns denn die glatten Steine / Beständig? die an nichts erinnern, nichts / Bezeichnen?"[1005] (Who gives us then the smooth stones / Always? /which do not remind us of anything, Sig-

1004 Helga Slessarev, "Doppelte Moral in der Sozialisation der Töchter bei Joachim Campe und Gotthold Ephraim Lessing," *Lessing und die Toleranz* 347-356 at 348. For the quotation from the letter, see FA11/2, 351-353 at 352.

1005 FA 9, 516. Because of the ban in Islam of producing figures which represent human beings or animals, Lessing assumes that Saladin is playing chess with marked stones for the pieces.

nify?) The question is not only where the stones come from. It is rather who handles them and what is the positioning of the donor is in the context of the transaction. The lack of distinction in the chess pieces seems to be something that may not always have to be the case. Although Saladin is a very experienced player he loses a game with his sister Sittah. The shape of the chess figures says very little about their name yet it is noticeable that the female, the queen, is missing. So how to win?

The dialogue between Sittah and Saladin draws attention to a problem which may have relevance beyond the chess game. What these figures look like is less important than what they do. Such stones have no clear distinctions; they represent culturally engrained meanings and easily lose such a meaning and so may be designated as something else. The dilemma must not be permanent, the agents can change. But even after Sittah mentions that he had forgotten his queen, Saladin keeps ignoring her:

> Nein, nein, nimm nur die Königin.
> Ich war mit diesem Steine nicht ganz glücklich.
> SITTAH Bloß mit dem Stein? SALADIN Fort damit![1006]
>
> [No, no go ahead and take the queen.
> I was never completely lucky with that stone.
> SITTAH: Only the stone? SALADIN: Take it!].

Saladin seems to give up his control and lets almost voluntarily Sittah win for a change. Whereas his mind is elsewhere and apparently lost in reverie and mourning, the dialogue makes us made aware of a missing stone indicating that the game was not a fair play or correct from the start. The most important thing is exactly what is missing. There are three motifs in the context of *Nathan der Weise* that are interconnected: the exclusion of the female, the endless search for the ring, and the problem of to whom Recha belongs. Nathan does not talk about any daughters in the story he tells Saladin. As we know from another level of fiction, he adopted one. Whether or not this could indicate a return of the repressed, a change in the levels of repression, or a kind of liberation, will be open for discussion. We may notice that the exclusion of the female is restricted to only one level of the plot. Recha motivates the entire action of the play, the interaction among the main (male) figures. She is the one whom Nathan adopted as his daughter and who is rescued from the fire. She means everything to him. In the Ringparabel there are three sons but no daughter. We may ask: What has been forgotten?

On the action level of the play everything aims at defining Recha, allocating her in terms of degrees of belonging. It is also about the question who is her legitimate guardian, in charge of her protection and control. Everyone among the three men in question has his own agenda for her and attempts to label her from his own point of view. Curd von Stauffen rescued her from the fire and then wants to marry her. He cannot understand Nathan's resistance not knowing yet that he is her brother. He is self-centered to the point that he threatens Nathan's life by trying to manipulate his actions. He talks to the Patriarch about him, the most vicious character. Saladin tells Curd von Stauffen: "Was du gerettet, ist / Deswegen nicht dein Eigentum. Sonst wär'

1006 FA 9, 515.

/ Der Räuber, den sein Geiz ins Feuer jagt, / So gut ein Held, wie du!"[1007] (What you have saved is therefore not your property. Otherwise, a thief who jumps into the fire out of his miserliness would be as much a hero as you!"). Earlier Saladin had told Recha: "Sobald der Väter zwei / Sich um dich streiten:–laß sie beide; nimm / den dritten!–Nimm dann mich zu deinem Vater!"[1008] (As soon as the two fathers fight about you: leave them both; take a third. Take me then as your father). In the end, none of the three gets her exactly, at least not at all in the terms they wanted. No substitution or replacement works really in Lessing's context. At least not on this level of the action as presented. Recha's signification changes for everyone involved in the action. In fact, she does not correspond to any given assumptions, not even to her own expectations. The couple who are about to get married turn out to be siblings. New names are introduced (Recha as Blanda, etc.) and new family relations are revealed. The ending cuts off the vision of the audience, the curtain falls abruptly, and the viewers are left with a sense of uncertainty and puzzlement. Gestures finally replace words: "*Unter stummer Wiederholung allseitiger Umarmungen fällt der Vorhang*" (During silent repetition of mutual embraces the curtain falls).[1009]

This silence in the end shifts attention to gaps, to multiple meanings of signs, and to changes. The ending remains boldly open, parabolic, and indeterminable. It makes us aware of differences between gestures and words, signs and objects, expectations and results. It challenges the notions of control, logocentricity, and brings to awareness that the search for the ultimate ring may only bring results if we look now where we are expected to. Recha resists terminological restriction, confinement, and closed definition. She is–and I use a term coined by the theorist language philosopher Drucilla Cornell–"beyond accommodation."[1010] Recha stands for both the incommensurable and the female.

## 6. The Ring: Context Matters

The parable of the ring is an intertext. We know from the larger context of the play that it is the strategic reply offered by Nathan in response to Saladin's tricky question about the correct faith, the eternal law, or what is the essence of truth. Nathan's answer is a piece of fiction, not a religious or philosophical argument as expected. And Nathan, on the other hand, comes to make a trade with Saladin, wants to engage in business and the latter is pleasantly surprised about this quest for "truth" and enjoys having to hear a fairy tale. What follows is not just a dialogue between Nathan and Saladin. Nor is it exclusively a story about the dynamics between a father and his three

1007 Act V, scene viii, FA 9, 622.
1008 Act V, scene vii. FA 9, 620.
1009 FA 9, 627.
1010 See Drucilla Cornell, *Beyond Accommodation: Ethical Feminism, Deconstruction, and the Law* (New York: Routledge, 1991) especially her comments on mimesis (149-152).

sons as some critics argue.[1011] By using the imperative, attention shifts to everybody who hears or reads the story, the audience of the play, male and female.

> Es eifre jeder seiner unbestochnen
> Von Vorurteilen freien Liebe nach!
> Es strebe von euch jeder um die Wette,
> Die Kraft des Steins in seinem Ring' an Tag
> Zu legen! Komme dieser Kraft mit Sanftmut,
> Mit herzlicher Verträglichkeit, mit Wohltun,
> Mit innigster Ergebenheit in Gott,
> Zu Hülf"! Und wenn sich dann der Steine Kräfte
> Bei euren Kindes-Kindeskindern äußern:
> So lad ich über tausend Jahre
> Sie wiederum vor diesen Stuhl. Da wird
> Ein weiserer Mann auf diesem Stuhle sitzen,
> Als ich; und sprechen. Geht! – So sagte der
> Bescheidne Richter![1012]

> [Let everyone strive for uncompromised
> Love free of prejudice!
> Let everyone compete in striving with each other
> To bring into the light the power of the stone
> In their own ring! Come help this power with gentleness
> With sincere openness, with doing good things
> With innermost devotion to God.
> And when then the stone's powers express themselves
> In your children's grandchildren:
> Then I invite you again before this chair. Then
> A wiser man than I shall sit on this chair
> And say: Go! – thus spoke the
> Modest judge!].

Everybody is being asked to reproduce the radiance of the ring's stone by striving for the characteristic features that were initially associated with its original wearer. The power of the opal which used to be associated with the object has become detached from it. It may be rediscovered in different terms. It may disappear for generations but be rescued if its attributes can still be carried out by anyone who hears this or knows about this potential power of the ring. Wolfram Mauser wrote that Lessing created a kind of audience which did not yet exist at his time. Lessing makes "a conspiracy" with such an audience or the people he encourages to get involved in the construction of the meaning.[1013] Lessing was realistic enough to know that it would take generations to have the audience

---

1011 See Michael Morton, "Verum est factum: Critical Realism and the Discourse of Autonomy," *German Quarterly* 64.2 (1991): 149-165. He argues: "The parable is structured in such a way that we elucably find ourselves simultaneously in the position of the judge and the sons, which is to say that for us comprehension and (moral) activity are henceforth one" (158).

1012 FA 9, 559-560.

1013 "Diese Positions-Bekundung wendet sich nicht primär an der Widersacher der Fachdisziplinen, sondern zielt auf ein Publikum, d.h auf eine Öffentlichkeit, die Lessing (noch) nicht vorfindet, sondern erst herstellen muß." See Wolfgang Mauser, "Toleranz und Frecheit: Zur Strategie von Lessings Streitschriften," Freimark et al., ed., *Lessing und die Toleranz* 276-290 at 201. Also, see Friedrich Niewöhner, *Veritas sive Varietas. Lessings* be receptive of this task. He called for modesty and devotion to ideals that could not be propagated loudly and with the language of power. He suggested that only by means of differentiated use of signs things could change. In this context the metaphors could be characterized as ones associated with an "interaction model."[1014]

Lessing indicates in his *Ringparabel* that the quest for the original may be obsolete, but a purposeful striving must continue. The magic power of the ring is represented by attributes that can also be regarded as first being detached from the one ring they used to belong to before they may recall the same. Perhaps these attributes can in that sense be "rediscovered" or recreated on another level of the discourse or by someone else. The construction of meaning is no longer limited to reproduction, the formula of mimesis. Nathan's apparently evasive answer to Saladin's question is suggestive but leaves space for many options. The problem of belonging, or, to put it differently, the problem of "mehrfache Zuordnungsfunktionen" (multiple significations), is constructional not only in the parable of the rings. We find it also relevant in the larger context of the play. Lessing's struggle for tolerance and against prejudices has language-theoretical implications. His metaphor-based approach to language and seeing provides effective strategies and tactical responses to the challenge of censorship during his time.

On August 13, 1778, the infamous "Goeze-Streit" had escalated to the point that Lessing was no longer allowed to publish anything that could threaten religious dogmatism and authority.[1015] The shift from the pulpit to the stage was a successful political move for Lessing to avoid being silenced, In the process of this shift between media and types of language, Lessing moved away from monocausal, linear-deductive ways of reasoning and began to conceptualize truth no longer as the opposite of fiction. It is always intertextually connected. It seems that Lessing had already discovered the danger of language to destroy meanings by defining them too closely.[1016] Sittah expresses concern about this aspect of language when she refers to naming as an act of devouring or usurpation:

Seine Tugend nicht; sein Name
Soll überall verbreitet werden; soll
Die Namen aller guten Menschen schänden,

---

*Toleranzparabel und das Buch von den drei Betrügern, Veröffentlichung der Lessing-Akademie Wolfenbüttel* (Heidelberg: Verlag Lambert Schneider, 1988).

1014 These terms are used by Mark Johnson, "Introduction: Metaphor in the Philosophical Tradition," Mark Johnson, ed., *Philosophical Perspectives of Metaphor* 3-47. See also Frank Schlossbauer, "Nathans Witz: Zur Neubestimmung des witzigen Formprinzips bei Lessing," *German Quarterly* 62.1 (Winter 1989): 15-26.

1015 On Lessing's problems with censorship and on the historical-political background, see Wilfried Barner and Gunter E. Grimm, ed., *Lessing: Epoche-Werk-Wirkung*, 5th ed. (Munich: Beck, 1987), 309-313; Nisbet, *Lessing: Eine Biographie* 701-744; *Gotthold Ephraim Lessing* 537-570.

1016 Goethe expressed this same dilemma when he wrote in §754 of his *Farbenlehre: Didaktischer Teil* (*Color Theory: Didactic Section*): "Jedoch wie schwer ist es, das Zeichen nicht an die Stelle der Sache zu setzen, das Wesen immer lebendig vor sich zu haben und es nicht durch das Wort zu töten" (Yet how hard it is not to substitute the sign in the place of the thing, to keep its essence still living before one and not to kill it by means of the word). GFA 1: 23/1, ed. Manfred Wenzel, 245. Lessing's Recha is in this sense, I argue, not "Sache," but "Zeichen." She is a sign both for the metaphoric, the incommensurable, and for the female which is lacking elsewhere in the context.

Verschlingen. Um den Namen, um den Namen
Ist ihnen nur zu tun.[1017] [2.1.876-79]

[Not his virtue; his name
Shall become spread over everything
To harm, to devour, the name
Of all good people. The name, the name,
Is all that matters to them].

Lessing counteracts this tendency of naming and in doing so of erasing what the word is supposed to signify. When language becomes a matter of terminology and definitions, it can absorb what is being signified by the words. Lessing offers a type of language that opens up and he chooses a parable to give an example on how to pursue such counteracting by approximation of meaning, so that truth is not to be captured or claimed as a "possession" in any fixed terms. He anticipated Nietzsche's answer to the question "What is truth?" by referring to the metaphoricity of language.[1018] Nathan makes not only Saladin but also us, the recipients of Lessing's play think:

Hm! Hm!–wunderlich!–wie ist
Mir denn?–Was will der Sultan? was?–Ich bin
Auf Geld gefaßt, und er will Wahrheit. Wahrheit!
Und will sie so,–so bar, so blank,–als ob
Die Wahrheit Münze wäre.[1019] [3.6.1868-75]

[Hm!Hm!–strange!–How am I then?
What does the Sultan want? what? I am
Expecting money and he wants truth. Truth!
And wishes it so–so empty, so bare,[1020]–as if
The truth were a coin].

---

1017 FA 9, 517.

1018 Friedrich Nietzsche, "Über Wahrheit und Lüge" 314: "Was ist also Wahrheit? Ein bewegliches Heer von Metaphern, Metonymien, Anthropomorphismen, kurz eine Summe von menschlichen Relationen, die poetisch und rhetorisch gesteigert, übertragen, geschmückt wurden und die nach langem Gebrauch einem Volke fest, kanonisch und verbindlich dünken: die Wahrheiten sind Illusionen, von denen man vergessen hat, daß sie welche sind, Metaphern, die abgenutzt und kraftlos geworden sind, Münzen, die ihr Bild verloren haben und nun als Metall, nicht mehr als Münzen in Betracht kommen" ("What, then, is truth? A mobile army of metaphors, metonyms, and anthropomorphisms–in short, a sum of human relations, which have been enhanced, transposed, and embellished poetically and rhetorically, and which after long use seem firm, canonical, and obligatory to a people: truths are illusions about which one has forgotten that this is what they are; metaphors which are worn out and without sensuous power; coins which have lost their pictures and now matter only as metal, no longer as coins.") "*From* On Truth and Lie in an Extra-Moral Sense," *The Portable Nietzsche,* trans. Walter Kaufmann (New York: Viking Press, 1982). 42-47 at 46-47. Nathan's poetic response to the sultan's inquiry what "truth" is and his remark that it is much easier to believe one's own fathers than others, that truth therefore depends always on history, on cultural transmission, allows for comparison between Lessing's rings and Nietzsche's coins both of which share important elements in common.

1019 FA 9, 554.

1020 Or perhaps: "And wishes it as–as cash, as shiny."

Simplistic dualisms are ridiculed in the context of Nathan's dialogue with Recha:

> Er wird
> Nicht fett durch euer Fasten; wird nicht reich
> Durch eure Spenden; wird nicht herrlicher
> Durch eur Entzücken; wird nicht mächtiger
> Durch eur Vertraun. Nicht wahr? Allein ein Mensch![1021]" [1.2.312-18]
>
> [He will not become
> Fat through your fasting; will not become
> Rich through your charity; will not become more noble
> Through your reveries; will not become more powerful
> Through your confidence. Isn't that so? Only a human!].

## 7. Some random conclusions

Lessing who is considered a major representative of the Enlightenment movement, is actually also one of this movement's most challenging critics. Concepts as logocentricity, binarisms, didacticism, and the Cartesian scopic regime, are traditionally attributed to the Enlightenment discourse[1022] Lessing goes out of his way to deconstruct them.[1023] He anticipates a "Deleuzean fold" when he writes: "Es ist nicht wahr, daß die kürzeste Linie immer die gerade ist." (It is not true that the shortest line is always the straight one).[1024] Lessing offers the model of "language" as a building with many doors. In the context of *Eine Parabel vom brennenden Palast* (1778)—which is embedded in a text titled "Eine Parabel"—the image of a burning palace is a metaphor for

1021 FA 9, 495.

1022 Martin Jay, "Scopic Regimes of Modernity," Hal Foster, ed., *Vision and Visuality,* Dia Art Foundation Discussions on Contemporary Culture 2 (Seattle: Bay Press, 1988), 2-23. Reprinted in Martin Jay, Force Fields: *Between Intellectual History and Cultural Critique* (London: Routledge, 1993), 114-133 argues that there are at least three competing scopic regimes or ways of looking that characterize Western culture, the Baconian, the Cartesian, and the Baroque. Given these three Lessing definitely shifted away from the Cartesian and offered the multiple perspectives and non-linear ways of seeing as have been associated to the a baroque regime. Baroque in Jay's meaning is not only in a sense of a style or mode of seeing typical to the Baroque era in history but also to the modern and postmodern ways of looking. See Allert, "Hidden Aspects of Goethe's Writings" 156-160.

1023 The essays in Ursula Goldenbaum and Alexander Košenina, ed,. *Berliner Aufklärung. Kulturwissenschaftliche Studien* vol. 1-2 (Hannover: Wehrhahn 1999-2003) provide detailed accounts of the Enlightenment discourse and its margins. See Ursula Goldenbaum, "Im Schatten der Tafelrunde: Beziehungen der jungen Berliner Zeitungsschreiber Mylius und Lessing zu französischen Aufklärern," *Berliner Aufklärung* 1 (1999): 69-100 and "Universal oder Plural? Zum scheinbaren Gegensatz von Lessing und Mendelssohn über die Erziehung des Menschengeschlechts." *Lessing Yearbook* 39 (2010-2011): 241-260. Also see Armin Gebhard, *Gotthold Ephraim Lessing: Bühnendramatiker, Bühnenkritiker, theologischer Polemiker* (Marburg: Tectum Verlag, 2007).

1024 *Die Erziehung des Menschengeschlechts*, § 91 (FA 10, 98). See Gilles Deleuze, *The Fold: Leibniz and the Baroque,* trans. Tom Conley (Minneapolis: University of Minnesota Press, 1993), 14-26.

language which renders the search for the original ground plan obsolete and instead calls for ethical intervention. Lessing's work has self-referential and critical dimensions in correlating images with actions and words with the historical contexts and circumstances in which they are being applied.[1025] The *Ringparable* calls for sympathy and compassion to everyone who represents their culture in ethical ways. Moreover, this play brings to awareness co-existing meanings which do not cancel or absorb each other. In this late work the verbal must precede the visual as the meaning of the ring must yet be established by creating its attributes. Only then will language be able to document the authenticity of truth which Lessing associates with Ekphrasis from the visual to the verbal. Ekphrastic hope and the utopian power of language will have to come together so that one can articulate a great vision. Lessing finds that it is best to use understatement and poetic language. He finally turns to a parable that projects the truth to be found in another era and to be brought about by ethical human action and by compassion.

1025 Cf. Renate Homann, *Selbstreflexion der Literatur: Studien zu Dramen von G. E. Lessing und H. von Kleist* (Munich: Fink, 1986) 170-236.

# Chapter 14
# *The Education of Humankind* (1780): Why Lessing Chose the Left Hand

Abstract: It was a significant move in Lessing's *Duplik* when the protagonist opted for the left hand when both hands by the father were offered to him. The right hand would have provided the recipient the possession of the Truth. But instead, the choice to take the left hand meant all that was offered was the desire to honestly search for the Truth with the proviso that the search could involve error and never be completed. This selection of the left hand also indicates a choice for "Bilderschrift" (writing of images) over "Buchstabenschrift" (fixed terms). When choosing the left hand, there was then no claim to be made to possess and to hold meaning once and for all, as if it could be identified with any one singular "Wahrheit" (Truth). Such a notion must have become suspect to Lessing, long before Jean Paul and Friedrich Schlegel. It was superseded by an acute awareness for the metaphoricity of language, the multiplicity of truths, and possibilities. There was also the question of the timing of images. Images may be visions, or concepts only, but they cannot be transferred readily, or without any metaphoric procedure, into verbal claims, as if they were coins with a face value that one could enact business with. This gesture and the resistance to the all too naïve equation between signs and signifiers matters to Lessing. *Die Erziehung des Menschengeschlechts* (The Education of Humankind) serves as a marvelous document of this poetic constellation and as a self-reflective commentary on Lessing's own approach in his late work, whether on serious issues of religion and philosophy as has already been the focus of a great deal of scholarship, or on poetic language, images, and words which belong to "poesy" and motivate further exploration.[1026]

## 1. How to define content in *Die Erziehung des Menschengeschlechts*?

Friedrich Schlegel commented admiringly upon Lessing's "Durchdringung von Vernunft und Phantasie" (merging of reason and fantasy).[1027] He wrote about Lessing's "philosophische[n] Tendenz" (philosophical tendency),[1028] especially in his late writings. There he found "transcendentale–sokratische Ironie" (transcendental-Socratic

1026 On Lessing's "Selbstdeutungsbilder" (images of self-interpretation) and "Doppelreflexion und Ironie" (double reflection) see Ingrid Strohschneider Kohrs, *Poesie und Reflexion:* 139-158 and 159-195 respectively.

1027 Schlegel, "Lessings Gedanken und Meinungen," *Charakteristiken und Kritiken* II (1802-1829, ed. Hans Eichner, KFSA 3 (1974): 46-102 at 85.

1028 "Über Lessing" 117.

irony)."[1029] The poetic "I" of *Die Erziehung des Menschengeschlechts* tries to counteract the normal development from images to words, or from to what Jean Paul in 1804 referred to as the development from "Bilderschrift" (writing of images) to "Buchstabenschrift" (writing of terminologies or discursive language) by using heuristic metaphors in the poetic realm that have a healing function. They offer something of another, second nature, albeit perhaps only as Jean Paul explained them as "nachklingende Bilder von Urbildern–fremde, zerschnittene Gemälde werden zu musaischen Stiften neuer Bilder zusammengereiht–und man geht mit fremden poetischen Bildern um, wie im Mittelalter mit heiligen, von welchen man Farben loskratzte, um solche im Abendmahlwein zu nehmen" (echoing images of of original images. The cut-up pictures of others are arranged as tesserae for new pictures. Poetic images are now used as some were used in the Middle Ages, from which one scratched away flakes of color, to be taken in sacramental wine).[1030] Already for Lessing one singe "Truth" appears to be impossible to grasp because it is a matter of a meta-perspective that no living human could lay claim to. Lessing indicates that he intends to opt for a modest approach in his late philosophical and theological works and resists, even fights with great vigor, any all too grandiose claims. His plea for understatement which was noticeable throughout his works is now after a long reception history more clearly actualized.[1031] There is what we can call a "Lessingian style," a kind of poetic handwriting that draws attention not only to the question of what is given or presented but also to how it is to be communicated. It draws attention to the medium.

*Die Erziehung* is a text that has been debated with respect to its genre and the degree to which it contains levels of history and theology. To what extent are fictionality and vivid speculation the necessary ingredients to any vision of history? How

1029 Schlegel, "'Zur Philosophie. B. 1797.' Ende der ersten und Uebergang zur Moralischen Epoche," *Philosophische Lehrjahre 1796-1806,* ed. Ernst Behler, 2 vols., KFSA 18-19 (1963-1971), 1: 79-117 at 79 (#604).

1030 Jean Paul, *Vorschule der Ästhetik,* course 1 §2, 34; *Horn of Oberon,* 18. Jean Paul defines already in his first paragraph what "poesy" is for him and explains why it is more adequate to present life than any terminological discursive language: "[...] 'die Poesie ist die einzige *zweite* Welt in der hiesigen;–oder wie Singen zum Reden, so verhält sich die Poesie zur Prose [...]' Wenigstens würde in Bildern sich das verwandte Leben besser spiegeln als in toten Begriffen–nur für jeden anders; denn nichts bringt die Eigentümlichkeit der Menschen mehr zur Sprache als die Wirkung derer, welche die Dichtkunst auf sie macht; und daher werden ihrer Definitionen ebenso viele sein als ihrer Leser und Zuhörer" (*Vorschule der Ästhetik*, course 1 § 1, 30): "Poetry is the only *second* world in this world. [...] singing is to speaking so poetry is to prose [...] At least images would mirror kindred life better than do dead concepts, though differently for every man. Nothing brings out better the individuality of men than the effect that poetry has on them. Hence there will be just as many definitions of poetry as readers and listeners") (*Horn of Oberon* 15). Jean Paul adds: "Bei Individuen, wie bei Völkern, ist [...] *Bilderschrift* eher als *Buchstabenschrift*" (*Vorschule der Ästhetik*, course 1 §2, 33) ("With individuals as with peoples [...] *hieroglyphic* [the writing of images] precedes *alphabetic* [the writing of terminologies] writing") (*Horn of Oberon* 17).

1031 Achim Aurnhammer, Giulia Cantarutti, Friedrich Vollhardt, ed., *Die Drei Ringe. Entstehung, Wandel und Wirkung der Ringparabel in der Europäischen Literatur und Kultur* (Berlin: Walter de Gruyter, 2016). Compare with the notion of four rings: Bruno Buike, *Die Fabel von den vier Ringen und andere Ungereimtheiten,* Edition Wissenschaft Reihe Germanistik 9 (Marburg: Tectum Verlag, 1996).

does Lessing's late work contribute to the Enlightenment by challenging religion?[1032] Whereas some critics claim it Lessing's oeuvre *Die Erziehung* is ultimately a tentative representation of things that happened, others emphasize its hypothetical mode and draw attention to certain poetic features of this text which are helping to decode the content. The style is inseparable from the content and, as we remember in distinction to painting in *Laokoon*, according to Lessing the poet must provide free range to the imagination.[1033] If the arbitrary signs of language were to appear as if natural and images could fluidly transpose into words then poesy would have reached a goal Lessing had articulated in his *Laokoon*. The complete text of *Die Erziehung des Menschengeschlechts* (The Education of Humankind) was first published by Voß in Berlin in 1780. It is a complex work, almost a palimpsest of voices, a collage of sorts that articulates a cohesive vision but is associated with understatement and a plurality of meanings. We can detect a deconstructionist tendency and an ongoing quest with many references to other writers, so that it is very difficult to trace Lessing's own voice in this text. He refers to world religions and many other writers to such an extent that what we read depends on the context of each paragraph. Nevertheless, *Die Erziehung* has often been interpreted as Lessing's final stance on religion and philosophy, as if this text–consisting of one hundred paragraphs and being a collage of writings–summarized his ultimate credo. But it is also an example of poesy.

As Toshimasa Yasukata following in the footsteps of the theologian Helmut Thielicke, has eloquently shown, in this text lies "an intrinsically well-rounded system of [...] thought."[1034] Yasukata offers an astute and fascinating analysis of Lessing's "eso-

1032 Arno Schilson, *Geschichte im Horizont der Vorsehung. G. E. Lessings Beitrag zu einer Theologie der Geschichte*, Tübinger Theologische Studien 3 (Mainz: Matthias-Grünewald-Verlag, 1974) and Martin Bollacher, *Lessing. Vernunft und Geschichte. Untersuchungen zum Problem religiöser Aufklärung in den Spätschriften* (Tübingen: Niemeyer, 1978). For another excellent study on an approach to Lessing's horizon, see Karl Guthke, *Lessings Horizonte. Grenzen und Grenzenlosigkeit der Toleranz*, Kleine Schriften zur Aufklärung 12 (Göttingen: Wallstein, 2003).

1033 Jean Paul explains poesy also in these terms: "Ungleich der Wirklichkeit, die ihre prosaische Gerechtigkeit und ihre Blumen in unendlichen Räumen und Zeiten austeilet, muß eben die Poesie in geschlossenen beglücken; sie ist die einzige Friedensgötttin der Erde und der Engel, der uns, und wär' es nur auf Stunden, aus Kerkern auf Sterne führt: wie Achilles' Lanze muß sie jede Wunde heilen, die sie sticht" (*Vorschule der Ästhetik*, course 1 § 3, 35) ("Unlike reality which achieves a distribution of the flowers of poetry through infinite spaces and times, poetry must grant her favors within limitations, She is the only Goddess of peace on earth; she is the angel who leads us, if but for a few hours, out of our prisons up to the stars: like Achilles' lance, she must heal every wound she herself inflicts") (*Horn of Oberon* 19). And whereas Jean Paul warns that there can be nothing more dangerous than a poet who wants to encircle our already restricted reality with his personal second one, Lessing is similarly concerned with offering freedom and not restriction to the readers and spectators of the poetic realm while providing endless unrestricted possibilities of reading.

1034 Yasukata, *Lessing's Philosophy of Religion and the German Enlightenment* 89. He adds: "Furthermore, this work is regarded by many as foundation of modern philosophy of religion and the beginning of a deeper observation of history." See also Christoph Bultmann, "Lessings *Axiomata* (1778) als eine hermeneutische Programmschrift," Christoph Bultmann and Friedrich Vollhardt, ed., *Lessings Religionsphilosophie im Kontext. Hamburger Fragmente und Wolfenbütteler Axiomata*, Frühe Neuzeit 159 (Berlin: De Gruyter, 2011), 242–260.

teric theology, that is his normative attitude in the conflict between religious faith in the transcendent and adhesion to the immanent."[1035] He cites the theologian Paul Tillich who perceives in this work "the most genuine spirit of Lessing, a really Lessingian mode" and interestingly argued that this text is "the manifesto of Lessing's theological and religious-philosophical thought,"[1036] This raised interest in the rhetorical Lessing-specific way of argumentation. It will yet need to be explored.

Hugh Nisbet says that this text is a contribution to the attempts to rationalize the Holy Trinity.[1037] Arno Schilson and Axel Schmitt warn against any all too specific or even narrow interpretation of this work "in der einen oder anderen Richtung einer Lessingschen Weltanschauung oder eines ihm eigenen systematischen ausgearbeiteten Standorts" (in one or the other direction of a world view by Lessing or one of his personally and systematically worked out perspectives).[1038] Instead they emphasize the style of layering multiple references without clearly positioning one firm point of view. Ralph Häfner insists that *Die Erziehung* is in fact a manifesto of Lessing's anthropological turn, his search for the "ganzen Menschen" (the complete human) and that it reads as an attempt to bring mind and body into one, or to conceptualize the human soul so "daß die Seele in einer organischen Materie sich wieder verkörpert, oder, wie Herder sagen würde, daß sie sich einen Körper in dem sie wirksam in Erscheinung treten kann, 'baut'" (that the soul embodies itself again in an organic matter and, as Herder would say, that it "builds" itself in a body in which it can be effective).[1039] Häfner sees this as developing out of a "Pantheismus kabbalistischer Provinienz" (pantheism of a kabbalistic provenience).[1040] What matters are questions of freedom and mortality in the age of reason.[1041] It has been questioned in scholarship whether or not Lessing believed in palingenesis and whether he thought of a transmigration of souls from one state of being to another but in any case it has been argued that Lessing believed in the possibility of transformation or qualitative change, despite all apparent continuity across the ages, and in distinct modes of human existence.[1042]

---

1035 Yasukata, *Lessing's Philosophy of Religion* 89.

1036 Yasukata, *Lessing's Philosophy of Religion* 89.

1037 Hugh Barr Nisbet, "The Rationalisation of the Holy Trinity from Lessing to Hegel," *Lessing Yearbook* 31 (1999): 65-89 at 71.

1038 FA 10, 848.

1039 Ralph Häfner, "Das Menschengeschlecht im Zeitalter des Heiligen Geistes: Eine Hypothese zu Ursprung und Gestalt von Lessings Anthopologie," Bultmann and Vollhardt ed., *Lessings Religionsphilosophie im Kontext,* 126-137 at 136.

1040 Häfner, "Das Menschengeschlecht" 127.

1041 Klaus Hammacher, "Lessings Spinozismus aufgezeigt an seinem Beitrag zur Wandlung der philosophischen Grundfragen nach Gott, Freiheit und Unsterblichkeit in der Aufklärung," *Tijdschrift voor de Studie van de Verlichting en van het vrije Denken* 10 (1982): 87-110 at 91.

1042 Alexander Altmann, "Lessings Glaube an die Seelenwanderung," *Lessing Yearbook* 8 (1976): 7-41, reprinted in *Die Trostvolle Aufklärung. Studien zur Metaphysik und politischen Theorie Moses Mendelssohns,* Forschungen und Materialien zur deutschen Aufklärung II: Monographien 3 (Stuttgart-Bad Cannstatt: Frommann-Holzboog, 1982), 109-134; Heidrun Drescher-Ochoa, *Kultur und Freiheit. Ein Beitrag zu Lessings Kulturkritik und-Philosophie,* Europäische Hochschulschriften I: Deutsche Sprache und Literatur 1670 (Frankfurt am Main: Peter Lang, 1997). Also see Klaus Bohnen, "Lessings *Erziehung des Menschengeschlechts* (§4) und Bonnets *Palingénésie*, ein Zitat-Hinweis," *Germanisch-Romanische Monatsschrift* 62 (1981): 362-365.

Although Lessing's *The Education of Humankind* can still be regarded as a treatise consisting of various parts, the first one, containing paragraphs 1-53, was published in 1777.[1043] The other parts were added later and there are numerous questions concerning the treatise's content and form. This work's complicated publication history may explain some of the problems. When the text appeared in Berlin in 1780 Lessing's name was on the title page as the editor, not the author of the material included. Lessing claimed to have found this anonymous text which he was merely editing in the Wolfenbüttel library. It was not until 1804 that Reimarus' son, Johann Albert Hinrich Reimarus, "explained" the puzzle by attributing this work to Lessing's personal "interventions," if not to his complete authorship. It is usually interpreted as an important document of Lessing's detailing final beliefs, even though Lessing never claimed he was the author. The section published in 1777 was part of the counterproposal to Reimarus' statements, and so it became part of the controversy with pastor Goeze of Hamburg. It seems unsatisfactory to think that all that was at stake was merely a religious controversy. But it certainly has much to do with Lessing's advocacy of uncensored speech and critical thinking. The question why Lessing published it anonymously has most recently not only been identified with Lessing's need to avoid censorship, but moreover as being related to his emotional state after the death of his wife Eva in 1778 and his son Traugott the year before, so that the tone of confidence and hope in the early section no longer match his personal mood.[1044]

A third possibility for Lessing's preference to remain anonymous has been hinted at most recently by Friedrich Vollhardt. The treatise which is written from a Deist perspective articulates respect for all world religions in various cultures and eras. It is ultimately a celebration of reason that will lead to ethical human behavior, even to the point that people will act ethically without anyone or any institution having to tell them to do so. In other words, the work suggests the possibility that all the world religions are helpful only as long as they promote learning to act more humanly; but when humanity has achieved the goal of ethical perfection, then these religions will be superfluous. This was of course a rather heretical notion, although similarly ideas were expressed by Leibniz, Adam Ferguson (or Ferguson the Raith), and Spinoza to all of whom Lessing's text references, while also referring to older utopian ideals developed Joachim de Fiore and St. Augustine.[1045]

At one point, Monika Fick found *Die Erziehung* characterized by Lessing's "karge, nüchterne Begrifflichkeit" (meagre, sober terminology).[1046] She emphasized the complex scholarly academic format with all the many paragraphs, the differentiations of a wide array of terminologies, making it a historically immense undertaking. Lessing seems to have gathered information from early Patristic literature down to the most recent philosophical debates. But in the 4th edition of her *Handbuch* she acknowledges:

1043 They appeared *Zur Geschichte und Literatur* 4 (1777) which contained the Reimarus fragments as part of the editor's "Gegensätze" (objections). Lessing directed these 53 paragraphs to counter Reimarius' proposition that the books of the Old Testament were not written to reveal a religion (FA 8, 333-346).

1044 Nisbet, *Lessing: Eine Biographie* 763; *Gotthold Ephraim Lessing* 585.

1045 Friedrich Vollhardt, "'Enthusiasmus der Spekulation': Zur fehlenden Vorgeschichte von Lessings Erziehungslehre," Bultmann and Vollhardt, ed., *Lessings Religionsphilosophie im Kontext* 104-125.

1046 Monika Fick, *Lessing Handbuch* (Stuttgart, Weimar: Metzler, 2000), 425.

"Man sieht in ihm nicht länger ein abschließendes Bekenntnis und Vermächtnis Lessings, sondern einen bewußt offen gehaltenen Diskussionsbeitrag, in dem ein spezifisches Problem der Religionsdebatte durchgespielt wird" (One sees in it no longer a final confession and testament by Lessing, but rather a consciously left open contribution to a debate on religion in which a specific problem is being tested).[1047]

## 2. From content to rhetoric: A commentary on poesy

The religious debate surrounding *Die Erziehung* is intricate and not of an immediate concern here. What is of interest here is the way in which the work can be acknowledged for its dialogue-structure and its open-endedness. Perhaps it is even a parody of any "treatise" that would claim definite or all too simple answers to the questions raised. I shall pursue a rather specific line of thought with focus less on the religious and philosophical content than on the rhetorical implications of the text for the visual-verbal debate. Friedrich Vollhardt drew attention to the fictional mode of writing in the work identifying Lessing's style and rhetoric as the text's most important features:

> Auch die *Erziehung des Menschengeschlechts* trägt, was oft vergessen wird, poetische Züge. Das lässt sich etwa am Gebrauch der rhetorischen Stilmittel zeigen, mit denen Lessing die Eindeutigkeit zugunsten einer starken Anschaulichkeit zurückstellt, woraus sich nur der Schluss ziehen lässt, dass ihm an Eindeutigkeit hinsichtlich der angeführten Offenbarungsinhalte nicht gelegen war. Bereits das Motto[1048]–wiederum ein Augustinus-Zitat–stellt den Text unter das Argumentationsprinzip der Uneigentlichkeit, so wie auch die Analogie zwischen Erziehung und Offenbarung als literarisches Gleichnis interpretieren läßt. Die Organisation in genau einhundert Paragraphen könnnte ein Formzitat sein, mit dem der Gelehrte Traktat parodiert wird, und das Spiel mit den Rollen von Verfasser und Herausgeber verleiht der Schrift einen fiktionalen Modus. Mehr noch: Bei der Betrachtung der biblischen Elementarbücher wird ausführlich über deren "Einkleidung und den Stil" (§ 48) nachgedacht und es werden die literarischen Techniken der Anspielung untersucht, die Neugier auf höhere Einsichten wecken sollen. Denn das Alte und das Neue Testament sind nur "Vorübungen" (§ 47) für das kommende dritte Zeitalter; am Ende setzt sich bei Lessing die Vernunftreligion durch, die positive Religionen haben ihre erzieherische Rolle erschöpft.[1049]

1047 Fick, *Handbuch* 4th ed. (2016), 427-444 at 427. The 4th ed. gives a more thorough and updated account of this complex work, addresses its history of publication, elaborates on its publication history, the sources, the context, and its key terms "Vernunft" (reason) and "Offenbarung" (revelation). Fick further elaborates on Lessing's use of Spinoza's *Tractatus Theologico-Politicus* as a matrix and gives an informative account of the scholarship about it.

1048 "Haec omnia inde esse in quibusdam vera, inde in quibusdam falsa sunt" (Augustine, *Soliloquies* II: 10). Yasukata, *Lessing's Philosophy of Religion* 172 notes that there is some disagreement about how this should be translated and gives the standard English translation: "That all these things are in certain aspects true, by this very thing, that they are in certain aspects false."

1049 Friedrich Vollhardt, *Gotthold Ephraim Lessing* (Munich: Beck, 2016), 113.

[Also the *Education of Humankind* carries poetic features though these have often been forgotten. This can be shown in the use of rhetorical style with which Lessing ranks disambiguation into a lower position for the sake of a striking vividness. One can draw the conclusion that he was not interested in firmly defined meanings with respect to the contents of what will be revealed. Already the motto–once more a citation from Augustine–signifies the text under the header of a principle of argumentation with has an as-if mode, so as to be metaphorically speaking only, similar to the analogy between education and revelation, which itself can be interpreted as a literary parable. The organization into exactly one hundred paragraphs could be a citation of form with which the genre Educated Treatise is being parodied and the play with the roles of author and editor add to the script the modus of fictionality. Furthermore: In the reflection about the biblical elementary books much thought is given to the "wrapping and the style" (§48) and the literary techniques of allusion are being examined in order to awaken the curiosity for higher insights. Because the Old and the New Testament are only "Preliminary Exercises" (§47) for the coming third age; in the end for Lessing a religion of reason prevails, the positive religions seem to have exhausted their educational function].

While Vollhardt finds elements of a "starke[n] Anschaulichkeit" (striking vividness) in *Die Erziehung,* he does not explain how such "Anschaulichkeit" can best be characterized. It is the matter of an ekphrastic strategy which is not to be traced only from the visual to the verbal but also from the verbal to the visual, marked by multi-directional possibilities and important discrepancies that seem to be engrained in the medium. Vollhardt finds clarity of content also lacking a bit in the text and instead emphasizes its enhanced visual style. He notes that in *Die Erziehung* Lessing surprisingly combines the most diverse topics and aspects for arguments and speculations, thereby avoiding any stable definite terminologies. He diagnoses ambiguity as far as the content of this work is concerned and also affirms that it is hard to give any concrete summary of it. These must have been the features which attracted Jean Paul to the work:

Was Jean Paul besonders an der *Erziehung des Menschengeschlechts* angezogen haben muß, war außer der Verbindung von Theologie und Philosophie darin der einprägsame Stil, den Elise Reimarus nach der Lektüre der *Erziehung* in einem Brief an Lessing vom 25. April 1780 so beschrieben hat: "Überhaupt sind sie der einzige Philosoph, den ich kenne, der Wahrheiten auf diese Art, wie einen elektrischen Schlag, fühlbar zu machen und durch Mark und Bein zu führen weiß."[1050]

[What must have attracted Jean Paul to *The Education of Humankind* was, in addition to the link between theology and philosophy the most poignant style, which Elise Reimarus

1050 Wulf Koepke, "Jean Paul als ein früher Leser der *Erziehung des Menschengeschlechts,*" *Lessing Yearbook* 2 (1970): 90-114 at 94 refers to the letter by Elise Reimarus to Lessing (FA 12, 320-322 at 321). Koepke explains that such essays as "Übungen im Denken" (Exercises of Thinking" and "Lob der Dummheit" (Praise of Folly) by Jean Paul are modeled after this *Erziehungsschrift* by Lessing, especially Jean Paul's *Rhaspodien* which underwent numerous editions and reworking by the author and which were finally titled "Raffinerien für raffinierte Theologen" (94) (refiner matters for refined theologians), a work that is playful, and which presents itself like a riddle and a bit as a parody. It contains a slightly modified quote directly from this work by Lessing: "Gott hätte bei allem seine Hand im Spiele; nur bei unseren Irrthümern nicht?" (God should have his hand always in the game, only not when it comes to our errors?) (112, fn. 20). Lessing's version of the quote comes at the end of the editor's introduction to *Die Erziehung* (FA 10, 74). I find it significant that Jean Paul picks up on Lessing's humor, his mode of questioning and leaving things open.

described after having read *The Education* in a letter to Lessing on April 25, 1780 as follows: Generally speaking: "You are the only philosopher who I know who is capable to make truths sensible, so that they hit you through blood and bone."].

*Die Erziehung* is a text that has had a stark effect on its readers, overwhelming them with sense impressions and visual language. It is a text that has delicate shifts between focus and frame in the metaphoric process so that metaphors lead to a transformation of ideas in complete ways. One may link this with what Philip Wheewright defined as "diaphoric" metaphors, in the process of which multiple levels of meaning are imagined in terms of a sequencing from one point to the next without being merely additive or accumulative but rather "going through" (diaphoric) from one meaning to another, letting go one meaning for another. This allows for qualitative change in the metaphoric process.[1051] Thus they allow for change of imagery in the metaphoric process.

## 3. A "Fugue"?

*The Education of Humankind* is a collage of references ranging from Augustine to Adam Ferguson, from the Bible to Leibniz and Spinoza. It is characterized by a laconic style in an attempt to combine everything, no matter how remote into a single viewpoint. It is characterized by an effortless and fluid mode. Monika Fick suggests that Lessing's writing imitates the musical genre of "Engführung" (a fugue) which brings the dispersed and polyphone voices into harmony with each other while dissolving hierarchies between them. Such a fugue-like composition is able to link completely disparate ideas into a strict reduction, even to the point of ultimate dissolution and stunning silence.[1052] The tension, however, seems to remain. Lessing leaves us with gaps, puzzles, and no transitions between citations. Whatever definitions are alluded to, they seem to no longer cohesively grasp widely shared meanings. It has been pointed out that Lessing also in terms of his religious beliefs adopted esoteric ideas on palingenesis and metempsychosis, the transmigration of the soul.[1053] He both engaged with various world religions,[1054] and shifted attention to the end of didacticism, finding that the essence of religion is to promote ethical behavior. To him not what we believe matters but how we act, and to what degree our actions are contributing towards ethical humanity. Before this script could be published in one piece, the opening section was featured along with a series of fragments written by Hermann Samuel Reimarus, the

1051 Philip Wheelwright, *Metaphor and Reality* (Bloomington: Indiana University Press, 2nd ed. 1964, first 1962), 78-91.

1052 Fick, *Handbuch* 423-430.

1053 Palingenesis is the doctrine of continual rebirths and in Christian theology sometimes used to refer to baptism. The term is often conflated with metempsychosis or the transmigration of the soul, in which the soul at death passes into another body, human or animal.

1054 Daniel Cyranka, "Warum nicht? Lessings Äußerungen zur Seelenwanderung," Hans-Edwin Friedrich, Wilhelm Haefs, and Christian Soboth, ed., *Literatur und Theologie im 18. Jahrhundert: Konfrontationen–Kontroversen–Konkurrenzen,* Hallesche Beiträge zur Europäischen Aufklärung 41 (Berlin: De Gruyter, 2011), 122-138.

*Apologie oder Schutzschrift für die vernünftigen Verehrer Gottes* (The Apology or Protective Writing for the reasonable Admirers of God).[1055] But this work by Reimarus, professor for Hebrew and Oriental Languages at the Gymnasium in Hamburg, was not published during his life time.

*Die Erziehung* is sometimes taken to be Lessing's final credo about world religions, about the project of the Enlightenment, and about a notion of progress that cannot be conceptualized as one-sided linear straight line from point A to point B, or from a childhood stage or early civilization to advanced adulthood and enlightened humankind. On the one hand it is associated in Lessing's rational terms with wisdom, divine understanding, and but on the other hand Lessing introduces what he considers is a necessary adjustment, the notion of "Akkommodation" (accommodation), a realigning or attuning to the temporality of what can be learnt in a given time period. The central idea expressed in this work, with all its highly theological and philosophical ramifications, seems to be that the world religions are all valuable for learning ethical behavior on earth. This is what matters most and reason will ultimately lead to the same effect, whether educated consciously towards a specific goal, or on its own accord.

Lessing remained carefully guarded and always maintained the modus of narration in fiction. Of particular interest are Lessing's poetic strategies in presenting a world view guided by "Accommodation" according to which only that can be understood which is at the same time being revealed. Learning, reading, and understanding truth is then conceptualized in terms of interactive processes which are multi-directional, a give and take. These processes have been associated with an anthropological turn on Lessing's part, involving the idea that the divine becomes human to the extent that the human becomes divine. Lessing makes us reflect on changes of meaning through semantic movements (*phora*). These involve the use of metaphor so that through certain particulars something appears in a previously unknown and hence apparently fresh and significant way.

## 4. Lessing's approach to humanistic education

Lessing's *Die Erziehung* questions the notion of institutionalized knowledge and refers to Islam, Judaism, Christianity, and all of them as systems of knowledge and ways to understand truth as available at a certain time in history and in the context of a given culture. There seems to be an inclusive vision of an educated and tolerant society that implies a meta-perspective similar to Spinoza's *Tractatus Theologico-Politicus* (1670) where there is a plurality of paths with each of them leading to truth albeit from very diverse vantage points.[1056] They simply won't fit on any single map. Human education is the ultimate goal yet the "Erfüllung" (fulfillment) of such shared hopes may also occur by

---

1055 Hermann Samuel Reimarus, *Apologie oder Schutzschrift für die vernünftigen Verehrer Gottes*, ed. Gerhard Alexander (2 vols. Frankfurt am Main: Insel 1972).

1056 Monika Fick, "Religion der Vernunft: Spinoza's 'Tractatus Theologico-Politicus' als Folie," *Lessing Handbuch. Leben–Werk–Wirkung*, 4th ed. (Stuttgart: Metzler, 2016), 437-440. Also Spinoza, *Theological-Political Treatise*, trans. Michael Silverstone and Jonathan Israel means of an "Offenbarung" (revelation). Yet such revelation would have to be timed so perfectly that whatever is visible can in fact be comprehended and assimilated in the process of perception. Whereas the idea of "Offenbarung" seems to be related to visibility and seeing, it requires perception skills to able to actualize it and to transform that knowledge into action. Karl Eibl suggested that *Die Erziehung* dissolves the binary between theology and rationalism while oscillating between the senses.[1057] Influenced by John Locke, Leibniz, Adam Ferguson, and others, Lessing traces a multi-step development of all humans from one world religion to the next, up the ladder or in the development across centuries until insights, fulfillment, and completion were to become realized. This could potentially happen through conscious learning and by means of great effort through "Glaubenswahrheiten" (truths of faith) but it could also happen through "Vernunftwahrheiten" (truths of reason). Religions could be very helpful in educating people but they are not the only way for everyone to become ethically human.

## 5. Questions on revelation, education and "Akkommodation"

We have no access to Lessing's "intentions" in composing *Die Erziehung* and it would be presumptuous to claim knowledge about what Lessing may have had in mind when completing this late and most abstract work. As someone with an addiction to gambling, he was not someone who played with open cards. He had many secrets as a writer. His late works contain an abundance of levels of metaphor and abstraction.[1058] His questions about the ends of education were not new at the time and his curiosity about such concepts as palingenesis, metempsychosis, reincarnation, transmigration, the soul's progression, and the transindividual dimensions of human existence were esoteric, rather than being mainstream, although related ideas had been discussed in works by such diverse writers as Baruch Spinoza, John Locke, Gottfried Leibniz, Adam Ferguson, Charles Bonnet, and Johann Gottfried Herder.[1059]

---

(Cambridge: Cambridge University Press, 2007). Israel points out that Spinoza is pathbreaking in terms of his "practical philosophy" (viii).

1057 Karl Eibl, "'... kommen würde' gegen '... nimmermehr gekommen wäre.' Auflösung des 'Widerspruchs' von § 4 und § 77 in Lessings *Erziehung des Menschengeschlechts*," *Germanisch-Romanische Monatsschrift* 65 (N. F. 34) (1984): 461-464.

1058 For some interesting observations see Patricia Hayden-Roy, "Refining the Metaphor in Lessing's 'Erziehung des Menschengeschlechts'," *Monatshefte* 95 (2003): 393-409.

1059 Spinoza who had similarly written about the idea of accommodation with respect to the preliminary nature of the scriptures which may at some point in the future become dispensable once the truth or the Divine will has revealed or established itself. As fragmentary as his *Tractatus Theologico-Politicus* (1670) may be, it has similar connotations to those that resurface in Lessing's work. With John Locke Lessing shares certain aspects of his theory of mind so that the mind was considered a blank slate or *tabula rasa* and contrary to pre-existing Cartesian philosophy, humans are not born with innate ideas but learn from experience through sense perception. Lessing was much influenced by this empiricist tradition and questioned given norms while focusing on an approach to learning via "Mitleid" and sense perception especially through theater. Also important was Locke's *The Reasonableness of Christianity* (1710) where he formulated the notion that

Yasukata characterizes the basic features of *Die Erziehung* as "eminently polemical," "anti-theoretical," "gymnastic," and "hypothetical."[1060] There is a dynamic at stake here which Lessing summarized himself: "Es ist nicht wahr, dass die kürzeste Linie immer die gerade ist" (It is not true that the shortest line is always the straight one").[1061] Just when the reader is perhaps about to think that a matter is closed, Lessing comes up with paradoxes and open endings, especially concerning the use of such notions as "Erziehung" (education) and "Offenbarung" (revelation). These terms are associated with rational understanding, learning and civilization, and with immediate sense perception, religion and ethics. Lessing's late writings negotiate a wide spectrum of ideas and positions concerning truth and hope. Lessing knows, as is obvious in *Nathan der Weise, t*hat the most important truths can often only be expressed by means of a fairytale.

On December 27, 1777, Lessing's infant son died two days after his birth, followed by the death of his wife Eva the following January 10. Nisbet has identified a marked change of tone in Lessing's late works depending whether they were written before or after these catastrophic events. The "Goezestreit" was gathering steam. In July 1778 Lessing's freedom from censorship and in publishing material from the ducal library in Wolfenbüttel was revoked. All of these matters had an enormous impact on Lessing's well-being.[1062] In contrast to the standard view which sees Lessing's last epoch as

revelation is a folkloric medium used by God to teach people ethical behavior. From the philosopher and polymath Gottfried Wilhelm Leibniz, Lessing had been inspired to take a great interest on the most minimal things and not to ignore the marginal. Leibniz suggested in his *Monadenlehre* an idea of metamorphosis, continuous change, while drawing attention to the importance of ongoing reflection and self-reflection. The Scottish philosopher and historian Adam Ferguson had, similar to Lessing, a great interest in history as a progress that is based more than anything external on human civil society and ethics. Ferguson was an avid poker player and Lessing was even addicted at times to playing cards and gambling. The Swiss naturalist or botanist Charles Bonnet studied reproduction by fusion and regeneration of small creatures in nature, such as insects and butterflies. Fick, *Handbuch* 428 notes that Lessing's ideas on metempsychosis go back to Joachim de Fiore and Origen. On the latter see: Wilhelm Schmidt-Biggemann, "Lessings origenistische Eschatologie," Bultmann and Vollhardt, ed., *Lessings Religionsphilosophie im Kontext,* 138-153 at 146. The influence of Lessing's *Erziehungsschrift* can be seen in Herder's 1782 essay "Über die Seelenwanderung" (FHA 4, 425-473). See: Kelly Barry, "Natural Palingenesis: Childhood, Memory, and Self-Experience in Herder and Jean Paul," *Goethe Yearbook* 14 (2007): 1-25 linking both Herder and Jean Paul with Lessing's approach; Daniel Cyranka, *Lessing im Reinkarnationsdiskurs. Eine Untersuchung zu Kontext und Wirkung von G. E. Lessings Texten zur Seelenwanderung* (Göttingen: Vandenhoeck & Ruprecht, 2005), "'Gehet hin und leset euren Lessing, den wir Spiritisten stolz den unseren nennen!' Lessings Wirkung in der modernen Esoterik." *Lessing Yearbook* 37 (2006/2007): 125-138, "'Warum nicht?' Lessings Äußerungen zur Seelenwanderung." Friedrich et al., ed., *Literatur und Theologie im 18. Jahrhundert* 122-138; Fick, *Handbuch* 427-442.

1060 Yasukata, *Lessing's Philosophy of Religion* 90.

1061 FA 10, 98.

1062 Also Kowalik, "Nathan as a Work of Mourning" separates *Nathan der Weise,* the writing of which began after the end of the "Goezestreit" in October 1778, from his earlier dramatic works by linking it to these personal events in Lessing's life. One may question the extent to which Lessing's personal experience with death may not only have led him to mourn and to let go of certain hopes but also to project onto life an existence beyond constituted of three major works (*Die Erziehung des Menschengeschlechts, Ernst und Falk,* and *Nathan der Weise).* Nisbet makes a more careful distinction among them:

> It therefore follows that if there is such a thing as Lessing's philosophical testament–often identified with *The Education of Human Race*–we must not overlook the biographical hiatus which separates the two works discussed here [The *Education of Humankind* and *Ernst and Falk*] from the later *Nathan the Wise.*[1063]

We can increasingly observe in Lessing's work a move from didacticism to metaphor, from narrative to philosophical statement, and from description to the use of poetic reference, illustration, and ongoing reflection. Yet these shifts occur in a progression, so that by the end Lessing departs from his previous fondness for fables and stories to a pronounced preference for open-ended parables and the projection of unfinished ideas. *Nathan der Weise* and some related texts, such as the Ringparable included in this play and *Eine Parabel vom brennenden Palast* each are writings about ideas on what could happen or might have happened, along with speculations about the future. He shifts attention to vague possibilities, invokes images associated with fire and water, invents scenarios which are no longer grounded in any specific time or location but situated ultimately somewhere in the realm of the subjective, characterized by paradoxes and riddles.

Since Lessing failed to identify himself as the author of *Die Erziehung,* this has led to the so-called "Thaer Legend" which questions Lessing's authorship of the treatise and raises important issues about the specifics of his works. A complicated reception history then draws more attention to the "style" of the paragraphs since only it can reveal true authorship. Apparently Lessing never signed the text nor made a clear statement about its authorship. Albrecht Daniel Thaer, who had visited Lessing in 1780, claimed in a letter written in 1785 that during his student years he had developed and written out a "new system" for the defense of Christianity and that "ein grosser Mann" (a great man) had subsequently taken it and published it after having made stylistic changes. The second part was published later. For many years, it was assumed that Lessing must have been this "great man." However, in a letter written in 1777 which was first published in 1945 it seems that this "great man" may actually have been Jakob Mauvillon who had published a systematic of Christianity in 1787.[1064] Not everyone has been convinced by this and Nisbet observes that it is not at all clear that the matter has been solved: "What is known as the 'Thaer legend' has never been conclusively refuted."[1065] Nisbet on the other hand accepts the arguments that confirm the work to be Lessing's because of its unique poetic style which he argues is consistent with Lessing's other late works. They were written in response to the attacks of Haupt-Pastor Goeze and address the limits of education where the real issue is how people act and not only what they think. But why did Lessing prefer not to be identified as the author of *Die Erziehung?*

---

death similar to that Spinoza argued for, who equated duration with continuation but rather with timelessness.

1063 Nisbet, *Lessing: Eine Biographie* 745–746; *Gotthold Ephraim Lessing* 571 (quoted).

1064 Nisbet, *Lessing: Eine Biographie* 746; *Gotthold Ephraim Lessing* 572.

1065 Nisbet, *Lessing: Eine Biographie* 746; *Gotthold Ephraim Lessing* 572.

Although he apparently wrote an anonymous preface to the second edition in 1780 Lessing avoided making this work look like his last word on the matters. I think he did this because he had dealt with the same issues much more poetically. It seems therefore understandable that Lessing preferred to have *Nathan der Weise* be regarded as his final word and not *Die Erziehung* since *Nathan* has more levels of reflection illustrated than *Erziehungsschrift*. Lessing was consistent in avoiding dogmatism, not only because of the censorship resulting from the infamous Fragmentenstreit but also because his own philosophical and cognitive approach to poesy necessitated radically open endings. These scripts further raise awareness for what Lessing calls a "Geheimnis" (hidden truth).[1066] The curtain seems to fall all too quickly not only in *Nathan der Weise* but perhaps also in the debate about *Die Erziehung*. Lessing resists showing everything and as a master of abbreviation indicates that reality is in process to become something else. It other words reality is itself metonymic revealing only *pars pro toto* relations. These late works share Lessing's insight that one's faith has a great deal to do with one's ability to change according to history and location. Truth can be achieved through education, but alternatively, it may at times be revealed sporadically, in unprecedented ways, not to be calculated.

There are limits to the Enlightenment, not everything can be visualized since something mysterious seems to remain hidden beyond the horizon and will perhaps only be unraveled in the future. "Offenbarung" (revelation) remains postponed to the future. It could perhaps come through in dramatic performance as an exceptional moment. To be part of such a revelation means tapping into the dynamics shared between nature and art. Lessing tries to do justice to the insight that the nature of truth remains pluralistic and partial and he borrows much from contemporary science where questions about speed, energy, the nature of light, seeing, sense perception, and cognition were becoming of considerable interest along with ancient ideas about enargeia. These insights may contradict Lessing's previous net of interwoven messages, but they also add nuances to it. *Eine Parabel* or, more precisely, his *Parable about the Burning Palace* and his last play *Nathan the Wise* with its inter- or meta-text Ringparable, are truly his very final works written after the catastrophes of 1778.

It is plausible that *Die Erziehung, Ernst und Falk,* and *Nathan der Weise* are all three works in which the wisdom of the late Lessing is articulated in final form ("grouped together as embodying the definitive wisdom of Lessing's final years"),[1067] concerning as they do complex relations between knowledge and experience, rationality and sense perceptions. Although the second part of *Die Erziehung* and the second part of *Ernst und Falk* were only published in 1780, both works had already been written well before Lessing's catastrophic crises of 1777-1778.

1066 The word occurs nine times in *Ernst und Falk* and seven times in *Nathan der Weise.*
1067 Nisbet, *Lessing: Eine Biographie* 745; *Gotthold Ephraim Lessing* 571.

## 6. Back to the sources? On the provisional nature of scripts

Erasmus of Rotterdam wrote: "At homines, mihi crede, non nascuntur, sed finguntur" ("But man certainly is not born but made man").[1068] With his dictum: "Sed in primis ad fontes ipsos properandum" ("But first and foremost, however, recourse must be had to the sources themselves").[1069] Erasmus tried to give everyone access to literature and first-hand understanding of writing, including the Scriptures that were even then not widely available. He tried to emancipate people and considered education a power for access to the truth. Education to him was everything. The belief in humankind is also a belief in education. Didacticism was thought to be a strong powerful instrument for improving the world. This position still plays an important role in Lessing's early work but by the end of his life Lessing was prepared to reject it for a less rigid position on learning. *Eine Parabel vom brennenden Palast* seems to make fun of those who debate over the so-called "ground plans" of a building while it is at the same time in the process of burning down. Lessing questions people who waste their time with arguing over the blue prints and ownership-slips of a building which might in fact be the palace of truth, associated with religion, language, and the testament of the Divine. His text consists of multiple voices and indicates that there is no outside perspective. One must go inside in order to understand it. Instead of being preoccupied with scripts, the spectators should better get the water needed to extinguish the fire and help out with ethical actions that would be true to history, to a lived situation. Lessing may still be an advocate for education but he increasingly valued imagination over words. Especially in his last work he refrains from didacticism. While Lessing is certainly to be considered an Enlightenment writer, he questions already some of the fundamental underpinnings of that movement.[1070] He distanced himself from Kant in order to be more in line with Herder and those for whom truth is best mediated via symbols, analogies, metaphors, and metonymies. Lessing challenged the authority of institutionalized religions and is nevertheless a devout deist, continuously trying to find wisdom. He is aware that truth is anchored in history, integrated into all physical sense perceptions, and not only a matter of any isolated seeing. He no longer thought of education in terms of a linear progression but rather as a movement that is interactive and dynamic in multidirectional and often unpredictable ways.

---

1068 Desiderius Erasmus, *De pueris statim ac liberaliter instituendis*, ed. Jean-Claude Margolin, ASD I.2 (1971): 1-78 at 31; "A Declamation on the Subject of Early Liberal Education for Children," trans. Beert C. Verstraete, *Literary and Educational Writings* 4, ed. J.K. Sowards, CWE 26 (1985): 291-346 at 304. A more gender-inclusive translation would be: "But, as I believe, you are not born a human being, but you become one through education."

1069 Desiderius Erasmus, *De ratione studii,* ed. Jean-Claude Margolin, ASD I.2 (1971): 78-151 at 120; "On the Method of Study," trans. Brian McGregor, *Literary and Educational Writings,* 2nd ed. Craig R. Thompson, CWE 24 (1978): 661-691 at 673.

1070 See the essays in Robinson, ed., *Lessing and the German Enlightenment.* On Lessing's critical and poetic stance, see Hans Mayer, "Lessings poetische Ausdrucksform," *Lessing und die Zeit der Aufklärung* (Göttingen: Vandenhoeck & Ruprecht, 1968), 130-147.

Hans Blumenberg claims in *Die Lesbarkeit der Welt* that Lessing later influenced Novalis, Schlegel, Schleiermacher and others.[1071] Friedrich von Hardenberg alias Novalis, a German Romantic at the core of the Jena circle, found in reading Lessing that perhaps even the Holy Scriptures may not be exclusively the final word by God but, as he calls them, they are most likely "provisorisch" (provisional). Therefore, there exists always a possibility of further unprecedented Divine intervention.[1072] Even the ultimate book of truth appears to be one that may be edited later. Just like the apprentice of Sais it is a gift and talent of the artist often to see connections in the universe where others don't and in that sense to contribute to a new science that pays much attention to everyone's specific place in the universe and one's stage in the cultural development. This idea caused a great controversy and set in motion heated discussions among theologians, poets, philosophers, educators, and social historians which were much to continue. It has gained a new impetus in the most recent discussions surrounding Lessing's last works concerning education and revelation. Lessing still believed in the continuous progress of humankind but nevertheless was prepared to give equal value to change, contingency, and what he called "Offenbarung" (revelation). Only a bit later Moses Mendelssohn wrote:

> Ich habe keinen Begriff von der Erziehung des Menschengeschlechts, die sich mein verewigter Freund Lessing von, ich weiss nicht, welchem Geschichtsforscher der Menschheit hat einbilden lassen [...] Ihr wollt erraten, was für Absichten die Vorsehung mit der Menschheit hat? Schmiedet keine Hypothesen; schauet nur umher auf das, was wirklich geschiehet [...] Nun findet ihr in Absicht auf das gesamte Menschengeschlecht keinen beständigen Fortschritt.[1073]

> [I have no concept of the education of humankind which my eternally documented friend Lessing has imagined, according to, I do not know which historian [...]. You want to guess what intentions the fate of humankind has? Do not formulate any hypotheses, look around and see what really happens [...]. Now you will find no consistent progress regarding humanity as a whole].

Lessing was already careful and perhaps he let go, even before Mendelssohn, of a certain optimism concerning education. He seemed to have worried more about using too many words than not enough but this is, as I have tried to show here, consistent with his earlier approach giving importance to minimalist style and freedom of imagination. Lessing expressed statements that suggest a pervasive nature of truth beyond all human efforts of education and hinted at the possibility that the slow path of linear

1071 Hans Blumenberg, *Die Lesbarkeit der Welt* (Frankfurt am Main: Suhrkamp, 1981), 233-266.

1072 Blumenberg, *Die Lesbarkeit der Welt* 239: "Novalis könnte den Grundgedanken der unvollendeten Bibel aus Lessings 'Erziehung des Menschengeschlechts' entnommen haben, wo die Gewissheit verkündet worden war, es werde die Zeit eines neuen ewigen Evangeliums kommen. Dies war auf den provisorischen Charakter der bisher kanonischen Bibel bezogen, denn jedes neue Evangelium sei in den Elementarbüchern des Neuen Bundes nur versprochen gewesen" (Novalis could have taken the basic idea from the unfinished Bible of Lessing's *Education of Humankind* where a certainty had been announced implying that a new eternal gospel were to come. This was in reference to the provisional character of the hitherto canonical Bible, because each new gospel would have been only promised in the elementary books of the covenant).

1073 Moses Mendelssohn, "*Jerusalem* oder über religiöse Macht und Judentum," *Gesammelte Schriften* 8, 99-204 at 162-165. First published, Berlin: Friedrich Maurer, 1783.

logic is not all we have to depend on. He writes in *Die Erziehung* § 4: "Also gibt auch die Offenbarung dem Menschengeschlechte nichts, worauf die menschliche Vernunft, sich selbst überlassen, nicht von selbst gekommen würde" (Therefore revelation does not give anyhthing to humankind which human reason, left alone, might not have also been able to find out by itself).[1074] What "revelation" or discovery means in this context has been much debated among theologians, philosophers, and literature scholars.[1075] It may range from perceptions of "lower senses" as in Leibniz' in his *Monadenlehre* up to the highest wisdom. Whereas in § 4 Lessing emphasizes the importance of human reason and the education of humankind, he writes in § 77: "Und warum sollten wir nicht auch durch eine Religion [...] auf nähere und bessere Begriffe vom göttlichen Wesen [...] geleitet werden können, auf welche die menschliche Vernunft von selbst nimmermehr gekommen wäre?" (And why shouldn't we be able to be led also by means of religion [...] to closer and to better concepts of the Divine truth, [...] upon which human reasoning would have never been able to arrive on its own?)[1076] In this statement he seems to back-paddle from his earlier sentence while putting all education into question for the sake of revelation which cannot be predicted at any time. What to do with this apparently irrational move by Lessing?

Karl Eibl comments on how Lessing shifts importance to images, metaphors, and rhetorical features in his late work, so that what eventually matters is only the poetics of the text.[1077] He claims that content does not matter to Lessing, so that all the intense theological and philosophical battles fought over the interpretation have now for Lessing become obsolete. But content and style are still connected. This stark poeticism in his latest work may well have to do with renewed plea for freedom, religious or otherwise. It is true that Lessing challenges the word "education" and rescues the notion of "revelation" as a belief in intuition, knowledge beyond any given culture and history.

Already in *Laokoon* Lessing argues for the importance of imagination when he writes "Je mehr wir sehen desto mehr müssen wir uns dazu denken können" (The more we see, the more we must be able to imagine).[1078] Lessing challenges the notion of pre-given meanings and hoped to actively emancipate those participating in the construction on meaning. His final texts refer to multiple voices. Lessing's *Erziehungsschrift* is, as many times asserted by his readers, a pedagogical, religious, philosophical, and ethical treatise on the question to what extent humanity can or cannot be educated through words alone. Lessing discovers that all teaching is limited and the best teaching is reached when didacticism has become superfluous. When it will finally be obsolete, the grandiose vision Lessing shared with Spinoza, John Locke, Leibniz,

---

1074 FA 10, 75. See also the edition: Louis Ferdinand Helbig, ed., *Gotthold Ephraim Lessing: Die Erziehung des Menschengeschlechts*. Historisch-kritische Edition mit Urteilen Lessings und seiner Zeitgenossen, Einleitung, Entstehungsgeschichte und Kommentar, Germanic Studies in America 38 (Bern: Peter Lang, 1980), 10.

1075 See in Bollacher, *Lessing. Vernunft und Geschichte and in Willi Goetschel, Spinoza's Modernity: Mendelssohn, Lessing, and Heine* (Madison: University of Wisconsin Press, 2004).

1076 FA 10, 95; Helbig, *Die Erziehung 24.*

1077 Karl Eibl, "Lauter Bilder und Gleichnisse. Lessings religionsphilosophische Begründung der Poesie," *Deutsche Vierteljahrsschrift für Literaturwissenschaft und Geistesgeschichte* 59 (1985): 224–252.

1078 FA 5/2, 32; *Laocoön,* trans. McCormick 19.

and Adam Ferguson, then truth will have manifested itself culturally and individually. It can then convince on its own accord, visually and through sense perceptions. Ultimately for Lessing, knowledge is not the result of discursive language and can only be expressed poetically.[1079] Lessing's late work has, what Ingrid Strohschneider-Kohrs calls, "Doppelreflexion."[1080] Moreover, through its multiple levels of signification it always hints at its own possibility of failure but remains firm in maintaining that what really matters are not words but actions. Problems and injustices are vanishing or already in the process of being diminished "aufgehoben," or suspended and replaced by something qualitatively better. It is a term much used to describe history in terms of Hegelian dialectics. As for Lessing the present communicative situation requires ethical intervention, even if that means the suspension of previous arguments.

Lessing seems to think that the main purpose of religions is to educate ethical behavior and in that regard all world religions are respectable and helpfully. In the long run, there seems to be a possibility that reason would reach that same ultimate goal or turning point via revelation, insights beyond education without external intervention, from the individual within. There is a message embedded in his style that speaks through its style of representation and through rhetoric features. It is nevertheless a message that has enormously wide-ranging implications, perhaps most immediately for a daring and censor-prone critique of religious beliefs, rejection of dangerous self-righteousness and bigotry, and the abstinence of any inflated notions of one's own cultural and theological identity. It is always limited and bracketed in time. *Die Erziehung* expresses a hope of reaching someday a peaceful society. Wilhelm Schmidt-Biggemann explains that Lessing accepted a thesis by the theologian Johann August Eberhard (1739-1808) who drew consequences from Leibniz in his *Neue Apologie des Sokrates* (1772) (New Apology of Socrates), and challenged any notion of a narrow self-complacent community.[1081] There is an image of increasing improvement of the world. It should not end with the life of an individual or one culture. There is the idea of metempsychosis for all. Lessing suggests that one should allow oneself to step outside from one's place and time in and reflect on one's limited setting.

Such a reality would make one's own upbringing seen from afar rather relative and religion less of a matter of concern compared to what really happens on earth. Lessing is not interested in any such notion such as eternal punishment but as Schmidt-Biggemann summarizes: "Der Wiederaufstieg, das heißt die Entkörperlichung in den Glücksstatus der Primordialität–das gilt auch für die Materie selbst, die sich verzehren muß und als Kristall sublimiert wird" (The repeated rising, that is the disembodiment into the blissful state of premordiality–that applies to the material itself, which must consume itself and become sublimated into crystal).[1082]

---

1079 Robert S. Leventhal, "The Parable as Performance: Interpretation, Cultural Transmission, and Political Strategy in Lessing's *Nathan der Weise*," *German Quarterly* 61 (1988): 502-527.

1080 Ingrid Strohschneider-Kohrs, "Doppelreflexion und Ironie bei Lessing," *Poesie und Reflexion* 159-195. See also her "Zur Logik der Erziehungs-Schrift: Widerspruch oder Kohärenz," Bultmann and Vollhardt, ed., *Lessings Religionsphilosophie im Kontext* 155-178.

1081 Schmidt-Biggemann, "Lessings origenistische Eschatologie," Bultmann and Vollhardt, ed., *Lessings Religionsphilosophie im Kontext* 149-150.

1082 Schmidt-Biggemann, "Lessings origenistische Eschatologie," Bultmann and Vollhardt, ed., *Lessings Religionsphilosophie im Kontext* 152.

In *Die Erziehung* there are images and ideas cited and referred to, yet they may be resistant to theorizing and to definite verbalness. Lessing draws attention to the powers of change that are intrinsic to nature. In his dramatic pieces he had shifted attention away from the visible events onstage to the inner actions and interpersonal dynamics that are the driving forces in his plays. He associated them with sense perceptions, emotions, and thoughts at the core of what we think and what we do. As he suggests, poetic writing and catharsis may turn readers into spectators and spectators into compassionate observers. These writings, however theological and philosophical their ramifications may be, are constructed of allusions, hints, or partial images that cannot be cogently grasped or completely verbalized. Lessing requires an awareness of careful sense perceptions and offers non-imposing readings that challenge institutionalized beliefs. The visual is expressed verbally, but an Enlightenment process is interactive and incomplete. Lessing's readers become dialogue partners who may reflect on personal and cultural liminality, on historicity, and on ethical actions but forget about rewards. They may have to simply trust that what they do with compassion will have an impact beyond given spaces and beyond each one's allotted life span.

# Bibliography


Adler, Hans. *Die Prägnanz des Dunklen: Gnoseologie, Ästhetik, Geschichtsphilosophie bei J.G. Herder.* Studien zum achtzehnten Jahrhunderts 13. Hamburg: Meiner, 1990.

–. "Fundus Animae–der Grund der Seele. Zur Gnoseologie des Dunkeln in der Aufklärung." *Deutsche Vierteljahrsschrift für Literaturwissenschaft und Geistesgeschichte* 62 (1988): 197-220.

–. "Was ist Ästhetische Wahrheit?" *Zeitschrift für Ästhetik und allgemeine Kunstwissenschaft.* Sonderheft 15. Hamburg: Meiner Verlag, 2016. 49-66.

– and Rainer Godel, ed. *Formen des Nichtwissens in der Aufklärung.* Munich: Fink, 2010.

– and Sabine Gross, ed. *Anschauung und Anschaulichkeit: Visualisierung im Wahrnehmen, Lesen und Denken.* Munich: Fink, 2016.

– and Lynn L. Wolff, ed. *Aisthesis und Noesis. Zwei Erkenntnisformen vom 18. Jahrhundert bis zur Gegenwart.* Munich: Fink, 2013.

– and Ulrike Zeuch, ed. *Synästhesie. Interferenz–Transfer–Synthese der Sinne.* Würzburg: Königshausen & Neumann, 2002.

Adorno, Theodor W. *Ästhetische Theorie.* GS 7.

–. "Prismen." *Kulturkritik und Gesellschaft,* GS 10, 2 vols. 1: 9-287.

Aesop (Ésope). *Fables.* Ed. Émile Chambry. 7th Printing. 1927. Paris: Les Belles Lettres, 2012.

–. *Fabularum Aesopicarum collectio.* Ed. Johann Gottfried Hauptmann. Leipzig: Johann Christian Martinus, 1741.

*Aesop's Fables.* Ed. and intro. Laura Gibbs. Oxford World's Classics. Oxford: Oxford University Press, 2002.

Aichele, K. Porter. *Paul Klee, Poet/Painter.* Rochester, NY: Camden House, 2006.

–. *Paul Klee's Pictorial Writing.* Cambridge: Cambridge University Press, 2002.

Albert, Claudia. *Der melancholische Bürger. Ausbildung bürgerlicher Deutungsmuster im Trauerspiel Diderots und Lessings.* Frankfurt am Main: Peter Lang, 1982.

Albes, Claudia and Christiane Frey, ed. *Darstellbarkeit. Zu einem ästhetisch-philosophischen Problem um 1800.* Würzburg: Königshausen & Neumann, 2003.

Albrecht, Wolfgang. *Gotthold Ephraim Lessing.* Stuttgart: Metzler, 1997.

– and Richard E. Schade, ed. *Mit Lessing zur Moderne: Soziokulturelle Wirkungen des Aufklärers um 1900.* Erbepflege in Kamenz 24. Kamenz: Lessing-Museum, 2004.

–, Dieter Fratzke, and Richard E. Schade, ed. *Aufklärung nach Lessing. Beiträge zur gemeinsamen Tagung der Lessing Society und des Lessing-Museums Kamenz aus Anlaß seines 60jährigen Bestehens.* Erbepflege in Kamenz 12/13. Kamenz: Lessing-Museum, 1992.

Alexander, Gerhard. "Wie kam Lessing zur Handschrift der Wolfenbütteler Fragmente?" *Philobiblon* 16 (1972): 160-173.

Allert, Beate. "Heine's *Doctor Faust:* A Ballet Poem." Lorna Fitzsimmons, ed. *Faust Adaptations from Marlowe to Aboudoma and Markland.* West Lafayette: Purdue University Press, 2017. 66-77.

–. "About a Burning Building in Eco and Lessing, or: How to Process Messages." *Lessing Yearbook* 29 (1997): 57-86.

–. "Ekphrasis und die Kunst der Verstehens: Möglichkeiten und Grenzen im Kontext Lessings." Košenina and Stockhorst 161-181.

–. "Hidden Aspects of Goethe's Writings on Color, Seeing, and Motion and Their Significance for a Feminist Visual Theory." Laura Doyle, ed., *Bodies of Resistance: New Phenomenologies of Politics, Agency, and Culture.* Evanston: Northwestern University Press, 2001. 144-191, 287-302.

–. "Horaz–Lessing–Mitchell: Ansätze zu Bild-Text-Relationen und kritische Aspekte zur weiteren Ekphrasis-Debatte." Monika Schmitz-Emans and Gertrud Lehnert, ed. *Visual Culture*. Heidelberg: Synchron 2008. 37-48.

–. "Lessing im Kontext kunsttheoretischer Debatten." *Lessing Yearbook* 32 (2000): 371-387.

–. "Lessing, Novalis, Schiller: Romantisierung und Medienspiel." Fisher 223-245.

–. "Lessings Grenzen der Anschaulichkeit." Zeuch 65-80.

–. "Lessing's Poetics as an Approach to Aesthetics." Fischer and Fox 104-130.

–. "Pluralisierung der Ringe oder Ringverlust? Lessings Beitrag zur Metaphorisierung und/oder Politisierung der Sprache." Mauser and Saße 113-120.

–. "The Poignant Moment: From G. E. Lessing to Film Theory." *Forum for World Literature Studies* 3.3 (2011): 399-409.

–. "Reconceptualizing a Pictorial Turn: Lessing, Hoffmann, Klee and Elements of Avant-Garde Language." Marsha Meskimmon and Martin L. Davies, ed., *Breaking the Disciplines: Reconceptions in Knowledge, Art, and Culture.* London: Tauris Press, 2003. 187-222.

–. "Roxalana in German Baroque and Enlightenment Dramas: Lohenstein, Haugwitz, Lessing, and Weisse." Yermolenko 89-108, 239-242.

–. "Strohschneider-Kohrs, Ingrid. *Poesie und Reflexion: Aufsätze zur Literatur.* 480 pages. Tübingen: Niemeyer, 1999." *Monatshefte* 92.4 (Winter 2000): 499-500 [Review].

–."Wie farbig darf die Dichtung sein? Lessings Beitrag zum Farbendiskurs im 18. Jahrhundert." *Lessing Yearbook* 37 (2008): 139-149.

– and Christina Weiler. "Herder Orphaned as Kant's Intellectual Child but Father of an Innovative Metaphorology before Blumenberg." *E-WOR(L)DS*-Electronic Journal in Comparative Literature, Semiotics, and Cultural Studies (April 2016). www.orfandade.ufba.br

–, ed. *J. G. Herder: From Cognition to Cultural Science / Von der Erkenntnis zur Kulturwissenschaft.* Heidelberg: Synchron, 2016.

–, ed. *Languages of Visuality. Crossings between Science, Art, Politics, and Literature.* Detroit: Wayne State University Press, 1996.

Alt, Peter-André. *Tragödie der Aufklärung.* Tübingen: Francke, 1994.

– and Alexander Košenina, ed. *Prägnanter Moment. Studien zur deutschen Literatur der Aufklärung und Klassik. Festschrift für Hans-Jürgen Schings.* Würzburg: Königshausen & Neumann, 2002.

Althaus, Horst. *Laokoon. Stoff und Form.* 2nd ed. Tübingen: Francke, 2000.

Althaus, Thomas. *Das Uneigentliche ist das Eigentliche: Metaphorische Darstellung in der Prosa bei Lessing und Lichtenberg.* Literatur als Sprache: Literaturtheorie–Interpretation–Sprachkritik 8 Münster: Aschendorff, 1991.

Altmann, Alexander."Lessings Glaube an die Seelenwanderung." *Lessing Yearbook* 8 (1976): 7-41; reprinted in: *Die Trostvolle Aufklärung. Studien zur Metaphysik und politischen Theorie Moses Mendelssohns.* Forschungen und Materialien zur deutschen Aufklärung II: Monographien 3. Stuttgart-Bad Cannstatt: Frommann-Holzboog, 1982, 109-134.

Andreae, Bernard. *Laokoon und die Kunst von Pergamon. Die Hybris der Giganten.* Frankfurt am Main: Fischer Taschenbuch Verlag, 1991.

Aristotle. *The "Art" of Rhetoric.* Trans. John Henry Freese. Loeb Classical Library 193. 1926. Cambridge: Harvard University Press, 2006.

–. *On the Soul. Parva naturalia. On Breath.* Trans. W. S. Hett. Rev. ed. Loeb Classical Library 288. Cambridge: Harvard University Press, 1957.

–. *Poetics.* Ed. and trans. Stephen Halliwell. Aristotle *Poetics,* Longinus *On the Sublime,* Demetrius *On Style,* trans. Stephen Halliwell et al., corr. ed. Loeb Classical Library 199. Cambridge: Harvard University Press, 1999.

Arnold, Antje. *Rhetorik der Empfindsamkeit. Unterhaltungskunst im 17. und 18. Jahrhundert.* Quellen und Forschungen zur Literatur- und Kulturgeschichte 73. Berlin: De Gruyter, 2012.

Arons, Wendy and Natalya Baldyga, "The Hamburg Dramaturgy in the Digital Age: A New and Complete Translation. With Critical Introductory Essays by Wendy Aarons, Natalya Baldyga, and Michael Chemers." *Lessing Yearbook* 41 (2014): 303-305. (http://mcpress.media-commons.org/hamburg/essay-).

Assmann, Jan, ed. *Kultur und Gedächtnis.* Frankfurt am Main: Suhrkamp 1988.

Auerbach, Erich. *Mimesis. Dargestellte Wirklichkeit in der abendländischen Literatur.* 9th ed. Sammlung Dalp 90. Bern: Francke, 1994.

Aurnhammer, Achim, Giulia Cantarutti, and Friedrich Vollhardt, ed. *Die Drei Ringe. Entstehung, Wandel und Wirkung der Ringparabel in der Europäischen Literatur und Kultur.* Frühe Neuzeit 200. Berlin: De Gruyter, 2016.

Babrius and Phaedrus. *Fables.* Ed. and trans. Ben Edwin Perry. Loeb Classical Library 436. Cambridge: Harvard University Press, 1965.

Bahr, Ehrhard. "Die Bild- und Sinnbereiche von Feuer und Wasser in Lessings *Nathan der Weise.*" *Lessing Yearbook* 6 (1974): 83-96.

Bann, Stephen, *The True Vine. On Visual Representation and Western Tradition.* Cambridge: Cambridge University Press, 1989.

Baran. H. and A.W. Halsall. "Anthropology." *The Princeton Encyclopedia of Poetry and Poetics.* 4th ed. Ed. Roland Greene et al. Princeton: Princeton University Press, 2012. 55-56.

Bark, Joachim. "Brandstifter Reimarus." Mauser and Saße 147-156.

Barner, Wilfried. *Produktive Rezeption. Lessing und die Tragödien Senecas.* Munich: Beck, 1973.

–."'Zu viel Thränen-nur Keime von Thränen.' Über *Miß Sara Sampson* und *Emilia Galotti* beim zeitgenössischen Publikum." Rainer Gruenter, ed. *Das weinende Saeculum.* Beiträge zur Geschichte der Literatur und Kunst des 18. Jahrhunderts 7. Heidelberg: Winter, 1993. 89-105.

–."'Laut denken mit einem Freunde.' Anmerkungen zu Lessings *Ernst und Falk.*" Gutjahr et al. 1-12.

– and Gunter E. Grimm, Helmut Kiesel, Martin Kramer et al. *Lessing: Epoche–Werk–Wirkung.* 5th ed. Munich: Beck, 1987.

Barry, Kelly. "Natural Palingenesis: Childhood, Memory, and Self-Experience in Herder and Jean Paul." *Goethe Yearbook* 14 (2007): 1-25.

Barthes, Roland. *Image. Music. Text.* Trans. Stephen Heath. New York: Noonday Press, 1977.

Bätschmann, Oskar. "Pygmalion als Betrachter: Die Rezeption von Plastik und Malerei in der zweiten Hälfte des 18. Jahrhunderts." Wolfgang Kemp, ed. *Der Betrachter ist im Bild. Kunstwissenschaft und Rezeptionsästhetik.* Cologne: DuMont, 1985. 183-224; 2nd ed. Berlin: Dietrich Reimer, 1992. 237-278.

Battenfeld, Katja, et al., ed. *Gefühllose Aufklärung. Anaisthesis oder die Unempfindlichkeit im Zeitalter der Aufklärung.* Bielefeld: Aisthesis, 2012.

Baumgärtel, Bettina. "Die Attitüde und die Malerei. Paradox der stillen Bewegtheit in Synthese von Erfindung und Nachahmung." *Zeitschrift des deutschen Vereins für Kunstwissenschaft* 46 (1992): 21-42.

Baumgarten, Alexander Gottlieb. *Ästhetik.* Ed. and trans. Dagmar Mirbach. 2 vols. Philosophische Bibliothek 572. Hamburg: Meiner, 2007.

Baxmann, Inge, et al., ed. *Das Laokoon-Paradigma. Zeichenregime im 18. Jahrhundert.* Berlin: Akademie Verlag, 2000.

Bayerdörfer, Hans-Peter. "Markante Signale: Zur Bühnengeschichte von Lessings Dramen seit 2000." *Lessing Yearbook* 37 (2006/2007): 67-78.

Becker, Andrew Sprague. *The Shield of Achilles and the Poetics of Ekphrasis.* Lanham, MD: Rowman and Littlefield, 1995.

Becker-Cantarino, Barbara. "Patriarchy and German Enlightenment Discourse: From Goethe's *Wilhelm Meister* to Horkheimer and Adorno's *Dialectic of Enlightenment* in Germany." Wilson and Holub 48-64.

–. *Der lange Weg zur Mündigkeit: Frauen und Literatur in Deutschland von 1500-1800.* Munich: Deutscher Taschenbuch Verlag, 1989.

Bedenk, Jochen. *Verwicklungen. Wilhelm Hogarth und die deutsche Literatur des 18. Jahrhunderts (Lessing, Herder, Schiller, Jean Paul).* Würzburg: Königshausen & Neumann, 2004.

Bender, John F. "Ikonenbildung und Affirmation: Lessing in der Theaterpublizistik des 18. Jahrhunderts." *Lessing Yearbook* 33 (2001): 79-96.

– and David E. Wellbery. "Rhetoricality: On the Modernist Return of Rhetoric." Bender and Wellbery 3-39.

– and David E. Wellbery, ed. *The Ends of Rhetoric: History, Theory, Praxis.* Stanford: Stanford University Press, 1990.

Bennett, Benjamin. *Beyond Theory: Eighteenth Century German Literature and the Poetics of Irony.* Ithaca, NY: Cornell University Press, 1993.

–. *Modern Drama and German Classicism: Renaissance from* Lessing *to* Brecht. Ithaca, NY: Cornell University Press, 1979.

Benjamin, Walter. "Das Kunstwerk im Zeitalter seiner technischen Reproduzierbarkeit." *Gesammelte Schriften.* Ed. Rolf Tiedemann and Hermann Schweppenhäuser. 7 vols. in 14. Frankfurt am Main: Suhrkamp, 1974-1989. 1.2/3 431-508, 983-1063.

–. *Ursprung des deutschen Trauerspiels. Gesammelte Schriften.* Ed. Rolf Tiedemann and Hermann Schweppenhäuser. 7 vols. in 14. Frankfurt am Main: Suhrkamp, 1974-1989. 1.1. 202-430.

Bentham, Jeremy. *The Panopticon Writings.* Ed. and intro. Miran Božovič. Wo es war series. London: Verso, 1995.

Berghahn, Klaus L. "Lessing the Critic: Polemics as Enlightenment." Fischer and Fox 67-87.

–. "Zermalmende Beredsamkeit." Lessings Literaturkritik als Polemik. Ein Essay." *Lessing Yearbook* 24 (1992): 25-44.

Berger, Renate and Inge Stephan, ed. *Weiblichkeit und Tod in der Literatur.* Cologne: Böhlau, 1987. 69-86.

Besançon, Alain. *The Forbidden Image. An Intellectual History of Iconoclasm.* Trans. by Jane Marie Todd. Chicago: University of Chicago Press, 2000.

Binczek, Natalie. *Kontakt: Der Tastsinn in Texten der Aufklärung.* Studien zur deutschen Literatur 182. Tübingen: Niemeyer, 2007.

–. "Das veränderliche Gewebe. Zur Empfindungstheorie in Lessings *Laokoon.*" *Zeitschrift für Ästhetik und allgemeine Kunstwissenschaft.* 49.2 (2004): 219-235.

Black, Max. "Metaphor." *Proceedings of the Aristotelian Society* 55 (1954-1955): 273-294. Reprinted in Johnson 63-87.

–. *Models and Metaphors: Studies in Language and Philosophy.* Ithaca, NY: Cornell University Press, 1962.

–. "More about Metaphor." *Dialectica* 31 (1977): 431-57. Rev. rpt: Andrew Ortony, ed. *Metaphor and Thought.* 2nd ed. Cambridge: Cambridge University Press, 1993. 19-41.

Blumenberg, Hans. *Die Lesbarkeit der Welt.* Frankfurt am Main: Suhrkamp, 1991.

–. "Paradigmen zu einer Metaphorologie." *Archiv für Begriffsgeschichte* 6 (1960): 7-142; *Paradigmen zu einer Metaphorologie.* Bonn: Bouvier, 1960; paperback Frankfurt am Main: Suhrkamp, 1997.

–. *Paradigms for a Metaphorology.* Trans. Robert Savage. Ithaca, NY: Cornell University Press, 2010.

Boehart, William. *Politik und Religion: Studien zum Fragmentestreit Reimarus, Goeze, Lessing.* Schwarzenbeck: Rüdiger Martienss, 1988.

Boehm, Gottfried. "Die Wiederkehr der Bilder." G. Boehm, ed. *Was ist ein Bild?* Munich: Fink, 1994. 11-38.

–. "Jenseits der Sprache? Anmerkungen zur Logik der Bilder." Christa Maar and Hubert Burda, ed. *Iconic Turn. Die neue Macht der Bilder.* 2nd ed. Cologne: DuMont, 2004. 28-43.

–. *Wie Bilder Sinn erzeugen. Die Macht des Zeigens.* Berlin: Berlin University Press, 2007.

– and Helmut Pfotenhauer, ed. *Beschreibungskunst–Kunstbeschreibung. Ekphrasis von der Antike bis zur Gegenwart.* Munich: Fink, 1995.

Bohnen, Klaus. "Lessing zu Feier: Über den 'Nachruf' auf einen unbequemen Autor in Geschichte und Gegenwart." Klaus Bohnen, ed. *Lessing: Nachruf auf einen Aufklärer. Sein Bild in der Presse der Jahre 1781, 1881 und 1981.* Munich: Fink, 1982. 175-182

–. "Lessings *Erziehung des Menschengeschlechts* (§ 4) und Bonnets *Palingénésie*, ein Zitat-Hinweis." *Germanisch-Romanische Monatsschrift* 62 (1981): 362-365.

–. "Nathan der Weise. Über das Gegenbild einer Gesellschaft bei Lessing." *Deutsche Vierteljahrsschrift für Literaturwissenschaft und Geistesgeschichte* 53 (1979): 394-416. Rpt. Bohnen 374-401.

–."Von den Anfängen des 'Nationalsinns': Zur literarischen Patritiotsmusdebatte im Umfeld des Siebenjährigen Krieges." Helmut Scheurer, ed. *Dichter und ihre Nation.* Frankfurt am Main: Suhrkamp, 1993. 121-137.

–, ed. *Lessings Nathan der Weise.* Wege der Forschung 587. Darmstadt: Wissenschaftliche Buchgesellschaft, 1984.

Bollacher, Martin. *Lessing. Vernunft und Geschichte. Untersuchungen zum Problem religiöser Aufklärung in den Spätschriften.* Studien zur deutschen Literatur 56. Tübingen: Niemeyer, 1978.

–."Tradition und Selbstbestimmung. Lessings *Emilia Galotti* in geistesgeschichtlicher Perspektive." *Literatur und Geistesgeschichte. Festschrift für Richard Brinkmann.* Ed. von einem Red.-Kollegium. Tübingen: Niemeyer, 1981. 99-118.

Bonn, Kristina. *Vom Schönen: Schönheitskonzeptionen bei Lessing, Goethe und Schiller.* Bielefeld: Aisthesis, 2008.

Breidbach, Olaf. *Neuronale Ästhetik. Morpho-Logik des Anschauens.* Munich: Fink, 2013.

Breithaupt, Fritz. "Wie ist Gesellschaft möglich? Geld und Medien bei Lessing und Simmel." Albrecht and Schade 67-77.

Brenner, Peter J. *Gotthold Ephraim Lessing.* Stuttgart: Reclam, 2000.

Brewer, Daniel. "Diderot and the Culture of Belatedness." Ogée and Strugnell 183-196.

Breth, Andrea (Director, Inszenierung). *Emilia Galotti von Gotthold Ephraim Lessing, Aufführung des Wiener Burgtheaters.* The Theater Edition by BelAir Edition GmbH & Friedrich Berlin Verlagsgesellschaft GmbH, ZDFE 2005 (ISBN 7000000621925).

Brilliant, Richard. *My Laocöon. Alternative Claims in the Interpretation of Artworks.* Berkeley: University of California Press, 2000.

Brodsky Lacour, Claudia. "Is that Helen? Contemporary Pictorialism, Lessing, and Kant." *Comparative Literature* 45.3 (Summer 1993): 230-257.

Brummack, Jürgen. "Herders Theorie der Fabel." Sauder 251-266.

Bryson, Norman. *Word and Image: French Painting of the Ancien Régime.* Cambridge: Cambridge University Press, 1981.

Buch, Hans Christoph. *Ut Pictura Poesis. Die Beschreibungsliteratur und ihre Kritiker von Lessing bis Lukács.* Munich: Hanser, 1972.

Buike, Bruno. *Die Fabel von den vier Ringen und andere Ungereimtheiten.* Edition Wissenschaft Reihe Germanistik 9. Marburg: Tectum Verlag, 1996.

Bultmann, Christoph, "Lessings 'Axiomata' als eine hermeneutische Programmschrift." Bultmann and Vollhardt 242-270.

– and Birka Siwczyk, ed. *Tolerant mit Lessing: Ein Lesebuch zur Ringparabel.* Leipzig: Evangelische Verlagsanstalt, 2013.

– and Friedrich Vollhardt, ed. *Lessings Religionsphilosophie im Kontext: Hamburger Fragmente und Wolfenbütteler Axiomata.* Frühe Neuzeit 159. Berlin: De Gruyter, 2011.

Burgard, Peter. "Schlangenbiß und Schrei." Mauser and Saße 194-202.

Burwick, Frederick. *Mimesis and its Romantic Reflections.* University Park: The Pennsylvania University Press, 2001.

–."Ekphrasis and Theories of Reading Visual Representation." Wagner 78-104.

–."Verbal and Visual Modes." Frederick Burwick and Jürgen Klein, ed. *The Romantic Imagination. Literature and Art in England and Germany.* Studies in Comparative Literature 6. Amsterdam: Rodopi, 1996. 1-16.

–. "Lessing's *Laokoon* and the Rise of Visual Hermeneutics." *Poetics Today* 20.2 (Summer 1999): 219-272.

Busch, Stefan. "Blasphemisches Lachen in Klopstocks *Messias* und Lessings *Minna von Barnhelm*. Zur Herausbildung eines literarischen Leitmotivs der Moderne." *Lessing Yearbook* 33 (2001): 27-54.

Butler, Elizabeth M. *The Fortunes of Faust.* Magic in History. College Station: Pennsylvania State University Press, 1998.

–. *Ritual Magic.* Cambridge: Cambridge University Press, 1949.

Butt, Lydia. "Mitleid ex machina: Die Disproportion der Affekte in Sophokles' *Philoktet* im Spiegel von Lessings Theorie der Tragödienwirkung." Katja Battenfeld et al., ed. *Gefühllose Aufklärung: Anaisthesis oder die Unempfindlichkeit im Zeitalter der Aufklärung.* Bielefeld: Aisthesis, 2012. 117-139.

Caylus, Comte de. *Tableaux tirés de l'Iliade, et de l'Odyssée d'Homère, et de l'Eneide de Virgile, avec des observations générales sur le costume.* Paris: Tilliard, 1757.

Cheeke, Stephen. *Writing for Art. The Aesthetics of Ekphrasis.* Manchester: Manchester University Press, 2008.

Chodowiecki, Albert, *Vom Reißbrett der Loge 'Lessing' Or. Valparaiso. Auswahl von Reden und Vorträgen von Johanni 1870 bis 1882.* Zusammengestellt vom Schriftführer der Loge. Leipzig: Findel, 1883.

–. *Loge Lessing. Vortrag gehalten in der Trauerloge am 15. Februar 1881 zum Andenken an G. E. Lessing.* Bern: Francke, 1975, 1981.

Cocalis, Susan. "Der Vormund will Vormund sein: Zur Problematik der weiblichen Unmündigkeit im 18. Jahrhundert." Marianne Burkhard, ed. *Gestaltet und Gestaltend: Frauen in der deutschen Literatur.* Amsterdamer Beiträge zur neueren Germanistik 10. Amsterdam: Rodopi, 1980. 33-55.

Cohen, Michael. "Lessing on Time and Space in the Sister Arts: The Artist's Refutation." Ugarinsky 13-23.

Collins, Christopher. *Reading the Written Image. Verbal Play, Interpretation, and the Roots of Iconophobia.* Philadelphia: University of Pennsylvania Press, 1991.

–. "Writing and the Nature of the Supernatural Image." Allert, *Languages* 242-261.

Connon, Derek R. *Innovation and Renewal: A Study of the Theatrical Works of Diderot.* Studies on Voltaire and the Eighteenth Century 258. Oxford: The Voltaire Foundation, 1989.

Cornell, Drucilla A. *Beyond Accommodation: Ethical Feminism, Deconstruction, and the Law.* New York: Routledge, 1991.

–. *Transformations: Recollective Imagination and Sexual Desire.* New York: Routledge, 1993.

Cosgrove, Brian. "Murray Krieger: Ekphrasis as Spatial Form, Ekphrasis as Mimesis." Morrison and Krobb 25-31.

Craig, Charlotte M. "Four Enlighteners and the Devils." *Lessing Yearbook* 20 (1988): 45-60.

Critchfield, Richard. "Lessing, Diderot, and Theatre." Richard Critchfield and Wulf Koepke, ed. *Eighteenth Century German Authors and their Aesthetic Theories.* Columbia, SC: Camden House, 1988. 11-28.

Crowther, Louise. *Diderot and Lessing as Exemplars of a Post-Spinozist Mentality.* MHRA Texts and Dissertations 78. London: Manley, 2010.

Culler, Jonathan. *Framing the Sign: Criticism and its Institutions.* Oklahoma Project for Discussion and Theory 3. Norman: University of Oklahoma Press, 1988.

Cyranka, Daniel. *Lessing im Reinkarnationsdiskurs. Eine Untersuchung zu Kontext und Wirkung von G. E. Lessings Texten zur Seelenwanderung.* Göttingen: Vandenhoeck & Ruprecht, 2005.

–. "'Gehet hin und leset euren Lessing, den wir Spiritisten stolz den unseren nennen!' Lessings Wirkung in der modernen Esoterik." *Lessing Yearbook* 37 (2006/2007): 125-138.

–"'Warum nicht?' Lessings Äußerungen zur Seelenwanderung." Hans-Edwin Friedrich,, Wilhelm Haefs, and Christian Soboth, ed. *Literatur und Theologie im 18. Jahrhundert: Konfrontationen–Kontroversen–Konkurrenzen.* Hallesche Beiträge zur Europäischen Aufklärung 41. Berlin: De Gruyter, 2011. 122-138.

Daemmrich, Horst S. "Illusion: Möglichkeiten und Grenzen eines Begriffs." *Lessing Yearbook* 1 (1969): 88-98.

Danesi, Marcel. *Vico, Metaphor, and the Origin of Language.* Advances in Semiotics. Bloomington: Indiana University Press, 1993.

Daunicht, Richard. *Die Enstehung des Bürgerlichen Trauerspiels in Deutschland.* 2nd ed. Berlin: De Gruyter, 1965.

–, ed. *Lessing im Gespräch: Berichte und Urteile von Freunden und Zeitgenossen.* Munich: Fink, 1971.

Davies, Owen. *Grimoires: A History of Magic Books.* Oxford: Oxford University Press, 2009.

Deleuze, Gilles. *Cinema 1: The Movement-Image.* Trans. Hugh Tomlinson and Barbara Habberjam. Minneapolis: University of Minnesota Press, 1986.

–. *Cinema 2: The Time-Image.* Trans. Hugh Tomlinson and Robert Galta. Minneapolis: University of Minnesota Press,1989.

–. *The Fold: Leibniz and the Baroque.* Trans. Tom Conley. Minneapolis: University of Minnesota Press, 1993.

– and Felix Guattari, *A Thousand Plateaus: Capitalism and Schizophrenia.* Trans. Brian Massumi. Minneapolis: University of Minnesota Press, 1987.

Diderot, Denis. *Diderot on Art.* I: *The Salon of 1765* and *Notes on Painting,* II: *The Salon of 1767.* Trans. John Goodman. Intro. Thomas Crow. New Haven: Yale University Press, 1995.

–. *Le Fils naturel ou les Épreuves de la Vertu, Comédie en cinq Actes, et en Prose, avec l'Histoire véritable de la Pièce.* Amsterdam [Paris]: n.p., 1757.

–. *Lettre sur les Aveugles A l'Usage de Ceux qui Voyent.* London [Paris]: n.p., 1749.

–. Lettre sur les sourds et muets A l'Usage de ceux qui entendent & qui parlent. Addressée à M**. [Paris]: n.p. 1751.

–. *Le Père de famille, Comédie en cinq Actes, et en Prose, avec un Discours, sue la Poésie dramatique.* Amsterdam [Paris]: n.p. [Michel Lambert], 1758.

Dithmar, Reinhard, ed. *Texte zur Theorie der Fabeln, Parabeln, und Gleichnisse.* Munich: Deutscher Taschenbuch Verlag, 1982.

Dönike, Martin. *Pathos, Ausdruck und Bewegung. Zur Ästhetik des Weimarer Klassizismus 1796-1806.* Quellen und Forschungen zur Literatur- und Kulturgeschichte 34. Berlin: De Gruyter, 2005.

Dörr, Volker C. "Offenbarung, Vernunft, und 'fähige Individuen'. Die positiven Religionen in Lessings *Erziehung des Menschengeschlechts.*" *Lessing Yearbook* 26 (1994): 29-54.

*Doctor Fausts großer und gewaltiger Höllenzwang.* Graz: Geheimes Wissen, 2009.

–. *The Black Book of Doctor Faust. Doctor Johannes Faust's Miracle and Magic Book, or The Black Raven or also Named The Three-Fold Coercion of Hell.* Trans. Robert Blanchard. 2nd ed. Palm Springs, CA: International Guild of Esoteric Sciences, 1992.

Drescher-Ochoa, Heidrun. *Kultur der Freiheit: Ein Beitrag zu Lessings Kulturkritik und -philosophie.* Europäische Hochschulschriften I: Deutsche Sprache und Literatur 1670. Frankfurt am Main: Peter Lang, 1998.

Drügh, Heinz. *Ästhetik der Beschreibung. Poetische und kulturelle Energie deskriptiver Texte (1700-2000).* Studien und Texte zur Kulturgeschichte der deutschsprachigen Literatur 5. Tübingen: Narr, 2006.

Dubos, Abbé. *Réflexions critiques sur la poésie et sur la peinture*, 2 vols. Paris: Jean Mariette, 1719; 4th ed., corr. and enl. 3 vols. Paris: Pierre-Jean Mariette, 1740.

Dülmen, Richard van, ed. *Der Geheimbund der Illuminaten.* Neuzeit im Aufbau 1. Stuttgart-Bad Cannstatt: Frommann-Holzboog, 1975.

Düsing, Wolfgang. "Wandlungen des Literaturbegriffs in der *Laokoon*-Debatte zwischen Lessing und Herder." Alt and Košenina 63–78.

Dusch, Johann Jakob. *Vermischte, kritische und Satyrische Schriften nebst einigen Oden auf gegenwärtige Zeiten.* Altona: David Iversen, 1758.

Dvoretzky, Edward. *Lessing. Dokumente zur Wirkungsgeschichte 1755-1968.* Göppingen: Kümmerle, 1971.

–. *The Enigma of Emilia Galotti.* The Hague: Martinus Nijhoff, 1963.

Dziergwa, Roman. *Lessing und die Freimaurerei: Untersuchung zur Rezeption von G. E. Lessings Spätwerk* Ernst und Falk. Gespräche für Freymäurer *in den freimäurerischen und antifreimäurerischen Schriften des 19. und 20. Jahrhunderts (bis 1933).* Europäische Hochschulschriften I: Deutsche Sprache und Literatur 1332. Frankfurt am Main: Peter Lang, 1992.

Eckardt, Jo-Jacqueline. "Das Lessingbild im Dritten Reich." *Lessing Yearbook* 23 (1991): 69–78.

Eco, Umberto. *Einführung in die Semiotik.* Authorized German version by Jürgen Trabant. Munich: Fink, 1972.

–. *The Limits of lnterpretation.* Bloomington: Indiana University Press, 1990.

–. *A Theory of Semiotics.* Bloomington: Indiana University Press, 1976.

Eibl, Karl. "Lauter Bilder und Gleichnisse. Lessings religionsphilosophische Begründung der Poesie." *Deutsche Vierteljahrsschrift für Literaturwissenschaft und Geistesgeschichte* 59 (1985): 224–252.

–."Identitätskrise und Diskurs. Zur thematischen Kontinuität von Lessings Dramatik." *Jahrbuch der Deutschen Schillergesellschaft* 21 (1977): 138–191.

–. "'... *kommen würde' gegen '... nimmermehr gekommen wäre.*' Auflösung des 'Widerspruchs' von §4 und §77 in Lessings *Erziehung des Menschengeschlechts.*" *Germanisch-Romanische Monatsschrift* 65 (N.F. 34) (1984): 461–464.

–. *Gotthold Ephraim Lessing: Miss Sara Sampson–Ein bürgerliches Trauerspiel.* Frankfurt am Main: Athenäum, 1971.

Eichner, Siglinde. *Die Prosafabel Lessings in seiner Theorie und Dichtung.* Bonn: Bouvier, 1974.

Eisenstein, Sergej. *Film Form.* Orlando: Harcourt Brace Jovanovich, 1969.

Elkins, James. *The Object Stares Back. On the Nature of Seeing.* San Diego: Harcourt Brace, 1996.

Elm, Theo and Peter Hasubek, ed. *Fabel und Parabel: Kulturgeschichtliche Prozesse im 18. Jahrhundert.* Munich: Fink, 1994.

Elon, Amos. *The Pity of it All: A Portrait of the German-Jewish Epoch 1743-1933.* New York: Picador, 2002.

Emde, Ruth B. "Die Schauspielerin im 'Kennerblick.' Gefühls- und Verstandes-Schauspiel als Neuformation der Geschlechterdifferenz." Erika Fischer-Lichte and Jörg Schönert, ed. *Theater im Kulturwandel des 18. Jahrhunderts. Inszenierung und Wahrnehmung von Körper–Musik–Sprache.* Göttingen: Wallstein, 1999. 449-462.

Engel, Eva J. and Claus Ritterhoff, ed. *Neues zur Lessing-Forschung. Ingrid Strohschneider-Kohrs zu Ehren.* Tübingen: Niemeyer, 1998.

Erasmus Desiderius. "A Declamation on the Subject of Early Liberal Education for Children." Trans. Beert C. Verstraete. *Literary and Educational Writings,* 4. Ed. J.K. Sowards. CWE 26 (1985): 291-346.

–. *De pueris statim ac liberaliter instituendis.* Ed. Jean-Claude Margolin. ASD I.2 (1971): 1-78.

–. *De ratione studii.* Ed. Jean-Claude Margolin. ASD I.2 (1971): 78-151.

–. "On the Method of Study." Trans. Brian McGregor. *Literary and Educational Writings,* 2. Ed. Craig R. Thompson. CWE 24 (1978): 661-691.

Erlemann, Kurt, Irmgard Nickel-Bacon and Anika Loose. *Gleichnisse–Fabeln–Parabeln. Exegetische, literaturtheoretische und religionspädagogische Zugänge.* UTB 4134. Tübingen: Francke, 2014.

Fauser, Markus, ed. *Gotthold Ephraim Lessing. Neue Wege der Forschung.* Darmstadt: Wissenschaftliche Buchgesellschaft, 2008.

Ferry, Luc. *Homo Aestheticus: The Development of Taste in the Democratic Age.* Trans. Robert de Laoiza. Chicago: University of Chicago Press, 1993.

Fick, Monika. *Lessing Handbuch: Leben–Werk–Wirkung.* 1st ed. Stuttgart: Metzler, 2000.

–. *Lessing Handbuch: Leben–Werk–Wirkung.* 4th ed. Stuttgart: Metzler, 2016.

–. *Lessings* Nathan der Weise *und das Bild vom Orient und Islam in Theatertexten aus der zweiten Hälfte des 18. Jahrhunderts.* Wolfenbüttler Vortragsmanuskript 29. Wolfenbüttel: Lessing Akademie, 2016.

–."Verworrene Perzeptionen. Lessings *Emilia Galotti.*" *Jahrbuch der Deutschen Schillergesellschaft* 39 (1993): 113-129.

Fischer, Barbara. "Lösungsansatz 'Raum' versus 'Zeit': Jüdische Reaktionen auf Lessings *Nathan der Weise* im Vor-Shoah Deutschland." *Lessing Yearbook* 32 (2000): 324-339.

–. *Nathans Ende? Von Lessing bis Tabori. Zur deutsch-jüdischen Rezeption von* Nathan der Weise. Göttingen: Wallstein, 2000.

– and Thomas C. Fox, ed. *A Companion to the Works of Gotthold Ephraim Lessing.* Rochester, NY: Camden House, 2005.

Fischer, Bernhard. "Von der Ars bis zur literarischen Evidenz. Überlegungen zur Entwicklung der Poetologie von Gottsched bis Lessing." *Zeitschrift für deutsche Philologie* 109.4 (1990): 481-502.

Fischer-Lichte, Erika. *Kurze Geschichte des deutschen Theaters.* Tübingen: Francke, 1993.

–. *The Show and the Gaze of Theatre: A European Perspective.* Iowa City: University of Iowa Press, 1997.

– and Jörg Schönert, ed. *Theater im Kulturwandel des 18. Jahrhunderts: Inszenierung und Wahrnehmung von Körper–Musik–Sprache.* Göttingen: Wallstein, 1999.

Fisher, Richard, ed. *Ethik und Ästhetik. Werke und Werte in der Literatur vom 18. bis zum 20. Jahrhundert. Festschrift für Wolfgang Wittkowski zum 70. Geburtstag.* Forschungen zur Literatur- und Kulturgeschichte 52. Frankfurt am Main: Peter Lang, 1995.

Fitzsimmons, Lorna, ed. *Adapting Faust from Marlowe to Aboudoma.* West Lafayette: Purdue University Press, 2016.

Flaherty, Gloria. "The Art of Dying on Stage." *Lessing Yearbook* 21 (1989): 103-121.

Flax, Neil. "From Portrait to Tableau Vivant: The Pictures of Emilia Galotti." *Eighteenth-Century Studies* 19.1 (1985): 39-55.

Forester, Vera. *Lessing und Moses Mendelssohn: Geschichte einer Freundschaft.* Hamburg: Europäische Verlagsanstalt, 2001.

Forsey, Jane. "The Aesthetic Force of the Unpleasant." *Eventual Aesthetics* 5.1 (2016): 15-24.

Freimark, Peter, Franklin Kopitzsch, and Helga Slessarev, ed. *Lessing und die Toleranz.* Sonderband zum *Lessing Yearbook.* Detroit: Wayne State University Press, 1986,

Fried, Michael. *Absorption and Theatricality: Painting and Beholder in the Age of Diderot.* Chicago: University of Chicago Press, 1980.

Flusser, Vilém. *Für eine Philosophie der Fotographie.* 11th ed. Berlin: Edition Flusser, 2011, first published 1983.

Gaiger, Jason. "The Contemporaneity of Lessing's Aesthetics." Robertson 97-117.

Garrett, Jeffrey. "'Teichoscopy' in the Wall Novels of Peter Schneider and Uri Orlev." Allert, *Languages* 215-225.

Gaunt, Berys and Dominic McIver Lopes, ed. *The Routledge Companion to Aesthetics.* London: Routledge, 2001.

Gebauer, Gunter. "Die Beziehungen von Bild und Text in Lessings *Laokoon.*" Sybil Dümchen and Michael Nerlich, ed. *Texte–Image, Bild–Text.* Berlin: Institut für Romanische Literaturwissenschaft, Technische Universität Berlin, 1990. 17-27.

–, ed. *Das Laokoon-Projekt: Pläne einer semiotischen Ästhetik.* Studien zur Allgemeinen und Vergleichenden Literaturwissenschaft 25. Stuttgart: Metzler, 1984.

Gebhardt, Armin. *Gotthold Ephraim Lessing: Bühnendramatiker, ästhetischer Kritiker, theologischer Polemiker.* Marburg: Tectum Verlag, 2007.

Geitner, Ursula. *Die Sprache der Verstellung. Studien zum rhetorischen und anthropologischen Wissen im 17. und 18. Jahrhundert.* Communicatio 1. Tübingen: Niemeyer, 1992.

Gessinger, Joachim. *Auge und Ohr. Studien zur Erforschung am Menschen 1700-1850.* Berlin: De Gruyter, 1994.

–. "Visible Sounds and Audible Colors: The Ocular Harpsichord of Louis-Bertrand Castel." Allert, *Languages of Visuality* 89-110.

Göbel, Helmut. *Bild und Sprache bei Lessing.* Munich: Fink, 1971.

–. "Die Bildlichkeit im *Nathan.*" Bohnen, *Lessings Nathan der Weise* 229-266. First published in *Bild und Sprache bei Lessing* 154-195.

Goethe, Johann Wolfgang. *Aus meinem Leben. Dichtung und Wahrheit.* Ed. Peter Sprengel. GMA 16 (1985).

–. *Farbenlehre: Didaktischer Teil.* Ed. Manfred Wenzel. GFA 1: 23/1 (1991).

–. *Faust.* Ed. Albrecht Schöne. GFA I: 7/1 (1994), *Texte*; I: 7/2 (1994), *Kommentare.*

–. "Regeln für Schauspieler." GFA I: 18 (1998), *Ästhetische Schriften 1771-1805.* Ed. Friedmar Apel. 857-860.

–. "Über Laokoon." GFA I: 18 (1998), *Ästhetische Schriften 1771-1805.* 489-500. 1253-1258.

–. "Weimarisches Hoftheater," GFA I: 18, (1998), *Ästhetische Schriften 1771-1805.* 842-850.

Goetschel, Willi. *Spinoza's Modernity: Mendelssohn, Lessing, and Heine.* Madison: University of Wisconsin Press, 2004.

–. "Lessing and the Jews." Fischer and Fox 185-208.

Goldenbaum, Ursula. "Im Schatten der Tafelrunde: Beziehungen der jungen Berliner Zeitungsschreiber Mylius und Lessing zu französischen Aufklärern." *Berliner Aufklärung* 1 (1999): 69-100.

–. "Universal oder Plural? Zum scheinbaren Gegensatz von Lessing und Mendelssohn über die Erziehung des Menschengeschlechts." *Lessing Yearbook* 39 (2010-2011): 241-260.

– and Alexander Košenina, ed. *Berliner Aufklärung. Kulturwissenschaftliche Studien,* vol. 1. Hannover: Wehrhahn, 1999.

– and Alexander Košenina, ed. *Berliner Aufklärung. Kulturwissenschaftliche Studien,* vol. 2. Hannover: Wehrhahn, 2003.

Goldman, Alan. "The Aesthetic." Gaunt and Lopez 181-192.

Gombrich, E.H. "Lessing: Lecture on a Master Mind." *Proceedings of the British Academy* 45 (1957): 133-156.

Gottsched, Johann Christoph. *Versuch einer Critischen Dichtkunst.* 4th ed. Leipzig: Bernhard Christoph Breitkopf, 1751.

Graf, Fritz. "Ekphrasis: Die Entstehung der Gattung in der Antike." Boehm and Pfotenhauer 143-155.

Grant, Deena E. "Fire and the Body of Yahweh." *Journal for the Study of the Old Testament* 40.2 (2015): 139-161.

Grassi, Ernesto. *Die Macht der Phantasie: Zur Geschichte abenländischen Denkens.* Königstein im Taunus: Athenäum, 1979.

Greiner, Bernhard. *Streitkultur des Als Ob: Die Komödie als transzendentale Bedingung des Streitens in* Minna von Barnhelm. Tübingen: Niemeyer, 1983.

Gross, Sabine. "Image and Text: Recent Research in Intermediality." *Monatshefte* 93. 3 (2001): 355-366.

–. "Malen, Dichten, Schildern, Sehen: Lessing und Herder im Streit über Homer und Vergil." Adler and Gross 107-130.

Groys, Boris. *Einführung in die Anti-Philosophie.* Munich: Hanser, 2009.

Grubmüller, Klaus. "Fabel, Exempel, Allegorese: Über Sinnbildungsverfahren und Verwendungszusammenhänge." Walter Haug and Burghart Wachinger, ed. *Exempel und Exempelsammlungen.* Fortuna vitrea: Arbeiten zur literarischen Tradition zwischen dem 13. und 16. Jahrhundert 2. Tübingen: Niemeyer, 1999. 58-76.

Gruenter, Rainer, ed. *Das weinende Saeculum.* Beiträge zur Geschichte der Literatur und Kunst des 18. Jahrhunderts 7. Heidelberg: Winter, 1993.

Guderian-Driesen, Astrid. *Die Stimme in der Kunst. Schweigen ist Silber. Reden ist Gold.* Ebringen: Bannstein Verlag, 1989.

Gustafson, Susan E. *Absent Mothers and Orphaned Fathers. Narcissism and Abjection in Lessing's Aesthetic and Dramatic Production.* Detroit: Wayne State University Press, 1995.

–. "Windungen und Wendungen in Lessings *Laokoon.*" Albrecht, Fratzke, and Schade 21-36.

Guthke, Karl S. *Das deutsche bürgerliche Trauerspiel.* 6th revised and expanded edition. Stuttgart, Weimar: Metzler, 2006.

–. *Gotthold E. Lessing.* 3rd expanded edition. Stuttgart: Metzler, 1979.

–. "Lessings Faust-Dichtung." *Wege zur Literatur: Studien zur deutschen Dichtungs- und Geistesgeschichte.* Bern: Francke, 1967. 247-255. First published as: "Problem und Problematik von Lessings Faust-Dichtung." *Zeitschrift für Deutsche Philologie* 79 (1960): 141-149.

–. *Lessings Horizonte. Grenzen und Grenzenlosigkeit der Toleranz.* Kleine Schriften zur Aufklärung 12. Ed. Lessing-Akademie. Göttingen: Wallstein, 2003.

–."Lessings *Sechstes Freimaurergespräch.*" *Literarisches Leben im achtzehnten Jahrhundert in Deutschland und in der Schweiz.* Bern: Francke, 1975. 315-332. First published in: *Zeitschrift für deutsche Philologie* 85 (1966): 576-597.

–, ed. and "Nachwort." Gotthold Ephraim Lessing: *D. Faust, Die Matrone von Ephesus. Fragmente.* Stuttgart: Reclam, 1968.

Gutjahr, Ortrud, et al., ed. *Gesellige Vernuft: Zur Kultur der literarischen Aufklärung. Festschrift für Wolfram Mauser.* Würzburg: Königshausen & Neumann, 1993.

Häfner, Ralph. "Das Menschengeschlechts im Zeitalter des Heiligen Geistes: Eine Hypothese zu Ursprung und Gestalt von Lessings Anthopologie." Bultmann and Vollhardt 126-137.

Hammacher, Klaus. "Lessings Spinozismus aufgezeigt an seinem Beitrag zur Wandlung der philosophischen Grundfragen nach Gott, Freiheit und Unsterblichkeit in der Aufklärung." *Tijdschrift voor de Studie van de Verlichting en van het vrije Denken* 10 (1982): 87-110.

Harreld, Donald J. *A Companion to the Hanseatic League.* Brill's Companions to European History 8. Leiden: Brill, 2015.

Hart, Gail. *Tragedy in Paradise: Family and Gender Politics in German Bourgeois Tragedy 1750-1850.* Columbia, SC: Camden House, 1996.

Harth, Dietrich. *Gotthold Ephraim Lessing. Oder die Paradoxien der Selbsterkenntnis.* Becksche Reihe Autoren. Munich: Beck, 1993.

Hassauer, Friederike. *Textverluste. Eine Streitschrift.* Munich: Fink, 1992.

Haßelbeck, Otto. *Illusion und Fiktion: Lessings Beitrag zur poetologischen Diskussion über das Verhältnis von Kunst und Wirklichkeit.* Theorie und Geschichte der Literatur und der schönen Künste 49. Munich: Fink, 1979.

Hasubek, Peter, ed. *Die Fabel: Theorie, Geschichte und Rezeption einer Gattung.* Berlin: Erich Schmidt, 1982.

–, ed. *Fabelforschung.* Wege der Forschung 572. Darmstadt: Wissenschaftliche Buchgesellschaft, 1983.

Hausman, Carl R. *Metaphor and Art: Interactionism and Reference in the Verbal and Nonverbal Arts.* Cambridge: Cambridge University Press, 1989.

Hayden-Roy, Patricia. "Refining the Metaphor in Lessing's *Erziehung des Menschengeschlechts.*" *Monatshefte* 95 (2003): 393-409.

Heffernan, James A. W. *Cultivating Picturacy. Visual Art and Verbal Interventions.* Waco, TX: Baylor University Press, 2006.

–. *Museum of Words. The Poetics of Ekphrasis from Homer to Ashbery.* Chicago: University of Chicago Press, 1993.

Hegel, Georg Wilhelm Friedrich. *Vorlesungen über die Ästhetik,* ed. Heinrich Gustav Hotho. Vol 3. 3rd ed. (= *Sämtliche Werke: Jubiläumsausgabe,* ed. Hermann Glockner et al., vol. 14). Stuttgart-Bad Cannstatt: Frommann-Holzboog, 1964.

Helbig, Louis Ferdinand, ed. *Gotthold Ephraim Lessing: Die Erziehung des Menschengeschlechts. Historisch-kritische Edition mit Urteilen Lessings und seiner Zeitgenossen, Einleitung, Entstehungsgeschichte und Kommentar.* Germanic Studies in America 38. Bern: Peter Lang, 1980.

Heller, Peter. *Dialectics and Nihilism: Essays on Lessing, Nietzsche, Mann and Kafka.* Amherst: University of Massachusetts Press, 1966.

Herder, Johann Gottfried. "Aesop and Lessing." *Schriften zu Philosophie, Literatur, Kunst und Altertum 1774-1778.,* ed. Jürgen Brummack and Martin Bollacher. FHA 4 (1994): 1311-1322.

–. "Fabel." *Adrastea* 2.3 (1802). *Adrastea,* ed. Günter Arnold. FHA 10 (2000): 235-241, 242-255.

–. "Alte Fabeln.mit neuer Anwendung." SWS 29: *Herders poetische Werke,* ed. Carl Redlich, 5 vols. Berlin: Weidmann, 1885-1889, 5: 379-416, 737-740.

–. "Fabeln."*Der Teutsche Merkur vom Jahr 1776* (May 11, 1776): 201-203; SWS 29, 60-62.

–. "Über die Seelenwanderung." FHA 4: (1994), 425-473.

–. "Von der aesopischen Fabel." In "Über Bild, Dichtung und Fabel." FHA 4 (1994). 631-677 at 648-669.

Hermes De Fonseca, Lieselotte. "Wachsfigur-Mensch-Plastinat: Über die Mitteilbarkeit von Sehen, Nennen und Wissen." *Deutsche Vierteljahrsschrift für Literaturwissenschaft und Geistesgeschichte* 73.1 (1999): 43-68.

Hess, Jonathan M. *Germans, Jews and the Claims of Modernity.* New Haven: Yale University Press, 2002.

–. Lessing and German Jewish Culture: A Reappraisal." Robertson 179-204.

Hess-Lüttich, Ernest W. B. "Medium–Prozeß–Illusion: Zur rationalen Rekonstruktion der Zeichenlehre in Lessings *Laokoon.*" Gebauer 103-136.

Heßelmann, Peter. *Gereinigtes Theater? Dramaturgie und Schaubühne im Spiegel deutschsprachiger Theaterperiodika (1750-1800).* Das Abendland, N. F. 31. Frankfurt am Main: Vittorio Klostermann, 2002.

Hiebel, Hans Helmut. "Mißverstehen und Sprachlosigkeit im 'Bürgerlichen Trauerspiel.' Zum historischen Wandel dramatischer Motivationsformen." *Jahrbuch der deutschen Schillergesellschaft* 27 (1983): 124-153.

Hoesterey, Ingeborg. "*Laokoon* und Modernität. Eine Rettung." *Lessing Yearbook* 15 (1983): 165-176.

Höyng, Peter. "Lessing's Drama Theory: Discursive Writings on Drama, Performance, and Theater." Fischer and Fox 211-229.

Hoff, Dagmar von, and Helga Meise. "Tableaux vivants-Die Kunst-und Leben Kultform der Attitüden und lebenden Bilder." Dagmar von Hoff and Helga Meise, ed. *Weiblichkeit und Tod in der Literatur.* Cologne: Böhlau, 1987. 69-86.

Hofmannsthal, Hugo von. "Ein Brief." *Brief des Lord Chandos. Poetologische Schriften, Reden und erfundene Gespräche.* Ed. Hansgeorg Schmidt-Bergmann. Frankfurt am Main: Insel, 2000. 127-138.

–."A Letter," *The Lord Chandos Letter and Other Writings.* Trans. Joel Rotenberg. New York: New York Review of Books, 2005. 117-128.

Holmström, Kirsten Gram. *Monodrama. Attitudes. Tableaux Vivants. Studies on some Trends of Theatrical Fashion, 1770-1815.* Stockholm Studies in Theatrical History 1. Stockholm: Almquist and Wiksell, 1967.

Honold, Alexander and Ralf Simon, ed. *Das erzählende und das erzählte Bild.* Munich: Fink, 2010.

Huber, Gerlinde. *Das Motiv der "Witwe von Ephesus" in lateinischen Texten der Antike und des Mittelalters.* Mannheimer Beiträge zur Sprach- und Literaturwissenschaft 18. Tübingen: Gunter Narr, 1990.

Huizinga, Johan. *Homo Ludens: A Study of the Play Element in Culture.* Boston: Beacon Press, 1955.

Israel, Jonathan I. *Radical Enlightenment. Philosophy and the Making of Modernity 1650-1750.* Oxford: Oxford University Press, 2001.

–. *Democratic Enlightenment. Philosophy, Revolution, and Human Rights 1750-1790.* Oxford: Oxford University Press, 2011.

Jacobs, Carol. "The Critical Performance of Lessing's *Laokoon.*" *Modern Language Notes* 102. 3 (1987): 483-521.

–. *Telling Time: Lévi-Strauss, Ford, Lessing, Benjamin, de Man, Wordsworth, Rilke.* Baltimore: Johns Hopkins University Press, 1993.

Jahn, Gunter. *Lessings Fabelabhandlungen: Ein Elementarbuch der Didaktik und Methodik.* Bielefeld: Aisthesis, 2000.

Jameson, Fredric. *The Prison-House of Language: A Critical Account of Structuralism and Russian Formalism.* Princeton: Princeton University Press, 1972.

Jay, Martin. "Scopic Regimes of Modernity." Hal Foster, ed. *Vision and Visuality.* Dia Art Foundation Discussions on Contemporary Culture 2. Seattle: Bay Press, 1988. 2-23; Rpt. Martin Jay. *Force Fields: Between Intellectual History and Cultural Critique.* London: Routledge, 1993, 114-133.

Jean Paul (Johann Paul Friedrich Richter). *Horn of Oberon: Jean Paul Richter's School for Aesthetics.* Trans. Margaret R. Hale. Detroit: Wayne State University Press, 1973.

–. *Vorschule der Ästhetik.* Ed. Norbert Miller. Intro. Wolfhart Henckmann. Philosophische Bibliothek 425. Hamburg: Meiner, 1990.

Johnson, Mark. "Introduction: Metaphor in the Philosophical Tradition." Johnson 3-47.

–, ed. *Philosophical Perspectives on Metaphor.* Minneapolis: University of Minnesota Press, 1981.

Jooss, Birgit. *Lebende Bilder: Körperliche Nachahmung in der Goethezeit.* Berlin: Reimer, 1999.

Jusdanis, Gregor. "Parabasis." *The Princeton Encyclopedia of Poetry and Poetics.* 4th ed. Ed. Roland Greene et al. Princeton: Princeton University Press, 2012. 996.

Kaiser, Herbert. "Die Pädagogisierung der Fabel am Ende des 18. und zu Beginn des 19. Jahrhunderts." Hasubek, *Die Fabel* 163-179.

Kandinsky, Wassily. *Punkt und Linie zu Fläche. Beitrag zur Analyse der malerischen Elemente.* 7th ed. Intro. Max Brill. Bern: Bentili Verlag, 1955.

—. *Über das Geistige in der Kunst.* 10th ed. Intro. Max Brill. Bern: Benteli Verlag, 1952.

Käuser, Andreas. "*Ut pictura poesis–ut musica poesis.* Modifikation und Modalitäten von Anschaulichkeit um 1800." Schneider, Simon and Wirtz 229-247.

Kelly, Veronica and Dorothea von Mücke, ed. *Body and Text in the Eighteenth Century.* Stanford: Stanford University Press, 1994.

Kemp, Wolfgang. "Die Kunst des Schweigens." Koebner 96-119.

–, ed. *Der Betrachter ist im Bild. Kunstwissenschaft und Rezeptionsästhetik.* Cologne: DuMont, 1985. 2nd ed. Munich: Reimer, 1992.

Kenkel, Karen J. "Monstrous Women, Sublime Pleasure, and the Perils of Reception in Lessing's Aesthetics." *PMLA* 116.3 (May 2001): 545-561.

Kim, Eun-Ae. *Lessings Tragödientheorie im Licht der neueren Aristotelesforschung.* Epistemata 374. Würzburg: Königshausen & Neumann, 2002.

Kittler, Friedrich A. "'Erziehung ist Offenbarung:' Zur Struktur der Familie in Lessings Dramen." *Jahrbuch der Deutschen Schillergesellschaft* 21 (1977): 111-137.

Klarer, Mario. *Ekphrasis: Bildbeschreibung als Repräsentationstheorie bei Spenser, Sidney, Lyly und Shakespeare.* Buchreihe der Anglia 35. Tübingen: Niemeyer, 2001.

Klee, Paul. *Diaries 1898-1919.* Ed. Felix Klee. Trans Pierre B. Schneider et al. Berkeley: University of California Press, 1964.

—. "Schöpferische Konfession." *Kunst-Lehre. Aufsätze, Vorträge, Rezensionen und Beiträge zur bildnerischen Formlehre.* Ed. Günther Regel. 3rd ed. Leipzig: Reclam, 1995. 60-66.

—. *Tagebücher 1898-1918.* Ed. Felix Klee. Cologne: DuMont, 1957.

Knaller, Susanne. "Verschiebungen im Kunstsystem. Zum Verhältnis von Sprachkunst und Bildkunst in den ästhetischen Diskursen des 18. und 19. Jahrhunderts." *Komparatistik: Jahrbuch der Deutschen Gesellschaft für Allgemeine und Vergleichende Literaturwissenschaft.* Heidelberg: Synchron: 2013. 55-72.

Koebner, Thomas, ed. *Laokoon und kein Ende: Der Wettstreit der Künste.* Munich: Text + Kritik, 1989.

Koepke, Wulf. "Jean Paul als ein früher Leser der *Erziehung des Menschengeschlechts.*" *Lessing Yearbook* 2 (1970): 90-114.

Kohle, Hubertus. *Ut pictura poesis non erit. Denis Diderots Kunstbegriff. Mit einem Exkurs zu J. B. S. Chardin.* Studien zur Kunstgeschichte 52. Hildesheim: Georg Olms, 1989.

Koopmann, Helmut. "Lessing: Das Allgemeine im Besonderen. Aufklärung als Denkfigur und Fabeltheorie." Elm and Hasubek 51-63.

Kornmeyer, Evert, ed. *Gotthold Ephraim Lessing: Ernst & Falk, Gespräche für Freimaurer 1-5.* Modernisierte Sprachfassung mit zwei weiteren bisher verschollenen Gesprächen für Freimaurer. Vorwort des Meisters vom Stuhl der Loge Lessing in Frankfurt am Main. Frankfurt am Main: Edition Königliche Kunst, 2011.

Korzeniewski, Uta. "*Sophokles! Die Alten! Philoktet!*" *Lessing und die antiken Dramatiker.* Konstanz: UVK Universitätsverlag, 2003.

Košenina, Alexander. *Anthropologie und Schauspielkunst: Studien zur 'eloquentia corporis' im 18. Jahrhundert.* Theatron 11. Tübingen: Niemeyer, 1995.

—. Augenbühne versus Hörbuch. Was leisten die Sinne aus Lessings Theater?" Košenina and Stockhorst 213-230.

–. *Ernst Platners Anthropologie und Philosophie: Der 'philosophische Arzt' und seine Wirkung auf Johann Karl Wezel und Jean Paul.* Epistemata: Reihe Literaturwissenschaft 35. Würzburg: Königshausen & Neumann, 1989.

–. "Die anthropologische Neubegründung der *eloquentia corporis.*" Fauser 95-105.

–. "Bühnen-Bilder. Von den Grenzen der Malerei und Dramaturgie bei Lessing." *Lessing Yearbook* 41 (2014): 175-190.

– and Stefanie Stockhorst, ed. *Lessing und die Sinne.* Hannover: Wehrhahn, 2016.

Kowalik, Jill Anne. "*Nathan* as a Work of Mourning." *Lessing Yearbook* 21 (1989): 1-18.

Kraft, Helga. "Gotthold E. Lessings Marwood in *Miss Sara Sampson.*" Kraft and Liebs 35-36.

– and Elke Liebs, ed. *Mütter, Töchter, Frauen. Weiblichkeitsbilder in der Literatur.* Stuttgart: Metzler, 1993.

Krieger, Murray. *Ekphrasis: The Illusion of the Natural Sign.* Baltimore: Johns Hopkins University Press, 1992.

–. "Das Problem der Ekphrasis: Wort und Bild, Raum und Zeit–und das literarische Werk." Boehm and Pfotenhauer 41-57.

–. "The Problem of Ekphrasis: Image and Words, Space and Time–and the Literary Work." Robillard and Jongeneel 3-20.

Kuschel, Karl-Josef. *"Jud, Christ und Muselmann vereinigt"? Lessings* Nathan der Weise. Düsseldorf: Patmos, 2004.

Lakoff, George and Mark Johnson. *Metaphors We Live By.* Chicago: University of Chicago Press, 1980.

Lamport, J.J. "The Death of Emilia Galotti–A Reconsideration." *German Life and Letters* 44 (1990): 25-33.

Lee, Rensselaer W. *Ut Pictura Poesis: The Humanistic Theory of Painting.* New York: Norton, 1967.

Lehmann, Johannes Friedrich. *Der Blick durch die Wand. Zur Geschichte des Theaterzuschauers und des Visuellen bei Diderot und Lessing.* Freiburg im Breisgau: Rombach, 2000.

Lessing, Gotthold Ephraim. *Äsopische Fabeln mit moralischen Lehren und Betrachtungen.* Aus dem Englischen übertragen und mit einer Vorrede von Gotthold Ephraim Lessing nach der Ausgabe von Samuel Richardson. Ed. Walter Pape. Zürich: Diogenes, 1999.

–. *Emilia Galotti: Ein Trauerspiel in fünf Aufzügen. Historisch-kritische Ausgabe.* Ed. Elke Monika Bauer. Tübingen: Niemeyer, 2004.

–. *Die Erziehung des Menschengeschlechts. Werke 1778-1781.* Ed. Arno Schilson and Axel Schmitt. FA 10 (2001): 73-99, 794-879.

–. *Fables and Epigrams; with Essays on Fable and Epigram from the German of Lessing.* London: John and H.L. Hunt, 1825.

–. *Hrn. Samuel Richardsons Verfassers der Pamela, der Clarissa, des Grandisons Sittenlehre für die Jugend in den auserlesenden Aesopischen Fabeln mit dienlichen Betrachtungen zur Beförderung der Religion und die allgemeinen Menschenliebe vorgestellet.* Leipzig: Wiedemann, 1757.

–. *Laocoon: An Essay on the Limits of Painting and Poetry.* Trans. with intro. and notes by Edward Allen McCormick. 3rd ed. Baltimore: Johns Hopkins University Press, 1992.

–. *Laokoon oder Über die Grenzen der Malerei und Poesie. Laokoon: Werke 1766-1769.* Ed. Wilfried Barner. FA 5/2 (1990): 9-206.

–. *Laokoon oder Über die Grenzen der Malerei und Poesie. Studienausgabe.* Ed. Friedrich Vollhardt. Stuttgart: Reclam, 2012.

–. *D. Faust. Die Matrone von Ephesus.* Ed. Karl S. Guthke with "Nachwort". Stuttgart: Reclam, 1968.

–. *Die Matrone von Ephesus–Eine Komödie.* Ed. Gerhard Kirchhoff with an appendix, "Die Fabel des Petronius Arbiter." Munich: Max Hueber, 1969.

–. *Nathan der Weise. Die Erziehung des Menschengeschlechts.* Ed. Philippe Wellnitz, Strasbourg: Presses Universitaires de Strasbourg, 2000.

Leibfried, Erwin. *Die Fabel.* 4th ed. Stuttgart: Metzler, 1982.

L'Estrange, Roger. *Fables, of Aesop and other eminent mythologists: with morals and reflections.* London: R. Sare et al., 1692.

Leventhal, Robert S. "The Parable as Performance: Interpretation, Cultural Transmission, and Political Strategy in Lessing's *Nathan der Weise.*" *German Quarterly* 61 (1988): 502-527.

Lewis, Jayne Elizabeth. *The English Fable: Aesop and Literary Culture 1651-1740.* Cambridge Studies in Eighteenth-Century English Literature and Thought 28. Cambridge: Cambridge University Press, 1996.

Longinus. *On the Sublime.* Ed. and trans. W.H. Fyfe, rev. Donald Russell. Aristotle *Poetics,* Longinus *On the Sublime,* Demetrius *On Style,* trans. Stephen Halliwell et al., corr. ed., Loeb Classical Library 199. Cambridge: Harvard University Press, 1999.

Luckhurst, Mary. "Revolutionising Theatre: Brecht's Reinvention of the Dramaturge." Peter Thomson and Glendyr Sacks, ed. *The Cambridge Companion to Brecht.* 2nd ed. Cambridge: Cambridge University Press, 2006. 193-208.

Lützeler, Paul Michael. "Die marxistische Lessing-Rezeption. Darstellung und Kritik am Beispiel der *Emilia Galotti*-Interpretation in der DDR." *Lessing Yearbook* 8 (1976): 42-60.

–. *Geschichte inder Literatur. Studien zu Werken von Lessing bis Hebbel.* Munich: Piper, 1987. 15-39.

Lupke, Johannes von. *Wege der Weisheit: Studien zu Lessings Theologiekritik.* Gottinger theologische Arbeiten 41. Gottingen: Vandenhoeck und Ruprecht, 1989.

Maar, Christa and Hubert Burda, ed. *Iconic Turn: Die Neue Macht der Bilder.* 2nd ed. Cologne: DuMont, 2004.

Mahal, Günther."Lessings Faust: Planen, Ringen, Scheitern." *Faust-Blätter* 11 (1972): 525-551.

Malebranche, Nicolas. *The Search after Truth.* Trans. and ed. Thomas M. Lennon and Paul J. Olscamp. Cambridge: Cambridge University Press, 1997.

Margolis, Joseph. "Medieval Aesthetics." Gaunt and Lopes 27-36.

Markschies, Hans-Lothar. "Lessing und die äsopische Fabel." *Wissenschaftliche Zeitschrift der Karl-Marx-Universität Leipzig.* Gesellschafts- und Sprachwissenschaftliche Reihe 4.1/2 (1954-1955): 129-142. Hasubek, *Fabelforschung* 129-164.

Martinec, Thomas. "Musik und Sprache." *Lessing Yearbook* 41 (2014): 209-224.

–. "Lessing und Aristoteles? Versuch einer Grenzbestimmung in Lessings Interpretation des aristotelischen Tragödienansatzes." Zeuch 82-100.

–. "Lessings Ästhetischer Sensualismus." Košenina and Stockhorst 141-160.

–. "Lessing's Dramatic Theory." Robertson 119-137.

–. *Lessings Theorie der Tragödienwirkung. Humanistische Tradition und aufklärerische Erkenntniskritik.* Untersuchungen zur deutschen Literaturgeschichte 116. Tübingen: Niemeyer, 2003.

Martinson, Steven D. *Projects of Enlightenment. The Work of Gotthold Ephraim Lessing: Cultural, Intercultural, and Transcultural Perspectives.* Hermeia 11. Heidelberg: Synchron, 2013.

Mauser Wolfram. "'Ich stehe für nichts'. Zur Uraufführung von G.E. Lessings *Emilia Galotti* im Hoftheater zu Brauschweig." Gerd Biegel, ed. *Lessing in Braunschweig und Wolfenbüttel.* Braunschweig: Braunschweigisches Landesmuseum, 1997. 111-123.

–. "Toleranz und Frecheit: Zur Strategie von Lessings Streitschriften." Freimark, Kopitzsch and Slessarev 276-290.

– and Günter Saße, ed. *Streitkultur: Strategien des Überzeugens im Werk Lessings.* Tübingen: Niemeyer, 1993.

Mayer, Hans. *Außenseiter.* Frankfurt am Main: Suhrkamp, 1975.

–. "Der weise Nathan und der Räuber Spiegelberg. Antinomien der jüdischen Emanzipation in Deutschland," *Jahrbuch der Deutschen Schillergesellschaft* 17 (1973): 253-272.

– "Lessings poetische Ausdrucksform." *Lessing und die Zeit der Aufklärung*. Göttingen: Vandenhoeck & Ruprecht 1968. 130-147.

Mazur, Ronald M. "Gotthold Ephraim Lessing's Fables: Theory and Practice." Ugrinsky 53-57.

McClain, Jeoraldean. "Time in the Visual Arts: Lessing and Visual Criticism." *Journal of Aesthetics and Art Criticism* 44 (1985): 41-58.

Mehring, Franz. *Die Lessing-Legende. Eine Rettung.* 1893. Rpt. Frankfurt am Main: Ullstein, 1972.

Mendelssohn, Moses. "Betrachtungen über die Quellen und Verbindungen der schönen Künste und Wissenschaften." *Bibliothek der schönen Wissenschaften und der freyen Künste* I.2 (1757): 231-268. Reprinted *Gesammelte Schriften* 1: 165-90.

–. *Gesammelte Schriften. Jubiläumsausgabe.* Ed. Fritz Bamberger et al. 24 vols. in 35. Stuttgart: Friedrich Frommann Verlag [Günther Holzboog], 1929 [1971]-2005.

–. "Jerusalem oder über religiöse Macht und Judentum." Berlin: Friedrich Maurer, 1783. Reprinted *Gesammelte Schriften* 8: 99-204

–. "Ueber die Hauptgrundsätze der schönen Künste und Wissenschaften." *Philosophische Schriften.* 2 vols. (Berlin: Christian Friedrich Voß, 1761; rev. ed. 1771. 2: 95-152. Reprinted *Gesammelte Schriften* 1: 425-452.

Meise, Jutta. *Lessings Anglophilie.* Europäische Aufklärung in Literatur und Sprache 10. Frankfurt am Main: Peter Lang, 1997.

Merrell, Floyd A. *Peirce's Semiotics Now. A Primer.* Toronto: Canadian Scholar's Press, 1995.

–. *Semiosis in the Postmodern Age.* West Lafayette, IN: Purdue University Press, 1995.

–. *Semiotic Theory of Texts.* Approaches to Semiotics 70. Berlin: Mouton de Gruyter, 1985.

Meyer-Kalkus, Reinhart. "Schreit Laokoon? Zur Diskussion pathetisch-erhabener Darstellungsformen im 18. Jahrhundert." Gérard Raulet, ed. *Von der Rhetorik zur Ästhetik: Studien zur Entstehung der modernen Ästhetik im 18. Jahrhunderts.* Rennes: Centre de Récherche PHILIA, Université de Rennes 2, 1992. 64-107.

Michelsen, Peter. *Der unruhige Bürger. Studien zu Lessing und zur Literatur des achtzehnten Jahrhunderts.* Würzburg: Königshausen & Neumann, 1990.

–."Die Verbergung der Kunst. Über die Exposition in Lessings *Minna von Barnhelm.*" *Jahrbuch der Deutschen Schillergesellschaft* 17 (1973): 192-252.

–. "Die 'wahren Taten' der Freimaurer. Lessings *Ernst und Falk.*" *Der unruhige Bürger,* 1990. 221-280.

–. "Lessing, mit den Augen Goezes gesehen." Mauser and Saße 378-391.

Mitchell, P.M. "Aspekte der Fabeltheorie im 18. Jahrhundert vor Lessing." Hasubek, *Die Fabel* 119-134.

Mitchell, W.J.T. *Picture Theory: Essays on Verbal and Visual Representation.* Chicago: University of Chicago Press, 1994.

–. *On Narratives.* Chicago: University of Chicago Press, 1981.

–. "Space and Time: Lessing's Laocoon and the Politics of Genre." *Iconology: Image, Text, Ideology.* Chicago: University of Chicago Press, 1986. 95-115.

–. *What Do Pictures Want? The Lives and Loves of Images.* Chicago: University of Chicago Press, 2005.

Mönch, Cornelia. *Abschrecken oder Mitleiden. Das deutsche bürgerliche Trauerspiel im 18. Jahrhundert. Versuch einer Typologie.* Studia Augustana 5. Tübingen: Niemeyer, 1993.

Morrison, Jeff, and Florian Krobb, ed. *Text to Image: Image to Text. Proceedings of the Interdisciplinary Bicentenary Conference held at St. Patrick's College Maynooth (The National University of Ireland) in September 1995.* Internationale Forschungen zur Allgemeinen und Vergleichenden Literaturwissenschaft 20. Amsterdam: Rodopi, 1997.

Moser-Rath, Elfriede. "Die Fabel als rhetorisches Element in der katholischen Predigt der Barockzeit." Hasubek, *Die Fabel* 59-75.

Motte, Houdar de la. *Fables nouvelles, dédiées au Roy ... avec un discours sur les fables.* Paris: Grégoire Dupuis, 1719.

–. "La Matron d' Ephèse." *Oeuvres,* 11 vols. Paris: Chez Prault L'ainé, 1754. 5: 469-510.

Mülder-Bach, Inka. "Bild und Bewegung: Zur Theorie bildnerischer Illusion in Lessings Laokoon." *Deutsche Vierteljahrsschrift für Literaturwissenschaft und Geistesgeschichte* 66 (1992): 1-30.

–. *Im Zeichen Pygmalions. Das Modell der Statue und die Entdeckung der Darstellung im 18. Jahrhundert.* Munich: Fink. 1998.

–. "Sichtbarkeit und Schriftlichkeit. Goethes Laokoonaufsatz." Baxmann et al. 465-479.

Müller, Paul. *Untersuchungen zum Problem der Freimaurerei bei Lessing, Herder und Fichte.* Sprache und Dichtung, N.F. 12. Bern: Paul Haupt, 1965.

Müller Nielaba, Daniel. "'Die arme Recha, die indes verbrannte!' Zur Kombustibilität der Bedeutung in Lessings *Nathan der Weise.*" Engel and Ritterhoff 105-125.

Multhammer, Michael. *Lessings 'Rettungen'. Geschichte und Genese eines Denkstils.* Frühe Neuzeit 183 Berlin: De Gruyter, 2013.

Nadler, Steven. "Introduction." Nadler 1-8.

–, ed. *Causation in Early Modern Philosophy: Cartesianism, Occasionalism, and Preestablished Harmony.* University Park: Pennsylvania State University Press, 1993.

Neumann, Peter Horst. *Der Preis der Mündigkeit. Über Lessings Dramen.* Stuttgart: Klett Cotta, 1977.

Niekerk, Carl. "Lessings Körperlichkeits-Entwürfe zwischen Richardson und Diderot." Košenina and Stockhorst 99-121.

Nietzsche, Friedrich. *Werke in drei Bänden.* Ed. Karl Schlechta. 1954-1956. Reprint in 4 vols. Darmstadt: Wissenschaftliche Buchgesellschaft, 1997-

–. *Die Fröhliche Wissenschaft. Werke* 2: 7-274.

–. "*From* On Truth and Lie in an Extra-Moral Sense." *The Portable Nietzsche.* Trans. Walter Kaufmann. New York: Viking Press, 1982. 42-45.

–. "Über Wahrheit und Lüge im außermoralischen Sinn." *Werke* 3: 309-322.

Niewöhner, Friedrich. *Veritas sive Varietas. Lessings Toleranzparabel und das Buch von den drei Betrügern.* Veröffentlichung der Lessing-Akademie Wolfenbüttel. Heidelberg: Verlag Lambert Schneider, 1988.

Nisbet, Hugh Barr. *Gotthold Ephraim Lessing. His Life, Works, and Thought.* Oxford University Press, 2013.

–. *Lessing: Eine Biographie.* Trans. Karl S. Guthke. Munich: Beck, 2008.

–. "Lessing and Misogyny: *Die Matrone von Ephesus.*" John L. Hibberd and H.B. Nisbet, ed. *Texte, Motive und Gestalten der Goethezeit. Festschrift für Hans Reiss.* Tübingen: Niemeyer, 1989. 13-31.

–."Laokoon in Germany: The Reception of the Group since Winckelmann." *Oxford German Studies* 10 (1979): 22-63.

–. "The Rationalisation of the Holy Trinity from Lessing to Hegel." *Lessing Yearbook* 31 (1999): 65-89.

Noel, Thomas. *Theories of the Fable in the Eighteenth Century.* New York: Columbia University Press, 1975.

Nölle, Volker. *Subjektivität und Wirklichkeit in Lessings dramatischem und theologischem Werk.* Philologische Studien und Quellen 87. Berlin: Erich Schmidt 1977.

Ogée, Frédéric and Anthony Strugnell, ed. *Diderot and European Culture.* SVEC 2006 vol 9. Oxford: Voltaire Foundation, 2006.

O'Neil, John. "Diderot and the Enlightenment's poetics of confusion in the 'Lettre sur les aveugles'." Ogée and Strugnell 159-169.

O'Neill, Eileen. "Influxus Physicus." Nadler 27-55.

Ortony, Andrew, ed. *Metaphor and Thought*. 2nd ed. Cambridge: Cambridge University Press, 1993.

Osterkamp, Ernst. *Im Buchstabenbilde. Studien zum Verfahren Goethescher Bildbeschreibungen*. Germanistische Abhandlungen 70. Stuttgart: Metzler, 1991.

Ott, Karl August. "Lessing und La Fontaine: Von dem Gebrauche der Tiere in der Fabel." *Germanisch-Romanische Monatsschrift*, N.F. 9, (40) (1959): 235-266. Rpt. Hasubek, *Fabelforschung* 165-206.

Overath, Angelika, Navid Kermani, Robert Schindel. *Toleranz. Drei Lesarten zu Lessings Märchen vom Ring*. Göttingen: Wallstein, 2003.

Perry, Ben Edwin. *Aesopica: A Series of Texts Relating to Aesop or Ascribed to Him or Closely Connected with the Literary Tradition that Bears his Name*. New ed. Urbana: University of Illinois Press, 2007.

– "Introduction." Babrius and Phaedrus, *Fables*, ed. Perry (1965), xxxv-xlvi.

Petsch, Robert, ed. *Lessings Briefwechsel mit Mendelssohn und Nicolai über das Trauerspiel. Nebst verwandten Schriften Nicolais und Mendelssohns*. Darmstadt: Wissenschaftliche Buchgesellschaft, 1967.

–, ed. *Lessings Faustdichtung mit erläuternden Beigaben*. Germanische Bibliothek II: Untersuchungen und Texte 4. Heidelberg: Winter, 1911.

Petronius. *Satyricon*. Ed. Michael Heseltine. Rev. and corr. ed. Loeb Classical Library 15 Cambridge: Harvard University Press, 1987.

Pfotenhauer, Helmut."Winckelmann und Heinse. Die Typen der Beschreibungskunst im 18. Jahrhundert oder die Geburt der neuen Kunstgeschichte." Boehm and Pfotenhauer 313-340.

Pikulik, Lothar. *"Bürgerliche Trauerspiele" und Empfindsamkeit*. Cologne: Böhlau, 1966.

Pizer, John. "Lessing and the Fable." Fischer and Fox 89-104.

Politzer, Heinz. "Lessings Parabel von den drei Ringen." *German Quarterly* 31 (1958): 161-177. Reprint: Gerhard Bauer and Sibylle Bauer, ed. *Gotthold Ephraim Lessing*. Wege der Forschung 211. Darmstadt: Wissenschaftliche Buchgesellschaft, 1968. 343-361. Revised version: *Das Schweigen der Sirenen: Studien zur deutschen und österreichischen Literatur*. Stuttgart: Metzler, 1968. 339-372 and 425-428.

Potolsky, Matthew. *Mimesis. The New Critical Idiom*. New York: Routledge, 2006.

Poynter, John. "The Pearls of Emilia Galotti." *Lessing Yearbook* 9 (1977): 81-96.

Prager, Brad. *Aesthetic Vision and German Romanticism: Writing Images*. Rochester, NY: Camden House, 2007.

Primavesi, Oliver. "Bild und Zeit: Lessings Poetik des natürlichen Zeichens und die Homerische Ekphrasis." Jürgen Paul Schwindt, ed. *Klassische Philologie inter disciplinas: Aktuelle Konzepte zu Gegenstand und Methode eines Grundlagenfaches*. Bibliothek der Klassischen Altertumswissenschaften, N.F. 2. Reihe 110. Heidelberg: Winter, 2002. 187-211.

Prutti, Brigitte. *Bild und Körper: Weibliche Präsenz und Geschlechterbeziehungen in Lessings Dramen* Emilia Galotti *und* Minna von Barnhelm. Würzburg: Königshausen & Neumann, 1996.

–. "Coup de Theatre–Coup de Femme or: What is Lessing's Emilia Galotti dying from?" *Lessing Yearbook* 26 (1994): 1-27.

Pütz, Peter. *Die Leistung der Form. Lessings Dramen*. Frankfurt am Main: Suhrkamp, 1986.

Quintilian. *The Orator's Education* [*Institutio Oratoria*]. Ed. and trans. Donald A. Russell. 5 vols. Loeb Classical Library 124-27, 494. Cambridge: Harvard University Press, 2001.

Raaberg, Gwen. "Laokoon Considered and Reconsidered: Lessing and Comparative Criticism of Literature and Art." Ugrinsky 67-110.

Ragno, Tiziana. *Il teatro nel racconto: Studi sulla fabula scenica della matrona di Efeso.* Tyche 3. Bari: Palomar, 2009.

Ratkowitsch, Christine, ed. *Die Poetische Ekphrasis von Kunstwerken. Eine literarische Tradition der Großdichtung in Antike, Mittelalter und früher Neuzeit.* Österreichische Akademie der Wissenschaften, philosophisch-historischen Klasse, Sitzungsberichte 735. Vienna: Verlag der Österreichischen Akademie der Wissenschaften, 2006.

Redekop, Benjamin W. *Enlightenment and Community: Lessing, Abbt, Herder, and the Quest for a German Public.* Montreal: McGill-Queens University Press, 2000.

Reh, Albert M. "Emilia Galotti–'großes Exempel der dramatischen Algebra' oder 'Algebra der Ambivalenz'?" *Lessing Yearbook* 28 (1997): 83-104.

Rehermann, Ernst Heinrich, and Ines Köhler-Zürich. "Aspekte der Gesellschafts- und Kirchenkritik in der Fabeln von Martin Luther, Nathanael Chytraeus and Burkhard Waldis." Hasubek, *Die Fabel* 27-42.

Reimarus, Hermann Samuel. *Apologie oder Schutzschrift für die vernünftigen Verehrer Gottes.* Ed. Gerhard Alexander. 2 vols. Frankfurt am Main: Insel, 1972.

Reinitzer, Heimo and Walter Sparn, ed. *Verspätete Orthodoxie: Über D. Johann Melchior Goeze (1717-1786).* Wolfenbüttler Forschungen 45. Wiesbaden: Harrassowitz, 1989.

Rennie, Nicholas, "Lessing's 'Lethotechnics': Memory and Perspective in Laokoon." *Lessing Yearbook* 42 (2015): 103-124.

Richardson, John, trans. *Fables from the German of Lessing.* York: C. Etherington, 1773.

Richardson, Samuel. "Aesop's Fables." *Early Works.* Ed. Alexander Pettit. The Cambridge Edition of the Works of Samuel Richardson 1. Cambridge: Cambridge University Press, 2012. 99-320.

Richert, Hans-Georg. "Die *Declaration of Independence* und Lessings *Ernst und Falk*: Eine bare Koinzidenz?" Uwe Faulhaber et al., ed. *Exile und Enlightenment. Studies in Comparative Literature in honor of Guy Stern.* Detroit: Wayne State University Press, 1987. 77-86.

Richter, Simon. *Laocoon's Body and the Aesthetics of Pain: Winckelmann, Lessing, Herder, Moritz, Goethe.* Detroit: Wayne State University Press, 1992.

–. "The End of Laocoön: Pain and Allegory in Goethe's 'Über Laokoon'." *Goethe Yearbook* 6 (1992): 123-141.

Ricœur, Paul. "Narrative Time." W.J.T. Mitchell, ed. *On Narrative.* Chicago: University of Chicago Press, 1980. 165-195.

Robert, Jörg and Friedrich Vollhardt, ed. *Unordentliche Collectanea. Gotthold Ephraim Lessings* Laokoon *zwischen antiquarischer Gelehrsamkeit und ästhetischer Theoriebildung.* Frühe Neuzeit 181. Berlin: De Gruyter, 2013.

Robertson, John George. *Lessing's Dramatic Theory: Being an Introduction to and Commentary on his Hamburgische Dramaturgie.* Cambridge: Cambridge University Press, 1939. Rpt. New York: Benjamin Bloom, 1965.

Robertson, Richard. *The "Jewish Question" in German Literature, 1749-1939: Emancipation and its Discontents.* Oxford: Oxford University Press, 2001.

–. ed. *Lessing and the German Enlightenment.* SVEC 2013 09. Oxford: Voltaire Foundation, 2013.

Robillard, Valerie and Els Jongeneel, ed. *Pictures into Words. Theoretical and Descriptive Approaches to Ekphrasis.* Amsterdam: VU University Press, 1998.

Rohde, Carsten. *Doppelte Vernunft: Lessing und die reflexive Moderne.* Hannover: Wehrhahn, 2013.

Rousseau, Jean Jacques. Émile. Trans. Barbara Foxley. Everyman's Library 518. 1911. London: Dent, 1955.

Rubin, Gayle. "The Traffic in Women: Notes on the 'Political Economy' of Sex." Rayna R. Reiter, ed. *Toward an Anthropology of Women.* New York: Monthly Review Press, 1975. 157-210, 396-416.

Rudowski, Victor, Anthony. "Action as the Essence of Poetry: A Revaluation of Lessing's Argument." *PMLA* 82 (1967): 333-441.

–. "Lessing Contra Winckelmann." *The Journal of Aesthetics and Art Criticism* 44.3 (1986): 235-243.

–. *Lessing's* Aesthetica in Nuce: *An Analysis of the May 26, 1769, Letter to Nicolai.* University of North Carolina Studies in the Germanic Languages and Literatures 69. Chapel Hill: University of North Carolina Press, 1971.

Ruskin, John: *The Two Paths. The Works of John Ruskin.* New. ed. vol. 10. Sunnyside, Orpington: George Allen, 1884.

Saße, Günter. "Das Besondere und das Allgemeine. Lessings Auseinandersetzung mit Diderot über Wahrheit und Wirkung des Dramas." Gutjahr et al. 263-276.

–. *Die Ordnung der Gefühle: Das Drama der Liebesheirat im 18. Jahrhundert.* Darmstadt: Wissenschaftliche Buchgesellschaft, 1996.

–. *Liebe und Ehe. Oder: Wie sich die Spontaneität des Herzens zu den Normen der Gesellschaft verhält. Lessings* Minna von Barnhelm. Studien und Texte zur Sozialgeschichte 40. Tübingen: Niemeyer, 1993.

Sauder, Gerhard. *Empfindsamkeit.* Vol. 1: *Voraussetzungen und Elemente*; Vol. 3: *Quellen und Dokumente.* Stuttgart: Metzler, 1974-1980–no more published.

–. "Sinnliche Erkenntnis: Der Kontext von Herders Abhandlung 'Vom Erkennen und Empfinden der menschlichen Seele' (1778)." Allert, *Herder* 137-155.

–, ed. *Johann Gottfried Herder: 1744-1803.* Studien zum achtzehnten Jahrhundert 9. Hamburg: Meiner, 1987,

Sauerland, Karol. "Lessings Palast-Parabel–ein literarisches Kleinod, das über das Streitobjekt hinauswuchs." Mauser and Saße 457-461.

Schade, Richard E. and Dieter Sevin, ed. *Practicing Progress. The Promise and Limitations of Enlightenment: Festschrift for John A. McCarthy.* Internationale Forschungen zur Allgemeinen und Vergleichenden Literaturwissenschaft 106. Amsterdam: Rodopi, 2007.

Schenkel, Martin. "Wer über gewisse Dinge den Verstand nicht verliert, der hat keinen zu verlieren. Zur Dialektik der bürgerlichen Aufklärung in Lessings *Emilia Galotti.*" *Zeitschrift für deutsche Philologie* 195 (1986): 181-186.

Scherpe, Klaus. *Gattungspoetik im 18. Jahrhundert: Historische Entwicklung von Gottsched bis Herder.* Studien zur Allgemeinen und Vergleichenden Literaturwissenschaft 2. Stuttgart: Metzler, 1968.

Schilson, Arno. "Glanz der Wahrheit oder blendender Stil? Überlegungen zu Gegenstand und Methode in Lessings Streit mit Goeze." Mauser and Saße 56-77.

–. *Geschichte im Horizont der Vorsehung. G. E. Lessings Beitrag zu einer Theologie der Geschichte.* Tübinger Theologische Studien 3. Mainz: Matthias-Grünewald-Verlag, 1974.

Schiller, Friedrich. *Über die Ästhetische Erziehung des Menschen. Theoretische Schriften.* Ed. Rolf-Peter Janz et al. FSA 8 (1992): 556-676.

Schings, Hans-Jürgen. *Die Brüder des Marquis Posa. Schiller und der Geheimbund der Illuminaten.* Tübingen: Niemeyer, 1996.

–. *Der mitleidigste Mensch ist der beste Mensch: Poetik des Mitleids von Lessing bis Büchner.* Munich: Beck, 1980. 2nd rev. ed. Würzburg: Königshausen & Neumann, 2012.

– ed. *Der Ganze Mensch. Anthropologie und Literatur im 18. Jahrhundert. DFG-Symposion 1992.* Stuttgart: Metzler, 1994.

Schlegel, Karl Wilhelm Friedrich. "Lessings Gedanken und Meinungen." *Charakteristiken und Kritiken II (1802-1829).* Ed. Hans Eichner. KFSA 3 (1974): 46-102.

–. "Über Lessing." *Charakteristiken und Kritiken I (1796-1801).* Ed. Hans Eichner. KFSA 2 (1967): 100-125.

–. *Vorlesungen über dramatische Kunst und Literatur: Kritische Ausgabe.* Ed. Giovanni Vittorio Amoretti. 2 vols. Bonn: Kurt Schröder, 1923.

–. "'Zur Philosophie. B. 1797.' Ende der ersten und Übergang zur Moralischen Epoche." *Philosophische Lehrjahre 1796-1806.* Ed. Ernst Behler, 2 vols. KFSA 18-19 (1963-1971). 1: 79-117.

Schlipphacke, Heidi M. "The Dialectic of Female Desire in G.E. Lessing's *Emilia Galotti.*" *Lessing Yearbook* 33 (2001): 55-78.

Schmeling, Manfred and Monika Schmitz-Emans, ed. *Das visuelle Gedächtnis der Literatur.* Würzburg: Königshausen & Neumann, 1999.

Schmidt, Erich. *Lessing: Geschichte seines Lebens und seiner Schriften.* 4th ed. 2 vols. Berlin: Weidmann, 1923.

Schmidt-Biggemann, Wilhelm. "Lessings origenistische Eschatologie." Bultmann and Vollhardt 138-153.

Schmiesing, Ann. "Remembering and Forgetting in *Miß Sara Sampson.*" *Lessing Yearbook* 27 (1995): 19-37.

–. "Lessing and the Third Reich." Fischer and Fox 261-280.

Schmitz-Emans, Monika. "Boccaccio, Lessing, and Pavic, Variationen der Ringparabel." Zeuch 197-222.

–."Das visuelle Gedächnis der Literatur. Allgemeine Überlegungen zur Beziehung zwischen Texten und Bildern." Schmeling and Schmitz-Emans 17-34.

–."Der Augenblick und das Transitorische: Lessings Medienästhetik und ihre Bedeutung für die literarische Bildinterpretation." *Die Literatur, die Bilder und das Unsichtbare. Spielformen literarischer Bildinterpretation vom 18. bis zum 20. Jahrhundert.* Saarbrücker Beiträge zur vergleichenden Literatur- und Kulturwissenschaft 7. Würzburg: Königshausen & Neumann, 1999. 39-42.

– and Gertrud Lehnert, ed. *Visual Culture.* Hermeia 10. Heidelberg: Synchron, 2008.

Schneider, Helmut J. "Deconstruction of the Hermeneutical Body: Kleist and the Discourse of Classical Aesthetics." Kelly and von Mücke 209-226.

–, Ralf Simon and Thomas Wirtz, ed. *Bildersturm und Bilderflut um 1800. Zur schwierigen Anschaulichkeit der Moderne.* Bielefeld: Aisthesis, 2001.

Schrader, Monika. *Sprache und Lebenswelt: Fabeltheorien des 18. Jahrhunderts.* Germanistische Texte und Studien 38. Hildesheim: Georg Olms, 1991.

–. *Laokoon–"eine vollkommene Regel der Kunst": Ästhetische Theorien der Heuristik in der zweiten Hälfte des 18. Jahrhunderts: Winckelmann, Mendelssohn, Lessing, Herder, Schiller, Goethe.* Hildesheim: Georg Olms, 2005.

Schröder, Jürgen. *Gotthold Ephraim Lessing: Sprache und Drama.* Munich: Fink, 1972.

Schulz, Georg-Michael. "Das 'Lust-und Trauerspiel' oder Die Dramaturgie des doppelten Schlusses. Zu einigen Dramen des ausgehenden 18. Jahrhunderts." *Lessing Yearbook* 23 (1991): 111-126.

Schweizer, Niklaus R. *The Ut Pictura Poesis Controversy in Eighteenth-Century England and Germany.* European University Papers, Series 18: Comparative Literature 2. Bern: Herbert Lang, 1972.

Sedgwick, Eve Kosofsky. *Between Men: English Literature and Male Homosocial Desire.* New York: Columbia University Press, 1985.

Sha, Richard C. *The Visual and Verbal Sketch in British Romanticism.* Philadelphia: University of Pennsylvania Press, 1998.

Siebert, Jr., Donald T. "Laocoön and Polymetis: Lessing's Treatment of Joseph Spence." *Lessing Yearbook* 3 (1971): 71-84.

Siegert, Bernhard. "Schüsse, Schocks, und Schreie. Zur Undarstellbarkeit der Diskontinuität bei Euler, d'Alembert und Lessing." Baxmann et al. 291-305.

Siegrist, Christoph. "Fabel und Lehrgedicht: Gemeinsamkeiten und Differenzen." Hasubek, *Die Fabel* 106-118.

Simon, Ralf. "Ein falsches Bild. Oder: Was passiert, wenn Katharsis Form wird? Zu Lessings *Emilia Galotti.*" Adler and Godel 249-262.

–. *Die Idee der Prosa. Zur Ästhetikgeschichte von Baumgarten bis Hegel mit einem Schwerpunkt bei Jean Paul.* Munich: Fink, 2013.

–. *Der poetische Text als Bildkritik.* Munich: Fink, 2009.

–, ed. *Herders Rhetoriken im Kontext des 18. Jahrhunderts.* Heidelberg: Synchron, 2014.

Singer, Rüdiger. "Intermediale Anschaulichkeit: *Enargeia* als rhetorisches Wirkungsideal von Text, Bild und *actio.*" Adler and Gross 157-177.

Söntgen, Beate and Geraldine Spiekermann, ed. *Tränen.* Munich: Fink, 2008.

Sørensen, Bengt Algot."Lessings Laokoon und Winckelmann." *Lessing Yearbook* 36 (2004/2005): 69-78.

Spence, Joseph. *Polymetis or: An Enquiry Concerning the Agreement between the Works of the Roman Poets, and the Remains of the Ancient Artists: Being an Attempt to Illustrate them Mutually from one Another in 10 Books.* London: R. Dodsley, 1747.

Stafford, Barbara M. *Body Criticism. Imaging the Unseen in Enlightenment Art and Medicine.* Cambridge, MA: MIT Press, 1991.

Staege, Max. *Die Geschichte der deutschen Fabeltheorie.* Sprache und Dichtung 44. Bern: Paul Haupt, 1929.

Starr, G.G. "Ekphrasis." *The Princeton Encyclopedia of Poetry and Poetics.* 4th ed. Ed. Roland Greene et al. Princeton: Princeton University Press, 2012, 393

Steinmetz, Horst. "Die Sache, die Person, und die Verselbständigung des kritischen Diskurses. Offene und verdeckte Antriebe in Lessings Streitschriften." Mauser and Saße 483-493.

–. "Verstehen, Mißverstehen, Nichtverstehen. Zum Problem der Interpretation, vornehmlich am Beispiel von Lessings *Emilia Galotti.*" *Germanisch-Romanische Monatsschrift,* N.F. 37 (1987): 378-398.

–, ed. *Gotthold Ephraim Lessings* Minna von Barnhelm: *Dokumente zur Rezeptions- und Interpretationsgeschichte.* Königstein im Taunus: Athenäum, 1979.

–, ed. *Lessing–ein unpoetischer Dichter. Dokumente aus drei Jahrhunderten zur Wirkungsgeschichte Lessings in Deutschland.* Frankfurt am Main: Athenäum, 1969.

Stenzel, Jürgen and Roman Lach, ed. *Lessings Skandale.* Tübingen: Niemeyer, 2005.

Stephan, Inge. "'So ist die Tugend ein Gespenst'. Frauenbild und Tugendbegriff im bürgerlichen Trauerspiel bei Lessing und Schiller." *Lessing Yearbook* 17 (1985): 2-20. Reprint in Freimark, Kopitzsch and Slessarev 357-374.

Strathman, Christopher A. *Romantic Poetry and the Fragmentary Imperative: Schlegel, Byron, Joyce, Blanchot.* Albany: State University of New York Press, 2006.

Strohschneider-Kohrs, Ingrid. *Historische Wahrheit der Religion: Hinweise zu Lessings Erziehungsschrift.* Kleine Schriften zur Aufklärung 16. Göttingen: Wallstein, 2009.

–. *Vernunft als Weisheit. Studien zum späten Lessing.* Tübingen: Niemeyer ,1991.

–. "Zur Logik der Erziehungs-Schrift: Widerspruch oder Kohärenz." Bultmann and Vollhardt 155-178.

Sutcliffe, Adam. "Lessing and Toleration." Robertson 205-225.

Szondi, Peter. *Die Theorie des bürgerlichen Trauerspiels im 18. Jahrhundert.* Ed. Gert Mattenklott. 3rd ed. Studienausgabe der Vorlesungen 1. Frankfurt am Main: Suhrkamp, 1977.

–."Tableau und coup de théatre. Zur Sozialpsychologie des bürgerlichen Trauerspiels bei Diderot. Mit einem Exkurs über Lessing." *Schriften,* vol. 2. Frankfurt am Main: Suhrkamp, 1978. 205-232.

Ter-Nedden, Gisbert. *Lessings Trauerspiele: Der Ursprung des deutschen Trauerspiels aus dem Geist der Kritik.* Stuttgart: Metzler, 1986.

Thalheimer, Michael, Director and Wolfgang Bergmann, ed. *Deutsches Theater Berlin. Gotthold Ephraim Lessing. Emilia Galotti.* ZDfB Enterprises GmbH, DvD ZDFE 2008 (www.theateredition.de) (ISBN 4 280000101129).

Tolkien, J.R.R. *On Fairy-stories. Expanded Edition.* Ed. Verlyn Flieger and Douglas A. Anderson. London: HarperCollins, 2008.

Trop, Gabriel. "The Fable as Aesthetic Exercise: Lessing's Philosophy of Poetic Form." *Lessing Yearbook* 43 (2016): 55-76.

Ugrinsky, Alexej, ed. *Lessing and the Enlightenment.* Westport, CT: Greenwood Press, 1986.

Utz, Peter. *Das Auge und das Ohr im Text. Literarische Sinneswahrnehmung in der Goethezeit.* Munich: Fink, 1990.

Van der Laan, J.M. "Lessings 'Lost Faust' and Faustus Socinus." *Lessing Yearbook* 38 (2008-2009): 53-65.

Van Laak, Lothar. "Synästhesie und Sinnlichkeit. Überlegungen zu einer Hermeneutik der Synästhesie in der Literatur des 18. Jahrhunderts." Adler and Zeuch 225-238.

–. "'Seine von sich selbst arbeitende Phantasie.' Zum Stellenwert der Einbildungskraft in Lessings *Laokoon.*" Robert and Vollhardt 309-319.

Van Stockum, Theodorus. C. "Lessings Dramenentwurf 'Die Matrone von Ephesus'." *Neophilologus* 46 (1962): 125-134.

–. "Lessing und Diderot." *Neophilologus* 39 (1955): 191-202.

Veraldi D. and S. Cushman. "Paralipsis," *The Princeton Encyclopedia of Poetry and Poetics.* 4th ed. Ed. R. Greene et al. Princeton: Princeton University Press, 2012, 997.

Vierhaus, Rudolf. *Was war Aufklärung?* Kleine Schriften zur Aufklärung 7. Göttingen: Wallstein, 1995.

Vollhardt, Friedrich. "Die Ringparabel in G.E. Lessings Drama *Nathan der Weise.* Aktualität–Historizität–Kontiguität." Aurnhammer, Cantarutti, and Vollhardt 205-234. Also in: Jan-Heiner Tück, and Rudolf Langthaler, ed. *"Es strebe von euch jeder um die Wette": Lessings Ringparabel–ein Paradigma für die Verständigung der Religionen heute?* Freiburg i.Br.: Herder, 2016. 223-244.

–. "'Enthusiasmus der Spekulation': Zur fehlenden Vorgeschichte von G.E. Lessings Erziehungslehre." Bultmann and Vollhardt 104-125.

–. *Gotthold Ephraim Lessing.* Munich: Beck, 2016.

–. ed. *G.E. Lessing. Laokoon oder Über die Grenzen der Malerei und Poesie. Studienausgabe.* Stuttgart: Reclam, 2012.

Von Lüpke, Johannes. *Wege der Weisheit. Studien zu Lessings Theologiekritik.* Göttingen: Vandenhoeck & Ruprecht, 1989.

Wagner, Peter, ed. *Icons–Textes–Iconotexts: Essays on Ekphrasis and Intermediality.* European Cultures: Studies in Literature and the Arts 6. Berlin: De Gruyter, 1996.

–. "Introduction: Ekphrasis, Iconotexts, and Intermediality–the State(s) of the Art(s)." Wagner 1-40.

Wallach, Martha Kaarsberg. "Emilia und ihre Schwestern: Das seltsame Verschwinden der Mutter und die geopferte Tochter." Kraft and Liebs 53-72.

Walzøe-Engel, Ingrid. *Fathers and Daughters: Patterns of Seduction in Tragedies by Gryphius, Lessing, Hebbel and Kroetz.* Columbia, SC: Camden House, 1993.

Wandhoff, Haiko. *Ekphrasis: Kunstbeschreibungen und virtuelle Räume in der Literatur des Mittelalters.* Trends in Medieval Philology 3. Berlin: De Gruyter, 2003.

Watson, Richard A. "Malebranche, Models, and Causation." Nadler 75-91.

Webb, Ruth. *Ekphrasis. Imagination and Persuasion in Ancient Rhetorical Theory and Practice.* Burlington, VT: Ashgate, 2009.

Wehrli, Beatrice. *Kommunikative Wahrheitsfindung. Zur Funktion der Sprache in Lessings Drama.* Hermaea, N.F. 46. Tübingen: Niemeyer, 1983.

Weigand, Hermann J. "Warum stirbt Emilia Galotti?" Hermann John Weigand and Amos Leslie Willson, ed. *Fährten und Funde: Aufsätze zur deutschen Dichtung.* Bern: Francke, 1967. 39-50. First published in *JEGP* 28.4 (October 1929): 467-481.

Wellbery, David E. *Lessing's Laocoon: Semiotics and Aesthetics in the Age of Reason.* 1984. Cambridge: Cambridge University Press, 2009.

–."Das Gesetz der Schönheit: Lessings Ästhetik der Repräsentation." C.L. Hart Nibbrig, ed. *Was heißt 'Darstellen'?* Frankfurt am Main: Suhrkamp, 1994. 175-204.

–. "The Pathos of Theory in *Laokoon* Revisited." Ingeborg Hoesterey and Ulrich Weisstein, ed. *Intertextuality: German Literature and Visual Art from the Renaissance to the Twentieth Century* Columbia, SC: Camden House, 1993. 47-63.

Wells, G.A. "What is wrong with Emilia Galotti?" *German Life and Letters* 37.3 (1984): 163-173.

Wenzlaff-Mauderer, Isabelle. *Wenn statt des Mundes Augen reden. Sprachlosigkeit und nonverbale Kommunikation in* Miss Sara Sampson *(1755),* Düvall und Charmille *(1788),* Kabale und Liebe *(1784) und* Penthesilea *(1808).* Munich: Iudicium, 2001.

Wessell, Leonard P. *G.E. Lessing's Theology. A Reinterpretation: A Study in the Problematic Nature of the Enlightenment.* The Hague: Mouton, 1977.

Wessels, Hans-Friedrich. *Lessings* Nathan der Weise. Königstein im Taunus: Athenäum, 1979.

Wheelwright, Philip. *Metaphor and Reality.* 2nd ed. Bloomington: Indiana University Press, 1964.

Wiedemann, Conrad. "Ein schönes Ungeheuer. Zur Deutung von Lessings Einakter 'Philotas'." *Germanisch-Romanische Monatsschrift,* N.F. 17 (1967): 381-397.

Willems, Gottfried. *Anschaulichkeit: Zu Theorie und Geschichte der Wort-Bild Beziehungen und des literarischen Darstellungsstils.* Studien zur deutschen Literatur 103. Tübingen: Niemeyer, 1989.

Willems, Marianne. "Der 'herrschaftsfreie Diskurs' als 'opus supererogatum'. Überlegungen zum Interaktionsethos des 'bloß Menschlichen'." Mauser and Saße 540-551.

Wilson, W. Daniel and Robert C. Holub, ed. *Impure Reason: Dialectic of Enlightenment in Germany,* Detroit: Wayne State University Press, 1993.

Winckelmann, Johann Joachim. *Gedanken ueber die Nachahmung der griechischen Werke in der Malerey und Bildhauerkunst.* 2nd enlarged edition (1756). *Reflections on the Imitation of Greek Works in Painting and Sculpture. Complete German Text.* Ed. and trans. Elfriede Heyer and Roger C. Norton. La Salle, IL: Open Court, 1987. 1-69.

–. *Geschichte der Kunst des Altertums.* Bibliothek klassischer Texte. Darmstadt: Wissenschaftliche Buchgesellschaft, 1993. First published in this edition: Cologne: Phaidon Verlag, 1972.

–. "Gedanken ueber die Nachahmung der griechischen Werke." *Kleine Schriften, Vorreden, Entwürfe.* Ed. Walther Rehm. 2nd ed. Berlin: De Gruyter, 2002. 27-89.

Witte, Karsten. "How Nazi Cinema Mobilizes the Classics: Schweikart's 'Das Fräulein von Barnhelm'." Eric Rentschler, ed. *German Film and Literature: Adaptations and Transformations.* New York: Methuen, 1986. 103-116.

Wittgenstein, Ludwig. *Philosophische Untersuchungen. Philosophical Investigations.* Ed. and trans. G.E.M. Anscombe. 2nd ed., rev. Malden, MA: Blackwell, 1997.

Wittkowski, Wolfgang. "Bürgerfreiheit oder -feigheit? Die Metapher des 'langen Weges' als Schlüssel zum Koordinatensystem in Lessings politischem Trauerspiel *Emilia Galotti.*" *Lessing Yearbook* 17 (1985): 65-87.

Woesler, Wilfried. "Lessings *Miß Sara Sampson* und Senecas *Medea.*" *Lessing Yearbook* 10 (1978): 75-93.

Wolf, Norbert Christian. "'Fruchtbarer Augenblick'–'prägnanter Moment:' Zur medienspezifischen Funktion einer ästhetischen Kategorie." Alt and Košenina 373-404.

Wolff, Christian. *Philosophia practica universalis.* Part 2, new edition. Frankfurt am Main: Officina libraria Rengeriana, 1739.

–. *Psychologia Empirica.* Frankfurt am Main: Officina libraria Rengeriana, 1738.

Worvill, Romira M. *'Seeing Speech': Illusion and the Transformation of Dramatic Writing in Diderot and Lessing.* SVEC 2005 vol 9. Oxford: Voltaire Foundation, 2005.

Wurst, Katrin A. *Familiale Liebe ist die 'wahre Gewalt'. Die Repräsentation der Familie in G. E. Lessings dramatischem Werk.* Amsterdamer Publikationen zur Sprache und Literatur 75. Amsterdam: Rodopi, 1988.

–. "Spellbinding: The Body as Art/Art as Body in the Cultural Practice of 'Attitüden'." *Lessing Yearbook* 33 (2001): 151-181.

Yasukata, Toshimasa. *Lessing's Philosophy of Religion and the German Enlightenment: Lessing on Christianity and Reason.* New York: Oxford University Press and The American Academy of Religion, 2002.

Yermolenko, Galina, ed. *Roxalana in World Literature.* Burlington, VT: Ashgate Publishers, 2010.

Zammito, John. *Kant, Herder, and the Birth of Anthropology.* Chicago: Chicago University Press, 2002.

Zelle, Carsten. *Die doppelte Ästhetik der Moderne. Revisionen des Schönen von Boileau bis Nietzsche.* Stuttgart: Metzler, 1995.

Zeuch, Ulrike, "*Sensus communis, imaginatio* und *sensorium commune* im 17. Jahrhundert." Adler and Zeuch 167-184.

–. *Umkehr der Sinneshierarchie: Herder und die Aufwertung des Tastsinns seit der frühen Neuzeit.* Communicatio 22. Tübingen: Niemeyer, 2000.

–. ed. *Lessings Grenzen.* Wolfenbütteler Forschungen 106. Wiesbaden: Harrassowitz, 2005.

Zimmermann, Christian von. "Verinnerlichung der Trauer. Publizität des Leides." Achim Aurnhammer et al., ed. *Gefühlskultur in der bürgerlichen Aufklärung.* Frühe Neuzeit 98. Tübingen: Niemeyer, 2004. 47-74.

Zymner, Rüdiger. "'Der Stein war ein Opal ...' Eine versteckte Kunst-Apotheose in Lessings morgenländischer Ringparabel?" *Lessing Yearbook* 24 (1992): 77-96.

# Index

Contains names referred to in the main text, but footnotes are excluded. Dates are only given for Lessing's contemporaries and those individuals no longer living.